MUSIC SINCE 1900

MUSIC SINCE 1900

Nicolas Slonimsky

THIRD EDITION
REVISED AND ENLARGED

COLEMAN-ROSS COMPANY, Inc.

NEW YORK • 1949

Third Edition

MANUFACTURED IN THE UNITED STATES OF AMERICA

CONTENTS

vi · · CONTENTS · ·

Introduction

This is a book in the first place of materials, in the second of evaluation. The main body of the book, a Descriptive Chronology, is intended to be a sort of newsreel reflecting the "inner headlines" of musical events that may not be at the moment of their occurrence of any seeming importance, but do contain elements of evolutionary power that subtly but surely influence the entire future of music. Thus, the date of completion of *Le Sacre du Printemps* or of *Pierrot Lunaire,* while quite unnoticed by the music world at large, is an inner headline of extreme importance; such dates, when ascertainable, are given particular attention. Usually a brief description of the work accompanies the date of its completion, but when such a date is not available, a description is given under the date of the first performance. Selection of important dates has been governed exclusively by the musical importance of the event. Spectacular performers, great singers, big impresarios have been left out of the picture almost entirely, although their power in the musical world and their hold on the "outer headlines" is incomparably superior to that of a composer-innovator. Sometimes the outer and inner headlines coincide, as in the case of the production of Alban Berg's opera, *Wozzeck.* At other times the sensationalism of a musical event, such as a concert of futurist music or a demonstration of Dadaists, obscures the musical significance, be it only of a destructive nature, of the event itself.

This Descriptive Chronology is here unrolled without national subdivisions. An event of musical importance may happen today in America, tomorrow in Russia; it is their contiguity in time alone that places them one after another. This method has the disadvantage of lumping together unrelated phenomena, but so has every chronology. On the other hand, this temporal juxtaposition frequently gives an interesting sidelight on this or that period.

A history of the modern musical idiom is yet to be written. Here we may cautiously draw a general outline of musical evolution since 1900, and post its milestones. We must remember only one very important thing: that all musical innovation, no matter how extreme, is useful in that it indicates potentialities heretofore overlooked. Thus, composers thoroughly averse to the spirit of the twelve-tone technique may finds its methods of great value within the tonal framework. The exploration of quarter-tone music may remain an isolated phenomenon, and yet subtilize our perception of chromatic scales. The growing independence of the percussion section in the orchestra calls our attention to the varied timbres of percussion even when they are used as symphonic background.

Similarly, esthetic trends and fashions, even when completely outmoded in the process of evolution, remain potent as influences in the new art. "Repudiations" and movements "back to the old music" are only partial repudiations. The repudiated element remains in the new art as an ingredient. Thus the new classicism of the thirties of our century is classicism plus pandiatonicism (i.e., the use of all seven tones of a given tonality in free melodic or harmonic array) where the older classicism was confined to concords and permissible discords.

Changes in artistic trends are often signaled by events the dates of which it is possible to ascertain. Thus, impressionism in painting may be dated from an article in the French paper *Charivari* of 25 April 1874, in which Monet and his followers were derisively dubbed "impressionists." Futurism was launched by Marinetti in a manifesto published in the Paris *Figaro* of 20 February 1909. The famous Group of Six was designated as such in an article published in the Paris daily, *Comoedia,* on 16 January 1920. According to an eminent Dadaist, the word "Dada" was invented at six o'clock in the evening of 8 February 1916. The progress of jazz as a musical phenomenon can be traced almost day by day since its beginnings in New Orleans and its conquest of, consecutively, Chicago, New York, and Europe. (We have the exact date of the first jazz-band concert in Paris, 17 November 1918.) An example of change of trend by decree is the dissolution, by the Soviet government on 23 April 1932, of the Russian Association of Proletarian Musicians, so marking a turn toward free exercise of the composer's functions without the necessity of injecting a proletarian element.

The selection of landmarks in the history of modern music is perforce arbitrary, but no more so than the choosing of historical landmarks. It was not announced in Rome in A.D. 476 that the Middle Ages had then and there begun; yet historians have accepted this date as a convenient chronological landmark. Similarly, we are justified in selecting an important event in 20th-century music as a chronological symbol of esthetic evolution. The first performance of Debussy's *Pelléas,* on 30 April 1902, was such a symbol, signalizing the advent of impressionist opera. The outbreak of World War I brought about a musico-psychological realignment, with the romance of the machine replacing the old romance. The era of machine music flourished until the economic collapse of October 1929, when musicians abandoned the cult of the discredited machine and turned to composing pure music in a neo-classical manner. As if by general consent, pictorial and descriptive titles disappeared from the pages of musical scores, and were replaced by the impersonal forms of Suite and Symphony. Thus, Honegger's first "mouvement symphonique," composed in December 1923, is subtitled *Pacific 231,* to glorify the mighty American locomotive; his second "mouvement" was *Rugby,* in 1928, the musical picture of a fashionable game; but his third work in the same genre, written between October 1932 and January 1933, is entitled simply *Mouvement Symphonique.*

The process of forming a new technique is illuminated in an important letter to the author from Schoenberg (in the section Letters and Documents) regarding the origin of the twelve-tone method of composition. Schoenberg's letter shows how an idea latent in a musician's mind crystallizes, by the logic of true intuition, into a definite formula, at a definite time. We may now assign the birth of the twelve-tone technique to December 1914. However, the first work in the twelve-tone technique, Schoenberg's *Serenade*, op.24 (the fourth movement of which presents the first instance of melody building in twelve non-repeated notes), was not published until ten years later, on 1 March 1924, to be exact.*

The first use of polyrhythmy is found in an orchestral movement by Charles E. Ives, composed on 4 July 1904. The first comprehensive exposition of the quarter-tone system was completed by Richard H. Stein on 22 May 1909, and he was regarded as the pioneer of quarter-tone music until recently, when evidence has been adduced that Julián Carrillo, the Mexican musician, experimented with quarter-tone music as early as 1895.

The beginning of polytonal technique may also be assigned to a definite date, 26 May 1911, when Stravinsky completed the score of *Petrouchka* which contains the first bitonal chord, C major with F-sharp major. Before Stravinsky, Mozart used polytonality in his *Musikalischer Spass* (composed on 14 June 1787), with its quadritonal ending, but that, after all, was a joke!

I wrote the foregoing pages (herein somewhat reworded) in the Introduction to the First Edition of *Music Since 1900*, published in 1937. In the present edition the purposes of the book remain unaltered. It adds a newsreel—or a television broadcast —of an eventful decade in modern music. As in the first edition, the coverage is, by intention, worldwide, listing dates of performances of important new works, taking note of the passing of great figures of music, detailing the programs of interna-

---

* Herbert Eimert in his *Atonale Musiklehre*, published in 1924, gives a detailed account of the "12-Tondauer-Musik" by the Russian expatriate composer Jef Golyscheff, developed, according to Eimert's claims, as early as 1914. Golyscheff's *Trio*, written in an integral twelve-tone system, was published on 30 March 1925.

tional festivals, and entering occasional items that throw interesting light on musical manners and morals.

Musical events that have taken place in America during the period 1937-1948 have come in for the greater part of attention in the Descriptive Chronology. This pro-American partiality is accounted for not alone by the obvious fact that this book is published in America, and is designed primarily for American readers, but by the objective truth that during the last decade the center of creative music has gradually shifted from Europe to the United States. This shift has been evidenced in the migration to America of great European figures in modern music. As authoritative preceptors, they have influenced young American musicians and have been themselves influenced by native American music. The big three of modern music, Stravinsky, Schoenberg and Hindemith are now American citizens working in this country as members of the American confraternity of music. So are Toch and Krenek. Kurt Weill, the erstwhile composer of an "anti-American" opera, *Mahagonny*, in which American life was represented as a palimpsest of skyscrapers and gangsters, has now discovered the America of the countryside and is writing folk operas of a genuinely American flavor. Béla Bartók wrote some of his best works in America before his death in 1945. Rachmaninov lived in the United States and became an American citizen shortly before he died. Among the figures of old Russian music, Gretchaninov has also become an American citizen.

Skeptical European musicians are beginning, however grudgingly, to recognize the coming of age of American music. Thus, *Le Guide du Concert* of 30 January 1948 runs this delectable item: "L'Amérique n'est plus une nation a-musicale: elle compte une cinquantaine de compositeurs de talent." Time marches on!

The second edition of *Music Since 1900*, published in 1938, brought the Descriptive Chronology up to the end of the year 1937. The present edition retains the text for the years 1900 to 1936 virtually intact, except for the necessary corrections of typographical errors in the original plates. On the other hand, the entries for 1937 have been completely revised.

The perspective of musical events has, of course, changed considerably since the appearance of the first edition of the book. Many names and musical events that loomed large on the musical horizon of 1937 are now dimmed into relative obscurity. Yet, it is astonishing to consider how many young beginners with an uncertain future, whose names are included in the first edition of *Music Since 1900,* have shown a sturdy growth and have, in some instances, risen to the stature of masters of modern music.

The Descriptive Chronology, by its very nature, requires the consecutive listing of exact dates of musical events. It is not always easy to establish these dates. Even printed concert programs are not necessarily conclusive evidence that a given composition was actually performed on the date listed. Performances are often put off to a later date, or even canceled altogether after the printed program is issued. Numerous instances can be given of such stillborn announcements, and a musical chronicler must be extremely careful not to set down such anticipated events as facts of musical chronology. There are recorded cases when a music critic has reported the performance of a new work which never took place. One of such embarrassing *scandales* was the devastating review written by Leonid Sabaneiev in a Russian musical journal about a performance (that never took place) of Prokofiev's *Scythian Suite* in Moscow, which the reader will find in the Descriptive Chronology under the date 25 December 1916.

The dates of the Russian old-style calendar have been adjusted to correspond to the Western (Gregorian) style. Before 1900 the Russian calendar was twelve days behind the Western calendar. The year 1900 was a leap year in Russia but not in the West.* By having an extra day in February 1900, the Russian old

* Centesimal years are leap years in the Western reckoning only if exactly divisible by 400, which 1900 is not.

style increased the difference to thirteen days. Consequently, all Russian dates after 29 February 1900, old style (13 March 1900, new style), should be adjusted by adding thirteen days; before that date, by adding twelve days. The old style was abolished and the new style established by the Soviet government in February 1918, when 1 February, old style, officially became 14 February.

Philip Hale once said that he would accept a date as accurate if he found it in two independent sources. But two sources, seemingly independent of each other, may be derived from a third source which contains an original error. There are migrating wrong dates familiar to every musicographer. Thus, the death date of Albéniz is correctly given in the Descriptive Chronology as 16 June 1909, instead of 18 May 1909, as in almost all music dictionaries, although the same dictionaries list in the bibliographies to their Albéniz articles Henri Collet's book *Albéniz et Granados,* which gives not only the exact day, but the hour of the composer's death.

Frequently the day and the month are correct, while the year is wrong. In such instances it is more than likely that the error is clerical in its origin. For example, the date of Napravnik's death is incorrectly given in the *Encyclopaedia Britannica* as 10 November 1915, instead of 10 November 1916, old style. The error first appears in Hull's *Dictionary of Modern Music and Musicians,* published in 1924. Grove and the *Encyclopaedia Britannica* must have copied Hull; Rieman copied Grove; the Dutch *Muzieklexicon* copied Riemann, and several other dictionaries copied each other. Exceptionally, the American Supplement to Grove had the correct year, but revoked it in the Appendix.

In the Descriptive Chronology, the dating of deaths is always given in local time. Rachmaninov died at 1:30 a.m. on the night of 27-28 March 1943; his date of death is then given as 28 March. Alban Berg died at 1:15 a.m. on 24 December 1935, Vienna time, which was still 23 December in America, but the Vienna date is given here. Ippolitov-Ivanov was found dead by his wife at 2:30 a.m., Moscow time, on 28 January 1935. Presumably, he died after midnight, Moscow time, but before midnight, Western European and American time, i.e., technically, on the 27th, Western time. Nevertheless, the date is here given as 28 January 1935. Enrico Bossi died at sea, on his voyage home from America, and the day and the hour of his death are given in Greenwich Mean Time. It occurred, according to the log of the S.S. *de Grasse,* at one o'clock in the afternoon on 20 February 1925. Philip Heseltine committed suicide by gas, and was found in his London flat at seven o'clock in the morning of 17 December 1930. He was pronounced dead upon arrival at the hospital. As he presumably lived after midnight, London time, the date is given as 17 December 1930.

When the famous prima donna Melba died in Melbourne on 23 February 1931, her death was reported in New York newspapers of 22 February, that is, according to the calendar, one day before her death! But this was of course due to the fact that she died in Australia, west of the international date line.

The first and the second editions of *Music Since 1900* carried a Concise Biographical Dictionary of Twentieth-Century Musicians, and also extensive lists of corrections of dates in other music dictionaries, viz., *A Dictionary of Modern Music and Musicians* (1924), Grove's *Dictionary of Music and Musicians* (1927 edition), Riemann's *Musik-Lexikon,* (1929 edition) and H. J. Moser's *Musik-Lexikon* (1935). Having served its purpose, this lexicographical section of the book has been left out of the present edition. The corrections have been incorporated into virtually all music dictionaries published during the last decade, among them the supplementary volume to Grove's *Dictionary* (1940), the fourth edition of Baker's *Biographical Dictionary of Musicians* (1940), and Oscar Thompson's *International Cyclopedia of Music and Musicians* (First Edition, 1939).

In the Descriptive Chronology the author has attempted to define the style of each musical work under consideration in two or three verbal symbols. This has entailed the use of rather formidable sesquipedalian Graeco-Latin word formations. Yet, these terms, in the author's mind, convey the exact meaning of the esthetic and technical concepts which they define. One of these terms, first used in *Music Since 1900,* has been widely adopted. It is described by Paul Rosenfeld, in his *Discoveries of a Music Critic,* as "a new sort of diatonism—pandiatonism, in Nicolas Slonimsky's happy nomenclature." The form in which the author uses the term is, however, pandiatonicism.

A new feature has been added to the present edition. It is a Tabular View of Stylistic Trends in Music Since 1900. Its purpose is to give a graphic synopsis of important musical events, arranged in stylistic categories, such as impressionism, neo-classicism, neo-romanticism, futurism, luxuriant nationalism, operatic naturalism and sophisticated folk music.

These new styles and techniques are further elucidated and defined in the section Explanation of Terms. In the Third Edition this section has been revised and, in the treatment of new techniques, considerably expanded.

The section Letters and Documents gives the texts of significant documents related to various aspects of 20th-century music. The documents published in the early editions of *Music Since 1900* have been retained in the present edition and some new material has been added, namely, excerpts, related to music, from the papal encyclical, *Mediator Dei* of 20 November 1947, and—on the opposite pole of musical philosophy—the text of the resolution of the Communist Party of the USSR of 10 February 1948 denouncing the symptoms of "decadent formalism" in Soviet music. A further addition is the text of the Manifesto issued by the Second International Congress of Composers and Musicologists, meeting in Prague, 20-29 May 1948.

For the preparation of the Third Edition heartfelt thanks are hereby extended to Clare Alexander of Boston, whose mental alertness in research, and indefatigable energy in tracking down the facts of music, have been of tremendous help. The author is greatly indebted to G. E. Kaltenbach of Santa Fe, whose intimate knowledge of European languages and wide experience in editing copy have contributed greatly to the elimination of avoidable errors and misprints. Acknowledgment is also due to the

Music Department of the Boston Public Library, Richard Appel, Chief, for lending library facilities for research work. Last but not least, the author is grateful to his new publisher, Herbert Coleman, whose knowledge of contemporary musical activities has been a rich reservoir of information for compiling the entries in the Descriptive Chronology.

31 January 1949

Boston, Massachusetts   NICOLAS SLONIMSKY

Explanation of Terms

ABSOLUTE music is an inclusive term for all forms of non-programmatic music. It is practically coincidental with neo-classical music, with this difference—that while NEO-CLASSICISM is committed to classical forms and titles, ABSOLUTE music may be couched in any musical idiom.

ABSTRACT music chooses non-pictorial abstract concepts for its subject matter, often of mathematical or philosophical origin. In contradistinction to ABSOLUTE music, ABSTRACT music is usually couched in an atonal idiom and avoids fixed themes, replacing them by expressive motifs, in which usage it approaches EXPRESSIONISM.

DADAISM in music is a nihilistic movement which stands in opposition to IMPRESSIONISM and NEO-PRIMITIVISM alike; to IMPRESSIONISM because of its poetic spirit, to NEO-PRIMITIVISM because of its snobbistic crudity and urbanistic philosophy. DADAISM stands nearest to FUTURISM, but has nothing of the futurist idea of building a new world. DADAISM is primarily intent on destroying values and creating a vacuum for a spontaneous generation of any form of human activity that could not possibly be called art. It proclaims machine art, but the machine in DADAISM is a grotesque symbol. The word "DADA" was first used in print on 26 February 1916.

EXPRESSIONISM stands in opposition to IMPRESSIONISM inasmuch as the latter depends on the inspiration from the world outside, whereas the former is guided exclusively by inner soul-events. If IMPRESSIONISM tends to be geographic, exotic, programmatic, EXPRESSIONISM is utopian, introspective, metaphysical. IMPRESSIONISM depends in melody on modal constructions, clothed in harmonies built in thirds and moving in parallel block chords. EXPRESSIONISM rejects modality, tonality, or polytonality. Its melody is constructed parabolically, away from the tonic, in fourths and fifths rather than in thirds. This quartal construction serves as a starting point first for vague atonality, then for the conscious and logical twelve-tone method. If IMPRESSIONISM is an integrating movement, then EXPRESSIONISM is a differentiating movement. Thus in instrumentation, EXPRESSIONISM individualizes each instrument, bringing to light the subtlest points of orchestral color. In rhythm, EXPRESSIONISM tends toward polymetric construction, asymmetry, extreme shortness of musical phrase. Geographically and racially, IMPRESSIONISM is the product of the Gallic spirit, EXPRESSIONISM of the Germanic.

FUTURISM was proclaimed in a manifesto published in the Paris *Figaro* on 20 February 1909. It aimed at complete annihilation of all accepted forms in favor of a future music created according to some imagined law of machine-like perfection. In reality, it is a weak imitation of IMPRESSIONISM, with the whole-tone scale as its mainstay. With some futurists, however, a real disintegration of musical matter takes place, with melody and harmony reduced to rudimental forms. Such extreme FUTURISM reduces melody to homonymous iteration, harmony to simultaneity of heterogeneous sounds, rhythm to tripudiary singultation, and orchestration to contrasted use of onomatopoeic instruments, such as snorers, gurglers, rufflers, fracasseurs.

GEBRAUCHSMUSIK, or UTILITARIAN music, originated shortly after World War I. An early mention of it is found in an article in *Die Signale* in December 1918, in relation to the UTILITARIAN opera. The emergence of GEBRAUCHSMUSIK was due to the sudden realization by modern composers that their music was doomed to remain unknown to the musical masses. In harmony and form, it approximates the Mozartian aspect of NEO-CLASSICISM. Nearest of all, GEBRAUCHSMUSIK comes to the spirit of the eighteenth-century divertissement and easy pieces composed for home playing. New music for children, spiced with dissonance, but quite easy to play, is a by-product of GEBRAUCHSMUSIK.

IMPRESSIONISM is of pictorial origin. The name "IMPRESSIONISTS" was used in print for the first time by Louis Leroy in the French paper, *Charivari*, of 25 April 1874, semi-derisively applied to Monet and his followers. In music, IMPRESSIONISM was applied by analogy with pictorial IMPRESSIONISM, and derives its literary and programmatic inspiration from SYMBOLISM in poetry. (The word "SYMBOLISM" as applied to literature was used for the first time in print in an article in the Paris daily, *Le Figaro*, of 18

September 1886.) Analogously to pictorial IMPRESSIONISM and
literary SYMBOLISM, musical IMPRESSIONISM integrates fragments
of musical phrases, suggestions of instrumental color, inferred
tonalities, into a musical poem with a programmatic or pictorial
title. The melodic and harmonic style of IMPRESSIONISM is characterized by the following uses: In melody, (1) affectation of Greek
modes, particularly ecclesiastical Dorian; (2) whole-tone scale
constructions; (3) pentatonic scales. In harmony, (1) chords of
piled-up thirds used en bloc as indivisible units, e.g., consecutive triads, consecutive seventh chords, ninth chords, chords with
an added sixth; (2) root progressions by equal division scales,
that is, scales produced by the division of the octave into two
equal parts, resulting in tritones; three equal parts, resulting in
augmented triad harmonies; four equal parts, resulting in diminished seventh harmonies; the whole-tone scale; chromatic scales;
(3) intertonal harmonization, with no three successive chords
belonging to any given tonality, specifically harmonization in
major triads only, the melody in contrary motion to the bass, and
in melodic positions following the row: 358358 . . . [example:
the descending whole-tone scale in the bass, beginning with C,
harmonized, C major, B-flat major, A-flat major, F-sharp major,
E major, D major, C major, with the derivative melody being C
(8), D (3), E-flat (5), F-sharp (8), G-sharp (3), A (5), C (8)].
An early instance of intertonal harmonization by major chords is
found in Moussorgsky's *Boris Godunov,* in Gregory's prophetic
vision in the second scene, composed on 23 October 1871, where
the melodic row B, C-sharp, E, F-sharp, G, is harmonized respectively, E major, C-sharp major, A major, F-sharp major, E-flat
major (enharmonic). In rhythm: (1) use of a short appog-
giatura-like ictus on the strong part of the measure, analogous to
the daubs of color of the stipplers' school of painting; (2) rapid
uniform non-symmetric groups of notes, mostly in prime numbers, 3, 5, 7, 11, 13, 17, . . . in strict time (opposed to Chopin's
rubato passages). In orchestration: (1) progressive individuali-
zation of instrumental colors, and virtual abandonment of group
orchestration; (2) exploration of the extreme registers; (3)
larger use of percussion instruments, including exotic instruments; (4) use of the piano as a percussion instrument, also
other percussion keyboard instruments, such as the xylophone.

JAZZ originated in New Orleans. One of the earliest uses of the word is found in the trade weekly, *Variety*, of 27 October 1916. JAZZ reached New York in January 1917, and the first JAZZ band abroad opened in Paris on 17 November 1918. In melody, JAZZ follows a tonal design essentially not different from any folk song. In harmony, JAZZ introduces "blue" notes as unresolvable consonances. (The first "blue" note, chronologically speaking, was the minor seventh of the tonic, approximating the seventh overtone. Later the twenty-seventh overtone came into use in the form of an added sixth. Also the ninth and the fifteenth overtones are frequently used as extensions of the tonic chord.) In rhythm, JAZZ derives from the counterpoint of the fourth species, greatly ornamented, often approaching *imbroglio* (cross meters). In the 1930's, JAZZ underwent a rhythmic change in the technique of SWING, which, by syncopating the syncopation of the classical JAZZ formula, re-transferred the main accent onto the strong beat, at the same time introducing a greater freedom into intra-mensural rhythm, with a constant sum of variable note-values in each measure. In 1947, the new technique of BEBOP (or Rebop, or simply Bop) re-syncopated the SWING rhythm, returning it to the spirit of earlier JAZZ music, modernized by dissonant harmonies of the polytonal brand. The special technique of BOOGIE-WOOGIE, introduced in 1938, is represented by an *ostinato* bass, with a rather rigid harmonic scheme, the characteristic feature of which is a modulatory digression into the subdominant.

NEO-CLASSICISM is essentially a return to eighteenth-century simplicity, as a reaction against pregnant programmaticism of the nineteenth century. In melody, it differs from the classics in that NEO-CLASSICISM makes use of larger intervals in a larger melodic compass; in harmony, it makes use of a pandiatonic extension of tonality. Contrary motion and sustaining tones replace the parallel harmonies of IMPRESSIONISM. In rhythm, NEO-CLASSICISM preserves eighteenth-century simplicity, but favors unsymmetric bar periods. In orchestration, it cultivates the harsher instruments of the orchestral palette, in opposition to pictorial instrumentation.

NEO-MYSTICISM is the product of supercharging music with religious content. It is neo-Wagnerian in melody and orchestration; in rhythm, it tends toward differentiated short phrases; in harmony it affects the tempered higher harmonics (8, 9, 10, 11, 13, 14, in Scriabin's *Prometheus*) .

NEO-PRIMITIVISM is an attempt to recreate in a stylized form the elemental power of primitive music. It is characterized in melody by simple symmetric tunes with folk-song flavor, clear tonal structure, limited compass, usually of a fifth; in harmony, by block chords in parallel motion; in rhythm, by crude iterative beat; in orchestration, by return to group instrumentation.

NEO-ROMANTICISM embraces general trends prevalent in post-Wagnerian music. Its principal characteristics are a heavy programmatic design and hugeness of symphonic or operatic dimensions.

PROLETARIAN music aims to serve the musical needs of the working masses. Its prerequisites are accessibility of musical idiom and simplicity of principal lines. Technically, PROLETARIAN music is built on the axes of the tonic and dominant (or subdominant in plagal melos) . Historically, PROLETARIAN music became significant after the Russian Proletarian Revolution of 6 November 1917. An Association of Proletarian Musicians was formed in Russia in 1924 for the purpose of disseminating the ideology of PROLETARIAN music. It was disbanded by the Soviet government on 23 April 1932. (See text of the declaration of the Association in Letters and Documents section)

PSEUDO-EXOTICISM developed after visits of Far Eastern musicians and dancers to the Paris Exposition of 1900. PSEUDO-EXOTICISM enters as part of the impressionistic palette, but is disdained by composers leaning toward NEO-PRIMITIVISM. PSEUDO-EXOTICISM transcribes the non-tempered scales of the East into the tempered scales of the West, affecting particularly the pentatonic scale ("black-key scale") . In melody it pursues simple designs within non-heptatonic scales; in harmony, bare fourths and fifths; in rhythm, non-symmetric groups of prime numbers, 5, 7, 11; in orchestration, emphasis on percussion color, often imitating native instruments.

URBANISM is the music of the city. Its source of inspiration is the machine, urban (factory, automobiles, moving pictures, newspapers) and interurban (locomotive, airplane), also city sports (rugby, football, prize fighting) . Because URBANISM depends on program, urbanist music is characterized by onomatopoeic stylization. It flourishes best in operas or symphonic poems. The text of an urbanist song may be a newspaper advertisement or a catalogue. Urbanist music was championed in the Futurist Manifesto of 20 February 1909. URBANISM flourished at about the same time as DADAISM and EXPRESSIONISM, roughly between 1915 and 1930.

VERISM (from *vero,* true) is operatic naturalism, the emergence of which may be dated from Mascagni's opera *Cavalleria Rusticana,* first performed in Rome, 17 May 1890. Veristic operas often propound an ironically tragic moral, as in the prologue to *Pagliacci.* VERISM is Wagnerian insofar as it accepts Wagner's continuity of music drama; Verdian insofar as it cultivates flowing melody and melodramatic effectiveness; Moussorgskyan insofar as it employs speech-like prosody. Operatic VERISM integrates these elements into a realistic tragi-comedy, with the subject matter historical or topical rather than legendary.

TECHNIQUES.

Atonality is the negation of tonality, a systematic avoidance of the keynote and the dominant. An intervallic contraction takes place in atonal melodies whereby the basic tonal intervals of the octave and the fifth are reduced by a semitone, the octave shrinking to a major seventh, and the fifth to an augmented fourth. The differential interval, the perfect fourth (major seventh minus augmented fourth equals perfect fourth), plays an important role in atonal structure, in quartal melodic progressions. For general esthetics, see Alban Berg, *What is Atonality?* in Letters and Documents.

Polytonality is the simultaneous use of several tonalities. In actual practice, *Bitonality* is the most common application of the simultaneity of different keys; and the most frequent use of *Bitonality* is the simultaneous sounding of two major triads whose keynotes are polar in the cycle of keys, as C major and F-sharp major. It is notable that these keynotes are at the distance of a tritone, which interval is basic also in *Atonality.*

A diminishing intervallic series of 9, 8, 7, 6, 5, 4, and 3 semitones results in the formation of a major bitonal chord with tonics related by a tritone; an increasing intervallic series, 3, 4, 5, 6, 7, 8, 9, results in the formation of a minor bitonal chord with tonics also at the distance of a tritone.

Theoretically, it is possible to form a polytonality of four mutually exclusive triads, two major and two minor, without duplicating a note. C major, D minor, F-sharp major and G-sharp minor is an instance of such a quadritonal combination. The two major triads stand here in the relationship of a tritone; the same relationship exists between the paired minor triads.

The nature of both *Polytonality* and *Atonality* leads to the development of the *Twelve-Tone Technique,* based on the principle of non-repetition of thematic tones. Its historic concept is given in the letter from Arnold Schoenberg, the originator of the technique, in the section Letters and Documents.

The designation *Twelve-Tone System* is commonly applied to Schoenberg's method as well as the *Twelve-Tone Technique.* The terms *Dodecuple Scale* and *Twelve-Note Music* are used in the writings of English musicologists; in France, Schoenberg's method is known as *Dodécaphonie,* and in Italy as *Dodecafonia.* Schoenberg deprecates the usage *Twelve-Tone System,* and prefers *Method of Composing With Twelve Tones,* as stated in the opening sentence of his letter in the section Letters and Documents. He reaffirms this designation in a letter published in the *Saturday Review of Literature* of 1 January 1949, in which he protests against the treatment of the method by Thomas Mann. He writes: "In his novel *Doctor Faustus,* Thomas Mann has taken advantage of my literary property. He has produced a fictitious composer as the hero of his book; and in order to lend him qualities a hero needs to arouse people's interest, he made him the creator of what one erroneously calls my 'system of twelve tones,' which I call 'method of composing with twelve tones.' "

479,001,600 combinations and transpositions of a twelve-tone row are possible. The basic row selected by the composer is applied in four forms: basic, melodically inverted, retrograde (crab), and in retrograde inversion.

The extension of the principle of non-repetition to intervallic structure of a melody leads to tone-rows in which not a single interval is used twice. In such a row, all twelve different notes and eleven different intervals are present. A chord based on such a row was first used by Fritz Klein in his work *Die Maschine,* subtitled "an extonal self-satire," and published under the nom de plume Heautontimorumenus (Self-Torturer). Klein called this chord a *Mutterakkord,* to indicate its capacities as a matrix.

A chord containing all twelve tones and all eleven intervals, capable of inversion, and furthermore forming an intermittent series of arithmetical progressions in odd and even numbers, 11, 2, 9, 4, 7, 6, 5, 8, 3, 10, 1, indicating the intervals in semitones, has been constructed by the author of the present volume, and dubbed *Grossmutterakkord.* Further enlightenment on the subject is found in the author's technical volume, *Thesaurus of Scales and Melodic Patterns* (Coleman-Ross, 1947).

The *Whole-Tone Scale* is produced by the division of the octave into six equal intervals. By its nature, it is atonal, for there is no dominant or subdominant. Two mutually exclusive whole-tone scales aggregate to the twelve tones of the chromatic scale. Whole-tone scales are employed by the Impressionist School to create an atmospheric effect.

Pandiatonicism is the technique of free use of all seven notes of the diatonic scale in melodic, contrapuntal and harmonic combinations, with the bass, the fifth from the bass, and the tenth from the bass determining the prevalent harmony. The chords are built in tertian harmony in the lower strata, in quartal harmony in the higher tones. The fourth from the bass is avoided, and cadential pandiatonic formations favor the inclusion of the second, sixth and seventh from the bass. Roy Harris uses a pandiatonic chord containing all seven notes in the ending of his *Little Suite* for piano. Major tonalities are by far more frequent in pandiatonic usage, and C major is the favorite key. As a consolidation of tonality, *Pandiatonicism* is often applied in NEO-CLASSICISM.

Displaced Tonality is a system of sudden modulation by semitones directly into the new key, at strong metrical points, approaching a cadence, or on the final chord of a harmonic section. A displacement of the cadential formula is made upwards by a semitone when an increase of tension is desired; downwards by a semitone when a drooping effect is the aim. The resulting displaced tonality may be either major or minor. Thus, an ascending scale in C major in the eighteenth measure of

Prokofiev's fairy tale *Peter and the Wolf* is displaced a semi-tone up, and thenceforth continues in the new key of C-sharp minor. The modern Russian composers are making an especially persistent practice of *Displaced Tonality,* as a twentieth-century counterpart of the deceptive cadence in classical music.

Polymetry is the simultaneous use of two or more different meters, such as 3/4 and 6/8, with coincidental bar-lines; or 2/4 and 3/4 with non-coincidental bar-lines. The latter type is the *imbroglio* (literally, entanglement).

Polyrhythmy, in effect identical with *Polymetry,* is technically limited to the simultaneous use of different rhythms within the same meter, resulting in strong cross-accents. Consistent *Polyrhythmy* is used by Charles E. Ives in the second movement of his symphonic suite *Three Places in New England,* composed on 4 July 1904, in which two march tunes are so combined that one runs 33 1/3% faster than the other. Polymetrically, this effect can be expressed by writing four measures against three measures, both in march time; polyrhythmically, the two melodies can be written within the same meter, by reducing the note-values of the faster march.

Fractional tones, or *microtones,* are divisions of the octave into 24, 36, 48, etc. equal parts. Quarter-tones were experimented with by John Herbert Foulds in 1898, and by Richard Stein in 1906. Quarter-tones and other fractional tones were exhaustively explored by Alois Hába in his theoretical work and practical teaching as early as 1914. The Mexican composer Julián Carrillo outlined the system of microtonal division in his *Sonido 13* (Thirteenth Sound, i.e. sound beyond the chromatic division of the tempered scale) in 1895, and later developed a system of number notation for division of the octave into as many as 96 equal parts.

Part One

TABULAR VIEW OF STYLISTIC TRENDS IN MUSIC: 1900-1948

Increasing Grandiosity of Musical Materials and Forms from the Turn of the Century to World War I

Musical pictorialism; impressionistic luxuriance of tone color. Auditory representation of visual arts. Landscape and travel music; pseudo-exoticism. Rapid spread of operatic naturalism and verism; cultivation of the short opera buffa, and concomitant decline of romantic grand opera and of Wagnerian music drama. The flowering of choreographic music of grandiose magnitude. Grafting of philosophical and mystical concepts onto musical forms.

Thinning-out of contrapuntal texture; gradual abandonment of polyphonic writing in favor of chordal harmony of great complexity. Legitimization of unresolved dissonances; increasing use of parallel formations of consonant or dissonant chordal units in static rows of block harmonies. Neo-archaism and revitalization of the old modes. Conscious regression to the pre-tertian harmony of fourths and fifths. Sophisticated appropriation of the pentatonic scale for the purposes of pseudo-exotic tone painting. The whole-tone scale, and its use to evoke an atmosphere of eeriness and mystery.

Stylization of primitive music in prime-numbers meters (5, 7, 11); asymmetric rhythms, percussive accentuation, and primitivistically crude instrumentation as an antinomial development to the super-refinement of the impressionistic palette.

DATE INDICATES FIRST PERFORMANCE

Impressionism	Neo-Romanticism	Operatic Naturalism	Luxuriant Nationalism
		La Tosca (melodramatic historicism) Puccini 14 January 1900	
		Louise (nostalgic Parisianism) Charpentier 2 February 1900	*Finlandia* (hymnal patriotism) Sibelius 2 July 1900
		Zaza (veristic Italianism) Leoncavallo 10 November 1900	*Tsar Saltan* (decorative Russianism) Rimsky-Korsakov 3 November 1900
		L'Ouragan (melodramatic verism) Bruneau 29 April 1901	
	Cockaigne Overture (stylized urbanism) Elgar 20 June 1901		
Nocturnes (evocative colorism) Debussy 27 October 1901	*Second Piano Concerto* (melancholy Russianism) Rachmaninov 27 October 1901		
	Fourth Symphony (introitive psychologism) Mahler 25 November 1901		

Pelléas et Mélisande
(dramatic symbolism)
Debussy
30 April 1902

Second Symphony
(post-classical romanticism)
Sibelius
8 March 1902

Le Jongleur de Notre Dame
(Parisian verism)
Massenet
18 February 1902

Kastchei the Immortal
(mythological Russianism)
Rimsky-Korsakov
25 December 1902

La Carmélite
(moralistic historicism)
Reynaldo Hahn
16 December 1902

The Apostles
(austere religionism)
Elgar
14 October 1903

Siberia
(Italianate pseudo-Russianism)
Giordano
19 December 1903

Jenufa
(operatic Bohemianism)
Janácek
21 January 1904

Estampes
(exotic imagism)
Debussy
9 January 1904

Sinfonia Domestica
(symphonic sentimentalism)
Strauss
21 March 1904

Madame Butterfly
(operatic pseudo-orientalism)
Puccini
17 February 1904

Shéhérazade
(pseudo-orientalism)
Ravel
17 May 1904

Valse Triste
(somber evocation)
Sibelius
25 April 1904

La Cabrera
(operatic pathetism)
Dupont
17 May 1904

Fifth Symphony
(impassionate megasymphonism)
Mahler
18 October 1904

Impressionism	Neo-Romanticism	Operatic Naturalism	Luxuriant Nationalism
	Piano Concerto (inflationary pianism) Busoni 10 November 1904		
	Divine Poem (mystical symphonism) Scriabin 29 May 1905		
La Mer (aquatic pictorialism) Debussy 15 October 1905	Violin Concerto (instrumental romanticism) Sibelius 19 October 1905	Salome (operatic eroticism) Strauss 9 December 1905	
Jour d'été à la Montagne (pastoral imagism) d'Indy 18 February 1906	Sixth Symphony (tragical Hamletism) Mahler 27 May 1906		
	Eighth Symphony (epic Russianism) Glazunov 21 December 1906		Pohjola's Daughter (evocative Suomianism) Sibelius 29 December 1906
			Tale of the Invisible City of Kitezh (operatic religionism) Rimsky-Korsakov 20 February 1907

Ariane et Barbe-Bleue
(uxoricidal psychologism)
Dukas
10 May 1907

Third Symphony
(introspective romanticism)
Sibelius
25 September 1907

Brigg Fair
(Anglican folklorism)
Delius
18 January 1908

Second Symphony
(somber psychologism)
Rachmaninov
8 February 1908

Rapsodie Espagnole
(stylized Hispanism)
Ravel
15 March 1908

First Symphony
(austere symphonism)
Roussel
22 March 1908

Seventh Symphony
(apocalyptic subjectivism)
Mahler
19 September 1908

Poem of Ecstasy
(symphonic solipsism)
Scriabin
10 December 1908

Elektra
(neo-mythological symbolism)
Strauss
25 January 1909

Island of the Dead
(symphonic necrophilism)
Rachmaninov
1 May 1909

Mass of Life
(vitalistic neo-ecclesiasticism)
Delius
7 June 1909

The Golden Cockerel
(phantasmal Russianism)
Rimsky-Korsakov
24 September 1909

Impressionism	Neo-Romanticism	Operatic Naturalism	Luxuriant Nationalism
	Third Piano Concerto (meditative pianism) Rachmaninov 28 November 1909		
Ibéria (Gallic Hispanism) Debussy 20 February 1910		*La Glu* (Parisian melodrama) Dupont 24 January 1910	
			Fire-Bird (coloristic folklorism) Stravinsky 25 June 1910
			Comedy Overture on Negro Themes (folkloric Afro-Americanism) Gilbert 17 August 1910
	Eighth Symphony (macrocosmic grandiosity) Mahler 12 September 1910		
Macbeth (operatic psychologism) Ernest Bloch 30 November 1910		*La Fanciulla del West* (pseudo-Americanism) Puccini 10 December 1910	
		Rosenkavalier (phantasmal realism) Strauss 26 January 1911	
	Prometheus (elemental neo-Luciferism) Scriabin 15 March 1911		
Daphnis et Chloé (sensuous neo-Hellenism) Ravel 2 April 1911	*Fourth Symphony* (extrospective colorism) Sibelius 3 April 1911		

Impressionism	Neo-Romanticism	Expressionism Futurism	Luxuriant Nationalism
Le Martyre de St. Sébastien (Parisian neo-ecclesiasticism) Debussy 22 May 1911	*Das Lied von der Erde* (pantheistic symphonism) Mahler 20 November 1911	*The Jewels of the Madonna* (melodramatic Italianism) Wolf-Ferrari 23 December 1911	*Petrouchka* (primitivistic Russianism) Stravinsky 13 June 1911
Mother Goose (sophisticated neo-infantilism) Ravel 21 January 1912			
La Péri (orientalistic exoticism) Dukas 22 April 1912	*Ninth Symphony* (neo-mystical grandiosity) Mahler 26 June 1912	*Five Orchestral Pieces* (subtilized harmonism) Schoenberg 3 September 1912	
Evocations (sublimated exoticism) Roussel 18 May 1912			
The Sea (aquamarine pictorialism) Bridge 24 September 1912			

Impressionism	Neo-Romanticism	Expressionism / Futurism	Luxuriant Nationalism
		Pierrot Lunaire (sublimated psychologism) Schoenberg 16 October 1912	
	Gurre-Lieder (coloristic vocalism) Schoenberg 23 February 1913		
		Six Orchestral Pieces (esoteric miniaturism) Webern 31 March 1913	
Le Festin de l'Araignée (animistic ballet) Roussel 3 April 1913			
			Le Sacre du Printemps (primitivistic Russianism) Stravinsky 29 May 1913
	On Hearing the First Cuckoo in Spring (avian vernalism) Delius 2 October 1913		
	London Symphony (extroitive urbanism) Vaughan Williams 27 March 1914		
		Networks of Noises (futuristic percussionism) Russolo 21 April 1914	
Le Rossignol (sinological exoticism) Stravinsky 26 May 1914			
	First Symphony (expansive subjectivism) Miaskovsky 2 June 1914		

PULVERIZATION OF GRANDIOSE FORMS AND THE WAVE OF RETRO-
GRESSIVE NEO-CLASSICISM FROM WORLD WAR I
TO THE EVE OF WORLD WAR II

Reaction against coloristic impressionism, pictorialism and mysticism in music. Flare-up of nihilistic futurism, Dadaism, and self-conscious musical infantilism. Rise of satire and grotesque as an antidote of musical romanticism. Search for negative beauty in the music of noises. Polyrhythmy and polymetry in dissonant counterpoint. Jazz as a source of neo-primitivistic inspiration.

Growth of political left-wing opera. Music for the masses, and self-styled proletarian music. Sophisticated use of folk songs as raw material of symphonic and operatic music. New luxuriance of entertainment music; formalistic utilitarianism and instrumental functionalism.

Expressionism. as a medium of exploring the musical microcosm. Atonality and its systemization in the twelve-tone technique. Fractional divisions of intervals: quarter-tones. Urbanistic music; glorification of the machine; abstract and scientific music.

Emergence of neo-classicism in the new guise of pandiatonicism. The refurbishing of classical forms of absolute music in the quest for new simplicity and classical lucidity.

Impressionism Neo-Romanticism	Neo-Classicism	Expressionism Machine-Music	Neo-Primitivism Grotesque & Jazz
Alpensinfonie (illustrative travel music) Strauss 9 February 1915			
Goyescas (pictorial Hispanism) Granados 28 January 1916			*Scythian Suite* (neo-pagan Russianism) Prokofiev 29 January 1916
Fountains of Rome (impressionistic Italianism) Respighi 11 March 1917			
Three Hebrew Poems (coloristic Hebraism) Bloch 23 March 1917	*Palestrina* (operatic historicism) Pfitzner 12 June 1917		*Parade* (nihilistic Parisianism) Satie 18 May 1917
	Classical Symphony (sophisticated stylization) Prokofiev 21 April 1918	*Die Gezeichneten* (operatic psychologism) Schreker 25 April 1918	*Histoire du Soldat* (phantasmal demonism) Stravinsky 28 September 1918

The Pleasure Dome
of Kubla Khan
(impressionistic pseudo-
orientalism)
Griffes
28 November 1919

Three-Cornered Hat
(folkloristic Hispanism)
Falla
22 June 1919

Le Boeuf Sur le Toit
(sophisticated Parisianism)
Milhaud
21 February 1920

Socrate
(Parisian neo-Grecianism)
Satie
14 February 1920

Pulcinella
(stylized Italianism)
Stravinsky
15 May 1920

The Planets
(astrological symphonism)
Holst
15 November 1920

L'Aviatore Dro
(operatic avio-futurism)
Pratella
4 September 1920

La Valse
(Gallic neo-Straussianism)
Ravel
12 December 1920

Chout
(choreographic Russianism)
Prokofiev
17 May 1921

Le Roi David
(neo-biblical dramatism)
Honegger
11 June 1921

Murder, Hope of Women
(operatic journalism)
Hindemith
4 June 1921

Pour Une Fête
de Printemps
(coloristic vernalism)
Roussel
29 October 1921

Krazy Kat
(journalistic grotesque)
Carpenter
23 December 1921

Love for Three Oranges
(operatic hedonism)
Prokofiev
30 December 1921

Impressionism Neo-Romanticism	Neo-Classicism	Expressionism Machine-Music	Neo-Primitivism Grotesque & Jazz
		Skating Rink (sublimated sportism) Honegger 20 January 1922	
Pastoral Symphony (contemplative folklorism) Vaughan Williams 26 January 1922			
			Sancta Susanna (miniature duodrama) Hindemith 26 March 1922
		Bluebeard's Castle (operatic uxoricidalism) Bartók 13 May 1922	
	Mavra (neo-archaic Russianism) Stravinsky 3 June 1922		
	Color Symphony (heraldic symbolism) Bliss 7 September 1922		
First Symphony (pessimistic subjectivism) Bax 4 December 1922			
Sixth Symphony (polyphonic objectivism) Sibelius 19 February 1923			
		Hyperprism (geometric symbolism) Varèse 4 March 1923	
Padmavati (operatic Hindustanism) Roussel 1 June 1923			
			Les Noces (orgiastic Russianism) Stravinsky 13 June 1923
		The Chinese Flute (sinological exoticism) Toch 24 June 1923	
	Fantasia Contrappuntistica (intervallic constructivism) Busoni 6 August 1923		
			Valses Bourgeoises (urbanist stylization) Lord Berners 5 August 1923

xl

Octet
(polyphonic stylization)
Stravinsky
18 October 1923

Psalmus Hungaricus
(jubilee oratorio)
Kodály
19 November 1923

La Création du Monde
(paleo-biological
pantomime)
Milhaud
25 October 1923

Les Biches
(choreographic neo-
Gallicism)
Poulenc
6 January 1924

Escales
(travel exoticism)
Ibert
6 January 1924

Rhapsody in Blue
(jazzified ceruleanism)
Gershwin
12 February 1924

Nordic Symphony
(romantic ancestralism)
Hanson
19 March 1924

Seventh Symphony
(post-classical Suomianism)
Sibelius
24 March 1924

Pacific 231
(romantic machinism)
Honegger
8 May 1924

Salade
(epicurean pantomime)
Milhaud
17 May 1924

Piano Concerto
(instrumental
neo-Bachianism)
Stravinsky
22 May 1924

They Are Seven
(Sumerian demonism)
Prokofiev
29 May 1924

Erwartung
(psychological monodrama)
Schoenberg
6 June 1924

Impressioni dal Vero
(vernal symphonism)
Malipiero
2 June 1924

Le Train Bleu
(hedonistic urbanism)
Milhaud
20 June 1924

Impressionism Neo-Romanticism	Neo-Classicism	Expressionism Machine-Music	Neo-Primitivism Grotesque & Jazz
Pines of Rome (coloristic Italianism) Respighi 14 December 1924		*Die Glueckliche Hand* (expressionist monodrama) Schoenberg 14 October 1924	
		Preludio a Cristóbal Colón (microtonal Pan-Americanism) Carrillo 15 February 1925	
	Concerto Grosso (functional instrumentalism) Bloch 1 June 1925	*Les Matelots* (urbanistic ballet) Auric 17 June 1925	
La Naissance de la Lyre (operatic Hellenism) Roussel 1 July 1925			
	Concerto Accademico (formalistic scholasticism) Vaughan Williams 6 November 1925		*Music for the Theatre* (sophisticated jazzification) Copland 28 November 1925
			Concerto in F (pianistic Americanism) Gershwin 3 December 1925
		Wozzeck (Freudianistic opera) Berg 14 December 1925	
			Skyscrapers (Americanistic stylization) Carpenter 19 February 1926

Pageant of P. T. Barnum
(Americanistic pictorialism)
Moore
15 April 1926

Façade
(urbanistic revue)
Walton
27 April 1926

Amériques
(technocratic
Americanism)
Varèse
9 April 1926

First Symphony
(hedonistic Russianism)
Shostakovitch
12 May 1926

Five Orchestral Pieces
(subtilized colorism)
Webern
23 June 1926

Háry János
(stylized Magyarism)
Kodály
16 October 1926

Creation
(stylized Afro-
Americanism)
Gruenberg
27 November 1926

Cardillac
(psychological opera)
Hindemith
9 November 1926

Tapiola
(Suomian evocation)
Sibelius
26 December 1926

Suite in F
(Gallic Bachianism)
Roussel
21 January 1927

Scarlattiana
(sophisticated neo-
Italianism)
Casella
22 January 1927

Jonny Spielt Auf
(operatic jazzification)
Krenek
11 February 1927

Lilacs
(coloristic evocation)
Hill
31 March 1927

Arcana
(Paracelsian symbolism)
Varèse
8 April 1927

Impressionism Neo-Romanticism	Neo-Classicism	Expressionism Machine-Music	Neo-Primitivism Grotesque & Jazz
Schwanda (operatic hedonism) Weinberger 27 April 1927	*Symphony in E minor* (scholastic constructivism) Sessions 22 April 1927	*Ballet Mécanique* (constructivist percussionism) Antheil 10 April 1927	*La Chatte* (felinophilic choreography) Sauguet 30 April 1927
	Oedipus Rex (medievalistic oratorio) Stravinsky 30 May 1927	*Flivver 10,000,000* (symphonic Fordism) Converse 15 April 1927	
		Pas d'Acier (mechanistic ballet) Prokofiev 7 June 1927	
October Symphony (revolutionary programmaticism) Shostakovitch 6 November 1927		*Mahagonny* (satirical Americanism) Weill 17 July 1927	*Hin und Zurueck* (operatic palindrome) Hindemith 17 July 1927
		Iron Foundry (mechanistic onomatopeia) Mossolov 4 December 1927	
Feste Romane (pictorial Romanism) Respighi 21 February 1929	*Apollon Musagète* (neo-Hellenistic choreosophy) Stravinsky 27 April 1928		*African Dances* (negroid equatorialism) Villa-Lobos 5 April 1928

Rebambaramba
(orgiastic Afro-Cubanism)
Roldan
12 August 1928

An American in Paris
(sophisticated
transatlanticism)
Gershwin
13 December 1928

Amazonas
(jungle pictorialism)
Villa-Lobos
30 May 1929

Rugby
(glorified sportism)
Honegger
19 October 1928

Machinist Hopkins
(mechanistic opera)
Brand
13 April 1929

Neues vom Tage
(operatic journalism)
Hindemith
8 June 1929

The First Airphonic Suite
(electronic
instrumentalism)
Schillinger
28 November 1929

*Accompaniment to a
Cinema Scene*
(dodecaphonic stylization)
Schoenberg
14 February 1930

The Rio Grande
(European jazzification)
Lambert
12 December 1929

The Nose
(rhinological burlesque)
Shostakovitch
13 January 1930

Bolero
(choreographic Hispanism)
Ravel
22 November 1928

America
(panoramic
continentalism)
Bloch
20 December 1928

Capriccio
(neo-classical
constructivism)
Stravinsky
6 December 1929

Second Symphony
(coloristic subjectivism)
Bax
13 December 1929

Third Symphony
(contemplative Nordicism)
Bax
14 March 1930

Impressionism Neo-Romanticism	Neo-Classicism	Expressionism Machine-Music	Neo-Primitivism Grotesque & Jazz
		Christopher Columbus (symbolic historicism) Milhaud 6 May 1930	*Transatlantic* (hemispheric opera) Antheil 25 May 1930
			The Golden Age (anti-Fascist choreography) Shostakovitch 27 October 1930
May First Symphony (revolutionary programmaticism) Shostakovitch 7 November 1930			
Romantic Symphony (constructivist emotionalism) Hanson 28 November 1930	*Symphony of Psalms* (neo-Handelian ecclesiasticism) Stravinsky 13 December 1930		
Peter Ibbetson (nostalgic melodramatism) Taylor 7 February 1931			
		Die Mutter (microtonal opera) Hába 17 May 1931	*Bolt* (anti-capitalist ballet) Shostakovitch 8 April 1931
	Wir Bauen Eine Stadt (scholastic utilitarianism) Hindemith 25 July 1931	*Synchrony* (scientific symphonism) Cowell 6 June 1931	

xlvi

Belshazzar's Feast
(neo-Babylonian oratorio)
Walton
10 October 1931

Violin Concerto
(instrumental
functionalism)
Stravinsky
23 October 1931

Yamba-O
(ritualistic Afro-Cubanism)
Caturla
25 October 1931

Rebus
(choreographic
constructivism)
Markevitch
15 December 1931

Ionisation
(atomistic percussionism)
Varèse
13 November 1931

Fourth Symphony
(externalized austerity)
Bax
16 March 1932

Second Symphony
(functional emotionalism)
Randall Thompson
24 March 1932

H.P.
(mechanistic choreography)
Chávez
31 March 1932

The Emperor Jones
(operatic Afro-
Americanism)
Gruenberg
7 January 1933

Mouvement Symphonique
(non-programmatic
motricity)
Honegger
27 March 1933

Arctic Symphony
(geographic Russianism)
Vassilenko
5 April 1933

Fifth Symphony
(Sibelian pantheism)
Bax
15 January 1934

Symphony 1933
(proclamatory
Americanism)
Harris
26 January 1934

Four Saints in Three Acts
(sophisticated
paradoxicalism)
Virgil Thomson
8 February 1934

Lady Macbeth of the
Mzensk District
(melodramatic
psychologism)
Shostakovich
22 January 1934

Merry Mount
(American folklorism)
Hanson
10 February 1934

Impressionism / Neo-Romanticism	Neo-Classicism	Expressionism / Machine-Music	Neo-Primitivism / Grotesque & Jazz
	Mathis der Maler (Germanic neo-ecclesiasticism) Hindemith 12 March 1934		
	Persephone (Hellenistic choreosophy) Stravinsky 30 April 1934	*Union Pacific* (machinistic Americanism) Nabokov 6 April 1934	
		Maschinenmensch (robot symphonism) Zador 9 June 1934	*Lieutenant Kije* (satirical stylization) Prokofiev 8 July 1934
			Sinfonia Proletaria (revolutionary programmaticism) Chávez 29 September 1934
Iceland (Arctic pictorialism) Leifs 23 January 1935	*Concerto for Two Pianos* (formalistic neo-academism) Stravinsky 1 September 1935	*Dialectic* (leftist polyphony) Bush 2 September 1935	*Porgy and Bess* (operatic Americanism) Gershwin 30 September 1935
Fourth Symphony (Gallic neo-romanticism) Roussel 19 October 1935			

Impressionism Neo-Romanticism	Neo-Classicism	Expressionism Machine Music	Sophisticated Folk Music and Political Music
			Quiet Flows the Don (operatic Sovietism) Dzerzhinsky 22 October 1935
Fifteenth Symphony (extroitive lyricism) Miaskovsky 28 October 1935			
			The Limpid Stream (collectivistic ballet) Shostakovitch 30 November 1935
	Second Symphony (assertive Americanism) Harris 28 February 1936		
		Violin Concerto (dodecaphonic lyricism) Berg 19 April 1936	
			Czar Kalojan (Bulgarian opera) Vladigerov 20 April 1936
			Peter and the Wolf (symphonic fairy tale) Prokofiev 2 May 1936
	Partita (polyphonic Germanism) David 22 October 1936		
Third Symphony (nostalgic Russianism) Rachmaninov 6 November 1936			
			Pinocchio Overture (stylized infantilism) Toch 10 December 1936

Impressionism Neo-Romanticism	Neo-Classicism	Expressionism Machine-Music	Sophisticated Folk Music and Political Music
Second Symphony (elegiac evocation) Malipiero 25 January 1937			
L'Aiglon (operatic Napoleonism) Honegger & Ibert 10 March 1937			
	Amelia Goes to the Ball (operatic neo-Rossinism) Menotti 1 April 1937		
			The Second Hurricane (junior melodramatism) Copland 21 April 1937
	The Card Party (aleatory symbolism) Stravinsky 27 April 1937		
			Il Deserto Tentato (imperialist opera) Casella 8 May 1937
Te Deum (romantic neo-ecclesiasticism) Vaughan Williams 12 May 1937			
		Lulu (Freudianistic psychologism) Berg 2 June 1937	
		Checkmate (chessboard choreosophy) Bliss 15 June 1937	
			The Cradle Will Rock (operatic leftism) Blitzstein 16 June 1937
	Concertino (neo-classical constructivism) Piston 20 June 1937		
			Dreadnaught Potemkin (operatic revolutionarism) Tchishko 21 June 1937
Piano Concerto (rhapsodic instrumentalism) Khatchaturian 5 July 1937			
		Mekhano (robot ballet) Castro 17 July 1937	

1

Anti-Fascist Symphony
(political Sovietism)
Mokrousov
1 August 1937

El Salón México
(folkloric Mexicanism)
Copland
27 August 1937

Filling Station
(stylized motorism)
Virgil Thomson
6 January 1938

The Incredible Flutist
(stylized hedonism)
Piston
30 May 1938

A Poem About Stalin
(symphonic Sovietism)
Khatchaturian
29 November 1938

Time Suite
(metronomic experimentalism)
Harris
8 August 1937

Soil Upturned
(operatic Sovietism)
Dzerzhinsky
23 October 1937

Horoscope
(astrological choreosophy)
Lambert
27 January 1938

Second Piano Concerto
(dodecaphonic pianism)
Krenek
17 March 1938

Charles V
(dodecaphonic operatism)
Krenek
22 June 1938

Dumbarton Oaks Concerto
(neo-archaic instrumentalism)
Stravinsky
8 May 1938

Jeanne d'Arc au Bûcher
(epic oratorio)
Honegger
10 May 1938

Third Symphony
(polyphonic Americanism)
Harris
24 February 1939

Eighteenth Symphony
(lyrical Russianism)
Miaskovsky
1 October 1937

Fifth Symphony
(neo-Beethovenian Russianism)
Shostakovitch
21 November 1937

Peer Gynt
(operatic Nordicism)
Egk
24 November 1938

Impressionism Neo-Romanticism	Neo-Classicism	Expressionism Machine Music	Sophisticated Folk Music and Political Music
	The Old Maid and the Thief (operatic neo-Rossinism) Menotti 22 April 1939	*Violin Concerto* (expressionistic instrumentalism) Bartók 23 April 1939	*Ballad of Heroes* (militant democratism) Britten 5 April 1939
			Alexander Nevsky (historical Russianism) Prokofiev 17 May 1939
			The Devil and Daniel Webster (operatic Americanism) Moore 18 May 1939
			Billy the Kid (choreographic Americanism) Copland 24 May 1939
Seventh Symphony (symphonic lyrico-dramatism) Bax 9 June 1939			

ESTHETIC DISEQUILIBRIUM AND SEARCH FOR NEW STYLE FROM WORLD WAR II TO PRESENT TIME

Collapse of coordinated cosmopolitanism in world music. New esthetic isolationism. Lingering fires of neo-romanticism in national forms; neo-classicism of emphatic tonality in a pandiatonic technique, with occasional use of mild polytonalities. Sporadic survivals of atonality, and the adoption of a liberalized twelve-tone technique as a functional idiom of applied music. Upsurge of nationalistic music in the new form of sophisticated folk opera, and symphonic poems with narrated texts.

Quickened cultivation of the psychological opera and symbolic ballet. Choral music of political and national content. Symphonic and theatrical music on war themes. Neo-ecclesiasticism in the form of a religious oratorio. Practice of fugal counterpoint in a moderately dissonant style. Renascence of triad harmony in free concatenation of keys. Anticipations of a neo-romantic idiom as the esthetic resultant of divergent trends in mid-twentieth century music.

Neo-Romanticism	Neo-Classicism and Neo-Utilitarianism	Political and War Music	Sophisticated Folk Music
			American Festival Overture (metropolitan Americanism) Schuman 6 October 1939
		On the Field of Kulikov (oratorical Russianism) Shaporin 18 November 1939	
Peacock Variations (coloristic Magyarism) Kodály 23 November 1939			
		Emelian Pugatchov (historic Russianism) Koval 25 November 1939	
Sixth Symphony (non-programmatic Russianism) Shostakovitch 3 December 1939			
	Violin Concerto (constructivist instrumentalism) Hindemith 14 March 1940		
			Folk Song Symphony (Americanistic stylization) Harris 25 April 1940
			Xochipili-Macuilxochitl (mechanistic Mexicanism) Chávez 16 May 1940
		Simeon Kotko (operatic Sovietism) Prokofiev 23 June 1940	
Twenty-first Symphony (lyrical Russianism) Miaskovsky 16 November 1940			

Violin Concerto
(twelve-tone instrumentalism)
Schoenberg
6 December 1940

No For An Answer
(operatic leftism)
Blitzstein
5 January 1941

The Virgin of Sparta
(operatic Hellenism)
Kalomiris
12 January 1941

Dansa Brasileira
(tropical polyrhythmy)
Guarnieri
7 March 1941

Fantaisie Portugaise
(rhapsodic Iberianism)
Ernesto Halffter
23 March 1941

Tales of the Countryside
(modernistic folklorism)
Cowell
11 May 1941

Concierto Argentino
(South American
constructivism)
Ginastera
18 July 1941

Malazarte
(operatic Brazilianism)
Fernandez
30 September 1941

Czech Rhapsody
(patriotic folklorism)
Weinberger
5 November 1941

Symphony in E flat
(constructivistic
objectivism)
Hindemith
21 November 1941

Scottish Ballad
(Hebridean evocation)
Britten
28 November 1941

First Symphony
(neo-romantic infra-
modernism)
Diamond
21 December 1941

The Blood of the People
(operatic Russianism)
Dzerzhinsky
21 January 1942

Neo-Romanticism	Neo-Classicism and Neo-Utilitarianism	Political and War Music	Sophisticated Folk Music
Ramuntcho (operatic neo-romanticism) Taylor 10 February 1942	*Fourth Symphony* (constructivist lyricism) Schuman 22 January 1942		
The Island God (operatic symbolism) Menotti 20 February 1942		*Seventh Symphony* (patriotic Sovietism) Shostakovich 1 March 1942	*Strawberry Jam* (symphonic jazzification) McBride 16 March 1942
	Solomon and Balkis (operatic functionalism) Randall Thompson 29 March 1942		*A Lincoln Portrait* (symphonic Americanism) Copland 14 May 1942
Second Symphony (polyphonic constructivism) Honegger 18 May 1942		*Bataan* (patriotic illustrativeness) McDonald 3 July 1942	*Chóros No. 11* (grandiose Brazilianism) Villa-Lobos 18 July 1942
	Newsreel (cinematic stylization) Schuman 14 July 1942	*Fanfare for Airmen* (valedictory aviationism) Wagenaar 9 October 1942	*Rodeo* (stylized Americanism) Copland 16 October 1942
Fourth Symphony (polyphonic neo-classicism) Rubbra 14 August 1942		*Fanfare for Paratroopers* (polyharmonic aerialism) Creston 27 November 1942	*Gayane* (hedonistic Sovietism) Khatchaturian 9 December 1942
Cantata de los Rios de Chile (evocative Chileanism) Santa Cruz 27 November 1942			

1941 Suite
(anti-Fascist battalianism)
Prokofiev
21 January 1943

Fifth Symphony
(patriotic
    internationalism)
Harris
26 February 1943

The Testament of Freedom
(oratorical Jeffersonianism)
Randall Thompson
13 April 1943

Dunkirk
(evocative dramatism)
Damrosch
12 May 1943

The Four Freedoms
(symphonic
    Rooseveltianism)
Bennett
26 September 1943

The Prairie
(Americanistic evocation)
Foss
15 October 1943

Invasion
(premonitive historicism)
Rogers
17 October 1943

Fourth Symphony
(stylistic cosmopolitanism)
Berezowsky
22 October 1943

Memorial to Lidice
(commemorative
    patriotism)
Martinů
28 October 1943

Neo-Romanticism	Neo-Classicism and Neo-Utilitarianism	Political and War Music	Sophisticated Folk Music
Eighth Symphony (philosophic Russianism) Shostakovitch 4 November 1943		*Commando March* (militant functionalism) Barber 29 October 1943	
Second Symphony (somber Americanism) Gardner Read 26 November 1943			
Fourth Symphony (commemorative Nordicism) Hanson 3 December 1943		*March in Time of War* (stylized martialism) Harris 30 December 1943	
Jeremiah Symphony (biblical Hebraism) Bernstein 28 January 1944	*Piano Concerto* (twelve-tone instrumentalism) Schoenberg 6 February 1944		*Four Norwegian Moods* (Nordic stylization) Stravinsky 14 January 1944
	Ludus Tonalis (neo-medieval functionalism) Hindemith 15 February 1944		

Second Symphony
(American classicism)
Piston
5 March 1944

Second Symphony
(aviational symbolism)
Barber
3 March 1944

A Child of Our Time
(anti-Fascist symbolism)
Tippet
19 March 1944

Ballad of a Boy Who Remained Unknown
(assertive patriotism)
Prokofiev
21 March 1944

A Tale of the Battle for the Russian Land
(impassionate Russianism)
Shaporin
18 April 1944

Sixth Symphony
(Lincolnian symbolism)
Harris
14 April 1944

Theme and Variations according to the Four Temperaments
(neo-medieval symbolism)
Hindemith
3 September 1944

Second Symphony
(cosmopolitan lyricism)
Diamond
13 October 1944

Theme and Variations for Orchestra
(tonal functionalism)
Schoenberg
20 October 1944

Fugue on a Victory Tune
(jubilatory motricity)
Piston
21 October 1944

Chant de Libération
(jubilatory vocalism)
Honegger
22 October 1944

Letter from Home
(nostalgic domesticism)
Copland
17 October 1944

Appalachian Spring
(lyrico-dramatic Americanism)
Copland
30 October 1944

Neo-Romanticism	Neo-Classicism & Neo-Utilitarianism	Political & War Music	Sophisticated Folk Music
	Portraits (quasi-photographic psychologism) Virgil Thomson 17 November 1944	*Ode to Napoleon* (twelve-tonal anti-totalitarianism) Schoenberg 23 November 1944	*Symphony on a Hymn Tune* (Americanistic neo-ecclesiasticism) Virgil Thomson 22 February 1945
Fifth Symphony (lyric Russianism) Prokofiev 13 January 1945	*Concerto for Orchestra* (dramatic instrumentalism) Bartók 1 December 1944	*Toast to Stalin* (salutatory Sovietism) Prokofiev 21 December 1944	*Chóros No. 12* (luxuriant Brazilianism) Villa-Lobos 23 February 1945
		Thanksgiving for Victory (jubilatory gratulation) Vaughan Williams 8 May 1945	
	Peter Grimes (operatic psychologism) Britten 7 June 1945	*Victory Overture* (patriotic laetification) Glière 30 October 1945	
Ninth Symphony (hedonistic Russianism) Shostakovitch 3 November 1945		*Ode to the End of War* (martial valediction) Prokofiev 10 November 1945	*Le Bal Martiniquais* (Caribbean stylization) Milhaud 6 December 1945

Metamorphoses
(commemorative Germanism)
Strauss
25 January 1946

Symphony in Three Movements
(stylized eclecticism)
Stravinsky
24 January 1946

Danzón Cubano
(stylized Cubanism)
Copland
17 February 1946

Second Symphony
(thematic cosmopolitanism)
Moore
5 May 1946

The Medium
(spiritualistic theatricalism)
Menotti
8 May 1946

Airborne
(epical aviationalism)
Blitzstein
23 March 1946

Ebony Concerto
(stylized jazzification)
Stravinsky
25 March 1946

The Rape of Lucretia
(expressionistic psychologism)
Britten
12 July 1946

Songs from Captivity
(nostalgic lamentation)
Dallapiccola
8 July 1946

Symphonie Liturgique
(neo-ecclesiasticism)
Honegger
17 August 1946

Corroboree
(Australian neo-primitivism)
Antill
18 August 1946

Third Symphony
(lyrico-dramatic instrumentalism)
Copland
18 October 1946

Musique de Table
(gastronomic imagism)
Rosenthal
10 October 1946

Second Symphony
(psychological pictorialism)
Milhaud
20 December 1946

Ricercari
(constructivist neo-Italianism)
Dello Joio
19 December 1946

Moscow
(patriotic Muscovitism)
Shebalin
14 December 1946

Second Symphony
(polyphonic constructivism)
Sessions
9 January 1947

Neo-Romanticism	Neo-Classicism & Neo-Utilitarianism	Political & War Music	Sophisticated Folk Music
Symphonia Serena (rhapsodic polythematism) Hindemith 2 February 1947	*The Telephone* (hedonistic duodrama) Menotti 18 February 1947		
Hymne pour grand Orchestre (proclamatory neo-medievalism) Messiaen 13 March 1947	*Trial of Lucullus* (historistic symbolism) Sessions 18 April 1947		*The Mother of Us All* (Americanistic imagism) Virgil Thomson 7 May 1947
Danton's Death (operatic historicism) Einem 6 August 1947	*Les Mamelles de Tirésias* (existentialist theatricalism) Poulenc 10 June 1947		
	Fourth Symphony (philosophic atonalism) Krenek 27 November 1947		
Fourth Symphony (elegiac colorism) Malipiero 27 February 1948	*Third Symphony* (instrumental rationalism) Piston 9 January 1948		*Symphonie expiatoire* (neo-ecclesiastic programmaticism) Sauguet 8 February 1948

Sixth Symphony
(austere emotionalism)
Vaughan Williams
21 April 1948

Orpheus
(choreosophic Hellenism)
Stravinsky
28 April 1948

Third Symphony
(twelve-tonal
    functionalism)
Riegger
16 May 1948

Down in the Valley
(Americanistic folklorism)
Weill
15 July 1948

Magdalena
(theatrical tropicalism)
Villa-Lobos
26 July 1948

A Survivor of Warsaw
(apocalyptic ultra-realism)
Schoenberg
4 November 1948

Part Two

DESCRIPTIVE CHRONOLOGY
1900-1948

1900

1 JANUARY 1900

The first volume of the complete edition of the works of Hector
BERLIOZ, precursor of modern developments in music, is issued by
Breitkopf and Haertel, under the joint editorship of Felix WEIN-
GARTNER and Charles MALHERBE, archivist of the Paris Opéra.

6 JANUARY 1900

Pierre Octave FERROUD, French composer of neo-romantic, often
programmatic, music, in an advanced tonal idiom, with an ener-
gizing rhythmic sense, is born at Lyons.

14 JANUARY 1900

La Tosca, Sardou's Napoleonic melodrama, music by Giacomo
PUCCINI, written in the most effective manner of Italian verismo,
with harmonic innovations in the orchestra, such as use of consecutive triads, whole-tone scales, etc., is performed for the first
time at the Constanzi Theatre in Rome.

"Last evening at the Constanzi Theatre the first performance of Puccini's new opera was given before an immense audience, the largest
that ever filled that theatre. Early in the evening the crowd began to
assemble. Every seat and every ticket had been sold for days previous,
so that when the curtain rose, the house was packed from top to bottom
to its fullest capacity, even standing room being at a premium. The
boxes were filled with a dazzling array of richly dressed women, while
celebrities of all kinds—the court, diplomats, artists, literary men, critics, clerics, army and navy men, musicians—were seen on every side.
Never has such interest been shown in any first representation as upon
this occasion. . . . After the close of the first act the composer was called
out eight times in response to the demands of the audience." (*Musical
Courier,* February 1900)

"The great musical event of the New Year in Rome is over, and Giacomo Puccini, the young composer, has launched a new opera. . . . The
general opinion seems to be that the story is somewhat too dramatic
for an opera, that the music is lost in the general interest of the development of the plot. However, difficult as the situations are from a

3

musical standpoint, the 'maestro' has handled them in a masterly manner." *(Pall Mall Gazette,* London)

"Signor Puccini's *La Tosca* originally produced at the Constanzi Theatre, Rome, on 14 January 1900 is a typical example of the proclivity of Italian composers to seek inspiration in the crudest forms of elemental passion, and of their apparent inability to perceive that ignoble sentiment is a fatal bar to the creation of noble music. In *La Tosca* another degradation has certainly been put on Music by seeking to make it express physical torture. Although the music consists of little more than growls and screams from the orchestra and declamatory passages of little meaning from the soloists, the gruesomeness of this portion of the play is invested with peculiar objectionableness by force of contrast." (A London paper, 1900)

27 JANUARY 1900

After forty-nine and a half years of existence, the old Bachgesellschaft (founded on the hundredth anniversary of Bach's death, 28 July 1850) declares its task completed with the publication of the concluding volume, and a new Bach Society (Neue Bachgesellschaft) is formed with Hermann Kretzschmar, president, Gustav Schreck, secretary, Breitkopf and Haertel, treasurers.

31 JANUARY 1900

RIMSKY-KORSAKOV completes the composition of his opera, *Tsar Saltan.*

"Today I finished the score and transcription of the *Saltan.* At last! I am glad it is over, I feel so tired. All that is left is to correct a few things and put in a few instruments here and there." (From a letter to his son, Andrey, dated 18 January 1900, old style, that is 30 January 1900, new style, published in the 1935 Russian edition of *My Musical Life;* the manuscript, however, has the date of 19 January 1900, old style, that is 31 January 1900, new style. It must be observed that all Russian dates before 12 March 1900, new style, are twelve days behind the Western calendar, and after that date thirteen days behind. The year 1900 was not a leap year in the Western World, but it was a leap year in Russia. Thus, February had in 1900 twenty-nine days in Russia, and twenty-eight in the Western World. The increase of difference between the two calendars occurred when Russia counted that extra day. It is important to remember this in adjusting the dates of the Russian calendar. The new style was adopted in Russia on 1 February 1918, which was reckoned as 14 February)

2 FEBRUARY 1900

Louise, "musical romance" in four acts and five scenes by Gustave CHARPENTIER, the first and most significant opera of the
French "verism," entirely realistic in its theme and stage action,
is produced at the Opéra-Comique in Paris.

"It was Gustave Charpentier who in an article which appeared in the
Journal on 23 February 1896 wrote: 'I alone can judge the necessary
range for my work, and for me the universe is contained within the
town district where I live!' It is this maxim that guided the composition
of *Louise,* the first stage work of the young composer. Intoxicated with
the multitudinous voices of a large city, particularly with the street
noises, he has built a great symphony, in which the orchestra gathers
and proclaims all the cries that are daily launched by poor little street
vendors. 'Artichokes, big artichokes. Take the carrots, the best carrots.
. . . Give yourself a treat, madame. . . .' These are the leading themes
of his work. No one could make a better orchestral dish of all these
cries than the one who was early impassioned for an expression of
popular life. . . . Upon this orchestral framework is projected, on the
stage, a vocal recitative which expresses the dialogue with a singular
art." (H. Imbert in *Le Guide Musical,* Paris, 11 February 1900)

"Now is the moment to speak of a French work, the most significant of
the year 1900, a work of consummate art, penetrating intelligence,
vigorous originality. *Louise* by Victor [sic!] Charpentier. . . . Not only
did he find a way to please; he found it by means so bold that, before
the work proved a success, his daring was regarded with a frown.
Louise is an example of a new art, or at least, an art that is entirely
aware of its essentials. . . ." (Lionel Dauriac in *Zeitschrift der Interna-
tionalen Musikgesellschaft,* January 1901)

7 FEBRUARY 1900

Lancelot, lyric drama by Victorin DE JONCIÈRES, to the story of
King Arthur's time, with conventional music in Gounod's style
but without his melodic genius, is produced at the Opéra in
Paris.

2 MARCH 1900

Kurt WEILL, German composer of functional stage music, topical
in theme and neo-classical in treatment, ranging from twentieth-
century cantatas (*Lindbergh's Flight*) to satirical skits (*City of*

Mahagonny) and practical *Gebrauchsmusik* (radio and cinema music), is born in Dessau.

6 MARCH 1900

Carl BECHSTEIN, German founder of the Bechstein firm, manufacturing pianos of easy action and mellifluous tone, dies in Berlin, in his seventy-fourth year.

10 MARCH 1900

Johann HARTMANN, Danish romantic composer, dies in his native Copenhagen, at the patriarchal age of ninety-four years, nine months, and twenty-five days.

18 MARCH 1900

RIMSKY-KORSAKOV conducts a concert of Russian music in Brussels.

22 MARCH 1900

Hiawatha's Departure, third part of a trilogy by Samuel COLERIDGE-TAYLOR, British mulatto composer, is performed for the first time in London.

29 MARCH 1900

Fritz SCHEEL conducts at the Academy of Music in Philadelphia an orchestral concert "for the Relief of the Families of the Nation's Heroes Killed in the Philippines," which leads to the establishment of the Philadelphia Symphony Orchestra.

15 APRIL 1900

The 1900 Exposition Universelle opens in Paris, and presents, among other attractions, a theater featuring dancers and musicians of Cambodia, Annam, Java, Japan, and China, bringing exotic scales, translatable into Western music as pentatonic, and new rhythms, which were strongly to influence the entire course of modern French music.

15 MAY 1900

The Paderewski Fund of $10,000 is established in New York

with a view to encouraging American composers by the award
of annual prizes for the best orchestral works.

17 MAY 1900

Nicolai BEREZOWSKY, Russian-American composer of cosmopoli-
tan tendencies, ranging from neo-classicism (*Violin Concerto*) to
Gallic impressionism (*Wood-Wind Quintet*) and Borodinesque
Russian grandeur (*First Symphony*), is born in St. Petersburg.

28 MAY 1900

Sir George GROVE, English writer on music, first editor of the
dictionary bearing his name, dies in his native London two and
a half months before reaching eighty years of age.

17 JUNE 1900

Hermann REUTTER, German composer of neo-romantic music
with national folklore as melodic foundation, is born at Stuttgart.

1 JULY 1900

Breitkopf and Haertel issue the first volume of the *Denkmaeler
der Tonkunst in Bayern,* under the editorship of Adolf SAND-
BERGER, containing selected works of Evaristo Felice Dall'Abaco
(1675–1742). (Date of the preface)

2 JULY 1900

SIBELIUS' tone-poem, *Finlandia,* is performed for the first time in
Helsingfors, Robert Kajanus conducting.

"It was later that *Finlandia* was performed under its final title. At the
festival concert of the Helsingfors Philharmonic Orchestra before leaving for Paris, it was called *Suomi.* It was introduced by the same name
in Scandinavia; in German towns it was called *Vaterland;* and in Paris,
La Patrie. In Finland its performance was forbidden during the years
of unrest." (Karl Ekman, *Sibelius,* 1935)

2 JULY 1900

The Académie des Beaux-Arts in Paris awards the first Prix de
Rome to Florent SCHMITT for his "scène lyrique" *Semiramis,*

the score bearing a dedication "à mes chers Maîtres Massenet et Fauré—Hommages d'affectueuse reconnaissance."

"I had to compete five times for the *Prix de Rome* to get it. If I did not remain out in the cold, it was thanks to Gabriel Fauré who succeeded in winning enough votes among sculptors and painters to offset the animosity of musicians. For the latter, except Massenet, Reyer, and Saint-Saëns, had their thumbs down on me. But the important thing was the thirty thousand gold francs plus the trip and the lodging in the city of Mussolini." (Florent Schmitt in *Cinquante ans de musique française,* Paris, 1926)

8 JULY 1900

George ANTHEIL, American composer of music of the mechanized age, expressive of the modern world and modern man, is born at Trenton, New Jersey.

(Ezra Pound in his singular volume, *Antheil and the Treatise on Harmony,* Paris, 1924, which is neither a treatise on harmony nor an essay on Antheil, gives the wrong year, 1901. The Dutch *Muzieklexicon* gives the correct year but changes it to the wrong year, 1901, in the Addenda)

30 JULY 1900

The Helsingfors Philharmonic Orchestra gives its first Paris concert (presented in connection with the 1900 Exposition), with a program of orchestral works by Sibelius, Jaernefelt, and Kajanus.

10 AUGUST 1900

Alexandre MOSSOLOV, Russian Soviet composer of music glorifying the machine (*Steel Foundry*) and urban culture (*Advertisements*) in effectively discordant style, is born in Kiev.

23 AUGUST 1900

Ernst KŘENEK, composer of Czech extraction, who more than any contemporary reflects the three principal tendencies of modern music—absolute (*Atonal Symphony*), urban (the jazz opera, *Jonny Spielt Auf*), and satiric (*Der Diktator*)—is born in Vienna.

25 AUGUST 1900

Friedrich NIETZSCHE, whose scant music production lacks the virility that his philosophy glorifies, dies at Weimar, a victim of dementia praecox, in his fifty-sixth year.

12 SEPTEMBER 1900

The first monument to Stephen FOSTER is unveiled at Pittsburgh, with Victor HERBERT conducting the musical program.

1 OCTOBER 1900

Symphony in E Major, by Josef SUK, Czech continuator of the tradition established by his father-in-law, Antonin Dvořák, is performed for the first time in Prague.

3 OCTOBER 1900

The Dream of Gerontius, oratorio for soloists, chorus, and orchestra, expressly composed by Edward ELGAR for the Birmingham Festival—the score having been completed on 7 June preceding, five days after his forty-third birthday (according to Basil Maine, *Elgar: His Life and Work,* London, 1933)—is performed there for the first time, Hans RICHTER conducting.

"What every connoisseur of orchestration must have said at the first hearing (among other things) was, 'What a devil of a fortissimo.' Here was no literary paper instrumentation, no muddle, and noise, but an absolutely new energy given to the band by a consummate knowledge of what it could do and how it could do it." (G. B. Shaw, *Music and Literature,* 1920)

15 OCTOBER 1900

Symphony Hall is formally opened in Boston, and Major Higginson, founder of the Boston Symphony Orchestra, writes to the architect, Wallace Sabine: ". . . you have proved here that the Science of Acoustics certainly exists in a definite form. . . ."

15 OCTOBER 1900

Zdenek FIBICH, Czech composer of 376 works, including a trilogy of music dramas and a number of highly playable violin concert pieces, in a vaguely Tchaikovskian mood, dies at Prague, two months and six days before his fiftieth birthday.

(Grove gives the erroneous date, 10 October 1900)

2 NOVEMBER 1900

Vincent D'INDY reads his Inauguration Speech as new President of the Schola Cantorum in Paris.

"Where shall we find the quickening life that will give us fresh forms and formulas? The source is difficult to discover. Do not let us seek it anywhere but in the decorative art of the plain-song singers, in the architectural art of the age of Palestrina, and in the expressive art of the great Italians of the seventeenth century. It is there, and there alone, that we shall find melodic craft, rhythmic cadences, and a harmonic magnificence that is really new—if our modern spirit can only learn how to absorb their nutritious essence. And so I prescribe for all pupils in the School the careful study of classic forms, because they alone are able to give the elements of a new life to our music, which will be founded on principles that are sane, serious, and trustworthy." (Quoted from *Tribune de Saint-Gervais*, November 1900, by Romain Rolland in his *Musiciens d'aujourd'hui*)

3 NOVEMBER 1900

RIMSKY-KORSAKOV's opera from Pushkin's book, *Tsar Saltan,* belonging to the composer's "second period" (between the "Balakirev period" of apprenticeship and the "twentieth-century period" of advanced harmonies foreshadowing Stravinsky), is produced in Moscow. (Yastrebtzev, *Rimsky-Korsakov,* Moscow, 1908)

3 NOVEMBER 1900

Semiramis, the Prix de Rome composition of Florent SCHMITT, is performed for the first time in Paris.

10 NOVEMBER 1900

Zaza, four-act lyric comedy from theatrical life, words and music by Ruggiero LEONCAVALLO, is produced at the Teatro Lirico Internazionale in Milan, TOSCANINI conducting.

11 NOVEMBER 1900

SCRIABIN's *First Symphony* is performed for the first time, minus the sixth choral movement, at the Russian Symphony concerts in Moscow, Liadov conducting.

14 NOVEMBER 1900

Aaron COPLAND, American composer of strongly national music (often with jazz rhythms), within the formal design of symphony, suite (*Music for the Theatre*, 1923), concerto (*Piano Concerto,* 1924), or symphonic poem (*Symphonic Ode,* 1933), is born in Brooklyn.

16 NOVEMBER 1900

The Philadelphia Symphony Orchestra gives its first concert, under the direction of Fritz SCHEEL, with Ossip GABRILOVITCH (on his first American tour) as soloist.

19 NOVEMBER 1900

The *First Symphony* of SCRIABIN, E major, op. 26, in six movements, the last being a "Hymn to Art" with solo voices and chorus, is published in the Belaiev edition.

22 NOVEMBER 1900

Arthur SULLIVAN, English composer of Victorian comic operas to Sir William Gilbert's quasi-Shakespearean librettos, author of the celebrated ballade *The Lost Chord* and the hymn *Onward, Christian Soldiers,* dies in London after a brief illness.

"The death of Sir Arthur Sullivan in his fifty-ninth year may be said without hyperbole to have plunged the whole of the Empire in gloom; for many years he has ranked with the most distinguished personages rather than with ordinary musicians. Never in the history of the art has a position such as his been held by a composer. For all the English-speaking races, with the exception of a very small and, possibly unimportant class, Sullivan's name stood as a synonym for music in England." (London *Times,* 23 November 1900)

22 NOVEMBER 1900

Edward ELGAR is awarded the honorary degree of Doctor in Music by the University of Cambridge, England.

27 NOVEMBER 1900

Antonin DVOŘÁK completes the composition of his opera, *Russalka* (The Mermaid), begun on 19 May 1900.

9 DECEMBER 1900

The first two numbers of DEBUSSY's suite *Nocturnes: Nuages,* impressionist tone-poem of only 102 bars, opening in Moussorgskyan fifths and diaphanously scored for divided strings and paired wood-winds, and *Fêtes,* animated movement in ternary form, with a coda in vanishing diminuendo, until nothing but percussive rhythm remains of the festal sound—are performed for the first time at the Lamoureux concerts in Paris.

1901

4 JANUARY 1901

Vassily SHIRINSKY, Russian Soviet composer of neo-Scriabinesque music in all forms, is born at Ekaterinodar.

10 JANUARY 1901

Gian Luca TOCCHI, Italian composer of constructivist music, including music for the films, is born at Perugia.

"A pupil of Ottorino Respighi, Gian Luca Tocchi from the very start evinced a flair for the form of a symphonic poem, indued with strong literary suggestions. But soon finding a better and clearer path, he absorbed the spirit of popular rustic song, directly stemming from the popular musical imagination of the Italian people, in the music of the Tuscan country, rustic, amorous and gay. Thus he succeeded in writing a number of most subtle and savory songs in a popular vein. Between times, Tocchi has tried to recreate, through the medium of sonorities the mechanical miracles of our age. He has also tried successfully to apply music to the art of the cinema." (From an appreciation sent to the author by Gianandrea Gavazzeni of Milan)

11 JANUARY 1901

Vassili KALINNIKOV, Russian composer of melodious national music approaching, in a diluted form, the grandeur of Borodin's, dies at Yalta, Crimea, two days before his thirty-fifth birthday.

17 JANUARY 1901

Il Maschere, "lyric and gay comedy," by Pietro MASCAGNI is performed simultaneously in seven Italian cities: Milan, Venice, Verona, Naples, Turin, Genoa, and Rome.

"The general opinion is that *Il Maschere* is a fiasco. No originality, no progress, no ideas, great many reminiscences. So clear were they that the public shouted 'Ah! Puccini! Viva Puccini!!!' Mascagni and the artists had one call before the curtain, but when his friends tried to get him before the curtain a second time, hisses and shouting and a few whistles prevented his coming before the public again. . . . At Naples the tenor refused to sing the part. . . . At Genoa the public has declared they would abandon the theatre if the opera was repeated." *(Musical Courier,* 13 February 1901)

22 JANUARY 1901

Hans Erich APOSTEL, composer of atonal tendencies, pupil of Schoenberg and Berg, is born at Karlsruhe.

27 JANUARY 1901

Giuseppe VERDI, great Italian operatic composer, whose twenty-six operas range from the Bellinian formal simplicity of the early *Nabuchodonosor* to the modern symphonic design of his last opera, *Falstaff,* dies in Milan at the age of eighty-seven years, three months, and seventeen days.

"Rome, Jan. 27, Signor Verdi died at Milan today at 2:50 a. m. . . . The Senate was specially convoked this afternoon in order to commemorate the great musician to whom it was decided to grant the same honors as those paid in 1873 to Alessandro Manzoni—namely, a State funeral and the execution of a bust of Verdi for the Senate." (London *Times,* 28 January 1901)

"In person Verdi was the ideal of a well-bred Italian: the finely-cut features, the piercing black eyes, and the expressive face which are familiar to all, were associated with a figure of a height unusual among his countrymen and a bearing of the utmost dignity." *(Ibid.)*

"The maestro is dead. He carried away with him a great quantity of light and vital warmth. We had all basked in the sun of his Olympian old age. He died magnificently like a fighter redoubtable and mute. The silence of death fell on him a week before he died. With his head bent, his eyebrows set, he seemed to measure with half-shut eyes an unknown and formidable adversary, calculating in his mind the force that he could summon up in opposition. Thus he put up a heroic resistance. The breathing of his great chest sustained him for four days and three nights; on the fourth night the sound of his breathing still filled the room; but what a struggle, poor maestro! How magnificently he fought up to the last moment!" (Giacosa, quoted in Francis Toye, *Giuseppe Verdi and His Works,* New York, 1931)

2 FEBRUARY 1901

Jascha (properly Jacob, "Jascha" being a diminutive used only for children and intimates) HEIFETZ, celebrated child prodigy and violin virtuoso of the new school of "cold tonal beauty," is born at Vilna.

3 FEBRUARY 1901

Pelléas et Mélisande, orchestral suite by Gabriel FAURÉ, written in a formal tonal idiom neither romantic nor impressionistic, is performed for the first time at the Lamoureux concerts in Paris.

15 FEBRUARY 1901

Astarté, opera in four acts by Xavier LEROUX, is produced at the Grand Opéra in Paris.

"A work of undeniable merit by a musician of high talent has been welcomed with every mark of approval by a distinguished and critical audience at our Opera, yet I frankly confess that it bored me exceedingly. In the first place, the score is one of the noisiest ever heard, from the first note to the last it rattles along a ceaseless, interminable flow of ear-splitting, clangour and hulla-balloo, thundering, clanking, jangling, without a single moment of respite or instant's pause in the deafening clatter. Then the subject is repugnantly indecent." (*Era,* London, 23 February 1901)

17 FEBRUARY 1901

Ethelbert NEVIN, American composer of unpretentious songs and piano pieces of simple melodic invention and pleasing harmonies, dies in New Haven in his thirty-ninth year.

17 FEBRUARY 1901

Gustav MAHLER's *Das Klagende Lied,* a revised version of an early

musical setting of his youthful poem fraught with mystical introspection, is performed in Vienna for the first time.

20 FEBRUARY 1901

La Fille de Tabarin, lyric comedy in three acts by Gabriel
PIERNÉ, to a romanticized story of a famous seventeenth-century
mountebank, is produced at the Opéra-Comique in Paris.

(The title-page of the score gives 8 February 1901, probably the originally
scheduled date, also given in Grove. Clément & Larousse in their *Dictionnaire des opéras* give 20 January 1901, probably copying the misprint in *Le Ménestrel* in its issue of 24 February 1901, in the date-line of
Arthur Pougin's review, "Première représentation le 20 Janvier." We
have the corroborating authority for the correct date in the London
Era of 21 February 1901. The reviewer, giving the date on top of the
page, says, "A very eloquent work was presented to us *last night* by
M. Gabriel Pierné to mark the gifted and accomplished musician's entry
at the Opéra-Comique.")

6 MARCH 1901

Charlotte Corday, lyric drama in three acts on the story of Marat's
young murderess, by Alexandre GEORGES, written in the fin-de-
siècle manner, making use of rows of bare fifths, pseudo-archaic
modes, and free recitative, is produced by the Opéra Populaire
in Paris.

(Grove gives the erroneous date, 6 May 1901. The title-page of the
printed score gives the premature date, 16 February 1901. The correct
date, 6 March 1901, is given in *Le Ménestrel* of 10 March 1901 and is
further corroborated by the Paris dispatch of the London *Era*.)

8 MARCH 1901

Pierre BENOIT, Belgian-Flemish composer who wrote a Flemish
opera and a number of cantatas and other vocal and instrumental
music in the manner of his master César Franck, dies at Antwerp
in his sixty-seventh year.

17 MARCH 1901

Heinrich LITINSKY, Russian composer who combines musical science with profound feeling for the basic melos of the people, is
born in the Ukraine.

"I belong to a generation of Soviet musicians whose social and artistic ideals and views have been formed during the years of the Great October Revolution and under its direct influence." (From the composer's letter to the author)

21–23 MARCH 1901

The first Bach Festival organized by the Neue Bachgesellschaft is held in Berlin.

29 MARCH 1901

The first complete performance (including the choral Finale which was omitted at the performance of 11 November 1900 under Liadov) of SCRIABIN's *First Symphony,* in E minor, is given in Moscow, Safonov conducting.

31 MARCH 1901

Russalka (The Mermaid), "lyric tale" by Antonin DVOŘÁK, based on Slavonic folklore, is produced at the National Theatre in Prague.

1 APRIL 1901

DEBUSSY's first article on music appears in the *Revue Blanche,* under the signature "Monsieur Croche."

29 APRIL 1901

L'Ouragan, lyric drama in four acts by Alfred BRUNEAU, to Zola's story, is produced at the Opéra-Comique in Paris.

"Monday night at the Opéra-Comique was really a joy . . . *L'Ouragan,* the storm of nature, the storm and passion of human hearts rages in the Ile de Goël—'you will not find Goël on any map,' say the collaborators, 'it is the world about us, near to us in our hearts.' " (Paris letter in the *Musical Courier,* 22 May 1901)

"The public applauded vigorously, in some cases stormily. Of the critics some were enthusiastic, others scornful. Gustave Charpentier, the composer of *Louise* wrote a hymn of praise on the opera; Gauthier-Villars of the *Echo de Paris* found it tiresome and stupid. . . . Some say the music is no music . . . others find it epoch making." (Theodor Wolff in a Paris dispatch to *Berliner Tageblatt*)

17 MAY 1901

Pope Leo XIII publicly commends the Benedictine monks of Solesmes for their recovery of authentic Gregorian melos by collation of manuscript copies.

22 MAY 1901

Twenty days before his thirty-seventh birthday Richard STRAUSS completes in Berlin the score of *Feuersnot* (op. 50), to a "song-poem" of Ernst von Wolzogen—about a "fire-famine" that struck a Dutch town and was not relieved until a young maiden bared her phosphorescent spine from which the burghers lighted their candles—his third opera as yet in the Wagnerian tradition, but already employing wide-spaced melodic intervals, abandoned unresolved dissonances and free modulatory technique evolved in his earlier symphonic poems.

29 MAY 1901

Manru, opera by Ignace PADEREWSKI, is produced at the Dresden Royal Opera.

30 MAY 1901

Much Ado About Nothing, opera in four acts after Shakespeare, by Charles Villiers STANFORD, is produced at Covent Garden in London. (Date from the London *Era* of 1 June 1901)

"*Much Ado About Nothing* was strangled at birth. It was given twice in all at Covent Garden and then withdrawn. Judged on its merits, this was a rank injustice. Full of the loveliest tunes, sparkling with humour, beautifully scored, and sung and acted by a splendid cast it made a great hit. I was there and can testify to this." (Harry Plunket Greene, *Charles Villiers Stanford,* London, 1935)

1 JUNE 1901

Universal Edition, Austrian music publishing firm, is established in Vienna at the constitutional assembly of its members.

"From C major to the *Motherchord* (containing all 12 different tones and 11 intervals) runs the range of works published by Universal Edition." (Alban Berg in *Die Musik,* November 1929)

12 JUNE 1901

RIMSKY-KORSAKOV completes the composition of *Servilia,* his only large operatic work (with the exception of *Mozart and Salieri*) written on a non-Russian subject.

16 JUNE 1901

Conrad BECK, Swiss composer of orchestra and chamber music (but little for solo instruments) in a strong contrapuntal style, international and abstract, is born at Schaffhausen.

20 JUNE 1901

Eighteen days after his forty-fourth birthday, Edward ELGAR conducts at a Philharmonic concert, London, the first performance of his Overture, *Cockaigne (In London Town),* in descriptive sonata form, the first subject depicting the cheerful aspect of London; the second, a London romance; the development, a military band passing by and a church service; the recapitulation and coda, the streets in turmoil.

3 JULY 1901

Ruth CRAWFORD, the first American woman-composer to adopt a radical constructivist style of musical composition, is born in Chicago.

28 JULY 1901

Rudy VALLÉE (Hubert Prior Vallée), American protagonist of crooning (singing in head-tones, with blandly suggestive expression), is born in Vermont.

10–21 AUGUST 1901

RIMSKY-KORSAKOV composes an orchestral "prelude-cantata," *From Homer.* (Date in the fifth Russian edition of *My Musical Life,* 1935)

15 AUGUST 1901

Sulho RANTA, Finnish composer of neo-romantic orchestral and instrumental works (among them a *Sinfonia Programmatica,* in three "symphonic poems" instead of orthodox movements), is born in Helsingfors.

17 AUGUST 1901

Edmond AUDRAN, French composer of the *Mascotte* and other popular operettas, dies near Paris, in his sixtieth year.

SEPTEMBER 1901

The Benedictine initiators of the restoration of Gregorian chant settle on the Isle of Wight, after forced departure from the Abbey of Solesmes.

20 SEPTEMBER 1901

Die Musik, "an illustrated bi-monthly, edited by Kapellmeister Bernhard Schuster," begins publication in Berlin, the first issue containing 104 pages.

"Our publication was born out of a clear consciousness of the fact that there is lacking, in the art of Music to which hundreds of thousands pledge their devotion, an organ, that might favorably compare with the foremost magazines of literature, pictorial and applied arts. . . ." (From the "Praeludium" to the first issue)

23 OCTOBER 1901

Les Barbares, "lyrical tragedy" by SAINT-SAËNS to Sardou's story of a barbarian tamed by a beautiful captive, is produced at the Paris Opéra.

27 OCTOBER 1901

Serge RACHMANINOV (now twenty-eight and a half years old) plays in Moscow the solo part in the first performance of his *Second Concerto* in C minor, written in a novel, but eminently pianistic technique, in three movements: majestic Allegro, in C minor; nostalgic Andante, in E major; and brilliant Finale, in C major.

27 OCTOBER 1901

An integral performance of DEBUSSY's *Nocturnes,* including the third piece, *Sirènes,* omitted in a partial performance ten and a half months before, is given at a Lamoureux concert in Paris.

20 NOVEMBER 1901

Grisélidis, "lyric tale" in three acts, with a prologue, to Boccaccio's story of a perversely cruel husband and a humble wife, with melodious music by Jules MASSENET, is produced at the Opéra-Comique in Paris.

21 NOVEMBER 1901

Richard STRAUSS conducts the first performance of his third opera, *Feuersnot,* at the Dresden Opera.

25 NOVEMBER 1901

The *Fourth Symphony,* in G major, by Gustav MAHLER, in four orthodox movements, and as yet in the old romantic tradition, is performed for the first time in Munich, Felix WEINGARTNER conducting.

(Date from review in the *Allgemeine Zeitung,* Munich, *Abendblatt,* 26 November 1901, and in the advertisement in the same paper, on the day of the performance. Philip Hale's *Boston Symphony Programme Notes,* edited by John Burk, New York, 1935, gives the erroneous date, 28 November 1901)

"It is not fair to the readers of the 'Musical Courier' to take up their time with a detailed description of that musical monstrosity which masquerades under the title of Gustav Mahler's *Fourth Symphony.* There is nothing in the design, content, or execution of the work to impress the musician, except its grotesquerie. The only part of the Symphony which is bearable is the soprano solo at the end, and that is not Symphony." (*Musical Courier,* December 1901)

5 DECEMBER 1901

Walt DISNEY, originator of the Silly Symphonies, cinematographic animated cartoons with a synchronized musical score, as well as the inventor of the famous character, Mickey Mouse, is born in Chicago.

13 DECEMBER 1901

Georg RIMSKY-KORSAKOV, grandson of the composer, founder of the Quarter-Tone Society in Leningrad, foremost Russian exponent of the quarter-tone technique, is born at St. Petersburg.

20 DECEMBER 1901

On Henry HADLEY's thirtieth birthday, his *Second Symphony,* subtitled *The Four Seasons,* is performed by the New York Philharmonic Orchestra, Emil Paur conducting.

25 DECEMBER 1901

RACHMANINOV completes the composition of his *Sonata* for violoncello and piano, op. 19.

1902

4 JANUARY 1902

Los Pirineos, the first part of an operatic trilogy (the second being *La Celestina* and the third, *Raimundo Lulio*), by Felipe PEDRELL, the "Spanish Wagner," is produced at Barcelona.

12 JANUARY 1902

Till Eulenspiegel, opera by Emil REZNICEK, is produced in Karlsruhe.

18 JANUARY 1902

Filippo MARCHETTI, Italian operatic composer, Director of Liceo di Santa Cecilia in Rome, dies a month and eight days before his seventy-first birthday.

(Grove, in the second edition, published in 1907, establishes the date of Marchetti's birth as 26 February 1831, from the birth certificate, reproduced in *Gazetta musicale* of 6 February 1902; but in the same article, the writer, or the printer, makes another error, in giving 1901 instead of 1902 as the year of Marchetti's death. The error is carried into the third edition of Grove, 1927)

25 JANUARY 1902

SCRIABIN's *Second Symphony,* entirely orthodox in style and tonality, but containing already the characteristic trumpet-like melodic ascensions, premonitory of the "jeux divins" of the *Third Symphony,* is performed for the first time at the Russian Symphony concerts in St. Petersburg, Liadov conducting.

Most biographers, following Leonid Sabaneiev (who should have known better) cite a later performance under Safonov in Moscow on 3 April 1903—21 March, old style—as the first. The correspondence between Scriabin and Belaiev published in Russian in 1922 substantiates the authenticity of the above date (the following dates are given according to the old Russian calendar):

"13 December 1901 St. Petersburg. Dear Sacha! I spoke to Tolia [Anatol Liadov] and he consents to put your Symphony on the program of the second concert. The only question is whether the copyist will have time to finish the orchestral parts. . . . Your friend Mitrofan [Belaiev]."

"29 December 1901 Moscow. Dear Mitrofan Petrovitch! . . . I am very glad that the symphony will be performed on the 12th and that I will see you soon. . . . Lovingly, A. Scriabin."

14 FEBRUARY 1902

The Metropolitan Opera Company in New York gives the first American performance of PADEREWSKI's *Manru.*

"Paderewski's New Opera Sung—*Manru* Politely Received by Big Audience at the Metropolitan—Composer Dragged Before the Curtain—But the Work Written on Wagnerian Lines Failed to Make a Profound Sensation." (Headlines in the New York *World*)

18 FEBRUARY 1902

Le Jongleur de Notre Dame, a "miracle" in three acts by Jules MASSENET, from a medieval story of an exalted juggler's ascension to heaven at the summons of Mary, is produced at Monte Carlo.

5 MARCH 1902

The first concert exclusively composed of works by SCRIABIN is given in Moscow, with the composer playing his piano pieces and SAFONOV conducting the orchestral works.

8 MARCH 1902

Jan SIBELIUS conducts at Helsingfors the first performance of his *Second Symphony,* in D major, in four movements:

(1) Allegretto, in characteristic duple-triple time, sustained feeling of tonality, and a dying-off ending; (2) Andante rubato, opening in the Hypodorian mode, and then pursuing free modulatory course, at times forming harsh, angular chords; (3) Vivacissimo, in a gigue movement alternating with a Lento section; (4) Finale, based on running figuration and ending in a plagal cadence for full orchestra in triple forte.

10 MARCH 1902

Less than four months before his forty-second birthday, Gustav MAHLER marries Alma Maria Schindler.

"The opening of the fifth decade of Mahler's life proved from every point of view revolutionary. The year 1901 shows his symphonic labors suddenly interrupted. There is one reason—a woman; turning aside from a long-confirmed celibacy he begins to court the charming young step-daughter of the artist Carl Holl. At the home of the musically gifted and highly congenial Alma Maria Schindler he doffs his grey cloak of solitude and makes every effort to appear the jolly, sociable companion. Alma, at first just fascinated by the attention of the famous director, in the course of a few months knows that she loves him. At length he ventures and proposes and she agrees to become his wife. The marriage took place in March 1902." (Gabriel Engel, *Gustav Mahler, Song-Symphonist*, New York, 1932)

In the English translation of Paul Stefan's book on Mahler, New York, 1931, the erroneous year and day of Mahler's marriage is given, 9 March 1901; no date is found in the two German editions of Paul Stefan's book; Hull gives 1904 in an article on Mahler, but the correct year 1902 in a paragraph on Alma Mahler.

19 MARCH 1902

Heinrich SPITTA, German composer of choral works, son of Friedrich Spitta, the music historian, and nephew of Philipp Spitta, the Bach scholar, is born at Strasbourg.

29 MARCH 1902

William Turner WALTON, the English composer, who has brought Elizabethan freshness to English music in neo-classical oratorios (*Belshazzar's Feast*), illustrative overtures (*Portsmouth Point*),and urban comedy-revues (*Façade*), is born at Oldham, Lancashire.

5 APRIL 1902

Ricardo Viñés, the Spanish pianist, plays at the Société Nationale in Paris the first performance of Ravel's *Jeux d'Eau,* a work definitely establishing the new pianoforte technique of massed sonorities, harmonically derived from the counterposition of two rows of mutually exclusive scales of the white (heptatonic) and black (pentatonic) keys.

7 APRIL 1902

Lino Liviabella, Italian composer of neo-classical tendencies in the national Italian application of the term, is born in Macerata. (Date from *La Rassegna musicale,* July–August, 1936)

9 APRIL 1902

At the inauguration of the New Finnish Theatre in Helsingfors, Sibelius conducts *The Origin of Fire,* cantata for baritone, chorus, and orchestra, composed by him especially for the occasion, to the words from the Finnish epic, *Kalevala.*

14 APRIL 1902

Two weeks before the dress rehearsal of Debussy's opera, *Pelléas et Mélisande,* the Paris daily *Le Figaro* publishes an open letter from Maurice Maeterlinck, author of the drama, sharply denouncing both Carré's libretto and Debussy's setting and expressing a wish that the production should result in a "prompt and resounding failure," his wrath aroused because Debussy preferred Mary Garden in the title role to Georgette Leblanc, Maeterlinck's common-law wife.

Paris 13 April 1902

Dear Sir: The direction of the Opéra-Comique announces the impending performance of Pelléas et Mélisande. This performance will take place against my will, for Messrs. Carré and Debussy have ignored my legitimate rights.

I should have solved this difference in the courts, which would probably rule once more that a poem belongs to the poet, if a particular circumstance had not altered the *espèce* as they say in the courts.

Indeed, Monsieur Debussy, having first agreed with me on the choice of the interpreter whom I judged the sole person capable of creating the role of Mélisande in conformity with my intentions and desires, decided, when confronted with unjustifiable opposition to this choice on the part of Monsieur Carré, to deny me the right of intervention in the casting, by taking advantage of an all-too-confident letter I wrote him more than six years ago.

Bizarre practices followed this inelegant gesture, as proved by the receipt record of the work, manifestly antedated in an attempt to establish that my protests had been tardy.

Thus, they managed to oust me from my own work, and thenceforth it has been treated as conquered territory. Arbitrary and absurd cuts have been made in the play, rendering it incomprehensible; on the other hand, they have left intact the parts that I intended to delete or improve, as I did in a booklet just published, and from which one can see how much the text adopted by the Opéra-Comique differs from the authentic text.

In a word, the Pelléas under discussion is a piece which has become an almost enemy alien to me. Barred from all control of my work, I am compelled to wish that its failure should be resounding and prompt.

I beg you, dear Sir, to accept the expression of my highest regard.

Maurice Maeterlinck.

28 APRIL 1902

DEBUSSY's opera, *Pelléas et Mélisande,* is presented in the afternoon in public rehearsal at the Opéra-Comique in Paris.

"The theatre programs that the noisy boys are in the habit of peddling at the entrance usually expatiate on the merits of the production. Yesterday, at the rehearsal at the Opéra-Comique, those privileged to attend the first audition of Claude Debussy's work were not a little astonished at reading the program sold at the door which contained an ironic description of Maeterlinck's work. This little drama is a chef-d'oeuvre, and Maeterlinck is a genius. At least, they say so. Is it a mystification? Is there anything behind this? There was a great deal of talk about this and very singular stories have been heard with great curiosity in the lobby. Some propose to call the play *Pelléas et Médisances.*" (*Le Figaro,* Paris, 29 April 1902)

"The copyist was conscientious but very inexperienced; he wrote sharps for flats so that Debussy himself could not make out which was which; frequently the change of clef or time-signature after a rest was left out. Result: exasperating rehearsals; impossible to proceed; every time a stop. 'Is this a sharp?' . . . A first desk player declares that the music makes no sense, but after the twenty-first rehearsal admits that the enthusiasts were right. The trombone player, speaking for the brass sec-

tion opines: 'We have little to play here, but what we do play is great!'
. . . To gain time, the scenery is entrusted to two great specialists, Jus-
seaume and Ronsin. Catastrophe! Pelléas demands thirteen changes of
scenery, but it is impossible to accomplish in the hall. The stage technicians swear a thousand oaths, and, to save the situation, Debussy sits
down to compose, between two rehearsals, the necessary interludes; it is
a miracle that the stitches do not show. . . . After the end, the assistant
secretary of the Ministry of Education demands the deletion of fifteen
bars on account of the portion of the dialogue inadmissible on the stage
of a subsidized theatre:

    'Golaud: Et . . . et le lit? Sont-ils près du lit?
    Yniold: Le lit, petit père? Je ne vois pas le lit.' "
(Robert Jardillier, *Pelléas*, Paris, 1927)

"On the day of the dress rehearsal (and in Paris the guests at a dress
rehearsal comprise many hundreds of members of the general public)
hawkers sold, outside the theatre, an analytical programme giving a
clumsily jocular description of the play. . . . Naturally this pamphlet
was regarded by many people as a deliberate manoeuvre against Debussy.
Those people, I think, were wrong. It is obvious enough that it was
written by one of the hacks ordinarily employed to compile the un-
official programmes sold outside most Paris theatres—a hack who knew
very little about the play which he purported to describe." (M. D. Calvocoressi, *Musicians' Gallery*, London, 1934)

30 APRIL 1902

DEBUSSY's *Pelléas et Mélisande* is produced at the Opéra-Comique
in Paris, André MESSAGER conducting.

"The first performance of *Pelléas and Mélisande* in Paris, on 30 April
1902 was a very notable event in the history of French music; its importance can only be compared with that of the first performance of
Lully's *Cadmus et Hermione*, Rameau's *Hippolyte et Aricie*, and Gluck's
Iphigénie en Aulide; and it may be looked upon as one of the three or
four red-letter days in the calendar of our lyric stage." (Romain Rolland
in *Musiciens d'aujourd'hui*)

"A rear-guard Wagnerite saw nothing in Pelléas but a sign to neuras-
thenia and impotence, another critic spoke of 'musical hashish and
kaleidoscope of sounds.' The king of periodicals *L'Illustration* devoted
to Pelléas ten lines at the bottom of the last page. . . . From on high,
in the *Revue des Deux Mondes*, Camille Bellaigue judged that the drama
is both mysterious and mystifying; he saw in the music 'neither melody,
rhythm, leitmotiv, nor charm,' and concluded with this anathema:

'Everything is destroyed and nothing is created in the music of Monsieur Debussy. It contains the elements not of life and progress, but of decadence and death.' " (Robert Jardillier, *Pelléas,* Paris, 1927)

"Pelléas c'est encore de la musique à écouter la figure dans les mains. Toute musique à écouter la figure dans les mains est suspecte. Wagner c'est le type de la musique qui s'écoute dans les mains." (Jean Cocteau, *Le coq et l'arlequin,* 1918)

"The music is such as one could expect from the composer of L'Après-Midi d'un Faune, the Damoiselle Élue, the Nocturnes, etc., i.e., indefinite, strange, escaping, full of harmonic hardness, particularly in the preludes and post-ludes of the orchestra. . . . We know too well that one shouldn't be scandalized by *notes not in the harmony,* for examples of such attempts one might find in the works of the greatest masters. But, with them, it is an exception, and the ear relishes their bold innovations as long as they are tempered by tonalities pure of all accidents. With Debussy, it is exactly the reverse: harmonic simplicity is a rare thing in his score." (H. Imbert in *Le Guide musical,* 4 May 1902)

"Music is the final religion of these last centuries without faith. The disciples of Wagner were at least sincere. They were recruited from all classes of society, and the poverty of their dress, the ugliness, sometimes sublime, of their drawn faces, bore witness to the fervor and fury of their faith. The religion of Mr. Claude Debussy has more elegance. The neophytes affect especially the orchestra fauteuils, the first boxes, the orchestra stalls; they are found by the side of the young blonde girls, too delicate, too white, too blonde, in evident imitation of the type to which Mary Garden belongs.

" '*Je regardais Lucie, elle était pâle et blonde.*' And turning over with a lazy hand the score placed on the rail of the box there is a whole class of beautiful young men (nearly all the Debussyites are young, O, so young), ephebes with long hair cunningly brought in stringy locks over the forehead, with dull, smug faces, with deep-sunken eyes. Their dress coats have a velvet collar and puffed sleeves; their frock-coats are a little too pinched in the waist; their satin cravats are mussy over the neck or they float loosely, tied carelessly to the turn-over collar when the Debussy-ite is 'en veston.' They all wear on their little fingers (for they all have pretty hands) precious rings of Egypt or Byzantium, rings of turquoise or of twisted greenish gold. Thus adorned, they go in couples. Orestes and Pylades commune together, or the model son accompanies his mother. They are archangels with visionary eyes, and under the spell of an impression they whisper in each other's ears, and their whispers go to the lowest depth of the soul. 'The Pelléastres!' " (Jean Lorrain in *Le Journal,* 1902)

"The public is tired of hearing music which is not music; it is weary of this heavy, continuous declamation, without air and light; it is sated with this unsupportable abuse of chromatics, thanks to which all sense of tonality disappears along with the melodic sense. . . . Rhythm, melody, tonality—these are three things that are unknown to M. Debussy. His music is vague, without color or nuance, without motion, without life. It is not even declamation, but a continual dolorous melopoeia, without vitality or vigor, deliberately shunning all semblance of precision. . . . And what a delightful series of false relations! What adorable progressions of consecutive triads, with the inevitably resulting fifths and octaves! What a collection of dissonances, sevenths and ninths, ascending even by disjunct intervals! I recommend to music lovers a ninth chord on page ten of the full score, where the voice sings the fifth of that ninth, so that only one note is missing to complete the scale in this chord. Very pretty! No, I will never have anything to do with these musical anarchists!" (Arthur Pougin in *Le Ménestrel*, 4 May 1902)

"The vocal parts are written without any attention being paid to the characteristics of the singing voice. In fact the singers recite their role to notes without the composer's having cared as to whether the sequence of these notes shall prove agreeable to the ear. Of melody there is not the slightest pretension. In fact, the same results would be obtained exactly if the singers were to declaim their parts instead of singing them, provided they kept the pitch of the voice quite distinct from the tonality of the orchestra. D'Harcourt says, 'Debussy has a horror of the common chord, and if by accident he uses it, it is nearly always in another tonality,' as if to say, 'This is a common chord, it is true, but you will admit that it doesn't sound like one.' " (*Musical Courier*, 28 May 1902)

"In Debussy's opera consecutive fifths, octaves, ninths, and sevenths abound in flocks, and not only by pairs but in whole passages of such inharmonious chords. . . . Such progressions sound awful and as they come out in the strings, one gives an involuntary start, as when the dentist touches the nerve of a sensitive tooth." (Arthur Bles in the *Musical Courier*, 16 July 1902)

"M. Debussy's score defies description, being such a refined concatenation of sounds that not the faintest impression is made on the ear. The composer's system is to ignore melody altogether, and his personages do not sing, but talk in a sort of lilting voice to a vague musical accompaniment of the text. No solo, no detached phrase ever breaks the interminable flow of commonplace sound. The effect is quite bewildering, almost amusing in its absurdity." (Paris dispatch in *Era*, London, May 1902)

"Through the intellectual refinement of a crazy pursuit for novelty, Debussy has arrived at the greatest negation of every doctrine. He disowns melody and its development, and despises the symphony with all its resources. The opinion of the best musical critics is unanimous in declaring *Pelléas et Mélisande* a work of musical decline. . . . France may be still congratulated upon possessing Reyer, Massenet, Saint-Saëns, and Charpentier. They cannot certainly prevent the decline of the musical art; but they will delay it for a while." (S. Marchesi in the *Monthly Musical Record,* London, June 1902)

"Debussy is not a stylist, but an impressionist. Like Claude Monet he seems to delight in giving us the complementary hue of every tone. There are purples on his palette—no blacks. His colors occasionally screech, so 'high' are they, and their vibrations never cease. If the Western World ever adopted Eastern tonalities, Claude Debussy would be the one composer who would manage its system, with its quarter-tones and split quarters. Were it not that the pun is so shudderingly bad I should call Claude Debussy the greatest of living De-composers! Every musical idea he touches thaws and resolves itself into everlasting notes. His future should be viewed with suspicion from all the critical watch towers." (James Huneker in the New York *Sun,* 19 July 1903)

6 MAY 1902

Vincent D'INDY conducts the orchestra of the Société Nationale de Musique in the first performance of *Nymphes au Crépuscule* by Déodat DE SÉVERAC.

27 MAY 1902

Konsertfoerening, Stockholm's Symphony Orchestra Society, is officially formed, with John May as president, Wilhelm Stenhammar as vice-president, and Tor Aulin as conductor.

(Date from the *Stockholms Konsertfoerening, 1902–1927,* an anniversary booklet, Stockholm, 1927)

30 MAY 1902

La Troupe Jolicoeur, "comédie musicale" in three acts by Arthur COQUARD, French composer of Wagnerian tendencies, is produced at the Opéra-Comique in Paris.

10 JUNE 1902

Horatio PARKER is awarded the honorary degree of Doctor in

Music by the University of Cambridge. (Date from a letter from the University's Registrar's clerk to the author)

11 JUNE 1902

Vissarion SHEBALIN, Russian Soviet composer, whose magnum opus is a dramatic symphony, *Lenin,* for chorus, four soloists, narrator, and orchestra, to the text by Mayakovsky, is born at Omsk, Siberia.

12 JUNE 1902

Twenty-five days before his forty-second birthday, Gustav MAHLER conducts, at a Tonkuenstler meeting at Crefeld, the first complete performance of his *Third Symphony,* surnamed (in the program book of the first performance, though not in the printed score) *A Summer Morning Dream,* with the following program given for the six movements (but omitted from the printed score):

(1). *Summer enters.* (2). *What the flowers of the meadow tell me (Minuet).* (3). *What the animals in the forest tell me (Rondo).* (4). *What man tells me (alto solo).* (5). *What the angels tell me (female chorus).* (6). *What love tells me (Adagio).*

1 AUGUST 1902

Oscar SONNECK, American musicologist, librarian, and music publisher, is called to organize the Music Division of the Library of Congress in Washington, D. C.

14 OCTOBER 1902

RIMSKY-KORSAKOV's opera *Servilia* is produced at the Maryinsky Theatre at St. Petersburg. (Date from the fifth Russian edition of *My Musical Life,* Leningrad, 1935)

21 OCTOBER 1902

Tor AULIN conducts the inaugural concert of the Stockholm Symphony Orchestra.

1 NOVEMBER 1902

The charter of the Philadelphia Orchestra Association is adopted, with the articles stipulating that the said corporation is to exist perpetually and that its object is to encourage the performance of first-class orchestral music in Philadelphia.

(Date from Appendix A, in Wister's *Twenty-Five Years of the Philadelphia Orchestra, 1900–1925*)

1 DECEMBER 1902

Carl NIELSEN conducts in Copenhagen the first performance of his *Second Symphony,* surnamed *The Four Temperaments.*

3 DECEMBER 1902

Feodor STRAVINSKY, bass of the Imperial Opera, father of Igor Stravinsky, dies at Wildungen, Germany, in his sixtieth year.

16 DECEMBER 1902

La Carmélite, "comédie musicale en quatre actes" by Reynaldo HAHN, Venezuelan-born French symbolist composer, is produced at the Opéra-Comique in Paris.

25 DECEMBER 1902

Michael IPPOLITOV-IVANOV conducts at the Solodovnikov Theatre in Moscow RIMSKY-KORSAKOV's opera *Kastchei the Immortal,* written in a new harmonic idiom (to quote from Rimsky-Korsakov's *My Musical Life,* fifth Russian edition, Leningrad, 1935), with "cross-relations formed by consecutive major thirds . . . deceptive cadences on dissonant chords and a host of passing chords."

1903

1 JANUARY 1903

DEBUSSY receives the Cross of Chevalier de la Légion d'Honneur, through the efforts of the musicographer Combarieu, then a member of the government.

7 JANUARY 1903

L'Étranger, opera by Vincent d'INDY, is produced at the Théâtre de la Monnaie in Brussels.

"*L'Étranger* is what dogmatic people call an example of pure and lofty art, but in my humble opinion it is more than that. It is the working out of formulas which are admittedly pure and lofty, but which have the coldness, blueness, delicacy, and hardness of steel. Beautiful music is there, but it is, as it were, cloaked; and the mastery is so amazing that one hardly ventures to feel anything so incongruous as emotion. Say what you will, Wagner's influence on Vincent d'Indy was never really profound. If *Fervaal* owes something to the influence of the Wagnerian tradition, it is protected from it by its conscientious scorn of the grandiloquent hysteria which ravages the Wagnerian heroes." (Debussy, *Monsieur Croche, Anti-Dilettante,* Paris, 1933)

14 JANUARY 1903

Die Genossenschaft deutscher Komponisten, successor to Die Genossenschaft deutscher Tonsetzer, is founded by Richard STRAUSS, Hans SOMMER, and Friedrich ROESCH.

19 JANUARY 1903

Erwin NYIREGYHAZI, Hungarian child prodigy of the piano, possessed of absolute pitch to the rarest degree, and the subject of a solemn and erudite monograph published by the International Library of Psychology, Philosophy, and Scientific Method in New York, is born in Budapest.

20 JANUARY 1903

Titania, "drame musical" in three acts by Georges HÜE, winner of the Prix de Rome of 1879, is produced at the Opéra-Comique in Paris.

28 JANUARY 1903

Four French musicians die on the same day: Augusta Mary HOLMÈS, Parisian-Irish composer and pupil of Franck, pianistic wonder-child of the Second Empire, in Paris in her fifty-sixth year; Robert PLANQUETTE, composer of celebrated operettas, among them *Les Cloches de Corneville* (The Chimes of Nor-

mandy), in his native Paris in his fifty-fifth year; Edmond NEU-
KOMM, writer on music, in Paris in his sixty-third year; and one
AUGUEZ, a singer, in his fifty-sixth year.

"Funereal, indeed, is this week, which had borne the news on the same
day, Wednesday, of the death of four artists meriting recognition! Our
poor friend Augusta Holmès is gone. . . . She was older than it was believed. The year 1854 was given for her birth. But, it was in 1847 that
she was born. I am absolutely certain of this. . . . It is quite a distance
to the author of *Cloches de Corneville*. They rejuvenated him, too, making him appear in this world in 1850. The truth is, he was born on July
31, 1848. . . . I must also give the final farewell to my old comrade,
Edmond Neukomm, who was nephew of the famous Austrian composer,
Neukomm, friend of the two Haydns. . . . His most curious and original work is the one he will not see accomplished: *Le Tour de France en
musique*. . . . He was a gentleman and an artist of rare talent, this excellent Auguez. . . . Ah! If only his voice had equalled his talent!"
(Arthur Pougin in *Le Ménestrel,* 1 February 1903)

11 FEBRUARY 1903

Six and a third years after BRUCKNER's death his unfinished *Ninth
Symphony*, dedicated "an meinem lieben Gott," is performed in
Vienna for the first time, with his *Te Deum* in place of the un-
written *Finale*.

22 FEBRUARY 1903

Hugo WOLF, the Wagner of the Lied, who was to the last quarter
of the nineteenth century what Schubert was to the first, dies nineteen days before his forty-third birthday in an insane asylum in
Vienna.

"Early in 1900 the lesions in the nervous system extended. His powers
of speech were now affected, but he could still recognize his friends
though he could hardly pronounce their names. In August 1901, however, the paralysis spread alarmingly; all he could do now was to lie
in his cage-bed day and night, refusing nourishment so far as he could,
already almost blind and deaf to everything around him. The doctors
gave him up at the beginning of 1902, but the heart was quite sound,
and he still lived on. At last in February 1903, the deliverance came. On
the 16th he was attacked by an affection of the lungs, to which his body
was now too weak to offer any resistance, though there was still enough
sensation left in the nerves for him to suffer agonies from paralytic

cramps. . . . He passed away at three o'clock in the afternoon of Sunday, 22 February 1903." (Ernest Newman, *Hugo Wolf*, London, 1907. Romain Rolland in all editions of his *Musiciens d'aujourd'hui* gives 16 February 1903 for Wolf's death, an error that has been preserved in all editions of the English translation of the book)

27 FEBRUARY 1903

SCRIABIN's *Second Symphony*, in C, op. 29, in five movements, composed in 1901–1902, is published in the Belaiev edition.

15 MARCH 1903

Two weeks before his thirty-first birthday Sergei VASSILENKO conducts in Moscow the first performance of his first orchestral work *Poème Épique*, op. 4, written in a mixed style of Russian ecclesiastical modality and Tchaikovskian emotivity.

(Date from Moscow daily, *Russkiya Vedomosti*, of 4/17 March 1903, also given in Victor Belaiev's monograph, *Sergei Vassilenko*, Moscow, 1927. Fleisher's Catalogue gives the old-style date, 2 March 1903)

16 MARCH 1903

Nicolas LOPATNIKOV, Russian composer of forceful contrapuntal music in classical form, is born in Reval.

17 APRIL 1903

Nicolas NABOKOV, Russian composer in the neo-Dargomizhskian style, is born in St. Petersburg.

1 MAY 1903

Luigi ARDITI, famous Italian composer of waltz tunes, *Il Bacio* and *L'Estasi,* dies in Brighton, England, in his eighty-first year.

2 MAY 1903

Richard STRAUSS completes in Berlin the score of *Taillefer* for orchestra and chorus to Uhland's martial ballad of the Battle of Hastings. (Date in Richard Specht, *Richard Strauss,* 1921)

20 MAY 1903

Jerzy FITELBERG, Polish composer of neo-classical music virtually uninfluenced by Polish folklore, is born in Warsaw.

25 AUGUST 1903

The *Second Symphony* by Cyril SCOTT is performed for the first time a month and two days before his twenty-fourth birthday at a Promenade concert in London under the direction of Sir Henry Wood.

SEPTEMBER 1903

Erik SATIE writes *3 Morceaux en Forme de Poire avec une Manière de Commencement, une Prolongation du même et un en plus suivi d'une Redite* for piano four-hands, caricaturing the classical pedantry as well as impressionist preciosity.

"Impressionist composers cut a pear in twelve pieces and gave each of them the title of a poem. Then Satie composed twelve poems and entitled the whole: *Morceaux en forme de poire.*" (Jean Cocteau, *Le Rappel à l'ordre,* Paris, 1926)

"This title, Satie explained, had been given to them because Debussy had declared them shapeless: 'So I called them "pear-shaped"—and *that* ought to show him and everybody that they are *not* shapeless.' " (M. D. Calvocoressi, *Musicians' Gallery,* London, 1935)

6 SEPTEMBER 1903

Paul KADOSA, Hungarian composer of neo-classical and neo-romantic music strongly imbued with native flavor, is born at Léva, Hungary. (Date from the composer's letter to the author)

1 OCTOBER 1903

RIMSKY-KORSAKOV composes a *Serenade for Cello* dedicated to his son, Andrey.

(Date from the annotations of Andrey Rimsky-Korsakov to his father's *Musical Life,* fifth Russian edition, Leningrad, 1935)

10 OCTOBER 1903

Vladimir DUKELSKY, Russian-American composer of ballets, symphonies, and songs in a neo-Glinkian style, also writing American popular music under the name of Vernon Duke, is born in the railroad station at Parfianovka, during his mother's trip to Pskov.

14 OCTOBER 1903

The Apostles, by Edward ELGAR, oratorio on the calling of the Apostles, their teaching, their mission, and the establishment of the church among the Gentiles, making use of an authentic Hebrew melody harmonized in the orthodox fashion of Western harmony, is produced at the Birmingham Festival.

26 OCTOBER 1903

Victorin DE JONCIÈRES, whose real name was Félix Ludger Rossignol, French composer of operas in a style touched with Wagnerian ideas, dies in Paris in his sixty-fifth year.

30 OCTOBER 1903

The Christmas Tree, children's opera by the Russian composer, Vladimir REBIKOV, in a poetic quasi-Tchaikovskian style, is produced in Moscow.

31 OCTOBER 1903

Alexander SILOTI inaugurates the first season of his symphony concerts in St. Petersburg.

(Date from Siloti's original program, 18 October, old style)

15 NOVEMBER 1903

Tiefland, opera by Eugen D'ALBERT, is produced in Prague.

16 NOVEMBER 1903

At the invitation of the Coleridge-Taylor Society of Washington, D. C., Samuel COLERIDGE-TAYLOR, British mulatto composer, conducts in Washington his choral trilogy, *Hiawatha,* with Negro singers.

22 NOVEMBER 1903

Pope Pius X issues the encyclic *motu proprio* sanctioning restoration of Gregorian chant according to the method of the Benedictine monks of Solesmes. (See full text in Part III)

27 NOVEMBER 1903

Le Donne Curiose, opera by Ermanno WOLF-FERRARI, is produced in Munich.

8 DECEMBER 1903

Pope Pius X addresses a letter to Cardinal Respighi, Vicar-General of Rome, on the restoration of sacred music, condemning the "endless musical compositions on the words of the Psalms . . . in the style of the old theatrical works, most of which are of such small value as works of art that they would not be borne even in second-rate secular concerts," urging their suppression, and a return to the liturgical tradition.

11 DECEMBER 1903

A century has passed since the birth of Hector BERLIOZ.

19 DECEMBER 1903

Siberia, opera to a pseudo-Russian story by Luigi ILLICA, with pseudo-Russian music by Umberto GIORDANO, is produced at La Scala, Milan.

23 DECEMBER 1903

La Reine Fiamette, "conte dramatique" by Xavier LEROUX, in four acts and six scenes to a story by Catulle Mendès, is produced at the Opéra-Comique in Paris.

"M. Leroux resolutely searches for pale tones. He is the Whistler of music." (Moreno in *Le Ménestrel,* January 1904)

26 DECEMBER 1903

Nicolas TCHEREPNIN conducts the first performance (from manuscript) of the dances from his *Pavillon d'Armide* at the Siloti concerts in St. Petersburg. (Date of original program, 13 December 1903, Russian old-style calendar)

31 DECEMBER 1903

Richard STRAUSS completes in Charlottenburg the score of his *Sinfonia Domestica,* op. 53, a thoroughly literal domestic musicorama—down to the seven strokes of the clock, the child's happy lallation, and a proud "just like his father" from paternal, "just like his mother" from maternal relatives—the thematic material of the score containing sixty-seven interplaying motifs.

(Date at the end of the score, also given in Max Steinitzer's *Richard Strauss* and Schattmann's monograph on *Sinfonia Domestica* in the Musikführer series. But Specht gives 21 December 1903 in his authoritative two-volume work, *Richard Strauss und Sein Werk,* published in 1921, vol. II, p. 388; apparently a misprint.)

1904

2 JANUARY 1904

Peter JURGENSON, founder of the Russian publishing house bearing his name, publisher and friend of a pleiad of Russian composers from Tchaikovsky to Scriabin, dies in Moscow in his sixty-ninth year.

8 JANUARY 1904

In a decree of the Congregation of Rites Pope Pius X sanctions the *cantus traditionalis* as rediscovered by the Benedictine monks of Solesmes, in contradistinction to the reformed choral.

9 JANUARY 1904

At the Société Nationale in Paris Ricardo VIÑÉS, Spanish pianist, plays the first performance of DEBUSSY's *Estampes,* written in the style of French orientalism inspired by the Cambodian dancers at the Paris Exposition of 1900.

10 JANUARY 1904

Mitrofan Petrovitch BELAIEV, Russian publisher of Balakirev, Borodin, Rimsky-Korsakov, Cui, Scriabin, Glazunov, and their musical satellites, dies in St. Petersburg in his sixty-eighth year.

(Hull gives the misconstrued date 10/23 Jan. 1903 [sic], an all-round error. Belaiev died 28 December 1903, old style, i.e., 10 January 1904, new style. Grove gives the date of Belaiev's birth 10 February 1836, which is the correct date according to the Russian calendar. It should be adjusted by adding 12 days)

"The Christmas holidays came. M. P. Belaiev, who had not been feeling well for a long time, made up his mind to undergo a serious operation. The operation was performed successfully, but two days later his heart gave way, and he died in his sixty-eighth year. One can easily imagine what a blow this was for the whole circle whose center had gone with him. In his detailed last will and testament, after providing for his family, Belaiev bequeathed all his wealth to the cause of music; he divided it into funds for the Russian Symphony Concerts; the publishing business and composers' fees; prizes in memory of Glinka; prize-competitions in chamber music and relief of needy composers." (Rimsky-Korsakov in *My Musical Life,* 1935)

21 JANUARY 1904

Jeji Pastorkyňa (literally, *Her Daughter-in-Law,* generally known under the heroine's name, *Jenůfa*), the third and greatest opera by Leoš JANÁČEK, written in a dynamically prosodic Moussorgskyan style, is performed for the first time at Brno.

(Date from the photographic reproduction of the program in Daniel Muller's book on Janáček, Paris, 1930. The title-page of the printed score also gives the correct date)

28 JANUARY 1904

Modest ALTSCHULER conducts, in Cooper Union Hall, New York City, the first concert of the Russian Symphony Orchestra, founded by him.

1 FEBRUARY 1904

The first number of *Revista Musical Catalana,* a monthly musical publication in the Catalan language, is issued in Barcelona.

3 FEBRUARY 1904

Luigi DALLAPICCOLA, Italian composer of neo-Palestrinian tendencies, polyphonic in texture and rhapsodic in essence, pursuing neither the neutral European modern idiom, nor intensely national folklore style, is born at Pisino, Istria.

"In his early years Luigi Dallapiccola used means of expression belonging to diverse schools and tendencies. But soon he determined the limits of his creative orientation through profound national assimilation, and performed an evolution in the cultural plane, that was nurtured mainly by the great past of Italian art. In fact his compositions, beginning with the first maturity, disclose a flair for the poetical and musical art of the Italian Renaissance, for the old polyphonic and instrumental forms. His self-expression invariably turns towards choral works; and it is in his works for chorus and for chorus with orchestra that the native subjects which are a source of his inspiration, find their most felicitous expression, in an idiom terse and direct, but at the same time vibrant with life. At present his style seems to veer towards a general European idiom, but his true nature reflects images of Italian national art." (An appreciation sent to the author by Gianandrea Gavazzeni)

17 FEBRUARY 1904

La Scala in Milan produced Giacomo PUCCINI's opera, *Madame Butterfly*, melodrama of Japanese-American love, desertion, and hara-kiri, set to music in a quasi-Japanese pentatonic idiom, with block harmonies in parallel progressions, or powerful orchestral unisons when maximum expression is required.

"First performance of Madame Butterfly . . . growls, shouts, groans, laughter, giggling, the usual single cries of *bis,* designed especially to excite the audience: these sum up the reception given by the public of *La Scala* to Giacomo Puccini's new work. . . . This is a true account of the evening, after which the authors, Puccini, Giacosa, and Illica with the approval of the publishers, withdrew *Madame Butterfly* and returned the fee for rights of performance to the management." (*Musica e musicisti*)

"You will be horrified by the vile words of the envious press, Never fear! *Butterfly* is alive and real, and will soon rise again. I say it and believe it with an inalterable faith." (Puccini in a letter to Don Panichelli)

"Sad to relate, after many grand triumphs of Puccini, a genuine fiasco must be recorded of his *Madame Butterfly*. Fiasco in every sense of the word, and fiasco so profound that the opera has been withdrawn after its first and only performance. The music is not at all moving. When the curtain fell, there followed an absolute silence." (*Musical Courier,* 9 March 1904)

"One cannot imagine how complicated is this affair of *Madame Butterfly*. First of all, this French opera written by Italians after an American play derived from an English short story, has a French novel as a point of departure, viz. 'Madame Chrysanthème' by Pierre Loti; for one can bet anything that without this first Madame the second Madame would have never seen the light of day. . . . So an English writer, Mr. John Luther Long, published a short story under the title of *Madame Butterfly*. Seeing this, an American playwright, Mr. David Belasco, undertook to draw from this short story a one-act play which was performed in New York with colossal success, a success which did not tarry to cross the ocean and repeat itself in London. . . . Mr. Puccini having had occasion to see the play did not fail to be enraptured with it and decided to make it into opera. He then asked his librettists, Messrs. Luigi Illica and Giuseppe Giacosa to write a libretto for him. This accomplished and the score finished, the opera was performed at *La Scala* of Milan as a 'Japanese Tragedy.' Mr. Puccini being the darling of Milan, a success equal to that of the original play was anticipated. But thunder and lightning! instead of the expected success there was a colossal fiasco, fiasco so annihilating that the authors judged it opportune to withdraw the work after this first performance which was bespattered with shouts and hisses. But this contretemps did not undermine the authors' confidence in their work. They applied themselves courageously to it, arranged it in three acts instead of two, cutting here, adding there, and, their work done, launched *Madame Butterfly* once more before the public, in Brescia, not in Milan. This time the about face was complete. Madame Butterfly was acclaimed at Brescia, shone upon all Italy, made a trip to London, and finally arrived in Paris." (Arthur Pougin in *Le Ménestrel*, 5 January 1907)

23 FEBRUARY 1904

Richard STRAUSS sails on his first American tour. (Date from Richard Specht's *Richard Strauss*, Munich, 1921)

26 FEBRUARY 1904

The *Second Symphony*, in B-flat major, by Vincent d'INDY, highly chromatic in texture, with occasional whole-tone runs, is performed for the first time at the Lamoureux concerts in Paris.

3 MARCH 1904

RIMSKY-KORSAKOV conducts at the Russian Symphony concerts in St. Petersburg the first performance of *On the Tomb*, composed by him in commemoration of the death of Belaiev.

5 MARCH 1904

The Schola Cantorum in Paris presents at its concert in Paris the first performance of RAVEL's *String Quartet* in F, which replaces the traditional sonata form by the principle of continual thematic mutation.

21 MARCH 1904

Eighty-two days before his fortieth birthday STRAUSS conducts in New York the first performance of his *Sinfonia Domestica,* and also *Don Juan* and *Thus Spake Zarathustra.*

"Monday evening, 21 March 1904, Carnegie Hall was the scene of a musical event so important that by comparison everything else pales into insignificance that has been done here in music since the first production of the Wagner 'Niebelungen' operas. On Monday evening, 21 March—the date will play a role in history—a vast auditorium full of enthusiastic men and women heard the first public performance on any concert stage of Richard Strauss' latest and greatest work of orchestra, his *Sinfonia Domestica.* The conductor was Richard Strauss, and the players were the Wetzler Symphony Orchestra." (*Musical Courier,* 23 March 1904)

"The *Symphony Domestica—Home Sweet Home* as Written by Richard Strauss—Papa and Mama and Baby Celebrated in a Huge Conglomeration of Orchestral Music." (Headlines in the New York *Sun*)

23 MARCH 1904

Dunja, one-act opera from Russian life by the German-Russian, Ivan KNORR, is produced at Coblenz.

26 MARCH 1904

Armida, Antonin DVOŘÁK's last opera, is produced at the National Theatre in Prague, five weeks before the composer's sudden death.

30 MARCH 1904

Koanga, opera by Frederick DELIUS, based on negro themes culled while he was an orange planter in Florida, is produced at Elberfeld, Germany. (Date from *25 Jahre Neue Musik,* Universal Edition, Vienna, 1926)

7 APRIL 1904

SCRIABIN's *Two Poems,* op. 32, for piano, in which the use of the altered ninth chord foreshadows his evolution toward the autochthonous *Promethean Chord,* are published by the Belaiev publishing firm.

8 APRIL 1904

SCRIABIN's *Four Preludes* for piano, op. 33, with such marks as "vagamente" or "ardito, bellicoso," indicative of the programmatic design despite the unprogrammatic titles, are published by the Belaiev firm.

15 APRIL 1904

SCRIABIN's *Fourth Sonata,* in F-sharp minor, in which the building up of perfect and augmented fourths presages his *Promethean Chord,* and the ecstatic melodic leaps give premonitions of the *Poem of Ecstasy,* is published by the Belaiev firm.

20 APRIL 1904

SCRIABIN's *Four Preludes* for piano, op. 31, significant for the transition from Chopin-influenced melodies to disjunct melodies in acrid chromaticized harmonies, are published by the Belaiev firm.

21 APRIL 1904

SCRIABIN's *Three Preludes* for piano, op. 35, reflecting the style of his transition period, are published by the Belaiev firm.

25 APRIL 1904

Pope Pius X issues a second papal *motu proprio,* indicating the rules for the use of the Vatican edition of Gregorian chant.

25 APRIL 1904

SIBELIUS conducts in Helsingfors the first performance of the chamber-orchestra version of his *Valse Triste.* (In the original incidental music to Jaernefelt's play, *The Death,* it was orchestrated for strings only)

28 APRIL 1904

Richard STRAUSS returns to Germany from his first American tour.

1 MAY 1904

Antonin DVOŘÁK, great Czech composer, the Verdi of Bohemia, who by his art of harmonic Europeanization of primitive material let the world learn and cherish the simple beauties of his native folk songs and dances, and who did similar service for American musical folklore in his *Fifth Symphony,* "From the New World," dies suddenly, at the dinner table in his house in Prague, at the age of sixty-two years, seven months, and three weeks.

4 MAY 1904

Belaiev publishes SCRIABIN's *Poème Satanique,* op. 36, for piano, the only work of his which bears the name of Satan.

17 MAY 1904

RAVEL's *Shéhérazade,* three poems for voice and orchestra, the subtlest revelation of French orientalism, and Albert ROUSSEL's first symphonic work, *Resurrection,* after the theme of Tolstoy's novel, are performed for the first time at a concert of the Société Nationale de Musique in Paris.

28 MAY 1904

PUCCINI's opera *Madame Butterfly* is performed at Brescia in a new version, in three acts instead of the original two, and reverses the Milan fiasco, marking a first success.

"It went exactly as I had wished: a real and unqualified triumph." (Puccini in a letter to his sister, 11 June 1904)

9 JUNE 1904

The first concert of the London Symphony Orchestra takes place under the direction of Hans Richter.

28 JUNE 1904

Daniel Decatur EMMETT, composer of *Dixie,* dies at his native Mt. Vernon, Ohio, in his eighty-ninth year.

4 JULY 1904

The American composer Charles E. IVES sketches a *March 1776* (later incorporated in the second movement of *Three Places in New England*), polymetrically constructed so that there are two march rhythms in the velocity ratio of 4:3. (Date of the manuscript, lent by the composer to the author)

14 JULY 1904

Debussy's first wife, Rosalie ("Lily") Texier, deserted by Debussy for the more intelligent, more artistic, and more comfortably situated Madame Bardac, shoots herself, inflicting a grave though not fatal wound in the region of the heart.

"Debussy loved few women. Each brought him what he needed spiritually at the moment of their meeting. In Lily Texier Debussy loved her ravishing beauty, boyish vivacity, ardor of devotion. This *midinette* was, according to the opinion of those who had known her, a model of patience, tact, discretion. When Debussy seemed perturbed and preoccupied, she always managed to divert him with a pleasantry and never spared an effort to bring him cheer. None the less Lily Texier's spirit of a *petite Parisienne* could not make up for the almost complete absence of culture. Very soon Debussy began to suffer from her lack of refinement and intellectual poverty. . . . Against his will, he ceased to love her. Her voice became repulsive to him to the point that his blood congealed in his veins when he heard it. It was in this state of mind that he met the woman who was to become the second Madame Debussy. She was an accomplished *femme du monde,* brilliant conversationalist, a singer of compelling talent. She presented a complete contrast to Lily. . . . As Debussy would leave the salon of Madame Bardac to join Lily, silent and brooding, suspicious, ready to burst into the violent passions of a woman of the people that she always remained, he could measure the chasm that separated them. He hesitated a long time. Several times he left her and then came back, until he finally decided to abandon his ruined household forever. For those who have followed this psychological crisis there cannot be any question of cold calculation on Debussy's part. It is beyond doubt that he suffered cruelly even as he made suffer." (Henry Prunières in an article *Autour de Debussy* in *La Revue Musicale,* May 1934)

16 JULY 1904

Goffredo PETRASSI, Italian composer of neo-classical music, in a pan-diatonic idiom, making free use of all seven diatonic steps over a functional bass, is born in Rome.

"Goffredo Petrassi is inspired by the great Italian tradition of the eighteenth century. He has made a rapid evolution, liberating himself from the influences of Hindemith and Casella and finding his own subjects, gradually acquiring a style of tense and strong lyricism. He possesses contrapuntal ability and judicious harmonic sense, evolving into individual specific values, integrating into a new concrete subjectivism. His musical language tends towards absolute sonorities, free of foreign literary connotations." (An appreciation sent to the author by Gianandrea Gavazzeni)

23 JULY 1904

Adone ZECCHI, Italian composer of neo-classical tendencies, is born in Bologna. (Date in Zecchi's letter to the author)

3 AUGUST 1904

Ferruccio BUSONI finishes the complete full score of his pianoforte *Concerto* in four movements. (Date from Edward J. Dent, *Busoni,* London, 1933)

6 AUGUST 1904

Eduard HANSLICK, Austrian music historian, who earned unenviable fame mostly through his bitter criticism of the moderns of his day—Wagner, Bruckner, Hugo Wolf (Wagner's Beckmesser was modeled after Hanslick, and in the first version of the *Meistersinger,* the name of the giftless caviller was Hans Lick)—dies in Vienna in his seventy-ninth year.

12 SEPTEMBER 1904

Gabriel POPOV, Russian Soviet composer of polyphonic music in dissonant counterpoint, is born at Novotcherkask.

29 SEPTEMBER 1904

Sigurd LIE, Norwegian composer of precocious and versatile gifts, who wrote Grieg-like music, with contrapuntal elaborations acquired during his Leipzig apprentice days, dies in his thirty-fourth year.

(Date from Norlind's *Allmänt Musik-Lexikon,* in Swedish, 1926. Hull gives the tardy 30 September)

1 OCTOBER 1904

Vladimir HOROWITZ, pianist of the modern school, with emphasis on technique and dynamics rather than romanticized interpretation, is born in Kiev, Russia.

18 OCTOBER 1904

Gustav MAHLER's *Fifth Symphony,* in C-sharp minor ("The Giant," as it was surnamed, although its orchestra is not exorbitant), is performed for the first time at Cologne.

"When the symphony was performed in certain German cities, the programme books contained no analytical notes and no argument of any sort. The compilers thus obeyed the wish of the composer. Mr. Ludwig Schiedermair tells us this pleasant anecdote. Mahler conducted a performance of his symphony in C minor at a concert of the Munich Hugo Wolf Society. After the concert there was a supper, and in the course of the conversation some one mentioned programme books. Mahler sprang from the table and exclaimed: 'Away with programme books which breed false ideas. The audience should be left to its own thoughts. If a composer by his music forces on his hearers the sensations which streamed through his mind, then, he reaches his goal.' And Mahler raised his glass and emptied it with 'Pereat den Programmen.' " (Philip Hale's notes in the Boston Symphony program book, 24–25 February 1906)

27 OCTOBER 1904

Djemal RECHID, Paris-bred Turkish composer of many orchestral and instrumental works, inspired by the folk songs of his native land and clothed in Parisian dress, is born in Constantinople.

(Date communicated by the composer)

10 NOVEMBER 1904

BUSONI plays in Berlin the first performance of his *Concerto* for piano with orchestra and male chorus.

"Ferruccio Busoni provided his friends with a surprise. He appeared without his beard and with a great pianoforte concerto, or rather with a long one." (Dr. Adolf Weissmann in the *Roland von Berlin,* 17 November 1904)

"During five movements we were submerged in a flood of cacophony; a *pezzo giocoso* painted the joys of barbarians lusting in war, and a tarantella, the orgies of absinthe-drinkers and harlots." (*Taegliche Rundschau,* November 1904)

1905

4 JANUARY 1905

Theodore THOMAS, German-born American conductor, founder of the Chicago orchestra, and pioneer of American orchestral music, dies in Chicago, in his seventieth year.

7 JANUARY 1905

Vincent D'INDY conducts the Boston Symphony Orchestra in the first American performance of his *Second Symphony,* in B-flat major.

"D'Indy's symphony (????) is so unutterably shocking to us that we hesitate to express our frank opinion. It is evident that harmony books are now mere waste paper, that there are no more rules, that there is to be an 11th commandment for the composer—'Thou shalt avoid all beauty.'" (Louis Elson, in the Boston *Advertiser,* 8 January 1905)

"It contains deep and impressive thoughts, pages of beauty that is almost unearthly. We believe this symphony to be one of the most important works of modern times." (Philip Hale in the Boston *Herald,* 8 January 1905)

8 JANUARY 1905

Le Palais Hanté, symphonic poem after Edgar Poe, by Florent SCHMITT, laden with somber harmonies of unresolved discords in a post-Lisztian manner, is performed for the first time at a Lamoureux concert in Paris.

15 JANUARY 1905

Hugues IMBERT, French music critic charitable to modern ideas, himself a composer of some harmless unnecessary music, dies in Paris four days after his sixty-third birthday.

16 JANUARY 1905

Ernesto HALFFTER, composer of the modern Spanish school, distinguished by greater condensation and brilliance than the older generation, is born in Madrid.

26 JANUARY 1905

SCHOENBERG conducts in Vienna the first performance of his *Symphonic Poem, Pelléas and Mélisande,* to Maeterlinck's play, at a concert organized by the Society of Creative Musicians, with the *Orchestral Fantasy* and *Five Orchestral Songs* by Oskar POSA on the same program.

"The three leaders of the *Verein der Schaffenden Tonkuenstler,* Arnold Schoenberg, Alexander von Zemlinsky and Oskar Posa, have devoted an entire evening to their cause. The most talented of them—Schoenberg— was the most unpalatable. Fully fifty minutes are needed for his continuous Symphonic Poem, *Pelléas and Mélisande.* Here and there a speck of common sense. Otherwise, for the whole fifty minutes one deals with a man either devoid of all sense or who takes his listeners for fools. . . . Schoenberg's *Opus* is not merely filled with wrong notes, in the sense in which Strauss' *Don Quixote* is, but is itself a fifty-minute-long protracted wrong note. This is to be taken literally. What else may hide behind this cacophony is impossible to ascertain." (Ludwig Karpath in *Die Signale,* 1 March 1905)

"A trombone glissando was used for the first time by Schoenberg in his symphonic poem *Pelléas and Mélisande,* full score, p. 51. Here the note E and its octave are fixed as basis of the 6th position by the lips, and the tube is pushed through all the positions in such a way that the intervals of half and quarter tones can be clearly heard." (Egon Wellesz in Hull, London, 1924)

2 FEBRUARY 1905

Robert EITNER, German musicographer, founder in 1868 of the Gesellschaft fuer Musikforschung and author of the ten-volume encyclopedia, *Biographisch-Bibliographisches Quellenlexikon der Musiker und Musikgelehrten,* dies at Templin, in his seventy-third year. (Grove gives the erroneous date 22 January 1905)

12 FEBRUARY 1905

Edward DANNREUTHER, Alsace-born British-American musicologist, whose two-volume treatise *Musical Ornamentation* deals with the entire development of musical graces, from Diruta to Wagner, registering all the exacerbating vagaries and inconsistencies with scholarly patience, dies in London in his sixty-first year.

14 FEBRUARY 1905

Chérubin, "comédie chantée" in three acts, to a story about a seventeen-year-old Don Juan and his elder rival, with gay and melodious music by Jules MASSENET, is produced at the Monte Carlo Theatre.

(Date in the telegraphic dispatch from Monte Carlo by Gabriel Fauré, published in *Le Figaro* of 15 February 1905. The same date is given on the title-page of the printed score. Grove also gives the correct date)

22 FEBRUARY 1905

Luis SANDI, Mexican composer of the young national school, is born in Mexico City.

"I studied violin, singing and composition at the *Conservatorio Nacional.* I was for a time chief of the Music Department of the Secretariat of Public Education. In that capacity I propagandized indigenous music of the country, which is almost entirely unknown in the urban centers. I am at present engaged in writing a ballet on the theme 'exploitation of the workers of the hinterland.' With this work begins a new era of my production, an effort to write music that shall in some way contribute to the struggle for an equitable distribution of wealth." (From the composer's letter to the author)

24 FEBRUARY 1905

Guillaume LANDRÉ, Dutch composer, son of Willem Landré, is born at The Hague. (Date from Keller's *Muzieklexicon,* 1932)

2 MARCH 1905

Marc BLITZSTEIN, American composer of modern, versatile talents, capable of effective composition in all styles from austere atonality to simple tonal harmony, and for all purposes, from symphony to political satire of leftist tendencies, is born in Philadelphia.

5 MARCH 1905

At six o'clock in the evening, Claude DEBUSSY completes the orchestral score of his symphonic suite, *La Mer,* the greatest work of impressionist pictorialism, in three illustrative movements:

(1) *De l'aube à midi sur la mer* (coruscating sonorities of tremolo strings as a background for characteristic jogging rhythms of melodic appogiaturas in the wind instruments); (2) *Jeux de vagues* (staccato rhythms in triple time with ninth-chord harmonies in exceedingly fluid tonality); (3) *Dialogue du vent et de la mer* (animated and tumultuous, with poignant, insistent melody of constantly changing harmonic implications, converging ultimately upon the parent harmony of D-flat major). (Date from Léon Vallas, *Claude Debussy et son temps,* Paris, 1932)

16 MARCH 1905

Amica, two-act opera by Pietro MASCAGNI, is produced at Monte Carlo. (Date in De Angelis' *Dizionario dei musicisti,* 1928)

1 APRIL 1905

Rimsky-Korsakov is discharged from professorship at the St. Petersburg Conservatory for his public protest (in a letter to the newspaper *Russia,* published on 19 March 1905) against the high-handed actions of the government-appointed directorate in the students' strike.

(Dates from the fifth Russian edition of Rimsky-Korsakov's *My Musical Life,* 1935, pp. 366 and 368)

1 APRIL 1905

Goeteborgs Orkesterfoerening, Orchestral Society of Goeteborg, Sweden, is officially formed.

(Date from an anniversary publication of the Society, *Goeteborgs Orkesterfoerening, 1905–1915,* Goeteborg, 1915)

14 APRIL 1905

Die Heirat Wider Willen (The Forced Marriage), comic opera in three acts, by Engelbert HUMPERDINCK, libretto adapted from a comedy by Alexandre Dumas, is produced at the Royal Opera House in Berlin.

15 APRIL 1905

The first demonstration of the method of eurythmics of Jaques-Dalcroze is given at the Conservatory of Geneva "to create with the help of rhythm a rapid and regular current of communication between brain and body." (See Part III for the history of the Dalcroze movement)

22 APRIL 1905

Belaiev publishes SCRIABIN's *Third Symphony* (*Divine Poem*), his first work of theosophic meaning, subdivided into three continuous movements, with expressive titles: *Luttes,* with an introductory Lento, marked "divin, grandiose," and the main movement, "mystérieux, tragique," in sonata form, with the second subject proclaiming the divine élan in upward trumpet tones; *Voluptés,* slow and tense, heavy with suspensions and vibrating trills, with expression marks from "sublime" to "sensuel, passionné, caressant"; *Jeu Divin,* marked "avec une joie éclatante," and written in clear C major, with a harmonically figurated plagal cadence ending on a sustained unison on the keynote (which is also the designated key of the symphony).

9 MAY 1905

Ernst PAUER, Viennese musicologist and composer, known principally by his editions of piano literature, dies at Jugenheim in his seventy-ninth year.

15 MAY 1905

Le Mercure musical, a fortnightly review, later the official journal of the Société Internationale de Musique, starts publication in Paris.

17 MAY 1905

Vilhelm RAVN, Danish music historian who did some interesting research on English instrumentalists at the Danish Court (one of whom, William Kemp, might have enlightened Shakespeare on the topography of Kronborg Castle), dies in Copenhagen in his sixty-seventh year.

20 MAY 1905

The first musical festival of Alsace-Lorraine begins at Strasbourg, featuring three orchestral concerts conducted by Richard STRAUSS, Gustav MAHLER, and Camille CHEVILLARD in programs of French and German works.

"It was a splendid ambition for Alsace—the eternal field of battle—to inaugurate these European Olympian games. But in spite of good intentions, this meeting of nations resulted in a fight, on musical ground, between two civilizations and two arts—French and German." (Romain Rolland, *Musiciens d'aujourd'hui*)

22 MAY 1905

Le Matin publishes an article by COVIELLE condemning the Prix de Rome Jury for failing the second time to award the Grand Prix to RAVEL, who had applied for it in 1903 and again in 1905.

25 MAY 1905

The Schola Cantorum in Paris gives a concert, entirely devoted to compositions by Déodat DE SÉVERAC.

29 MAY 1905

Arthur NIKISCH conducts in Paris the first performance of SCRIABIN's *Third Symphony* (*Divine Poem*) the fullest expression of his musico-theosophic faith (as *Poem of Ecstasy* is of the panegoistic and *Prometheus* of the pantheistic).

31 MAY 1905

Franz STRAUSS, Royal Kammermusikus in the Munich Court Orchestra, horn player, father of Richard Strauss, and himself a composer (ten trios for Bavarian postillion horns), dies in Munich in his eighty-fourth year.

4 JUNE 1905

Albert LOESCHHORN, German composer of famous pianoforte studies and exercises, dies in Berlin twenty-three days before reaching the age of eighty-six.

20 JUNE 1905

Nine days after his forty-first birthday, Richard STRAUSS completes in Berlin his one-act opera *Salome,* after Oscar Wilde, op. 54, in which he reduces Wagner's ideal of music drama to a one-movement symphonic tragedy of tense, uninterrupted action, with the music in an idiom established in his symphonic poems and characterized by extreme fluidity of harmonic centers, melodic scaling of wide-spaced intervals, and acervative suspensions, resolving at critical moments into six-four major chords, suggesting cadential finality; all this against a background of definite rhythmic pulse, free from imbroglios, and coruscating orchestration.

17 JULY 1905

RIMSKY-KORSAKOV begins his book on orchestration with examples taken exclusively from his own works. (Date from the fifth Russian edition of *My Musical Life,* 1935)

2 AUGUST 1905

Claude DEBUSSY signs a contract with the publisher, Durand, for all his future works.

8 AUGUST 1905

André JOLIVET, French composer, of decidedly anti-tonal tendencies, striving to restore to music the magical, incantational powers it possessed in primitive humanity, disciple of Edgar Varèse in his belief in cosmic universality of abstract music, and member of the group La Jeune France, is born in Paris.

11 AUGUST 1905

The Sacred Congregation of the Rites at the Vatican issues a decree approving the Vatican edition of Gregorian melodies and establishing the rules for the use of this edition.

23 AUGUST 1905

Constant LAMBERT, brilliant, facile, and inventive English composer, talented in all the allied fields of music and literature, and susceptible to transatlantic rhythms of jazz, is born in London.

27 AUGUST 1905

Leopold GODOWSKY writes his polyphonic but pianistic arrangement of Rameau's *Tambourin*. (Date on the printed score)

13 SEPTEMBER 1905

Lilia, opera by the twenty-five-year-old futurist musician, Francesco Balilla PRATELLA, is produced at the Teatro Rossini at the composer's birthplace, Lugo. (Date from *Francesco Balilla Pratella, appunti biografici e bibliografici*, Ravenna, 1931)

11 OCTOBER 1905

The first concert of the Goeteborg Orchestra, Sweden (Goeteborgs Orkesterfoerening) is given under the direction of Heinrich Hammer.

15 OCTOBER 1905

Camille CHEVILLARD conducts, at the first concert of the Paris season at the Lamoureux concerts, the first performance from the manuscript of DEBUSSY's symphonic suite *La Mer*.

19 OCTOBER 1905

The revised and final version of SIBELIUS' *Violin Concerto* is performed for the first time in Berlin, Carl Halir playing the solo part, Richard Strauss conducting the orchestra accompaniment.

(The first version was performed in Helsingfors, Victor Nováček playing the solo part, and Sibelius conducting, 8 February 1904)

21 OCTOBER 1905

Ferruccio BUSONI conducts in Berlin the first performance of his suite in eight divisions to Gozzi's Chinese fairy tale, *Turandot*, quite Western in texture, diatonic or chromatic, free from pseudo-sinological pentatonicity.

7 NOVEMBER 1905

Miarka, The Bear's Daughter, opera in four acts by Alexandre

GEORGES, after Jean Richepin's fairy tale, written in free modal style, with open fifths in the chromatic series and consecutive triads as the chief innovation, is produced at the Opéra-Comique in Paris.

10 NOVEMBER 1905

Willem MENGELBERG conducts the New York Philharmonic Orchestra, in his first appearance in America.

27 NOVEMBER 1905

At the first distribution of prizes of the Glinka Prize Fund, established by the publisher, Belaiev, the following awards are made: Anton ARENSKY—500 rubles for his *Trio in D Minor;* Serge LIAPUNOV—500 rubles for the *Second Piano Concerto;* Serge RACHMANINOV—500 rubles for two sonatas; and Serge TANEIEV—1000 rubles for his *Symphony in C Minor.*

5 DECEMBER 1905

Cassandra, "tragedy in two acts and a prologue" by Vittorio GNECCHI, quasi-Straussian in its harmonic and orchestral dress, is produced at Bologna, Toscanini conducting.

9 DECEMBER 1905

Ernst SCHUCH conducts at the Dresden Opera, the first performance of STRAUSS' *Salome,* from Oscar Wilde's drama of sensual love. (At this performance the Heckelphone, a baritone oboe invented by W. Heckel, was used for the first time in an orchestral score)

"For a long time no work has been awaited here with such expectancy as Strauss' *Salome.* It has been an open secret that the censor's prohibition in Vienna has only served as a cloak wherewith to hide the real reason for abandoning the performance—i.e., the refusal of the singers to devote themselves to its insane difficulties. It was expected that a similar condition might arise here even at the eleventh hour, but no obstacle intervened and everything went off in perfect order. The singers and orchestral musicians who accomplished almost supernatural deeds received full reward. First the public accorded them an ovation that lasted ten minutes by actual count, and culminated in twenty recalls, and secondly, the triumph was witnessed by all the managers of Germany's largest opera houses and by the most representative audience, intellectually, that could be gathered together in this country." (*Musikalisches Wochenblatt*)

"Seldom has the première of a new opera been expected more eagerly than the first performance of Richard Strauss' *Salome* at the Dresden Royal Opera. It was considered almost certain that the intelligent and educated Dresden public, accustomed as it is to the best in art, would protest angrily and loudly at an opera whose story exceeds in gruesomeness and perverted degeneracy anything that has ever been offered in a musical work for the stage. These fears were not realized, for the opera had a thunderous, stormy and unanimous success." (*Allgemeine Musik-Zeitung*)

"Richard Strauss' new work, *Salome,* has elicited more comment than any other opera produced in Europe since Verdi's *Falstaff.* Opinions vary as to its merits but it is certain that no other opera has created such a sensation in recent years.

"It is improbable that the larger opera houses will immediately accept the work in spite of its great success in Dresden. The German Emperor has, indeed, decided that it shall not be sung at the Royal Opera House in Berlin. . . .

"The music seems to differ in no important particular from the scores of the two earlier operas by Strauss. There is the same lack of melody—'economy of thematic construction' his admirers call it." (The New York *Sun*)

17 DECEMBER 1905

At the first meeting of the Autonomous Artistic Council of the St. Petersburg Conservatory, Alexandre GLAZUNOV is unanimously elected Director of the Conservatory.

(Date communicated by Maximilian Steinberg. Grove, Hull, and the *Encyclopaedia Britannica* give the erroneous year 1906)

"The provisional regulations for the Conservatory authorized the Artistic Council to engage instructors and elect a director from their midst. . . . The first act of the Council under the new law was to ask me and all those who had left with me to rejoin the faculty. The expelled students were reinstated. But it was impossible to resume classes because of the students' decision not to go back until the University and other institutions would open." (Rimsky-Korsakov in his *Musical Life*)

1906

1 JANUARY 1906

The Pipe of Desire, "romantic grand opera in one act" by Frederick S. CONVERSE, his first operatic work, is produced at Jordan Hall, Boston, four days before his thirty-fifth birthday.

(Date from *Analytical Notes* of the opera by Olin Downes, New York, 1906)

11 JANUARY 1906

Igor STRAVINSKY marries his first cousin, Catherine Nossenko, in St. Petersburg.

21 JANUARY 1906

Édouard COLONNE conducts in Paris the first performance of Georges ENESCO's *Symphony in E-Flat Major.*

5 FEBRUARY 1906

Maurice RAVEL affirms his priority in evolving new piano technique in the following letter, addressed to Pierre LALO, music critic of *Le Temps:*

"You have commented at great length upon a rather special method of writing for piano, the invention of which you attribute to Debussy. I wish to point out that my *Jeux d'Eau* appeared early in 1902, when there were no other piano works by Debussy than his three pieces *Pour le Piano,* which I admire very much but which contain nothing new from the pianistic point of view." (Quoted in *Le Temps* of 9 April 1907)

8 FEBRUARY 1906

Gustavo PITTALUGA, Spanish composer of modernistic *zarzuelas* (musical comedies) and neo-romantic chamber music, is born in Madrid.

18 FEBRUARY 1906

Édouard COLONNE conducts the first performance of Vincent D'INDY's *Jour d'Été à la Montagne,* subdivided into three symphonic movements: *Aurore, Jour, Soir,* and written in an evocative, rather than literally pictorial style, in an early impressionistic harmonic idiom.

24 FEBRUARY 1906

L'Ancêtre, lyrical drama in three acts, by Camille SAINT-SAËNS, is produced at Monte Carlo.

25 FEBRUARY 1906

Anton ARENSKY, Russian composer of the Tchaikovsky-Rubinstein school, limner of twilight moods in minor keys, poet of nostalgic indetermination, dies at Terjoki, near St. Petersburg, in his forty-fifth year.

(Date from the obituary in the St. Petersburg Daily, *Novoye Vremya,* of 13 February 1906, old style. Arensky died on 12 February, old style, which corresponds to 25 February, new style, and this is the date given by the German dictionaries. Grove, in the article on Arensky, and M. D. Calvocoressi, in his article in Hull, give the mistaken date 11 March 1906, adding 13 more days to the also erroneous date of 26 February 1906, which latter date appears in Baker)

"In the autumn [sic] death carried off Arensky. A former pupil of mine, upon being graduated from the St. Petersburg Conservatory, he had become professor at the Moscow Conservatory and had lived in Moscow a number of years. According to all testimony, his life had run a dissipated course between wine and card-playing, yet his activity as a composer was most fertile." (Rimsky-Korsakov, *My Musical Life,* American edition, New York, 1935)

26 MARCH 1906

La Figlia di Jorio, opera by Alberto FRANCHETTI, is produced at La Scala, Milan.

27 MARCH 1906

Aphrodite, opera by Camille ERLANGER, to Pierre Louÿs' tale of a pagan and sensual Alexandria, is produced at the Paris Opéra-Comique. (Grove gives the erroneous date, 23 March 1906)

25 APRIL 1906

John Knowles PAINE, American composer and educator, founder of the music faculty at Harvard University, dies at Cambridge, in his sixty-eighth year.

29 APRIL 1906

➤ Eleven days after the earthquake in San Francisco, musical activities are resumed, and a concert of miscellaneous music is given for the first time since the disaster.

8 MAY 1906

Le Roi Aveugle, opera by Henri FÉVRIER, dedicated "À mon cher Maître Gabriel Fauré," with music that technically justifies the dedication (there are whole-tone scales, freely used modalities, consecutive melodic fourths, and other Fauréisms), is produced at the Paris Opéra-Comique.

21 MAY 1906

Willy FERRERO, precocious orchestral conductor, world sensation of prewar years, is born of Italian parents at Portland, Maine.

27 MAY 1906

Six weeks before his forty-sixth birthday, Gustav MAHLER conducts in Essen the first performance of his autobiographical "tragic" *Sixth Symphony,* in the classical four movements:

(1). *Allegro energico,* in A minor, with a quasi-Brahmsian first subject and quasi-Straussian second subject. (2). *Scherzo,* with the eighth note as a constant unit in a changing meter; chromatic in melody and harmony, and curiously orchestrated, with agile trombones and other brass doing passage work. (3). *Andante moderato,* in a modified E-flat harmonic major, with a pastoral E-major middle section, where cowbells are introduced. (4). *Finale,* antithesis of the first three movements, equaling their combined duration and overshadowing them in elemental force, of which a Berliozian orchestra, including the use of a heavy hammer, is the embodiment.

29 MAY 1906

Oxford University awards Edvard GRIEG the degree of Doctor of Music *honoris causa.*

14 JUNE 1906

Samuel COLERIDGE-TAYLOR, British mulatto composer, conducts in London the first performance of his symphonic *Variations on an African Air.*

16 JUNE 1906

The International Music Trades Exhibition is held at the Crystal Palace in London.

27 JUNE 1906

The Canadian Musical Festival is held in London with a program of music written either by Canadians or on subjects bearing on life in Canada.

1 JULY 1906

Manuel GARCIA, Madrid-born teacher of the "Swedish Nightingale," the lyric soprano-singer, Jenny Lind, father of the Paris-born dramatic soprano-singer, Pauline Viardot, and inventor of the laryngoscope, dies in London at the record age of one hundred and one years, three months, and two weeks, the only musician of any renown to have lived over a century.

14 JULY 1906

Sergei TANEIEV completes in Klin, near Moscow, his magnum opus, *Moving Counterpoint in Strict Style,* a textbook on counterpoint based on a mathematical method of analysis.

"Taneiev warned us that in order to understand his system of counterpoint one has to 'know algebra.' But what mathematics Taneiev had to introduce into his course was of a very elementary nature, and only the fact that our musical world is too far removed from any science whatsoever can account for the confusions and holy terror with which this 'algebra' and 'erudition' inspired most musicians." (Leonid Sabaneiev, *Serge Taneiev,* Paris, 1930, in Russian)

24 JULY 1906

On the eve of his twenty-third birthday Alfredo CASELLA completes, in Prascorsano, the composition of his *Symphony in B Minor,* op. 5, dedicated to his teacher, Xavier Leroux, and conceived along the broad lines of post-romantic symphonic music. (Date at end of manuscript)

AUGUST 1906

Gustav MAHLER, with his *Seventh Symphony* still unperformed, finishes his *Eighth Symphony* known as the "Symphony of a Thousand" because of the numbers of singers its choruses require.

"I have just finished my *Eighth!* It is the greatest thing I have as yet done and so individual in content and form that I cannot describe it in words. Imagine that the whole universe begins to sound in tone. The result is not merely human voices singing, but a vision of planets and suns coursing about." (From Mahler's letter to Willem Mengelberg, quoted in Gabriel Engel's book, *Gustav Mahler, Song-Symphonist,* New York, 1932)

23 AUGUST 1906

The first *Norfolk Rhapsody,* in E minor, by VAUGHAN WILLIAMS, based on folk songs, collected by the composer at Kings Lynn, Norfolk, is performed for the first time at a Promenade concert in London.

4 SEPTEMBER 1906

RIMSKY-KORSAKOV finishes his *Musical Life* with the following words: "The chronicle of my musical life has been completed. It is not orderly, it is uneven in details, written badly, and often dry, but it contains nothing that is not true."

7 SEPTEMBER 1906

Wolfgang GRAESER, precocious composer, mathematician, orientalist, and Bach scholar, who edited the Neue Bachgesellschaft edition of the *Art of the Fugue,* and in addition made an orchestral transcription of this great work, is born at Zurich.

25 SEPTEMBER 1906

Dmitri SHOSTAKOVITCH, Russian Soviet composer of operas, symphonies, and instrumental pieces in a fresh melodic style, is born in St. Petersburg.

10 OCTOBER 1906

RIMSKY-KORSAKOV finishes the orchestration of his opera, *Tale of the Invisible City of Kitej*, the Russian *Parsifal*.

(Date from Andrey Rimsky-Korsakov's annotations to the fifth Russian edition of *My Musical Life*, 1935, p. 319)

23 OCTOBER 1906

Vladimir STASSOV, Russian critic, champion of the national school, dies in St. Petersburg in his eighty-third year.

27 OCTOBER 1906

Camille SAINT-SAËNS arrives in New York on his American tour.

31 OCTOBER 1906

Ariane, opera in five acts, by Jules MASSENET, to the book of Catulle Mendès, is produced at the Paris Opéra.

"The season at the Paris Opéra has opened with an event of the first order. It is Massenet's new piece, *Ariane*. Critics may be left to wrangle as to the music's merit; the already old master has evidently striven to rise above the prettinesses of his prime." (Special Correspondence of the New York *Evening Post*, 13 November 1906)

"*Ariane* will rank high in the composer's works. The sensitive, seductive, sensual music of Massenet we have heard a great deal about. A hundred passages give us the familiar, fascinating Massenet, the feminine Massenet, one might say. Even in Hades, he cannot help charming us. But he does not only charm, he moves and thrills, also. In none of his previous operas has he proved himself as strong a dramatic composer as in *Ariane*." (London *Telegraph*, November 1906)

11 NOVEMBER 1906

The Wreckers, opera by Dame Ethel SMYTH, is performed for the first time at Leipzig.

1 DECEMBER 1906

Jean CARTAN, French composer of austere neo-classical chamber music, is born in Paris.

3 DECEMBER 1906

The Manhattan Opera House opens in New York City under the general management of Oscar HAMMERSTEIN.

8 DECEMBER 1906

A month and a half after the death of Vladimir STASSOV, a memorial concert of orchestral works dedicated to him—among them Rimsky-Korsakov's *Scheherazade*—is given at St. Petersburg, Felix Blumenfeld conducting.

11 DECEMBER 1906

Das Christ-Elflein, a "Christmas fairy story" in three acts, by Hans PFITZNER is produced at the Court Theatre in Munich.

(Date from *Musikalisches Wochenblatt* of 20 December 1906; Riemann and Moser give 1917. Grove mentions both 1906 and 1917. The *Universal Edition Jahrbuch,* 1926, gives 11 December [?] 1917, omitting the 1906 date)

14 DECEMBER 1906

The French Chamber of Deputies votes not to tax automobiles, but instead imposes a tax on pianos, as being more numerous than motor cars.

21 DECEMBER 1906

The *Eighth* and last symphony by Alexandre GLAZUNOV, "Ormazd-Ahriman," as it might be surnamed, the four movements alternating in joyful or foreboding moods, is performed for the first time at St. Petersburg.

24 DECEMBER 1906

Julio Cesare SONZOGNO, Italian composer of effective orchestral and vocal music, mostly of programmatic design, is born at Milan.

26 DECEMBER 1906

The Bohemian Club, a musicians' society, is founded in New York, with membership including persons of wealth and influence in society.

27 DECEMBER 1906

Psalm XLVI, for orchestra, chorus, and organ, by Florent SCHMITT, is performed for the first time at a Prix de Rome concert in Paris.

"Certainly this score of 120 pages, written on 32 staves generously blackened with notes, has not been filled with a dropper. The performers have no time to read their newspapers between two forte. . . . But this music is so well balanced that it ought not to frighten anybody." (Émile Vuillermoz)

29 DECEMBER 1906

Three weeks after his forty-first birthday, SIBELIUS conducts the first performance of his orchestral work, *Pohjola's Daughter,* at the Siloti concerts in St. Petersburg.

(Karl Ekman writes in his book on Sibelius, Helsingfors, 1935: "In the autumn *Pohjola's Daughter* was completed, the first performance taking place under the leadership of the composer in St. Petersburg shortly before Christmas, 1906." The author must have meant the Russian Christmas which occurs thirteen days later than in the Western countries. The date, taken from Siloti's original program, is 16 December, old style, i.e., 29 December, new style)

30 DECEMBER 1906

Eugene GOOSSENS, Belgian-born operatic conductor, father of Eugene Goossens, French-born operatic conductor, and grandfather of Eugene Goossens, London-born composer and conductor, dies at Liverpool in his sixty-first year.

1907

12 JANUARY 1907

At a concert of the Société Nationale in Paris, Maurice RAVEL's songs to the animal fables of Jules Renard, under the general title of *Histoires Naturelles,* are presented for the first time, arousing a great deal of wonderment, derision, and indignation.

"The Société Nationale had been very useful to French art, but since about 1900 it found itself under the influence of Vincent d'Indy. While pieces by mediocre students of the Schola Cantorum were performed at the Society's concerts, works of real value were often rejected. Even Ravel was accepted with suspicion, and at the first performance, the whole clan of the Schola was hostile to the point of impoliteness." (From a letter to the author from Charles Koechlin, one of the secessionist spirits of the Société Nationale and founder of the Société Indépendante)

14 JANUARY 1907

RIMSKY-KORSAKOV begins the composition of the entrance of the eunuch Astrologer in his opera, *The Golden Cockerel,* assigning the part to a tenor falsetto, an octave above the natural tenor register.

15 JANUARY 1907

The *Bulletin français de la S.I.M.,* edited by Écorcheville, succeeds the *Mercure musical,* continuing in its tradition of learned liberalism and aesthetic internationalism.

17 JANUARY 1907

Heink BADINGS, Dutch composer of symphonic music, pupil, in Amsterdam, of Sem Dresden and Willem Pijper, is born at Bandong, Java.

19 JANUARY 1907

Beniamino CESI, Italian pianist, pedagogue, and author of numerous teaching exercises and studies, dies in his native town of

Naples, in his sixty-second year, after long years of paralysis which had spared only his right hand and his speech.

22 JANUARY 1907

Salome, by Richard STRAUSS, is performed for the first time in America by the Metropolitan Opera Company in New York, creating dissension over the sensual plot of the heroine's heathen love for a decapitated saint.

"Operatic stories are as a rule quite dreadful enough to satisfy the most jaded fancy, and Wagner has outraged family relations sufficiently without our having to go into the history of the detestable Herod family. What with *Semiramida* and *Fedora* and *Tosca* and a few other tidbits, we certainly have enough of the seamy side of life on the operatic stage." (New York *Sun*)

"As to the mind and morals, they were diseased. Not to emphasize disgust, their state was one of decomposition far advanced. As to the music, it fits. It makes worse that to which nothing but music could give added degradation." (Brooklyn *Eagle*)

"Why, I know an old lady in Germany who has heard the opera twenty-seven times, and she likes it very much. It never did her any harm." (New York *Tribune*)

"Mark Twain's secretary said Mr. Clemens had never been able to sit through any production of grand opera, and that *Salome* was one of the very least of the author's troubles." (New York *Herald*)

26 JANUARY 1907

The Directors of the Metropolitan Opera and Real Estate Company of New York protest to the Director of the Opera against the continuation of STRAUSS' *Salome.*

"*Salome* Is Barred In New York
"Metropolitan Opera House Directors Denounce Production—Call It 'Detrimental to House's Interest'—Public Condemnation of Oscar Wilde Play Cause of Action—Audience Disgusted by Severed Head Scene—Disapproval of Critics Finds Prompt Response and Presentation is Doomed." (Headlines in the New York *Sun,* 27 January 1907)

"*Salome* Too, Too Dreadful–Strauss-Wilde Eroticism Is Protested by Directors of Metropolitan." (Headlines in the Boston *Herald,* 27 January 1907)

27 JANUARY 1907

Yielding to protests of the Directors of the Metropolitan Opera and Real Estate Company, the executive committee of the Metropolitan Opera in New York announces that no further performances of STRAUSS' *Salome* will be given.

"*Salome* Not Immoral Says Its Composer—Strauss Amazed at the Opposition Raised to his Play in New York." (Headlines in a Boston paper)

"Declares New York Wicked—Unfit to Judge *Salome*—The Noted Composer Emil Paur Attacks New York in Defending Strauss' Opera—Says City Pretends to Virtue But Is Rotten to Core." (Headlines in the Boston *Herald*)

"Shaw, Praising *Salome* Says People Don't Understand Him or Wilde." (Headlines in the Boston *Post*)

28 JANUARY 1907

The New England Watch and Ward Society starts an investigation into the inherent obscenity of the action and music of STRAUSS' *Salome,* with a view to preventing its possible performance in Boston.

"Boston Anxious to Hear *Salome*." (Headline in the Boston *Herald*) "*Salome* Named an Indecent Opera—The Rev. Dr. McElveen Condemns Music Which Appeals to Beast in Man." (Boston *Herald*) "Clergy Opposed to *Salome*—Strauss' Opera Disgrace to Civilization Is View of Dr. Henson—Dragging Sacred Things Down to Mire—Its Production an Insult, says Dr. Mann—Bishop Jaggar Also Disapproves—Mayor Intimates That Show May Not Come—Doubts If Theatre Will Do Anything Offensive to Public Opinion." (Headlines in a Boston paper)

"No *Salome* For Boston—Too Many Stumbling Blocks Stops Presentation." (Headline in the Boston *Post)*

3 FEBRUARY 1907

At the National Theatre in Prague, the first performance is given of *Asrael,* second symphony in five movements, by Josef SUK, the MAHLER of Bohemia, written in a considerably enlarged tonal style, with the inclusion of whole-tone scales, and sustained in a funereal, fatalistic mood, explainable by a personal loss: SUK's wife, Antonin DVOŘÁK's daughter, had died during the composition of this symphony.

"Dvořák severely censured his son-in-law for attempting this pentagonal monument. When he was asked once what he thought of symphonic form, he said: 'God gave us five fingers. Why not four or six? Beethoven gave four movements to a symphony. Three is too few; five is too many.' " (William Ritter in Chronique Tchèque, *Mercure musical et S.I.M.*, 15 January 1907)

5 FEBRUARY 1907

Ludwig THUILLE, German composer of music in neo-Brahmsian style, dies in Munich in his forty-sixth year.

9 FEBRUARY 1907

At Siloti's concert in St. Petersburg, celebrating the twenty-five years of GLAZUNOV's musical career, RIMSKY-KORSAKOV conducts his own symphonic sketch, *Toast to Glazunov*.

"The anniversary concert was a great success. The hall was full. The program was as follows: (1). The First Symphony (I conducted), then (2). Liadov's 'Processional,' with which Glazunov appeared on the podium. There were more than forty delegates with valedictory speeches, wreaths, etc. Towards the end, many telegrams from all over Russia and from abroad were read. Glazunov descended from the podium to the strains of my 'Toast,' which was repeated by request. Then Siloti conducted the *Eighth Symphony*, and for conclusion, Chaliapin sang Glazunov's *Bacchic Song*, with the orchestral accompaniment." (From Rimsky-Korsakov's letter to S. N. Kruglikov, published in the Chronograph in the fifth Russian edition of his *Musical Life*)

15 FEBRUARY 1907

The *Quartet in D Minor*, op. 7, by Arnold SCHOENBERG, entirely within a tonal frame, as the designation of the key clearly indicates, is performed for the first time in Vienna.

17 FEBRUARY 1907

Taijiro GOH, Japanese composer, founder of Hacsoh-ha, Composers' Society of Japan, is born in Manchuria.

(Date in the printed score of Goh's *Theme and Variations for String Trio*, Tokyo, 1933. See Goh's letter to the author in Part III)

20 FEBRUARY 1907

RIMSKY-KORSAKOV's mystic opera, *Tale of the Invisible City of Kitej,* is performed for the first time at the Maryinsky Theatre in St. Petersburg, Felix BLUMENFELD conducting.

21 FEBRUARY 1907

A Village Romeo and Juliet, opera by Frederick DELIUS, is produced in Berlin. (Date from *Universal Edition Jahrbuch,* 1926)

28 FEBRUARY 1907

La Faute de l'Abbé Mouret, opera by Alfred BRUNEAU to Zola's story, is produced at the Odéon Theatre, in Paris.

(Date from announcements in *Le Temps* of 28 February 1907 *seq.,* corroborated in Gabriel Fauré's review in *Le Figaro* of 1 March 1907. Also, Arthur Harvey in his monograph on Alfred Bruneau, London, 1907, gives 28 February 1907. The title-page of the printed score gives the erroneous date of 1 March 1907)

2 MARCH 1907

Sergei VASSILENKO conducts in Moscow the first performance of his *First Symphony,* in G minor, op. 10.

(Date from *Russkoe Slovo,* announcement in 17 February/2 March 1907. Fleisher gives the old-style date, 17 February 1907)

4 MARCH 1907

W. W. BESSEL, head of the Bessel Music Publishing House, publisher of the original edition of' MOUSSORGSKY's *Boris Godunov* (1874), dies in Zurich.

(Grove, Riemann, Baker, and Einstein in his *Musiklexikon,* 1926, all give the wrong date, 25 April 1907, obviously through confusion with the day and month of Bessel's birth, 25 April 1843. Whenever someone in a dictionary dies on his birthday, the alarm of dubiety should be instantly rung, as the odds against such an occurrence are 364 to one. The date, 4 March 1907, or 19 February 1907, old style, is taken from the highly reliable Chronograph to Andrey Rimsky-Korsakov's fifth Russian edition of his father's *My Musical Life,* 1935. *Die Signale* of 27 March 1907, page 403, has a note about Bessel's death, which definitely disposes of the April date)

4 MARCH 1907

The Congregational ministers of Boston appeal to Mayor Fitz-
gerald to prevent the possibility of STRAUSS' *Salome* ever being
staged in Boston, because of its "debauching and brutalizing effects."

5 MARCH 1907

Dr. Lee de Forest transmits Rossini's *William Tell* overture by
wireless from the Telharmonic Hall in New York City to the
Navy Yard, the first time that a musical composition has been
broadcast.

"There's music in the air about the roof of the Hotel Normandie these
days. A good deal of it is being collected by wireless telephone ready
for distribution to possible purchasers." (New York *Tribune*, 7 March
1907)

9 MARCH 1907

Arnold SCHOENBERG finishes the composition of his choral work,
Friede auf Erden, op. 13, and begins his work on the *F-Sharp
Minor Quartet,* designated op. 10, his last work (in time and by
opus number) to bear a key signature indicative of tonality.

9 MARCH 1907

Albert ROUSSEL composes his stylized neo-classical song *Ode à un
Jeune Gentilhomme.* (Date from Louis Vuillemin's monograph on
Roussel, Paris, 1919)

17 APRIL 1907

Tom Jones, comic opera by Edward GERMAN, written in the style
made familiar by Gilbert and Sullivan, is produced at the Apollo
Theatre in London.

10 MAY 1907

Ariane et Barbe-Bleue, opera in three acts to Maeterlinck's drama,
music by Paul DUKAS, written in an impressionist symphonic style,
with individualized instrumentation and great profusion of di-
aphanous tone-color, is produced at the Opéra-Comique in Paris.

"... The Maeterlinck drama might perhaps dispense with a musical commentary; but this music of Paul Dukas, so clearly delineated, so sharp and eloquent, does it not throw more light on the personages of the drama, who walk in a somewhat imprecise atmosphere and express themselves in a similarly imprecise manner? Does it not make their emotions more vivid, their sayings more vibrant and articulate? And what a marvelous subject for pictorial music is the cascade of scattered jewelry! What an admirable page has Dukas written! What magic sonority, what variety, what invention in this phantasmagoria of rich stones, falling in a cataract, emeralds, sapphires, pearls, rubies!" (Gabriel Fauré in *Figaro,* 11 May 1907)

16, 19, 23, 26, 30 MAY 1907

Five Historical Russian Concerts are given in Paris, at which RIMSKY-KORSAKOV conducts a suite from his opera *Christmas Eve; Introduction* and two songs from the opera *Snow-Maiden;* and the submarine scene from *Sadko.*

26 MAY 1907

The Bach House and Museum are opened at Eisenach.

27 MAY 1907

RACHMANINOV completes the composition of his first piano *Sonata,* op. 28.

30 MAY 1907

Richard STRAUSS gives Antoine MARIOTTE, French composer of an opera called *Salomé,* unconditional permission to have the opera performed, waiving his legal right to the exclusive use of Oscar Wilde's text. (Date from special Paris correspondence in the New York *Times,* 4 December 1908)

4 JUNE 1907

Agathe BACKER-GROENDAHL, Norwegian woman pianist and composer of some seventy works, mostly music for children, dies at Christiania in her sixtieth year.

(Date confirmed by the Library of Oslo in a communication to the author. Grove and Hull give the erroneous 6 June, Riemann gives 16 June)

12 JUNE 1907

Alexandre GLAZUNOV is awarded the honorary degree of Doctor in Music by the University of Cambridge, England. (Date from the University's Registrar's clerk to the author)

"Gaudium nostrum cumulauit hodie uir in arte musica insignis, qui Russorum in imperio maximo iam per annos quinque et uiginti in luce publica uersatus, primum abhinc annos decem Britanniae innotuit. Argumenta magna uir magnus aggressus, popularium suorum artis musicae hodiernae in 'Raymonda' praesertim documentum splendidum protulisse dicitur. Inter peritos uero constat, 'nympham pulchram dormientem' illam a Tschaikovskio, doctore olim nostro, musicis modis accommodatam, quasi statuarum elegantissimarum ordinem effingere; uiri huius autem 'Raymondam' figuris potius ex aere fusis immensis comparari. Iuuat nunc iterum ex imperio Russorum ad nos aduectum salutare magistrorum in arte musica magnorum aemulum, qui artis suae genus pulchrum, genus seuerum et sobrium repraesentat, patriaeque cantus populares non minus fideliter quam feliciter exprimit." (Text of the speech delivered by the Public Orator in presenting to the Chancellor the recipient of the honorary degree of Doctor in Music)

18 JUNE 1907

Alexandre GLAZUNOV is awarded the honorary degree of Doctor of Music by Oxford University.

26 JUNE 1907

Camille SAINT-SAËNS is awarded the honorary degree of Doctor of Music by Oxford University.

15 AUGUST 1907

Joseph JOACHIM, Hungarian-born violin virtuoso, leader of a famous string quartet, composer of violinistic pieces, and teacher of a generation of violinists, dies in Berlin at the age of seventy-six years, one month, and eighteen days.

4 SEPTEMBER 1907

Edvard GRIEG, the "Chopin of the North," whose style is rooted in the Norwegian folk song set in modal harmonies, dies at his native Bergen, at the age of sixty-four years, two months, and nineteen days.

"Edward Grieg, the famous composer, died here [Bergen] this morning. Mr. Grieg stayed at the Hotel Norge here during the last few days, and intended to leave for Christiania yesterday; his luggage had already been taken on board. At noon, however, he complained of feeling ill, and, as the symptoms appeared to be serious, the patient was removed to the hospital. His wife was with him all night, and at half-past three this morning he passed away peacefully." (London *Times*, 5 September 1907)

11 SEPTEMBER 1907

Nine months and ten days before his death, RIMSKY-KORSAKOV completes the score of his last opera, *The Golden Cockerel*, to Pushkin's tale of a lazy Tsar, wily astrologer, heartless princess, and fateful cockerel, in three acts with a prologue and epilogue, the music of the mock-funereal second act being extremely advanced, making use of whole-tone scales and diminished-seventh chords superimposed on augmented triads.

25 SEPTEMBER 1907

Jan SIBELIUS conducts in Helsingfors a concert of his compositions, including *Pohjola's Daughter,* the *Belshazaar Suite,* and the first performance anywhere of the *Third Symphony in C Major,* begun in September 1904 and completed in the summer of 1907.

27 SEPTEMBER 1907

Two *Norfolk Rhapsodies* (Nos. 2 and 3) by VAUGHAN WILLIAMS, based on the folklore of the countryside, are performed for the first time at the Cardiff Festival in England.

15 OCTOBER 1907

Gustav MAHLER conducts at the Vienna Opera House for the last time before his resignation and departure to America.

26 OCTOBER 1907

Die Rote Gret, first opera by the Viennese composer, Julius BITTNER, based on folklore of the Austrian countryside, is produced at Frankfort.

26 OCTOBER 1907

Giovanni SALVIUCCI, Italian composer of neo-romantic music, in

large forms and rich sonorities, pupil of Respighi at the Academy
of Santa Cecilia, is born in Rome.

"The first works of Giovanni Salviucci belong to the genre of symphonic
poem, and give no premonition of his future development. After several
experiments in this musical style, Salviucci turns to counterpoint, and in
it he finds his greater strength. He eventually forms a symphonic style,
well-balanced and distinguished by clarity and definiteness. His esthetic
position is not exactly neo-classical, and he is never completely attracted
by the ideal of absolute objectivism. In him there mingle elements of
instrumental classicism and imaginative romanticism, of the pictorial,
plastic quality characteristic of a Respighi. His true nature cannot however be determined by these two tendencies, and he remains an individual force in his architectonic design." (An appreciation sent to the
author by Gianandrea Gavazzeni)

27 OCTOBER 1907

Wilhelm Tappert, German musicologist, onetime editor of the
Allgemeine Deutsche Musikzeitung, and compiler of a lexicon of
abusive criticism of Wagner, under the title *The Dictionary of
Impoliteness,* dies in Berlin in his seventy-eighth year.

1 NOVEMBER 1907

Rimsky-Korsakov completes the composition of his *Neapolitan
song* for orchestra, a symphonic version of *Funiculi, funicula* by
Luigi Denza, which he had mistaken for a folk-song as Richard
Strauss did in his early symphonic poem, *Aus Italien.*

6 NOVEMBER 1907

Le Chemineau, a rustic opera by Xavier Leroux, based on French
peasant songs, is produced at the Paris Opéra-Comique.

"We do not find here that violence that made *Astarté* so painful to listen
to . . . harmonies are fine, modulations elegant without desire to make
the listener gnash his teeth. . . . Here are qualities to which—alas! we
have not been accustomed for a long time." (Arthur Pougin in *Le
Ménestrel,* 9 November 1907)

16 NOVEMBER 1907

Jan Sibelius conducts his *Third Symphony* at a Siloti Concert in
St. Petersburg. (Date from the original program)

21 NOVEMBER 1907

Gaetano BRAGA, Italian composer of eight operas and of the celebrated *Angel's Serenade,* by which he is chiefly known, dies in
Milan in his seventy-ninth year.

22 NOVEMBER 1907

A Pagan Poem, after Virgil, for orchestra with piano obbligato, by
the Alsatian-born American composer, Charles Martin LOEFFLER,
written in the poetic evocative style of French impressionism, is
performed for the first time in public by the Boston Symphony
Orchestra, Karl Muck conducting.

(The date 23 November 1927, given in Philip Hale's *Boston Symphony
Programme Notes,* New York, 1935, is a misprint)

9 DECEMBER 1907

Gustav MAHLER leaves Vienna for America.

15 DECEMBER 1907

The censor refuses to allow the production of STRAUSS' opera,
Salome, in London.

17 DECEMBER 1907

Arnold SCHOENBERG begins the composition of a suite of songs
to Stefan George's expressionist poems *Das Buch der Haengenden
Gaerten.*

1908

1 JANUARY 1908

Gustav MAHLER makes his first appearance in the United States,
conducting *Tristan and Isolde* at the Metropolitan Opera in New
York.

2 JANUARY 1908

Blanche SELVA plays the first performance, at Madame de Poli-
nac's home in Paris, of the third book (*El Albaicin, El Polo, La-
vapiés*) of *Iberia,* pianoforte suite by Isaac ALBÉNIZ.

"In *El Albaicin,* from the third book of *Iberia* one finds the atmosphere
of those Spanish nights that emanate the fragrance of carnation and
aguardiente. . . . It is like the muffled sounds of a guitar complaining
in the night." (Claude Debussy, in the *Bulletin français de la S.I.M.,*
Paris, 1 December 1913)

6 JANUARY 1908

Jack Frost in Midsummer, symphonic ballet, written according
to the Wagnerian leitmotiv system, by Edward Burlingame HILL,
his first orchestral work, is performed for the first time by the
Chicago Symphony Orchestra.

18 JANUARY 1908

Eleven days before Frederick DELIUS' forty-fifth birthday, his
Brigg Fair, character piece for orchestra based on English country
songs, is performed at Liverpool, for the first time anywhere.

22 JANUARY 1908

August WILHELMJ, famous German violin virtuoso and arranger
of numerous pieces for his instrument, dies in London in his
sixty-third year.

22 JANUARY 1908

The *First Symphony,* in E-flat major, by the twenty-five-and-a-half-
year-old Igor STRAVINSKY is performed for the first time, by the
Imperial Orchestra in St. Petersburg.

"This symphony was composed at a time when Glazunov was the absolute master in symphonic science. Each one of his works was accepted
as a musical event of the first magnitude, so greatly appreciated was
the perfection of his form, the purity of his counterpoint, the ease and
sureness of his writing. At that time, I, too, shared in this admiration,
fascinated by the astonishing mastery of this scholar. It was natural
then that along with other influences (Tchaikovsky) I should have espe-

cially taken his symphonies for a model." (Stravinsky, *Chroniques de ma vie*, Paris, 1935)

23 JANUARY 1908

Edward MacDowell, the first truly national composer of America, whose European technique never dulled his sense for native folklore, dies in New York at the age of forty-six years, one month and five days.

"E. A. MacDowell Dead—Noted Composer and Pianist Passes Away at Home Here.—Dr. Edward A. Macdowell, the composer and pianist, died about 8 o'clock last night in his apartment at the Westminster Hotel, Irving Place and 16th Street, following a long illness. . . . The end was not unexpected, as he had been unconscious for twenty-four hours. . . . In the spring of 1905 overwork and insomnia brought on what eminent medical specialists pronounced to be a hopeless case of cerebral collapse. This it proved to be. Under the devoted care of his wife, he lived on, spending the summer months at Peterboro, N. H., the winter at his apartments in the Westminster Hotel, N. Y. C., oblivious to all the things which had once occupied a peculiarly active and sensitive mind." (New York *Tribune*, Friday, 24 January 1908)

(Grove, British edition, Riemann, Moser, and the *Encyclopaedia Britannica* give erroneously 24 January. It may be argued, however, that MacDowell died at 1:00 a.m. London time [8:00 p.m. New York time], that is, technically on the 24th, European time.)

23 JANUARY 1908

Serge Koussevitzky conducts the Philharmonic Orchestra in Berlin in his first appearance as conductor abroad, where he was chiefly known as a double-bass virtuoso.

1 FEBRUARY 1908

Claude Debussy conducts, in Queen's Hall, London, his *Prélude à l'Après-midi d'un Faune* and *La Mer*.

"With all the wealth of picturesque orchestration and piquant harmony and rhythm, we are inclined to doubt whether a second hearing of *La Mer* pieces would make us feel that they are the equal to the Prelude in imaginative impression. . . . The breath of freshness that came with Schubert's 'Unfinished' Symphony, which Mr. Wood conducted immediately after Mr. Debussy's work, was a tribute to older methods of expression, and showed up one defect at any rate in the French composer's music, its monotonous orchestral coloring." (An unidentified London paper—not the *Times*—3 February 1908)

2 FEBRUARY 1908

Renzo ROSSELINI, Italian composer of music, rhapsodic and dramatic in subject matter and neo-Vivaldian in treatment, is born in Rome.

8 FEBRUARY 1908

Serge RACHMANINOV conducts the first performance of his *Second Symphony* at the Siloti concerts in St. Petersburg.

13 FEBRUARY 1908

Gerald STRANG, composer of rationalist music, such as the characteristic piano piece, *Mirrorrorrim* (the title being the doubled word "mirror" in mirror spelling), inspired by Bach's contrapuntal art and Schoenberg's composing technique, is born at Claresholm, Canada.

15 FEBRUARY 1908

Giuseppe MARTUCCI conducts the dedicatory program at the inauguration of the Augusteo Symphony concerts in Rome.

19 FEBRUARY 1908

DEBUSSY's *Pelléas et Mélisande* is performed for the first time in America at the Manhattan Opera House, in New York.

"Lyric Drama Dazes New York—Debussy's opera Exquisite But Creepy —Characters Do Not Sing, They Intone to Wonderful and Mystic Harmonies." (Headlines in the New York *American*)

"Preraphaelite Opera—Pelléas and Melisande a Study in Glooms—A Mass of Shifting and Inessential Details—The Fundamentals of Music Left Out of Account." (Headlines in the New York *Sun*)

26 FEBRUARY 1908

La Habanera, by Raoul LAPARRA, French-Pyrenean composer of veristic music in effective Spanish or Basque rhythms, is produced in Paris at the Opéra-Comique.

29 FEBRUARY 1908

Le Faune et la Bergère, suite for orchestra and mezzo-soprano, by Igor STRAVINSKY, written in the Glazunov-like style of his apprentice years, with a few Debussyan major thirds appearing in the second song, is performed for the first time anywhere, at the Russian Symphony concerts in St. Petersburg.

3 MARCH 1908

Riccardo NIELSEN, Italian composer of symphonic and chamber music in the polyphonic style of a neo-classical design, is born at Bologna. (Date communicated by the composer)

9 MARCH 1908

RIMSKY-KORSAKOV is notified that the dramatic censor would give permission for the production of the opera *The Golden Cockerel,* only if the epilogue and some of the text, such as the cock-crow motto: "Cock-a-doodle-do! Rule your Tsardom in your sleep," are deleted.

"Pushkin's verse 'Rule your Tsardom in your sleep' is not passed by the censor. The introduction is allowed unconditionally, but the epilogue is absolutely banned (?!!?). The censors cannot even read right: they thought that the concluding verses are sung by the Tsar Dodon, instead of the Astrologer. What idiots! So an entirely new text for the conclusion will have to be written. But if the censors will not agree even to this innocent verse, then I will publish the whole thing in the press. There is a limit to everything." (From Rimsky-Korsakov's letter to his publisher, Jurgenson, dated 21 March 1908, published in the fifth Russian edition of *My Musical Life,* 1935, p. 351)

13 MARCH 1908

Nikita BALIEV gives the first performance, for an invited public, of his intimate cabaret show, *Chauve-Souris,* in a house next to the Church of Christ the Savior in Moscow. (The date is the leap-year day 29 February 1908, old style)

15 MARCH 1908

Rapsodie Espagnole by Maurice RAVEL, suite in four movements, evocative *Prélude à la Nuit,* rhythmic *Malagueña,* slow *Habanera,* and joyous *Feria,* is performed for the first time at a Colonne concert, in Paris, eight days after the composer's thirty-third birthday.

"The Rhapsody was enthusiastically received; the second movement was repeated. The enthusiasm was manifested chiefly in the gallery, where some perfervid student shouted to the conductor after the Malagueña had been repeated, 'Play it once more for those downstairs who have not understood it.' At the end of the Rhapsody the same person shouted to the occupants of subscribers' seats, 'If it had been something by Wagner, you would have found it very beautiful.' " (From Philip Hale's program note in the Boston Symphony program book, 1929–1930)

"Not mere impressionism, but 'pointillisme' in music is Mr. Maurice Ravel's *Spanish Rhapsody.* Even Mr. Claude Debussy's musical poem, *La Mer,* is painted in broader strokes. Mr. Ravel throws tiny little dabs of colour in showers upon his canvas. There is not an outline nor an expanse in the sketch; everything is in spots. In the third part, a 'Feria,' or fête, the first Violins, literally mewing like a rather deep-voiced tom-cat, brought laughs from the audience." (From the Paris dispatch in a London paper)

(Fleisher's Catalogue, Philadelphia, 1932, gives the erroneous date, 19 March 1908)

22 MARCH 1908

First Symphony, op. 7, surnamed *Le Poème de la Forêt,* by Albert ROUSSEL, is performed for the first time anywhere at the Théâtre de la Monnaie in Brussels, Sylvain DUPUIS conducting.

6 APRIL 1908

Carl NIELSEN conducts in Copenhagen the first performance of his *Saga-Dream,* op. 39.

8 APRIL 1908

Pope Pius X gives official sanction to the *Editio Vaticana* as the only authentic edition of Gregorian chant.

18 APRIL 1908

Geschichte der Motette by Hugo LEICHTENTRITT, tracing the history of the motet from the thirteenth to the twentieth century, is published by Breitkopf and Haertel.

15 MAY 1908

Lars-Erik LARSSON, Swedish composer in an advanced neo-romantic idiom, pupil of Alban Berg, author of an opera, *The Princess on Cyprus,* is born in Akarp, Sweden.

13 JUNE 1908

"Blind Tom," Negro musician with a freakish musical memory, dies in New York in his fifty-ninth year.

"Tom was born in Georgia, owned by a man named Jones. He was an idiot from birth. His father and mother were offered for sale. Price: $1500 without Tom. $1200 with him." (From Dwight's *Journal of Music,* date uncertain)

15 JUNE 1908

Twenty-nine days after his forty-second birthday, Erik SATIE, French eccentric genius, obtains a diploma for three years' graduate work in counterpoint under Albert ROUSSEL at the Schola Cantorum with the mark "très bien."

17 JUNE 1908

Seventeen days before his twenty-fifth birthday, Maximilian STEINBERG marries RIMSKY-KORSAKOV's daughter in a village church near Kritzi, and Igor STRAVINSKY, on his own twenty-sixth birthday, dedicates his symphonic poem, *Fireworks,* to the newlyweds.

20 JUNE 1908

Federico CHUECA, Spanish composer of popular music, called by Pedro Morales the "barrel-organ of his generation," co-author with Joaquín Valverde of the international hit, the musical comedy, *La Gran Via,* dies in Madrid in his sixty-third year.

21 JUNE 1908

Daniel AYALA, Mexican-Mayan-Indian composer, whose music expresses, in its rhythm and melos, his three-fold cultural and racial heritage, is born in Yucatan.

21 JUNE 1908

RIMSKY-KORSAKOV dies of asthma at Lubensk, near St. Petersburg, during the night, after a short but strong electrical storm, at the age of sixty-four years, three months, and three days, survived only by BALAKIREV and CUI of the "Mighty Five."

JULY 1908

Claude DEBUSSY composes a suite of piano pieces dedicated to his daughter (*À ma chère petite Chouchou avec les tendres excuses de son père pour ce qui va suivre*) and entitled (in English) *Children's Corner:*

(1). *Doctor Gradus ad Parnassum,* brilliant stylization of Clementi, in C major with some acrid harmonic digressions. (2). *Jimbo's Lullaby,* elephantine swinging tune, spiced with secundal embellishments. (3). *Serenade of the Doll,* in pentatonic harmony, technically in E major. (4). *The Snow Is Dancing,* built on a Phrygian tetrachord, and sustained in a rapid movement of sixteenth notes. (5). *The Little Shepherd,* in the form of an aria. (6). *Golliwogg's Cake Walk,* stylized imitation of a popular American dance.

8 AUGUST 1908

Two weeks after his twenty-fifth birthday, Alfredo CASELLA completes in Paris the orchestral arrangement of BALAKIREV's *Islamey,* making use of all the resources of modern orchestra. (Date at end of score)

19 SEPTEMBER 1908

Gustav MAHLER conducts in Prague the first performance of his *Seventh Symphony,* in E minor, the "Song of the Night," or "Romantic" symphony (which concludes the symphonic trilogy of the "earthly" *Fifth Symphony* and the autobiographical "tragic" *Sixth Symphony*), in the following five movements:

(1). *Allegro con fuoco* with a funereal, foreboding introduction, in a Beethoven-like sonata form, with the second subject significantly built on fourths—Mahler's first incursion into quartal harmony. (2). *Night Music,* evocative tone-poem opening with a horn theme in C harmonic major, answered by another horn in C minor. (3). *Shadow-like,* a light scherzo in D minor and F major. (4). *Night Music,* in the nature of a serenade in duple time in F major. (5). *Rondo-Finale,* in brilliant C major, opening with a kettle-drum solo.

20 SEPTEMBER 1908

Pablo de SARASATE, celebrated Spanish violinist and composer of prestidigital concert pieces, dies in his villa at Biarritz at the age of sixty-four years, six months, and ten days.

(Date from the London *Times,* 22 September 1908, which specifically states that Sarasate "died suddenly last Sunday evening," i.e., 20 September. Riemann, 1929, Moser, 1935, Grove give the inaccurate date 21 September)

21 SEPTEMBER 1908

Nicolas MIASKOVSKY completes the full score of his *First Symphony* in C minor, op. 3, in three movements.

(Composition of piano score was completed 9 August 1908. Dates communicated by the composer)

30 OCTOBER 1908

Franco MARGOLA, Italian composer whose style reveals early neo-romantic, Pizzettian influences beneath a more sober and secure sonorous objectivism of the Casella school, is born at Orzinuovi, Brescia.

"Influenced at first by Pizzetti and his decidedly romantic outlook on music, Franco Margola experiences musical impressions more fully corresponding to the spirit of the times, and puts himself, uncompromisingly, under the guidance of Alfredo Casella. The mark of Casella's personality is clearly impressed upon Margola's more recent works. Margola combines musical objectivism with instrumental efficiency, and indues his musical invention with sonorous and rhythmic acridities." (An appreciation sent to the author by Gianandrea Gavazzeni)

9 NOVEMBER 1908

The Baptist and Methodist clergy of Philadelphia make a protest against any attempt to produce Strauss' *Salome* in their city.

16 NOVEMBER 1908

Arturo TOSCANINI makes his first appearance in America, conducting *Aïda* at the Metropolitan Opera in New York.

19 NOVEMBER 1908

Daniel-Lesur, French composer, member of the group, La Jeune France, professing to write music expressive of new France, is born in Paris. (Date in the *Dictionnaire national des contemporains,* Paris, 1936)

3 DECEMBER 1908

Hans Richter conducts in Manchester the first performance of Elgar's *First Symphony,* in A-flat major, dedicated "to Hans Richter, Mus. Doc., true Artist and true Friend," and composed in traditional four movements with no acknowledged program— and certainly not descriptive of General Gordon's life and death, as a spontaneously generated myth had it.

"You will find many subtle enharmonic relationships I think, and the widest *looking* divergencies are often the closest relationships." (From Elgar's letter to Jaeger, quoted in Basil Maine, *Elgar, His Life and Works,* London, 1933)

10 DECEMBER 1908

Olivier Messiaen, French composer of strong polyphonic music based on novel scales, is born in Avignon.

10 DECEMBER 1908

The Russian Symphony Orchestra of New York, conducted by Modest Altschuler, gives the world première of Scriabin's *Poem of Ecstasy,* op. 54, in one continuous movement, subdivided into the following sections:

Andante, Languido, serving as an introduction; *Lento, Soavamente,* in which the clarinet states the main subject built on ascending fourths over a tonic-dominant pedal point, forming an altered chord of the thirteenth; *Allegro volando,* rhythmically varying the main melodic and harmonic design; *Lento, Allegro non troppo,* where the trumpet imperiously enters for the first time, ascending in fourths, over ninthchord harmonies of the orchestra, with strong pedal points, "avec une noble et douce majesté"; *Moderato, avec délice,* of transitional character, gradually growing in dynamic power, with such expression marks as "avec une ivresse toujours croissante" and "presque en délire"; *Allegro dramatico,* marked "avec une noble et joyeuse émotion," where the trumpet intones the main subject anew in the modified recapitulation, culminating in a fifty-three bar *Maestoso* over a pedal point on C.

"It was a confident young man of 19 years who appeared at the Carnegie Hall platform last night to endeavor to make the name of Mischa Elman as well known and liked here as it is in England and Europe. . . . The nerves of the audience last night, as it happened, had been worn and racked just previous to Elman's appearance as nerves are seldom assailed even in these days. Scriabin's *Poème de l'Extase* was the cause. This composition was heralded as a foster-child of Theosophy. Certainly it conveyed a sense of eeriness. . . . A solo violin spoke occasionally, growing more and more plaintive, and finally being swallowed up in a chaos of acid harmonies with violins screaming in agony overhead. There were three such climaxes in the composition, all built upon a basis of cymbals, drums and inchoate blarings of the brass. It all seemed far more like several other things than ecstasy." (New York *Sun,* 11 December 1908)

24 DECEMBER 1908

François Auguste GEVAERT, Belgian composer and author of fundamental treatises on music, dies in Brussels in his eighty-first year.

25 DECEMBER 1908

Eva Wagner, step-daughter of Wagner, marries Houston Stewart Chamberlain, Germanized English Wagnerite.

25 DECEMBER 1908

Claude DEBUSSY completes the orchestral score of *Iberia,* second number of the suite, *Images,* and itself subdivided into three sections:

(1). *Par les rues et par les chemins,* in animated triple time, making use of characteristic parallel chord progressions and Lydian tetrachords as parts of a whole-tone scale. (2). *Les parfums de la nuit* in dreamy duple time. (3). *Le matin d'un jour de fête,* in march time, making use of violins pizzicato played under the arm, like guitars.

30 DECEMBER 1908

The *Berliner Tageblatt* publishes an article by Dr. Schmidt with a denial of the newspaper story that Richard STRAUSS demanded the destruction of the manuscript of the opera, *Salome,* by the

French composer, Mariotte, on the grounds that he, Strauss, possessed legal rights to Oscar Wilde's text.

1909

13 JANUARY 1909

Monna Vanna, lyric drama to Maeterlinck's play, by Henri FÉVRIER, in which he abandons the more advanced idiom of the Fauré school for pure operatic melos and traditional harmonies, is produced at the Opéra in Paris.

15 JANUARY 1909

Ernest REYER, French operatic composer who added two letters to his real name, Rey, out of admiration for Wagner, dies at Lavandou, France, in his eighty-sixth year.

21 JANUARY 1909

Hircus Nocturnus, symphonic poem by Sergei VASSILENKO, descriptive of magic on the Brocken Mountain in a neo-Moussorgskyan manner, is performed for the first time in Moscow, Emil COOPER conducting.

24 JANUARY 1909

The name of ROGER-DUCASSE appears for the first time on the program of an orchestral concert in Paris, when his *Variations Plaisantes sur un Thème Grave* is played at a Lamoureux concert. (Date from Laurent Ceillier, *Roger-Ducasse,* Paris, 1920)

25 JANUARY 1909

Ernst SCHUCH conducts at the Dresden Opera the first performance of Richard STRAUSS' *Electra,* tragedy in one act to Hugo von Hofmannsthal's libretto, which attains the ultimate complexity of the Wagnerian music drama, and reaches well into polytonality and atonality as a result of progressive chord alteration and use of pedal points.

(The date 25 January 1900 on page 244 of Henry T. Finck's *Richard Strauss*, Boston, 1917, is a misprint)

"*Electra*, Richard Strauss' newest operatic sensation, was produced for the first time on any stage before a brilliant international audience at the Saxon Royal Opera here tonight, with Mme. Krull as Electra, Mme. Schumann-Heink as Clytemnestra, and Perron as Orestes. With one act lasting an hour and forty minutes, and 122 players in the orchestra, for thrilling histrionic vocal and orchestral effects, *Electra* outrivals *Salome*. . . . It is a prodigious orchestral orgy, with nothing that can be called music in the score, and makes superhuman demands upon the physical and mental powers of the singers and players. The marvellous imitative effects of the orchestra are blood curdling, drastic and gruesome to the last degree. It is fortunate for hearers the piece is no longer for it would else be too nerve racking." (From cable dispatch to the New York *Times*)

"Violent, Lurid *Electra*—First impressions of Richard Strauss' new opera—A Remarkable Work Whatever May Be Thought of the Theme—*Salome* Outdone—Gruesome Expressions in Music of Mysterious Moments of Horror."

"*Dresden*, 26 January 1909. The most interesting if not the most important event in recent years in the musical world was the first performance last evening of Richard Strauss' *Electra* at the Royal Opera House of Dresden. If the orchestral apparatus was unprecedentedly ambitious in *Salome*, it has not grown less so for *Electra*. A body of instrumentalists that can with difficulty be placed in even our largest theatres, have tasks set them which rival in difficulty only those of the soloists on the stage. In the matter of exacting qualities of the new music all previous standards must be set aside. The seemingly impossible has been accomplished: *Salome* has been outdone." (Dispatch to the New York *Sun*)

31 JANUARY 1909

Édouard Louis François FÉTIS, French music scholar, son of the great François Fétis, dies in a street accident in Brussels, at the age of ninety-six years and eight and a half months.

3 FEBRUARY 1909

A century has passed since Felix MENDELSSOHN was born in Hamburg.

6 FEBRUARY 1909

STRAVINSKY's *Fantastic Scherzo* is performed for the first time at a Siloti concert. (Date from the original program)

"The performance of the *Fantastic Scherzo* and *Fireworks* marks an important date in my entire musical career. It is then that my close relationship with Diaghilev was established. Having heard these pieces in the orchestra, he entrusted me with the orchestration of two pieces by Chopin for the ballet *Sylphides* which was to be performed in Paris in the Spring of 1909." (Stravinsky, *Chroniques de ma vie*, Paris, 1935)

9 FEBRUARY 1909

The fourth and last book (containing *Malaga, Jerez, Eritaña*) of the suite *Iberia* for pianoforte by Isaac ALBÉNIZ is performed for the first time by Blanche SELVA in Paris, three months and nine days before ALBÉNIZ' death.

"*Eritaña,* in the fourth book of *Iberia,* is joy of the morning, a happy stop at an inn where wine is fresh. An incessantly changing crowd passes with peals of laughter, accentuated by the ringing rhythms of a tambourin. Never has music attained impressions so diverse, so colorful." (Claude Debussy in the *Bulletin français de la S.I.M.,* 1 December 1913)

9 FEBRUARY 1909

Quo Vadis, opera from Senkiewicz's book of early Christian drama, by Jean NOUGUÈS, French composer of facile melodic gifts and fine understanding of theatrical music, is produced at Nice.

12 FEBRUARY 1909

PADEREWSKI's *Symphony in B minor* is given its first public performance by the Boston Symphony Orchestra, with Paderewski playing, on the same program, the SAINT-SAËNS C-minor *Concerto,* Max FIEDLER conducting.

"Paderewski the Magnet—Attracts as Soloist and Composer—New Symphony a Monumental Work of Art." (Headlines in the Boston *Globe)*

"Paderewski's *Symphony*—Yesterday Its First Audience Heard It. The Disappointment That It Brought and a Lukewarm Reception for It . . . The Monotony of Mood and Color and the Lack of Vital Emotional Appeal." (Headlines in the Boston *Transcript)*

12 FEBRUARY 1909

F. T. MARINETTI publishes in the Paris *Le Figaro* the first Futurist Manifesto, proclaiming the new foundations of futurist art, literature, and music.

20 FEBRUARY 1909

Arnold SCHOENBERG composes the second piece of the three *Klavierstuecke,* op. 11, which marks the final departure from tonality and the beginning of atonality (not yet the twelve-tone system) with the keynote still remaining in the form of a basso ostinato.

"I am striving toward a goal that seems to be certain, and I already feel the opposition that I shall have to overcome. . . . It is not lack of invention nor of technical skill, nor of the knowledge of the other requirements of contemporary aesthetics that has urged me to this direction. . . . I am following an inner compulsion that is stronger than education, stronger than my artistic training." (Arnold Schoenberg in a program note)

22 FEBRUARY 1909

SIBELIUS conducts a concert of his music in the Queen's Hall, London.

1 MARCH 1909

The *Rivista musicale italiana* publishes an article by Giovanni TEBALDINI, entitled "Musical Telepathy," purporting to demonstrate, by collation of some fifty musical examples, that Richard Strauss in his opera, *Electra,* has used identifiable melodic and harmonic portions from *Cassandra,* opera by Vittorio GNECCHI, produced at Bologna three years and one and a half months before *Electra.*

"This article of Tebaldini was destined to attract extraordinary attention in the entire European press, which devoted a hundred articles to it. In Germany, friends of Strauss replied that the similarity was in appearance only, and that certain themes dressed in Straussian instrumentation are unrecognizable. Hartman, while breaking lances in defense of Strauss, published a letter in the *Dresdner Neueste Nachrichten* in which he admitted that Gnecchi had met Strauss in Turin and gave him a copy of the score of *Cassandra* with an inscription." (De Angelis, *Dizionario dei musicisti,* Rome, 1928)

16 MARCH 1909

Serge KOUSSEVITZKY and his wife, Natalie, formally establish the Russian Music Publishing House with a capital of 1,250,000 French francs, designed for publication of works by Russian composers.

19 MARCH 1909

Arnold SCHOENBERG composes No. 1 of the three *Klavierstuecke,* op. 11, in an idiom farther away from tonality than No. 2 of the same opus, composed twenty-five days before.

25 MARCH 1909

Ruperto CHAPÍ, Spanish composer of one hundred and sixty-eight works for the stage in a light vein and co-author of the international musical comedy hit *Gran Via,* dies in his native Madrid two days before his fifty-eighth birthday.

1 APRIL 1909

Governor Draper of Massachusetts writes to Manager Hammerstein of the Manhattan Opera Company asking him to omit an announced performance of STRAUSS' *Salome* in Boston,. in deference to the protests from Bishop Lawrence and other prominent Massachusetts personages.

2 APRIL 1909

Mayor Hibbard of Boston puts a ban on the production of STRAUSS' *Salome,* giving as a reason a telephone call from a woman acquaintance who had seen the opera in New York and thought it was not proper for Boston consumption.

8 APRIL 1909

Ivan DZERZHINSKY, Soviet composer of simple melodious music, accessible to the masses, author of the opera, *Quiet Flows the Don,* to Sholohov's epic of the Cossack land, is born at Tambov.

1 MAY 1909

A month after his thirty-sixth birthday, Serge RACHMANINOV conducts in Moscow the first performance of his *Island of the Dead*, symphonic poem for full orchestra inspired by Boecklin's famous painting, and couched in ⅝ meter expressive of the tranquil motion of mortuary waves.

5 MAY 1909

In a letter to Romain Rolland, Richard STRAUSS (1) ridicules the story of identifiable affinity between his opera *Electra* and GNECCHI's earlier *Cassandra;* (2) denies that he ever demanded the suppression of the French composer Mariotte's opera *Salomé.*

15 MAY 1909

Giuseppe BLANC, twenty-three-year-old Italian student, composes the song *Giovinezza,* destined to become the official Fascist hymn.

"On the fifteenth of May 1909 we students were to have a farewell dinner before we graduated, and that morning some of them came to me and said, 'You must write us a song to sing at the dinner tonight.' I said I would do it if some one else would write the words. Nino Oxilia sat down and in five minutes wrote the verse. It took me no longer than that to write the music." (From an interview with Giuseppe Blanc in the New York *Times,* 10 October 1934. The story is corroborated in Alberto de Angelis' *Dizionario dei musicisti,* third edition, Rome, 1930)

18 MAY 1909

Isaac ALBÉNIZ, Spanish composer who, with Granados and Pedrell, created the authentic national style of Spanish music, dies at Cambo, in the Pyrenees, eleven days before reaching his forty-ninth birthday.

"During the last days of April Albéniz suffered a grave uremic attack, and after that he could not stand up. . . . The disease made terrifying progress. Enrique Granados came to salute his dying friend and to bring him the Cross of the Légion d'Honneur from the French government. Albéniz understood and shed tears of joy . . . and sorrow. . . . The last day, the 18th of May, he suffered so that he could no longer speak. He died a few minutes before eight o'clock in the evening." (Henri Collet, *Albéniz et Granados,* Paris, 1926)

(With suspicious unanimity, Riemann, 1929, Grove, 1927, Moser, 1935, and Hull, 1924, give the wrong date of 16 June 1909. Moser and Riemann mention Collet's book in the bibliography without heeding the circumstantial report quoted above. Baker, 1918, and De Bekker, 1925, approximate the correct date by a day, giving 19 May 1909)

22 MAY 1909

Richard H. STEIN completes a detailed exposition of his quarter-tone system.

(The date at the end of the brochure is marked meaningfully, "am Geburtstage Rich. Wagners 1909," i.e., 22 May 1909. A briefer exposition is to be found in the introduction to his *Zwei Konzertstuecke* for cello and piano, making use of quarter-tones, and published in 1906)

1 JUNE 1909

Romain Rolland publishes an article in the *Bulletin français* de *la S.I.M.*, exposing the method of mosaic integration and collation by which Giovanni TEBALDINI, in the March 1909 issue of the *Rivista musicale italiana*, strives to demonstrate the identifiable similarity between STRAUSS' opera *Electra* and GNECCHI's earlier opera *Cassandra*.

1 JUNE 1909

Giuseppe MARTUCCI, grand figure of Italian music, who exerted a catalyzing influence on a generation of Italian musicians, conductor, pianist, and composer of symphonic and chamber music, dies at Naples in his fifty-fourth year.

2 JUNE 1909

Lucien HILLEMACHER, French composer, author of orchestral works written in collaboration with his brother, Paul, dies in Paris eight days before reaching forty-nine years of age.

29 JUNE 1909

In a letter to Romain Rolland, Antoine MARIOTTE, the composer of the opera *Salomé*, points out the ambiguous attitude of Richard STRAUSS in not insisting that his publishers should abide by his promise and allow the production of his opera to take place.

(Date and text in Romain Rolland's article in the 15 July 1909 issue of the *Bulletin français de la S.I.M.*)

1 JULY 1909

Section 28 of the Copyright Law of the U.S.A. comes into force, forbidding the copying of orchestral parts or a whole musical work by any process whatever.

4 JULY 1909

Erik SATIE is given an honorary academic degree at Arcueil-Cachan, near Paris, for civic services in local musical education, and adopts the long-winded title of *Président d'Honneur du Comité de Pupilles Artistes et Directeur du Service Intérieur du Patronage Laïque*. (Date from P. D. Templier, *Erik Satie*, Paris, 1932)

15 JULY 1909

The name of Igor STRAVINSKY appears for the first time in a European press review in a St. Petersburg correspondence of the *Bulletin français de la S.I.M.*:

"W. L. Senilov, J. Th. Stravinski et M. O. Steinberg: voilà les noms de jeunes auteurs qui ont à peine commencé leur carrière musicale, et déjà ont su attirer l'attention sur eux. . . . Le jeune Stravinski a été un élève particulier de Rimsky-Korsakov. Il est l'auteur de la symphonie en *mi bémol majeur* et de la suite *la Bergère et le Faune*. Dans l'ensemble la suite ne manque pas de pages intéressantes; elle fait remarquer son jeune auteur, dont le talent va encore se développer davantage."

25 JULY 1909

Gianandrea GAVAZZENI, Italian composer, disciple of Pizzetti, in his neo-romantic, folkloristic, and even narrowly ethnical style, is born in Bergamo.

"Shunning since his early beginnings the influence of international modernism, Gianandrea Gavazzeni became a disciple of Ildebrando Pizzetti. Soon he freed himself from Pizzetti's exclusive influence and acquired a simple and terse style, following the pattern of popular Lombardian music, the elements of which he integrated in a poetic and pastoral manner. The search for a perfect medium of expression in this purely ethnic style has become his greatest task. He narrates these mu-

sical images in an individual musical language and forceful rhythms."
(From the composer's letter to the author)

27 AUGUST 1909

Arnold SCHOENBERG begins the composition of his monodrama,
Erwartung, in which he subtilizes the means of expression to the
greatest degree, to correspond with the philosophical idea of
simultaneity of the course of life, as seen at the moment of death.
(Date from Egon Wellesz, *Arnold Schoenberg,* 1921)

12 SEPTEMBER 1909

Arnold SCHOENBERG completes the composition of his monodrama,
Erwartung.

14 SEPTEMBER 1909

Serge PROKOFIEV receives a diploma as graduate of the St. Peters-
burg Conservatory in the classes of composition and pianoforte.
(Date communicated by Maximilian Steinberg, Director of the
Leningrad Conservatory)

24 SEPTEMBER 1909

A year, three months, and three days after RIMSKY-KORSAKOV's
death, his last opera, *The Golden Cockerel,* is produced at the
Zimin Private Opera in Moscow.

6 OCTOBER 1909

Dudley BUCK, American organist and composer of numerous cantatas and other music in traditional style, dies at Orange, N. J.,
in his seventy-first year.

10 OCTOBER 1909

Der Merker, Austrian semi-monthly music periodical, dedicated
to the promotion of Straussian-Mahlerian tendencies, begins
publication at Vienna, under the editorship of Richard SPECHT.

15 OCTOBER 1909

Jan SIBELIUS finishes the composition of his music to *The Lizard.*
(Date in Karl Ekman's *Sibelius,* Helsingfors, 1935)

4 NOVEMBER 1909

Serge RACHMANINOV makes his first appearance in the United States as a pianist, in a recital at Smith College, Northampton.

8 NOVEMBER 1909

Charles BORDES, French composer and co-founder on the sixth of June 1894 of the Schola Cantorum in Paris, dies at Toulon in his forty-seventh year.

10 NOVEMBER 1909

Ludvig SCHYTTE, Danish composer, pupil of Liszt, author of many piano pieces and a *Children's Symphony,* dies in Berlin in his sixty-second year.

23 NOVEMBER 1909

Alexandre GLAZUNOV conducts the first performance of his *Cortège Solennel,* at the Russian Symphony concerts in St. Petersburg.

27 NOVEMBER 1909

Alexander SILOTI conducts, at his St. Petersburg concerts, the first performance of the *Second Symphony,* in B-flat minor, by Maximilian STEINBERG. (Date from the original program)

28 NOVEMBER 1909

Serge RACHMANINOV plays for the first time anywhere his *Third Piano Concerto,* in D minor, with the New York Symphony Orchestra.

4 DECEMBER 1909

The Secret of Suzanne, one-act musical comedietta or "intermezzo" by Ermanno WOLF-FERRARI, written in a Mozartian style, ornamented with Italianate arabesque, is produced at the Munich Opera.

5 DECEMBER 1909

Ebenezer PROUT, English encyclopedic scholar, author of standard textbooks on everything in music, himself a composer of sym-

phonies and chamber music in which no rule is ever broken, and
discoverer of the third copy of Bach's manuscript of the forty-
eight Preludes and Fugues, dies in London in his seventy-fifth
year.

8 DECEMBER 1909

Le Coeur du Moulin, opera by Déodat DE SÉVERAC, is produced at
the Opéra-Comique in Paris.

10 DECEMBER 1909

Chaliapin sings, at a Siloti concert in St. Petersburg, Beethoven's
Song of the Flea and Moussorgsky's *Song of the Flea*, accompaniment orchestrated by Igor STRAVINSKY.

26 DECEMBER 1909

Professor YAMADA conducts at the Uyeno School of Music in Japan
the first performance of his dramatic oratorio *The Star of Promise*.

"This oratorio is the first attempt to render a dramatic theme musically by a Japanese composer by means of Japanese orchestra, chorus,
and soloists." (Japan *Advertiser*, 28 December 1909)

1910

15 JANUARY 1910

Maia, opera by Ruggiero LEONCAVALLO to his own text, is produced at the Constanzi Theatre in Rome.

17 JANUARY 1910

Fritz STEIN conducts in Jena the first performance of Beethoven's
so-called *Jena Symphony*, in C major, from the score reconstructed
from the separate orchestral parts bearing Beethoven's name,
found by Stein in the archives of the Jena Musical College.

19 JANUARY 1910

Malbruck, operetta, text and music by Ruggiero LEONCAVALLO, is produced in Rome.

20 JANUARY 1910

Ennio PORRINO, Italian composer, pupil of Respighi, is born at Cagliari.

"Ennio Porrino, like all Sardinian composers, is particularly stirred by the popular songs and dance tunes of his native island. The musical language adopted by him recalls Pizzetti and even more so, Respighi, in his manner of building and carrying out a programmatic symphonic work. This conception is characterized by realistic interpretation of pictorial and sculptural aspects of the outside world, with frequent romantic digressions in a style expressive above all of emotional effusion. . . . Descriptive style and subjective emotionalism govern his music without, however, imparting a theatrical quality to it." (An appreciation sent to the author by Gianandrea Gavazzeni)

20 FEBRUARY 1910

Don Quichotte, "heroic comedy in five acts" by Jules MASSENET, is produced at the Theatre of Monte Carlo, with Chaliapin in the title role.

(Date of the printed score is 24 February, but the London *Telegraph* of 23 February 1910, carries a dispatch from Monte Carlo, dated "Monday," which refers to the première "last night," i.e., Sunday; the previous Sunday being 20 February, this must be the date. Grove gives 19 February, and so does *Le Ménestrel* of 26 February 1910)

20 FEBRUARY 1910

Gabriel PIERNÉ conducts at the Colonne concerts in Paris the first performance of DEBUSSY's symphonic poem, *Iberia.*

"The composer attaches importance only to tone color. He puts his timbres side by side, adopting a process like that of the *Tâchistes* or the *Stipplers* in distributing color. The Debussyites and Pelléastres wished *Iberia* repeated, but while the majority of the audience was willing to applaud, it did not long for a repetition." (From a review by Boutarel in a French newspaper)

22 FEBRUARY 1910

A century has passed since CHOPIN was born in Zelazowa-Wola. (The formerly accepted date of 1 March 1809 has been proved erroneous)

2 MARCH 1910

Claude DEBUSSY conducts at the third of the four Concerts de Musique Française, organized by the publisher Durand in Paris, the first performance of *Rondes de Printemps,* third piece of his second suite, *Images.*

"These are real pictures in which the composer has endeavored to convey aurally impressions received by the eye. He attempts to blend the two forms of sensation, in order to intensify them. The melody, with its infinitely varied rhythms, corresponds to the multiplicity of lines in drawing; the orchestra represents a huge palette where each instrument supplies its own color. Just as a painter delights in contrasts of tone, in the play of light and shade, so the musician takes pleasure in the shock of unexpected dissonances and the fusion of unusual timbres; he wants us to visualize what he makes us hear, and the pen he holds in his fingers becomes a brush. This is musical impressionism of a very special kind and of a very rare quality." (From a program note by Charles Malherbe, written for this concert)

10 MARCH 1910

Carl REINECKE, German composer and pianist, writer of cadenzas for classical concertos and editor of piano literature, dies in Leipzig in his eighty-sixth year.

28 MARCH 1910

Édouard COLONNE, French conductor, founder of the Colonne concerts, dies in Paris in his seventy-second year.

APRIL 1910

Erich Wolfgang KORNGOLD, not quite thirteen-year-old Austrian child prodigy, son of the Viennese music critic, Julius Korngold, completes his opus 1, a piano *Trio,* in a neo-Straussian idiom of surprising maturity. (Date on the printed score)

12 APRIL 1910

Der Musikant, second opera of Julius BITTNER, is produced in Vienna three days after the composer's thirty-sixth birthday.

13 APRIL 1910

Julius Ferdinand BLUETHNER, founder of the piano manufacture bearing his name, and patent-holder of the Aliquot system of increased vibration in the upper octaves, dies in Leipzig in his eighty-seventh year.

20 APRIL 1910

At the first concert of the secessionist Société Musicale Indépendante in Paris two children, Christine Verger, age six, and Germaine Durant, age ten, give the first performance of the original version for piano four hands of RAVEL's suite *Ma Mère l'Oye,* "5 pièces enfantines":

(1). *Pavane de la Belle au bois dormant,* in the Æolian mode. (2). *Petit Poucet,* in neo-faux-bourdon style, in the key of C minor, with a major tierce-of-Picardy cadence. (3). *Laideronnette Impératrice des Pagôdes,* march time, in the pentatonic mode on the black keys. (4). *Les Entretiens de la Belle et de la Bête,* in a slow waltz time, in contrasting registers, high for the Beauty, low for the Beast. (5). *Le Jardin Féerique,* in slow triple time, in a free pan-diatonic C major mode, i.e., with the seven tones freely superimposed on each other.

23 APRIL 1910

Alfredo CASELLA conducts a concert of his works at the Salle Gaveau in Paris, giving the first performance of his rhapsody *Italia* and his *Suite in C major.*

4 MAY–7 JUNE 1910

Serge KOUSSEVITSKY takes his orchestra on a tour of eleven towns on the Volga, giving concerts of old and new music, with SCRIABIN as soloist in his own *Piano Concerto.*

18 MAY 1910

One month before his twenty-eighth birthday, Igor STRAVINSKY finishes in St. Petersburg the score of the *Fire-Bird,* "conte dansé

en 2 Tableaux," dedicated to Andrey Rimsky-Korsakov, and depicting the tale of Kastchei the Immortal, the Princess-Irresistible-
Beauty, Ivan the Tzarevitch and the Fire-Bird who gives Ivan a
protecting feather as a ransom for her freedom, the score comprising the following sections:

(1). *The Magic Garden of Kastchei,* opening with a mysterious ostinato
figure within the compass of a tritone and containing the first use in
any orchestral work of a harmonics glissando in the strings over the
range of the first twelve overtones. (2). *The Supplications of the Fire-
Bird*—a poignantly chromatic instrumental song harmonized in open
fifths. (3). *The Princesses' Game with the Golden Apples,* a coruscating
rhythmic dance in attenuated orchestration. (4). *The Round Dance,* on
a Russian folk-song melody. (5). *The Infernal Dance of Kastchei's Kingdom,* starting with a syncopated figure, and leading to the final A in a
two-octave chromatic ascent.

"Towards the end of the summer (1909), I received a telegram which
upset all my plans. Diaghilev who had just arrived in St. Petersburg
asked me to write the music of the *Fire-Bird* for the season of Ballets
Russes at the Paris Opéra, in the Spring 1910. . . . The offer was flat-
tering. I was being chosen among musicians of my generation and was
asked to collaborate in an important enterprise. . . . I worked on the
score with frenzy and when I finished it in time I felt the need of rest
in the country before going to Paris for the first time in my life." (Stravinsky, *Chroniques de ma vie,* Paris, 1935)

18 MAY 1910

Pauline VIARDOT, French soprano, daughter of the Spanish cen-
tenarian Manuel Garcia, wife of a Paris impresario, and intimate
friend of Turgenev, dies in her native Paris, at the age of eighty-
eight years and ten months.

20 MAY 1910

Jean Baptiste WECKERLIN, Alsatian-French composer and musi-
cophile, prolific author of operatic and symphonic works with
programmatic titles, and collector of songs of his native Alsace,
dies at Trottberg, near his birthplace, in his eighty-ninth year.

(Riemann, 1929, Moser, 1935, and Baker, 1918, give the erroneous
date May 10. Hull cites 10 March, an obvious misprint for May. All
dictionaries give the wrong date of Weckerlin's birth—9 November in-

stead of 29 November 1821. The correct day of Weckerlin's birth and death is established by Arthur Pougin in his obituary of Weckerlin in *Le Ménestrel,* 28 May 1910, in which he states that Weckerlin died at Trottberg on 20 May, and his funeral took place at Gebweiler, on the 22nd. In the same article, Pougin quotes Weckerlin's own note addressed to him, in which he gives his birth date, 29 November 1821, at Gebweiler)

25 MAY 1910

At the Société Musicale Indépendante in Paris, Claude DEBUSSY plays his piano *Preludes,* among them the first performance of *Voiles,* based on the whole-tone scale, with the middle section in the pentatonic mode of the black keys.

29 MAY 1910

Mili BALAKIREV, dean of the Russian national school, protagonist of Russian orientalism with its characteristic harmonies, creator of the Russian type of the nineteenth-century symphoniç poem, friend and benevolent adviser of Moussorgsky, Borodin, Rimsky-Korsakov, dies in St. Petersburg at the age of seventy-three years, four months, and twenty-seven days, to be survived by the last of the "Mighty Five"—César Cui—by nearly eight years.

(The date is taken from the obituary in the St. Petersburg daily paper, *Novoye Vremya.* Grove, 1927, gives the erroneous date of 30 May; Riemann, 1929, and Moser, 1935, give 28 May, also erroneous. The date in Hull is correct but the German edition of Hull edited by Alfred Einstein, 1926, gives the erroneous 28 May)

30 MAY 1910

On ne Badine pas avec l'Amour, lyric comedy in three acts by Gabriel PIERNÉ, to the book of Alfred de Musset, is produced at the Opéra-Comique in Paris.

"With M. Pierné, delicacy and grace are not exclusive of vigor. Subtle harmonist, he does not deem it necessary to indulge in savage and grotesque eccentricities so dear to some who, in offending the ear, destroy the sense of tonality and transform music into a game of algebra. . . ." (Arthur Pougin in *Le Ménestrel,* 4 June 1910)

8 JUNE 1910

A century has passed since the birth of Robert SCHUMANN, at Zwickau.

25 JUNE 1910

One week after STRAVINSKY's twenty-eighth birthday, his first ballet, the *Fire-Bird,* is presented by DIAGHILEV's Ballet Russe, at the Opéra in Paris, conducted by Gabriel PIERNÉ.

"The spectacle was warmly acclaimed by the Paris public. Of course, I do not attribute this success solely to the music; it was equally due to the sumptuous scenery of the painter Golovin, the brilliant interpretation of Diaghilev's dancers and to the talent of the ballet master." (Stravinsky, *Chroniques de ma vie,* Paris, 1935)

4 JULY 1910

Louis BOURGAULT-DUCOUDRAY, French composer and enlightened aesthetician, one of the first Western theorists to make a first-hand study of non-European music and claim recognition for "all possible modes, old or new, European or exotic," dies in Paris in his seventy-first year.

17 AUGUST 1910

Comedy Overture on Negro Themes, by Henry F. GILBERT, containing a fugue on the Negro spiritual, *Old Ship of Zion,* is performed for the first time at an open-air Municipal Symphony concert in Central Park, New York.

(Date from Philip Hale's program note in the program book of the Boston Symphony Orchestra, 13 April 1911)

21 AUGUST 1910

Héliogabale, "lyric tragedy in three acts" by Déodat DE SÉVERAC, written in the traditional French style of the second half of the nineteenth century, except for an occasional Duparc-like melodic undulation and refreshing use of Catalan reeds in the orchestra, is produced at the Théâtre des Arènes in Béziers, France. (Date on the printed score)

31 AUGUST 1910

Pierre AUBRY, French musicologist and paleographer, collector of folk songs of many countries and codifier of oriental melodies, dies in Dieppe, victim of an accident, in his thirty-seventh year.

10 SEPTEMBER 1910

Charles E. IVES finishes, in New York, *Col. Shaw and his Colored Regiment,* the first movement of the orchestral set *Three Places in New England,* with evocative rather than literal use of Negro rhythms. (Date on the holograph)

12 SEPTEMBER 1910

Two months and five days after his fiftieth birthday, Gustav MAHLER conducts at the Munich Exposition his choral *Eighth Symphony,* surnamed because of a large number of performers required, "Symphony of the Thousand," in two parts: (1). *Veni, creator spiritus,* on a ninth-century hymn for two combined choruses, in clear E-flat major. (2). *Concluding Scene from "Faust,"* conceived as a symphonic poem with chorus, opening in E-flat minor and ending in E-flat major, very diatonic throughout, on a consciously reduced modulatory plan.

(Hull's *Dictionary* in the article on Mahler, and Philip Hale's *Boston Symphony Programme Notes,* New York, 1935, give the date two years off, 12 September 1908)

"The work marshals an orchestra such as no other symphonist in the history of music has required. In actual performance in Munich the vocal parts were sung by two mixed choruses of 250 members each, a children's choir of 350 and seven soloists. The orchestra has been augmented to 146 players." (Boston *Evening Transcript,* 29 September 1910)

26 SEPTEMBER 1910

Richard STRAUSS completes, at his home in Garmisch, the score of *Der Rosenkavalier,* "comedy with music in three acts" to Hugo Hofmannsthal's book, in a stylized eighteenth-century musical idiom, making use of a reduced classical orchestra without, however, abandoning the motif construction, one hundred and eighteen leading themes having been tabulated in the score by diligent musicographers.

(Composition of the opera begun on 1 May 1909)

(The date 26 September 1909, in the chronograph of Richard Specht's *Richard Strauss und sein Werk,* Vol. 2, p. 388, is a misprint. On page 214 of the same volume the correct year is given)

3 OCTOBER 1910

JAQUES-DALCROZE leaves Geneva with fifteen disciples to found his institute of eurythmics in Hellerau.

(Date obtained from the Secretariat of the Dalcroze school in Geneva. *See* history of the Dalcroze movement in Part III)

4 OCTOBER 1910

Der Schneemann, opera by the prodigiously precocious Erich Wolfgang KORNGOLD in Alexander Zemlinsky's orchestration, is performed in Vienna four months and five days after the composer's thirteenth birthday.

"The music to the pantomime *The Snow Man,* which at once made him famous, he wrote as a piano solo when he was eleven years old, never dreaming of its being scored by Herr Zemlinsky or performed. But when it had received a most favorable reception at some aristocratic houses here, the authorities of the Imperial Opera resolved to have it performed. Till then Dr. Korngold (father of Erich, musical critic at the Vienna *Neue Freie Presse,* successor of Hanslick) had purposely kept a knowledge of his prodigy from the public. Finally he came to the conclusion that he had no right any longer to conceal his son's marvelous achievements. . . . So extraordinary are they that they have been made the subject of theoretical study at the Berlin University, and Professor Arthur Seidl has lectured on them at the Leipzig Conservatoire." (Vienna dispatch in the *Musical Standard,* 5 November 1910)

8 OCTOBER 1910

An exhibition of paintings by Arnold SCHOENBERG is opened at the Heller bookstore in Vienna.

(Date from an announcement in the *Neue Freie Presse,* Vienna, 2 October 1910. E. Wellesz in his monograph on Schoenberg, 1921, gives the approximate date of September 1910)

"The exhibition of the collection of paintings by Arnold Schoenberg in Heller's bookstore has attracted large attendance. Three oil paintings have been purchased to date: a self-portrait, the artist's wife, and a portrait of a doctoress." (*Neue Freie Presse,* Vienna, 14 October 1910)

23 OCTOBER 1910

The Orquesta Sinfonica gives its inaugural concert at Barcelona.

29 OCTOBER 1910

Frederick S. CONVERSE completes at Westwood, Massachusetts, the full score of his "romantic grand opera" in three acts, *The Sacrifice,* to his own story from the period of the Mexican war in Southern California, 1846. (Date at end of manuscript score)

5 NOVEMBER 1910

STRAVINSKY's *Fire-Bird* is performed from manuscript for the first time in Russia, at a Siloti concert in St. Petersburg. (Date from the original program)

7 NOVEMBER 1910

Alexandre GLAZUNOV conducts, in Helsingfors, the first performance of his *Finnish Fantasy,* op. 88.

10 NOVEMBER 1910

Fritz KREISLER plays in London the first performance of the *Violin Concerto* of Edward ELGAR.

12 NOVEMBER 1910

Gabriel FAURÉ appears as guest conductor in a program of his own compositions at a Siloti concert in St. Petersburg. (Date from the original program)

30 NOVEMBER 1910

Macbeth, the first and only opera of Ernest BLOCH composed in 1903, is produced at the Opéra-Comique in Paris.

"This music is an indecipherable rebus, rhythmically as well as tonally, and I ask myself how the singers and the orchestra found their way through it. As to the rhythm, it is not only capricious but downright incoherent as a result of incessant changes of meter. Judge for yourself: In a certain place I find this succession: 3/4, 4/4, 3/4, 4/4, 6/4, 4/4; in another place I find a bar of 4/4, one of 5/4, 6/4 and 4/4. What becomes of rhythmic unity, and what accuracy of performance can be expected under such conditions? As to harmonic sequences, they are no less extraordinary, and one can qualify them as savage. . . . It is noise for the sake of noise and the abuse of trumpets would break the sturdiest ear drums." (Arthur Pougin in *Le Ménestrel,* 3 December 1910)

4 DECEMBER 1910

Claude DEBUSSY conducts a concert of his own works in Budapest.

10 DECEMBER 1910

La Fanciulla del West, an opera in three acts by Giacomo PUCCINI to David Belasco's drama of California life in 1848, is produced by the Metropolitan Opera Company in New York, Toscanini conducting.

"Puccini Tells How He Set a Game of Poker to Music—Strange and Curious Scene in·'The Girl' One of the Strong Features of the Opera.—All Written at Night." (Headlines in a New York paper)

"An International Premiere—America Proud of *The Girl of the Golden West*—Under Two Flags, a $20,000 House Riots over Puccini—Caruso as 'Mr. Johnson' Looks and Acts his Best and All His Admirers Will Have to Hear His Lynching Aria—Sheriff Amato Shares the Big Scene—Gold Miner Gilly and Red Squaw Mattfeld Not Forgotten on the Fifty Curtain Calls." (Headlines in the New York *Sun*)

28 DECEMBER 1910

Koenigskinder, fairy opera in three acts by Engelbert HUMPERDINCK, is produced at the Metropolitan Opera in New York.

1911

8 JANUARY 1911

Florent SCHMITT's symphonic poem *Tragedy of Salome,* written in an advanced harmonic idiom, and making use of compound meters such as $\frac{3 \pm \frac{1}{2}}{4}$, is performed for the first time at the Colonne concerts in Paris.

(Date from P. O. Ferroud, *Autour de Florent Schmitt*, Paris, 1927, p. 72. In its original version for small orchestra, *Tragedy of Salome* was given 9 November 1907)

26 JANUARY 1911

Four months after the completion of STRAUSS' opera *Rosenkavalier*, the first performance of it takes place at the Dresden Royal Opera, Ernst Schuch conducting.

12 FEBRUARY 1911

On the eve of the twenty-eighth anniversary of Wagner's death, his youthful *Symphony in C Major*, utterly orthodox, in the prevalent idiom of the time, is published by the Max Brockhaus Publishing House in Leipzig.

21 FEBRUARY 1911

Gustav MAHLER conducts the New York Philharmonic Orchestra for the last time, twelve weeks before his death.

25 FEBRUARY 1911

Natoma, opera by Victor HERBERT from Joseph Redding's book about an Indian-Spanish-American love triangle in the California of 1820, is produced in Philadelphia twenty-four days after the composer's fifty-second birthday.

"Philadelphia Certainly Did Enjoy Itself—At *Natoma's* Irish-American 'World Premiere.' " (Headlines in New York *Sun*)

"*Natoma* Performed—A Dull Text Set to Mediocre Music—The Comparative Failure of the First Performance in Philadelphia in Spite of the Able Cast and Thorough Preparation—An Antiquated 'Book' Written in Stilted Speech and Silly Verse That Contains Neither Operatic Drama nor Operatic Characters—The Mediocrity and the Dull Commonplace of Mr. Herbert's Music Except Where It Approximates Operetta—Its Undramatic and Untheatrical Quality—The Vivid Pictorial Side of the Opera and of Miss Garden's Indian Girl." (H. T. Parker's sub-headlines in the Boston *Evening Transcript*)

26 FEBRUARY 1911

Aux Étoiles, for orchestra, the second—and last—orchestral piece by Henri DUPARC, written in the atmospheric manner of his songs, is performed for the first time at the Lamoureux concerts in Paris.

3 MARCH 1911

The Sacrifice, second opera by Frederick S. CONVERSE, is produced for the first time anywhere at the Boston Opera House, Wallace Goodrich conducting.

11 MARCH 1911

Enrique GRANADOS plays, at the Palais de la Musique Catalane in Barcelona, the first performance of his pianistic chef-d'oeuvre *Goyescas.*

"In *Goyescas* I intended to give a personal note, a mixture of bitterness and grace . . . rhythm, color and life that are typically Spanish; and a sentiment suddenly amorous and passionate, dramatic and tragic, such as is seen in the works of Goya." (Granados quoted by Henri Collet in *Albéniz et Granados,* Paris, 1926)

12 MARCH 1911

The full score of SCRIABIN's *Prometheus* is published by the Édition Russe de Musique.

15 MARCH 1911

Serge KOUSSEVITSKY conducts in Moscow, with the composer at the piano, the first performance of SCRIABIN's *Prometheus, Poem of Fire* for large orchestra, piano, organ, choruses, and the keyboard of light (clavier à lumières), in one continuous movement, running through the following moods:

Lento, brumeux, establishing from the very first the quartal harmony of the "Promethean chord" (augmented, diminished, augmented and two perfect fourths); entrance of the solo piano, marked *impérieux,* followed by a swift alternation of moods: *voluptueux, presque avec douleur, avec délice, avec un intense désir, avec émotion et ravissement, voilé, mystérieux, avec enthousiasme, limpide, sourd, menaçant, étrange, charmé;* a rhythmic subject in the piano part, suddenly abandoned (*soudain très doux et joyeux,* then *avec un effroi contenu, avec défi belliqueux, orageux, avec un splendide éclat, déchirant, comme un cri*); a series of spasmodic, explosive splashes of instrumental color, in soft dynamics in triply triple time, driving to the coda in a cumulative assault, frustrated by relapse into sudden softness (*extatique, étincelant, de plus en plus large, avec un éclat éblouissant, ailé, dansant, flot lumineux, dans un vertige*), ending on a sustained F-sharp major chord in fortissimo.

"Sergius Kussewitzky's subscription concert took place on March 2 at the Hall of Nobles and was one of the most interesting and brilliant of the season. It had on its program two Symphonies of Scriabin, who is considered here to be a real genius. . . . Scriabin himself played the piano part. The audience cheered the conductor to the echo for his splendid and marvelous performance. Flowers rained down from the balconies upon the composer and the leader, both of whom were recalled many times, while the ovation lasted for more than half an hour after the concert was over." (*Musical Courier,* Moscow dispatch, 4 March 1911, old style)

16 MARCH 1911

Edward ELGAR completes at Tintagel the score of his *Second Symphony* in four movements, with a motto from Shelley: "Rarely, rarely comest thou, Spirit of delight!" and dedicated to the memory of Edward VII. (Date of the dedication on title-page of score)

20 MARCH 1911

The Russian government promulgates the copyright law protecting authors' and composers' rights against infringement.

29 MARCH 1911

Alexandre GUILMANT, French composer-organist, co-founder together with Charles BORDES and Vincent D'INDY of the Schola Cantorum of Paris on the sixth of June 1894, dies at Meudon seventeen days after his seventy-fourth birthday.

(Date from the obituary in *Le Figaro* of 30 March 1911. Marcel Dupré in his article on Guilmant in *La Revue musicale* of February–March 1937 gives the erroneous date, 22 March 1911)

1 APRIL 1911

Domenico ALALEONA publishes in the *Rivista musicale italiana* a treatise on "modernist harmony," "neutral tonality," and the "art of stupefaction" (by means of diminished 7th chords!).

2 APRIL 1911

The first suite drawn from RAVEL's ballet *Daphnis and Chloe* is performed for the first time at a concert conducted by Gabriel Pierné, in Paris.

"The *Nocturne* with its multiple *divisi* of various instrumental groups produces a strange effect of transparence and dreamlike atmosphere; the *Interlude* with its chorus behind the stage, coming with great tenderness, its trumpet calls and the adroitly wrought gradation leading up to a barbarically rhythmed *Warriors' Dance,* are curious pages of extreme complexity which will surprise, interest and please." (*Le Ménestrel,* 2 April 1911)

"Rather than pretending to give a synthetic presentation of the story of *Daphnis and Chloe,* the suite is a series of what the Futurists might call rhythmic pictures. There is no characterization and no drama, but the score pulsates with a life that is now sensitive and subtle, now vigorous and wild." (London *Times,* 3 August 1912)

"This score has strength, rhythm, brilliance. Voices mingle with the instruments, mysterious and fervid voices. . . . The liberty of form and of writing surpasses anything that can be imagined. Harmonic and polyphonic anarchy here reigns supreme, and I must confess that I do not accept it without hesitation." (Alfred Bruneau in *Le Matin*)

3 APRIL 1911

Jan SIBELIUS conducts at a concert of his music in Helsingfors the first performance of his *Fourth Symphony* in four movements:

(1). *Quasi Adagio,* which opens in a characteristic Lydian mode, with the low strings and bassoons in fortissimo, and, after six dynamic explosions alternating with brief spaces of piano, and a curious interlude for strings playing on the keyboard, vanishes towards a unison A. (2). *Allegro Molto Vivace,* as a scherzo. (3). *Il Tempo Largo,* in a nocturne style with solos of the wood-winds, making use of whole-tone scales, and ending on a pianissimo unison C. (4). *Allegro,* in a brusque style, with characteristic scale passages repeated without modification, and slowly rising dynamics in strings working up towards a sonorous climax, then subsiding into nothingness, and ending in eight funereal A-minor chords in the strings.

"Now he has joined the Futurists. He is as frankly dissonant as the worst of them. He has swallowed the whole-tone scale, the disjointed sequences, the chord of the minor second, the flattened supertonic and all the Chinese horrors of the forbidden fifths. Yet the new symphony is a noteworthy composition. It has elemental imagination, courage of utterance, fearlessness of style." (W. J. Henderson in the New York *Sun* writing on Sibelius' *Fourth Symphony)*

26 APRIL 1911

The cornerstone of the Jaques-Dalcroze Institute is laid at Hellerau-Dresden, the first German garden city designed for rhythmic education.

26 APRIL 1911

La Jota, two-act opera by Raoul LAPARRA, is produced at the Opéra-Comique.

16 MAY 1911

Six days before the production of DEBUSSY's musical setting of d'Annunzio's mystery play *Le Martyre de Saint Sébastien,* the Archbishop of Paris exhorts all Catholics to abstain from attending the play as irreligious.

17 MAY 1911

Josef STRANSKY is appointed conductor of the New York Philharmonic Orchestra, to succeed Gustav MAHLER.

18 MAY 1911

Gustav MAHLER, the last of the great romantic composers of Vienna, who strove to translate his spiritual struggle into symphonies of cosmic design, dies in Vienna of heart trouble, complicated by septic poisoning resulting from inflammation of the throat and pneumonia, fifty days before his fifty-first birthday.

"It was generally understood that Mr. Mahler had frequent struggles with the women managers of the N. Y. Philharmonic Orchestra who assembled the large guarantee fund which was needed to cover the deficits of the orchestra. His physical breakdown was said to be the result of these disagreements although this has been denied even by the conductor himself. His wife, however, repeated the charges when it was thought that Mr. Mahler was about to die in a Paris Sanitarium." (New York *Sun,* 20 May 1911)

"Worried by New York Women.—Mahler was taken gravely ill in Paris and went to a sanitarium in Neuilly. When an American correspondent called there on May 4 he met Madame Mahler, who said that she attributed her husband's illness to nervous prostration and its consequences caused by his unfortunate relations with the Philharmonic Society of New York.

" 'You cannot imagine,' she said, 'what he has suffered. In Vienna my husband was all-powerful. Even the Emperor did not dictate to him. But in New York, to his amazement, he had ten women ordering him about like a puppet. He hoped, however, by hard work and success to rid himself of his tormentors. Meanwhile he lost health and strength. Then, after an excursion to Springfield, he contracted angina pectoris. At his last concert in New York, rather than disappoint the public, he conducted while he was in a high fever.' " (New York *American,* 20 May 1911)

"He was looked upon as a great artist, and possibly he was one, but he failed to convince the people of New York of the fact, and therefore his American career was not a success. . . . In his treatment of the simple melodies of his symphonies (some of them borrowed without acknowledgment) he was utterly inconsiderate of their essence. . . . We cannot see how any of his music can long survive him." (New York *Tribune,* 21 May 1911)

" 'It is easy to kill a man through witchcraft, provided it be helped out with a little arsenic.' So said Voltaire. 'Nobody dies of a broken heart,' say we, unconvinced when we are not able to find the germ or 'bug.' There were some expressions of derision when it was reported that Gustav Mahler, late of this city, was dying in Europe of 'worry'—His wife was the authority for the statement.

"Mahler, Tchaikovsky, Dvořák and Richard Strauss were the most distinguished men to conduct in our Carnegie Hall. Perhaps if the first had had some amiable peculiarities, if he had used no baton in conducting, or had had a huge family, or had gone to afternoon teas, he would have been more popular, and would be alive today." (Editorial in the New York *Evening Sun,* 20 May 1911)

19 MAY 1911

L'Heure Espagnole, one-act opéra bouffe, by Maurice RAVEL is performed for the first time at the Paris Opéra-Comique.

20 MAY 1911

The Orchestra of the Société Nationale de Musique in Paris gives the first performance of Déodat DE SÉVERAC's *Fête des Vendanges,* and *Danse des Treilles et du Chevalet,* the latter being a ballet drawn from Séverac's opera *Coeur du Moulin.*

22 MAY 1911

Le Martyre de Saint Sébastien, DEBUSSY's evocative miracle-drama to Gabriele d'ANNUNZIO's play, is produced at the Opéra in Paris.

"Debussy's score is characteristic in its expression of religious respect, discretion, mystic contemplation. It seems that it disappointed certain 'Debussyites.' . . . They expected infinite subtleties of nuance, strange refinements of sonorities, morbid curiosity for rare effects. But Debussy is not a slave of a formula. . . . His manner is always the same, but here it is magnified, grown, ennobled. . . . It expands gloriously in the orchestra, flows in powerful waves in the voices. . . ." (Special issue of *Le Théâtre,* June 1911)

"The dress rehearsal was to take place on Sunday, 21 May. On that very day, in the morning, during an airplane contest at Issy-les-Moulineaux, a member of the French government, minister of war, was hit and killed by the propeller of one of the planes. Official mourning was declared, and the announced performance became impossible." (Léon Vallas, *Claude Debussy et son temps,* Paris, 1932)

24 MAY 1911

Nine days before his fifty-fourth birthday Edward ELGAR conducts the first performance of his *Second Symphony* in E-flat major at the London Musical Festival.

26 MAY 1911

Three weeks before his twenty-ninth birthday, STRAVINSKY completes, in Rome, the composition of *Petrouchka,* "burlesque scenes in 4 Tableaux":

FIRST SCENE: *Popular Festivities at Mardi Gras,* built on four tones D—E—G—A in rapid rhythmic movement; *Dance of the Drunken Crowd* in heavy duple time, in a Dorian mode; *The Organ-Grinder and a Ballerina,* interfered with by a music box, ringing off Italianate city tunes, while the organ-grinder (paired clarinets) plays a sentimental romance; *The Fair Attracts the Crowds Again,* with the four tones D—E—G—A returning as part of a complete Dorian tone-row; *The Return of the Drunken Crowd,* recapitulation of the first section, with the constant eighth-note unit within changing meters, 2, 3, 4 and 5 eighth-notes in a bar; the entire movement ending with a solo of the percussion; *The Magician Plays the Flute,* bringing to life three dolls: Petrouchka, a Moor and a Ballerina. *Russian Dance* of the revived dolls, with the piano on the white keys joining the orchestra in a rhythmic dance on a dominant pedal, alternating, as in a rondo, with songful themes, usually within the compass of a fifth. SECOND SCENE: *At Petrouchka's,* a poignant improvisatory interlude, in which the bitonal chord of C major and F-sharp major is outlined, in arpeggio form, for the first time in music, in the paired clarinets and the piano cadenza; *Adagietto,* on a tritone base, implying a Lydian mode; *The Entrance of the Ballerina,* and the despair of the rejected Petrouchka, expressed by a piercing clarinet cadenza, and then full orchestra in the bitonal triple forte, ending on a sudden plagal cadence. THIRD SCENE: *At the Moor's,* starting with a drum call and going into a syncopated dance; *Ballerina's Dance,* introduced by a cornet flourish accompanied by a drum; *Waltz,* to mock-sentimental city tunes in crude harmonies; *Appearance of Petrouchka and His Quarrel with the Moor, While the Ballerina Faints,* to the accompaniment of frictional bitonal harmonies. FOURTH SCENE: *Mardi Gras in the Evening,* in pan-diatonic harmony, with all seven tones of the D major scale in free intercourse and juxtaposition, but with the four principal tones, D—E—G—A as in the first scene, clearly dominant. *Nurses' Dance,* with the sentimental romance of the organ-grinder appearing again, in a Mixolydian mode, followed by the popular song, "Oh, my gates, my brand-new gates," wryly harmonized in tritones; *Moujik with a Dancing Bear* introduced by a clarinet in the highest register over lumbering syncopation in the low register of the orchestra; *Merchant on a Spree,* with two gypsy women, playing the accordion while the gypsies dance, in rapid duple time and Dorian mode, alternating with the Mixolydian; *Dance of the Coachmen,* in stamping duple time and Mixolydian mode, in crude syncopation; *Nurses' Dance with the Coachmen,* with the sentimental romance, accompanied by brassy explosions marking time, the coachmen's tune finally prevailing; *The Maskers,* in an animated marching dance, changing to a five-eighth meter with a rhythmic twelve-note motto in an Æolian hexachord, going over to the *General Dance,* which stops when Petrouchka runs out of the theatre, pursued by the Moor, and falls with a cracked skull to the bitonal outcries of the orchestra.

"Before tackling *Le Sacre du Printemps,* I wanted to amuse myself with an orchestral work in which the piano would play a preponderant rôle, a sort of *Konzertstück.* While composing this music, I had a definite vision of a clown, suddenly let loose, who, with a cascade of devilish arpeggios, exasperates the orchestra, which in its turn, replies to him in menacing fanfares. There is a terrible brawl ending in a dolorous and pathetic debacle of the poor clown. This bizarre piece finished, I sought, for hours, walking by the lake of Geneva, a title that would express in one word the character of my music. . . . One day, I started with joy. Petrouchka! The eternal and unlucky hero of all the fairs, in all countries! I had found my title!" (Stravinsky, *Chroniques de ma vie*, Paris, 1935)

2 JUNE 1911

MASCAGNI's opera *Isabeau*, based on a modified story of Lady Godiva's ride (in the opera the ride is undertaken with the object of securing an heir), is produced at Buenos Aires.

13 JUNE 1911

Silence, symphonic poem after Edgar Allan Poe, by Nicolas MIASKOVSKY, is performed for the first time in Moscow, Constantin Saradjev conducting.

(Composition completed 17 October 1909; orchestration completed 20 February 1910. Dates communicated by the composer)

13 JUNE 1911

Four days before STRAVINSKY's twenty-ninth birthday, his ballet *Petrouchka* is performed at DIAGHILEV's Ballet Russe, at the Châtelet Theatre in Paris, Pierre MONTEUX conducting the orchestra.

14 JUNE 1911

Johan SVENDSEN, neo-romantic Norwegian composer of facile melodious music in all forms, dies in Copenhagen, his home since 1883, in his seventy-first year.

21 JUNE 1911

The Ballet Russe under the direction of its founder, Serge DIAGHILEV, makes its first appearance in London.

22 JUNE 1911

At the end of the ceremony of the coronation of King George and Queen Mary, Edward ELGAR's specially composed *Coronation March*, op. 65, is performed for the first time.

JULY 1911

Two months before his thirty-seventh birthday, Arnold SCHOEN-
BERG completes in Vienna his *Harmonielehre* dedicated to the
memory of Gustav Mahler.

"No art has been so hindered in its development by teachers as music,
since nobody watches more closely over his property than the man who
knows that, strictly speaking, it does not belong to him." (From the
opening chapter)

19 JULY 1911

Anton VON WEBERN writes in Vienna the shortest piece of orchestral literature, the fourth of his *Five Pieces for Orchestra,* op.
10, scored for clarinet, trumpet, trombone, mandoline, celesta,
harp, small drum, violin, and viola, six and one-third bars in
¾ time, the whole lasting nineteen seconds according to the
metronome mark.

(The date of composition of No. 1 of the *Five Pieces* is 28 June 1911; of
No. 2, 13 September 1913; of No. 3, 8 September 1913; of No. 5, 6
October 1913. All these dates communicated by the composer)

15 AUGUST 1911

Nazib ZHIGANOV, composer of the first national Tartar opera, *The
Deserter,* based on the story of Pugatchev's rebellion, is born at
Uralsk.

26 AUGUST 1911

RACHMANINOV composes the last of his six *Études-Tableaux,* op.
33, a supremely pianistic set of well-contrasted, now elegiac, now
impetuous pieces.

(The non-consecutive dates of the first five *Études-Tableaux* are: No. 1,
24 August 1911; No. 2, 29 August 1911; No. 3, 5 September 1911; No. 4,
30 August 1911; No. 5, 28 August 1911. All these dates are given in new
style, by adding thirteen days to the dates listed in *Rachmaninoff's
Recollections Told to Oskar von Riesemann,* New York, 1934)

27 AUGUST 1911

Three centuries have passed since the death of Tomás Ludovico
DA VICTORIA, the Palestrina of Spain.

14 SEPTEMBER 1911

Nicolas MIASKOVSKY receives a diploma as graduate in the class of composition of the St. Petersburg Conservatory.

(Date communicated to the author by Maximilian Steinberg, Director of the Leningrad Conservatory)

7 OCTOBER 1911

Three and a half weeks after his thirty-seventh birthday, Arnold SCHOENBERG marries Alexander Zemlinsky's sister.

8 OCTOBER 1911

Ferruccio BUSONI completes in Berlin the composition of his opera *Die Brautwahl*, a complex, romantic, and at the same time mock-romantic score.

"Die Brautwahl is suffering from constipation like the composer himself." (Busoni in a letter quoted in Edward J. Dent's *Ferruccio Busoni, a Biography*, London, 1933)

22 OCTOBER 1911

A century has passed since the birth, at Raiding, of Franz LISZT.

4 NOVEMBER 1911

E. H. Crump is re-elected Mayor of Memphis, Tennessee, after a hard campaign, for which W. C. HANDY, the Negro composer, wrote a song, *Mr. Crump,* later renamed *Memphis Blues,* that has created a new style in American popular music.

"Blues in their original vocal form are distinguished chiefly by their peculiar structure—three lines of verse—although they take their name from their most common motif, that of depression. Originating among the illiterate Southern negroes, they were first brought before the notice of the general public in 1909. In that year a mayoral contest was taking place in Memphis in which three candidates were competing, assisted by as many coloured bands. Mr. W. C. Handy, the son and grandson of Methodist ministers, was in charge of one of these. His candidate was a Mr. E. H. Crump, and one of the airs which he devised for his orchestra was named after his employer. So popular did it become that Mr. Crump was elected mayor, Mr. Handy became locally famous, the term 'Blues' appeared out of nowhere, and 'Mr. Crump,' rechristened

'Memphis Blues,' started the avalanche of this form of music that has since swept over the country." *(Encyclopaedia Britannica,* 14th edition)

The following statement from Mr. Crump's secretary, furnished the author by Mrs. Frances Fink, casts doubt on this accepted story. "Mr. Crump did not use Handy's song in either of his elections. The song was written a couple of years after Mr. Crump was elected Mayor the first time. . . . He was elected the second time in November, 1911, and again in November, 1915. I do not think Handy wrote the song as a campaign song, but simply used Mr. Crump's name in the composition of same." But from Mr. W. C. Handy comes a rejoinder: "I did not write the 'Memphis Blues' as a campaign song for Mr. Crump but wrote 'Mr. Crump' as a campaign song for Mr. Crump and then changed the title for publication to the 'Memphis Blues' and published it in 1912 myself. Later sold it to Theron C. Bennett who copyrighted it in 1913. . . . I then followed that with the 'St. Louis Blues' copyrighted 14 September 1914."

7 NOVEMBER 1911

After ten and a half years of intermittent work, Arnold SCHOEN-BERG completes, in Zehlendorf, near Berlin, the composition of *Gurre-Lieder* to the poems by the Danish poet Jens Peter Jacobsen, for five solo voices, three four-part male choirs and a mixed choir of eight parts, a narrator and large orchestra, in three parts:

Part 1: Beginning with an orchestral introduction in E-flat major, in sextuple and dodecuple time, vaguely Brucknerian and Straussian in character, also showing selective affinity with Mahler and including nine solos alternately sung by Waldemar IV of Denmark and his beloved, Tove. *Part 2:* Slow and short, in B-Flat minor, containing Waldemar's lament. *Part 3: The Wild Hunt,* the longest, and the most chromatic, but never breaking the bounds of tonality, with the choruses shouting hunting cries, then lamenting the lost peace, and ending in a joyous diatonic hymn to the rising sun with a twenty-eight-bar coda in inergotistic C major. (The date is marked at the end of the manuscript score)

"The whole composition was finished, I should say, in April or May 1901. Only the final chorus was still in rough sketches. . . . Indications for the orchestration were, in the original composition, not very numerous. . . . In finishing off the score I rewrote only a few passages. Everything else, even a good deal that I would willingly have had otherwise, remained as it was at first." (From Schoenberg's letter to Alban Berg, quoted in Berg's *Guide to Gurre-Lieder*)

9 NOVEMBER 1911

Julius BITTNER's opera, *Der Bergsee,* based on Austrian folk music is produced in Vienna.

11 NOVEMBER 1911

The aerophor, a tone-sustaining instrument, consisting of a rubber bulb and a tube appliance which enables the player on a wind instrument to hold a note indefinitely, is given first demonstration by its inventor, Bernard SAMUELS, in Berlin.

20 NOVEMBER 1911

Six months and two days after Gustav MAHLER's death, Bruno Walter conducts in Munich the first performance of his pantheistic song-symphony, *Das Lied von der Erde,* to the texts of a Chinese poet of the eighth century, for tenor, contralto, and orchestra, in six parts:

Part 1: The Drinking Song of Earthly Woe, with a pentatonic horn motto, the movement maintained in swift triple time, and fluid but well delineated tonality, the tenor singing the poem. *Part 2: The Solitary Soul in Autumn,* sung by the contralto to a florid contrapuntal accompaniment in a concertizing instrumental style, with a Phrygian close. *Part 3: Of Youth,* sung by the tenor, to a wood-wind accompaniment in rhythmically patterned duple-time figures, in a Mixolydian mode with pentatonic connotations. *Part 4: Of Beauty,* sung by the contralto, in a broad dynamic style, with the pentatonic melos clearly indicated by exclusive use of the E—G—A—B—D pattern in the orchestra. *Part 5: The Drunkard in Springtime,* in gay march-like time, sung by the tenor. *Part 6: Farewell,* sung by the contralto, accompanied by an orchestra of a few instruments in extreme registers, with frequent instrumental cadenzas, rising towards the middle of the song and relapsing to the initial low C, in a ternary form, characteristic of every song of the cycle. (Date from an advertisement in the *Allgemeine Zeitung,* Munich, 18 November 1911, which also mentions a public rehearsal of *Das Lied von der Erde* on the day before the first performance, i.e., the nineteenth. Philip Hale's *Boston Symphony Programme Notes,* New York, 1935, gives the erroneous date, 10 November 1911)

3 DECEMBER 1911

Nino ROTA, Italian composer, pupil of Pizzetti and Casella, adherent of the national school of music in form and essence, is born in Milan.

"Even in his infancy, Nino Rota was prodigiously precocious. At eleven, he composed an oratorio which was publicly performed. His musicianship, however, did not suffer from early exhibitions, and evolved in discretion and earnestness. His musical language does not follow internationalist tendencies, and remains strictly diatonic, in the spirit of true Italian art." (An appreciation sent to the author by Gianandrea Gavazzeni)

14 DECEMBER 1911

Arthur Nikisch conducts at the ninth Gewandhaus concert in Leipzig the first performance of the *Schauspiel Overture,* op. 4, by Erich Wolfgang KORNGOLD, six and a half months after the composer's fourteenth birthday.

"The Overture deserves an honorable place in the Museum of Infant Prodigies. If Master Korngold could make such a noise at fourteen, what will he not do when he is twenty-eight? The thought is appalling." (Philip Hale in the Boston *Herald,* 16 February 1914)

23 DECEMBER 1911

The Jewels of the Madonna, opera in three acts from contemporary Neapolitan life by Ermanno WOLF-FERRARI, in veristic orchestration of guitars, mandolins, wooden clappers, etc., is produced at the Berlin Opera.

29 DECEMBER 1911

The San Francisco Symphony Orchestra gives its initial concert as a permanent organization, Henry Hadley conducting.

1912

21 JANUARY 1912

The orchestral version of RAVEL's *Mother Goose* suite (*Ma Mère l'Oye*) is performed for the first time in Paris.

30 JANUARY 1912

Eight days after his twenty-sixth birthday, John J. BECKER, American composer, completes the composition of his *First Symphony,* subtitled *Etude Primitive.*

(Date communicated by the composer. The date of completion of his *Second Symphony,* subtitled *Fantasia Tragica,* is 1 April 1920; that of his *Third Symphony,* subtitled *Sinfonia Brevis,* 20 June 1929)

7 FEBRUARY 1912

La Lépreuse, "legendary tragedy" of a leper girl's contagious love, set to quasi-Wagnerian music by the Tyrolian-born French composer Silvio LAZZARI, is produced at the Opéra-Comique. (Date from *Cinquante ans de musique française,* Paris, 1926)

5 MARCH 1912

Rochus LILIENCRON, grand old man of German musicography, editor-in-chief of the *Denkmaeler der Deutschen Tonkunst,* dies at Coblenz, in his ninety-second year.

11 MARCH 1912

An imperial masque, *The Crown of India,* by Henry Hamilton with music by Edward ELGAR, written on the occasion of King George the Fifth's visit to India, is produced at the London Coliseum.

12 MARCH 1912

At the San Francisco Music Club Henry COWELL performs for the first time in public, on the day after his fifteenth birthday, piano tone-clusters, on white or black keys, struck with the forearm.

13 MARCH 1912

The full score of STRAVINSKY's *Petrouchka* is published by the Édition Russe de Musique.

14 MARCH 1912

Mona, opera by Horatio PARKER, the winner of the Metropolitan Opera prize of $10,000, is produced by the Metropolitan Opera in New York.

"One device which I have used is that of associating the different personalities of the drama with definite tonalities. For instance, Gwynn, the hero, is associated with the key of B major. With Mona herself I have carried the idea still further, assigning separate keys to the two distinct aspects of her personality. In her character of Druid priestess she is associated with the key of E minor, while in her character as a woman she is assigned to the key of E-flat major." (Horatio Parker in a statement to the press)

30 MARCH 1912

Arnold SCHOENBERG writes the first song of the cycle of "Three Times Seven" poems, opus (significantly!) 21, under the general title *Pierrot Lunaire,* to the symbolist texts by Albert Giraud translated into German by Hartleben, and scored for a small ensemble of instruments—flute (also piccolo), clarinet (also bass-clarinet), violin, interchangeable with viola, cello, piano, and a singing-speaking voice (contralto)—the first song being thirty-nine unequal bars in length.

6 APRIL 1912

A thousand years have passed since the death of NOTKER (Balbulus), the St. Gall monk who was one of the earliest composers to develop the ecclesiastical sequence.

13 APRIL 1912

Die Brautwahl, "musically-fantastic comedy after E. T. A. Hoffman's short story," a modern "magic opera" by Ferruccio BUSONI, is produced in Hamburg.

22 APRIL 1912

Natacha TROUHANOVA gives a dance recital in Paris at which four French composers conduct their own works: Paul DUKAS the first performance of his symphonic poem *La Péri,* a score of rarefied exoticism with a fluid enharmonic modulatory chord employed as a sonorous "block"; Vincent D'INDY his orientalistic *Istar;* Florent SCHMITT his barbaric *Tragédie de Salomé;* and Maurice RAVEL his delicate orchestral version of *Les Valses Nobles et Sentimentales,* under the title of *Adelaïde ou le Langage des Fleurs.*

(The printed score of *La Péri* gives June 1911 as the date of the first performance; indeed the première was announced for 13 June 1911 by Diaghilev's Ballet Russe with Trouhanova as the chief ballerina, but something intervened, Trouhanova did not dance, and Rimsky-Korsakov's *Scheherazade* was played instead)

24 APRIL 1912

Richard STRAUSS completes the score of his one-act opera, *Le Bourgeois Gentilhomme,* to Hoffmansthal's text after Molière.

18 MAY 1912

Evocations, orchestral triptych by Albert ROUSSEL, poetic impressions of his Eastern journey, is performed for the first time, at a concert of the Société Nationale de Musique in Paris.

23 MAY 1912

Jean FRANÇAIX, composer of new France, writing in a healthy, rhythmic neo-classical style, is born in Paris.

26 MAY 1912

Jean BLOCKX, Belgian composer, follower of the Antwerp school founded by Benoit, author of numerous operas and ingratiating songs deeply rooted in Flemish folklore, dies in his native Antwerp in his sixty-second year.

8 JUNE 1912

RAVEL's ballet *Daphnis and Chloe* is performed in stage form by DIAGHILEV's Russian Ballet in Paris.

(An extraordinary diversity of wrong dates of this performance exists in various sources. Roland-Manuel in his book *Maurice Ravel et son oeuvre,* 1914, gives one wrong date, 8 March 1912, on p. 27, and another wrong date, 18 June 1912, on p. 46. Philip Hale's *Boston Symphony Programme Notes,* 1935, gives the erroneous 5 June 1912. Hull and, after him, Einstein in *Das Neue Musik-Lexikon* give the outlandish date, 8 March 1921, probably a misprint of Roland-Manuel's first wrong date. The correct date, 8 June 1912, is given in the official *Annales du Théâtre* for the year 1912, and is definitely confirmed by the reviews in *Le Figaro* of 9 June 1912 and *Excelsior* of the same date)

15 JUNE 1912

The Children of Don, a Cymric music drama in three acts and a prologue by T. E. Willis, music by Joseph HOLBROOKE, is produced at the London Opera House.

(Date in Lowe, *Josef Holbrooke and His Work*, London, 1920)

20 JUNE 1912

Twenty-five days after his nineteenth birthday, Eugene GOOSSENS conducts at a students' concert at the Royal College of Music in London, his first orchestral piece, *Variations on a Chinese Theme.*

"In the middle of the students' orchestral concert which Sir C. V. Stanford conducted at the Royal College of Music last night came a set of Variations on a Chinese melody by Mr. E. Goossens, an exhibitioner of the College. This work had the rather unusual distinction among students' compositions of being conducted by the composer, who evidently not only knows what to do with his orchestra when he is writing for it but is well able to get it done when it is written. He took command with complete assurance and yet without any ostentation, and his clear beat and simple indications to the players secured an admirable performance. The work, too, has the qualities of clearness and simplicity— there is a quantity of pleasant melody, a vein of sentiment which is not afraid of being obvious, and sufficient harmonic variety to suggest that there is plenty of interesting work to come from him in the future." (London *Times*, 21 June 1912, p. 9)

26 JUNE 1912

A year, a month, and eight days after the death of Gustav MAHLER, Bruno WALTER conducts, during the Festival Week in Vienna, the first performance of MAHLER's posthumous *Ninth Symphony,* in four movements:

(1). *Andante commodo,* in D major-minor, starting with a foreboding pianissimo on the unison A in the low register and building toward a triple forte, repeating this dynamic pulsation in increasingly shorter intervals of time, like a "dynamic stretto," and ending on a unison D, thus encasing the whole movement in a dominant-tonic clause. (2). *Im Tempo eines gemaechlichen Laendlers,* a stylized dance, predecessor of the waltz, in a Chopinesque amplified ternary form, with C major as chief tonality. (3). *Rondo, Burlesque,* in rapid country-dance movement, duple time. (4). *Adagio,* with a simple symmetric theme in D-flat major as the principal key, dying away in an attenuated coda.

1 JULY 1912

The English Copyright Act is promulgated as a result of two years' investigation by the international copyright committee, and in accordance with the preliminary statute of 1911.

24 JULY 1912

The *Second Symphony* in C-sharp minor, op. 11, in three movements, by Nicolas MIASKOVSKY, is performed for the first time in Moscow, Constantin Saradjev conducting.

(The first movement completed 30 September 1910; the second and third, 5 July 1911. Orchestration completed 22 December 1911. All these dates communicated by the composer)

"All my works of this period bear the imprint of deep pessimism. It is difficult for me to analyze the reason for this. . . ." (Miaskovsky, in *Autobiographical Notes, Sovietskaya Musica,* No. 6, 1936)

27 JULY 1912

Igor MARKEVITCH, Russian-Parisian composer of music in a sober neo-classical manner, without any romantic or programmatic connotations, is born in Kiev.

12 AUGUST 1912

Erik SATIE composes *Sévère Réprimande,* the first of his three piano pieces, *Véritables Préludes Flasques* (assonance for Basque), with a subtitle *pour un chien,* in barless notation.

13 AUGUST 1912

Jules MASSENET, French composer of songful operatic music, marvelously effective on the stage, dies in Paris at the age of seventy years, three months, and a day.

17 AUGUST 1912

Erik SATIE composes *Seul à la Maison,* the second of his piano pieces *Véritables Préludes Flasques* in barless notation with expression marks in barbarous Latin.

18 AUGUST 1912

Der Ferne Klang, opera with text and music by Franz SCHREKER, is produced at Frankfurt.

23 AUGUST 1912

Erik SATIE composes *On Joue,* the third of his piano pieces *Véritables Préludes Flasques,* in barless notation.

1 SEPTEMBER 1912

Samuel COLERIDGE-TAYLOR, British mulatto composer, dies at Croyden, sixteen days after his thirty-seventh birthday.

"He left his home on Wednesday afternoon intending to visit the Crystal Palace, but was taken ill near West Croydon Railway Station and fell. Recovering sufficiently to return home by tram, he at once went to bed, and a doctor who was called, stated that he was suffering from influenza. Pneumonia supervened and Mr. Coleridge-Taylor died at 6 o'clock last evening. His father was a native of Sierra Leone, and his mother an Englishwoman. His mixed descent cannot be forgotten in any study of his music, since it makes his work an interesting example to all who are concerned with the appearance of racial characteristics in music." (London *Times,* 2 September 1912)

3 SEPTEMBER 1912

Sir Henry Wood conducts at Queen's Hall in London the first performance of Arnold SCHOENBERG's *Five Orchestral Pieces,* op. 16:

(1) *Vorgefuehl,* rapid movement melodically based on fourths, fifths, and tritones in canonical construction; (2) *Vergangenes,* in measured slow time, highly individualized instrumentation with solo passages suggesting, Strauss-like, faces seen and events lived; (3) *Der wechselnde Akkord,* thematically stationary chord in quartal harmony enveloped in constantly changing instrumental colors; (4) *Peripatetik,* in rapid tempo, in a more astringent, secundal harmony; (5) *Das Obbligato Recitativ,* in which a special sign to indicate the principal theme is introduced for the first time.

"This music seeks to express all that dwells in us subconsciously like a dream; which is a great fluctuant power, and is built upon none of the lines that are familiar to us; which has a rhythm, as the blood has its pulsating rhythm, as all life in us has its rhythm; which has a tonality, but only as the sea or the storm has its tonality; which has harmonies, though we cannot grasp or analyze them nor can we trace its themes. All its technical craft is submerged, made one and indivisible with the content of the work." (From the program book)

"The program of last Tuesday's Promenade Concert included *Five Orchestral Pieces*, op. 16, by Arnold Schoenberg, who evidently revels in the bizarre. According to Dr. Anton von Webern, his music 'contains the experience of his emotional life,' and that experience must have been of a strange, not to say unpleasant character. . . . Is it really honest music or merely a pose? We are inclined to think the latter. If music at all, it is music of the future, and we hope, of a distant one. There is plenty of interesting and noble music to enjoy. Why, then, should the ears of the Promenade audience be tortured with scrappy sounds and perpetual discord?" (London *Daily Mail*, 7 September 1912)

"It was like a poem in Tibetan; not one single soul could possibly have understood it at a first hearing. We can, after all, only progress from the known to the unknown; and as the programme writer, who had every reason to know, said, there was not a single consonance from beginning to end. Under such circumstances the listener was like a dweller in Flatland straining his mind to understand the ways of that mysterious occupant of three dimensions, man. . . . At the conclusion half the audience hissed. That seems a too decisive judgment, for after all they may turn out to be wrong; the other half applauded more vehemently than the case warranted, for it could hardly have been from understanding." (London *Times*, 4 September 1912)

"It is impossible to give an idea of the music. The endless discords, the constant succession of unnatural sounds from the extreme notes of every instrument, and the complete absence of any kind of idea, which, at one hearing at least, one can get hold of, baffle description. Herr Schoenberg, in short, is to Strauss at his wildest what Strauss is to Mozart, and he is never for a bare space normal. He does not even end his pieces with recognizable chords. He is a Futurist painter, and he scores as he paints." (The *Manchester Guardian*, 5 September 1912)

"Imagine the scene of the bleating of sheep in 'Don Quixote,' the sacrificial procession in 'Electra,' and the scene of the opponents in 'Heldenleben' all played together and you will have a faint idea of Schoenberg's idea of orchestral color and harmony. As to theme or subject, it must be supposed that he would consider it an insult to be told that he has any traffic with such things. . . . The pieces have no programme or poetic basis. We must be content with the composer's own assertion that he has depicted his own experiences, for which he has our heartfelt sympathy." (The *Daily News*, London, 4 September 1912)

"Schoenberg's music is a return to an elemental condition. It is a collection of sounds without relation to one another. It is the reproduction of the sounds of nature in their crudest form. Modern intellect has advanced beyond mere elementary noise: Schoenberg has not. If the mind of man is superior to that of beast then it should be able to improve and not rest content with imitation. The course adopted by Schoenberg is retrograde." (The *Morning Post,* 4 September 1912)

"It is not often that an English audience hisses the music it does not like; but a good third of the people at Queen's Hall the other day permitted themselves that luxury after the performance of the five orchestral pieces of Schoenberg. Another third of the audience was not hissing because it was laughing, and the remaining third seemed too puzzled either to laugh or to hiss. . . . Nevertheless, I take leave to suggest that Schoenberg is not the mere fool or madman that he is generally supposed to be. . . . May it not be that the new composer sees a logic in certain tonal relations that to the rest of us seem chaos at present, but the coherence of which may be clear enough to us all some day?" (Ernest Newman in the London *Nation,* September 1912)

8 SEPTEMBER 1912

Bernhard ZIEHN, German theorist and promulgator of the enharmonic law which treats not only diminished seventh chords, but all "tonal" chords as stepping-stones to an immediate modulation, dies in his sixty-eighth year in Chicago, his home since 1868.

9 SEPTEMBER 1912

After one hundred and sixty-three days of intermittent work, Arnold SCHOENBERG completes, four days before his thirty-eighth birthday, the cycle of "Three Times Seven" songs, *Pierrot Lunaire,* opus (significantly!) 21, containing $[39 + 41 + 31 + 18 + 44 + 24 + 27 = 224] + [26 + 20 + 20 + 29 + 13 + 36 + 22 = 166] + [31 + 27 + 32 + 19 + 53 + 30 + 30 = 222] = 612$ unequal bars in quarter-note meters (except in *Parodie* and *Heimfahrt*).

11 OCTOBER 1912

Leopold STOKOWSKI conducts his first concert in Philadelphia as conductor of the Philadelphia Symphony Orchestra.

"Leopold Stokowski made his début yesterday afternoon at the Academy as conductor of the Philadelphia Orchestra, in the opening concert of its thirteenth season. Every seat was taken and the extra chairs had been placed within the orchestra rail. There was much enthusiasm, manifesting itself at the beginning in prolonged applause as Stokowski came forward with bowed head, evidently pondering the content of his musical message. Those who went forth to see a hirsute eccentricity were disappointed. They beheld a surprisingly boyish and thoroughly business-like figure, who was sure of himself, yet free from conceit, who dispensed with the score by virtue of infallible memory, and held his men and his audience from first note to last firmly in his grasp." (*Public Ledger*, Philadelphia, 12 October 1912)

14 OCTOBER 1912

The Firefly, comic opera by Rudolf FRIML, is produced at the Empire Theatre in Syracuse, N. Y.

16 OCTOBER 1912

After forty rehearsals, *Pierrot Lunaire*, "set to tones" (*vertont*) for speaking voice and chamber orchestra by Arnold SCHOENBERG, is performed for the first time anywhere, in the Choralionsaal in Berlin, with Albertine Zehme, to whom the work is dedicated, as singing narrator.

"Hermann Helmholtz speaks somewhere about so-called 'metamathematical spaces,' that is, spaces wherein the known axioms of Euclid's geometry are not valid. I think of these remarkable spaces when I tread on the tone-space of the latest Schoenberg: I feel translated into 'metamusical spaces.' To breathe in this new atmosphere, one must leave behind all that is considered axiomatic in things musical. One must first learn the new alphabet to approach this new frightful Schoenberg, to get the bearings of this 'Prose of Music,' as Herr von Webern calls it. . . . Outwardly the evening in the Choralionsaal was very, very interesting. And there was virtually no hissing. Perhaps the audience was an invited one. . . ." (Pisling in *Die Signale*, 2 November 1912)

"Schoenberg's music to Albert Giraud's fantastical poems entitled *The Songs of Pierrot Lunaire* [sic] is the last word in cacophony and musical anarchy. Some day it may be regarded as of historical interest, because it represents the turning point, for the outraged muse surely can endure no more of this. Such noise must drive even the moonstruck Pierrot back to the realm of real music. Albertine Zehme, a well-known Berlin actress, dressed in a Pierrot costume, recited the 'Three Times Seven'

poems, while a musical, or, rather, unmusical ensemble, consisting of a
piano, violin, viola, cello, piccolo, and clarinet, stationed behind a black
screen and invisible to the audience, discoursed the most ear-splitting
combinations of tones that ever desecrated the walls of a Berlin music
hall." (Berlin correspondent of the *Musical Courier,* November 1912)

"If this is music of the future, then I pray my Creator not to let me live
to hear it again." (Otto Taubmann in the *Boersen Courier,* Berlin,
November 1912)

"In Berlin I had occasion to hear Schoenberg's music for the first time,
when he invited me to attend a performance of his *Pierrot Lunaire.*
I was not at all enthusiastic over the estheticism of this work which
seemed to me a reversion to the superannuated cult of Beardsley. But,
as an instrumental achievement, the score of *Pierrot Lunaire* is unquestionably a success." (Stravinsky, *Chroniques de ma vie,* Paris, 1935)

25 OCTOBER 1912

Richard Strauss conducts at Stuttgart the first performance of his
opera *Le Bourgeois Gentilhomme,* to the play by Molière, elaborated by Hofmannsthal, with the inclusion of incidental music to
Ariadne auf Naxos, as a play within a play.

26 OCTOBER 1912

Gustave Charpentier is elected a member of the Académie des
Beaux-Arts in Paris, as Massenet's successor.

(Date from Marc Delmas, *Gustave Charpentier et le lyrisme français,*
Paris, 1931)

1 NOVEMBER 1912

The government of Holland promulgates the copyright law protecting authors and composers from infringement of their rights.

DECEMBER 1912

C. A. Martienssen, editor of the Neue Bachgesellschaft, publishes,
in the second book of the thirteenth volume of the Society, Bach's
Solo Cantata for soprano, *Mein Herze Schwimmt im Blut,* the
manuscript of which, in Bach's handwriting, was found by Martienssen in the Royal Library of Copenhagen. (Preface date)

21 DECEMBER 1912

Arnold SCHOENBERG conducts the first Russian performance of his symphonic poem *Pelleas und Melisande,* at a Siloti concert in St. Petersburg.

1913

7 JANUARY 1913

La Forêt Bleue, "lyric tale" in three acts by Louis AUBERT, is produced at the Grand Théâtre in Geneva.

(Louis Vuillemin in his monograph, *Louis Albert, son oeuvre,* Paris, 1921, states that the Boston performance of 8 March 1913 was the first "integral performance which strictly conformed with the composer's wishes." Grove cites the Boston performance as the first, without mentioning the earlier Geneva production)

11 JANUARY 1913

The French government bestows upon SAINT-SAËNS the Grand Cross of the Legion of Honor, the highest decoration of the order.

(Date from Arthur Dandelot, *La Vie et l'oeuvre de Saint-Saëns,* Paris, 1930)

29 JANUARY 1913

La Festa dei Fiori, "idyllic operetta" by Giuseppe BLANC, composer of *Giovinezza,* the future Fascist hymn, is produced at the Apollo Theatre in Rome.

(Date from the first edition of *Dizionario dei musicisti* by Alberto de Angelis, Rome, 1918)

23 FEBRUARY 1913

Fifteen and a half months after the completion of the score of Arnold SCHOENBERG's *Gurre-Lieder,* Franz Schreker conducts in Vienna the first performance of the work.

"There was an orchestra of one hundred and forty pieces, including chimes, calls, gongs, weird sounding trumpets and even a huge iron chain. Four choruses were called into action—three of men's voices and one of mixed voices—making in all a total of nearly four hundred persons on the stage." (*Musical Courier,* Vienna dispatch, March 1913)

27 FEBRUARY 1913

Cyrano, opera in four acts by Walter DAMROSCH to the book by W. J. Henderson after Rostand's drama, is produced by the Metropolitan Opera in New York.

"Rostand's Play Made Opera—The High Merits of Mr. Henderson's Text—Music That Succeeds Far Less Well—Its Lack of Individuality, Imagination and Communicating Force—Skill and Suitability for Compensation." (H. T. Parker's headlines in the Boston *Evening Transcript,* 28 February 1913)

4 MARCH 1913

Pénélope, a "lyric poem" in three acts by Gabriel FAURÉ, is produced at Monte Carlo.

"Fauré conceived the opera almost as a Grecian relief made animate and articulate upon a twentieth century stage: that is to say, he wrote the music in chaste and sensitive line, with subtle inflections, suffused coloring, reticent emotion." (H. T. Parker in the Boston *Evening Transcript*)

5 MARCH 1913

Julian KREIN, Russian composer of precocious talent in a neo-romantic vein, son of Gregory and nephew of Alexander Krein, composers both, is born in Moscow.

"Tendencies: emotionalism, expanded tonality, clarity. Have attempted to express pacifist ideas in music (symphonic prelude, *Destruction,* written in 1929). I adore Puccini's music. I do not follow the mechanists or formalists in music." (From composer's note to the author)

8 MARCH 1913

Three months and nine days before his thirty-first birthday, Igor STRAVINSKY completes, at Clarens, Switzerland, the score of his "Scenes of Pagan Russia," *Spring the Sacred,* known mostly under its French title *Le Sacre du Printemps,* a ballet-musicorama in two parts:

Part 1: Kiss of the Earth, opening with a high-register bassoon solo, the tune being derived from a Lithuanian song; *Spring Fortune-telling,* in stamping duple time; *Dance of the Womenfolk,* on a melody within the range of a fifth, characteristic of Stravinsky's stylized Russian thematics; *The Game of Kidnaping,* brusque and crude, with unperiodic explosive chords; *Spring Rounds,* a syncopated march-tune, opening and closing with six bars of serene folk song in unison; *Game of Two Cities,* polytonal and polyrhythmic; *Procession of the Oldest and Wisest Men,* with a stultifying persistent figure in the brass; *Dance of the Earth,* in triple time with unperiodic blasts against a quartal motto on a firm pedalpoint C. *Part 2: The Great Sacrifice,* opening with a tortuous introduction in subdued orchestral colors; *Mysterious Games of Young Maidens,* in a polyharmonic major-minor mode, in soft coloring, ending in an eleven-times-repeated chord in heavy beats; *The Glorification of the Chosen,* in uneven meters, with the eighth-note as a constant, dynamically and rhythmically vitalized into a frenzied dance; *Evocation of the Ancestors,* slow and elementally crude; *Rites of Old Men, Human Forebears,* on D as a keynote, with a sinuous chromatic English-horn solo against a rhythmic duple-time motion; *Great Sacred Dance,* in ternary form with a sixteenth-note as a constant in the first and third part and eighth-note rhythm in the middle section; *Sostenuto e Maestoso,* with a quarter note as a unit, in triplets or duplets, interrupted by a quotation from the *Sacred Dance,* which finally returns in constantly changing meters of 1, 2, 3, 4, 5 sixteenth-notes in a bar, until, after a scratch of a Cuban *guiro,* used here for the first time in European orchestral music, and a fertilizing run of the piccolo, the orchestra comes to rest on the key-note D, with the tritone-note G sharp on top.

11 MARCH 1913

Luigi Russolo, Italian futurist musician, issues in Milan a manifesto establishing the fundamental laws of the Art of Noises. (See full text in Part III)

31 MARCH 1913

The Academic Society for Literature and Music in Vienna presents a concert of first performances of music by Arnold Schoenberg's pupil Anton von Webern (*Six Orchestral Pieces*); Schoenberg's teacher and brother-in-law, Alexander Zemlinsky (*Four Orchestral Songs to Poems of Maeterlinck*); Schoenberg himself (*Kammersymphonie,* op. 9, for fifteen solo instruments, in one continuous movement, well within the indicated tonality of E major, and thematically based on rows of perfect fourths); and Schoenberg's pupil Alban BERG (*Two Orchestral Songs to Picture-Postcard Texts*).

"The Grosser Musikvereinsaal audience has an air of expectancy. Vienna prides itself on being 'advanced,' and this is no joke either. There are more things possible with the modern orchestra, so we find out, than Strauss ever dreamed of. These strange whimpers and sighs, the growls of the basses underneath the peculiar wheezes which the clarinetist can produce if he presses his lower lip in a certain way—can they be the birth pangs of a new art, these zoological expressions that would make the real menagerie seek cover with drooping tails and ears in their general disgust at nature's provision to them of such inadequate vocal talents? As for the key,—gracious! people wrote in 'keys' far back in 1910. We thought we knew all the discords which human ingenuity could devise, but here even the wisest can learn something. It is without doubt 'original' music. It is, to be specific, the music of some of Schoenberg's pupils being performed at the concert of March 31 given under the auspices of the *Akademischer Verband fuer Literatur und Musik* with the master himself conducting. They may be called 'Ultralists,' though by any other name they could by no means lose any of their fragrance.

"If this concert was intended to be a 'memorable occasion' it surely succeeded, for it occasioned the greatest uproar which has occurred in a Vienna concert hall in the memory of the oldest critics writing. Laughter, hisses and applause continued throughout a great part of the actual performance of the disputed pieces. After the Berg songs the dispute became almost a riot. The police were sought and the only officer who could be found actually threw out of the gallery one noisemaker who persisted in blowing on a key for a whistle. But this policeman could not prevent one of the composers from appearing in a box and yelling to the crowd, '*Heraus mit der Baggage!*' ('Out with the trash!'). Whereat the uproar increased. Members of the orchestra descended from the stage and entered into spirited controversy with the audience. And finally the president of the Akademischer Verband came and boxed the ears of a man who had insulted him while he was making an announcement." (Vienna dispatch in the *Musical Courier*, 23 April 1913)

1 APRIL 1913

La Vida Breve, two-act opera of socially incompatible love, betrayal, and death, by Manuel DE FALLA, composed in 1905, is performed for the first time at the Casino Municipal in Nice.

3 APRIL 1913

Le Festin de l'Araignée, ballet-pantomime by Albert ROUSSEL, written in a harmonic idiom based on tritones and fourths in syncopated rhythmic treatment, is performed for the first time in Paris, two days before Roussel's forty-fourth birthday.

11 APRIL 1913

L'Amore Dei Tre Re, three-act opera by Italo MONTEMEZZI, to an Italian story of medieval love, by Sem Benelli, is produced at La Scala, Milan, Tullio Serafin conducting.

"Montemezzi has done in an Italian way for an Italian drama what Debussy in an ultra-modern French way did for the Belgian Maeterlinck." (Philip Hale in the Boston *Herald,* 15 February 1914)

18 APRIL 1913

At the 400th concert of the Société Nationale in Paris, *Au Jardin de Marguerite,* symphonic poem by ROGER-DUCASSE, is performed for the first time.

21 APRIL 1913

Erik SATIE writes the first of his *Descriptions Automatiques* for piano, in barless notation, entitled *Sur un Vaisseau,* with humorous remarks in the score, such as *Le Capitaine dit: Très beau voyage.*

"The public is shocked by the charming ridicule of the titles and marks of Satie but it respects the formidable ridicule of the libretto of Parsifal. The same public accepts the craziest titles of François Couperin: *Le tic-toc choc ou Les Maillotins, Les Culbutes JXCXBXNXS, Les Coucous bénévoles, Calotins et Calotines ou la Pièce à tretous, Les Vieux Galants, Les Tresorières surannées.*" (Jean Cocteau, *Le Rappel à l'ordre,* Paris 1926)

22 APRIL 1913

Erik SATIE composes the second of his *Descriptions Automatiques* for piano in barless notation, entitled *Sur une Lanterne,* with expression marks such as *Nocturnement, N'allumez pas encore: vous avez le temps.*

26 APRIL 1913

Three weeks before his forty-seventh birthday, Erik SATIE composes the third and last piano piece of the suite *Descriptions Automatiques,* in barless notation, entitled *Sur un Casque,* with remarks in the music such as: *Que de monde! C'est magnifique! Léger comme un oeuf,* etc. (Date at end of printed music)

11 MAY 1913

One month before his forty-ninth birthday, Richard STRAUSS completes in Garmisch the score of the *Zwischenspiel, Das Festliche Praeludium,* for orchestra and chorus written for the inauguration of the Vienna Konzerthaus, and first performed on that occasion five months and eight days hence (19 October 1913), making use of the aerophor for sustained notes in the brasses.

22 MAY 1913

A century has passed since the birth, in Leipzig, of Richard WAGNER.

29 MAY 1913

Twenty days before STRAVINSKY's thirty-first birthday, his ballet, *Le Sacre du Printemps,* is performed for the first time by the Diaghilev Ballet Russe, at the Théâtre des Champs-Elysées in Paris, Pierre Monteux conducting.

(Date from the advertisement in *Le Temps,* 29 May 1913, and *ante.* Stravinsky in his *Chroniques de ma vie,* Paris, 1935, gives the incorrect date, 28 May)

"I left the theatre from the very first bars of the prelude, which evoked laughter and mockery. I was outraged. These outbursts at first isolated, soon became general and provoked counter-protests, quickly transforming into a terrible uproar. During the entire performance, I remained behind the scenes with Nijinsky. . . . I had to hold him, he was furious and was ready to jump at any moment on the stage and start a riot. Diaghilev, intending to stop the disturbance, gave orders to the electricians to turn the lights off and on. This is all that I recall about this performance." (Stravinsky, *Chroniques de ma vie,* Paris, 1935)

"*Le Sacre du Printemps* was performed in a new hall, too comfortable and too cold for a public accustomed to rub elbows in red and golden velvet. I do not mean to say that *Le Sacre* would have had a more polite reception in a less pretentious theatre; but this luxurious hall symbolized the error of pitching a work of power and youth at a decadent public. An exhausted public, seated amid the Louis XVI garlands, Venetian gondolas, soft divans and cushions of an orientalism which makes us resent the Ballet Russe. . . . The public played the rôle that it had to play. It laughed, spat, hissed, imitated animal cries. They might have eventually tired themselves of that if it had not been for the crowd of esthetes and a few musicians, who, carried by excess of zeal, insulted and even pushed the public of the boxes. The riot degenerated into a fight. Standing in her box, her diadem askew, the old Countess de Pourtales brandished her fan and shouted all red in the face: 'It is the first time in sixty years that anyone has dared to make a fool of me!' The good lady was sincere, she thought it was a mystification." (Jean Cocteau, *Le Rappel à l'ordre*, Paris, 1926)

"A certain part of the audience thrilled by what it considered a blasphemous attempt to destroy music as an art, and swept away with wrath, began very soon after the rise of the curtain to whistle, to make catcalls, and to offer audible suggestions as to how the performance should proceed. Others of us, who liked the music and felt that the principles of free speech were at stake, bellowed defiance. It was war over art." (Carl Van Vechten, in *Music After the Great War*, New York, 1921)

"The cult of the false note has never been practiced with such zeal and persistence as in this score; from the first measure to the last whatever the note you expect, it is never that one which comes, but the next one to it; whatever chord may seem to be involved by a preceding chord, it is always another that follows; and these notes and chords often give an impression of sharp, almost atrocious discord." (Pierre Lalo in *Le Temps*, 3 June 1913)

2 JUNE 1913

Julien, sequel to *Louise*, story of Montmartre passion in a realistic setting, by Gustave CHARPENTIER, is produced in an afternoon dress rehearsal at the Opéra-Comique.

"Paris Sees Charpentier's *Julien*—Enthusiasm Evoked by Sheer Beauty and Lyric Passion of the Music and Superb Stage Setting. Long Expected Continuation of *Louise* Is a Success—Critics Disappointed, However, by Failure of the Composer to Produce Any Really New Note." (Headlines in New York *Sun*, 3 June 1913)

"*Julien* New Work of Charpentier Dazzles Paris—Opera, or Lyrical Poem, as Composer Pleases to Call It, Has Public Rehearsal—Promise of

Louise Fully Carried Out—Music Critic of the Excelsior Writes Enthusiastically of the Merits of Work and Its Beauties." (Headlines, New York *Herald,* 4 June 1913)

"Charpentier's New Opera *Julien* Sequel to *Louise* a Triumph—The Long-Awaited Opera Enthusiastically Received at Its Dress Rehearsal —'Daring Lyric Symbolism' 'The Best French Work of Its Generation'— A Strange Libretto Mingling Reality, Poetry, and Dreams." (Headlines in Boston *Evening Transcript,* 3 June 1913)

(The title-page of the score reads: *Représenté pour la première fois sur le Théâtre National de l'Opéra-Comique, à Paris le 4 Juin 1913.* Grove, 1927, in an article on Charpentier, gives 3 January 1913 as the date of the production of *Julien,* an obvious misprint for June)

2 JUNE 1913

A month and a day after his twenty-eighth birthday, Luigi Russolo, the futurist musician, gives the first public presentation, at the Teatro Storchi in Modena, of the *intonarumore* (noise instruments) invented by him and constructed in collaboration with Ugo Piatti.

(The date of the year, 1903, in *L'Arte dei rumori,* by Luigi Russolo, Futurista, Edizioni Futuriste di "Poesia," Milan, 1916, is a misprint. In the appendix to de Angelis' *Dizionario dei musicisti,* 1928, we find the wrong date of 2 January 1913. See Russolo's manifesto, *The Art of Noises,* in Part III)

2 JUNE 1913

Erik Satie composes *Danse Maigre,* the second in order of the *Croquis et Agaceries d'un gros Bonhomme en Bois,* for piano in barless notation, the title of the piece being an obvious assonance of the much composed Danse Nègre. (Date at end of printed music)

"It is often asked why Satie gives funny titles to the most beautiful of his works which confuse the least hostile public. These titles protect his music against people who are prey to the 'sublime' and allow those who do not see their import to laugh: besides, they are explained by the Debussyst abuse of precious titles. Perhaps there is good-natured moodiness, a malice against the *Lunes descendant sur le temple qui fût,* the *Terrasses des audiences du clair de lune,* and the *Cathédrales englouties.*" (Jean Cocteau, *Le Rappel à l'ordre,* Paris, 1926)

10 JUNE 1913

Tikhon KHRENNIKOV, Soviet Russian composer writing in a clear healthy rhythmical style, unobscured by the pre-revolutionary gloom, is born at Eletz. (Date communicated to the author by the composer)

11 JUNE 1913

La Pisanella, drama by Gabriele D'ANNUNZIO with incidental music by Ildebrando PIZZETTI, is produced at the Châtelet Theatre in Paris.

30 JUNE 1913

Erik SATIE composes *Holothurie,* in barless notation, the first of his three piano pieces under the general title *Desiccated Embryos* with his customary expression marks such as *"comme un rossignol qui aurait mal aux dents"* (like a nightingale with the toothache).

1 JULY 1913

Erik SATIE composes *Edriophthalma,* his second "Desiccated Embryo," with a quotation from Chopin's Funeral March, waggishly labeled: *"citation de la célèbre mazurka de Schubert."*

4 JULY 1913

Erik SATIE composes *Podophthalma,* the third and last of the series of his *Desiccated Embryos* for piano in barless notation, with an "obligatory cadence" in humorously trite F-major arpeggios and chords.

6 JULY 1913

At the annual hearing of prize compositions, the Académie des Beaux-Arts in Paris awards the Grand Prix de Rome to Lili BOU-LANGER, nineteen years and ten and a half months old, the first woman to receive it.

"The Academy of Fine Arts assembled yesterday for the final audition of cantatas submitted for the *Grand-Prix de Rome* in music. The contestants, five in number, were to set to music the text by Eugène Adenis: *Faust and Helen,* after Goethe. After the required drawing of lots, the cantata of Claude Delvincourt was heard first; the cantata of Marc Delmas followed. Mademoiselle Lili Boulanger, pupil of Paul Vidal came next. Her cantata was accompanied by her sister, Nadia Boulanger. Then cantatas of Marcel Dupré and Edouard Mignan were performed. After a long deliberation, the Academy adjudged the *Grand-Prix de Rome,* by 31 votes to 5, to Mlle. Lili Boulanger and the *Second Grand-Prix* to Claude Delvincourt by 29 votes to 7. Marc Delmas received the first *Second Grand-Prix.* The result was received with a long ovation. Mlle. Boulanger, who is not quite twenty is the first woman to receive the *Grand-Prix de Rome* in music. Her elder sister, Nadia Boulanger, had also entered the competition for the *Grand-Prix.* She obtained the *Second Grand-Prix* in 1908, but was less fortunate than her younger sister and did not succeed in carrying the *Grand-Prix* in 1909." (*Le Temps,* 7 July 1913, p. 5, col. 2)

18 JULY 1913

Nine centuries have passed since the birth of Hermannus CONTRACTUS (Count of Vehringen), enlightened musical scientist and inventor of a system of interval notation that anticipated equal temperament.

28 JULY 1913

Erik SATIE writes *Tyrolienne Turque* [sic] for piano, the first in order of the three *Croquis et Agaceries d'un gros Bonhomme en Bois,* in barless notation with humorous expression marks, *Avec précaution, Très turc,* etc.

7 AUGUST 1913

David POPPER, Austrian violoncellist and composer of virtuoso pieces, dies at Baden in his seventieth year.

9 AUGUST 1913

Serge RACHMANINOV completes the composition of *The Bells,* sonorous and effective choral symphony for solo soprano, tenor, and baritone, female and male chorus, and orchestra, to Poe's poem, Russianized by Constantin Balmont.

20 AUGUST 1913

Eugen D'ALBERT completes in Vienna the composition of his opera, *Die Toten Augen,* to the story of Hanns Ewers, dealing with

the miraculous cure of a blind Greek woman on Palm Sunday,
A.D. 29.

25 AUGUST 1913

Erik SATIE composes *Españaña,* the third of the series of piano
pieces in barless notation, entitled *Croquis et Agaceries d'un gros
Bonhomme en Bois,* a sarcastic bisyllabilization of "España," the
music containing caricatured quotations from Chabrier's *España.*

18 SEPTEMBER 1913

The Gesellschaft der Musikfreunde at Donaueschingen is established at a meeting of founder members.

12 OCTOBER 1913

The Gesellschaft der Musikfreunde at Donaueschingen presents its
first concert. (Date from *Neue Musik-Zeitung,* 2 August 1923)

26 OCTOBER 1913

Erik SATIE composes three piano pieces, under the general title,
Peccadilles Importunes: (1). *Être jaloux de son camarade qui a
une grosse tête.* (2). *Lui manger sa tartine.* (3). *Profiter de ce qu'il
a des cors aux pieds pour lui prendre son cerceau,* all on white
keys, with humorous text over the music, as for instance: *Si le
Bon Dieu voit cela, il sera furieux.* (Date at end of printed music)

18 NOVEMBER 1913

Two months and five days after his thirty-ninth birthday, Arnold
SCHOENBERG completes the score of *Die Glueckliche Hand,* expressionist monodrama, to his own text, making use of color dynamics,
crescendo in the orchestra being accompanied by a *crescendo*
of colors: red—brown—green—dark blue—purple. (Date at end of
printed music)

19 NOVEMBER 1913

The *Violoncello Concerto* by Johann Cristoph MONN, freely arranged by Arnold Schoenberg with cembalo and small orchestra
accompaniment, is performed for the first time at a concert in

honor of the twentieth anniversary of the Denkmaeler der Tonkunst in Oesterreich, with Pablo Casals playing the cello solo.

28 NOVEMBER 1913

Felix Weingartner conducts in Vienna the first performance of
the *Sinfonietta* for full orchestra, op. 5, by Erich KORNGOLD, sixteen-
and-a-half-year-old Viennese wonder-boy, a score of Straussian
complexity with a motto of ascending fourths, "motif of the cheerful heart," on the title-page.

"Occasion: the third Philharmonic concert. Scene: the great concert hall
of the Musikvereinshaus. Prophets to the right, prophets to the left, and
the wonder-child, young Korngold, in the middle. . . . His *Sinfonietta*
performed for the first time before what is perhaps the most critical
audience in the world went the way of most productions destined to out-
live the praise or blame of a day: it evoked storms of applause and protest." (*Musical Courier,* December 1913)

4 DECEMBER 1913

L'Amore Medico, opera by Ermanno WOLF-FERRARI to Molière's
play, is produced at the Dresden Opera.

9 DECEMBER 1913

Richard Strauss' opera *Rosenkavalier* is presented by the Metropolitan Opera in New York for the first time in America.

"Richard Strauss Turns His Hand to a Comedy Opera.—Von Hofmanns-
thal's Sprightly Libretto Filled with Music Which Is Mozartian in
Terms of the Modern Orchestra—The Altogether New and Different
Strauss of This Score—Its Waltz Tunes Not Distinguished: Its Humor
Often Exaggerated, but Remarkable in His Union of Intricacy and
Simplicity." (Headlines in the Boston *Evening Transcript,* 10 December
1913)

"*Rosenkavalier* at Metropolitan.—A Vapid and Salacious Comedy Given
with Great Earnestness—From Necrophilism to Lubricity—The Policy of
Such a Production at the Opera Questioned." (Headlines in the New
York *Tribune*)

9 DECEMBER 1913

Franz KULLAK, German piano pedagogue and editor, son of Theodor Kullak, nephew of Adolf Kullak, and first cousin of Ernst

Kullak, all pianists and pianologists, dies in Berlin in his seventieth year.

10 DECEMBER 1913

Claude DEBUSSY conducts KOUSSEVITZKY's orchestra in Moscow in a program of his works: *Nocturnes, Clarinet Rhapsody, La Mer, L'Après-midi d'un Faune, Images,* and *Marche Écossaise.*

15 DECEMBER 1913

Eight days after Pietro MASCAGNI's fiftieth birthday, his four-act opera *Parisina,* to the book of Gabriele D'Annunzio, is produced at La Scala in Milan.

21 DECEMBER 1913

Arione, poem for cello and orchestra, by Francesco MALIPIERO, the prize work in the competition of the city of Rome, is performed for the first time at the Augusteo.

1914

5 JANUARY 1914

Siegfried LANGGAARD, Danish composer, pupil of Liszt, and himself a piano virtuoso of no mean order, dies in his native Copenhagen in his sixty-second year.

17 JANUARY 1914

Arnold SCHOENBERG conducts his *Five Orchestral Pieces* in his first appearance in London.

"London Baffled by Schoenberg's Orchestral Pieces—Composer Himself Conducts His Work and He at Last Is Pleased—Reminiscent of a Nightmare." (*Musical America,* February 1914)

"Critics in London Rap Futurist Music—Herr Schoenberg's Composition Called 'Vague, Scrappy and Incoherent.'—'Incomprehensible Noise'—

Viennese Composer Writes in Hieroglyphics, Says One Newspaper."
(New York *Sun,* February 1914)

"To the Editor of 'The Daily Telegraph': Sir: Any one acquainted with
music history would find little cause for surprise at the incoherent criticism following on the performance of the Schoenberg compositions at
Queen's Hall. The vulgarity of the writer who stated that 'long hair used
to be indispensable has now been superseded by the bald head' (an
obvious and disgraceful attack on the personality of Herr Schoenberg)
and the even more stupid remark of the other person who wrote that
'they (the Schoenberg pieces) were so ridiculous in their chaotic form-
lessness that the orchestra sometimes laughed down their instruments
instead of blowing down them,' may be dismissed as examples of ignorance and lack of decency. It is, however, surprising to find . . . this bewilderment on the part of our most sincere critics. May I venture to
suggest that it is a lack of constructive vision in regard to musical psychology." (From a letter by Leigh Henry to the editor of the *Daily
Telegraph,* 17 February 1914)

24 JANUARY 1914

Madeleine, lyric opera in one act by Victor HERBERT, is produced
at the Metropolitan Opera in New York.

"Herbert's *Madeleine* Has Its Metropolitan Première. A One-Act Description of a Lonely and Temperamental Prima Donna Whose Friends
Insist upon Spending New-Year's Day with Their Mothers. Sixteen Curtain Calls for Composer and Principals." (Headlines in *Musical America,*
February 1914)

5 FEBRUARY 1914

Las Golondrinas, opera by the not quite twenty-seven-year-old
Basque composer, José Maria USANDIZAGA, written in an effective
Puccini-like style, is produced at Teatro Price, Madrid, some
twenty months before the composer's untimely death.

7 FEBRUARY 1914

The Academy of Santa Cecilia in Rome confers honorary membership on DEBUSSY, ELGAR, GLAZUNOV, GOLDMARK, HUMPERDINCK,
Felipe PEDRELL, SAINT-SAËNS, and Richard STRAUSS.

23 FEBRUARY 1914

A year and a half after MASSENET's death, his posthumous opera,

Cléopatre, "drame passionel" in four acts, is produced at Monte Carlo.

"The speech of M. Viviani, Minister of Public Instruction, surveyed the composer's life and work in admirable fashion. The Minister declared Massenet's music to be a poem in honor of women—the full expression of woman as a temptress and consoler." *(Musical America,* March 1914)

1 MARCH 1914

Tor AULIN, Swedish violinist and composer of virtuoso pieces, dies in his native Stockholm in his forty-eighth year.

7 MARCH 1914

Akira IFUKBE, Japanese composer of rhythmic music with native coloring, is born at Kushiro.

11 MARCH 1914

La Fille de Figaro, opera by Xavier LEROUX, is produced at the Apollo Theatre in Paris.

11 MARCH 1914

At Carnegie Hall, New York, Jim EUROPE conducts a Negro symphony orchestra in an instrumentation anticipatory of jazz, without oboes, bassoons, or second violins, but with numerous clarinets, trombones, banjos, and ten pianos.

27 MARCH 1914

A London Symphony, metropolitan musicorama by VAUGHAN WILLIAMS, is performed for the first time at Queen's Hall, London.

"The composer of the London Symphony understood that music begins where realistic noise leaves off. If his thoughts are not all pleasant or all hopeful individually, in their relations to one another he builds up something which is beautiful in its entirety." (London *Times,* 28 March 1914)

"The man that has written the mysterious introduction of this symphony, expressed loneliness and tragic shabbiness in the second movement, the cruelty of the great city in the finale, is more than an accomplished musician; he is a rare poet of tones." (Philip Hale in the Boston *Herald,* 16 April 1921)

29 MARCH 1914

At the Concerts Colonne in Paris Alfredo CASELLA conducts the first performance of his *Notte di Maggio,* a work in which his "second style"—polytonal and polymodal—is definitely established.

29 MARCH 1914

Variations for Orchestra, the first important work by the Dutch composer, Sem DRESDEN, is presented in the first performance by the Concertgebouw Orchestra at Amsterdam, under the direction of Willem Mengelberg.

30 MARCH 1914

The term "polyharmony," instead of polytonality, is suggested by Émile VUILLERMOZ in his article in *Comoedia,* in Paris, to describe the superposition of two or more chords or melodic figures in different keys.

2 APRIL 1914

Five months before his tragic death Albéric MAGNARD conducts the first performance of his magnum opus, the *Fourth Symphony,* at the Concerts de l'Union des Femmes Professeurs et Compositeurs, in Paris.

5 APRIL 1914

STRAVINSKY'S *Sacre du Printemps* is performed for the first time as an orchestra piece, without stage action, at the Casino de Paris, Paris, Pierre MONTEUX conducting.

21 APRIL 1914

F. T. MARINETTI and Luigi RUSSOLO give a concert of futurist music at the Teatro dal Verme in Milan, presenting for the first time in public a complete set of noise instruments, invented by Russolo.

"The notice announced the first concert of *4 networks of noises* of which the titles are:
 1. Awakening of Capital
 2. Meeting of automobiles and aeroplanes

3. Dining on the terrace of the Casino
4. Skirmish in the oasis

Russolo himself conducted the orchestra, composed of 19 noise-instruments:

3 bumblers	2 gurglers
2 exploders	1 fracasseur
3 thunderers	2 stridors
3 whistlers	1 snorer
2 rufflers	

"An enormous crowd. Loges, pit, balcony, chock full. Deafening uproar of the 'pastists' who wished to break up the concert at any price. For an hour the futurists resisted passively. At the beginning of the fourth network of noise, an extraordinary thing happened: suddenly five futurists—Boccioni, Carra, Amando Mazza, Piatti and I—were seen to come down from the stage. They crossed the orchestra and, in the full center of the circle, with punches, sticks, and walking-sticks attacked the pastists, drunk with stupidity and traditional rage. The battle lasted in the pit for half an hour, while Luigi Russolo impeturbably continued to direct his nineteen noisters on the stage.

"Amazing accord of bloody faces and noisy discords, pellmell in an infernal hubbub. The battle over *Hernani* seems child's play in comparison with this mêlée.

"All our riots hitherto had taken place in the streets, in the corridors of the theatres and after performances. For the first time the artists having played an hour on the stage were brusquely divided into two groups —one continuing to perform their art, while the other went down into the pit to attack a hostile and hissing public. Thus the escort of a caravan in the desert defends itself against the Touaregs. Thus the infantry, set out as sharpshooters, sometimes defends the construction of a military bridge.

"Our knowledge of boxing and our enthusiasm for fighting enabled us to emerge from the struggle safe and sound, with two or three scratches. The pastists had *eleven wounded* who had to be taken to the first aid station." (F. T. Marinetti, *L'Intransigeant,* Paris, 29 April 1914)

10 MAY 1914

Ernst VON SCHUCH, Austrian conductor of most first performances of Richard STRAUSS' operas, dies in Dresden in his sixty-eighth year.

14 MAY 1914

Richard STRAUSS conducts in Paris the first performance of his first ballet score, *Josephslegende,* at the Russian Ballet's presentation in Paris.

"The *réclame* had done its work and the opera house was crowded . . . not even a 'strapontin' remained and no one appeared to find seats at $8 too much to ask to witness a Strauss ballet. . . . Melodies sometimes sensuous, sometimes naïve, work up to a long and majestic climax which brought the $13,000 first-night house down." (The Boston *Post,* 24 May 1914)

15 MAY 1914

Marouf, Cobbler of Cairo, opéra-comique in five acts, from the Arabian Nights, by Henri RABAUD, is produced at the Paris Opéra-Comique.

16 MAY 1914

Jan SIBELIUS leaves Helsingfors on his voyage to America.

26 MAY 1914

Le Rossignol, opera-ballet by Igor STRAVINSKY, a score of mixed tendencies, heterochronically evolved, to Andersen's fairy tale, is produced at DIAGHILEV's Ballet Russe in Paris, Emil Cooper conducting.

27 MAY 1914

Jan SIBELIUS arrives in New York.

1 JUNE 1914

The fifth, and last, Congress of the International Music Society is held in Paris, two months before the war.

2 JUNE 1914

Nicolas MIASKOVSKY's *First Symphony,* op. 3, is performed for the first time at a summer concert at Pavlovsk, near St. Petersburg, Aslanov conducting.

(Composition completed 9 August 1908, orchestration finished 21 September 1908. These dates are communicated by the composer)

"The summer of 1908 brought the First Symphony and, with this work, the free scholarship (had I not received that scholarship, I would have been forced to leave the Conservatory, for I could not raise 250 rubles for tuition). The composition of the First Symphony has decided my future. Before that I was afraid of orchestral writing. Theatre music never attracted me, either in the opera or in the ballet." (N. Miaskovsky, *Autobiographical Notes* in *Sovietskaya Musica*, No. 6, 1936)

2 JUNE 1914

The second part of *Metamorphoses*, suite by Maximilian STEIN-BERG, is performed for the first time anywhere at the Ballet Russe presentation at the Paris Opéra.

4 JUNE 1914

On his visit to America SIBELIUS conducts, at the twenty-eighth meeting and concert of the Litchfield County Choral Union, held in the Music Shed at Norfolk, Conn., his works: *Pohjola's Daughter, King Christian II, The Swan of Tuonela,* and *Oceanides.*

14 JUNE 1914

Seven weeks before the war, the French government confers the Légion d'Honneur on Richard STRAUSS.

17 JUNE 1914

The degree of Doctor of Music is conferred upon SIBELIUS by Yale University, with the following summary of his position in the music world made by President Hadley:

"By his music, intensely national in inspiration, and yet in sympathy with the mood of the West, Doctor Jan Sibelius long since captured Finland, Germany, and England, and on coming to America to conduct a symphonic poem found that his fame had already preceded him, also. Still in the prime of life, he has become, by the power and originality of his work, one of the most distinguished of living composers. What Wagner did with Teutonic legend, Dr. Sibelius has done in his own impressible way with the legends of Finland as embodied in her national epic. He has translated the Kalevala into the universal language of music, remarkable for its breadth, large simplicity, and the infusion of a deeply poetic personality."

22 JUNE 1914

Gino GORINI, Italian composer, pupil of Malipiero, and concert pianist, is born in Venice.

"Malipiero's influence manifests itself in Gino Gorini's music in the spirit of vivacity. A sharp and direct idiom evolved by Gorini is a compromise between melodic texture of Malipiero and the inflexible rhythmic spirit of Casella." (A short appreciation sent to the author by Gianandrea Gavazzeni)

25 JUNE 1914

Erik SATIE composes *Obstacles Vénimeux,* the first of his suite of three barless piano pieces, *Heures Séculaires et Instantanées,* with the following text over the music:

"This vast part of the world is inhabited but by one man: a Negro. He is bored to the point of dying of laughter. The shadow of millennial trees marks 9:17 o'clock. The toads call each other by name. For better thinking, the Negro holds his cerebellum in his right hand, with out-stretched fingers. From afar he looks like a distinguished physiologist. Four anonymous serpents hold him captive, suspended on the tails of his uniform, deformed by chagrin and solitude. On the bank of the river, an old mangrove-tree slowly laves its repugnantly filthy roots. It is not the shepherd's hour." (A footnote reads: "To whom it may concern: I forbid to read the text aloud during the musical performance. Failure to comply shall entail my just indignation against the trans-gressor")

27–28 JUNE 1914

The XV Tonkuenstler-Fest is held in Switzerland, at which per-formances of works by Otto BARBLAN, Friedrich NIGGLI, Walter COURVOISIER, Emil FREY, Hans HUBER, Émile JAQUES-DALCROZE, Gustave DORET, Volkmar ANDREAE, Hermann SUTER, and Frank MARTIN are given.

2 JULY 1914

Two centuries have passed since the birth at Erasbach of Christoph Willibald GLUCK.

3 JULY 1914

A month before the war, Erik SATIE writes *Crépuscule Matinal* (*de midi*), second of his suite of three barless piano pieces, *Heures Séculaires et Instantanées,* with the following text over the music:

"The sun rose early and in good humour. The heat is going to be above normal, for it is prehistorical times. The sun is high in the sky, he

looks like a good fellow. But let us not trust him. Mayhap he will burn
the harvest or administer a hard stroke: a sun-stroke. Behind the hangar,
a bull eats himself sick."

4 JULY 1914

Marcel DUPRÉ, French organist, composer, and unique improviser
of polyphonic music, is awarded the first Grand Prix de Rome at
an annual meeting of the Académie des Beaux-Arts in Paris.

4 JULY 1914

Dylan, second part of an operatic trilogy, by Joseph HOLBROOKE, is
produced at the Drury Lane, London.

10 JULY 1914

SIBELIUS arrives in Finland on his return from the American tour.

3 AUGUST 1914

Gabriel DUPONT, French composer of operatic music in an effective
and individualized style, dies in war-touched Paris, during the rehearsals of his last and best opera, *Antar,* at the age of thirty-six
years, five months, and two days.

12 AUGUST 1914

Die Signale prints an editorial announcement to the effect that it
will continue to be published each Wednesday, though reduced in
size owing to wartime economy.

15 AUGUST 1914

The Promenade Concerts in Queen's Hall, London, open the first
war season with the playing of national hymns of the allied powers,
a novelty by ELGAR, *Sospiri* for strings, harp, and organ, and
TCHAIKOVSKY's *Capriccio Italien,* replacing the previously announced *Don Juan* of Richard STRAUSS.

17 AUGUST 1914

A Franco-Russian program is substituted for an all-WAGNER evening at the Promenade concerts in London.

"The taboo of Wagner is much to be regretted. Apparently, the directors of the Queen's Hall and of the Orchestra feared a demonstration by non-musical super-patriots." (The *Musical Times,* London, September 1914)

28 AUGUST 1914

Anatol LIADOV, composer of miniature symphonic poems in the harmonic idiom of the Russian national school, dies at Novgorod, in his sixtieth year.

28 AUGUST 1914

Arnold SCHOENBERG composes in Berlin the fourth in order of the *Four Songs* for voice and orchestra, op. 22, *Vorgefuehl,* to a poem by Rainer Maria Rilke, twenty-seven unequal bars in length, making use of vocal harmonics (head-tones).

(The non-consecutive dates of composition of the first three songs are: No. 1, 6 October 1913; No. 2, 1 January 1915; No. 3, 3 December 1914. In these songs, published in 1917, Schoenberg applies for the first time his method of notation in simplified score, in three, four, or more staves to indicate homogeneous instrumental groups, and with themes designated by the signs, H ⌐ ⌐ *Hauptstimme,* principal theme; and N ⌐: ⌐, *Nebenstimme,* secondary theme)

30 AUGUST 1914

The Deutsches Opernhaus in Charlottenburg opens its season despite the war.

2 SEPTEMBER 1914

At a special meeting in Paris, the Société Messager, Broussan & Cie., decides to dissolve the society founded for the management of the Paris Opéra, in view of the closing of all theatres after the outbreak of the war.

3 SEPTEMBER 1914

Albéric MAGNARD, French composer of four symphonies, three operas, and many minor works of Franckian harmonies and passionate dramatic quality, is killed by the advancing German troops in his house on the Marne.

(Riemann definitely says, "von deutschen Soldaten erschossen" but see the following story)

"When the Germans reached Baron, near Nanteuil le-Haudouin, where Magnard lived for twelve years, Mme. Magnard and the rest of the family were sent away, while Magnard and his son-in-law who assumed the dress of a gardener, remained. The Germans tried to enter the grounds and Magnard from a window fired two shots, wounding one and killing another. Then the Germans set the house on fire. When the flames reached the first floor a shot was heard. Magnard had killed himself. . . . A few days before he showed an automatic pistol to a friend and said 'This pistol has five bullets; four are for the Germans if they break into my home, the fifth for myself.' " (Digest of the dispatch to the New York *Sun,* 15 January 1915, based on a story by Frédéric Masson in the Paris *Gaulois)*

5 SEPTEMBER 1914

The French musical weekly, *Le Ménestrel,* announces suspension of publication in the following statement:

"Now that as a result of departures to the front, our forces are more and more scattered, musical news is rare, and its interest appears truly insignificant compared with the drama being so tragically enacted in Europe, we are compelled, to our regret, to suspend the publication of the *Ménestrel."*

14 SEPTEMBER 1914

St. Louis Blues is copyrighted by its composer, W. C. HANDY.

30 SEPTEMBER 1914

The publishing house of Breitkopf & Haertel in Berlin issues a statement dissolving the International Musical Society, because of the impossibility of any international activity during the war.

12 OCTOBER 1914

The Berlin Philharmonic Orchestra opens its first war season with Beethoven's *Egmont Overture* and *Violin Concerto,* and Brahms' *Fourth Symphony,* conducted by Arthur NIKISCH.

13 OCTOBER 1914

Perseus, the second symphonic work by Eugene GOOSSENS, is performed for the first time at the Promenade concerts in London.

22 OCTOBER 1914

Cyril Scott's *Britain's War-March* is performed for the first time in London, at the Promenade concerts.

18 NOVEMBER 1914

Alastor, symphonic poem after Shelley, op. 14, by Nicolas Miaskovsky, is performed for the first time in Moscow, Koussevitzky conducting.

(Composition completed 13 November 1912; orchestration completed 6 February 1913. All these dates communicated by the composer)

DECEMBER 1914

Arnold Schoenberg sketches a symphonic work in which he applies for the first time the principle of composition in accordance with the twelve-tone system. (See Schoenberg's letter in Part III)

6 DECEMBER 1914

Musicians not of military age, members of the Lamoureux and Colonne orchestras in Paris, give their initial concert of the first war season in Paris, under the auspices of both orchestras.

7 DECEMBER 1914

Edward Elgar's orchestral piece, *Carillon,* to the patriotic poem by Émile Cammaerts, is performed at Queen's Hall.

14 DECEMBER 1914

Giovanni Sgambati, Italian composer, remarkable pianist, one of the founders of the Academy of Santa Cecilia, dies in his native Rome in his seventy-fourth year.

(Date from the cable dispatch in the New York *Times* of 15 December 1914. Grove, Riemann, Moser, and the *Encyclopaedia Britannica* give the erroneous date 15 December 1914)

20 DECEMBER 1914

A century and a half has passed since the completion of the *Dictionnaire de musique,* by Jean Jacques Rousseau. (Preface date is marked 20 December 1764)

27 DECEMBER 1914

The Academy of Santa Cecilia in Rome confers honorary membership on Vincent D'INDY.

1915

1 JANUARY 1915

The first issue of the *Musical Quarterly,* a publication with a touch of imagination and which devotes its pages to both the human and theoretical aspects of music, is published in New York under the editorship of O. G. Sonneck, Chief of the Music Division of the Library of Congress.

"Publisher and editor are agreed not to throttle *The Musical Quarterly* at birth with a 'program.' . . . The policy of the magazine? That may best be defined by this subtle alteration of a good, old doctrine: *Audietur et altera pars.* The foundations of this magazine were laid months before the European War broke out. Since then many foreign collaborators have been called to the colors, and the editor suddenly found himself under the necessity of changing the distribution of his forces and of adjusting his plans to unwelcome circumstances.

"While the war lasts, of necessity, articles by continental contributors will be fewer than were solicited and promised. Indeed the editor fears that the pen of more than one valued contributor rests for ever." (From the preface to the first issue)

1 JANUARY 1915

Florent SCHMITT conducts his *Chant de Guerre* at the matinee for convalescent soldiers at Toul, France.

2 JANUARY 1915

Karl GOLDMARK, Austrian composer of effective orchestral and operatic music, in an idiom between Wagnerian ideals and conventional nineteenth-century practice, dies in Vienna in his eighty-fifth year.

12 JANUARY 1915

Sergei TANEIEV finishes, in Moscow, his last work, a cantata, *Upon Reading the Psalms,* which gives supreme expression to Taneiev's Bach-like religious and musical faith.

(Date from the symposium *S. Taneiev, His Life and Work,* Moscow, 1935. Abraham and Calvocoressi in *Russian Music,* 1935, give the date 31 December 1914, old style, 13 January 1915, new style)

24 JANUARY 1915

Sinfonia Drammatica in three movements, by Ottorino RESPIGHI, is performed for the first time at the Augusteo Theatre in Rome, MOLINARI conducting.

25 JANUARY 1915

Madame Sans-Gêne, opera in three acts (taking place respectively on 10 August 1792 in Madame's laundry, in September 1811 at the Compiègne Castle, and in Napoleon's study), to the play of Victorien Sardou, music by Umberto GIORDANO in the transitional musical idiom of the Italian operatic verismo, is performed for the first time at the Metropolitan Opera in New York.

5 FEBRUARY 1915

Max REGER conducts in Berlin the first performances of his *Variations on a Mozart Theme,* op. 132, and *Eine Vaterlaendische Overture,* op. 140, a patriotic *pièce d'occasion,* dedicated to the German army.

9 FEBRUARY 1915

Richard STRAUSS completes, in Berlin, the composition of *Eine Alpensinfonie,* op. 64, a "hundred days' symphony," for it has taken Strauss exactly one hundred days to write this gigantic musicorama, a Baedeker in tones, the most literal piece of program music in orchestral literature, embanked within one continuous movement and subdivided into the following sections:

(1). *Night,* a peaceful descent of the B-flat minor scale over the entire bassoon range, while the strings tarry in pan-diatonic clusters covering the seven notes of the scale. (2). *The Sunrise,* in triple forte, on the A pedal point. (3). *The Ascent,* in fanfare-like harmonies with hunting horns behind the stage, in pure E-flat major. (4). *The Entrance into the Forest,* in broad C minor. (5). *Wandering by the Brook,* in shimmering A-flat major. (6). *At the Waterfall,* with the ascending fanfare in D major, in the high register of the orchestra, without basses, lower brass, or wood-winds. (7). *The Apparition,* in diminished-seventh-chord harmonies, alternating with D and A major, with violin groups in constant glissando. (8). *On the Blossoming Meadows,* with edelweiss springing staccato in the upper wood-winds. (9). *On the Mountain Pastures,* in horn-like E-flat major passages. (10). *Through Thickets and Underbrush,* on a Beethoven-like diatonic figure. (11). *On the Glacier,* in D minor, in broad harmonic figuration. (12). *Perilous Moments,* with menacing chromatic avalanches leaving behind a cluster of semitones in the violins. (13). *On the Summit,* in F major, and later in proclamatory C major. (14). *The Vision,* with a two-and-a-half octave chromatic ascent, stopped without consummation. (15). *Mists Rising,* in a low rumbling of B-flat minor tones. (16). *Gradual Darkening of the Sun,* with the tonality shifting to F-sharp minor. (17). *Elegy,* with the organ intoning a contemplative song. (18). *Stillness before the Storm,* with the descending B-flat minor scale coming back again, with foreboding loud drops of pizzicato strings and pan-diatonic clusters in the wind instruments. (19). *The Thunderstorm and the Descent,* with the wind machine and thunder machine rolling in the orchestra, flutes flutter-tonguing in downward runs toward the parent B-flat minor on a powerful dominant pedal, but unexpectedly resolving into the submediant G-flat major. (20). *The Sunset,* with the ascent motif inverted, chromatic and diatonic figures interweaving in a counterpoint of leading motifs. (21). *Ausklang,* in E-flat major in pure harmony. (22). *The Night,* descending as at the outset, along the parent B-flat minor scale, with the strings again tarrying at the diatonic steps, forming thick pan-diatonic clusters which remain until the very last bar of the score. (Richard Specht gives the date of 9 February 1915 in his preface to the Eulenburg edition of the score, and 8 February in the chronograph of his two-volume essay on Strauss)

16 FEBRUARY 1915

Emil WALDTEUFEL, the Alsatian-born waltz composer and ball director at the court of Napoleon III, dies in Paris in his seventy-eighth year.

(Date from the New York *Times* dispatch of 17 February 1915. Grove gives the altogether erroneous date 12 February 1912)

19 FEBRUARY 1915

Jules ÉCORCHEVILLE, French musicologist, co-founder, with Dauriac and J. G. Prod'homme, of the French section of the International Society of Music, editor of the complete music catalogue
of the Bibliothèque Nationale in Paris, musicologist of the modern
school, falls in Champagne, while leading his company in a French
counter-offensive, twenty-six days before his forty-third birthday.

27 FEBRUARY 1915

The *Third Symphony,* op. 15, in A minor, by Nicolas MIASKOVSKY,
in two movements, composed in March 1914 and orchestrated
in July 1914, is performed for the first time in Moscow, Emil
Cooper conducting.

(Dates of composition communicated by the composer. Date of performance from an announcement in the Moscow paper, *Russkiya Vedomosti* of 14/27 February 1915)

12 MARCH 1915

Jan SIBELIUS completes the composition of the *Sonata* in E major
for violin and piano. (Date in Karl Ekman's *Sibelius,* Helsingfors,
1935)

19 MARCH 1915

Adventures in a Perambulator (1. *En voiture!* 2. *The Policeman.*
3. *The Hurdy-Gurdy.* 4. *The Lake.* 5. *Dogs.* 6. *Dreams*) by John
Alden CARPENTER, a gay suite of obvious but effective program
music, is performed for the first time by the Chicago Symphony.

20 MARCH 1915

The Russian Symphony Orchestra of New York directed by Modest
ALTSCHULER gives the first American performance of SCRIABIN's
Prometheus with the part of *Luce* (light) executed on a "color
organ."

23 MARCH 1915

Debussy's mother dies in Paris, at one-thirty in the afternoon,
three years and two days before Debussy's own death.

(Date from Debussy's letter to Durand of 23 March 1915, in *Lettres de Claude Debussy à son éditeur*, Paris, 1927)

9 APRIL 1915

La Chasse aux Boches, military operetta by F. PERPIGNAN, is staged at the Folies-Bergère, in Paris. (Date from *Cinquante ans de musique française*, Paris, 1926)

15 APRIL 1915

El Amor Brujo, ballet-pantomime built on Andalusian folk songs, by Manuel DE FALLA, is produced at the Teatro de Lara in Madrid, in a small orchestra version.

15 APRIL 1915

Twelve days before his death, Alexander SCRIABIN plays his last piano recital of his own works in the Conservatory Hall in Petrograd, in a program including his last composition, opus 74.

25 APRIL 1915

Nicola D'ARIENZO, Italian opera composer, teacher of LEONCAVALLO and a generation of younger Italian composers, dies at Naples in his seventy-third year.

(The date is taken from the obituary article by Corte in *La Rivista musicale italiana*, June 1915. Grove gives the erroneous date, 24 April; also the correct date of d'Arienzo's birth is 24 December 1842, not 23 December, as in Grove. Hull gives the wrong year, 1843, while the day and month are given correctly)

27 APRIL 1915

Alexander SCRIABIN, great Russian composer, prophet of universal music, creator of meta-harmony of higher overtones, dies in Moscow, at the age of forty-three years, three months, twenty days, and eighteen hours.

"On April 7 Scriabin remained in bed with a small furunculus on the upper lip. At first this did not cause alarm, particularly since he had a similar eruption a year before in England which passed without ill results. But the malignancy of the abscess grew. The temperature rose threateningly. . . . Large incisions were made on the face and other measures were taken to prevent the spread of the infection. But the temperature did not fall. The pustule spread all over the face. . . . One more incision was made. . . . On the 13th, the swelling diminished and the patient felt comparatively well. But at noon he began to complain of pains in the chest, and the doctor found symptoms of pleurisy. The patient grew more and more restless. . . . At one o'clock a. m. he began to lose consciousness. At three he was given the last Sacrament and on 14 April, at 8:05 in the morning, Scriabin passed away." (Y. Engel in the *Musical Contemporary*, Moscow, December 1915. *Dates in the quotation are according to old style.* For some reason all dictionaries give wrong dates for both the birth and the death of Scriabin. Riemann, 1929, Grove, 1927, *Encyclopaedia Britannica*, Moser, 1935, all give 14 April, without allowing for the thirteen days' difference between the Russian and the Western calendars. Yet the news of Scriabin's death was cabled to all countries, and the dispatches printed on the next day in the principal newspapers of the world. Scriabin's birth is variously given as 6 January and 10 January 1872. 6 January is the correct date. Scriabin was born on Christmas Day and made much of this coincidence. The Christmas Day of the Russian calendar in 1871 coincided with 6 January of the following year 1872. Here is an authoritative account of Scriabin's birth, taken from the article quoted above:

"In December 1871 the young couple went to Moscow. . . . Liubov Petrovna approached the term of her first childbirth. She fell ill when she arrived in Moscow, and on that same date, at two o'clock in the afternoon, was delivered of a boy, the future composer. It happened on 25 December, Christmas Day. Scriabin used to point out this coincidence ascribing to it some special mystical significance.")

14–26 MAY 1915

The Boston Symphony Orchestra, conducted by Karl MUCK, gives thirteen daily concerts at the Panama-Pacific International Exposition in San Francisco, in programs of music of all nations.

21 MAY 1915

Camille SAINT-SAËNS arrives in San Francisco with the score of his jubilee piece *Hail, California!* dedicated to the Panama-Pacific Exposition.

2 JUNE 1915

Botho SIGWART, Count of Eulenburg, German composer of orchestral and instrumental music, is killed in Galicia, during a German-Austrian retreat, in his thirty-second year.

19 JUNE 1915

Sergei TANEIEV, great Russian contrapuntist, who cherished a dream of reducing music to pure science, but wrote in expansive romantic manner, dies in Moscow, in his fifty-ninth year.

(*Encyclopaedia Britannica* gives the erroneous date of 15 June 1915; Hull gives 18 June, also incorrect)

1 JULY 1915

Horatio PARKER's opera, *Fairyland,* the winning work in the prize contest of the National Federation of Women's Clubs of America, is produced in Los Angeles.

6 JULY 1915

Polonia, orchestral poem by ELGAR, written for the benefit of the Polish Relief Fund, is performed at a special concert at Queen's Hall, London.

15 JULY 1915

The West Virginia Folklore Society is organized with the purpose of ascertaining the possible derivation of Negro spirituals from the songs of the illiterate mountain whites.

23 AUGUST 1915

Erik SATIE writes *Idylle à Debussy,* the first of his three piano pieces in barless notation under the general title *Avant-dernières Pensées,* with a mocking text over the music:

"What do I see? The rivulet is all wet and the woods are inflammable like matches. But my heart is very small. The trees resemble crooked combs, and the sun has pretty gilded rays. But my heart has a cold in the back. The moon has quarrelled with her neighbours and the rivulet is wet to the bone."

1 SEPTEMBER 1915

The first issue of the *Musical Contemporary,* a Russian publication modeled after the best European art magazines, rich in informative material and attractive in its typography, appears in

Moscow, under the editorship of Andrey RIMSKY-KORSAKOV, son of the composer.

25 SEPTEMBER 1915

Fritz JUERGENS, German composer of songs, in the romantic vein of Hugo Wolf, is killed in action, on the Champagne front, at the age of twenty-seven years, five months, and three days.

26 SEPTEMBER 1915

Max VON SCHILLINGS conducts at Stuttgart the first performance of his symbolical opera *Mona Lisa.*

29 SEPTEMBER 1915

Rudi STEPHAN, German composer of neo-classical music with "objective titles," such as *Music for Seven String Instruments, Music for Orchestra,* etc., is killed on the Eastern front, near Tarnopol, at the age of twenty-eight.

29 SEPTEMBER 1915

Claude DEBUSSY completes the copy of his twelve *Études* for piano which treat problems of modern piano playing from five-finger exercises "according to Czerny" to exercises in double-thirds, fourths, sixths, octaves, chromatic degrees, embellishments, repeated notes, altered arpeggios, opposed sonorities and chords.

3 OCTOBER 1915

Erik SATIE composes *Aubade à Paul Dukas,* the second of his three piano pieces in barless notation, under the general title *Avant-dernières Pensées,* with a humorous text printed between the staves: *Do not sleep, sleeping Beauty,* etc.

6 OCTOBER 1915

Erik SATIE composes *Méditation, à Albert Roussel,* the third of the three barless piano pieces under the general title, *Avant-dernières Pensées,* with a humorous text over the music.

12 OCTOBER 1915

The Jaques-Dalcroze Institute opens at Geneva, after the Hellerau Institute is closed at the outbreak of the war.

26 OCTOBER 1915

August BUNGERT, German composer, author of a tetralogy of Homeric music dramas, emulating Wagner's *Ring,* dies at Leutesdorf in his seventieth year.

28 OCTOBER 1915

Richard STRAUSS conducts the Berlin Philharmonic Orchestra in the first performance of his *Alpine Symphony,* op. 64. (Date from the original program)

14 NOVEMBER 1915

Theodore LESCHETIZKY, Polish-born Vienna pianist-pedagogue, protagonist of the *Kugelhand* (arched hand) method of piano playing, pupil of Czerny, teacher of Paderewski, and composer of transcendent concert pieces, dies in Dresden, in his eighty-sixth year.

(The *Encyclopaedia Britannica,* 14th edition, gives the erroneous date 17 November with Vienna instead of Dresden as the place of death. The Américan Supplement to Grove, 1928, and Baker's *Dictionary,* 1919, also give this erroneous date)

5 DECEMBER 1915

Poem for Piano and Orchestra by Darius MILHAUD is performed for the first time at the Lamoureux concerts in Paris.

8 DECEMBER 1915

On the occasion of his fiftieth birthday SIBELIUS conducts a concert of his music in Helsingfors giving the first performance of his *Fifth Symphony,* in the first version, and also *Oceanides* and two *Serenades.*

15 DECEMBER 1915

Enrique GRANADOS arrives in New York with his wife to supervise the production of his opera, *Goyescas,* by the Metropolitan Opera Company.

25 DECEMBER 1915

Les Cadeaux de Noël, "heroic tale" by Xavier Leroux, dedicated "à mon cher fils Gaston Leroux, sous-Lieutenant au cinquième Génie," is performed, fittingly on Christmas Day, at the Opéra-Comique in Paris. (Date on title-page of printed score)

1916

10 JANUARY 1916

Samuel Lucas Milady, the first Negro writer of popular ballads, composer of *Grandfather's Clock,* the hit of 1878, erroneously credited to H. C. Work, dies in New York in his sixty-ninth year.

14 JANUARY 1916

Le Poilu, a military operetta in two acts by M. Jacquet, is produced at the Paris Palais-Royal. (Date from *Cinquante ans de musique française,* Paris, 1926)

20 JANUARY 1916

Le Tambour, opera in one scene by Alfred Bruneau, is produced at the Paris Opéra-Comique.

22 JANUARY 1916

Nineteen days after his sixty-third birthday, Ivan Knorr, Prussian-born composer of conventional but solid music and teacher of a generation of modern composers, dies at Frankfort.

28 JANUARY 1916

Goyescas, opera by Enrique Granados, derived from the material of his similarly named piano suite, is performed for the first time anywhere, at the Metropolitan Opera, New York.

"*Goyescas* Seen for First Time—Standing Room at Premium—If Applause Counts for Aught Latest Production Will Be Palpable Hit." (Headlines in the New York *Times*)

"Opera in Spanish First Sung Fails to Impress—Goyescas a Series of Tapestry Pictures Lacking in True Character and Without Real Consistency." (Headlines in New York *World*)

(Henri Collet in his book, *Albéniz et Granados*, Paris, 1925, gives 26 January, apparently the date of the dress rehearsal)

29 JANUARY 1916

At the age of twenty-four years and nine months, Serge PROKOFIEV conducts in Petrograd the first performance of the *Scythian Suite* ("Alla and Lolly"), pictures of pagan Russia, his first work of symphonic proportions, written in an idiom of great originality, equally effective in rapid movement and in lyrical interludes.

(Date from a notice in Petrograd daily, *Novoye Vremia,* of 16/29 January 1916)

8 FEBRUARY 1916

Tristan TZARA invents the word "Dada," expressive of utter mental nihilism in the domain of art, literature, and music.

"*Dada* is something newer, different, a bewilderment that affected the art world of Europe for a few shell-shocked years during and immediately after the War. The object of dadaism was a conscious attack on reason, a complete negation of everything, the loudest and silliest expression of post-War cynicism. 'I affirm,' wrote early Dadaist Hans Arp, 'that Tristan Tzara discovered the word dada on the 8th of February, 1916, at 6 o'clock in the evening . . . in the Terrace Café in Zurich. I was there with my twelve children when Tzara pronounced for the first time this word, which aroused a legitimate enthusiasm in all of us.' (Later Dadaist Richard Huelsenbeck claimed: '. . . it was I who pronounced the word dada [hobby-horse] for the first time.') In moments of harmony and logic which they affected to despise, dadaists admitted that their object was 'to spit in the eye of the world.'" (*Time,* 14 December 1936)

18 FEBRUARY 1916

Symphony in C Minor by the American composer, Daniel Gregory

MASON, couched in a post-Brahmsian idiom, is performed for the first time, by the Philadelphia Orchestra.

26 FEBRUARY 1916

The word "Dada," magnificently meaningless slogan of a new anti-aesthetic movement, is used for the first time in print, in an advertisement of a soirée at the Cabaret Voltaire in Zurich.

"Grande soirée—poème simultané 3 langues, protestation bruit musique nègre / Hoosenlatz Hoosenlatz / piano Typerrary Lanterna magica démonstration proclamation dernière!! invention dialogue!! **DADA**!! dernière nouveauté!!! syncope bourgeoise, musique BRUITISTE, dernier cri, chanson Tzara danse protestations—la grosse caisse—lumière rouge, policemen—chansons tableaux cubistes cartes postales chanson Cabaret Voltaire—p o è m e   s i m u l t a n é breveté Tzara Hoosenlatz et van Hoddis Hülsenbeck Hoosenlatz tourbillon Arp-twostep réclame alcool fument vers les cloches / on chuchote: arrogance / silence Mme Hennings, Janco déclaration, l'art transatlantique—peuple se réjouit étoile projetée sur la danse cubiste en grelots.
"Collaborateurs: Apollinaire, Picasso, Modigliani, Arp, Tzara, van Hoddis, Hülsenbeck, Kandinsky, Marinetti, Cangiullo, van Rees, Slodky, Ball, Hennings, Janco, Cendrars, etc. Dialogue DaDada dada dadadadadada la vie nouvelle—contient un poème simultané; la critique carnivore nous plaça platoniquement dans la maison des vertiges de génies trop mûrs. Evite l'Appendicite éponge l'intestin. J'ai constaté que les attaques venaient de moins en moins et qui veut rester jeune évite les rhumatismes." (From *Dada Almanach*, Berlin, 1920)

5 MARCH 1916

Die Toten Augen, opera by Eugen D'ALBERT, to the story of a cripple's love for a sightless woman, written in a Wagnerized idiom with profuse employment of ninth-chords, is produced at the Dresden Opera.

13 MARCH 1916

Frank BRIDGE conducts in London the first performance of his tone-poem, *Summer*.

24 MARCH 1916

Enrique GRANADOS perishes in the sea with his wife, when the Channel steamer, *Sussex*, is torpedoed by a German submarine at 3 o'clock in the afternoon, between Folkestone and Dieppe.

"Granados was already on the raft, but he plunged into the water to rescue his wife. He had just enough strength to reach her, and they perished together. . . ." (Henri Collet, *Albéniz et Granados*, Paris, 1925)

"Abandon Hope For Goyescas Composer—Señor and Señora Granados Lost in Sussex Disaster, Friends Fear. No Trace of Either.—When last seen, Señor and Señora Granados were clinging to a small raft which, it is thought, was unable to weather the heavy seas or the couple was washed over board to drown. . . ." (*Morning Telegraph*, London, 28 March 1916)

3 MAY 1916

The Society of the Friends of Music presents in New York a concert of Ernest BLOCH's highly charged, racial music, including the *Israel Symphony,* and *Schelomo* for cello and orchestra, the latter in first performance.

11 MAY 1916

Max REGER, German composer of highly developed polyphonic music, believer in the absolute value of contrapuntal logic, yet at heart a romanticist, dies in Leipzig at the age of forty-three years, one month, and three weeks.

20 MAY 1916

Alfredo CASELLA completes, in Rome, the composition of his *Sonatina* for piano, in three movements, in three styles: the first, *Allegro,* highly chromatic; the second, *Minuetto,* diatonic and polytonal; the third, *Finale,* bitonal, the right hand playing on the white keys, the left on the black. (Date at end of printed music)

28 MAY 1916

Albert LAVIGNAC, French music scholar and popularizer, the first editor of the *Encyclopédie de la musique,* dies in his native Paris in his seventy-first year.

14 JULY 1916

The Dadaists present their first public show in Zurich.

"1916–14 Juillet.—Pour la première fois dans tout le monde.

Salle zur Waag

I. DADA-SOIRÉE

(Musique, danses, Théories, Manifestes, poèmes, tableaux, costumes, masques)
   "Devant une foule compacte, Tzara manifeste, nous voulons nous voulons nous voulons pisser en couleurs diverses, Huelsenbeck manifeste, Ball manifeste, Arp Erklärung, Janco meine Bilder, Heusser eigene Kompositionen les chiens hurlent et la dissection du Panama sur piano sur piano et embarcadère—Poème crié—on crie dans la salle, on se bat, premier rang approuve deuxième rang se déclare incompétant le reste crie, qui est plus fort on apporte la grosse caisse, Huelsenbeck contre 200, Hoosenlatz accentué par la très grosse caisse et les grelots au pied gauche—on proteste on crie on casse les vitres on se tue on démolit on se bat la police interruption.

   "Reprise du boxe: Danse cubiste costumes de Janco, chacun sa grosse caisse sur la tête, bruits, musique nègre / trabatgea bonoooooooo ooooooo / 5 expériences littéraires: Tzara en frac explique devant le rideau, sec sobre pour les animaux, la nouvelle esthétique: poème gymnastique, concert de voyelles, poème bruitiste, poème statique arrangement chimique des notions, Biribum biribum saust der Ochs im Kreis herum (Huelsenbeck), poème de voyelles a a ò, i e o, a i ï, nouvelle interprétation la folie subjective des artères la danse du coeur sur les incendies et l'acrobatie des spectateurs. De nouveau cris, la grosse caisse, piano et canons impuissants, on se déchire les costumes de carton le public se jette dans la fièvre puerperale interomprrrre. Les journaux mécontents poème simultané à 4 voix / simultané à 300 idiotisés définitivs." (From *Dada Almanach*, Berlin, 1920)

27 JULY 1916

Karl KLINDWORTH, German musical scholar, renowned editor of pianoforte literature, dies at Stolpe in his eighty-sixth year.

5 AUGUST 1916

George BUTTERWORTH, English composer of the orchestral poem *A Shropshire Lad* and other national-romantic music, is killed in action, as lieutenant of the Durham Light Infantry, after successfully taking an enemy trench at the head of a bombing party, twenty-four days after his thirty-first birthday.

12 OCTOBER 1916

Arrigo Boïto completes in Milan the full score of his four-act opera, *Nerone,* begun nearly fifty-four years before.

15 OCTOBER 1916

Das Hoellisch Gold, one-act opera by Julius Bittner, is produced at Darmstadt. (Date from *Universal Edition Jahrbuch,* 1926)

22 OCTOBER 1916

Alexander Siloti conducts at his concert in St. Petersburg the first performance of the *First Symphony,* in C minor, by Vladimir Stcherbatchev. (Date from the original program)

27 OCTOBER 1916

One of the earliest mentions of jazz is made in *Variety.*

"Chicago has added another innovation to its list of discoveries in the so-called 'Jazz Bands.' The Jazz Band is composed of three or more instruments and seldom plays regulated music. The College Inn and practically all the other high-class places of entertainment have a Jazz Band featured, while the low cost makes it possible for all the smaller places to carry their Jazz orchestra." (*Variety,* 27 October 1916, p. 18)

This item seems to be the first, or one of the first, mentions of the word "jazz" in print. It is possible that this word appeared on programs, posters, or advertisements before this date, but such evidence has not been uncovered. In this connection it will be interesting to quote from letters received from the founder of The Original Dixieland Jazz Band, D. Jas. La Rocca, obtained by the author from Mrs. Frances Fink, to whom the letters were addressed:

"Re. The Original Dixieland Jazz Band. This band was organized in New Orleans about the year 1912 and played under the 'Dixieland Band' and the word 'Jazz' was not added until after we played in Chicago in 1914 for Harry James at the Booster Club. He billed us as The Original Dixieland Jazz Band coming to Reisenwebers in New York City in 1916 to 1918. . . . Re. any information you wish I am the man that can give you same, being the leader and manager for this band till we disbanded in 1927 in New York City." (Letter dated 6 April 1936)

"The Original Dixieland Jazz Band was the first band in the world to be called a Jazz Band. Our first billing was in the year of 1914, month

of March, place Boosters Club, Chicago, Illinois, Manager Harry James.
. . . It occurred one night while we played for dancers, one frenzied
couple kept yelling for more jazz. Mr. James, hearing them call out play
some more jazz or jazz it up, gave him the idea to bill us as such a band.
. . . The word jazz is of northern origin. We never before had heard
this word jazz down south. It was used in the theatrical profession, meaning various things, one meaning pep or excite one. . . . The word was
not known widely until the release of our Victor Records around the
latter part of 1916 or first part of 1917. Our records sold in the millions."
(From letter dated 19 April 1936)

Inquiries from the Victor Company establish that the first jazz record
was issued in March 1917. The Columbia Phonograph Company issued
their first jazz records at an even later date. The following letter from
Mr. A. W. Roos, of the Columbia Phonograph Company, written in
reply to the author's inquiries, and dated 11 March 1937, states in part,
"In the Columbia record catalog issued October 1st, 1918, the following
record is listed, and it was not included in the previously issued catalog
dated January 1st, 1918, and accordingly, was released during that interval. Columbia 10" Record A–2297 DARKTOWN STRUTTERS
BALL (Brooks)—Fox Trot, coupled with INDIANA (Hanley)—One Step,
played by Original Dixieland Jass Band. . . . In the October 1st, 1919,
Columbia catalog, that is the next following complete catalog, the spelling of the artist for Record A–2297 is changed to Original Dixieland Jazz
Band. In that 1918 catalog and in many other places we have many uses
of the word Jazz but never any other of Jass. . . . I have carefully ex-
amined our record catalogs for 1914, 15, 16, and 17, but find no use of
the word jass or jazz before the entry of Record A–2297, evidently released by us about the middle of 1918."

13 NOVEMBER 1916

Frederick Septimus KELLY, Australian composer of versatile gifts,
popular athlete, and a prize-winning oarsman, is killed in action
at Beaucourt, on the Ancre, France, at the age of thirty-five.

19 NOVEMBER 1916

During the performance under the direction of TOSCANINI of
WAGNER's Siegfried Funeral Music at the Augusteo in Rome, a
soldier shouts from the gallery: "In memory of our battalions!"
which, interpreted as a protest, results in suppression of all German music in Italy during the war.

(Information and date obtained from Alfredo Casella)

23 NOVEMBER 1916

Eduard NAPRAVNIK, Russianized Czech composer of operas and other music in a poetically Tchaikovskian manner, and, since 23 September 1863, opera conductor in St. Petersburg, dies there in his seventy-eighth year.

(Hull, Grove, Riemann, and the *Encyclopaedia Britannica,* copying each other, give the wrong year, 1915, while giving correct day and month, old style. The Dutch *Muzieklexicon* and the usually accurate Spanish *Enciclopedia universal ilustrada* give the erroneous 10 November 1915, too. Exceptionally, the American Supplement to Grove gives the correct year, but revokes it in the Appendix)

5 DECEMBER 1916

Hans RICHTER, conductor of Hungarian extraction, champion of Wagner's music, but equally distinguished in his presentation of classical works, dies, at Bayreuth, in his seventy-fourth year.

14 DECEMBER 1916

Six days after his fifty-first birthday, SIBELIUS conducts in Helsingfors the second, revised version of his *Fifth Symphony.*

24 DECEMBER 1916

The Academy of Santa Cecilia in Rome confers honorary membership on FAURÉ, SIBELIUS, RAVEL, and STRAVINSKY.

25 DECEMBER 1916

Leonid SABANEIEV, Moscow critic, writes a devastating review of a performance (that never took place) of Prokofiev's *Scythian Suite.*

"At a current Koussevitzky concert one of the main attractions was the first performance of the 'Scythian Suite' by a young composer, Prokofiev, under his own direction. . . . If one says it's bad, that it is cacophony, that a person with a differentiated auditory organ cannot listen to it, they will reply, 'But this is a barbaric suite.' And the critic will have to retreat in shame. So I will not criticize this suite; quite to the contrary, I shall say that it is magnificent barbaric music, the world's best barbaric music. But if I am asked whether this music gives me pleasure or an artistic sensation, or produces a deep impression on me, I must categori-

cally say, 'No.' The composer himself conducted with a barbaric abandon." (*News of the Season,* Moscow)

"In preliminary programs of the Moscow Symphonic Concerts under
Koussevitzky's direction, it was announced that my *Scythian Suite* was
to be performed under the composer's direction on the 12th of December. In view of the impossibility in time of war of gathering the augmented orchestra required for the work, its performance was cancelled.
However, in the Moscow paper, *News of the Season,* whose musical department is in charge of Mr. Leonid Sabaneiev, there appeared the
following review signed L. S. [*follows quotation from the above review*].
I hereby testify (1) that I never conducted in Moscow, (2) that my suite
was not performed in Moscow, (3) that the critic could not acquaint
himself with the music even from the score, for the only manuscript
copy is in my hands. [signed] Serge Prokofiev." (*Musicalny Sovremennik,*
Petrograd, 30 January 1917)

1917

5 JANUARY 1917

Variety marks the progress of jazz (spelled jaz), in Chicago cabarets.

"The most popular attractions in Chicago cabarets are now the Jaz
Bands or Orchestras, and every cabaret, regardless of its size has a Jaz
aggregation. Bert Kelly is credited with the introduction of the Jaz
Orchestra in and around Chicago, Kelly featuring his own organization
at the College Inn—The College Inn Jaz combination is probably the
best of the local outfits, with Kelly at the banjo and Gus Mueller playing the saxophone. At Harry James' Casino on the North Side, the Jaz
Band is also a big drawing card, but James has strengthened his amuse-
ment end there with a so-called Jug-Band. The Jug-Band is a Jaz Band
with a 'Juggist' blowing bass notes into an ordinary whiskey jug. The
tone resulting resembles the music of a bass viol."

21 JANUARY 1917

Elegia Eroica, by Alfredo CASELLA, a symphonic tribute to the
soldiers of the allied armies, is performed at the Augusteo, Rome,
for the first time, Rhené-BATON conducting. (Date from Louis
Cortese's monograph on Alfredo Casella, Genoa, 1936)

22 JANUARY 1917

Yehudi MENUHIN, child prodigy of the violin, is born in New York.

26 JANUARY 1917

The Dixie Jass Band (so spelled) of New Orleans opens at Reisenweber's Cabaret in Chicago.

(Date from a notice in *Variety,* 2 February 1917, p. 8, *"The Dixie Jass Band,* five pieces, is at Reisenweber's, brought on by Max Hart. The band opened last Friday. It is said to have come from New Orleans.")

2 FEBRUARY 1917

Variety reports the first appearance of the jazz band in New York.

"The Jazz Band has hit New York at last, but just how popular it will become here is a matter that is going to be entirely in the hands of certain authorities that look after the public welfare. There is one thing that is certain, and that is that the melodies as played by the Jazz organization at Reisenweber's are quite conducive to making the dancers on the floor loosen up and go the limit in their stepping. Last Saturday night the Jazz musicians furnished the bigger part of the music for dancing at the 400 Club, and the rather 'mixed' crowd that was present seemed to like it, judging from the encores that were demanded, and from the manner in which the dancers roughened-up their stepping. The band carries its strongest punches in the trombone and the piccolo, the latter hitting all the blues."

10 FEBRUARY 1917

The Kairn of Koridwen, dance-drama for five wind instruments, celesta, harp, and piano, by Charles T. GRIFFES, written in an impressionist style, is performed for the first time in New York.

13 FEBRUARY 1917

Harry Ellis WOOLDRIDGE, English music editor, contributor to the *Oxford History of Music,* dies in London in his seventy-second year. (Date from the obituary in the London *Times*)

25 FEBRUARY 1917

Lazare SAMINSKY, thirty-four-year-old composer of the Russian-Hebraic school, conducts in Petrograd his *First Symphony,* surnamed *Symphony of the Great Rivers*, in a tonality designated as *E-frimoll* (free minor mode).

11 MARCH 1917

Antonio GUARNIERI conducts at the Augusteo in Rome the first performance of *Fountains of Rome*, symphonic poem by Ottorino RESPIGHI, in four sections:

(1). *The Fountain of Valle Giulia*, opening with a simple oboe tune in a minor-major mode, against an atmospheric background of tremolando strings and celesta chord drops. (2). *Fountain of the Triton*, spouting a violent quadrupled horn unison, then spending itself in a gradual rarefaction of sonority and frequency through varying moods. (3). *Fountain of Trevi at Midday*, with trumpet peals and trombone blasts, followed by undulating strings and harps. (4). *Fountain of the Villa Medici*, meditative and wistful, marking the end of the day in subdued sonorities. (Date obtained by the author from the Director of the Augusteo Theatre in Rome. The performance under Toscanini, on 10 February 1918, is erroneously listed as the first in the program notes of American symphony orchestras)

17 MARCH 1917

La Société Française de Musicologie is founded in Paris at a general meeting at the Maison Gaveau, with Lionel de la LAURENCIE as first president. (Exact date obtained by the author from the Secretary of the Society)

23 MARCH 1917

Ernest BLOCH conducts the Boston Symphony Orchestra in the first performance of his *Three Hebrew Poems* for orchestra, dedicated to the memory of his father:

(1). *Dance*, rhythmical evocation of a Jewish festival in terse harmonies. (2). *Rite*, stately diatonic melody, interrupted by sudden outcries of the orchestra. (3). *Cortège Funèbre*, funeral march in hollow harmonies of fourths and fifths, with trumpeted imprecations.

"Strange and Signal Music of Ernest Bloch.—Three Jewish Poems That Evoke a Composer of Remarkable Idiom and Procedure, Invention, Imagination and Power—Pieces of a Stinging Vehemence." (H. T. Parker's headlines in the Boston *Evening Transcript*, 24 March 1917)

28 MARCH 1917

La Rondine, opera by Giacomo PUCCINI to the libretto of Giuseppe Adami, is produced at the Monte Carlo Theatre, under the direction of Gino MARINUZZI.

"The production was accompanied by fierce political polemics, as a result of an article of Leon Daudet in the *Action Française,* in which he asserted that the opera was suggested to Puccini by the Vienna editor, Wielberger, and that the libretto was by another Viennese, Doctor Willer, and concluded with the demand that Puccini's French Impresario, Raoul Gunsbourg, be prosecuted for culpable commerce with the enemy. The polemics closed with a court sentence that exonerated Gunsbourg from Daudet's vehement accusation. From the artistic viewpoint the opera was criticised for its vacillating character between grand opera and operetta and for its numerous concessions to the waltz type of operetta in the style of Lehar and his followers." (Alberto de Angelis, *Dizionario dei musicisti,* Rome, 1918. A. Della Corte and G. M. Gatti in their *Dizionario di musica,* 1930, give the inaccurate indication of the date as April 1917. Grove gives 27 March)

3 APRIL 1917

Twenty-four days after his twenty-fifth birthday, Arthur HONEGGER conducts as a student in Vincent D'INDY's orchestration class, in a studio of the Paris Conservatoire, his first symphonic work, *Aglavaine et Selysette,* an overture to Maeterlinck's drama of the same name.

4 APRIL 1917

At an "abstract" dance recital ("métachorie") presented by Valentine de Saint-Point at the Metropolitan Opera House in New York, to the accompaniment of an orchestra conducted by Pierre MONTEUX, the first orchestral works of Dane RUDHYAR (under the name of Chennevière-Rudyard), French-American composer, *Poèmes Ironiques* and *Vision Végétale,* influenced by the primitive dynamism of early Stravinsky, are performed for the first time, twelve days after the composer's twenty-second birthday.

7 APRIL 1917

El Corregidor y la Molinera, pantomimic farce based on Alarcón's story, *The Three-Cornered Hat,* by Manuel DE FALLA, is performed for the first time at the Teatro de Eslava in Madrid, Joaquin TURINA conducting.

9 APRIL 1917

Igor STRAVINSKY's orchestration of the *Volga Boatmen's Song* for wind instruments is performed for the first time at a gala concert of the Ballet Russe at Rome. (Date from *Il Giornale d'Italia,* 10 April 1917)

"The season was opened at the Constanzi Theatre with a gala performance for the benefit of the Italian Red Cross. It was shortly after the Russian Revolution. The Czar had abdicated and the provisional government stood at the head of the country. In normal times a Russian gala performance would have been started with the national hymn, but now it would have been quite out of place to sing: 'God save the Czar.' We had to find a substitute. Diaghilev conceived the idea of opening the concert with a Russian folk song. He chose the celebrated *Volga Boatmen's Song.* But it had to be played by the orchestra, and there was no orchestration available. Diaghilev urged me to take care of it. I had to agree, and, on the eve of the performance, I sat up all night at the piano in Lord Berners' apartment and made the orchestration of this song for a wood-wind orchestra, dictating chord by chord, and interval by interval to Ansermet who put it down on paper." (Stravinsky, *Chroniques de ma vie,* Paris, 1935)

14 APRIL 1917

After many laborious revisions, Debussy completes in Paris, less than a year before his death, the final version of his *Sonata* for violin and piano. (Date from *Lettres de Claude Debussy à son éditeur,* Paris, 1927)

24 APRIL 1917

Richard WALLASCHEK, Austrian musicologist, investigator of problems concerned with emergence and development of primitive music and primitive instruments, dies in Vienna, in his fifty-seventh year. (Hull gives the erroneous date of 14 April 1917)

30 APRIL 1917

Lodoletta, lyric drama in three acts, music by Pietro MASCAGNI, is produced at the Teatro Constanzi in Rome.

8 MAY 1917

The Provisional government of Russia offers Serge KOUSSEVITZKY complete charge of the former Court Orchestra of Petrograd, which he accepts.

11 MAY 1917

Arlechino and *Turandot,* two one-act operas by Ferruccio BUSONI, are produced at Zurich. (Date from *Universal Edition Jahrbuch,* Vienna, 1926)

18 MAY 1917

On the day after Erik SATIE's fifty-first birthday, his ballet *Parade,* book by Cocteau, scenery by Picasso, with mock-serious music, opposed to both the refinement of Debussyism and the "fauvisme" of Stravinsky, is produced by the DIAGHILEV Ballet Russe, at the Théâtre du Châtelet in Paris, at a gala performance for a war benefit.

"It was a *scandale;* All Paris was at the Châtelet and rioted. Satie was delighted: they fought on account of him! . . . The press was charming, Satie, Cocteau and Picasso were called 'boches.' . . . One review provoked Satie to such an extent that he sent an insulting postcard to the critic. Dragged to the court, the author of *Parade* was condemned for eight days in jail for 'public insults and defamation of character.' " (P. D. Templier: *Erik Satie,* Paris, 1932. Satie did not go to jail; his sentence was suspended. The critic in question was Poueigh)

"The score of *Parade* was to be a musical background for suggestive noises, such as sirens, typewriters, airplanes, dynamos, put there as what Georges Braque so justly calls *facts.* Technical difficulties and the rush at the rehearsals prevented the instalment of these noises. We suppressed almost all of them. That is to say, the work was presented incomplete and without its *bouquet.*" (Jean Cocteau, *Le Rappel à l'ordre,* Paris, 1926)

12 JUNE 1917

Palestrina, musical legend by Hans PFITZNER, is produced in Munich under Bruno Walter's direction.

"In *Palestrina* he created a work which has not been paralleled, in substance and nobleness, since Wagner's *Parsifal;* here is the inner affinity with the old Netherland poliphony grown into a new stylistic development." (Moser's *Musik-Lexikon,* 1935)

12 JUNE 1917

Teresa CARREÑO, Venezuelan pianist, "the Valkyrie of the pianoforte," whilom *Wunderkind* of international renown, dies in New York in her sixty-fourth year.

(Date from obituary in New York *Times* of 13 June 1917. Riemann and Moser give erroneous date of 13 June 1917)

1 JULY 1917

The *Musical Contemporary,* Russian musical periodical, irregularly issued in Petrograd under the editorship of Andrey RIMSKY-KORSAKOV, ceases publication yielding to insurmountable technical difficulties.

8 SEPTEMBER 1917

Charles LEFEBVRE, French operatic composer in the conventional style of the nineteenth century, winner of the Prix de Rome in 1870, dies at Aix-les-Bains in his seventy-fifth year.

18 SEPTEMBER 1917

Ukuleles, "musical instruments made in Hawaii," are patented by the Honolulu Ad Club.

(Date from the U.S. Patent Files, Washington)

25 SEPTEMBER 1917

The first published composition by Paul HINDEMITH, *Three Pieces for Cello and Piano,* op. 8, is issued by Breitkopf and Haertel, a month and twenty-two days before Hindemith's twenty-second birthday. (Exact date obtained by the author from the publishers)

13 OCTOBER 1917

The New York City Board of Education rules that German operas shall not be discussed at its educational lectures, being products of enemy genius. (New York *Times,* 14 October 1917)

25 OCTOBER 1917

In an opening speech of the Symphony Society in New York, Walter DAMROSCH makes a plea that BACH, BEETHOVEN, and BRAHMS should not be regarded as alien enemies. (New York *Times,* 26 October 1917)

27 OCTOBER 1917

Jascha HEIFETZ, the not quite seventeen-year-old Russian-Jewish prodigy of the violin, makes his first appearance in America in a recital at Carnegie Hall, New York.

"During a pause Mischa Elman made a remark to Leopold Godowsky that the heat in the hall was excessive, to which Godowsky replied that it was hot for violinists, not for pianists." (Story confirmed by Godowsky)

24 NOVEMBER 1917

The Spirit of England, a setting of three patriotic poems by Laurence Binyon—*The Fourth of August, To Women,* and *For the Fallen*—by Edward ELGAR, is given for the first time in its entirety at the Albert Hall, London, by the Royal Choral Society.

23 DECEMBER 1917

RACHMANINOV leaves Russia.

26 DECEMBER 1917

Henry HADLEY conducts, in the Chicago Auditorium, the first performance of his opera *Azora, The Daughter of Montezuma,* in three acts, couched in a conventional operatic idiom, with no attempt at any exotic quality of melody or rhythm.

(Date from the Chicago *Tribune,* 27 December 1917; see also Chicago *Herald* of the same date, p. 4, Felix Borowski's review. Julius Mattfeld in *A Hundred Years of Grand Opera in New York,* 1927, gives a later performance as first. The title-page of the printed score gives the premature date 18 December 1917, also given in Hull)

1918

15 JANUARY 1918

The first significant public showing of the group of Nouveaux Jeunes, under the benevolent tutelage of Erik SATIE, is made at a concert in the hall of the intimate Vieux Colombier theatre, with a program of music by Germaine Tailleferre, Arthur Honegger, Georges Auric, Roland-Manuel, and Francis Poulenc.

(Date from René Dumesnil, *La Musique contemporaine en France*, Paris, 1930)

19 JANUARY 1918

A program composed entirely of chamber music by Arthur HONEGGER is presented for the first time in a Paris studio.

20 JANUARY 1918

The Deutsche Musikgesellschaft is founded in Berlin as a national substitute for the Internationale Musikgesellschaft dispersed by the war.

21 JANUARY 1918

The directors of the Philharmonic Society of New York issue a statement that no compositions by living Germans shall be performed by the orchestra. (New York *Times*, 22 January 1918)

22 JANUARY 1918

Mrs. William Jay directs the following letter of protest to Major Henry L. Higginson, founder of the Boston Symphony Orchestra, against the continuance of Karl MUCK as conductor of the orchestra.

"As a result of the intense feeling regarding a man who bears the German Emperor's decoration and whose sympathies are most palpably opposed to the United States, the Boston Symphony Concerts in New York have become a gathering place for everyone who hopes for a defeat of Allied arms. On the other hand, many loyal Americans do attend these concerts in the belief that 'art is international.' This is intolerable. But in our opinion even art must stand aside so that every possible influence can be brought to bear to terminate the war with an allied victory. To this end, there seems no swifter means of emphasizing the wholeheartedness of the United States than by terminating the German influence in musical affairs." (Reproduced from the *Chronicle,* March 1918)

27 JANUARY 1918

Pause del Silenzio, "seven symphonic expressions," by Francesco MALIPIERO, portraying the spirit of softness, crudity, melancholy, gaiety, mystery, war, and savagery, ending on a pause, is performed for the first time anywhere at the Augusteo in Rome, Bernardo MOLINARI conducting.

30 JANUARY 1918

Major Higginson answers the demand of Mrs. Jay that Dr. Karl MUCK's services as conductor of the Boston Symphony Orchestra should be rescinded.

"I have a letter of January 22nd signed by you and several others. By the same mail comes a letter from a well-known New York gentleman asking for more concerts in New York. . . . Dr. Muck is probably German in feeling, but he has done nothing wrong. He has been eminently satisfactory to me as a conductor and as a man. His industry, knowledge, and power are great, and his place cannot be supplied in this country." (Reproduced from the *Chronicle,* March 1918)

7 FEBRUARY 1918

Alexander Sergeivitch TANEIEV, Chief Chancellor of Tsar Nicholas' Court, composer of some operatic and symphonic music in a very conventional idiom, dies in a tsarless capital of Russia, three weeks after his sixty-eighth birthday.

17 FEBRUARY 1918

Walter DAMROSCH conducts the New York Symphony in the first performance of *Stevensoniana,* four pieces after poems from Stevenson's *A Child's Garden of Verses,* by Edward Burlingame HILL:

(1). *March,* in ternary form, in acrid chromaticized tonality. (2). *The Land of Nod,* a lullaby spiced with resolvable discord. (3). *Where Go the Boats,* a stylized tarantella. (4). *The Unseen Playmate,* a reverie alternating with a marching tune, in free modulatory style.

25 FEBRUARY 1918

Mrs. Jay writes another anti-MUCK letter to Major Higginson.

"Five representative cities—Pittsburgh, Detroit, Baltimore, Springfield, Massachusetts, and Washington—have already refused to permit Dr. Muck's presence, thereby reflecting the wishes of their citizens. You, over your signature, admit that Doktor Muck is pro-German in his sympathies and there is no doubt that he still bears proudly the Teutonic title, 'Koeniglich Preussischer General Musikdirektor.' . . . There seems to be only one point to be considered. Aren't aid and comfort being given to the enemy in retaining in such an important capacity a musician so terribly entangled with German Kultur? Are we to pour forth our blood and nerve and brain and treasure and still hold to German musical domination? Rather a thousand times that the orchestral traditions fade from our lives than one hour be added to the war's duration by clinging to this last tentacle of the German octopus!" (The *Chronicle,* March 1918)

14 MARCH 1918

Karl MUCK conducts the Boston Symphony Orchestra in Carnegie Hall, New York, despite the efforts made by certain ultra-patriotic elements to suppress the concert.

"City Is Confident Ban Will be Put On Doktor Muck—Loyal Foes of Prussian Direktor Expect Action Today——Dr. W. T. Manning Favors Ban on Muck Orchestra—Trinity Rector Writes Concert Should Be Prohibited—Condemns Tolerance——Mrs. William Jay Moves to Stop Muck's Concerts—Patronage of Boston Symphony Is Largely Pro-German, She Says, Moving to Silence Orchestra——Muck and His Enemy Aliens Here Tonight—Patriotic Societies and Loyal Citizens by Thousands Protest in Vain—Kaiser's Direktor and Band Reach City—Carnegie Hall Swings Wide Its Doors to German Doktor—Nine Austrians in Orchestra——Muck Plays Here Guarded by Police—Only Subscribers Admitted to Concert Which Was Not Interrupted—Opens with Our Anthem——New York Bows Head in Shame as Muck Leads—Kaiser's Favorite Is Permitted to Direct Symphony Concert Here—Germans Applaud Their Hero Loudly." (Headlines in New York papers)

15 MARCH 1918

Lili BOULANGER, French composer, the first woman ever to receive the Grand Prix de Rome, whose delicate talent expressed itself in the impressionist style of the turn of the century, dies in her native Paris at the early age of twenty-four years, six months, and three weeks—four years, eight months, and nine days after she received the award.

23 MARCH 1918

The Metropolitan Opera in New York produces two American works in one Saturday afternoon: *Shanewis, or The Robin Woman,* one-act opera by Charles Wakefield CADMAN, based on Indian folk songs in effective harmonic treatment, and *Place Congo,* ballet by Henry F. GILBERT, based on Creole melodies of the Southwest and imbued with strong feeling for homely American folklore.

23 MARCH 1918

The Paris Opéra cancels the evening performance of *Rigoletto* and *Coppelia* in view of the bombardment of Paris by the German long-range gun.

24 MARCH 1918

The Paris Opéra opens its doors despite the daily bombardment, with the performance of GOUNOD's *Faust,* taking in 8,262 francs, 10 centimes in the box office. (*Cinquante ans de musique française,* Paris, 1926)

24 MARCH 1918

César CUI, the last, and least, of the Mighty Five, as Stassov has christened MOUSSORGSKY, BORODIN, RIMSKY-KORSAKOV, BALAKIREV, and CUI, dies in Petrograd at the age of eighty-three years, two months, and six days, surviving Balakirev, the last of the Five to die before him, by nearly eight years, Rimsky-Korsakov by nearly ten, Borodin by thirty-one, and Moussorgsky by thirty-seven. (Hull gives the erroneous date of 14 March 1918)

25 MARCH 1918

Claude DEBUSSY dies of cancer in Paris, at the age of fifty-five years, seven months, and three days.

"It is one o'clock in the afternoon, 25 March 1918. His eyes are closed. The last reflex, a slight, almost imperceptible stirring animates him, and, from afar, the cannon thunders, punctuating each hour of his long, slow coma. . . . The day closes; there is not the least movement of his face. . . . Evening, ten o'clock. Then only they notice that he is dead. . . . On 25 March 1918, those who bought their evening paper to read the communiqué found mingled with war news, the following brief insertion: 'Claude Debussy, the composer, passed away tonight, at ten o'clock.' " (Lépine, _La Vie de Claude Debussy_, Paris, 1932. All music dictionaries and the _Encyclopaedia Britannica_ give the erroneous date of 26 March 1918)

25 MARCH 1918

Karl MUCK, German conductor of the Boston Symphony Orchestra, is arrested in Boston as enemy alien.

"Dr. Karl Muck Arrested as Alien Enemy—Symphony Conductor Taken As He Leaves Motor Car at His Home—Locked Up in Back Bay Police Station—Federal Authorities Silent Regarding Possible Recent Evidence.

"Dr. Karl Muck, director of the Boston Symphony Orchestra, was arrested at his home, 50 Fenway, at 11:30 o'clock last night, by policemen and agents of the department of justice. He was taken to the Back Bay police station and lodged there for the night. . . . The arrest was decided upon late last evening. Policemen and department of justice agents kept vigil on the Fenway residence from about 8:30 until 11:30. Dr. Muck, they learned, was either at a play or at some social affair. Immediately upon the arrival of his limousine at his home a policeman stepped to his side, identified him, and told him he was under arrest." (The Boston _Herald_, 26 March 1918)

"Seize Papers Belonging to Karl Muck—Officers Visit House and Two Other Places During Their Quest—Prisoner Consigned to Cambridge Jail." (The Boston _Herald_, 27 March 1918)

"Dr. Muck Faces Fresh Quizzing—Federal Attorneys Planning Reexamination of Prisoner—Director Learns to Smoke Pipe in Jail.

"It is evident that the federal authorities view Dr. Muck as an important prisoner. They consider it established that his Boston residence was part of the Kaiser's policy of some years ago of 'planting' musicians, college professors, and other men of great accomplishments and culture in various countries as part of his gorgeous scheme of eventual world-wide conquest. Dr. Muck, claiming Swiss citizenship was 'loaned' by the Kaiser to the Boston Symphony Orchestra and constantly expressed his pride in the fact that his orchestra was composed almost wholly of Germans and Austrians." (The Boston *Herald,* 28 March 1918)

26 MARCH 1918

Ernest SCHMIDT, assistant conductor of the Boston Symphony Orchestra, conducts BACH's *Matthew Passion* at the afternoon and evening performances of the Boston Symphony Orchestra, in place of Dr. Muck.

"Dr. Muck in the final rehearsals had so completed the preparation that Mr. Schmidt, called suddenly to conduct, found his task greatly lessened. Nevertheless, he should be warmly praised for carrying out so well Dr. Muck's intentions." (Philip Hale in the Boston *Herald,* 27 March 1918)

7 APRIL 1918

Karl MUCK is interned at Ft. Oglethorpe, Georgia, for the duration of the war.

"Dr. Muck's Boast in Berlin His Undoing—Letters Show His Propaganda Connection and Contempt for America and Boston—Written to a Young Boston Woman He Deceived by Promise of Marriage—Complete Wireless Outfit in Muck's House—Muck Active German Spy Many Years—Wrote of Conferences with Bernstorff and of Sending Reports and Figures to Berlin—Boston People Gave Cash to Dr. Muck to Help Germany in War—Dr. Muck was Audacious in Use of Cipher—Complained Code was Muddled by Telegraph Co.—Boasted of Secret Meeting at Copley Plaza—Muck Listed Women with Phone Calls—Kept Record of Names and Activities in German Cause—Calls Cambridge Nest of Hypocrites.'" (Assorted headlines in the Boston *Post*)

21 APRIL 1918

Two days before his twenty-seventh birthday, Serge PROKOFIEV conducts in Petrograd the first performance of his *Classical Symphony,* written in an eighteenth-century style with witty melodic and modulatory turns characteristic of the composer's own idiom, in classical four movements: *Allegro,* D major, 4/4, in sonata form, with the recapitulation in C major; *Larghetto,* A major, with a violin melody skipping over a two-octave span: *Gavotta,* D major, with a Musette in G major; *Finale,* in D major, alla breve, in spirited Haydn-like movement.

25 APRIL 1918

Die Gezeichneten (The Stigmatized), opera in three acts by Franz SCHREKER—dealing with unconsummated love between a cripple with a beautiful soul and a girl with a beautiful body, in sixteenth-century Genoa—with highly chromatic music, harmonically derived from Wagner but theatrically approaching expressionist drama, is performed for the first time at the Frankfort Opera.

18 MAY 1918

Toivo KUULA, Finnish composer, pupil of Enrico Bossi in Italy, whose music is based on national Finnish, or, more accurately, East-Bothnian melos, and embellished with Western-European technique of counterpoint and instrumentation, is murdered seven weeks before his thirty-fifth birthday, in Vyborg, three weeks after the capture of the city by the Finnish White Army.

(Exact date obtained by the author from Sulho Ranta, Finnish composer and musicologist)

1 JUNE 1918

Jaroslav NOVOTNÝ, Czech composer of impressionist songs strongly influenced by Debussy, is killed at the age of thirty-two in the Ural, in the early days of the rebellion of Czecho-Slovak war prisoners against the Soviet government.

(Date from Vl. Helfert and E. Steinhard, *Histoire de la musique dans la République Tchécoslavaque,* Prague, 1936)

10 JUNE 1918

Arrigo BOITO, Italian composer of operas and librettist-poet of almost Wagnerian powers but extreme slowness in composition, dies in Milan at the age of seventy-six years and three and a half months.

17 JUNE 1918

A century has passed since the birth in Paris of Charles GOUNOD.

JULY 1918

Alberto DE ANGELIS issues in Rome the first edition of his informative and reliable *Dizionario dei musicisti*.

"Destined to appear before the public in time of war this Dictionary would like to be a war book: a call to arms of all militant national forces of the musical Italy of today against all foreign wiles. And because in order to fight with legitimate faith in the victory it is necessary to know the number and quality of the combatants, and their respective weapons, we have decided to compile this roster of living Italian musicians. I deem it necessary to add that this Dictionary is dedicated almost exclusively to composers, and that interpreters are here listed only in their capacity as composers." (From the Preface)

JULY 1918

The People's Commissariat of Education of the Russian Soviet Republic forms a Music Division, with Arthur LOURIÉ as Commissar of Music.

1 AUGUST 1918

The third edition of Baker's *Biographical Dictionary of Musicians*, a work of fine assiduity, striving, if not always succeeding, to give tested information and correct dates, is completed by Alfred REMY, with editorial advice from Theodore Baker, the original editor.

(Date of the Preface. The mention of five editions of Baker's dictionary in the article *Lexika* in Moser's *Musik-Lexikon*, is a misapprehension. Only three editions have been published so far, and a fourth edition is in preparation, 1938)

16–18 SEPTEMBER 1918

One thousand, nine hundred, and twenty-five years after the death of Gaius MAECENAS, Mrs. Elizabeth Sprague Coolidge, an American encourager of arts, opens on her estate in the Berkshires, near Pittsfield, Massachusetts, a Temple of Music dedicated to concerts of classical and modern works by American and European composers.

18 SEPTEMBER 1918

Serge PROKOFIEV arrives in New York from Petrograd via Japan and declares that Russian musicians keep working despite the blockade and want. (New York *Times,* 19 September 1918)

18 SEPTEMBER 1918

Ernest Bristow FARRAR, English composer of fine-textured impressionist music in a national folklorist style, is killed during the battle of the Somme at the age of thirty-three.

19 SEPTEMBER 1918

Liza LEHMANN, English singer and song-composer, author of the popular and melodious song-cycle, *In a Persian Garden,* dies in her fifty-seventh year in her native London.

28 SEPTEMBER 1918

At Lausanne, Ernest Ansermet conducts the first performance of Igor STRAVINSKY's *Histoire du Soldat,* to the story of C. F. Ramuz, recited by a narrator, who is accompanied by an ensemble of a minimum of instruments with a maximum of efficiency—namely, for two string instruments, violin and bass; two wood-winds, clarinet and bassoon, and two brasses, cornet and trombone, each pair covering the entire useful range in a given timbre; and divers percussion manned by one player—the whole work divided in two compound parts:

(1). *The Soldier's March,* grotesque marching tune polymetrically projected on a steady "oom-pah" figure of the bass; a lyric interlude (music for the second scene), with meditative phrases of the solo wind instruments against the sustained notes of the strings. (2). *The Soldier's March* once more, with the narrator querying rhythmically: "Where is he going? Who knows?"; *The March Royal,* burlesque in a military band manner with the trombone and trumpet in melodic acrobatics against a steady common-time rhythm; *Petit Concert,* Russian in melos and rhythm, in full orchestration; *Three Dances: Tango,* for violin, clarinet, and percussion; a mock-serious C-major *Waltz; Ragtime,* in fractional meters with the sixteenth-note as a minimal unit; *Devil's Dance,* for the entire ensemble; an eight-bar modulatory *Little Chorale;* the *Devil's Song,* in a thumping rhythm as a background for the spoken text; *Grand Chorale,* with eight pauses, majestic in its Palestrinian polyphony; and the *Triumphant March of the Devil,* ending in a solo of assorted percussion in changing meters, 2, 3, 4, 5, and 6 eighth-notes to a bar.

"*L'Histoire du Soldat* was born of preoccupations of an entirely opportunist nature. The war was still going on; nobody knew when it would end. The frontiers were closing in on us more and more, a circumstance that made Stravinsky's situation increasingly difficult. The Ballets Russes had suspended their activities; the theaters were virtually at a standstill. I myself suffered greatly because of the impossibility of finding what is called in commerce 'an outlet' and I recall that one day not without naïveté we said to each other, Stravinsky and I: 'Why then not do something simple? Why not write together a piece which would dispense with a large hall or a vast public; a piece scored for a few instruments and employing but two or three actors? Since there are no more theaters, we would have a theater all of our own, that is, our own scenery which could be mounted without difficulty no matter where, even in the open; we would have resumed the tradition of the itinerant theaters. . . .' *L'Histoire du Soldat* was born of these practical considerations. It remained to find a subject: That was easy. . . . All we had to do was to go over one of the volumes of an enormous compilation by an illustrious Russian folklorist . . . ; and among a multitude of subjects (so-called folk tales, in which the devil almost invariably plays the principal role), we selected for a number of reasons, among them the very incoherence of the story, the one about a soldier and his violin." (C. F. Ramuz, *Souvenirs sur Igor Stravinsky,* Paris, 1929)

29 SEPTEMBER 1918

Kurt ATTERBERG completes at Stockholm his *Fourth Symphony,* based on Swedish folk melodies.

1 OCTOBER 1918

First issue of the *Archiv fuer Musikwissenschaft,* organ of the Fuerstliches Institut for musical research, is published at Bueckeburg.

7 OCTOBER 1918

Sir Hubert PARRY, English composer of an enormous number of

works in all forms, author of books on classical music, and scholar of profound erudition, dies at Rustington in his seventy-first year.

24 OCTOBER 1918

Charles LECOCQ, French composer of the celebrated operettas *Giroflé-Girofla* and *La Fille de Madame Angot,* dies in Paris in his eighty-seventh year.

30 OCTOBER 1918

The word *Gebrauchsoper* (practical opera music) is used for the first time in an article by Heinrich NOREN in *Die Signale.*

NOVEMBER 1918

The Verein Fuer Musikalische Privatauffuerungen, a society of private performances dedicated to repeated performances of neglected music, with applause forbidden and newspaper critics not invited, is formed in Vienna, with Arnold SCHOENBERG as president. (See Declaration of the Society in Part III)

3 NOVEMBER 1918

La Nave, opera in three acts by Italo MONTEMEZZI, on Gabriele d'Annunzio's tragedy, is produced at La Scala, Milan.

11 NOVEMBER 1918

On the morning of the Armistice Igor STRAVINSKY completes at Morges the composition of his *Ragtime* for eleven instruments, including a cembalo, and written in a stylized form of neo-classical dance with pseudo-American rhythmical contents.

12 NOVEMBER 1918

On the day after the Armistice, the Bouffes-Parisiennes gives the dress rehearsal of Christine's operetta, *Phi-Phi.* (Date from *Cinquante ans de musique française,* Paris, 1926)

13 NOVEMBER 1918

Eugene GOOSSENS conducts in Liverpool the first performance of the orchestral version of his *Four Conceits: The Gargoyle, Dance*

Memories, A Walking Tune, The Marionette Show, character pieces originally written for the pianoforte.

14 NOVEMBER 1918

A Provisional Central Musical Council is formed in Berlin after the revolution in Germany to take care of musical affairs. (Date from *Die Signale,* November 1918)

17 NOVEMBER 1918

A jazz band appears for the first time in Paris, under the direction of Harry PILCER, at the Casino de Paris. (Date communicated to the author by the management of the Casino de Paris)

"The latest foreign influence to descend on French music is American. In 1918, the first jazz-band arrived from New York, brought by Gaby Deslys and M. Pilcer. I recall the shock, the sudden awakening this staggering rhythm, this new sonority brought. . . . This influence from North America has given us the *Rag-Time du Paquebot* in Satie's *Parade,* and *Adieu, New York* of Georges Auric. In these works we have a picture of a rag-time and a foxtrot seen through a symphonic medium." (Darius Milhaud, *Études,* Paris, 1927)

30 NOVEMBER 1918

The Société de l'Orchestre de la Suisse Romande gives its inaugural concert at Geneva, under the direction of Ernest ANSERMET.

2 DECEMBER 1918

Le Dit des Jeux de Monde, incidental music to Paul Méral's play in the form of a suite of ten dances, two interludes, and coda, composed by Arthur HONEGGER, is performed at the Théâtre du Vieux-Colombier in Paris. (Date from André George, *Honegger,* Paris, 1926)

10 DECEMBER 1918

Serge PROKOFIEV makes his first appearance in America, as soloist in his second *Piano Concerto,* at a concert of the Russian Symphony Society in New York, Modest ALTSCHULER conducting.

14 DECEMBER 1918

Three one-act operas by Giacomo PUCCINI, *Il Tabarro, Sister Angelica,* and *Gianni Schicchi,* are produced for the first time on any stage by the Metropolitan Opera in New York.

19 DECEMBER 1918

The Council of People's Commissars of the Russian Socialist Confederate Republic decrees nationalization of all Russian music publishing houses.

27 DECEMBER 1918

V. V. ANDREEV, founder of the "Great Russian Orchestra" of balalaikas, domras, gusli, svireli, and nakri, dies in Petrograd in his fiftieth year.

1919

14 JANUARY 1919

Gismonda, lyric drama in three acts, by Henri FÉVRIER, is produced for the first time on any stage by the Chicago Opera Company, with the composer present. (Date from the Chicago *Herald and Examiner,* 15 January 1919)

16 JANUARY 1919

Jaroslav JEREMIÁŠ, Czech composer of the modern school influenced by Mahler's symphonic ideals, composer of an oratorio, *Jan Huss,* dies at the early age of twenty-nine years, five months, and two days.

(This date is found in Masaryk's *Slovník Naučný,* also in *Ottuv Slovník Naučný,* 1936, and in Vl. Helfert and E. Steinhard, *Histoire de la Musique dans la République Tchécoslovaque,* Prague, 1936. Riemann gives the right day and month, but the wrong year 1916)

17 JANUARY 1919

Two months after his fifty-eighth birthday, Ignace PADEREWSKI becomes Premier of Poland, the first musician to head a modern state.

26 JANUARY 1919

Poème de la Maison, oratorio by Georges Martin WITKOWSKI (real name Martin), written in an idiom suggesting early Flemish or the latest German polyphony, is produced at Lyons, France, twenty days after the composer's fifty-second birthday.

2 FEBRUARY 1919

Xavier LEROUX, French composer of effective operas in the orthodox though tasteful style, pupil of Massenet, teacher of Casella and other modernists, dies in Paris in his fifty-sixth year.

16 FEBRUARY 1919

Arnold SCHOENBERG issues a declaration of aims of the Verein fuer Musikalische Privatauffuerungen in Vienna. (See full text in Part III)

18 FEBRUARY 1919

Through the Looking Glass, five pictures from Lewis Carroll, music by Deems TAYLOR, is performed for the first time in its original form for flute, oboe, clarinet, bassoon, horn, piano, and strings, by the New York Chamber Music Society in New York.

27 FEBRUARY 1919

Five out of the seven *Planets,* symphonic suite by Gustav HOLST, are performed for the first time by the Royal Philharmonic Society in London, Adrian BOULT conducting.

8 MARCH 1919

Three character pieces for orchestra, *Chinoiserie, Valse Sentimentale, Cossack Dance,* by Lord BERNERS (Gerald Tyrwhitt), the Satie of England, are performed for the first time at the Hallé Concerts in Manchester, Eugene GOOSSENS conducting.

22 MARCH 1919

Habanera, by Louis AUBERT, brilliant orchestral dance in Parisian harmonies of bitonal implications, is performed for the first time at the Pasdeloup concerts in Paris, Rhené-Baton conducting.

11 APRIL 1919

The first concert of the New Symphony Orchestra, dedicated to modern music, is conducted by Edgar VARÈSE in New York.

24 APRIL 1919

Camille ERLANGER, French composer of operas, musically undistinguished but effective in their melodramatic élan, dies in Paris in his fifty-sixth year.

25 APRIL 1919

Augustus D. JUILLIARD, merchant and banker, dies in New York, leaving an endowment of twenty million dollars for aiding talented music students.

29 APRIL 1919

The Society for the Publication of American Music is formed in New York.

MAY 1919

Béla BARTÓK completes in Rakoskeresztur, after seven months of work, the composition of his one-act pantomime, *The Wonderful Mandarin,* to a story dealing with three thieves, a girl, an old cavalier, a youth, and an unquenchably libidinous mandarin.

6 MAY 1919

The *Notturno e Rondo Fantastico* for orchestra by the Italian neo-contrapuntist, Riccardo PICK-MANGIAGALLI, is performed for the first time in Milan.

9 MAY 1919

Jim EUROPE, Negro leader of the "Hell Fighters" jazz band, is stabbed in his dressing room at 9:15 p.m., during a concert at the

Mechanics Hall, Boston, by the drummer of his band, and dies two hours later at the City Hospital.

11 MAY 1919

Thirteen and a half months after DEBUSSY's death, the Société Nationale de Musique in Paris gives the first performance of his *Rhapsody* for saxophone, sketched at the behest of Mrs. Elisa Hall of Boston in 1903, and completed, after his death, by Roger-Ducasse.

12 MAY 1919

The *Royal Opera* at Covent Garden, London, reopens after the war.

21 MAY 1919

Mrs. William JAY forms in New York an Anti-German Music League to combat "this subtle and most appalling of all German propaganda." (New York *Herald,* 22 May 1919)

15 JUNE 1919

Poland issues a 20-pfennig (⅕ Zloty) postage stamp with PADE-REWSKI's head. (Date obtained from the Philatelic Division of the Warsaw Post Office)

17 JUNE 1919

The Three-Cornered Hat, suite by Manuel DE FALLA, is performed (in fragments only) in Madrid, for the first time in this form and under this title.

22 JUNE 1919

DIAGHILEV's Ballet Russe gives the first performance of the definite version of DE FALLA's *Three-Cornered Hat,* at the Alhambra Theatre in London. (Date in Roland Manuel's monograph on De Falla, Paris, 1930)

10 JULY 1919

Hugo RIEMANN, German musical encyclopedist of compelling erudition, embracing all branches of musical knowledge, author of fundamental books on Music History, Music Theory, Folk-Song Modes, Musical Logic, Harmony, Counterpoint, Fugue, Orchestration, and of the celebrated *Musik-Lexikon,* dies in Leipzig eight days before reaching seventy years of age.

14 JULY 1919

DEBUSSY's daughter, Chouchou, to whom he dedicated his *Children's Corner,* dies in Paris at the age of fourteen.

22 JULY 1919

The first complete performance of Manuel DE FALLA's ballet suite, *The Three-Cornered Hat,* is given by DIAGHILEV's Ballet Russe at the Alhambra Theatre in London.

9 AUGUST 1919

Ruggiero LEONCAVALLO, composer of *Pagliacci,* pioneer of Italian operatic verismo (realist, life-like, verist school of stage music, as opposed to the old artificial melodrama), dies at Montecatini at the age of sixty-one years, five months, and a day.

"Ruggiero Leoncavallo was a verist composer tremendously impressed with Mascagni. Let the composer-poet speak for himself, in the prologue of *Pagliacci: 'L'autore ha cercato pingervi uno squarcio di vita. Egli ha per massima sol che l'artista è un uom e che per gli uomini scrivere ei deve. Ed al vero ispiravasi.'* But he did not succeed in carrying out this precept; and the idea of a great trilogy, *Crepusculum,* remained but a project." (Mario Rinaldi, *Musica e verismo,* Rome, 1932)

22 AUGUST 1919

The Academy of Santa Cecilia in Rome is "regificated," that is, caused by the government to be named "Regio Conservatorio Musicale di Santa Cecilia in Roma." (Date from de Angelis' *Dizionario,* 1928, p. 10 of the Appendix)

27 SEPTEMBER 1919

Adelina PATTI, celebrated Italian coloratura singer, dies at Brecknock, England, in her seventy-seventh year.

5 OCTOBER 1919

Henry HADLEY completes the composition of his overture to Shakespeare's *Othello*.

(Date from *Henry Hadley, Ambassador of Harmony* by Herbert R. Boardman, 1932)

10 OCTOBER 1919

Die Frau ohne Schatten, opera in three acts, op. 65, by Richard STRAUSS, to Hugo Hofmannsthal's symbolist oriental story, is produced in Vienna.

17 OCTOBER 1919

Le Ménestrel, French music weekly, resumes publication after a suspension of five years and six weeks.

24 OCTOBER 1919

The Los Angeles Philharmonic Orchestra gives its initial concert under the direction of Walter ROTHWELL.

27 OCTOBER 1919

The *Violoncello Concerto,* op. 85, by Edward ELGAR, is performed for the first time, with Felix Salmond as soloist.

8 NOVEMBER 1919

Three days before the first anniversary of Armistice, WAGNER's music is played again in Paris, by the Pasdeloup Orchestra, after a vote in the audience gives 4,983 ballots for and 213 against its restoration.

22 NOVEMBER 1919

Gustav HOLST conducts at a symphony concert in Queen's Hall, London, three movements of his suite, *The Planets,* namely: *Venus,* "the bringer of peace," *Mercury,* "the winged messenger," and *Jupiter,* "the bringer of jollity."

24 NOVEMBER 1919

Sibelius conducts the Helsingfors Symphony in a concert of his works, including the first performance of six *Impromptus* for violin and orchestra, with Paul Cherkassky as soloist.

(Date from the semi-centennial book of the Helsingfors Orchestra, 1932)

27 NOVEMBER 1919

Ignace PADEREWSKI resigns as Premier of Poland, after ten months and ten days in office.

28 NOVEMBER 1919

The Pleasure Dome of Kubla Khan, the only composition of symphonic proportions by Charles Tomlinson GRIFFES, American composer of poetic music saturated with French impressionism, is performed for the first time at a concert of the Boston Symphony Orchestra, Pierre Monteux conducting.

6 DECEMBER 1919

Chant du Rossignol, symphonic suite from the opera *Rossignol* by Igor STRAVINSKY, is performed for the first time by the Orchestre de la Suisse Romande in Geneva, Ernest ANSERMET conducting.

(Date obtained by the author from the Direction of the Orchestre de la Suisse Romande. André Schaeffner in his monograph on Stravinsky, Paris, 1931, gives the erroneous date, 6 November 1919)

". . . I must mention a concert which had a certain importance for me insofar as my new orchestral experiments are concerned. On 6 December, the first performance of my score, *Chant du Rossignol,* took place at a concert of the *Orchestre de la Suisse Romande* under the direction of Ernest Ansermet. I say, a new experiment, because I treated this symphonic poem, written for an orchestra of normal dimensions, as a chamber orchestra, not only stressing the concertizing element in various instrumental soli, but also using whole groups of instruments in the capacity of concertanti. This orchestral principle suited well this music filled with cadenzas, vocalises and all sorts of melismata, where *tutti* are almost an exception." (Stravinsky, *Chroniques de ma vie,* Paris, 1935)

13 DECEMBER 1919

Si, operetta in three acts by Pietro MASCAGNI, is produced at the Teatro Quirino in Rome.

18 DECEMBER 1919

Horatio PARKER, American composer of music of rhapsodic power in large forms, and teacher of a generation of American composers, dies at Cedarhurst, New York, in his fifty-seventh year.

21 DECEMBER 1919

Darius MILHAUD completes in Paris the composition of his "cinema-symphony on South American airs," *Le Boeuf sur le Toit,* bitonally constructed, and sustained in square time, except for the *Policeman's Dance* in 3/8.

23 DECEMBER 1919

The Birthday of the Infanta, ballet-pantomime by John Alden CARPENTER, American composer and business man, based on Oscar Wilde's story of the same name, is produced by the Chicago Opera Association at the Auditorium, Chicago.

(Date from the Chicago *News.* The title-page of the printed score gives the erroneous date of 19 December 1919)

1920

JANUARY 1920

Music and Letters, English quarterly, begins publication in London under the editorship of Arthur Henry FOX-STRANGWAYS.

". . . It is just six years over the century since the first musical quarterly in the English language was born, and six since the last one died. Between these there have been half a dozen, but their united ages have amounted to a bare fifty years. So that a musical quarterly may have

a merry life but is evidently a thing that people get tired of in time."
(From an editorial in the first issue)

16 JANUARY 1920

Reginald DE KOVEN, American composer of comic operas, dies in
Chicago, in his sixty-first year.

16 JANUARY 1920

Henri COLLET writes in the Paris daily, *Comoedia,* an article on
La Musique chez soi, subtitled: *Les Cinq Russes, Les Six Français
et Erik Satie,* in which he draws a parallel between the Russian
Group of Five and that of six young French composers, Darius
MILHAUD, Louis DUREY, Georges AURIC, Arthur HONEGGER, Francis
POULENC, and Germaine TAILLEFERRE.

" 'I want a French music of France,' writes Jean Cocteau in that astonishing little volume called *Le Coq et l'Arlequin.* And we are happy to
have him say that, for it is exactly what we preach on the tribune of
Comoedia.

" 'Music that is not national does not exist,' writes Rimsky-Korsakov
in *My Musical Life.* 'Indeed, all music that we consider universal,
is nevertheless national.' The book of Jean Cocteau and Rimsky-
Korsakov's book tell us what no Conservatory will teach them: the necessity to be of the race and the obligation to unite.

"Russian music cultivated by the illustrious Five: Balakirev, Cui,
Borodin, Mussorgsky and Rimsky-Korsakov united in their aims, became
the object of universal admiration because they understood the example
of Glinka.

"The Six Frenchmen, Darius Milhaud, Louis Durey, Georges Auric,
Arthur Honegger, Francis Poulenc and Germaine Tailleferre, insep-
arable, as demonstrated by a curious album of the group of Six, have,
by magnificent and voluntary return to simplicity, brought about a
renaissance of French music, because they understood the lesson of Erik
Satie and followed the precepts, so pure, of Jean Cocteau.

"The above-mentioned album is a suite of six pieces: *Prélude* by
Georges Auric, *Romance sans Paroles* by Louis Durey, *Sarabande* by
Arthur Honegger, *Mazurka* by Darius Milhaud, *Valse* by Francis Poulenc and *Pastorale* by Germaine Tailleferre. The different temperaments of the six composers jostle without jarring, and their works, individual and distinct, reveal a unity of approach to art, in conformity
with the spokesman of the group: Jean Cocteau." (From Collet's article
of the above date)

23 JANUARY 1920

Henri COLLET writes a second article on new French music in *Comoedia,* entitled *La Musique chez soi.* *Les Six Français: Darius Milhaud, Louis Durey, Georges Auric, Arthur Honegger, Francis Poulenc et Germaine Tailleferre.*

"The production of these young musicians is already considerable. Their facility is perhaps bewildering to their elders, one of whom remarked to us: 'To compose a quartet every week-end is just a trifle.' But not one of the Six composes a quartet every week. The most prolific among them, who is also the oldest, has written four quartets in ten years." (From Collet's article of the above date)

24 JANUARY 1920

Der Schatzgraeber, opera in four acts, with prologue and epilogue, by Franz SCHREKER, dedicated "to the city of Frankfort and its Opera House, in gratitude," is produced at the Frankfort Opera House.

(In the article on Frankfort-on-the-Main, Grove gives the inaccurate date of 20 June 1924, although in the article on Schreker the date is given correctly)

27 JANUARY 1920

On his American visit, Maurice MAETERLINCK hears Debussy's *Pelléas and Mélisande* for the first time, presented by the Chicago Opera Company at the Lexington Theatre in New York, with Mary Garden in the title role, seventeen years and nine months after the original production in Paris. (*See* 14 April 1902)

31 JANUARY 1920

Cleopatra's Night, opera in two acts by Henry HADLEY, is produced by the Metropolitan Opera in New York.

1 FEBRUARY 1920

Melos, fortnightly magazine for modern music, starts publication in Berlin, under the general editorship of Hermann SCHERCHEN.

2 FEBRUARY 1920

STRAVINSKY's *Chant du Rossignol,* symphonic version of his opera *Rossignol,* is produced for the first time as a ballet, by DIAGHILEV's Ballet Russe at the Paris Opéra.

5 FEBRUARY 1920

Leopold GODOWSKY writes in New York the thirtieth and last piece of the collection for the piano, *Triakontameron,* named in analogy with Boccaccio's *Decameron,* each piece having been written on a single day.

(The non-consecutive dates of composition of each of the thirty numbers are: No. 1, 25 Aug. 1919; No. 2, 7 Aug. 1919; No. 3, 10 Aug. 1919; No. 4, 5 Feb. 1920; No. 5, 12 Aug. 1919; No. 6, 23 Aug. 1919; No. 7, 13 Oct. 1919; No. 8, 10 Aug. 1919; No. 9, 8 Jan. 1920; No. 10, 14 Jan. 1920; No. 11, 8 Aug. 1919; No. 12, 22 Aug. 1919; No. 13, 14 Aug. 1919; No. 14, 24 Aug. 1919; No. 15, 11 Aug. 1919; No. 16, 16 Aug. 1919; No. 17, 27 Aug. 1919; No. 18, 3 Sept. 1919; No. 19, 26 Aug. 1919; No. 20, 16 Oct. 1919; No. 21, 27 Oct. 1919; No. 22, 30 Jan. 1920; No. 23, 31 Aug. 1919; No. 24, 17 Aug. 1919; No. 25, 18 Oct. 1919; No. 26, 28 Aug. 1919; No. 27, 19 Aug. 1919; No. 28, 18 Aug. 1919; No. 29, 21 Oct. 1919; No. 30, 24 Oct. 1919. All these dates communicated by Leopold Godowsky)

19 FEBRUARY 1920

A special Division of Musical History is formed at the Institute of the History of Arts in Leningrad.

(Date from the Bulletin of the Division, *De Musica,* Leningrad, 1925)

21 FEBRUARY 1920

Le Boeuf sur le Toit, or *The Nothing Doing Bar* (subtitle in English), farce "imagined and arranged" by Jean COCTEAU, music by Darius MILHAUD, is produced at the Comédie des Champs-Élysées in Paris, Vladimir Golschmann conducting. (Date on title-page of printed score)

28 FEBRUARY 1920

Le Tombeau de Couperin, by Maurice RAVEL, orchestrations of four out of six piano pieces of the same title, and constituting slightly archaized evocations of Couperin's moods, is performed for the first time at a concert of the Pasdeloup Orchestra in Paris.

5 MARCH 1920

Fredric FRADKIN, concertmaster of the Boston Symphony Orchestra, refuses to stand up and acknowledge applause, along with the rest of the orchestra at the behest of the conductor, Pierre MONTEUX, and is discharged by the board of trustees of the orchestra as a result of his action.

6 MARCH 1920

Thirty-two members of the Boston Symphony Orchestra go on strike and refuse to play at the Saturday concert of this date in protest against the dismissal of concertmaster FRADKIN, forcing Conductor MONTEUX to change the program at the last moment and substitute a MOZART symphony for BERLIOZ' *Symphonie Fantastique*.

10 MARCH 1920

Thirty-two members of the Boston Symphony Orchestra are discharged as a result of their refusal to play at the concert of 6 March.

31 MARCH 1920

Mirra, melodrama in two acts by Domenico ALALEONA, composed in a style which approaches expressionism and contains novel nontempered scales, such as a "pentafonia" of five equal intervals, is produced at the Constanzi Theatre in Rome.

1 APRIL 1920

Pro Musica, American music society chiefly devoted to propaganda of modern music, with branches in many cities abroad, is formed in New York with Robert E. SCHMITZ, French-American pianist and conductor, as president.

8 APRIL 1920

Charles Tomlinson GRIFFES, American composer of refined impressionistic music with poetic and exotic titles, greatly influenced

by Ravel, dies of pneumonia in New York at the age of thirty-five
years, six months, and three weeks.

11 APRIL 1920

Ballata delle Gnomidi, symphonic poem by Ottorino RESPIGHI, is
performed for the first time at the Augusteo in Rome, Bernardo
Molinari conducting.

23 APRIL 1920

The Adventures of Mr. Broucek, by the Czech composer, Leoš
JANÁČEK, opera-grotesque, picturing a common man's experience
during the Hussite Wars, and written in modern harmony without
recourse to musical archaisms, is produced at Prague.

4 MAY 1920

The shortened final version of the *London Symphony* by VAUGHAN
WILLIAMS is performed for the first time at a concert of the British
Music Society in London, Albert Coates conducting.

6–21 MAY 1920

Nine years after Gustav MAHLER's death, a festival of his music
is organized in Amsterdam, with Mengelberg conducting before
an audience assembled from all over Europe and America.

15 MAY 1920

DIAGHILEV's Ballet Russe presents at the Opéra in Paris the first
performance of *Pulcinella,* one-act "ballet avec chant" by Igor
STRAVINSKY, based on Pergolese, and forming a classical suite:

(1). *Overture,* in a major mode, enriched by pan-diatonic harmonization, i.e., free use of all seven tones of the scale in the harmony, with
the bass determining the functional character of each chord. (2). *Serenata, Allegro, Andantino, Allegro* and *Presto.* (3). *Tarantella,* and
an *Aria,* in a minor pan-diatonic mode, followed by a *Toccata.* (4). *Gavotte,* with two Variations. (5). *Vivo, Minuetto* and *Finale,* in pan-
diatonic C major.

20–22–28–29 MAY 1920

A festival of music by Camille SAINT-SAËNS is given at Athens,

Greece, with the composer, now nearly eighty-five years old, taking part as conductor and pianist.

24 MAY 1920

Pablo Picasso makes his three-quarter drawing of Igor STRAVINSKY (seated figure in heightened perspective, hands larger than normal, left forefinger hooked around right middle finger).

(Date on the drawing. A profile drawing by Picasso of Stravinsky is dated 31 December 1920)

24 MAY 1920

The British Music Society votes to adopt the standard pitch A = 435.4 vibrations per second, at 59° Fahrenheit.

9 JUNE 1920

The Académie Nationale de Musique et de Danse in Paris presents the first performance of *La Légende de Saint-Christophe,* "sacred drama" in three acts by Vincent D'INDY, based on enharmony of remote keys insuring modulatory freedom, with recitative-like vocal line expressive of verbal accents.

18 JULY 1920

The *Fifth Symphony,* in D major, by Nicolas MIASKOVSKY, written in a more objective and optimistic style than the somber works of his previous years, is performed for the first time in Moscow, Nicolai Malko conducting.

20 JULY 1920

The first experiment in broadcasting music from a ship is made during the crossing of the S. S. *Victorian* to Canada.

1 AUGUST 1920

Two weeks before his twenty-fifth birthday Kaikhosru SORABJI, London-born Parsi composer, completes in London, at 1:35 p.m., the composition of his second *Concerto for Piano and Orchestra,* written in a polyrhythmic and polyharmonic idiom of the greatest complexity.

20 AUGUST 1920

The first commercial radio broadcast is opened by the Detroit Station WWJ.

"On the night of 20 August 1920, the first commercial radio broadcast station in all the world was opened. And every night and every day since that momentous beginning WWJ has maintained this service. . . . Not until eleven weeks after its founding did WWJ share the channels of the air with a rival broadcasting station. The honor of being second . . . fell to KDKA of Pittsburgh . . . and, though it has erroneously claimed and been credited with priority among broadcasters, it is still entitled to a place of distinction . . ." (From the announcement by Lee de Forest, inventor, on the occasion of the sixteenth anniversary of the broadcast, 20 August 1936)

27 AUGUST 1920

Alfredo Casella completes at L'Aubraie, in France, the composition of his *Five Pieces* for string quartet: *Preludio,* in vivacious duple time on a C pedal; *Ninna-Nanna,* a berceuse; *Valse Ridicule,* on C pedal with the violin playing off key; *Nocturne,* in an atonal treatment, and *Fox-Trot* in stylized syncopation.

4 SEPTEMBER 1920

L'Aviatore Dro, three-act opera by the futurist musician, Francesco Balilla Pratella, harmonically based on the whole-tone scale, is performed for the first time at the Teatro Comunale at Lugo. (Date from Pratella's *Appunti biografici e bibliografici,* Ravenna, 1931)

1 OCTOBER 1920

Henri Rabaud is appointed Director of the Paris Conservatory.

2 OCTOBER 1920

Max Bruch, prolific German composer of music in all forms in a romantic vein, and of virtuoso pieces for string instruments, dies in Berlin in his eighty-third year.

19 OCTOBER 1920

Alexander Lunatcharsky, People's Commissar of Education of the

Russian Soviet Republic, declares the maintenance of the Philharmonic Orchestra of Petrograd to be of state importance:

"I herewith serve notice that the Petrograd State Philharmonic Orchestra is the only exemplary symphonic institution of the Republic. Any
attempt to disorganize the activities of this orchestra is a criminal offense. The Petrograd Philharmonic must remain intact as an institution of prime national importance. All musicians who were in the per-
sonnel of the orchestra before January 1919 are considered original
members, whose principal work is with the Philharmonic, and all extra
employment of members is permissible only as an inevitable concession
to the prevailing conditions of the times." (Date and text from *The
Leningrad Philharmonic,* 1935)

19 OCTOBER 1920

The Eternal Rhythm, symphonic poem op. 27 by Eugene GOOS-
SENS, is performed for the first time at the Promenade concerts in
London.

24 OCTOBER 1920

At the Colonne concerts in Paris, the first performance is given of
Darius MILHAUD's *Second Orchestral Suite,* originally written as
incidental music to Paul Claudel's satirical drama, *Protée,* comprising the following movements:

(1). *Overture,* in effective bitonal idiom, with D major as an axis. (2).
Prelude and Fugue, on a grotesque iterative pattern starting in the low-
wind and brass. (3). *Pastorale* in a compound meter of $\frac{3+3+2}{8} = \frac{8}{8}$
alternating with 3/4. (4). *Nocturne,* in swinging 5/8 time. (5). *Finale,*
in square time, employing effective polytonal combinations, and concluding on a unison C.

30 OCTOBER 1920

The second version of *Das Spielwerk,* "mystery in one act" by
Franz SCHREKER, written in an idiom considerably removed from
Wagner, and experimenting with pan-diatonic use of all seven
tones of a mode, consecutive triads, and novel scales, is produced
at the Munich National Theatre.

31 OCTOBER 1920

Ritter Blaubart, opera by E. N. VON REZNICEK, an eclectic score embodying elements of Italian cantilena style and the technique of French impressionism, is produced at the Berlin State Opera.

NOVEMBER 1920

Alfredo CASELLA writes in Rome his *Eleven Pieces for Children,* for piano:

Preludio; Valse Diatonique, on white keys only; *Canon,* on black keys only; *Bolero; Homage to Clementi,* exercise for five fingers in distorted *diapente* compass; *Siciliana,* in Dorian mode; *Giga,* in Lydian mode; *Minuetto,* in Æolian mode; *Carillon,* with the left hand on black keys, right hand on white keys, in the treble; *Berceuse,* swaying thirdless tonics and dominants; *Galope Final,* on white keys. (Date on printed score)

1 NOVEMBER 1920

La Revue musicale, "revue mensuelle internationale d'art musical ancien et moderne," starts publication in Paris under the editorship of Henry PRUNIÈRES.

(Hull, in the article on Periodicals, gives the wrong year, 1918, although in the article on Prunières the year is given correctly. The Italian *Dizionario di musica* by Della Corte and Gatti gives, in the article on Prunières, the wrong year, 1919)

15 NOVEMBER 1920

Albert COATES conducts, in Queen's Hall, London, the first complete performance of Gustav HOLST's suite, *The Planets:*

Mars, "the bringer of war," in 5/4 meter, opening on a thirty-nine-bar string unison on G, with martial brass in loud clamor; *Venus,* "the bringer of peace," with a tender violin solo, introduced by soft harp chords in an aura of Greek modality; *Mercury,* "the winged messenger," in gigue-like time; *Jupiter,* "the bringer of jollity," in ponderous harmonies and alternating duple and triple time; *Saturn,* "the bringer of old age," harmonized by bare fifths and fourths, in tedious diatonic progression; *Uranus,* the magician, opening in staccato rhythms of coughing bassoons, reaching a considerable climax, with the organ glissando contributing to the general C-major roar, then suddenly vanishing into nothingness; and *Neptune,* the mystic, in 5/4, with discursive arpeggios against sustained notes of the wind instruments, with two wordless choruses behind the stage.

1 DECEMBER 1920

Der Auftakt, "Musikblaetter fuer die Tschechoslowakische Republik," in the German language, begins publication in Prague under the editorship of Felix ADLER.

"At a time when unprecedented revaluation is taking place in all branches of music, in which the formation of new concepts pursues its irresistible course, there is an increasing need to define musico-esthetic problems from theoretical and practical viewpoints. These considerations led the Prague pedagogical union to transform its former organ *Musiklehrer-Zeitung* into a musical publication of general interest." (From the preface to the first issue)

1 DECEMBER 1920

Vladimir REBIKOV, Russian composer, one of the first to experiment in modern innovations, such as rows of fourth and fifths, the whole-tone scale, unresolved dissonances, and "frictional" harmonies, dies in Jalta, Crimea, at the age of fifty-four.

4 DECEMBER 1920

Die Tote Stadt, opera by the twenty-three-and-a-half-year-old Viennese erstwhile child prodigy, Erich KORNGOLD, to Rodenbach's symbolist play, *Bruges la Morte,* is produced on the same day in Hamburg and Cologne.

6 DECEMBER 1920

The Academy of Santa Cecilia in Rome confers honorary membership on Paul DUKAS, Henri RABAUD, and RACHMANINOV.

6 DECEMBER 1920

Karel KOVAŘOVIC, Czech composer, conductor at the National Theatre at Prague, pupil of Fibich, and author of operas in Smetana's tradition, dies in Prague, three days before reaching his fifty-eighth birthday.

(Date from *Gazette de Prague* of 8 December 1920. Masaryk's *Slovník Naučný,* in the Czech language, gives the correct day and month, but the year is marked 1919, a misprint no doubt. *Ottuv Slovník Naučný, Dodatky,* 1930–1936, gives the correct day, month, and year. Grove and the *Encyclopaedia Britannica* give 9 December 1920, probably through assimilation with the birth date, 9 December 1862)

12 DECEMBER 1920

La Valse, "choreographic poem for orchestra in Viennese waltz tempo" by Maurice RAVEL, is performed from the manuscript for the first time at a Lamoureux concert in Paris, Camille CHEVILLARD conducting.

"Whirling clouds give glimpses, through rifts, of couples waltzing. The clouds scatter little by little. One sees an immense hall peopled with a twirling crowd. The scene is gradually illuminated. The light of the chandeliers bursts forth fortissimo. An Imperial Court about 1855." (From the "argument" of the score)

(In his monograph, *Maurice Ravel et son oeuvre dramatique,* Paris, 1928, Roland-Manuel gives the premature date 8 January 1920)

28 DECEMBER 1920

Arturo TOSCANINI conducts the first concert of his American tour with the orchestra of La Scala, Milan, in New York.

31 DECEMBER 1920

The Lithuanian National Opera is organized in Kaunas by a council of four members of the Association of Lithuanian Art Promoters: Petrauskas, Silingas, Talat-Kelpsa, and Zilevicius.

1921

5 JANUARY 1921

For the first time since the war, the Paris Opéra gives a WAGNER opera, *Valkyrie,* drawing the unprecedented sum of 35,977 francs.

10 JANUARY 1921

By order of the city authorities jazz music is banned in Zion City, Illinois, along with smoking and other sinful practices.

18 JANUARY 1921

The five hundredth performance of Gustave CHARPENTIER's opera *Louise* is given in Paris.

9 FEBRUARY 1921

James HUNEKER, American author of brilliant essays on music, defender of traditional aesthetics as possessing an absolute standard of beauty, self-confessed ironic "old fogey" (the expression which he selected as a title for one of his books), dies at Brooklyn, nine days after his sixty-first birthday.

13 FEBRUARY 1921

Per una Favola Cavalleresca, "symphonic illustration of legendary love-scenes, tournaments and battles" by Francesco MALIPIERO, written in a characteristic dual style of Italian modernism, affecting archaisms in pan-diatonic treatment, is performed for the first time at the Augusteo in Rome, Antonio GUARNIERI conducting.

25 FEBRUARY 1921

Arthur HONEGGER starts work on his oratorio *Le Roi David.*

11 MARCH 1921

Antar, "conte héroïque" in four acts by Gabriel DUPONT, to a book of Arabian legend, making use of stylized oriental scales, in traditional European harmonies, is produced at the Paris Opéra, some six and a half years after the death of the composer on the day of the declaration of war.

(The printed score gives the premature date of 23 February; Grove gives 14 March. The date 11 March 1921 is authenticated in an emphatic article of Henri Collet in *Le Ménestrel,* 18 March 1921: "Date mémorable que celle du 11 Mars 1921," etc.)

19 MARCH 1921

Two and a half centuries have passed since the opening of the first public theater for opera in Paris by the poet, Pierre Perrin, and the musician, Cambert.

24 MARCH 1921

Déodat DE SÉVERAC, French composer of delicate impressionist music in all forms, often inspired by rural folklore, but not entirely alien to the grand manner of the nineteenth-century romanticism, dies at Ceret in the French Pyrenees in his forty-eighth year.

"On the 19th, fully conscious and with great piety, he receives the last Sacrament. Soon after he enters into a coma. His body is gradually paralyzed. This state continues until Thursday of the holy week, 24 March, at 2:30. He seems to regain consciousness. An injection is attempted to relieve the heart. Déodat opens his eyes wide and passes away surrounded by his family and several friends. . . . He was dead as a result of a uremia attack consequent upon a chronic albuminuria." (Blanche Selva, *Déodat de Séverac,* Paris, 1930. Grove, 1927, Riemann, 1929, and Moser, 1935, give the erroneous date 23 March 1921; Hull gives the erroneous date 27 March 1921)

5 APRIL 1921

Alphons DIEPENBROCK, Dutch composer, creator of a neo-Flemish polyphonic style and teacher of a generation of modern composers in Holland, dies in his native Amsterdam in his fifty-ninth year.

22 APRIL 1921

Serge KOUSSEVITZKY conducts in Paris a concert of Russian music, the first of the series of annual "Koussevitzky Concerts" in Paris, and the first since his departure from Russia.

28 APRIL 1921

A month and a half after his twenty-ninth birthday Arthur HONEG-GER completes, in Zurich, the score of *Le Roi David,* "dramatic psalm" in three parts after the drama of René Morax, for chamber orchestra, chorus, soloists, and a narrator, in a novel oratorio style, making free use of "frictional" harmony and atonal melodic line but remaining within the framework of basic tonality.

"28 April, the last day. Honegger works at maximum speed. . . . Joyously, he inscribes on the bottom of the final page: *Du 25 Février au 28 Avril 1921.* The last package goes to the post office on the corner. . . . Hallelujah! . . ." (André George, *Arthur Honegger*, Paris, 1926)

2 MAY 1921

Pietro MASCAGNI conducts the first performance of his opera, *Il Piccolo Marat,* at the Teatro Constanzi in Rome.

13 MAY 1921

The Academic Center of the People's Commissariat of Education sanctions the formation of the State Philharmonic Orchestra in Petrograd.

17 MAY 1921

Three and a half weeks after PROKOFIEV's thirtieth birthday, Diaghilev's Ballet Russe gives the first performance, in Paris, of his ballet, *The Buffoon Who Outwitted Seven Other Buffoons,* known also under the title of *Chout* (French spelling of the Russian word for buffoon), in the following six scenes:

(1) *Buffoon's Chambers,* in brusque square time and pan-diatonic harmony; (2) *At the Seven Buffoons',* boisterous and discordant entrance of the buffoons who butcher their wives in the mistaken belief that killing would improve their character; (3) *The Buffoons' Backyard,* in an anxious chromatic mode, changing to the furious *prestissimo,* and then to *andante innocente;* (4) *Reception Room,* with a polka-like dance of the buffoons' daughters; (5) *Merchant's Bedroom,* in slow quasi-lyrical manner, changing to an agitated dance with a she-goat; (6) *Merchant's Garden,* the burial of the she-goat in mock-funereal treatment, and the irruption of the buffoons in a frenzied dance, abruptly ending on a unison C.

26 MAY 1921

Francesco MALIPIERO completes, in Parma, the score of *San Francesco d'Assisi,* choral mystery play, with orchestral interludes, in a strictly diatonic style, with deep pedal tones expressive of religious fervor, divided into four linked sections: *The Prelude; The Sermon to the Birds; The Supper and Divine Fire; The Death of Saint Francis.* (Date at end of manuscript score)

31 MAY 1921

Edgar VARÈSE founds in New York the International Composers' Guild with the purpose of giving performances of new works.

(The above is the date carried by the charter of the Guild, communicated to the author by Carlos Salzedo)

"The composer is the only one of the creators of today who is denied direct contact with the public. When his work is done, he is thrust aside, and the interpreter enters, not to try to understand the composition but impertinently to judge it. Not finding in it any trace of the conventions to which he is accustomed, he banishes it from his programs, denouncing it as incoherent and unintelligible. . . . In every other field, the creator comes into some form of direct contact with his public. The poet and novelist enjoy the medium of the printed page; the painter and sculptor the open doors of a gallery; the dramatist the free scope of the stage. The composer must depend upon an intermediary, the interpreter. . . . It is true that in response to public demand, our official organizations occasionally place on their programs a new work surrounded by established names. But such a work is carefully chosen from the most timid and anaemic of contemporary production, leaving absolutely unheard the composers who represent the true spirit of our times. . . . Dying is the privilege of the weary. The present day composers refuse to die. They have realized the necessity of banding together and fighting for the right of each individual to secure a fair and free presentation of his work. It is out of such a collective will that the International Composers' Guild was born. . . . [Its] aim is to centralize the works of the day, to group them in programs intelligently and organically constructed, and, with the disinterested help of singers and instrumentalists, to present these works in such a way as to reveal their fundamental spirit. . . . [It] refuses to admit any limitation, either of volition or action . . . disapproves of all 'isms'; denies the existence of schools; recognizes only the individual." (From the Manifesto of the Guild)

4 JUNE 1921

Two one-act operas by Paul HINDEMITH, *Murder, Hope of Women*, to an expressionist play by Oscar Kokoschka, and *Nusch-Nuschi*, to a play for Burmese marionettes by Franz Blei, are produced at Stuttgart.

10 JUNE 1921

Symphony for Wind Instruments by Igor STRAVINSKY, dedicated to the memory of Debussy, is performed for the first time at Koussevitzky's third concert of Russian music in London.

"This music was not made to please nor to excite passions. . . . It is an austere ceremony which revolves in brief litanies among different families of homogeneous instruments." (Stravinsky, *Chroniques de ma vie,* Paris, 1935)

"To us it spelt nothing but senseless ugliness." (London *Times,* 12 June 1921)

11 JUNE 1921

Le Roi David, "dramatic psalm" by Arthur HONEGGER, is performed for the first time in a dramatic version at Jorat, Switzerland.

(Date from the chronology of Honegger's works in André George's *Arthur Honegger,* Paris, 1926. Grove gives 12 June 1921)

14 JUNE 1921

The first concert of The British Music Society in London gives its inaugural concert in London, presenting *The Planets* by Gustav HOLST, Overture to *The Children of Don* by Joseph HOLBROOKE, *The Eternal Rhythm* by Eugene GOOSSENS, *Concerto for Piano and Orchestra* by Cyril SCOTT, and *The Lark Ascending* by VAUGHAN WILLIAMS. (Date from the London *Times,* 15 June 1921)

18 JUNE 1921

The Italian futurist, Luigi RUSSOLO, conducts at the Champs-Élysées in Paris an orchestral concert of noise instruments, such as Thunderclappers, Exploders, Crashers, Splashers, Bellowers, Whistlers, Hissers, Snorters, Whisperers, Murmurers, Mutterers, Bustlers, Gurglers, Screamers, Screechers, Rustlers, Buzzers, Cracklers, Shouters, Shriekers, Groaners, Howlers, Laughers, Wheezers, and Sobbers.

19 JUNE 1921

Les Mariés de la Tour Eiffel, ballet by Jean COCTEAU, with music by Arthur HONEGGER, Darius MILHAUD, Georges AURIC, Francis

POULENC, Germaine TAILLEFERRE—the only work written by these five of the French Group of Six in collaboration—is presented by the Ballet Suédois in Paris.

22 JUNE 1921

Three quarters of a century have passed since the patenting of the saxophone, invented by the French instrument-maker, Adolphe SAX.

24 JUNE 1921

The American Conservatory of Music opens at Fontaineblcau, near Paris.

20 JULY 1921

A pageant to commemorate the tercentenary of the Pilgrims' landing is given in Plymouth, Massachusetts, with music written by George CHADWICK, Henry F. GILBERT, Frederick CONVERSE, Arthur FOOTE, Edward Burlingame HILL, Edgar Stillman KELLEY, John POWELL, Leo SOWERBY, and Chalmers CLIFTON.

31 JULY 1921

The Gesellschaft der Musikfreunde at Donaueschingen gives its initial two concerts of contemporary chamber music, marking the opening of the Donaueschingen Festivals for Furtherance of Contemporary Music, under the protectorate of Fuerst zu Fuerstenberg:

(1) In the morning concert: the first performance of the *String Quartet* No. 4, making use of intervals of ¼, ½, ¾, 1, 1¼, and other multiples of the quarter-tone by the Czech exponent of quarter-tone music, Alois HÁBA; piano pieces by the Austrian, Wilhelm GROSZ, played by the composer, and the first performance of the *Serenade* for clarinet and string quartet by the not quite twenty-one-year-old Czech modernist, Ernst KŘENEK. (2) In the evening concert: *Piano Quartet* by the German neo-romanticist, Franz PHILIPP; *Lieder* by the Austrian contrapuntist, Carl HORWITZ; *Six Fugues* for piano by the German neo-classicist, Arthur WILLNER, and a *String Quartet* by the French-born Catalonian, Philipp JARNACH.

"While there exists today a lively discussion of new departures in the domain of plastic arts, narrative, lyric and dramatic literature, young composers are compelled to fight against overwhelming odds to get a chance to bring their works to public hearing. Interpreting musicians and publishers, on whom the composer depends for his self-expression, in most cases deny their aid to unknown composers. In these conditions the Gesellschaft der Musikfreunde at Donaueschingen has decided to contribute its modest share to the furtherance of the creative output of the young generation by giving an open hearing exclusively to debatable young musical talents at special concerts. . . . When these Chamber Music Performances for Furtherance of Contemporary Music were arranged in the little Schwarzwald town of Donaueschingen, it was not an artificially planted seed in an uncultivated soil, but in continuance of a fine tradition established by a 150-year old Ducal House. . . . The programs are selected without any partisan predilection. Only the inherent value of the work and its craftsmanship are the factors determining acceptance. Stress is laid, however, on giving an opening to unknown or little-known talents; mature works by already established composers will frequently be passed by in favor of younger struggling musicians, even if their efforts today show more ardor than accomplishment." (From a declaration of the Donaueschingen Committee for Furtherance of Contemporary Music, signed by Heinrich Burkard, Eduard Erdmann, and Joseph Haas, published in the *Neue Musik Zeitung* of 21 July 1921)

1 AUGUST 1921

At the third concert of the first Festival at Donaueschingen three chamber-music works are performed for the first time: a *Sonata for Violin and Piano* by the not yet twenty-year-old German composer, Rudolf PETERS, with the composer at the piano; a one-movement *Piano Sonata* by the Schoenberg disciple, Alban BERG; and the *Third String Quartet* by the not quite twenty-six-year-old Paul HINDEMITH.

(Information from the original programs, obtained from the Secretariat of the Gesellschaft der Musikfreunde at Donaueschingen)

2 AUGUST 1921

Enrico CARUSO, celebrated Italian tenor, dies in his native Naples at the age of forty-eight years, five months, and one week.

"Enrico Caruso Dies in Native Naples; End Came Suddenly—Famous Tenor Succumbs When Taken From Sorrento for New Operation—National Mourning in Italy. Tenor, It Is Now Disclosed, Had Undergone

Six Operations and Blood Transfusion.—*Naples, 2 Aug. 1921.* The great singer passed away at 9 o'clock this morning at the Hotel Vesuvius. Caruso was said to have become extremely weak yesterday afternoon. The operation was for an abscess between the liver and the diaphragm which caused acute peritonitis. Caruso's wife and his brother were at his bedside." (New York *Times,* 3 August 1921)

8 AUGUST 1921

Arthur POUGIN, French music critic, defender of the faith of nineteenth-century ideals and conscientious objector to modern vagaries, editor of the French music weekly, *Le Ménestrel,* dies in Paris two days after his eighty-seventh birthday.

27 AUGUST 1921

Four centuries have passed since the death in Condé of Josquin DESPRÈS, great precursor of modern polyphony.

25 SEPTEMBER 1921

State Institute of Musical Science is formed in Moscow and the first conference of the Scientific Council of the Institute is held.

(The date of the official opening of the Institute is 1 November 1921. Dates from Ivanov-Boretzky, *Five Years of Scientific Research of the State Institute of Musical Science,* Moscow, 1926)

27 SEPTEMBER 1921

Engelbert HUMPERDINCK, composer of fairy operas in an infantilized Wagnerian idiom, dies at Neustrelitz, twenty-six days after his sixty-seventh birthday.

1 OCTOBER 1921

Fanfare, "musical causerie," an unperiodical magazine of musical culture, conducted in a witty modern style, begins publication in London under the editorship of Leigh HENRY.

23 OCTOBER 1921

Katia Kabanova, opera by Leoš JANÁČEK, to Ostrovsky's drama, *The Thunderstorm,* dealing with a prematurely emancipated young adulteress, the music reflecting a Wagnerian-Moussorg-skyan tradition, is performed for the first time at Brno.

28 OCTOBER 1921

Alfredo CASELLA makes his first appearance in America with the Philadelphia Orchestra in the triple capacity of composer, conductor, and pianist.

29 OCTOBER 1921

Pour une Fête de Printemps, symphonic poem by Albert ROUSSEL, couched in consistent bitonal harmonies, is performed for the first time at a Colonne concert in Paris, Gabriel Pierné conducting.

25 NOVEMBER 1921

VAUGHAN WILLIAMS completes in London the composition of his *Pastoral Symphony* in four classical movements, melodically based on English folk music, making use of consecutive triads and other devices of modern harmony, and orchestrated in an austere style, suggestive of neo-romantic rather than impressionist technique.

16 DECEMBER 1921

Serge PROKOFIEV plays the solo part in the first performance of his *Third Concerto for Piano and Orchestra* with the Chicago Symphony Orchestra, Frederick Stock conducting.

16 DECEMBER 1921

Camille SAINT-SAËNS, celebrated French composer, symbol of the era of transition, apostle of clarity and musical effectiveness, prolific creator of music in all forms, dies at his winter home, at Algiers—where he had arrived on 4 December, on what proved to be his last journey—at the age of eighty-six years, two months, and seven days.

(The date, 16 December 1922 [sic!] in Hull's *Dictionary of Modern Music and Musicians* is a dangerous misprint which is carried into the German edition of the *Dictionary,* edited by Alfred Einstein, 1926)

"He attended on the 16th of December the performance of *Lakmé* at the Algiers Opera, whence he returned to his favorite domicile, Hotel de l'Oasis. It was there at about one o'clock in the morning that the great master of French music passed peacefully on, without pain, as he always hoped he would." (Dandelot, *La Vie et l'oeuvre de Saint-Saëns,* Paris, 1930) (This account differs from *Le Temps* of 18 December 1921, according to which Saint-Saëns attended the performance of *Lakmé* on 11 December, and died five days later at 11 o'clock at night)

23 DECEMBER 1921

The Suite from *Krazy Kat,* "jazz pantomime" by John Alden CARPENTER, is performed for the first time by the Chicago Symphony, Frederick Stock conducting.

24 DECEMBER 1921

Camille SAINT-SAËNS is buried at the Montparnasse cemetery in Paris, his body having been brought to France from Algiers.

"One after another, the orators, giving diverse reasons for our admiration for him, indicated a more profound, primordial reason . . . which may be summed up in a brief formula—Saint-Saëns was a French musician." (From the funeral oration of Léon Bérard, Minister of Education, printed in the brochure, *Funérailles de Saint-Saëns,* Paris, 1922)

25 DECEMBER 1921

Hans HUBER, Swiss composer and educator of a generation of Swiss musicians, dies at Locarno in his seventieth year.

26 DECEMBER 1921

La Scala of Milan, closed since 1917, reopens with Verdi's *Falstaff,* conducted by TOSCANINI.

30 DECEMBER 1921

Serge PROKOFIEV conducts at the Chicago Opera the first performance of his opera, *The Love for Three Oranges,* to Carlo Gozzi's fantastic tale, dealing with a prince doomed to seek mysterious cure in laughter and finding a princess in an orange, with rhythmic, clear, effective music, abounding in witty turns and brilliantly orchestrated.

1922

9 JANUARY 1922

Arthur NIKISCH conducts the Berlin Philharmonic Orchestra for the last time before his fatal attack of influenza.

(Date from *50 Jahre Berliner Philharmonisches Orchester,* by Alfred Einstein, 1932)

10 JANUARY 1922

The first demonstration of the clavilux, an instrument that throws colors on a screen according to the key struck, is given in New York by the inventor, Thomas Wilfred.

15 JANUARY 1922

Carl NIELSEN, Danish neo-romantic composer, completes at Copenhagen the composition of his *Fifth Symphony,* in two extensive movements: (1) *Tempo giusto,* concluding on a clarinet solo against a vanishing drum-beat; and (2) *Allegro,* a scherzo built on a thematic fourth, with an Andante middle section. (Date at the end of the manuscript score)

17 JANUARY 1922

Ferruccio BUSONI addresses an open letter to the editor of *Melos,* expressing his views on the neo-classical ideal in music.

"If a physician advises the use of wine, it is not with the intention of making the patient drunk. Anarchy is not liberty. Magnanimity must not become profligacy, and free love is not prostitution. A good idea is not yet a work of art, a talented man not at once a master; a grain, however fertile and vigorous, is not the harvest.

"Far from discouraging the use of every effective means in the workshop of our possibilities, I only ask that these means should be used in an esthetic manner, that the proportions of measure, sound and intervals should be skillfully applied, that a work of art, whatever its nature, should be elevated to the rank of classic art, in the original sense of final perfection."

23 JANUARY 1922

Arthur NIKISCH, great Hungarian-born orchestral conductor, pioneer of the subjective school of interpretation, dies at Leipzig, at the age of sixty-six years, three months, and eleven days.

26 JANUARY 1922

Luigi DENZA, Italian composer of over 500 songs, among them the overpopular *Funiculi-Funicula* used by Strauss in his early symphonic poem, *Aus Italien,* as a folk song, dies in London four weeks before his seventy-sixth birthday.

(Date from the London *Times* of 27 January 1922. Grove gives the erroneous date 27 January 1922; Riemann the erroneous 13 February 1922)

26 JANUARY 1922

The *Pastoral Symphony* of VAUGHAN WILLIAMS is performed for the first time by the Royal Philharmonic Orchestra of London, Adrian BOULT conducting.

4 FEBRUARY 1922

L'Amour en Quatrième Vitesse (Love in Fourth Speed), operetta by H. MORISSON, is produced at the Variétés Parisiennes.

(Date from *Cinquante Ans de Musique Française,* Paris, 1926)

13 FEBRUARY 1922

Persymfans (Pervyi Symphonitchesky Ensemble), the first conductorless orchestra, gives in Moscow its inaugural concert in a program of Beethoven's music.

(Date from *Five Years of the Persymfans,* Moscow, 1927)

14 FEBRUARY 1922

Romeo and Juliet, opera in three acts by Riccardo ZANDONAI, written in the traditional operatic fashion, without any attempt at modernity, and relying for its musically dramatic effect on modified diminished-seventh chord harmonies, is produced at the Constanzi Theatre in Rome.

(Date from the Appendix to the third edition of the *Dizionario dei musicisti* by Alberto de Angelis, Rome, 1928, corroborated by contemporary press dispatches. Grove in the article on Zandonai gives the correct day and month, but the wrong year, 1921)

MARCH 1922

Igor STRAVINSKY completes the composition of *Mavra,* opéra bouffe in one act, dedicated to the memory of Pushkin, Glinka, and Tchaikovsky, and written in a rhythmic tonal idiom, pan-diatonically enriched.

4 MARCH 1922

Symphony in B-flat major, by Albert ROUSSEL, written in a neo-romantic idiom with tangent tritones, fourths, and fifths, and explosive sonorities at climactic points, is performed for the first time at a Pasdeloup concert in Paris, Rhené-Baton conducting.

18 MARCH 1922

The Castle of the Voivod, opera by Ernst DOHNÁNYI, written in a rich, post-romantic idiom without much originality, is produced at Budapest.

26 MARCH 1922

Sancta Susanna, one-act opera by Paul HINDEMITH, written in fairly tonal style, with little stress on singing (two *dramatis personae* have *Sprechrollen*), is performed for the first time at Frankfort.

"The whole work is a modification of a single theme whose powerful line signifies perhaps a new melodic consciousness. . . . Withal, great economy of means, in sharp opposition to the hypertrophy of romantic music drama. The *Principle of Stylization* is here immediately recognized. The music lends itself to simple plastic treatment. The music determines the form. (Heinrich Strobel, *Paul Hindemith,* Mainz, 1931)

1 APRIL 1922

Ta Bouche, operetta by Maurice YVAIN, is produced at the Théâtre Daunou in Paris. (Date from *Cinquante ans de musique française,* Paris, 1926)

APRIL 1922

The Benedictine monks of Solesmes, restorers of authentic Gregorian usage, return to Solesmes after twenty-one years of exile on the Isle of Wight. (Date obtained from the Monastery of Solesmes)

4–6 MAY 1922

The Society of St. Gregory of America at its convention in Rochester, New York, issues a "Black List" of music disapproved for performance at sacred services. (*See* complete list in Part III)

13 MAY 1922

Two works by Béla BARTÓK, *Herzog Blaubarts Schloss,* legendary opera based on peasant folk song, and *Der Holzgeschnitzte Prinz,* ballet-pantomime, both touched with expressionist technique and embellished with atonal melos, are performed for the first time at the Frankfort Opera House.

3 JUNE 1922

Mavra and *Le Renard,* two one-act operas by Igor STRAVINSKY, are produced by Diaghilev's Ballet Russe, at the Paris Opéra.

JULY 1922

Eugene GOOSSENS composes in London his choral fragment for chorus and orchestra to a poem by Walter de la Mare, entitled *Silence* and reaching triple forte at the words, "Vainly 'gainst that thin wall the trumpets call."

11 JULY 1922

Alfred HERTZ conducts the opening concert at the newly-constructed open-air auditorium, built in a natural canyon in Hollywood, California, and named the Hollywood Bowl.

17 JULY 1922

The Scriabin Museum is opened in the house where he lived in Moscow.

30 JULY 1922

The second Chamber Music Festival for Furtherance of Contemporary Music, arranged by the Gesellschaft der Musikfreunde, opens at Donaueschingen, presenting two Sunday concerts of first performances:

Morning concert: *Symphonic Music for 9 Solo Instruments,* in an abstract formalist idiom by Ernst KŘENEK; *Michelangelo-Lieder* by the German composer, Edmund SCHROEDER; *Fuga Grotesca* for string quartet by Rudolf DINKEL; *Quintet,* in a Reger-like linear idiom, by Richard ZOELLNER; and *Trio Sonate* for violin, viola, and piano in a rather ordinary contrapuntal style by the Austrian-born Reger disciple, Hermann GRABNER.

Evening concert: *String Quartet* by Bernard VAN DIEREN, Dutch composer, resident in London and writing in a neo-Flemish, Sweelinkian polyphonic style; *Clarinet Sonata* by the twenty-eight-year-old Swiss-Italian Reinhold LAGUAI; *Lieder* by the Prussian composer, Hans VON DER WENSE; and *Sextet* for clarinet, string quartet, and piano, in one movement, rhythmically and atonally advanced in the direction of Schoenberg's ideals, by the Viennese Czech composer, Felix PETYREK.

31 JULY 1922

At the second Donaueschingen Chamber Music Festival the following program of chamber music is given:

One-movement *Quintet* for oboe, clarinet, violin, viola, and cello, in a thorough contrapuntal neo-classical style, by Max BUTTING; *String Quartet* by the Bohemian polyphonist Fidelio FINKE; and the first performance of the thematically tonal, but contrapuntally heterotonal *Kammermusik No. 1* for chamber orchestra by the not yet twenty-seven-year-old Paul HINDEMITH. (Programs and dates from the special Donaueschingen issue of the *Neue Musik-Zeitung,* 20 July 1922)

7 AUGUST 1922

The first International Festival of modern music opens at Salzburg with the following program:

Five Songs by Richard STRAUSS; a militant, hedonistic *Sonata* for flute, oboe, clarinet, and piano by the not quite thirty-year-old Darius MILHAUD; a *Song* with flute and piano, in a neo-romantic style, by the Austrian composer, Joseph MARX; a neo-classical, pan-diatonic *Passacaglia* for piano by the Czech-German composer, Felix PETYREK; *Rout,* a bril-

liant piece with cleverly concealed lyrical sentiment, for voice and chamber orchestra, by the English composer, Arthur BLISS; and a percussive
Sonata for violin and piano by Béla BARTÓK.

8 AUGUST 1922

Two concerts of modern chamber music take place in the course
of the first Festival at Salzburg, with the following program:

In the morning concert: *Quintet* for wood-wind and piano by Albéric
MAGNARD, in commemoration of his tragic death nearly eight years before; songs by modern Italians, Francesco MALIPIERO, Ildebrando PIZ-
ZETTI, and CASTELNUOVO-TEDESCO; *Six Impromptus* for piano, op. 8, by
Francis POULENC, played by the composer; *Rag-Music* for piano by Igor
STRAVINSKY; *La Flûte de Pan* for flute alone by Claude DEBUSSY; *Sonata
for Two Flutes* by Charles KOECHLIN; *Three Greek Folk-Songs* by Maurice RAVEL; *Five Spanish Songs* by Manuel DE FALLA; and a *Rhapsody*
for two flutes, clarinet, and pianoforte by Arthur HONEGGER, written
in his characteristic style of acrid harmonies, broad cantilena, fluid tonality, and stimulating not-too-involved rhythm.

In the evening concert: *Sonata* for violin and piano by the Danish
composer, Carl NIELSEN; *Four Songs* by the Swedish composer, Ture
RANGSTROEM; *Gaspard de la Nuit* by Maurice RAVEL; *Sonatina* for piano
by Ferruccio BUSONI; *Tantris* for piano by Karol SZYMANOWSKI; *String
Quartet* by the Schoenberg disciple, Egon WELLESZ; *Marionettes,* pleasing burlesque for piano by the Czech composer, Fidelio FINKE; *String
Quartet* in a contrapuntal atonal idiom by Anton VON WEBERN; and a
poetic quasi-atonal *Sonata* for violin and piano by the impressionistic
Dutch composer, Willem PIJPER.

9 AUGUST 1922

A "Viennese Matinee" is given at the Salzburg Festival presenting
songs and chamber music by moderns of Vienna: Walter KLEIN;
Ernst KANITZ; Hugo KAUDER; Egon LUSTGARTEN; Carl HORWITZ;
Karl ALWIN; Wilhelm GROSZ; and Karl WEIGL—all in an idiom
distinguished by anti-tonal tendencies, neo-romantic, post-Mahler
subjectivism, and a basic Viennese trait in the decided predilection for ternary form ultimately traceable to dance form.

9 AUGUST 1922

At the evening chamber concert of the Salzburg Festival the following program is given:

Piano music by Joseph MARX, Adolfo SALAZAR, Manuel DE FALLA, and
the Czech-German composer, Egon KORNAUTH; *Odelette* by Dame Ethel
SMYTH; Ernest BLOCH's *Schelomo* for cello, played with piano accompaniment, an orchestra being unavailable; *String Quartet* by Paul
HINDEMITH; and *Violin Sonata* by Ernest BLOCH.

10 AUGUST 1922

The two concluding concerts of the Salzburg Festival are given:

In the matinee: *Serenade* for two violins and viola by Zoltán KODÁLY;
Four Songs with violin by Gustav HOLST; *Song* by Gerrard WILLIAMS;
Three Songs by Arnold BAX; *Sonata* for violin and piano by the Ameri-
can, Leo SOWERBY; *Two Songs* by the Danish neo-romanticist, Paul
SCHIERBECK; *Summer,* song by the Danish neo-classicist, Ebbe HAM-
MERIK; *Nod,* song with string quartet by the English composer, Arm-
strong GIBBS, performed coincidentally on his thirty-third birthday; and
Two Songs with string quartet by Eugene GOOSSENS.

In the evening: *Variations and Fugue on a Theme by Schumann* for
piano by the German Regerite, Guido BAGIER; *Molly on the Shore,* for
string quartet, dance in a popular vein, by the Australian composer-
pianist, Percy GRAINGER; *Six Songs* by Rudolf RETI; *Three Songs* with
string quartet by the scholarly atonalist, Paul A. PISK; *Songs* by the
Czechs Jaroslav KŘIČKA and Ladislav VYCPÁLEK; and *Second String Quartet* by Arnold SCHOENBERG.

"It seems almost incredible that one can have heard so much music in
four days, but the programmes are there to vouch for it: Fifty-four composers of fifteen different nationalities! If we include Strauss who arrived later to conduct the Mozart operas, there were more than twenty
composers present. Beginning at seven o'clock, not any of the evening
concerts were over before ten, and the matinées, at the unearthly hour
of half past ten, made it difficult to keep luncheon appointments at one.
Twenty hours of music!" (Edwin Evans in the *Musical Times,* 1 September, 1922)

11 AUGUST 1922

At a meeting held after the conclusion of the Salzburg Festival, it
is decided that an International Society for Contemporary Music
be established, with the seat at London and Edward J. Dent as
president.

"The plan is that in each country either an existing body, or one to be
created for the purpose, shall draw to itself all those interested in new

music, that is to say contemporary music, regardless of tendency. These national organizations pledge themselves to mutual aid by the transmission of information, of books and music, of programmes, and of anything further that appears likely to spread the knowledge of contemporary music. . . . Each of them will elect a delegate to the committee of the International Society for New Music as the new concern is to be called. There will be an annual Festival, provisionally at Salzburg. Wherever it takes place, it will be under the control of the International, which will, however, delegate to the local section the duty of technical organization." (Edwin Evans in the *Musical Times*, London, 1 September 1922)

19 AUGUST 1922

The first wireless music concert is broadcast at the experimental station at Sheffield University, England.

19 AUGUST 1922

Felipe PEDRELL, the "Spanish Wagner," prolific composer and writer on music, ardent preacher of the doctrine that every country should build its musical art on the foundation of its folk songs, teacher of Albéniz and de Falla, dies in Barcelona at the age of eighty-one years and six months.

2 SEPTEMBER 1922

The overture, six entr'actes, and incidental music by Eugene GOOSSENS, to Somerset Maugham's play *East of Suez*, are performed in London for the first time.

"No Chinese instruments are used in the orchestra, and the harmonic idiom of the incidental music is Western throughout." (Composer's note in the score)

7 SEPTEMBER 1922

Arthur BLISS conducts at the Three Choirs' Festival at Gloucester, England, the first performance of his *Color Symphony,* in four movements suggesting four heraldic colors: (1) Purple, the color of amethysts, pageantry, royalty, and death; (2) Red, the color of rubies, wine, revelry, furnaces, courage, and magic; (3) Blue, the color of sapphires, deep water, skies, loyalty, and melancholy; (4) Green, the color of emeralds, hope, joy, youth, spring, and victory.

18 SEPTEMBER 1922

Darius MILHAUD completes at Enclos, France, the composition of his opera, *The Eumenides,* in three acts, to Paul Claudel's translation of Aeschylus' tragedy, written in an acrid polytonal style with a pan-diatonic Finale in parallel chords of the fifteenth.

16 OCTOBER 1922

Richard STRAUSS completes, at his home at Garmisch, Bavaria, after eleven months of work, the full score of his "heiteres Wiener Ballett," *Schlagobers* (Whipped Cream).

17 OCTOBER 1922

The German section of the newly organized International Society for Contemporary Music is formed in Berlin.

22 OCTOBER 1922

The Ballad of Reading Gaol, symphonic poem after Oscar Wilde, by Jacques IBERT, his first orchestral work, in a broad melodic idiom and astringent close-knit harmony, is performed for the first time, at a Colonne concert, in Paris, Gabriel Pierné conducting.

3 NOVEMBER 1922

The French Society of Composers issues protest against the jazzing up of Chopin's *Funeral March.* (New York *Times,* 4 November 1922)

6 NOVEMBER 1922

William BAINES, English composer of sensitive piano music with impressionist titles, such as *Silver-Points, Colored Leaves, Milestones,* in a lyric style suggesting early Scriabin, dies in London as a result of a lung affection sustained in the army, at the early age of twenty-three.

11 NOVEMBER 1922

Four years after the Armistice, the British Broadcasting Company officially commences transmission of musical programs by wireless.

16 NOVEMBER 1922

The *Second Symphony* by the Russian symphonist of the Rimsky-Korsakov school, Lazare SAMINSKY, subtitled "Symphony of the Summits," in a tonality designated as *H-fridur* (free major mode on B), is performed for the first time by the Concertgebouw Orchestra in Amsterdam, Willem Mengelberg conducting.

23 NOVEMBER 1922

After eighteen years of litigation between the brothers Pierre and Adolphe DEGEYTER over the authorship of the music to *The Internationale,* the workers' song, written in 1888, the Paris Appellate Court gives its decision in favor of Pierre.

(Date from Alexandre Zévaés, *Chants révolutionnaires, l'Internationale, ses auteurs, son histoire,* in a Paris publication, *Monde,* 27 April 1929)

4 DECEMBER 1922

The *First Symphony,* in E-flat major, by Arnold BAX, a work of gloomy introspection with overtones of mystical contemplation, is performed for the first time in London, Albert Coates conducting.

(Date from London *Times,* 5 December 1922. *A Handbook for Bax's Symphonies* by Robert Hull gives the erroneous date 2 December 1922)

7 DECEMBER 1922

Two Choral Preludes of Bach, orchestrated by Arnold SCHOENBERG, are performed for the first time by the New York Philharmonic Orchestra under the direction of Josef Stransky.

10 DECEMBER 1922

A century has passed since the birth in Liége of César FRANCK.

15 DECEMBER 1922

The British Broadcasting Company is incorporated under the Companies Act.

17 DECEMBER 1922

The International Composers' Guild gives in New York its first concert of modern music, presenting short works by Arthur HONEGGER, Dane RUDHYAR, Lazare SAMINSKY, François GAILLARD, Maurice RAVEL, Carl RUGGLES, and Arthur LOURIÉ.

1923

8 JANUARY 1923

Mozart's *Magic Flute* is broadcast direct from the concert hall in London by the British Broadcasting Company, marking the first performance of an opera on the air.

24 JANUARY 1923

Théodore REINACH, French musical Hellenist, completes in Paris his book, *La Musique grecque,* presenting a scientific account of what is definitely known about Greek melos and rhythm, and quoting all authentic fragments of Greek music, including the only extant specimen (circa 408 B.C.) of the enharmonic mode, with quarter-tones, from a chorus to *Orestes.* (Date of Preface)

19 FEBRUARY 1923

The *Sinfonietta* by Eugene GOOSSENS, in three linked movements in modified sonata form, more diatonic than Goossens' earlier works, is performed for the first time by the London Symphony.

19 FEBRUARY 1923

Jan SIBELIUS conducts in Helsingfors the first performance of his *Sixth Symphony,* op. 104, in the following four movements:

Allegro molto moderato, in 2/2, in clear diatonic style with characteristic Sibelian thirds; *Allegretto Moderato,* a scherzo in accelerated rhythm, 3, 6, 9, and 12 notes to a 3/4 bar; *Poco vivace,* in gigue style; *Allegro molto,* in vigorous square time, with a characteristic ending in pianissimo.

"The *Sixth Symphony* is wild and impassioned in character, sombre with pastoral contrasts . . . the end rising to a sombre roaring of the orchestra in which the main theme is drowned." (From a description of the symphony long before its composition was actually begun, in a letter from Sibelius to a friend dated 20 May 1918, and quoted by Ekman in his book on Sibelius, 1935, as a program of the composition)

22 FEBRUARY 1923

The Juilliard Musical Foundation of New York City receives a $10,000,000 fund bequeathed by Frederick A. Juilliard for furtherance of musical education. (New York *Times,* 23 February 1923)

23 FEBRUARY 1923

A Victory Ball, symphonic poem by Ernest SCHELLING, evoking the ghosts of the war dead at a joyous dance of the victorious living and dedicated "to the memory of an American soldier," is performed by the Philadelphia Orchestra, Stokowski conducting.

4 MARCH 1923

The International Composers' Guild of New York gives the first performance of *Hyperprism* for wind instruments and percussion, by Edgar VARÈSE, reaching into the field of musical infinities and exploring extreme registers and sonorities.

23 MARCH 1923

El Retablo de Maese Pedro, marionette show by Manuel DE FALLA for chamber orchestra, is performed in concert version for the first time in Seville.

27 MARCH 1923

Ernest BLOCH finishes in Cleveland the composition of his *Piano Quintet,* making use of quarter-tones to increase emotional tension. (Date at end of original manuscript in the Library of Congress, Washington, D. C.)

6 APRIL 1923

Igor STRAVINSKY completes in Monaco the full score of *Les Noces,* "Russian choreographic scenes with singing and music," for chorus, soloists, four pianos, and seventeen percussion instruments, in two parts and the following four scenes:

(1) *In the Bride's Room,* nostalgic song of the bride, broken by the boisterous irruption of her maiden friends, in angular rhythms, with an eighth-note as metrical constant; (2) *In the Groom's Room,* invocation in acrid harmonies, suggesting a modified organum, followed by the parents' lament in *diapente* compass, with a wavering major-minor third, this mood quickly changing to a rude, ritually solemn chorus; (3) *The Bride's Farewell,* against an *ostinato,* swinging within the range of a minor ninth; (4) *The Wedding Repast,* which includes a syncopated section in square-cut harmonies, with the metrical constant of an eighth-note, this soon brutalized into rhythmed pitchless parlando, ultimately subsiding into an orchestral postlude in slow, bell-like drops of wide-spaced chords. (The last page of the manuscript bears in Stravinsky's hand: *L'Instrumentation achevée à Monaco le 6 Avril 1923*)

7 APRIL 1923

Ciboulette, the first operetta by Reynaldo HAHN, Caracas-born Parisian, is produced at the Paris Variétés. (Date from *Cinquante ans de musique française,* Paris, 1926)

11 APRIL 1923

A group of composers in New York secedes from the radical International Composers' Guild, and forms a League of Composers, with the view of giving equal representation to all tendencies in modern music.

(Date carried by the charter, communicated to the author by Minna Lederman, editor of the League's organ, *Modern Music*)

"The presentation in America of contemporary music is an undertaking that has rapidly outgrown the capacities of existing musical organizations. The mediums recently formed to promote modern music have been adequate only to offer a special phase of the whole movement. No organization exists today which proposes to bring the entire range of modern tendencies before the public. . . .

"It is for this purpose that the League of Composers has been organized. It believes not only that the creative artist needs contact with the public, but that the public is willing to give him a hearing. . . .

"The League intends to encourage and give support to the production of new and significant works. It will promote the publication of new music. It will effect cooperation between composers of all nations, and it will give well planned performances of new music selected from every school. . . . While 'first performances' will be a feature of the League's concerts they will not exclude such modern works as may have been heard before, but which the executive board considers of sufficient importance to be given a rehearing. All programs are chosen by unanimous decision of the board. . . .

"The League of Composers is directed by a small group, including five composers who represent divergent phases of the modern movement. Six of the League's executive board were members of the council of eight which directed the International Composers' Guild during the last season. They were largely responsible for the first American presentation of Arnold Schoenberg's famous melodrama 'Pierrot Lunaire.' Convinced, after a year's association with the Guild, that there is need for a more flexible selection of modern music than has heretofore been offered to the public, the six seceding members have undertaken the formation of the League of Composers. Executive Board: Arthur Bliss, Stephan Bourgeois, Louis Gruenberg, Miss Minna Lederman, Leo Ornstein, Mrs. Arthur M. Reis, Lazare Saminsky, Mrs. Maurice Wertheim, Emerson Whithorne." (From the League's folder, *Foreword to the Season of 1923–1924*)

3 MAY 1923

Ravel's orchestration of Moussorgsky's *Pictures at an Exhibition,* commissioned by Koussevitzky for 10,000 francs payable in consideration of five years' exclusive performing rights, is performed for the first time at one of Koussevitzky's concerts in Paris.

(Henry Prunières in his article on Ravel in Hull erroneously states that the performance of 8 May 1924 was the first)

5 MAY 1923

A Society of Quarter-Tone Music is founded in Petrograd by Georg Rimsky-Korsakov, grandson of the composer.

14 MAY 1923

Eugene Goossens conducts in London at the opening night of the British National Opera Company's season, the comic opera by Gustav HOLST, *The Perfect Fool,* allegoric play, in a neo-Elizabethan style, with brusque harmonies and frequently asymmetrical rhythms.

30 MAY 1923

Camille CHEVILLARD, French conductor, son-in-law of Charles Lamoureux and his successor as permanent conductor of the Lamoureux concerts in Paris, also composer of orchestra and chamber music of no great distinction, dies in his native Paris at the age of sixty-three years and seven and a half months.

1 JUNE 1923

Padmavati, two-act opera-ballet by Albert ROUSSEL, to the oriental legend of a beautiful Hindu woman and a Mongolian Khan, written in an idiom free from pseudo-exoticism and couched in acrid modern harmonies, is produced at the Paris Opéra.

13 JUNE 1923

Four days before Igor STRAVINSKY's forty-first birthday, Diaghilev's Ballet Russe presents in Paris the first performance of his *Les Noces,* under the direction of Ernest Ansermet.

14 JUNE 1923

Erik Satie presents, at the Collège de France in Paris, four young musicians, Henri CLIQUET-PLEYEL, Roger DÉSORMIÈRE, Maxime JACOB, and Henri SAUGUET, members of a new sodality, named École d'Arcueil, in honor of Satie's suburban residence.

"They chose the name 'School of Arcueil' because of their affection for an old inhabitant of that suburban town. I shall not discuss their merits, being happily neither a sycophant nor a critic. The public must be their critic, for the public alone has real power to pass judgment upon them. Personally, I am happy at the arrival of this group in the musical arena: they replace the Six, some of whom have won renown in spite of the absurd cavillings of parlor-artists, envious second-raters, and criticasters." (From Satie's letter to Rolf de Mare, director of the Ballets Suédois in Paris)

17 JUNE 1923

Das Marienleben, a song-cycle to the verses of Rilke by Paul HINDEMITH, in a neo-medieval idiom of great harmonic restraint and high emotional content, is performed for the first time during the course of the third Festival of modern chamber music at Donaueschingen. (Date from *Neue Musik-Zeitung,* 2 August 1923)

12 JULY 1923

Asger HAMERIK, Danish composer of seven symphonies, four operas, two choral trilogies, and other music, brother of the Danish historian, Angul Hammerich (sic), dies at Frederiksberg in his eighty-first year.

2 AUGUST 1923

The first Festival of the International Society for Contemporary Music (*first* because the 1922 Festival took place *before* the formation of the ISCM) opens at Salzburg with the following program of chamber music:

String Quartet by Alban BERG; *Die Haengenden Gaerten,* cycle of fifteen songs by Arnold SCHOENBERG; *Second Sonata for Violin and Piano* by Béla BARTÓK.

3 AUGUST 1923

At the second concert of the ISCM Festival at Salzburg, the following program is given:

Sonata for Violin and Piano by Florent SCHMITT; *Hafislieder* by the Reger disciple, Othmar SCHOECK; *Sonata for Violin Alone* by Eduard ERDMANN; *Songs* by the Finnish Hugo Wolf, Yrjö KILPINEN; *String Quartet* by the not quite twenty-three-year-old Viennese modernist, Ernst KŘENEK.

4 AUGUST 1923

At the third concert of the ISCM Festival at Salzburg, the following program is given:

Overture on Hebrew Themes for clarinet, string quartet, and piano by Serge PROKOFIEV, in his most felicitous mood; *Délie,* three songs by ROLAND-MANUEL; *Reiterburlesque* for piano by the Czech composer, Fidelio FINKE; *Two Hafiz Songs* by Karol SZYMANOWSKI; *Two Songs* by Manuel DE FALLA; *Duo for Violin and Cello* by Maurice RAVEL; *Sonatine* for flute and piano by Philipp JARNACH; *Two Sacred Songs* with organ by Paul A. PISK; and *String Quartet* by William WALTON.

5 AUGUST 1923

At the fourth concert of the ISCM Festival at Salzburg, the following program is given:

Austere and deeply inspirational *Sonata* for violin and piano by Leoš JANÁČEK; brilliant and colorful *Rhapsody* for flute, english horn, string quartet, double-bass, and two voices by Arthur BLISS; *Divertissement* for five wind instruments and piano by Albert ROUSSEL; a Debussyan *Sonata* for flute and harp by the Dutch composer, Sem DRESDEN, with the composer playing the harp part on the piano; *Valses Bourgeoises* for piano four hands by the British musical wit, Lord BERNERS; *New York Nights and Days,* an impressionistic piano piece by the American, Emerson WHITHORNE; a piano piece, *Il Raggio Verde* by the Italian, CASTELNUOVO-TEDESCO; and *Three Pieces* and *Concertino* for string quartet by Igor STRAVINSKY.

6 AUGUST 1923

At the fifth concert of the ISCM Festival at Salzburg, the following program is given:

Sonata for viola and piano by Arthur HONEGGER; *Two Sonnets* by Francesco MALIPIERO; *String Quartet in Quarter Tones* by Alois HÁBA; *Sonata for Violin and Cello* by Maurice RAVEL; and the *Fantasia Contrappuntistica* for two pianos by Ferruccio BUSONI.

7 AUGUST 1923

At the sixth concert of the ISCM Festival at Salzburg, the following program is given:

String Quartet by Darius MILHAUD; *Promenades* for piano by Francis POULENC; *Piano Sonata* by Charles KOECHLIN; *Songs* by Manfred GURLITT, German composer of neo-romantic tendencies; *Sonata* for cello solo by Zoltán KODÁLY, with the C and G strings lowered a semitone so as to give a B-minor triad as basic harmony; and *Clarinet Quintet,* in five movements, of which the last is a free inversion of the first, by Paul HINDEMITH.

21 AUGUST 1923

Richard STRAUSS completes at Buenos Aires the score of *Intermezzo,* domestic comedy with symphonic interludes in two acts, op. 72, in an idiom between light opera, such as *Rosenkavalier,* and musical tragedy, such as *Electra.*

"When Richard Strauss was court conductor in Berlin, a letter came to his house one day during his absence, in which a 'bar-lady' asked him for the two tickets he had promised her for the next performance at the opera. Frau Strauss, a lady of very choleric temperament, reacted promptly upon this by entering on a suit for divorce of which the unfaithful husband was at once notified by telegraph. By the same means Strauss avowed his innocence, without, however, being believed by his wife. When at last he hastened home, the matrimonial sky had already cleared, as one of his colleagues, the legitimate addressee of the letter, had explained the misunderstanding. . . . When the curtain rises we see Court Conductor Robert Storch occupied with the final preparations for a journey, while as a parting gift his wife hurls some sweet remarks at him, and ends by saying that his predilection for a nomadic life seems to indicate that he has Jewish blood in his veins. . . . It is high time for the bar-lady's letter to arrive at the house. Thereupon boundless indignation, suit for divorce, and then a touching final scene, the sorrowing wife weeping at the bedside of their eight-year-old son. . . . The second act . . . Conductor Storch is wandering disconsolately about in a park, where he meets Conductor Stroh, the legitimate addressee of the bar-lady's letter, who explains the mistake and promises to make matters clear to Frau Storch. Finally, Storch returns to his wife who . . . promises to be kindness itself to him ever afterward." (Story told by Dr. Rudolf Felber of Vienna)

14 SEPTEMBER 1923

Albert ROUSSEL completes in Paris the score of his opera, *La Naissance de la Lyre,* to the book by Théodore Reinach. (Date at end of printed score)

21 SEPTEMBER 1923

La Corporazione delle Nuove Musiche, Italian section of the International Society for Contemporary Music, is founded by Gabriele d'Annunzio, Alfredo Casella, and Francesco Malipiero at a meeting at d'Annunzio's villa in Rome. (Date communicated to the author by Alfredo Casella)

17 OCTOBER 1923

Eugene GOOSSENS conducts his first concert as conductor of the Rochester Philharmonic Orchestra.

18 OCTOBER 1923

At a Koussevitzky concert in Paris, Igor STRAVINSKY conducts the first performance of his *Octet* for wind instruments, marking a new turn in his style in the direction of neo-classical economy and clarity; at the same concert Serge PROKOFIEV's *Violin Concerto,* in three lyrico-rhythmic movements, is performed for the first time, Marcel Darrieux playing the solo part.

"The reasons why I composed this kind of music for an octet of flute, clarinet, 2 bassoons, 2 trumpets, and 2 trombones, are the following: (1) because this ensemble forms a complete sonorous scale; (2) because the difference in volume of these instruments renders more evident the musical architecture. And this is the most important question in all my recent compositions. I have excluded from this music all sorts of shading which I have replaced by the play of these volumes. I have excluded all shadings between forte and piano; I have left only forte and piano. Therefore, forte and piano are in my *Octet* only the dynamic limit which determines the function of the volumes in play." (From Stravinsky's article in the magazine, *The Arts*)

(The date, 18 October 1913, for Prokofiev's *Concerto,* in Fleisher's Catalogue, Philadelphia, 1933, p. 408, is a misprint)

11 NOVEMBER 1923

At the inaugural concert of the League of Composers in New York, Ernest BLOCH's *Piano Quintet* is performed for the first time.

19 NOVEMBER 1923

At the Budapest Festival in celebration of the fiftieth anniversary of the Union of Buda and Pest, the *Psalmus Hungaricus* by Zoltán KODÁLY, scored for orchestra, and mixed choir, including a children's chorus, is performed for the first time, on the same program with Béla BARTÓK's *Dance Suite.*

DECEMBER 1923

Arthur HONEGGER completes in Zurich the composition of his "mouvement symphonique," *Pacific 231,* glorifying the modern American locomotive in action.

The composition starts in screeching strings *sul ponticello,* flutes flutter-tonguing in perfect onomatopoeia; the rhythmic pulsations are accelerated from the whole notes to dotted half-notes, undotted half-notes, half-notes in triplets, quarter-notes, and finally eighth-notes, the while horns and trumpets sing their angular song of the rails and switches, coming to a fugato with an iterative insistent subject; then at full speed in sixteenth-notes, the trombones chanting powerfully at the top of their register, the piccolos steam-whistling, the violins speeding *saltando,* marking the rapid rotation of the wheels; the entire orchestra is now puffing heavily, until the brakes are applied, causing deceleration of rhythmic pulsations from the sixteenth-notes to the eighths in triplets, simple eighths, quarter-notes in triplets, simple quarter-notes, half-notes, dotted half-notes, finally pulling in on a whole note on the unison C-sharp, a full stop.

"I have always had a passion for locomotives. To me they are living beings whom I love as others love women or horses. In *Pacific 231* I have not aimed to imitate the noise of an engine, but rather to express in terms of music a visual impression and physical enjoyment. The piece opens with an 'objective' contemplation, the quiet breathing of the engine at rest, the straining at starting, the gradually increasing speed, and finally reaches the lyrical pathetic state of a fast train, three hundred tons of weight, thundering through the silence of the night at a mile a minute. The subject of my composition was an engine of the 'Pacific' type number 231 used for heavy loads and built for great speed." (Honegger's statement in an interview)

8 DECEMBER 1923

Dom Joseph POTHIER, Benedictine scholar of Solesmes, author of classical works on the Gregorian chant, first editor of the *Editio Vaticana,* which superseded the Medici edition in restoring the seemingly lost art of neume-reading, dies at Conques, on the day after his eighty-eighth birthday.

(Date obtained by the author from the Benedictine Monastery of Solesmes. Grove, 1927, gives the erroneous date, 8 September 1923, which is also given by the usually accurate Spanish *Enciclopedia universal* and the *Enciclopedia italiana.* The German dictionaries give the correct date)

15 DECEMBER 1923

La Brebis Égarée, opera in three acts by Darius MILHAUD, a youthful work in a discursive quasi-impressionist manner, is performed for the first time at the Opéra-Comique in Paris.

1924

1 JANUARY 1924

Musical Culture, a Moscow monthly edited by Nicolas ROSLAVETZ, composer in an idiom far more advanced than that of most of his compatriots, issues its first number, with the slogan "Music is music, not ideology."

6 JANUARY 1924

At the Theatre of Monte Carlo, Monaco, Diaghilev produces on the eve of the composer's twenty-fifth birthday Francis POULENC's "ballet avec chant," *Les Biches,* based on French popular songs.

6 JANUARY 1924

Escales, triptych of geographic impressions, portraying Palermo, Tunis, and Valencia, by Jacques IBERT, French post-impressionist composer, is performed for the first time at the Concerts Lamoureux in Paris.

7 JANUARY 1924

Three months and twelve days after his twenty-fifth birthday, George GERSHWIN completes in New York, after three weeks of work, the piano score of his *Rhapsody in Blue,* for jazz band and piano, written in the grand Lisztian style, with the following subdivisions:

Molto Moderato, opening with a clarinet run from low F to high B-flat and stating the main subject in a Mixolydian mode with a lowered sixth; *Moderato assai,* with the subject appearing in G-flat, A, and C, followed by two new themes, a lively one in pure Mixolydian mode and a syncopated subject in the same mode with enharmonic developments; *Meno Mosso e poco scherzando,* with a dancing chromatic subject; a *recapitulation,* with the main subject successively in G, C, E-flat; a Piano Cadenza; *Andantino moderato* in E major, with a new rhapsodic theme in a hypo-Ionian compass, soon jazzed up in a whole-tone scale; *Agitato e misterioso,* in a $3/16 + 3/16 + 2/16 = 2/4$ rhythm; *Molto Stentando,* with a songful theme in pure C major; *Grandioso,* with the "scherzando" theme in diminution, on E-flat, followed by a coda based on the first subject in the parent key of B-flat, concluding in a pure Mixolydian mode. (Date communicated to the author by George Gershwin)

19 JANUARY 1924

Les Fâcheux, ballet after Molière by the youngest of the "Six," Georges Auric, written in the form of a danse suite, classical in meter and movement, bitonal or pan-diatonic in harmony, is produced by Diaghilev at Monte Carlo. (Date communicated by the Direction of the Opera of Monte Carlo)

4 FEBRUARY 1924

Francesco Malipiero completes in Asolo the score of the fairy tale, *The Princess Ulalia,* cantata for soli, chorus, and orchestra.

9 FEBRUARY 1924

Le Petit Elfe Ferme-l'Oeil, "ballet féerique" in one act after Andersen's tale, by Florent Schmitt, is produced at the Paris Opéra-Comique.

12 FEBRUARY 1924

At Paul Whiteman's concert of modern jazz in New York, George Gershwin plays the piano part in the first performance of his *Rhapsody in Blue.*

20 FEBRUARY 1924

Ernst Křenek completes the composition of his *Concerto Grosso II* in the purest style of the "back to Bach" movement. (Date at end of printed score)

25 FEBRUARY 1924

The first number of a quarterly, *The League of Composers' Review,* later renamed *Modern Music,* is issued in New York as official organ of the League of Composers.

"The idea of publishing the magazine originated with myself and Stephan Bourgeois, who at that time was a member of our board. It was my idea that because of the attitude taken by American newspaper critics at the time toward the whole contemporary music movement, it was necessary to have some more informed criticism and that it would be a proper function for the League of Composers to fulfill. . . . The first two issues were published of contributions made by distinguished composers and critics, none of whom received payment for their work. The magazine was sent only to members of the League. It was with the third volume that we decided to sell the magazine outside the League's subscription, both by single copies and by subscription. With this volume we entered the quarterly field and the name of the magazine was changed to *Modern Music* with Volume IV, number 1, November-December issue. The magazine never carried advertising but though it is subsidized by the League, is not a house organ." (Letter to the author from Minna Lederman, editor of *Modern Music,* dated 2 April 1937)

1 MARCH 1924

Serenade, opus 24, by Arnold SCHOENBERG, his first work which contains explicit use, in the fourth movement, of the twelve-tone system, is published by Wilhelm Hansen in Copenhagen.

(The manuscript, now in possession of the publishers, bears no indication of date of composition. The work was purchased by the publishers on 5 March 1923. See Arnold Schoenberg's letter in Part III)

2 MARCH 1924

Jan SIBELIUS completes the composition of his *Seventh Symphony,* op. 105, in one movement, in four contrasting sections, a work in which the composer's characteristic style appears crystal clear, from the opening scale-like motto in A minor, through the dynamic chromatic transition passages to the semi-final choral in somber, restrained harmonies and the ultimate conclusion in proclamatory C major.

"On the 2nd March 1924, at night, as I entered in my diary, I completed *Fantasia Sinfonica*—that was what I at first thought of calling my seventh symphony in one movement." (Sibelius, quoted by Ekman in his book on Sibelius, Helsingfors, 1936)

16 MARCH 1924

Alfredo CASELLA completes in Rome the composition of his *Concerto for String Quartet,* begun 28 November 1923.

"This Concerto belongs to my third style. I consider it to be the first work in which I have truly achieved what for fifteen years has been the goal of all my studies, a modern Italian style." (Casella's note in program of International Composers' Guild, 14 February 1926)

18 MARCH 1924

The August FOERSTER piano manufacturing firm obtains the first patent for a quarter-tone piano. (Date communicated by the manufacturer)

19 MARCH 1924

Howard HANSON conducts the Rochester Philharmonic Orchestra in the first performance of his *Nordic Symphony,* an austere work in a post-romantic idiom, in three movements: a dramatic *Allegro;* a wistful *Andante;* and an energetic *Finale.*

24 MARCH 1924

Jan SIBELIUS conducts in Stockholm the first performance anywhere of his *Seventh Symphony.* (Date communicated by the Stockholm Symphony)

25 MARCH 1924

Florent SCHMITT resigns as head of the Conservatory at Lyons, and G. M. WITKOWSKI is appointed his successor.

29 MARCH 1924

Sir Charles Villiers STANFORD, English composer of seven operas, seven symphonies, four Irish rhapsodies, a clarinet concerto, and many lesser works in a spirited national Irish style, dies in London in his seventy-second year.

"On the evening of 17 March (St. Patrick's Day), 1924, he had a stroke while dressing for a public dinner. He lived for another twelve days and died quietly on the morning of the 29th. He was buried in Westminster Abbey on the 3d of April. . . . His ashes were then laid in the North Choir Aisle under a stone inscribed with the words *A great musician.*" (Harry Plunket Greene, *Charles Villiers Stanford,* London, 1935)

31 MARCH 1924

Ernst KŘENEK completes in Zurich the composition of his *Concerto* for violin and orchestra, in one continuous movement, subdivided into three principal sections, *Presto, Larghetto,* and *Allegro Vivace,* in an energetic rhythmic style, with a curious 16-bar ending for the violin alone in an ascending mixed scale, *diminuendo.* (Date at end of score)

APRIL 1924

Igor STRAVINSKY completes in Biarritz the composition of his *Concerto* for pianoforte and wind instruments, in three movements, written in a strict classical form and idiom, definitely establishing a return to the spirit of old music.

10 APRIL 1924

L'Appel de la Mer, lyric drama in one act, by Henri RABAUD, is produced at the Paris Opéra-Comique.

18 APRIL 1924

Carl EITZ, German music instructor, author of an ingenious mnemonic system of solmization (*Tonwortsystem*) for singing in schools, dies at Eisleben in his seventy-sixth year.

25 APRIL 1924

Half a century has passed since the word "impressionism," applied to pictorial art, appeared in print for the first time, coined by Louis Leroy in the Paris paper, *Charivari.*

1 MAY 1924

Nearly six years after Arrigo BOITO's death, Toscanini conducts at La Scala in Milan the first performance of his opera *Nerone.* (Grove's *Dictionary* gives the erroneous date 2 May 1924)

"*Nerone* was performed at the Scala in Milan on the night of 1 May 1924. The enthusiasm of the audience was unprecedented and surpassed the famous premieres of Verdi's *Otello* and *Falstaff.* The price of the seats, very high, reached fantastic figures at the hands of the ticket speculators. The box office receipts reached a million. Some eighty critics from Europe and America attended the opera. Absolute silence concerning the plans of the production whetted the curiosity of the public." (Alberto de Angelis, *Dizionario dei musicisti,* 1928, Appendix, p. 38)

4 MAY 1924

The *Sixth Symphony,* op. 23, in E-flat minor, in four movements, by Nicolas MIASKOVSKY, is performed for the first time in Moscow, Golovanov conducting.

(Composed between April 1921 and 10 August 1922; orchestration completed 3 July 1923. These dates are communicated by the composer. Date of the performance from Moscow daily, *Izvestia,* of 4 May 1924. Fleisher's Catalogue gives correct day and month, but wrong year, 1925)

"Despite my instinctively correct ideological orientation, the absence of a theoretically fortified and rational world-outlook created in me some sort of an intelligentsia-like neurotic and sacrificial conception of the Revolution; it was naturally reflected in the embryo of my *Sixth Symphony*. The first stimulus was provided by accidental hearing of the French revolutionary songs *Ça ira* and *la Carmagnole* sung by a French artist. When, in 1922, the *Sixth Symphony* was planned, the themes of the songs rose in my mind. My somewhat chaotic state of mind at that time resulted in a conception, which appears so strange now, of a 'sacrificial victim,' 'parting of body and soul,' and some kind of apotheosis of glorified eternity at the end; but the ardor I felt during the composition of the symphony makes this work dear to me; even now it is apparently capable of stirring the listener, as far as I can judge from performances here and frequent hearings of the symphony abroad, particularly in America." (*Autobiographical Notes* by Miaskovsky in the Moscow monthly, *Sovietskaya Musica,* No. 6, 1936)

7 MAY 1924

A century has passed since the first performance in Vienna of Beethoven's *Ninth Symphony.*

8 MAY 1924

Pacific 231, "symphonic movement," by Arthur HONEGGER, is performed for the first time at a Koussevitzky concert in Paris.

9 MAY 1924

A month and two days before his sixtieth birthday, Richard STRAUSS conducts at the Vienna Staatsoper the first performance anywhere of his "Merry Viennese Ballet in Two Acts," *Schlagobers,* adventures in a Vienna pastry-shop, with chocolate-creams, ginger cookies, pralines, and other dainties dancing to pretty tunes, whipped-cream (in the shape of gauze-clad girls) waltzing, imported liquors tossing French, Polish, and Russian rhythms, and proletarian buns, Vienna batons, and matzoths staging a revolutionary upheaval.

12 MAY 1924

Hermann KRETZSCHMAR, German musical scholar, historian, analyst, and teacher of a generation of German musicologists, originator of the theory of hermeneutics as applied to music, in which musical materials—rhythms, intervals—are assumed to possess direct emotional significance, dies in Berlin at the age of seventy-six years, three months, and twenty-three days. (Hull's *Dictionary,* 1924, gives the erroneous date, 10 May 1924)

17 MAY 1924

Salade, "ballet chanté" by Darius MILHAUD, composed between 5 and 20 February 1924, is performed for the first time in the series "Soirées de Paris," at the Théâtre de la Cigale in Paris. (Date at end of printed score)

22 MAY 1924

Four weeks before his forty-second birthday, Igor STRAVINSKY plays at a Koussevitzky concert in Paris the first performance of his *Concerto* for piano, the rest of the program consisting of his works: *Le Sacre du Printemps,* the *Fire-Bird,* and excerpts from *Petrouchka.*

25 MAY 1924

The first concert of Latin-American music is broadcast from Washington under the auspices of the Pan American Union.

26 MAY 1924

Victor HERBERT, Irish-American creator of modern sentimental operetta, as expressive of the English-speaking people's musical mind as the Strauss waltzes are of the Viennese, dies in New York at the age of sixty-five years, three months, and twenty-five days.

"Victor Herbert, American composer and one of the world's first composers of light opera, died of heart-disease yesterday afternoon at 4
o'clock. He fell as he was walking up the stairs at 57 East Seventy-
Seventh Street to visit his physician, and in a few minutes he was dead.
"His health apparently had been of the best up to yesterday afternoon
an hour or two before his death. . . . After luncheon Mr. Herbert felt
ill. . . . Instead of sending for his doctor, he decided that he was well
enough to go there himself. He left his automobile unassisted, but
weighing over 250 pounds, the extra effort of walking up the stairs
caused him to collapse on the way." (New York *Times,* 27 May 1924.
Grove's *Dictionary* gives the erroneous date 27 May 1924)

29 MAY 1924

Alexandre GRETCHANINOV conducts in Kiev the first performance
of his hundredth opus, *Symphony in E Major.*

29 MAY 1924

They Are Seven, incantation for tenor, mixed chorus, and orchestra, by Serge PROKOFIEV, a score of extremely discordant texture
and powerful pulsing rhythm, is performed for the first time at a
Koussevitzky concert in Paris.

31 MAY 1924

The second Festival of the International Society for Contemporary
Music opens in Prague with the following orchestral program:

Introduction and Polonaise from SMETANA's unfinished *Prague Carni-
val;* a scholarly but attractive *Sinfonietta* by the Czech neo-romanticist,
Ottokar OSTRČIL; a cycle of songs by the Austrian, Carl HORWITZ, who
had the misfortune to lose his hearing, shortly before the Festival; *Concerto* for wind quintet and orchestra, a lively and neo-classical piece in
pan-diatonic texture, by the Casella disciple, Vittorio RIETI; the passionate and rich *Twenty-Second Psalm* by Ernest BLOCH; *Bacchanale*
from Florent SCHMITT's *Antoine et Cléopatre;* and Arthur HONEGGER's
locomotive piece, *Pacific 231.*

1 JUNE 1924

At the second orchestral concert of the ISCM Festival in Prague,
the following program is given:

Second Symphony by the Latvian-German neo-romanticist, Eduard ERD-
MANN, in a heavy contrapuntal and at times discordant style; Serge

PROKOFIEV's *Violin Concerto,* with Josef Szigeti as soloist; Igor STRAVINSKY's symphonic poem, *Chant du Rossignol;* and Arnold BAX's emotive, slightly Russianized *First Symphony.*

2 JUNE 1924

At the third orchestral concert of the ISCM Festival in Prague, the following program is given:

Ripening, an expansive, romantic symphonic poem by Dvořák's son-in-law, Josef SUK; *Violin Concerto* by Karol SZYMANOWSKI; *Impressioni dal Vero,* symphonic sketches in spring moods by Francesco MALIPIERO; and Albert ROUSSEL's austere and masterful *Symphony in B-flat.*

6 JUNE 1924

Erwartung, monodrama by Arnold SCHOENBERG, op. 17, in the form of an expressionist cantata, with a single acting part, is performed for the first time at the conclusion of the ISCM Festival in Prague.

8 JUNE 1924

The Orquesta Filarmonica of Havana, Cuba, opens its first season under the direction of Pedro SANJUÁN, Spanish conductor and composer. (Date from the original program)

9 JUNE 1924

Sprung ueber den Schatten, opera buffa in three acts and ten episodes by the not quite twenty-four-year-old Ernst KŘENEK, in an amalgamated neo-classical and constructivist style, encompassing all forms, from passacaglia to fox-trot, with the story written by the composer himself and featuring crooks, detectives, and charlatans, is produced at the Frankfort Opera House.

15 JUNE 1924

Mercure, ballet by Erik SATIE, with scenery and costumes by Picasso, is produced in the series "Soirées de Paris," at the Théâtre Cigale in Paris.

20 JUNE 1924

Le Train Bleu, "danced operetta" dealing with the doings of gigolos and "poules" at a fashionable beach, with an easy-going, melodious, and harmonious score by Darius MILHAUD, is produced in Paris at the Théâtre des Champs-Élysées.

23 JUNE 1924

Cecil SHARP, British collector of folk song and dance, dies in London in his sixty-fifth year.

(The *Encyclopaedia Britannica* and Hull's *Dictionary* give the wrong date, 22 June. An obituary printed in the London *Times* of 24 June says in part, "We regret to announce that Mr. Cecil James Sharp, the well-known collector of folk song and dance died yesterday [that is, 23 June] morning, after a short illness [cancer]." Cecil Sharp's biography by Fox-Strangways, 1933, corroborates the date in stating that Cecil Sharp died on the eve of Midsummer Day, in the early morning)

1 JULY 1924

Nicolas OBOUHOV, thirty-two-year-old Russian expatriate, completes in Paris the full score of his magnum opus, *Le Livre de Vie,* some 2,000 pages long, in the composer's own notation of twelve independent tones, Do-Lo-Re-Te-Mi-Fa-Ra-Sol-Tu-La-Bi-Si, and with expression marks in red ink symbolical of the blood shed in the Russian Revolution.

"Nicolas Obouhow m'a fait entendre des fragments du *Livre de Vie;* j'ai été frappé par la force pathétique géniale, à vrai dire, de cette oeuvre singulière. Sans doute l'idée conductrice en est bien loin des miennes, aussi bien que la mystique russe peut l'être du sensualisme français, mais je ne dois tenir compte ici que des qualités musicales qui sont d'une profondeur et d'une élévation des plus rares." (From Maurice Ravel's letter to the author)

14 JULY 1924

Hugh the Drover, or Love in the Stocks, "romantic ballad-opera" in two acts by VAUGHAN WILLIAMS, to the story of a boxing match, is produced in London.

20 JULY 1924

The Gesellschaft der Musikfreunde zu Donaueschingen presents in the course of the fourth Festival of chamber music the first public performance of Arnold SCHOENBERG's opus 24, the significant *Serenade* for violin, cello, clarinet, bass clarinet, mandolin, guitar, and deep voice, the first work in which the twelve-tone system is firmly established, the themes being built on twelve non-repeated notes, the form remaining that of the classical suite:

(1) *March;* (2) *Minuet;* (3) *Variations;* (4) *Sonnet* of Petrarch (in which the row of 12 tones appears in the voice as a melody, in the accompaniment as motifs, in the harmony as complete chords); (5) *Tanzszene;* (6) *Lied ohne Worte;* (7) *Finale,* a modified recapitulation of the introductory March.

22 JULY 1924

The Bayreuth Festival, the first after an interruption of ten years, opens with the production of *Die Meistersinger.*

27 JULY 1924

Ferruccio BUSONI, romantic Italian composer, pianist, editor, teacher, and writer, dies in Berlin, his second home, at the age of fifty-eight years, three months, and twenty-six days.

"At the time of Busoni's death and for some years previously so many unfounded rumors were in circulation as to his alleged intemperance that it is necessary to give a medical account of his last illness on the authority of his physician, Dr. Hans Meyer of Berlin. It was commonly reported in Switzerland that Busoni was taken home every night from the station restaurant at Zurich in a state of complete intoxication. Directly after his death Italian papers asserted that he had died of *delirium tremens* in an inebriates' home. It cannot be too emphatically stated that these stories were utterly untrue.

"Busoni was Italian by birth and breeding; he was naturally brought up from infancy to regard wine as his normal beverage. He was always fond of wine and appreciated wines of fine quality, but he never drank to excess at any time of his life. The disease of which Busoni died was chronic inflammation of the kidneys together with chronic inflammation of the muscles of the heart. It was of long standing and probably due to some accidental injury received much earlier in life." (Edward J. Dent, *Ferruccio Busoni,* London, 1933)

6 AUGUST 1924

At the first concert of the Supplementary Festival of the International Society for Contemporary Music at Salzburg, the following program is given:

Arnold Bax's *Viola Sonata;* Ildebrando Pizzetti's *Cello Sonata;* Heinrich Kaminski's *Drei Geistliche Lieder* for voice, clarinet, and violin, in the stylized ecclesiastical modes; *Frauentanz* for soprano, viola, flute, clarinet, horn, and bassoon, by the German constructivist composer, Kurt Weill; *Songs* by the Viennese composer, Ernst Kanitz; pre-war *Lieder* by Ladislav Vycpálek; the *String Quartet No. 4,* contrapuntal with a vengeance, by the just twenty-four-year-old Ernst Křenek.

7 AUGUST 1924

At the second concert of the ISCM Festival at Salzburg, the following program is given:

Septet for flute, oboe, clarinet, horn, double-bass, and piano by Willem Pijper, Dutch musician whose music glides on the confines of polytonality and atonality; *The Curlew,* song by Philip Heseltine, under the nom de plume of Peter Warlock; *On Wenlock Edge,* song with string-quartet accompaniment by Vaughan Williams; *Sonata* for cello and violin by Zoltán Kodály; a song by the Russian, Alexander Shenshin; and *String Trio* by Paul Hindemith.

8 AUGUST 1924

At the third concert of the ISCM Festival at Salzburg, the following program is given:

String Quartet, subtitled *Stornelli e Ballate,* by Francesco Malipiero; Erik Satie's *Socrate,* symphonic drama in three parts, to dialogues of Plato; *Four Pieces* for string quartet by Erwin Schulhoff; a hedonistic *Sonata* for clarinet and bassoon by Francis Poulenc; *Twelve Etudes* for piano by Karol Szymanowski; *Sonata* for cello by John Ireland; and *Gasellen* for baritone, flute, oboe, bass-clarinet, trumpet, drums, and piano by Othmar Schoeck.

9 AUGUST 1924

At the fourth concert of the ISCM Festival at Salzburg, the following program is given:

String Quartet by the French-born Catalan composer, Philipp Jarnach, highly contrapuntal and logically developed from homunculus-like mo-

tifs; post-romantic piano pieces by Boleslav VOMÁČKA, Karl Boleslav
JIRÁK, and Francis POULENC; *Catalogues des Fleurs* for voice and piano
by Darius MILHAUD; *Short Suite* for seven instruments by Egon WEL-
LESZ, a revival of the ancient suite in a pan-diatonic guise; *Songs* by
CASTELNUOVO-TEDESCO; and Igor STRAVINSKY's *Octet.*

22 AUGUST 1924

J. M. Dent & Sons of London publish *A Dictionary of Modern
Music and Musicians* under the general editorship of Arthur
Eaglefield HULL, with national sub-editors of all European countries, as well as America, Asia, and Australia; a volume of 560
pages, unique in its purpose and generally intelligent in execution,
despite the unjustifiable number of errors of fact, omissions, over-
sights, and printer's errors. (Exact date of publication obtained
by the author from the publishers)

27 AUGUST 1924

After six weeks of work, Alfredo CASELLA completes in Rome the
composition of his "choreographic comedy in one act," *La Giara,*
in an idiom of his "third style," based on horizontal and vertical
quartal-quintal harmony, in clear unchromaticized modality. (Date
at end of printed score)

4 SEPTEMBER 1924

A century has passed since the birth at Ansfelden, in Upper Austria, of Anton BRUCKNER.

13 SEPTEMBER 1924

Friends and disciples of Arnold SCHOENBERG publish a dedicatory
volume of 342 pages for his fiftieth birthday, containing articles
by Anton VON WEBERN, Alban BERG, and Paul BEKKER, and testi-
monials from Alfredo CASELLA, Francesco MALIPIERO, also samples
of abusive newspaper articles published without comment. On
the same day Universal Edition opens in Vienna an Arnold
Schoenberg-Bibliothek fuer Moderne Musik, placing at students'

disposal a number of modern scores otherwise inaccessible or too expensive; and, in the evening, SCHOENBERG's *Quintet* for flute, oboe, clarinet, bassoon, and horn, op. 26, written in the strictest twelve-tone code, and in an equally strict sonata form, is performed for the first time anywhere in Vienna.

(Grove's *Dictionary* gives the erroneous date of 16 September 1924 for the first performance of the *Quintet*)

10 OCTOBER 1924

Two and a half months after his fiftieth birthday, Serge KOUS-SEVITZKY leads in Boston his first concert as conductor of the Boston Symphony Orchestra.

"Crowded Hall Greets Koussevitzky as 44th Season Opens—The 44th season of the Boston Symphony Orchestra began yesterday afternoon in Symphony Hall. Mr. Koussevitzky conducted for the first time in the United States. . . . When Mr. Nikisch succeeded Mr. Gericke, he said after the first rehearsal, delighted by the technical proficiency and euphony of the Boston Orchestra, 'All I have to do now is to poeticize.' . . . Mr. Monteux left a superb instrument, the work of his own creation for Mr. Koussevitzky to play upon." (From Philip Hale's review in the Boston *Herald*, 11 October 1924)

"Four-fold Comes New Conductor to Boston Stage—The Quality and the Rank of Mr. Koussevitzky—Master of Line, Color, Tone, and Characterization in Music—The new conductor somewhat belied report oral, textual, pictorial. He is in the flower of middle years; but no lingering aura of youth seems to gild them; while to one pair of eyes he was less romantic presence than twentieth century musician in the unglamored practice of his profession. As he approaches or leaves the stand, his step is quick; his carriage erect; his manner serene; his tailor admirable. Gravely and simply he receives applause; likes not to tarry between numbers. . . . Otherwise Mr. Koussevitzky's gesture takes character from the music in hand. In an ancient Concerto, it curves the line and evens the accents. In Scriabin's 'Poem of Ecstasy' it is like the leap of the conductor's to the composer's intensities and fires. Then does Mr. Koussevitzky ply that characteristic gesture of ingathering arm for outpouring orchestra. Then does he visibly mould great crescendoes. Then does his figure rise and draw tense until the whole force of his being has launched the tonal thunderbolt. Koussevitzky Superbus, as the old Romans might have written; but Koussevitzky passioning for his music—not for himself." (H. T. Parker in Boston *Evening Transcript*, 11 October 1924)

14 OCTOBER 1924

Arnold Schoenberg's drama with music, *Die Glueckliche Hand,*
op. 18, is brought to performance in Vienna, nearly eleven years
after completion of the score. (*See* 18 November 1913)

16 OCTOBER 1924

Zwingburg, one-act opera by Ernst Křenek, is produced at Frankfort.

2 NOVEMBER 1924

Darius Milhaud completes the composition, begun 22 September
1924, of *Les Malheurs d'Orphée,* opera in three short acts, patterned after Italian opera in separate numbers, in a dissonant
neo-classical idiom.

4 NOVEMBER 1924

Gabriel Fauré, French composer of the transition period, creator
of the symbolist school of composition in archaizing modal harmony with an implied literary program, dies in Paris, in his
eightieth year.

(Grove, Hull, Riemann, Moser, Baker, the *Encyclopaedia Britannica,*
and other dictionaries and encyclopedias give the erroneous date, 13
May 1845, of Fauré's birth, instead of 12 May. Alfred Bruneau in his
La Vie et les oeuvres de Gabriel Fauré, Paris, 1925, says emphatically:
"Gabriel-Urbain Fauré vint au monde le 12 mai 1845—et non le 13,
comme on le croit généralement." Koechlin in his *Gabriel Fauré,* Paris,
1927, also gives 12 May)

6 NOVEMBER 1924

Stravinsky's *Concerto* for piano and orchestra is published by the
Édition Russe de Musique.

11 NOVEMBER 1924

Serge Liapunov, Russian composer, epigone of the Balakirev-
Glazunov school of composition, dies in Paris nineteen days before
reaching his sixty-fifth birthday.

16 NOVEMBER 1924

Liška Bystrouška (The Alert Fox), animal opera by Leoš JANÁČEK, utilizing onomatopoeic musical material, in the manner of a pantheistic fairy ballet with philosophic implications, is performed for the first time at Brno. (Date from Daniel Muller, *Janáček*, Paris, 1930)

29 NOVEMBER 1924

Giacomo PUCCINI, Italian composer, innovator of operatic craft in the direction of enlightened verismo, and modernizer of the harmonic idiom incorporating the whole-tone scale, parallel progression of massed chords, and individualized instrumentation, dies in Brussels of cancer of the throat twenty-four days before his sixty-sixth birthday.

(Baker gives Puccini's birth date as 23 Dec. 1858, stating that he had it in an autograph letter from Puccini himself; yet Riemann, 1929, states emphatically, "22 Dez. nicht 23." Arnaldo Fraccaroli in *La Vita di Giacomo Puccini*, Milan, 1925, gives Baker's date 23 Dec. 1858, but the Italian dictionaries and encyclopedias give 22 Dec. 1858. Grove, 1927, and *Encyclopaedia Britannica* give an altogether wrong date, 22 June 1858)

29 NOVEMBER 1924

Relâche, "instantaneous ballet," last work of Erik SATIE, scenario and scenery by Picabia, cinematography by René Clair, is produced at the Ballet Suédois in Paris, seven months before Satie's death.

"The scenery of the second act bore such inscriptions as *Erik Satie est le plus grand musicien du monde* or *Si vous n'êtes pas contents, on vous vendra des sifflets pour deux ronds.*" (R. D. Templier, *Erik Satie*, Paris, 1932)

14 DECEMBER 1924

Bernardino Molinari conducts at the Augusteo in Rome the first performance anywhere of *Pines of Rome,* symphonic poem by Ottorino RESPIGHI, in four divisions:

(1) *Pines of the Villa Borghese,* children's gathering place, portrayed in the orchestra by running passages, zigzagging harps in counter glissandos

over the entire range, *saltando* strings, *tremolo* in the winds, stamping brass and percussion; (2) *Pines by a Catacomb,* in a meditative Hypodorian mode, in slow tempo, changing to the shouting ecstasy of self-assertion; (3) *Pines of the Janiculum,* poetic and crepuscular, making use for the first time in orchestral music of a phonograph record reproducing the song of an actual nightingale; (4) *Pines of the Appian Way,* a rousing march, starting from measured beats in the deep orchestral register and mounting to an extraordinary climax of the entire orchestra.

1925

1 JANUARY 1925

Fritz KLEIN-LINZ publishes in *Die Musik* an article, *Frontiers of the Semitone World,* as part of his theory of "musical statics," suggesting new ways of combining tones and intervals, and giving the formula for a "mother-chord" (*Mutterakkord*), which includes all twelve different tones and all eleven different intervals, in the following invertible row, in semitones: 11, 8, 9, 10, 7, 6, 5, 2, 3, 4, 1. (This row is not the only matrix; the combination 3, 7, 4, 2, 1, 6, 9, 5, 8, 10, 11, also gives an invertible mother-chord)

8 JANUARY 1925

Igor STRAVINSKY makes his first appearance in America as conductor with the Philharmonic Orchestra of New York, in a program of his works.

11 JANUARY 1925

Symphony for organ and orchestra by Aaron COPLAND, his first orchestral work, is performed for the first time in New York, Walter Damrosch conducting and Nadia Boulanger, Copland's teacher during his apprenticeship period at Fontainebleau, playing the organ part.

23 JANUARY 1925

Igor STRAVINSKY makes his first American appearance as pianist, in a performance of his neo-classical *Piano Concerto,* with the Boston Symphony Orchestra, Serge Koussevitzky conducting.

31 JANUARY 1925

Three Ballet Pieces by Jacques IBERT (*Flower Girls,* graceful music in frictional harmonies and typical jogging rhythms; *Creoles,* in a lazy tango-like see-saw time; *Chatterboxes,* in quick quintuple time) are performed for the first time at a Pasdeloup concert in Paris, Rhené-Baton conducting.

31 JANUARY 1925

Zéphyr et Flore, the first ballet by the twenty-one-year-old Russian composer, Vladimir DUKELSKY, commissioned by Diaghilev, and written in the form of an old suite of dances, in a free diatonic style, receives its first semi-private hearing at the Palais de Monaco, at Monte Carlo.

8 FEBRUARY 1925

Two symphonies by Nicolas MIASKOVSKY, the *Fourth,* in E minor, subjective and brooding, but with an optimistic conclusion, and the *Seventh,* more extravert, particularly in the introduction and in the second movement, are performed for the first time in Moscow, at a concert conducted by Constantin Saradjev.

(The *Fourth Symphony* was composed intermittently with the *Fifth Symphony,* between 20 December 1917 and 5 April 1918; the *Seventh* from 10 to 20 August 1922, and orchestrated in December 1922. These dates are communicated by the composer)

17 FEBRUARY 1925

Leo ORNSTEIN, the twenty-nine-year-old Russian-born American modernist, bold experimenter in ultra-musical sonorities, plays the first performance of his meta-pianistic *Concerto,* at a concert in New York of the Philadelphia Symphony Orchestra, Stokowski conducting.

20 FEBRUARY 1925

Marco Enrico Bossi, Italian composer of many operas, oratorios, and much chamber music, all in post-Verdian traditional style, dies on board the S.S. *De Grasse* on his trip home from America, in his sixty-fourth year.

(Date from the following statement in a letter to the author from the Compagnie Générale Transatlantique: "Marco Enrico Bossi, de nationalité italienne, né le 25 Avril 1861, est décédé à bord du *De Grasse* le 20 Février 1925, à 13 heures (G.M.T.)." Grove gives the erroneous date, 24 February 1925)

22 FEBRUARY 1925

Gagliarda of a Merry Plague, one-act chamber opera by Lazare Saminsky, written in an aggressive discordant idiom, marking a change of style from his early Russian-Hebraic romanticism, is produced in New York at a concert of the League of Composers, on the same program with *Daniel Jazz,* for tenor voice and seven instruments, by Louis Gruenberg.

11 MARCH 1925

Johan Andréas Hallén, Nestor of Swedish music, propagandist of Wagner's music in Sweden, and himself a composer of operas in a grand Wagnerian manner, dies in Stockholm in his seventy-ninth year. (Moser's *Musik-Lexikon* gives the erroneous date, 11 December 1925)

21 MARCH 1925

L'Enfant et les Sortilèges, "lyric fantasy" by Maurice Ravel to Colette's story of maltreated toys coming to life to wreak vengeance on the naughty child, with an orchestra that includes whistles, wood-blocks, and cheese-graters, is produced at Monte Carlo.

30 MARCH 1925

Trio for violin, viola, and cello in four movements by Jef Golyscheff, Russian expatriate composer, named after their dynamic values, (1) *Mezzo Forte,* (2) *Fortissimo,* (3) *Piano,* (4) *Pianissimo,* and written according to the strict system of twelve non-repeated tones, developed independently from Schoenberg's (*12 Tondauer-Musik* in the composer's terminology), is published by Lienau in Berlin, over a year after the publication, on 1 March 1924, of of Schoenberg's twelve-tone *Serenade,* op. 24.

(Herbert Eimert in his *Atonale Musiklehre,* Leipzig, 1924, states that Golyscheff used his twelve-tone system of composition as early as 1914, but gives no documentary proof or accurate dates)

1 APRIL 1925

Three Soviet composers, Alexander Davidenko, Boris Schechter, and Victor Bieliy, organize in Moscow a society for encouragement of proletarian composers, under the abbreviated name Procoll (Production Collective of Composers).

30 APRIL 1925

At the Eastman School of Music, Howard Hanson conducts the first of a series of concerts devoted to performances of music by American composers.

1 MAY 1925

The musical saw, an instrument capable of producing continuous pitch of about three octaves' range, is demonstrated at the Gervex Booth at the Paris Fair.

15 MAY 1925

The third Festival of the International Society for Contemporary Music opens in Prague with the following program:

Ferruccio Busoni's *Serenade*, performed to commemorate his death nine and a half months before; *Five Pieces for Chamber Orchestra,* op. 33, by Ernst Toch, modal and lyrical in slow movement, boisterous and chromatic in rapid passages, finely rhythmed and diaphanously instrumentated; *Tempo di Ballo,* brilliant pastiche by Roland-Manuel; Suite from *Noah's Ark,* vivacious animal ballet by Vittorio Rieti; *Demon,* brooding allegorical symphonic poem by the Czech composer, Rudolf Karel; and *Concerto Grosso,* for double orchestra, in an expansive neoclassical idiom, by Heinrich Kaminski.

17 MAY 1925

At the second orchestral concert of the ISCM Festival in Prague, the following program is given:

A neo-classical, complex, and dissonant *Partita* by the Viennese Schoenberg disciple, Paul A. PISK; *Six Pieces for Orchestra*, with introvert titles, such as "Seul," "Prière Sceptique," "Sans Espoir," etc., by the Hungarian Georg KÓSA; formalistic *Concertino* for piano and orchestra by the Serbian-born Rudolf RETI; the neo-romantic, Straussian poem, *Les Adieux*, for soloists and orchestra by Fidelio FINKE; *Half-Time*, descriptive of a football game by the Czech contrapuntist, Bohuslav MARTINU; and the *Pastoral Symphony* by VAUGHAN WILLIAMS.

19 MAY 1925

At the third orchestral concert of the ISCM Festival in Prague, the following program is given:

Concerto Grosso by Ernst KŘENEK, in a bold neo-Bachian style; *Variations Without a Theme* by Francesco MALIPIERO; *Toman et la Nymphe*, orthodox piece of programmatic music by Vítězslav NOVÁK; two movements from the neo-contrapuntal suite, *Protée,* by Darius MILHAUD; and the racial and rhythmic *Suite of Dances* by Béla BARTÓK.

21 MAY 1925

Nine months and three weeks after Ferruccio BUSONI's death, his unfinished opera, *Doktor Faust,* is performed for the first time at the Dresden Opera, with the score completed by Busoni's pupil and disciple, the French-born Catalan, Philipp JARNACH.

23 MAY 1925

Concertino for piano and orchestra by Arthur HONEGGER, containing samples of jazz in the Finale, is performed for the first time at a Koussevitzky concert in Paris with Andrée Vaurabourg, Honegger's fiancée, at the piano.

27 MAY 1925

Alexandre TANSMAN, Polish-Parisian composer, plays at a Koussevitzky concert in Paris the first performance of his *Piano Concerto,* abounding in cumulative harmonies of polytonal implications and making use of stylized Polish folk songs, within orthodox sonata form.

1 JUNE 1925

Ernest BLOCH conducts at the Cleveland School of Music the first performance of his *Concerto Grosso* for piano obbligato and string orchestra, composed as an instruction piece for his students.

6 JUNE 1925

The *Second Symphony* of Serge PROKOFIEV is performed for the first time at a Koussevitzky concert in Paris.

11 JUNE 1925

Arthur HONEGGER conducts his incidental music to *Judith,* a Biblical drama by René Morax, at the first performance of that play, at Mézières, Switzerland.

14 JUNE 1925

At the Kiel Music Festival, Alexander LÁSZLÓ plays his music on a specially constructed "color pianoforte" (*Farblichtklaviers*), designed to show parallelism between sound and light, pitch and color.

17 JUNE 1925

At the Théâtre de la Gaîté-Lyrique in Paris, Diaghilev's Ballet Russe gives the first performance of *Les Matelots,* ballet by the twenty-six-year-old Georges AURIC in the following scenes: *Betrothal* (horn-pipe time); *Solitude* (meditative 4/4); *Return* (scherzo and sensuous waltz); *Temptation* (horn-pipe again); *Finale* (gigue).

22 JUNE 1925

Francesco MALIPIERO completes at Asolo his music drama in three parts, *Filomela e l'Infatuato.*

1 JULY 1925

La Naissance de la Lyre, opera-ballet in a subtly archaizing idiom by Albert Roussel, to the book of the French Hellenist, Théodore Reinach, is produced at the Paris Opéra.

1 JULY 1925

Erik Satie, surrealist French composer, whose life, like his art, was a staged series of wistfully poetic epigrams, dies at the Saint-Joseph Hospital in Paris at the age of fifty-nine years and one and a half months.

(Date communicated to the author in the following letter from the director of the Saint-Joseph Hospital in Paris, dated 20 May 1937: "Monsieur Erik Satie qui est entré dans notre Établissement le 20 Février 1925 y est décédé le 1er Juillet de la même année." Templier's monograph on Satie, Paris, 1932, the French Riemann *Dictionary*, 1931, and the *Enciclopedia italiana* give the correct date. Grove, Riemann, German edition, and Moser give the wrong date, 2 July)

4 JULY 1925

The Académie des Beaux-Arts under the presidency of Paul Chabas, and with the assistance of the "perpetual secretary," Ch. M. Widor, adjudges the first Grand Prix de Rome to Louis Fourestier for the prize cantata, *La Mort d'Adonis.* (*Le Temps,* 5 July 1925)

23 JULY 1925

Alban Berg completes the score of his *Kammer-Konzert* for piano, violin, and thirteen wind instruments, written in the strict twelve-tone system. (The piano score completed on Alban Berg's fortieth birthday, 9 February 1925)

20 AUGUST 1925

Alfredo Casella completes at Champoluc Valdostando the composition, begun in Rome on 20 June 1924, of his *Partita* for piano and orchestra in three parts: *Sinfonia,* with the exposition built on a powerful C pedal; *Passacaglia,* in twelve variations; and *Burlesca,* a gay Neapolitan dance tune. (Date at end of printed score)

24 AUGUST 1925

The first Festival of Old Music, founded by Arnold DOLMETSCH, opens at Haslemere, England.

3 SEPTEMBER 1925

The supplementary chamber music Festival of the International Society for Contemporary Music opens in Venice with the following program of chamber music:

String Quartet by Erwin SCHULHOFF; *L'Horizon Chimérique,* a song cycle by Gabriel FAURÉ, played in commemoration of his death ten months before; *Nocturnal Impression of Peking* and *Korean Sketch* for chamber orchestra by the fifty-five-year-old American oriental traveler and collector of Chinese instruments, Henry EICHHEIM; *Jazz Band* for violin and piano, a naïve attempt at American syncopation by the Austrian, Wilhelm GROSZ; *Songs* by the Brazilian, Hector VILLA-LOBOS; and *Concerto,* op. 36, No. 1, for pianoforte and twelve instruments by Paul HINDEMITH in four movements, with the eighth-note and quarter-note as metrical invariants.

4 SEPTEMBER 1925

At the second concert of the ISCM Festival at Venice, the following program of chamber music is given:

Sonata for piano and cello by the Catalan cellist, Gaspar CASSADÓ; the Scriabinesque *Piano Sonata* by Samuel FEINBERG; *Sonata* for violin alone by Zoltán SZEKELY; *Five Pieces* for string quartet by Max BUTTING; *Songs* by Ladislav VYCPÁLEK; *Duo* for violin and cello by the Schoenberg disciple, Hanns EISLER; and *String Quartet* by Leoš JANÁČEK.

5 SEPTEMBER 1925

At the third concert of the ISCM Festival at Venice, the following program of chamber music is given:

String Quartet, op. 16 by the whilom *Wunderkind,* now twenty-eight and one half years old, Erich KORNGOLD; *Two Movements* for two flutes, clarinet, and bassoon by Jacques IBERT; *Sonata* for cello and piano by Arthur HONEGGER; *Joueurs de Flûte,* four pieces for flute and piano by Albert ROUSSEL; *Tzigane* for violin and piano by Maurice RAVEL; and *Sonata* for piano, flute, oboe, and bassoon by Vittorio RIETI.

7 SEPTEMBER 1925

At the fourth concert of the ISCM Festival at Venice, the following program of chamber music is given:

String Quartet by Mario LABROCA, disciple of Respighi and Malipiero; *Piano Sonata,* composed in a quite advanced style by the celebrated pianist, Arthur SCHNABEL; *Merciless Beauty,* three rondels for tenor and strings by VAUGHAN WILLIAMS; and *Serenade* for clarinet, bass clarinet, mandolin, guitar, violin, viola, cello, and men's voices by Arnold SCHOENBERG, op. 24, the historical work which establishes within the frame of an old suite the laws of the twelve-tone system.

8 SEPTEMBER 1925

At the fifth and last concert of the ISCM Festival at Venice the following program of chamber music is given:

String Quartet, op. 31, by Karol SZYMANOWSKI; *I e Stagioni Italiche,* song cycle by Francesco MALIPIERO; *Angels* by the almost fifty-year-old Vermonter, Carl RUGGLES, for six trumpets in a crushing unison, soon bifurcated into frictional intervals; Igor STRAVINSKY's *Piano Sonata,* his second neo-classical work (the *Piano Concerto* being the first), performed by Stravinsky himself; and *Daniel Jazz* for Negro voice, string quartet, trumpet, piano, and percussion by the Russian-born American composer, Louis GRUENBERG.

16 SEPTEMBER 1925

No, No, Nanette, musical comedy by Vincent YOUMANS, featuring the song *Tea for Two,* is produced at the Globe Theatre in New York.

16 SEPTEMBER 1925

Leo FALL, Austrian composer of operettas, among them the celebrated *Dollar-Princess,* dies in Vienna in his fifty-third year.

18 SEPTEMBER 1925

The Deutsche Oper reopens in Berlin with a performance of *Die Meistersinger,* conducted by Bruno Walter.

7 OCTOBER 1925

The *First Choral Symphony* by Gustav HOLST is performed for the first time by the London Symphony Orchestra.

25 OCTOBER 1925

The centenary of the birth of Johann STRAUSS is observed by a gala performance of his operetta, *Zigeunerbaron,* in Vienna.

28 OCTOBER 1925

The first Festival of Chamber Music, under the auspices of the Elizabeth Sprague Coolidge Foundation, opens at the Library of Congress in Washington, with a program containing BACH'S *Choral Prelude;* first public performances of *Canticle of the Sun* for voice and chamber orchestra, by Charles Martin LOEFFLER, and *Rhapsodic Fantasy* for chamber orchestra by Frederick A. STOCK, both works specially written for the Festival; *Two Assyrian Prayers* by Frederick JACOBI for voice and chamber orchestra; and HAN-DEL's organ *Concerto.*

(The second, third, fourth, and fifth programs included: on 29 October, in the morning, BEETHOVEN's quartet music; 29 October, afternoon, English music; 30 October, morning, Italian music; 30 October, evening, the first performance anywhere of Howard HANSON's *String Quartet,* also DEBUSSY's *String Quartet,* and SCHUBERT's *Quintet)*

29 OCTOBER 1925

La Giara and *Partita* by Alfredo CASELLA are performed for the first time anywhere by the New York Philharmonic Orchestra, Willem Mengelberg conducting.

6 NOVEMBER 1925

The *Concerto Accademico* in D minor for violin and string orchestra by VAUGHAN WILLIAMS is performed for the first time in London.

19 NOVEMBER 1925

The Royal Philharmonic Society presents its gold medal to Edward ELGAR at a concert of his own works conducted by him.

21 NOVEMBER 1925

La Fête chez la Bergère by Georges MIGOT, orchestral version of his *Three Epigrams,* each one a triptych, with a middle section a "crab" imitation of the principal melodic subject, is performed for the first time at a Pasdeloup concert in Paris.

28 NOVEMBER 1925

Music for the Theatre, suite for chamber orchestra and piano by Aaron COPLAND in five contrasting movements (*Prologue; Dance; Interlude; Burlesque; Epilogue*), couched in austere classical form and making use of jazz technique in the *Dance,* is performed for the first time at a concert of the League of Composers in New York, conducted by Serge Koussevitzky, to whom the score is dedicated.

3 DECEMBER 1925

George GERSHWIN plays the solo part of the first performance anywhere of his *Piano Concerto in F,* with the New York Symphony Orchestra.

6 DECEMBER 1925

The Academy of Santa Cecilia in Rome confers honorary membership on Arnold SCHOENBERG and Manuel DE FALLA. (Date obtained by the author from the Academy)

8 DECEMBER 1925

The sixtieth birthday of Jan SIBELIUS is celebrated in Finland by the award of the highest order of the realm and the largest state pension ever given to a private Finnish citizen, and also by the publication of a special dedicatory volume, *Aulos.*

11 DECEMBER 1925

Barabau, one-act ballet with chorus by Vittorio RIETI, commissioned by Diaghilev, is performed for the first time at Diaghilev's Ballet Russe in London.

11· DECEMBER 1925

Carl NIELSEN, the sixty-year-old neo-romantic Danish composer, conducts in Copenhagen the first performance of his sixth and last symphony, *Symfonia Simplice.*

14 DECEMBER 1925

After one hundred and thirty-seven rehearsals, the State Opera in Berlin produces Alban Berg's expressionist opera *Wozzeck,* scored for an ensemble of orchestras—one in the pit, one on the stage, and including a whole military band, a restaurant orchestra of high-pitched fiddles, accordion, bombardon, and an upright piano out of tune, as well as a chamber orchestra composed of the same instruments as Schoenberg's *Kammersymphonie*—and built as a magnified *Symphony-Suite,* including: a complete ancient suite of dances (*Prelude, Sarabande, Gigue, Gavotte, Air,* and the *Prelude* in "crab"); a *Rhapsody-Fantasy* on three chords; a *Passacaglia* with twenty-nine variations; a *Symphony* in five movements; *Six Inventions;* a set of *Variations* (on a pedal point, on a rhythm, on a six-note chord, on a tonality, and on a *moto perpetuo);* and a *Fugue*—all this intimately bound with the action on the stage.

"Opera of Noisy Dissonance Gets Composer Called a Genius.—The State Opera at Berlin has become a storm center of musical discussion through its production of the opera *Wozzeck* by Alban Berg, which breaks all records for dissonance and cacophony. The composer is acclaimed by critics in terms varying from 'musical mountebank' to 'inspired genius.' Not content with having the orchestra attack the ears with noises so inharmonious that some listeners aver they suffer physical pain, the composer prescribes that the tin-pan piano used in one of the scenes must be out of tune and that the singers must sing off key." (Associated Press dispatch in the New York *Times,* 15 December 1925)

"It is entirely natural that the acoustic, optical, and spiritual impression of *Wozzeck* should have been a surprise for musical cognoscenti. Though a piece of formal music-making, its effect was made more by its content than by its form. It hazards the hardest, the most piercing combinations, but convinces by the instinctive perception with which it grasps spiritual values." (Adolf Weissman in *Die Musik,* January 1926)

"Berg is a creator of sounds which terrify the ear accustomed to all manner of excesses, a mixer of colors which betray a limitless imagination. Dissonance has been elevated to the principle of this music, forms resolve into continuity, colors coalesce, and there results something which, by its very oscillation and its nebulous atmosphere, is probably exactly the music which justifies the transformation of *Wozzeck* into an opera." (Max Marschalk in *Die Vossische Zeitung,* 15 December 1925)

"Wozzeck stabs his mistress. A throbbing drum-roll, a twofold breath-taking orchestral crescendo on a single note from *ppp* to *fff*. . . . A dance of drunken street-girls and tramps who with outstretched hands pursue the murderer. The listener attains an hypnotic state in which he believes the walls of the theater about to crash down upon him." (Erich Steinhardt in *Der Auftakt,* January 1926)

"As I was leaving the State Opera, I had the sensation of having been not in a public theater but in an insane asylum. On the stage, in the orchestra, in the stalls,—plain madmen. . . . *Wozzeck* might have been the work of a Viennese Chinaman. For all these mass attacks and in-strumental assaults have nothing to do with European music and musi-cal evolution. The perpetrator of this work must have relied on the stupidity and charity of his fellow-men and abandoned himself for the rest to the mercy of God Almighty and the Universal Edition. . . . One may ask oneself seriously to what degree music may be a criminal occupation. We deal here, from a musical viewpoint, with a capital offense." (Paul Zschorlich in *Deutsche Zeitung,* 15 December 1925)

"Berg's opera, born of tragic consciousness of reality, and grown out of expressionist transformation of living tissue, reflecting the hopelessness of human suffering in the clutches of the monstrously inhuman capital-ist culture, reveals the helplessness of the Western-European petty-bourgeois intelligentsia before oncoming fascistization, and demonstrates the crisis not only in the individual consciousness of the Western-European bourgeois composer, but in Western-European musical cul-ture in general." (Boris Asafiev, in the *Sovietskaya Musica,* 1934)

1926

1 JANUARY 1926

The Association of Contemporary Music is founded in Leningrad.

"The society believes that: (1) during the transitional period of So-cialist upbuilding, contemporary music can play a socially organizing role along with other forms of art; (2) our music should utilize all the technical and formal attainments of modern Western musical art in order to achieve its fullest expression and greatest mastery; . . . (3) absorption of Western cultural music must be effected by means of critical selection of useful products. Purely esthetical, decadent tendencies are strongly opposed by the Society. . . . With these reservations contemporary music may become a powerful factor of Socialist culture, and a medium of self-expression of the class responsible for that culture." (From the Declaration of the Society reprinted in a brochure by S. Korev, *Disposition of Class Forces on the Music Front*, Moscow, 1930)

8 JANUARY 1926

Émile PALADILHE, French composer who began his career as a child prodigy, won the Prix de Rome at sixteen, and remained true to musical orthodoxy in the Meyerbeer tradition, dies in Paris in his eighty-second year.

11 JANUARY 1926

Igor STRAVINSKY begins work on his opera-oratorio *Oedipus Rex*.

"Stravinsky conceived the idea of writing a work sung in a 'petrified' language, which has gone out of usage, such as Latin. He asked Jean Cocteau to draft an opera-oratorio on any subject of ancient tragedy. Stravinsky himself proposed Oedipus-Rex. In fact the words were not of any importance to Stravinsky; all he needed was the possibility of repeating them at will no matter how idiotic they might sound. . . . And just as the text possessed value as sonority only, the actors, too, were to be motionless like columns, disappearing and appearing mechanically; the chorus was to be placed behind a bas-relief with only the face visible; a narrator was to explain the action. On 11 January 1926, Stravinsky put down the first chord and its ternary time, under the word *serva;* on the next day, he began the solo of Oedipus, and between the 13th to 15th wrote the entire opening chorus." (A. Schaeffner, *Strawinsky,* Paris, 1931)

15 JANUARY 1926

Enrico TOSELLI, Italian composer of the celebrated *Serenade,* and some operatic music, dies in Florence in his forty-third year.

(The date 15 January 1925 in the Appendix to Alberto de Angelis' *Dizionario*, 1928, is a misprint)

21 JANUARY 1926

Walter STRARAM conducts in Paris the opening concert of his orchestra established as Orchestre Straram.

24 JANUARY 1926

The Proletarian Collective of Soviet Musicians (Procoll) rejects the proposal of the Leningrad Association of Contemporary Music to merge into one group serving both the ends of proletarian culture and modern musical culture.

30 JANUARY 1926

The Paris Prefect of Police forbids the playing of the *Marseillaise* in a jazzed-up form in dance halls.

6 FEBRUARY 1926

Quodlibet, eine Unterhaltungsmusik, a modern revival of early polyphonic "what-you-will," by Kurt WEILL, protagonist of easy music in acrid dressing, is performed for the first time at Coburg.

11 FEBRUARY 1926

The newly organized Circle of New Music in Leningrad gives its first semi-private concert-conference, with the writer-composer, Igor GLEBOV-ASAFIEV, as President of the Circle. (Date from *Five Years of New Music,* Leningrad, 1928)

13 FEBRUARY 1926

Arthur HONEGGER conducts at the Monte Carlo Opera House the first performance of his three-act opera, *Judith,* subtitled "opéra sérieux" and expanded from his incidental music to a play of that name by André Morax, produced nine months and two days before.

19 FEBRUARY 1926

Skyscrapers, "a ballet of modern American life," by John Alden CARPENTER, is produced by the Metropolitan Opera in New York, nine days before the composer's fiftieth birthday.

13 MARCH 1926

The League of Composers presents in New York a demonstration of quarter-tone, eighth-tone, and sixteenth-tone music played on

special instruments by the fifty-one-year-old Mexican composer
and theorist, Julián CARRILLO.

13 MARCH 1926

Saturday's Child, opera-oratorio in a slightly modernized idiom, by
Emerson WHITHORNE, is given for the first time in New York under
the auspices of the League of Composers.

13–14 MARCH 1926

Glavpolitprosvet (Political Bureau of the Department of Education of the Soviet Republic) votes to advise composers not to follow the folklore pattern in composition of choral works designed
for mass singing.

21 MARCH 1926

Foules, symphonic poem by the twenty-six-year-old Pierre Octave
FERROUD, is performed for the first time at the Pasdeloup concerts
in Paris.

26 MARCH 1926

Franz KNEISEL, Rumanian-born violinist, organizer in 1885 of the
Kneisel Quartet, dies in New York two months after his sixty-first
birthday.

27 MARCH 1926

The Protagonist, by Kurt WEILL, a one-act opera of the "surrealist"
type, conjugating the fantastic with the all-too-realistic in its stage
action, and rhythmic squareness with harmonic compositeness, is
produced at the Dresden State Opera.

9 APRIL 1926

Amériques, by Edgar VARÈSE, a symphonic poem, the title of which
indicates, by its characteristic plural, an abstract approach to all
possible new worlds open to an inquiring mind, written for a very
large orchestra in free dissonant counterpoint, and making use of
rigid mottoes as themes in place of developed motifs, is performed
for the first time anywhere by the Philadelphia Symphony Orchestra, Leopold STOKOWSKI conducting.

25 APRIL 1926

Nearly one and a half years after PUCCINI's death, his unfinished opera *Turandot* is produced for the first time at La Scala, Milan, with TOSCANINI conducting.

"Puccini loved no opera so much as this *Turandot* which was born out of the composer's ardent desire to detach himself from the so-called 'bourgeois drama.' " (G. Adami, librettist of *Turandot*)

27 APRIL 1926

Façade, suite for orchestra, after poems by Edith Sitwell, by the barely twenty-four-year-old white hope of English music, William WALTON, is performed for the first time at the Chenil Galeries in London.

"How much I enjoyed the fun may be estimated from the fact that I— a critic—actually not only stayed to the end but added my voice and my umbrella to the clamor for encores. . . . All I knew of this young man's was a horrible quartet of his that was given at the Royal College three or four years ago. On the strength of this I take leave to dislike intensely Mr. Walton's serious music—if indeed, that quartet was serious and was music, both of which I doubt. But as a musical joker he is a jewel of the first water. . . . Here is obviously a humorous musical talent of the first order; nothing so good in the mock-serious line of music has been heard for a long time as the *Waltz*, the *Polka*, the *Yodelling Song*. . . . At its best, *Façade* was the jolliest entertainment of the season." (Ernest Newman in the London *Times*)

4 MAY 1926

Romeo and Juliet, the first ballet by the not quite twenty-one-year-old English composer, Constant LAMBERT, is given for the first time by DIAGHILEV's Ballet Russe at Monte Carlo.

5 MAY 1926

The Société Musicale Indépendante in Paris presents a concert of chamber music by American composers, students of Nadia Boulanger:

Aaron COPLAND (violin pieces and "As It Fell Upon a Day" for soprano, flute, and clarinet); Virgil THOMSON (Sonate d'Église-Choral, Tango-Fugue for wind instruments plus viola); G. H. ELWELL (piano pieces);

George ANTHEIL (string quartet); Theodore CHANLER (violin sonata); and piano sonata by the neo-classical Bostonian, Walter PISTON.

7 MAY 1926

Les Malheurs d'Orphée, mock-serious opera in three short acts by Darius MILHAUD, with Orpheus described as "having long hair and wearing a sheepskin cloak" and Eurydice as a "jeune Bohémienne," is performed for the first time anywhere at the Théâtre Royal de la Monnaie in Brussels.

12 MAY 1926

The *First Symphony,* by the nineteen-and-a-half-year-old Soviet composer, Dmitri SHOSTAKOVITCH, written in a neo-academic style vitalized by rhythmic invention, is performed in Leningrad, for the first time, on the same program with *March of the Orient* by the scientific composer, Joseph SCHILLINGER, and a symphonic cantata, *The Twelve,* after the poem of Block by Julia WEISSBERG, wife of Rimsky-Korsakov's son, Andrey.

15 MAY 1926

The Colonne Orchestra in Paris, conducted by Gabriel PIERNÉ, gives the first performances of works by the Greek composer, Petro PETRIDIS, in a neo-modal vein: *Danse de Kleftes, Prélude de Zemfira, Berceuse,* and *Le Petit Vaisseau.*

23 MAY 1926

The *Eighth Symphony,* in A major, by Nicolas MIASKOVSKY is performed for the first time in Moscow, Saradjev conducting.

(The *Eighth Symphony* was completed 1 September 1924, the orchestration finished 29 June 1925. These dates are communicated by the composer)

"In the design of my Eighth Symphony I received a true stimulus towards the objective mood I was seeking. First I conceived the idea of the Finale on a theme which I thought was a song about Razin, and which I decided to develop in juxtaposition with a number of other Volga Songs, and connect with the fate of despoiled peasantry. But the song proved unyielding, the original form did not develop, and only elements of it remained in the character of the first movement (steppe refrain), in the subject matter of the second movement (two Russian songs about a drake and a duck), in the third movement (on a Bashkir song about a deserted soldier's wife), and in the impetuous driving Finale, with a tragic end." (Miaskovsky in *Sovietskaya Musica,* 1936, No. 6)

29 MAY 1926

La Pastorale, constructivist ballet featuring movie stars, telegraph clerks, etc., by the twenty-seven-year-old French composer, Georges AURIC, is produced by DIAGHILEV's Ballet Russe in Paris. (Date in printed score)

3 JUNE 1926

Serge KOUSSEVITZKY conducts in Paris the first performance of the *Preface to the Book of Life,* by the Russian expatriate, Nicolas OBOUHOV, a religious work for orchestra, two pianos, and four soloists, making use of hushing, shrieking, and hissing sounds as well as straight singing.

5 JUNE 1926

A century has passed since the death in London of Carl Maria VON WEBER.

(Moser, 1935, gives the incorrect date of Weber's death, 5 July 1826. The following extract from the obituary in the London *Times* of 6 June 1826, establishes the correct date beyond any doubt: "DEATH OF M. VON WEBER. M. von Weber, the distinguished composer of *Der Freischütz, Euryanthe, Oberon,* and other musical works of the first order, died yesterday morning at the house of Sir George Smart, in Great Portland Street, where he has resided since his arrival from the continent. . . . A friend and countryman who paid him constant attention supped with him, and left him at 11 o'clock on the night before his death, apparently cheerful, and in no immediate danger. He was found in a lifeless state at seven o'clock yesterday morning, and though medical aid was promptly resorted to, it was too late, the vital spark being quite extinct.")

18 JUNE 1926

The fourth annual Festival of the International Society of Contemporary Music opens at Zurich, presenting at its first concert

two modern oratorios: KODÁLY's *Psalmus Hungaricus* and HO-
NEGGER's *King David.*

19 JUNE 1926

Two months and four days before his twenty-sixth birthday, Ernst
KŘENEK completes the text and music of his jazz opera *Jonny
Spielt Auf,* portraying in dissonant counterpoint adventures of
various modern personages: a Negro fiddler, in amatory misce-
genation with a chambermaid of a Parisian hotel; romantic composer Max; long-haired virtuoso violinist, Daniello, owner of an
instrument coveted and won (by theft) by Jonny; a diva of easy
morals and accessible emotions; an American manager, and others, against a background of railroad terminals, police stations,
glaciers, hotels, radio loudspeakers, etc., with a triumphant
apotheosis of Jonny, standing on the North Pole of a revolving
globe and dancing jazz.

19 JUNE 1926

At the Zurich Festival (ISCM) the following program of chamber
music is presented:

The neo-classical string *Trio* by the Swiss composer, Walther GEISER;
SCHOENBERG's *Wind Quintet* (hard on untutored ears because of the un-
familiar twelve-tone system, here attaining its logical peak); and *String
Quartet,* with some authentic Indian themes, by the American composer, Frederick JACOBI.

21 JUNE 1926

At the Zurich Festival (ISCM) two choral works are presented:

Le Miroir de Jésus, a work of religious fervor with aesthetic harmonies
by the French composer, André CAPLET, who had died fourteen months
before, and the neo-medieval *Litanies* for a chorus of boys, singing in
their low register and accompanied by two trumpets, two harps, and
percussion, by the Czech composer, Felix PETYREK.

22 JUNE 1926

At the Zurich Festival (ISCM) the following orchestral program
is presented:

Portsmouth Point, pictorial overture, full of musical brine, by William WALTON; *Concerto for Orchestra,* op. 38, by Paul HINDEMITH, in a neo-classic idiom with modern rhythm; Alfredo CASELLA's neo-Bachian *Partita;* the long and grandiose (in an obsolescent manner) *Fifth Symphony* by the Swiss composer-pianist, Ernst LEVY; *Foules,* symphonic poem written in a healthy non-impressionist style by the French composer, P. O. FERROUD; and *Danse de la Sorcière,* theater music in attractive harmonies built on fourths by the Parisian-Polish composer, Alexandre TANSMAN.

22 JUNE 1926

Hermann SUTER, Swiss conductor and composer of post-romantic near-Brahmsian music, dies at Basel, in his fifty-seventh year.

23 JUNE 1926

At the Zurich Festival (ISCM) the following program of chamber music is presented:

Piano Sonata by the Russian post-romanticist, Nicolas MIASKOVSKY; the Ravelesque *Septet* for soprano, flute, piano, and strings, by the Parisian-Belgian Arthur HOERÉE; *Five Orchestral Pieces* by the Austrian, Anton von WEBERN, containing but $12 + 14 + 11\frac{1}{2} + 6\frac{1}{3} + 32 = 75\frac{5}{6}$ bars of music, scored for the most uncommon instrumental constituency, and written in pointillist manner, each instrument playing alone, and very little, so that the changing timbre assumes melodic value (Schoenberg says about this "timbre-melody": "subtle, indeed, are the senses that can differentiate here; fine is the mind that is capable of finding pleasure in things so recondite"); *Concerto for Violin and Wood-Wind Instruments* in a frivolous pseudo-classical vein by the apostle of German *Gebrauchsmusik,* Kurt WEILL; and *Pastorale* and *March* in a spirited dissonant fashion by the Czech composer, Hans KRASA.

6 AUGUST 1926

The first "hundred per cent sound" picture, *Don Juan,* issued by the Vitaphone Company and featuring Henry HADLEY, American composer of moderate tendencies, conducting the New York Philharmonic Orchestra, is shown for the first time in New York City.

(An invitation performance was given at the Warner Theatre, New York City, on 5 August 1926. See J. N. Kane, *Famous First Facts,* New York, 1933)

21 AUGUST 1926

Albert ROUSSEL completes the score of his first work in a neo-classical form, devoid of all programmatic implications, and entitled, simply, *Suite en Fa,* in three movements, Prelude, Sarabande, and Gigue.

24 AUGUST 1926

Serge PROKOFIEV completes at Samoreau, near Paris, the first version of his *Overture for Seventeen Instruments,* op. 42. (Date communicated by the composer)

29 AUGUST 1926

Six days after his twenty-sixth birthday, Ernst KŘENEK finishes the text and music of his political opera, the first part of a trilogy, *The Dictator.* (Date at end of manuscript)

29 AUGUST 1926

Five weeks after his forty-third birthday, Alfredo CASELLA completes in Rome his neo-modal *Concerto Romano* in three movements for organ and orchestra, begun on 12 July 1926.

1 SEPTEMBER 1926

The first number of the *Bollettino bibliografico musicale,* a monthly publication of musical bibliography, is issued in Milan.

3 SEPTEMBER 1926

Deems TAYLOR, American composer of operas in a general Wagnerian style, completes, in Paris, the composition of his first opera, *The King's Henchman.* (Date at end of printed score)

7 SEPTEMBER 1926

Three days after his thirty-fourth birthday, Darius MILHAUD completes, in Paris, the composition, begun on 26 August 1926, of his ballet, *Le Pauvre Matelot,* "complaint in three acts," in an unsophisticated neo-Gluckian manner. (Date at end of printed score)

11 SEPTEMBER 1926

Ernst EULENBURG, German music publisher, who, on 1 February 1874, began the publication of the Eulenburg series of miniature orchestra scores, dies in Leipzig in his seventy-ninth year.

26 SEPTEMBER 1926

Reinhold GLIÈRE, Russian composer of symphonic poems based on Russian folklore, conducts in Moscow the first performance of his opera, *Zaporozhtzi* (the Dnieper Cossacks), based on Ukrainian folklore.

1 OCTOBER 1926

Henry T. FINCK, American music critic, inveterate hater of Brahms and champion of neo-romantic music, particularly Grieg and MacDowell, author of a journalistically witty book on Richard Strauss (treated as a professional cacophonist), dies at Rumford Falls, Maine, at 6:30 p.m., nine days after his seventy-second birthday.

(Date and hour communicated by Rumford Hospital. Riemann gives erroneous date 29 September 1926, and also places Rumford Falls in Minnesota)

16 OCTOBER 1926

Háry János, opera by Zoltán KODÁLY, based on Hungarian folk-song material, is produced at the Royal Opera in Budapest.

25 OCTOBER 1926

The New Music Society of California, founded by Henry Cowell, gives its first concert in San Francisco.

28 OCTOBER 1926

The *Third Symphony,* by the thirty-two-year-old Dutch modernist Willem PIJPER, is performed for the first time by the Concertgebouw Orchestra at Amsterdam, MONTEUX conducting.

29 OCTOBER 1926

Tzigane, symphonic poem by the Rumanian composer Filip LAZAR, is performed for the first time anywhere by KOUSSEVITZKY, to whom the score is dedicated, and the Boston Symphony Orchestra.

1 NOVEMBER 1926

Der Kraemerspiegel, self-satirizing pastiche written by Richard Strauss, containing a medley of motifs from his entire symphonic and operatic output, is played for the first time, at a semi-private entertainment in Berlin.

3 NOVEMBER 1926

Alfredo Casella completes, in Rome, the composition of *Scarlattiana,* a "divertissement on the music of Domenico Scarlatti for piano and small orchestra."

4 NOVEMBER 1926

André Wormser, French Prix de Rome winner in 1875 and composer of operas—among them one, *Le Fils Perdu,* written for vocalization without words—dies in his native Paris three days after reaching seventy-five years of age.

5 NOVEMBER 1926

Eighteen days before his fiftieth birthday Manuel de Falla conducts in Barcelona the first performance of his neo-classical *Concerto* for harpsichord, flute, oboe, clarinet, violin, and cello, with Wanda Landowska, for whom the work was written, at the harpsichord.

9 NOVEMBER 1926

Cardillac, stylized neo-Handelian opera by Paul Hindemith to Hoffmann's tale about a customer-slaying goldsmith, marking a turning point away from Wagner's endless melody and action and back to Handel's and Verdi's theatrical convention, is produced at the Dresden Opera, a week before the composer's thirty-first birthday.

10 NOVEMBER 1926

Nearly two hundred and eighty-three years after the death of

Claudio MONTEVERDI, the first volume of his complete works is issued in Italy, under the editorship of Francesco MALIPIERO.

10 NOVEMBER 1926

Two Pieces for Orchestra, by the Russian composer, Leonid POLO-VINKIN, written in a simple post-romantic manner with extra-tonal ornamentation, are performed for the first time by the Leningrad Philharmonic Orchestra.

13 NOVEMBER 1926

Symphony in F Minor, first major work by the twenty-four-and-a-half-year-old Soviet composer Vissarion SHEBALIN, and *Revolutionary Episode,* symphonic poem by the twenty-eight-year-old Soviet composer, Lev KNIPPER, are performed for the first time by the Leningrad Philharmonic Orchestra, Constantin SARADJEV conducting.

27 NOVEMBER 1926

Creation, a Negro sermon for baritone voice and eight instruments, of spiritual frenzy with near-jazz exultation, by the Russian-born American composer, Louis GRUENBERG, is performed for the first time at a concert of the League of Composers in New York.

29 NOVEMBER 1926

The municipal authorities in Prague order the production of Alban BERG's opera, *Wozzeck,* stopped at the National Theatre, in view of demonstrations and protests requiring police intervention during the performance.

3 DECEMBER 1926

The Triumph of Neptune, "English pantomime in ten tableaux," book by Sacheverell Sitwell, music by Lord BERNERS, is produced by DIAGHILEV's Ballet Russe at the Lyceum Theatre in London.

8 DECEMBER 1926

A Witch of Salem, American opera by Charles Wakefield CAD-
MAN, is produced by the Chicago Opera Company.

18 DECEMBER 1926

The Makropulos Affair, the last opera by the seventy-two-and-a-
half-year-old "Moussorgsky of Bohemia," Leoš JANÁČEK, to Capek's
fantastic play of that name, is produced at the National Theatre of
Brno.

26 DECEMBER 1926

Walter DAMROSCH conducts in New York the world première of
SIBELIUS' tone-poem, *Tapiola* (from Tapio, the forest god of Finnish mythology), composed between March and May 1926, in a
daringly iterative style which attains dynamic effects of great
power by sheer cumulative drive, as in the fifty-six-bar string crescendo before the coda.

29 DECEMBER 1926

The department of Oriental Music at the Turkish National Conservatory is abolished and teaching of Turkish music is stopped
in the public schools, as part of systematic Europeanization of
Turkey by Mustafa Kemal Pasha.

1927

9 JANUARY 1927

Houston Stewart CHAMBERLAIN, English Wagnerite naturalized
in Germany (and married to Cosima Wagner's daughter), who
expanded into a full-fledged doctrine Wagner's philosophical
views on the superiority of the German race and the inferiority of
the Hebrews, dies in his spiritual birthplace, Bayreuth, at seventy-

one, only six years and three weeks before the advent of the millennium he awaited in Germany.

16 JANUARY 1927

Fonctionnaire MCMXII: Inaction en Musique, a musical satire by Florent SCHMITT, is performed for the first time by the Lamoureux Orchestra in Paris.

21 JANUARY 1927

Suite in F, first neo-classical work by Albert ROUSSEL, is performed for the first time anywhere, by the Boston Symphony Orchestra, under the direction of Serge KOUSSEVITZKY, to whom the score is dedicated.

22 JANUARY 1927

Scarlattiana, divertissement on themes of Domenico Scarlatti, by Alfredo CASELLA, for piano and thirty-two instruments, is performed for the first time by the New York Philharmonic Orchestra, conducted by KLEMPERER, with the composer at the piano.

28 JANUARY 1927

Aaron COPLAND, twenty-six-year-old Brooklyn-born composer, plays the solo part with the Boston Symphony Orchestra, Serge KOUSSEVITZKY conducting, in the first performance of his *Concerto for Piano and Orchestra* in two connected movements, the second of which is a bold essay in jazz rhythms within the form of a sonata allegro.

29 JANUARY 1927

The second movement of the *Fourth Symphony* by the New England composer, Charles E. IVES, employing polymetrical notation, ad libitum instrumental passages, counterpoint of two orchestral units, and the freest use of dissonance within essentially simple tonality, is performed for the first time at a Pro Musica concert in New York, Eugene GOOSSENS conducting.

31 JANUARY 1927

A month and three days after his thirtieth birthday, Roger SES-SIONS finishes in Florence, Italy, his *Symphony in E Minor* in three movements: *Giusto,* with an eighth-note constant as rhythmic unit through changing meter, in the manner of an orchestral toc-cata; *Largo,* in ternary form, opening in the Locrian mode; and *Allegro Vivace,* E major, in syncopated polyphony, bravura fashion. (Date at end of manuscript)

6 FEBRUARY 1927

The Leningrad Association of Contemporary Music at a general meeting votes to merge with the Circle of New Music in Leningrad. (*Five Years of New Music,* Leningrad, 1927)

11 FEBRUARY 1927

Jonny Spielt Auf, jazz opera by Ernst KŘENEK, receives its world première at the Leipzig Opera.

17 FEBRUARY 1927

The King's Henchman, the first opera by Deems TAYLOR, is produced by the Metropolitan Opera in New York.

17 FEBRUARY 1927

Ernst KŘENEK completes his opera in one act, *The Mysterious Kingdom,* second in his politico-satiric trilogy.

21 FEBRUARY 1927

Le Poirier de Misère, first opera by the French neo-romantic composer, Marcel DELANNOY, is produced at the Opéra-Comique in Paris.

25 FEBRUARY 1927

Vetrate di Chiesa, by Ottorino RESPIGHI, a work based on ecclesiastical modes and calculated to convey the atmosphere of a medieval church, as in the stained glass windows, is performed for the first time anywhere by the Boston Symphony Orchestra, conducted by KOUSSEVITZKY.

4 MARCH 1927

Concertino by the fifty-two-year-old Mexican theorist, Julián CARRILLO, with special instruments to produce fractional tones (quarter-tones, eighth-tones, and sixteenth-tones), is performed for the first time anywhere by the Philadelphia Orchestra, Leopold STOKOWSKI conducting.

12 MARCH 1927

Eugene GOOSSENS conducts, at Rochester, New York, the first performance of his *Rhythmic Dance,* a one-hundred-and-nineteen-bar-long animated scherzo in duple time.

14 MARCH 1927

Igor STRAVINSKY completes in Paris the vocal score of *Oedipus Rex,* opera-oratorio in two acts, to the libretto of Jean COCTEAU, after Sophocles, translated into Latin by J. Danielou, the music following separate scenes in the manner of medieval mystery plays, in stark stripped harmonies, suggesting stylized and ornamented faux-bourdon.

18 MARCH 1927

Two weeks before his fifty-fourth birthday, RACHMANINOV plays in Philadelphia, with the Philadelphia Orchestra, STOKOWSKI conducting, the first performance of his *Fourth Concerto* for piano and orchestra, in three movements: characteristically rhapsodic, in minor or major harmonic modes.

18 MARCH 1927

Symphony in A Minor, in four contrasted movements, by Alexandre TANSMAN, classical in form, tonal in essence, with characteristic bitonal excursions of the chord type C, G, E, B-flat, E-flat, G-flat, is performed for the first time anywhere by the Boston Symphony Orchestra, conducted by KOUSSEVITZKY, to whom the score is dedicated.

26 MARCH 1927

A century has passed since the death of BEETHOVEN in Vienna.

31 MARCH 1927

Lilacs, poem for orchestra (after Amy Lowell) by Edward Bur-lingame HILL, written in a free modulatory, impressionist, but not over-chromaticized style, is performed for the first time by the Boston Symphony Orchestra in Cambridge, KOUSSEVITZKY conducting.

5 APRIL 1927

John the Soldier, opera by Clement KORTCHMAREV, is produced at the State Experimental Opera House in Moscow.

6 APRIL 1927

Impressions de Music-Hall, Ballet à l'Américaine by Gabriel PIERNÉ, is produced at the Paris Opéra.

8 APRIL 1927

STOKOWSKI conducts in Philadelphia the first performance of *Arcana,* symphonic poem by the French-American, Edgar Varèse, scored for a large orchestra "in fives" (including five choirs of percussion) and built on a scale of absolute sonorities, wherein harmony (dissonant, with the exception of two bars of pure C-G fifth), but ultimately reducible to the overtone series, rhythm (entirely free but precise, within a variable meter), timbre (extended to the extremes of instrumental registers), and melody (at wide-spaced intervals, and only approximately twelve-tonal) are parts of one higher-dimensioned musical continuum.

10 APRIL 1927

Shortly after his return from Europe, George ANTHEIL gives a concert of his works at Carnegie Hall, New York, with a program including a *Jazz Symphony,* a *String Quartet,* a *Sonata* for violin, piano, and a drum, and *Ballet Mécanique* for ten pianos.

"Antheil Art Bursts on Startled Ears—First Performance of Ballet Mécanique in This Country Draws Varied Response—Hisses, Cheers Greet

Him—Concatenation of Anvils, Bells, Horns, Buzzsaws Deafens Some, Pleases Others." (Headlines in the New York *Times*)

"I personally consider that the Ballet Mécanique was important in one particular and that it was conceived in a new form, that form specifically being the filling out of a certain time canvas with musical abstractions and sound material composed and contrasted against one another with the thought of time values rather than tonal values. . . . In the Ballet Mécanique I used time as Picasso might have used the blank spaces of his canvas. I did not hesitate, for instance, to repeat one measure one hundred times; I did not hesitate to have absolutely nothing on my pianola rolls for sixty-two bars; I did not hesitate to ring a bell against a certain given section of time or indeed to do whatever I pleased to do with this time canvas as long as each part of it stood up against the other. My ideas were the most abstract of the abstract. Still I was totally misunderstood by the morons who listened to the Ballet Mécanique in 1926. Although I had very clearly published exactly what I had intended way back in 1923 and 1924 in many advance-guard magazines, practically all of the dumb-bells in New York went to listen to the Ballet Mécanique expecting to see me grind out pictures of the machine age! Some imbeciles expected to see a kind of Buck Rogers fantasy of the future. I was totally misunderstood, so deeply misunderstood that I have never made any attempt whatever of explanation what I was after in America. I realized that it was hopeless. Today, almost ten years afterwards, I am making my first explanation to you." (From Antheil's letter to the author, dated 21 July 1936)

15 APRIL 1927

Flivver 10,000,000, a Joyous Epic; Fantasy for Orchestra Inspired by the Familiar Legend "The Ten Millionth Ford Is Now Serving Its Owner" by Frederick CONVERSE, written in a free, humorous, dissonance-touched style, is performed for the first time anywhere by the Boston Symphony Orchestra, KOUSSEVITZKY conducting.

17 APRIL 1927

The International Composers' Guild presents in New York the first performance of the *Concerto* for harp and seven wind instruments by the French-American, Carlos SALZEDO, with the composer performing the solo part which includes new harp sonorities (percussion effects on the frame, novel harmonics, etc.).

22 APRIL 1927

The *Symphony in E Minor* by Roger SESSIONS is performed for the first time by the Boston Symphony Orchestra, under the direction of KOUSSEVITZKY.

27 APRIL 1927

Schwanda, the Bagpipe Player, first light opera by the Czech composer, Jaromir WEINBERGER, is produced at the National Theatre in Prague.

28 APRIL 1927

The first Jazz Band to appear in Russia is presented at a concert of miscellaneous jazz music in Leningrad. (Date from original program)

5 MAY 1927

Madonna Imperia, lyric comedy in one act by Franco ALFANO, written in free diatonic and occasionally pan-diatonic style, is produced at Turin.

10 MAY 1927

A month and a week before his forty-fifth birthday, STRAVINSKY completes, at four o'clock in the morning, the instrumentation of his oratorio, *Oedipus Rex.*

30 MAY 1927

Eighteen days before his forty-fifth birthday, Igor STRAVINSKY conducts in Paris, at DIAGHILEV's Ballet Russe, the first performance in concert form of his opera-oratorio, *Oedipus Rex.*

7 JUNE 1927

Pas d'Acier, ballet of Soviet heavy industry by Serge PROKOFIEV, is produced at the DIAGHILEV Ballet Russe in Paris.

14 JUNE 1927

Red Poppy, ballet of the Revolution by Reinhold GLIÈRE, is produced at the Moscow State Opera.

14 JUNE 1927

At Kassel, Ernst Křenek finishes the third of his chamber-trilogy, the one-act "burlesque operetta," *Heavyweight, or Pride of the Nation,* its subject drawn from a diplomat's assertion that "a prize-fighter or channel swimmer does more for the glory of the German nation than all the artists and scientists put together."

15 JUNE 1927

Pedro Sanjuán, Spanish composer and conductor of the Philharmonic Orchestra in Havana, Cuba, conducts there the first performance of his forceful, melodious, and strongly Hispanic suite *Castilla.*

26 JUNE 1927

Bach's *Kunst der Fuge,* arranged for orchestra by the young and brilliant Swiss musician, mathematician, and orientalist, Wolfgang Graeser, is performed for the first time in Leipzig, less than a year before Graeser's tragic suicide.

29 JUNE 1927

Doktor Faust, posthumous opera of Busoni, is performed at the closing night of the Frankfort Opera season, also serving to open the fifth Festival of the International Society for Contemporary Music.

30 JUNE 1927

The first concert of the fifth Festival of the International Society for Contemporary Music at Frankfort presents the following program of chamber music:

String Quartet, in very effective and personal polyphony by the Soviet composer, Alexandre Mossolov; the subtle post-impressionist *Sonata for Flute and Piano* by the Dutch composer, Willem Pijper; *Concertino* for piano, two violins, viola, clarinet, horn, and bassoon, by the almost seventy-three-year-old Czech composer, Leoš Janáček; and *The Dances of King David,* a Hebrew rhapsody in a stylized neo-paleographical style by the Italian, Mario Castelnuovo-Tedesco.

1 JULY 1927

The second concert of the Frankfort Festival presents the following program of orchestral music:

The Dance in Place Congo, symphonic poem based on Creole rhythms and tunes, by the New Englander, Henry F. GILBERT; the *Seventh Suite,* a piece of absolute music based on a system of mutually exclusive tropes, by the Viennese methodologist, Josef Matthias HAUER; *Concerto* for piano and orchestra in a highly dynamic, strongly national style, by Béla BARTÓK; and the *Fifth Symphony* by the Danish composer, Carl NIELSEN.

2 JULY 1927

The third concert of the Frankfort Festival presents the following program of chamber music:

The third *String Quartet* by the Swiss neo-polyphonist, Conrad BECK; *String Quartet* by the Russian-born neo-romanticist, Vladimir VOGEL; the logical, austere, and yet emotionally tense *Chamber Concerto* for piano, violin, and thirteen wind instruments by Alban BERG, based on the modified musical letters, in German notation, of the names of SCHOENBERG (A D S C H B E G for ArnolD SCHönBErG, where S = Es = E-Flat), WEBERN (A E B E for Anton wEBErn), and his own (A B A B E G for AlBAn BErG), and on their inversions (cancrizans and mirror), treated according to the twelve-tone system; and the neo-theological *Magnificat* by the German-born Heinrich KAMINSKI.

3 JULY 1927

The Lives and Memory of the Holy Brethren and Apostles to the Slavs, Cyril and Methodius, an oratorio a capella by the Croatian composer Božidar ŠIROLA, is performed at a morning concert of the Frankfort Festival; in the evening, an orchestral concert is given, presenting the following program:

A *Choregraphic Poem* in pleasant none-too-modern harmonies by the French composer, Claude DELVINCOURT; the *Canticle to the Sun of St. Francis* by the Parisian composer, Raymond PETIT; the dynamic and transcendently technical *Piano Concerto* by Ernst TOCH; and the academic *Second Symphony* by Emil AXMAN.

3 JULY 1927

Two days before her fiftieth birthday, Wanda LANDOWSKA inaugurates, at her summer home in Saint-Leu-la-Forêt, near Paris, a series of concerts of old music.

4 JULY 1927

The last concert of the Frankfort Festival presents the following program of chamber music:

Fourth String Quartet in a neo-Flemish contrapuntal style by the Dutch-born Bernard VAN DIEREN; *Sonatina* for flute, clarinet, and bassoon, by the Danish composer Joergen BENTZON, pupil of NIELSEN; the tuneful and attractive piano *Trio* by the Spaniard, Joaquin TURINA; *Psalm 139,* a capella, by the English composer, William WHITTAKER; the logical, in an atonal direction, *Sonata* for violin and piano by the Hungarian composer, Alexander JEMNITZ; and *Music for the Theatre* for chamber orchestra by Aaron COPLAND.

15 JULY 1927

La Revista de musica, a monthly, modeled after *La Revue musicale* of Paris, starts publication in Buenos Aires.

16 JULY 1927

STRAVINSKY starts composition of *Apollon Musagète,* noting down the motto-chord of Apollo's birth: C, F, B, D, F-sharp. (André Schaeffner, *Strawinsky,* Paris, 1931)

17 JULY 1927

Four very short chamber operas are produced at the Baden-Baden Festival of New Music:

Hin und Zurueck by Paul HINDEMITH, a "film sketch" in which the story is run backwards after the denouement (hence the title): the adulteress, killed by her husband, comes back to life, the attending physician backs out of the door, the husband pockets the revolver and the scene ends in status quo ante; *Mahagonny* by Kurt WEILL, a skit pretending to idealize degeneration of life in some country very like New York, set to music of jazzy accent similarly pretending to be ideal; *Die Prinzessin auf der Erbse,* a musical fairy tale by Ernst TOCH; and *Rape of Europa,* a condensed pseudo-classical one-act opera by Darius MILHAUD.

12 AUGUST 1927

Half a century has passed since the day Edison patented the phonograph.

27 AUGUST 1927

We, a symphonic poem by the American composer, James DUNN,
celebrating Lindbergh's transatlantic flight, is played in first performance at the New York Stadium.

8 SEPTEMBER 1927

Alfredo CASELLA completes, in Rome, the composition of his *Sonata* for violoncello and piano in two movements, each subdivided into two sections, *Preludio* plus *Bourrée* and *Largo* plus
Rondo, in the key of C major pan-diatonically treated, the seven
tones of the scale being freely superimposed on each other, the
bass determining the ultimate harmonic function. (Date at end
of score)

11 SEPTEMBER 1927

After two years of work, Ildebrando PIZZETTI completes, at L'Al-
pino, nine days before his forty-seventh birthday, the composition
of his opera, *Fra Gherardo.* (Date at end of score)

19 SEPTEMBER 1927

The *Third String Quartet* by Arnold SCHOENBERG, op. 30, based
on the system of twelve tones in free style (repetition of notes admitted in transitional or introductory passages), is performed for
the first time in public by the Kolisch String Quartet in Vienna,
six days after Schoenberg's fifty-third birthday.

20 SEPTEMBER 1927

The International Society for Musical Research is founded in
Basel, with the aim of resuming the activities of the International
Music Society, disrupted by the European war.

20 SEPTEMBER 1927

Edward Burlingame HILL completes in Cambridge, Massachusetts, the composition of his *First Symphony,* in B-flat, op. 34, in three movements. (Date communicated by the composer)

8 OCTOBER 1927

Richard STRAUSS completes at his country home in Garmisch, Bavaria, the score of *The Egyptian Helen,* opera in two acts, op. 75, written in his "higher level" style but in an idiom less complex than that of *Electra* or even *Salome.*

12 OCTOBER 1927

The Bund deutscher Komponisten is founded in Berlin.

15 OCTOBER 1927

New Music, a quarterly of modern American music, founded in California by Henry COWELL, composer and pioneer, publishes its first issue, the full score of *Men and Mountains,* "symphonic ensemble" in a poignantly atonal idiom by the Vermonter, Carl RUGGLES.

"*New Music* affords a means of publication of ultra-modern works, and also insures their distribution among its subscribers. It publishes works for orchestra, piano, voice, violin, chamber music, etc., specializing in the music of Americans, but not excluding occasional foreign works. It is not a profit-making plan, and any profits which may accrue will be equitably divided among the contributing composers." (From the publisher's statement)

30 OCTOBER 1927

Sergei VASSILENKO, Russian composer of stylized ethnological music, conducts in Leningrad the first performance of his *Chinese Suite,* op. 60, composed according to the pseudo-Chinese "black key" pentatonic system.

4 NOVEMBER 1927

The *Third Symphony* by the Russian-American, Lazare SAMINSKY, in free fluctuating tonality, is performed for the first time by the New York Symphony, Fritz BUSCH conducting.

5 NOVEMBER 1927

The Salle Pleyel, the largest concert-hall in Paris, is officially opened to the public.

6 NOVEMBER 1927

On the occasion of the tenth anniversary of the Proletarian Revolution, *Symphonic Movement,* musicorama of the years between the two revolutions 1905–1917, by the neo-romanticist, Michael GNIESSIN, and *Symphonic Dedication to October Revolution* by the twenty-one-year-old white hope of Soviet music, Dmitri SHOSTAKOVITCH, are performed for the first time anywhere at a concert of the Leningrad Philharmonic.

7 NOVEMBER 1927

In an open letter to the New York *Times,* Edgar VARÈSE announces the dissolution of the International Composers' Guild, founded by him in New York some six years before, as having accomplished its purpose of awakening interest in new music.

27 NOVEMBER 1927

Les Euménides, the last part of a musical setting to Aeschylus' *Orestes,* by Darius MILHAUD, is performed for the first time at Anvers.

7 DECEMBER 1927

Alfredo CASELLA completes in Rome the composition of his *Serenade for Five Instruments* (clarinet, bassoon, trumpet, violin, and cello), begun on 19 September, and written in six sections: a traditional *March* in buffo style; a *Minuet;* a *Nocturne* based on a stylized Neapolitan folk song with a *Minore* middle part; a *Gavotte* for the three wind instruments; a *Cavatina* for violin and cello, a *tour de force* of four-part writing for two instruments; and a brilliant *Tarantella.* (Manuscript date)

11 DECEMBER 1927

Francesco MALIPIERO completes at Asolo his oratorio *La Cena* (The Last Supper) in a neo-medieval style, with melos of quasi-

Gregorian simplicity, and polymodal harmony in gradual progressions.

22 DECEMBER 1927

Horizons, four western pieces for orchestra (1. *Westward;* 2. *The Lone Prairie*, which begins with the song, "The Dying Cowboy" for saxophone solo; 3. *The Old Chisholm Trail*, on a merry cowboy tune of that name, and a Dogie song; 4. *Canyons*) by the Idahoan Arthur SHEPHERD, written in broad rhapsodic fashion, is performed for the first time anywhere by the Cleveland Symphony Orchestra, the composer conducting.

22 DECEMBER 1927

Stowarzyszenie Mlosych Muzykow Polakow W Paryzu (Association of Young Polish Musicians in Paris) is founded by Felix LA-BUNSKI, Stanislaw CZAPSKI, Piotr PERKOWSKI, Stanislaw WIECHO-WICZ, and M. KONDRACKI. (Date from *Philarmonia*, organ of the Chopin Committee, published at Palma, Mallorca)

1928

1 JANUARY 1928

La Rassegna musicale, scholarly, informative Italian monthly, thoroughly modern in style and typography, begins publication in Turin, under the editorship of Guido GATTI.

8 JANUARY 1928

Demetri KIRIAC, Rumanian composer, conductor, and harmonizer of Rumanian folk songs (in thoroughly orthodox style), dies in his native Bucharest, in his sixty-second year.

16 JANUARY 1928

Angelo, Tyrant of Padua, "lyric drama" in five acts by the French operatic composer, Alfred BRUNEAU, now nearly seventy-one years old, is produced at the Opéra-Comique in Paris.

31 JANUARY 1928

Ol-Ol, opera after Andreyev's drama, *Days of Our Life,* by the Russian expatriate composer, Alexander TCHEREPNIN, son of the composer, Nicolas TCHEREPNIN, written in a moderately stylized manner, and in an idiom of some originality, is produced at Weimar.

12 FEBRUARY 1928

On the thirtieth birthday of Roy Harris, the League of Composers presents in New York the first American performance of his op. 2, *Concerto for Piano, Clarinet and String Quartet* in four contrasting movements: *Fantasia,* opening with a falling phrase of three notes, C, B, A-flat, establishing a major-minor mode, which gives way to a row of tritones, atonally and polytonally treated; *Vivace,* with an eighth-note minimal unit, in polyrhythmic counterpoint; *Andante,* thematically related to the major-minor phrase of the first movement; *Finale,* with a sixteenth-note minimal unit within changing sub-meters.

16 FEBRUARY 1928

More than fifty-eight years after MOUSSORGSKY completed the full score and instrumentation of *Boris Godunov* on 15 December 1869, old style, the opera is performed in Leningrad in its original orchestration and harmonies, without cuts or revisions.

18 FEBRUARY 1928

The Czar Allows Himself to be Photographed, satiric sketch by Kurt WEILL, with a fantastic surrealist story and light music liberally sprinkled with dissonance, is performed for the first time at Leipzig.

28 FEBRUARY 1928

The thereminovox, an apparatus for the electrical generation of sounds to follow the motion of the hand in space, is patented in

Washington by Leo Theremin, Russian inventor. (Date from the files of the U. S. Patent Office)

3 MARCH 1928

The Cuban government lifts its ban against the *bongo,* ritual drum used by the Negroes to "telegraph" messages of war through the jungle.

6 MARCH 1928

Serge PROKOFIEV completes in Paris the revised score of his opera, *The Gambler,* originally sketched in 1916.

11 MARCH 1928

Lied der Sturmkolonnen, Hitlerite hymn to the tune of the *Internationale,* is sung for the first time at Bernau, with a new set of words extolling the Nazis' fight for freedom, work, and bread. (*Die Musik,* December 1936, p. 174)

20 MARCH 1928

Chirurgie, one-act opera by the "French Hindemith," P. O. FERROUD, to Chekhov's story of painful dentistry, with music expressive of the action in a naturalistic Moussorgskyan style, is produced at the Monte Carlo Opera.

21 MARCH 1928

A group of conscientious objectors to modern music and jazz throw a stink bomb in the Budapest Opera Theatre during the Hungarian première of KŘENEK's *Jonny Spielt Auf.*

23 MARCH 1928

Symphonic Piece, by the Boston neo-classicist, Walter PISTON, written in a dissonantly contrapuntal "absolute idiom," is performed for the first time by the Boston Symphony Orchestra, KOUSSEVITZKY conducting, on the same program with the first performance of a similarly conceived but quite differently executed programless *Music for an Orchestra* by the Rumanian composer, Filip LAZAR.

27 MARCH 1928

Armand GIVELET, Vice-President of the Radio-Club of France, gives the first public demonstration of a heterodyne keyboard instrument capable of producing tones of a determined pitch as an improvement over Theremin's method of changing the pitch by the movement of the hand. *(Le Ménestrel,* Paris, November 1928)

27 MARCH 1928

Leslie STUART, English composer of celebrated hits, among them *On the Road to Tipperary* (which became universally popular during the war, several years after its publication), *Louisiana Lou,* and others, dies at Richmond, England, in his sixty-fifth year.

29 MARCH 1928

The new harp, invented by Carlos Salzedo (in relation to which the old harp is said to be "as an ox to an airplane"), is presented for the first time at the eighth annual National Harp Festival in Philadelphia.

30 MARCH 1928

Symphony in B-Flat, by Edward Burlingame HILL, in three movements with "no descriptive basis, no dramatic conflict or spiritual crisis," in a free modulatory style, is performed for the first time anywhere by the Boston Symphony Orchestra, under the direction of KOUSSEVITZKY, to whom the score is dedicated.

APRIL 1928

Nine centuries have passed since Guido D'AREZZO presented to the Church in Rome his teaching methods: the Guidonian Hand and the movable Ut-Re-Mi-Fa-Sol-La hexachords.

4 APRIL 1928

Danses Africaines, neo-primitive orchestral tone-poems by the Brazilian-Parisian composer, Hector VILLA-LOBOS, are performed for the first time by the Straram Orchestra in Paris.

7 APRIL 1928

The first performance of MIASKOVSKY's *Tenth Symphony,* op. 30, in F minor, is given in Moscow, by the Persimfans (Pervyi Symfonitchesky Ansamble = First Symphonic Ensemble), the conductorless orchestra.

(The *Tenth Symphony* was completed on 29 April 1927 in piano score; orchestration finished on 29 December 1927. These dates are communicated by the composer)

"The Tenth Symphony was an answer (unfortunately not very articulate) to an urge which I had felt for a long time—to give utterance to the scenes of anxiety and confusion of the hero of Pushkin's *Knight of Brass.*" (Miaskovsky, *Autobiographical Notes* in *Sovietskaya Musica,* No. 6, 1936)

20 APRIL 1928

Ondes musicales, electric musical wave instrument, invented by MARTENOT, is demonstrated for the first time in public in Paris.

25 APRIL 1928

René BERTRAND presents in Paris an orchestra of six dynaphones (ether-wave instruments), capable of changing pitch and timbre.

27 APRIL 1928

STRAVINSKY's *Apollon Musagète,* ballet in two tableaux, commissioned by the Library of Congress, is performed for the first time anywhere at the first concert of the Festival of Chamber Music, at the Library of Congress in Washington, under the auspices of the Elizabeth Sprague Coolidge Foundation.

29 APRIL 1928

The *Ninth Symphony,* op. 28, in E minor, in four movements, by Nicolas MIASKOVSKY, is performed for the first time in Moscow, Constantin Saradjev conducting, nine days after the composer's forty-seventh birthday.

(Piano score completed 9 September 1926, orchestration finished 21 July 1927. These dates are communicated by the composer)

"The *Ninth Symphony* was conceived on a lyric and serene plane. I regard it as my symphonic Intermezzo." (Miaskovsky, *Autobiographical Notes, Sovietskaya Musica,* No. 6, 1936)

1 MAY 1928

Musicalia, a bimonthly music magazine in the Spanish language under the editorship of Maria Muñoz DE QUEVEDO, starts publication in Havana, Cuba.

"Programs and declarations are rarely justified by the results. For this reason *Musicalia* will not carry a predetermined or dogmatic program: it will shape itself as it goes along like an airplane that goes up as soon as it gathers speed. In one respect only it establishes a norm: fidelity to its epoch. *Musicalia* will be a publication of its time. It will consider the music of the past as a living art without adopting a fetishist attitude towards it, and it will assume a critical attitude towards present day art, while accepting enthusiastically all artistic innovation." (From the preface of the first issue)

6 MAY 1928

Ernst KřENEK's trilogy of one-act political satires, *The Dictator, The Mysterious Kingdom,* and *Heavyweight, or Pride of the Nation,* is performed for the first time at a festival of modern music at Wiesbaden.

7 MAY 1928

Alexandre SPENDIAROV, Russian composer of orchestral and other music in a typical pseudo-oriental Russian idiom, common to Rimsky-Korsakov's disciples, dies at Erivan, in the Caucasus, in his fifty-seventh year.

16 MAY 1928

TOSCANINI conducts at La Scala, in Milan, the first performance of the opera, *Fra Gherardo,* by Ildebrando PIZZETTI, a story of a medieval flagellant in love with an alleged witch, set to neo-modal music in a style evocative rather than veristic.

19 MAY 1928

Henry F. GILBERT, American composer of forceful native-flavored music drawing upon Negro, Indian, Creole, or white folklore, the "Uramerikaner" as the Germans dubbed him, a man who never wanted to be a colonial of the art of Europe and instead elaborated his own technique and science, dies at his Cambridge home in his sixtieth year.

25 MAY 1928

The original vocal score of MOUSSORGSKY's *Boris Godunov* is published by the State Music Publishers, Moscow.

6 JUNE 1928

The Egyptian Helen, the ninth opera of Richard STRAUSS, is given for the first time anywhere at the Dresden Opera, Fritz BUSCH conducting.

11 JUNE 1928

On his sixty-fourth birthday Richard STRAUSS conducts the first Vienna performance of his ninth opera, *The Egyptian Helen.*

13 JUNE 1928

Wolfgang GRAESER, youthful Swiss composer and musicologist, editor of *Die Kunst der Fuge* in the Neue Bachgesellschaft edition, kills himself in Berlin, at the age of twenty-one years, nine months, and six days.

15 JUNE 1928

Alexandre GLAZUNOV leaves Leningrad for Vienna as a delegate at the Schubert Centennial, never to return.

(Exact date obtained from Maximilian Steinberg, Glazunov's successor as Director of the Leningrad Conservatory)

2 JULY 1928

Alfredo CASELLA completes in Boston during his term as conductor of the "Pops" (popular concerts by the Boston Symphony Orchestra) the score of his *Violin Concerto* in A minor, begun in Rome on 13 February 1928.

19 JULY 1928

Virgil THOMSON completes the musical score of his opera, *Four Saints in Three Acts,* to Gertrude Stein's glossolalia for a libretto.

"The idea of doing an opera together was conceived by Miss Stein and myself at the house of Miss Nathalie Barnez, 20 rue Jacob, Paris, on February 6, 1927. . . . Act I was scored between July 1 and 15. Acts II, III, and IV were scored between August 1 and September 20, which date marks the termination of the present orchestral score. If a single date must be given for the termination of the entire work, that date is July 19, 1928, when the musical composition of the work actually came to an end." (From composer's letter to the author)

24 JULY 1928

The Oxford Press issues the first volume of a three-volume edition of the complete works of Chopin according to the original manuscripts. (Date of the preface by the editor Édouard Ganche, President of the Société Frédéric Chopin)

10 AUGUST 1928

In a public address Mustafa Kemal Pasha urges adoption of gay Western dance rhythms and jazz to relieve the traditional homophony of Turkish music.

12 AUGUST 1928

Leoš JANÁČEK, the MOUSSORGSKY of Bohemia, animator of a new Czech school of composition built on realistic conception of melody as spoken music and harmony as product of moving voices, dies at Ostrava in his seventy-fifth year.

17 AUGUST 1928

The International Grand Jury, consisting of Franz SCHALK (Austria), Donald Francis TOVEY (England), Alfred BRUNEAU (France), Max VON SCHILLINGS (Germany), Franco ALFANO (Italy), Emil MLYNARSKI (Poland), Alexandre GLAZUNOV (Russia), Carl NIELSEN (Scandinavia), Adolfo SALAZAR (Spain), and Walter DAMROSCH (United States), awards the $10,000 prize in the International Composers' Contest instituted by the Columbia Phonograph Company

of New York as part of the Schubert Centenary Celebration to Kurt
ATTERBERG, Swedish composer, for his *Symphony in C Major* as
being nearest to the main stipulation of the contest: to write a work
conceived as "an apotheosis of the lyrical genius of Schubert."

28 AUGUST 1928

The publishing firm of J. M. Dent & Sons, Ltd., withdraws from
circulation A. Eaglefield HULL's book, *Music, Classical, Romantic
and Modern* (published on 8 April 1927), in which the author admittedly borrows large sections from other books without acknowledgment. (Exact dates obtained from the publishers)

"This book I have made for my own pleasure; I have taken stones
for my walls, and tiles for my floors, wherever good material came to
hand, without always troubling to acknowledge it when the lifting is as
apparent as the use of the stones and columns from Hadrian's Wall by
the church-builders of Northumberland. Such an adaptation of warlike
material to peaceful ends I hold entirely justifiable." (From the Preface)

10 SEPTEMBER 1928

The sixth Festival of the International Society for Contemporary
Music opens at Siena, Italy, under the auspices of the Corporazione Delle Nuove Musiche, with a program of old Italian music
performed by the Augusteo Orchestra, under the direction of Bernardino MOLINARI.

11 SEPTEMBER 1928

The first concert of the Siena Festival (ISCM) presents the follow-
program of chamber music:

String Quartet by the Italian quasi-modernist, Vincenzo TOMMASINI; a
neo-romantic *Sonata for Flute and Piano* by Karel HÁBA, brother of
the tonal fractionalist, Alois HÁBA; a *Suite for Piano,* op. 37, by Paul
HINDEMITH; RAVEL's *Sonata for Violin and Piano,* influenced by his
American tour as its slow movement, entitled *Blues,* demonstrates; and
a *String Quartet* by Alexander ZEMLINSKY.

12 SEPTEMBER 1928

At the Siena Festival (ISCM), E. F. BURIAN, conductor and composer from Prague, gives a demonstration of his "voice band,"

with the accompaniment of piano and drums, creating harmonic effects by adroit combinations of vowels (as concords) and consonants (as discords).

13 SEPTEMBER 1928

The second chamber concert of the Siena Festival (ISCM) presents the following program:

String Quartet by the English post-romanticist, Frank BRIDGE; *Duo* for piano and violin by the German composer of neo-Wagnerian tendencies, Heinz TIESSEN; *String Trio,* in an evocative and terse idiom, by the Austrian, Anton VON WEBERN; *Concerto* for harpsichord and five instruments by Manuel DE FALLA; and *Music for Eight Instruments* by the Swiss composer of absolute music in a modern idiom, Robert BLUM.

14 SEPTEMBER 1928

At the Siena Festival (ISCM) Alfredo CASELLA conducts, in the morning concert, a double performance of *Façade* by William WALTON, and, in the afternoon concert, his own *Serenade* for five instruments and STRAVINSKY's *Les Noces.*

15 SEPTEMBER 1928

At the third and last chamber concert of the Siena Festival (ISCM) the following works are performed:

Second Quartet by the Czech neo-polyphonist Bohuslav MARTINU; the florid *Sonata for Cello and Piano* by Franco ALFANO; and the *Piano Quintet* (with quarter-tones) by Ernest BLOCH. (A *Quintet* by PROKO-FIEV was announced in the program, but not performed, owing to an unforeseen defection)

18 SEPTEMBER 1928

Dr. Arthur Eaglefield HULL, British musicologist and editor of the *Dictionary of Modern Music and Musicians,* jumps under the train at the Huddersfield Railway Station, in a suicide attempt, sustaining a fractured rib and loss of memory.

19 SEPTEMBER 1928

The first "hundred-percent all-talking, all-singing" motion picture, *The Singing Fool,* featuring Al Jolson, with a companion piece, *Steamboat Willie,* animated cartoon with synchronized music presenting Mickey Mouse for the first time, opens at the Colony Theatre in New York.

20 SEPTEMBER 1928

A week after his fifty-fourth birthday SCHOENBERG completes at Roquebrune, France, the score of his *Variations for Orchestra,* op. 31, on a theme of twelve different tones (the "row": B-flat, F-flat, G-flat, E-flat, F, A, D, C-sharp, G, G-sharp, B, C) treated in inversion, retrograde motion, and vertical integration. (Date at end of manuscript)

2 OCTOBER 1928

Eduardo GRANADOS, Spanish composer of theater music, son of the great Spanish composer, Enrique GRANADOS, dies in Madrid, in his thirty-fifth year, some twelve and a half years after his father's tragic death on a torpedoed channel steamer.

10 OCTOBER 1928

L'Eau du Nil, the first French "film sonore," is demonstrated for the first time in Paris.

15 OCTOBER 1928

Symphony in C Major, by Kurt ATTERBERG, the winner of the $10,000 Schubert Memorial Prize, offered by the Columbia Phonograph Company of New York, is performed for the first time in public at Cologne, Hermann ABENDROTH conducting.

19 OCTOBER 1928

At its inaugural concert, the Orchestre Symphonique de Paris gives the first performance of *Rugby,* "symphonic movement" by Arthur HONEGGER, descriptive of the game in a suggestive rather than onomatopoeic manner.

20 OCTOBER 1928

Celibacy is declared no longer *conditio sine qua non* for the Prix de Rome applicants in France.

28 OCTOBER 1928

Théodore REINACH, French Hellenist who codified the known facts concerning Greek modes and published authentic fragments of ancient monody, dies in Paris in his sixty-ninth year.

30 OCTOBER 1928

O. G. SONNECK, American writer on music, first Chief of the Music Division of the Library of Congress, dies in New York twenty-four days after his fifty-fifth birthday.

1 NOVEMBER 1928

The National Opera House is founded in Tashkent, capital of the Uzbek Soviet Republic in Central Asia.

4 NOVEMBER 1928

Dr. Arthur Eaglefield HULL, English encyclopedist, champion of modern music, dies in London, in his fifty-third year, of injuries sustained in his suicide attempt a month and a half before.

"Hull's suicide was the result of my exposure of his thefts in his book *Music, Classical, Romantic and Modern*. He threw himself under a train." (Percy A. Scholes in a letter to the author dated 21 March 1948)

11 NOVEMBER 1928

The eleventh edition of Riemann's *Musik-Lexikon* in two volumes, covering theory and biography of ancient and modern music and musicians, is completed by Alfred EINSTEIN as editor-in-chief. (Preface date)

16–17 NOVEMBER 1928

Igor STRAVINSKY conducts the Orchestre Symphonique de Paris in two programs of his own music on two consecutive days, featuring the first performance of the orchestral version of the *Étude for Pianola*, composed in 1917.

18 NOVEMBER 1928

Eight weeks after his thirtieth birthday, George GERSHWIN completes the score of his "orchestral tone poem," *An American in Paris,* portraying the gay nostalgia of a European trip in realistic orchestration, including taxi horns. (Date communicated by the composer)

18 NOVEMBER 1928

Ernest Newman reviews, in the Sunday *Times,* the first London performance of Kurt ATTERBERG's *Symphony,* the winning work of the Columbia contest, and suggests for the first time that the borrowings in the *Symphony* may have been deliberate.

"Every one was busy spotting reminiscences in the Symphony; and it can not be denied that they are plentiful and obvious. There may be two possible explanations of these. Atterberg may have looked down the list of judges, and slyly made up his mind that he would put in a bit of something that would appeal to each of them in turn—a bit of *Sheherazade* for the Russian, Glazunov, a bit of *Cockaigne* for Mr. Tovey, a bit of the *New World Symphony* for Mr. Damrosch, a bit of *Petrouchka* for the modernist Alfano, a bit of Granados for Salazar. . . . But I wonder if there may not be another explanation. . . . Atterberg is not merely a composer. He is a musical critic. . . . Suppose he looked round with the cynical smile that, as all the world knows, all critics wear, and decided to pull the world's leg? The tribute paid to certain other works in this symphony is so obvious that it would indeed be a strange thing if the composer himself (who, I repeat, is also a critic) should be the one man in the world of music to be unaware of them. . . . And if my theory is correct, the laugh is Atterberg's today." (London *Times,* 18 November 1928)

19 NOVEMBER 1928

A century has passed since Franz SCHUBERT died at his brother's house in Vienna, at the age of thirty-one.

22 NOVEMBER 1928

Bolero, the wildfire hit of modern music, by Maurice RAVEL, consisting of eighteen repetitions of a binary subject, in C major throughout, except for a momentary digression into E major in the coda, is performed for the first time, Walter STRARAM conducting, at Ida Rubinstein's dance recital at the Paris Opéra, along with music of BACH orchestrated by HONEGGER and music of LISZT orchestrated by MILHAUD.

27 NOVEMBER 1928

Igor STRAVINSKY conducts at Ida Rubinstein's dance recital at the Paris Opéra the first performance of his *Le Baiser de la Fée,* "allegorical ballet in four scenes, inspired by the muse of Tchaikovsky."

2 DECEMBER 1928

FURTWAENGLER conducts in Berlin the first performance of SCHOEN-BERG's *Variations for Orchestra,* op. 31.

"The majority of the audience was silent, but two excited minorities engaged in combat. The give-and-take of remarks for and against the piece grew to greater dimensions and took more unfortunate forms than we have ever experienced at a Schoenberg première. And we are accustomed to almost anything." (Max Marschalk in *Die Vossische Zeitung*)

11 DECEMBER 1928

The Society of the Friends of Music in the Library of Congress is organized "to provide a link among serious lovers of music in our country by associating them, through the national library, in musical activities devoted to artistic and educational ends."

(Date from the stenographic report of the first meeting of the Society; but the Society's brochure issued in 1930 gives the date of the formation of the Society as 16 December 1928)

13 DECEMBER 1928

An American in Paris, symphonic poem descriptive of nostalgia and joy of European travel, by George GERSHWIN, is performed for the first time under the direction of Walter DAMROSCH in New York.

14 DECEMBER 1928

La Symphonie by the thirty-eight-year-old Czech composer, Bohuslav MARTINU, in one continuous non-symphonic movement, written in commemoration of the giving of the first Czechoslovakian flag to the first Czechoslovakian regiment at Darney, France, in June 1918, is performed for the first time anywhere by the Boston Symphony Orchestra, KOUSSEVITZKY conducting.

20 DECEMBER 1928

America, "an epic rhapsody in three parts" for orchestra, a national American musicorama by the Swiss-American composer Ernest BLOCH, winner of the *Musical America* prize, is performed by the New York Philharmonic Orchestra for the first time anywhere.

"This Symphony has been written in love for this country—in reverence for its past—in faith in its future. It is dedicated to the memory of Abraham Lincoln and Walt Whitman whose vision has upheld its inspiration. I. 1620, The Soil—The Indians— (England)—The Mayflower—The Landing of the Pilgrims. II. 1861–1865, Hours of Joy—Hours of Sorrow. III. Turmoil of Present Time—Material 'prosperity'—Speed—Noise—'Man Slave of the Machines'—America's call of Distress—The Inevitable Collapse—Man's Introspection—Reconstruction—The Mastery of Man over the Machines, his Environment and . . . Himself—The Call of America to the Nations of the World—The Fulfilment—Anthem: 'America! America! Thy Name is in my heart; / My love for thee arouses me to nobler thought and deeds. / Our fathers builded a nation / To give us Justice and Peace, / Toward higher aims, toward brighter goals, / Toward Freedom of all mankind. Our hearts we pledge, America, / To stand by thee, to give to thee our strength, our faith and our lives.' " (Program of printed score)

21 DECEMBER 1928

The Boston, Chicago, Philadelphia, and San Francisco Symphony Orchestras present Ernest BLOCH's *America* on the same day, in local first performances.

23 DECEMBER 1928

At a Pasdeloup concert in Paris Maurice MARTENOT plays on his electrical (heterodyne) instrument, ondes musicales (musical waves), a work specially written for the instrument by the

Greek composer, Dimitri LEVIDIS, *Poéme Symphonique pour Solo d'Ondes Musicales et Orchestre.*

29 DECEMBER 1928

Domenico ALALEONA, Italian composer whose style combines expressive nationalism with aspirations after a new aesthetics built on non-tempered scales, dies at his native Montegiorgio, a month and thirteen days after his forty-seventh birthday.

(Date from *Il Giornale d'Italia* of 30 December 1928, p. 5. Moser, 1935, gives the erroneous date of 18 December 1928)

1929

1 JANUARY 1929

The *Proletarian Musician,* organ of the Association of Proletarian Musicians, begins publication in Moscow.

"The Marxist ideology of the Association, the necessity of ideological struggle on the musical front, all this makes imperative the existence of a special publication. . . . The Proletarian Musician will (1) fight the influence of decadent bourgeois music among young musicians, (2) impress the necessity of absorbing the best, the healthiest, and ideologically acceptable elements of the musical legacy of the past, (3) prepare the ground for the formation of a new proletarian music." (From the preface of the first issue of the *Proletarian Musician*)

19 JANUARY 1929

KŘENEK's "jazz opera," *Jonny Spielt Auf,* is presented by the Metropolitan Opera in New York with the miscegenating Negro band-leader converted into a black-faced white in deference to the sensibilities of southern patrons.

30 JANUARY 1929

Albert ROUSSEL completes in Paris his *Petite Suite* in neo-romantic, post-neoclassical style. (Manuscript date)

1 FEBRUARY 1929

Kurt ATTERBERG publishes, in the *Musical Digest,* an article entitled "How I Fooled the Music World," in which he admits that the last movement of his prize symphony for the Columbia competition is a satire on would-be connoisseurs of SCHUBERT, but denies intentional slight on the jury or competition itself.

10 FEBRUARY 1929

The Academy of Santa Cecilia in Rome confers honorary membership on Ernest BLOCH and Arthur HONEGGER.

21 FEBRUARY 1929

TOSCANINI conducts in New York the first performance of RESPIGHI's *Feste Romane,* in four movements: *Circus Maximus, Jubilee, October Festival, Epiphany,* making use of universal means, from old Greco-Roman modes to modern altered-chord formations.

24 FEBRUARY 1929

André MESSAGER, French composer of gay comic operas in the best tradition of AUBER, AUDRAN, and LECOCQ, conductor and champion of new music, dies in Paris in his seventy-sixth year.

3 MARCH 1929

Maximilian STEINBERG conducts in Leningrad the first performance of his *Third Symphony,* in which Russian folk melos is ingeniously wrought into complex harmonies. (Date communicated by the composer)

4 MARCH 1929

L'Éventail de Jeanne, "ballet d'enfants" to music by ten French composers—Florent SCHMITT, Albert ROUSSEL, Maurice RAVEL, Jacques IBERT, Roland-MANUEL, Darius MILHAUD, Marcel DELANNOY, Francis POULENC, Georges AURIC, and P. O. FERROUD, each of whom wrote a stylized dance in classical form—is performed for the first time in public, at the Paris Opéra.

(A performance in a private home took place in Paris on 16 June 1927; it was then that the name, *Jeanne's Fan,* was thought of, each dance by each composer being a "plait" of the fan)

24 MARCH 1929

Sir John in Love, opera in four acts, based on Shakespeare's *Merry Wives of Windsor,* music by VAUGHAN WILLIAMS, is produced at the Royal College of Music.

"Any comparison with Verdi's 'Falstaff' is, of course, out of the question. . . . Vaughan Williams has tried for something different. His score is based very largely on folk-tunes which he often treats very delightfully. . . . Where it fails as an opera is in characterization. None of the music seems to express the characters." (London *Post*)

6 APRIL 1929

The seventh Festival of the International Society for Contemporary Music in Geneva opens with the following program of orchestral music:

Neo-classical *Symphony in E Minor* by the New Englander, Roger SESSIONS; *Concertino* for piano and orchestra by the Dutch lady composer, Henriette BOSMANS, in a refined idiom of RAVEL-PIJPER parentage; *Le Fou de la Dame,* a neo-medieval "chanson de geste" by the French composer, Marcel DELANNOY; and *Rythmes,* ingenious orchestral movement by the Genevan, Frank MARTIN. (In the advance programs of the Festival, SESSIONS' symphony was scheduled to be performed on 9 April, and BUTTING's symphony on 6 April)

7 APRIL 1929

Two concerts are given at the Geneva Festival (ISCM), one in the morning with the following program of chamber music:

String Quartet in one slow movement by the Viennese composer, Julius SCHLOSS; *Sonatina* for piano by the English composer, John IRELAND, played by the composer; *Songs to the Virgin Mary* by the Parisian-Russian, Nicolas NABOKOV; *Five Variations and a Double Fugue* by the Prague atonal composer, Victor ULLMAN; and a *Sonata* for violin and piano by the Prague neo-classicist, Erwin SCHULHOFF;

and one in the afternoon presenting choral works by Karl MARX, Krsto ODÁK, and Leoš JANÁČEK.

8 APRIL 1929

At the Geneva Festival (ISCM) a concert of chamber music is given in the afternoon, with the following program:

Serenade for violin, viola, and cello by the Hungarian composer, Alexander JEMNITZ, in a highly economical (maximum sonority with minimum of means) atonal fashion; *Sonatina* for two violins and piano, diatonic, sprinkled with Parisian dissonance, by Manuel ROSENTHAL; *Piano Sonata* by a SCHREKER pupil, Berthold GOLDSCHMIDT; *Seven Hai-Kais,* cycle of Japanese songs with chamber orchestra, by the RAVEL disciple, Maurice DELAGE, in reticent orientalized style; and the *Second String Quartet* by the Polish composer, Jerzy FITELBERG, in clear tonality, pan-diatonically treated. (In the evening of the same day performances of works of MONTEVERDI, CIMAROSA, and LUALDI were given)

9 APRIL 1929

At the Geneva Festival (ISCM) the last concert is given, presenting the following program of orchestral music:

Flos Campi, for viola solo, chamber orchestra, and small chorus in an impressionist neo-romantic style by VAUGHAN WILLIAMS; *Concerto for Piano and Chamber Orchestra* by Johannes MUELLER; *Dance* for clarinet and orchestra by the Dutch lady composer, Emmy HEIL-FRENSEL-WEGENER; and the ponderous *Third Symphony* by Max BUTTING.

13 APRIL 1929

Machinist Hopkins, lurid music drama by Max BRAND, dealing with the hypnotic power of the machine which draws the guilty adulteress to the same death in its whirling cogs as that of her legitimate husband, with music of the constructivist genre, is produced in Duisburg.

(Date communicated to the author by the composer. The performance on 10 July 1929, during the fifty-ninth Tonkuenstlerfest des Allgemeinen Deutschen Musikvereins in Duisburg, usually given as the first, is the second)

19 APRIL 1929

Lazare SAMINSKY, Russian-American composer, conducts in Berlin the first performance of his *Fourth Symphony,* with thematic emphasis on fourths, in free modulatory style, and with a "musical motto" in place of the programmatic subtitle customary with Saminsky. (Date from *Lazare Saminsky, Composer and Civic Worker,* New York, 1930)

25 APRIL 1929

Twenty days after Albert ROUSSEL's sixtieth birthday, and in celebration of that event, an orchestral concert of his music is arranged in Paris, featuring the first performance of his *Psalm 80* for tenor solo, mixed chorus, and orchestra, op. 37.

29 APRIL 1929

The Gambler, opera in four acts after Dostoievsky's novel of that name, by Serge PROKOFIEV, is performed for the first time at the Théâtre Royal de la Monnaie in Brussels, five days after the composer's thirty-eighth birthday.

7 MAY 1929

German Hitlerite students throw stink bombs at the Berlin State Opera Theatre during the performance of Kurt WEILL's *Dreigroschenoper* to express disapproval of the new *Gebrauchsmusik.*

17 MAY 1929

Serge PROKOFIEV's *Third Symphony* is performed for the first time by the Orchestre Symphonique de Paris, directed by MONTEUX.

20 MAY 1929

Prodigal Son, ballet by Serge PROKOFIEV, is performed for the first time by DIAGHILEV's Ballet Russe in Paris.

21 MAY 1929

Les Enchantements d'Alcine, ballet in three scenes by Georges AURIC, inspired by Ariosto's heroic tales of amorous knights and the age of exaggerated chivalry, is produced at the Paris Opéra. (The work was misattributed to Roussel in the first two editions of *Music Since 1900*)

8 JUNE 1929

Neues vom Tage, journalistic *Gebrauchsoper* by Paul HINDE-
MITH, featuring an aria in the bathtub with cotton suds, rhythmically clicking typewriters, chorus reciting a business letter, etc.,
is produced in Berlin.

19 JUNE 1929

The first performance of *Aubade, a Choreographic Concerto for
Piano and Eighteen Instruments,* by Francis POULENC, is given at
the Paris home of Viscount and Viscountess de Noailles, to whom
the work is dedicated. (Date on printed score)

21 JUNE 1929

Hermann SCHERCHEN completes in Koenigsberg, on his thirty-
eighth birthday, the *Lehrbuch des Dirigierens,* a most thorough,
modern, and intelligent textbook of conducting, covering the entire range of orchestral literature up to polymetrical works like
STRAVINSKY's *History of a Soldier.* (Date of Preface)

25 JUNE 1929

A month after his thirty-sixth birthday Eugene GOOSSENS conducts at the Covent Garden Royal Opera House in London the
first performance of his one-act opera, *Judith,* to the book of Arnold Bennett, a score of powerful characterization without attempting particularly Assyrian effects, opening with a virtually
atonal motto (ten different tones before a repetition).

1 JULY 1929

The first book on STRAVINSKY in the Russian language, written by
the Russian critic-composer, Igor GLEBOV (real name, Boris Asafiev), is published in Leningrad. (Date of Preface)

15 JULY 1929

Eusebius MANDYCZEWSKI, Rumanian-born music editor of complete editions of SCHUBERT and HAYDN, dies in Vienna in his
seventy-third year.

3 AUGUST 1929

Arnold SCHOENBERG completes his one-act opera, *Von Heute Auf Morgen,* to the expressionist text by Max Blonda, the score using saxophones and a flexaton in addition to the usual orchestra.

3 AUGUST 1929

Emile Berliner, German-born American inventor of the microphone and the gramophone disc in its present form, dies in New York in his seventy-ninth year.

18 AUGUST 1929

Frank Van DER STUCKEN, American composer and conductor, Texan by birth, the first to give a full concert of American music abroad (12 July 1889, at the Paris Exposition), dies in Hamburg in his seventy-first year.

19 AUGUST 1929

Serge DIAGHILEV, the great modern impresario, animator of dancers, composers, and painters, creator of the Russian Ballet in foreign lands, magister elegantiarum of Europe, lover of artistic magnificence and tasteful splendor, dies at Venice, at the age of fifty-seven years and five months.

"In Venice . . . he was well and in excellent spirits. . . . Then suddenly he became very ill, with a temperature that mounted steadily, and he sank into a coma. . . . Towards dawn his breathing ceased. . . . At that moment the sun rose, and lit up his tranquil face. He had died on the water—in Venice, his favored resting place. The following night, as he lay in his room, surrounded by flowers, a violent thunderstorm came over the lagoon—grandiose and dramatic, as he himself would have chosen." (*Diaghileff, His Artistic and Private Life,* by Arnold Haskell, New York, 1935)

"At the beginning of my career he was the first to single me out for encouragement. . . . Not only did he like my music and believe in my development, but he did his utmost to make the public appreciate me. . . . I was not entirely unprepared for his death. I knew that he was diabetic, though I did not know that it was so serious as to be dangerous, especially as at his age his robust constitution should have enabled him to combat the disease for some years. His physical condition had not, therefore, caused me any alarm. But, of late, in watching the usual activities of his everyday life, I had formed the impression that his moral forces were rapidly disintegrating, and I was haunted by the thought that he had reached the limit of his life. That is why his death, though it caused me acute grief at our final parting, did not greatly surprise me." (Igor Stravinsky, *Chronicle of My Life,* English translation, London, 1936)

7 OCTOBER 1929

The Moscow Conductorless Orchestra, Persymfans, gives the first performance of MIASKOVSKY's *Serenata* in E-flat major, op. 32, No. 1, and *Concertino Lirico* in G major, op. 32, No. 3, both for small orchestra.

(The *Serenata* was completed 15 December 1928, the orchestration finished 24 June 1929. The *Concertino Lirico* was completed 24 January 1929; orchestrated between 11 and 20 May 1929. All these dates communicated by the composer)

"While working at the Tenth Symphony I had the idea of writing several orchestral suites of folk-song and dance character. . . . Thus were written the suites of the op. 32: a *Serenade* for small orchestra; *Sinfonietta* for string orchestra; and *Lyric Concertino* for a mixed ensemble." (Miaskovsky, *Autobiographical Notes* in *Sovietskaya Musica,* No. 6, 1936)

10 OCTOBER 1929

Souvenirs sur Igor Stravinsky by his friend and collaborator, C. F. RAMUZ, comes off the press at a Lausanne printing shop—a rambling book addressed in the second person plural to STRAVINSKY in a mood of mutual recollection of the war days in Switzerland. (Colophon date)

12 OCTOBER 1929

The festival of music of Frederick DELIUS opens in London under Sir Thomas BEECHAM's direction, with the following program:
Brigg Fair, A Late Lark (first performance), the second *Dance Rhapsody, Sea Drift, In a Summer Garden,* and excerpts from the opera *A Village Romeo and Juliet.*

1 NOVEMBER 1929

DELIUS' *Mass of Life* is performed at the conclusion of the festival of his music in London, six concerts in all.

4 NOVEMBER 1929

A new building for the Chicago Opera is opened by Samuel Insull, utility magnate.

10 NOVEMBER 1929

Anton VON WEBERN conducts in Vienna the first performance of SCHOENBERG's orchestration of BACH's *Prelude and Fugue* for organ, in E-flat major.

21 NOVEMBER 1929

Alexandre GLAZUNOV conducts his *Sixth Symphony* with the Detroit Symphony Orchestra, at his first appearance before an American audience.

29 NOVEMBER 1929

The Stephen Foster Society is organized in New York for the purpose of collecting and publishing unknown American folk songs.

5 DECEMBER 1929

Otto KLEMPERER conducts in Berlin the first concert performance of Kurt WEILL's radio-cantata, *Lindbergh's Flight,* for soloists, mixed chorus, and orchestra, in simple song style presenting the personified Ocean (monodically), Lindbergh himself (in *Blues* tempo), New York radio station asking ships to be on the lookout, the mist (canonically), the snowstorm (?) (Scherzando), Sleep (insidiously), the American newspapers (jazzily), the French papers (a capella), the motor (tremolando), the sighting of Scotch fishermen (à la gigue), the Bourget field in Paris at 10 p.m., 21 May 1927 (fox-trot-like), the arrival (marchingly), the report on the "Unattainable" (chorally and orchestrally).

6 DECEMBER 1929

STRAVINSKY's *Capriccio* for piano and orchestra is performed for the first time by the Paris Orchestre Symphonique, conducted by Ansermet.

"This form gave me the possibility of arranging my music in juxtapositions of episodes in varied genres which succeed each other and, by their nature, impart to the piece the capricious character wherefrom it takes its name." (Stravinsky, *Chroniques de ma vie,* Paris, 1935)

12 DECEMBER 1929

The Rio Grande (the Brazilian, not the Texan-Mexican Rio Grande) for chorus, orchestra, and solo pianoforte, by the twenty-four-year-old English composer, Constant LAMBERT, brilliant jazzified score to a poem by Sacheverell Sitwell, beginning thus: "By the Rio Grande they dance no Sarabande," is produced for the first time at Manchester, England.

13 DECEMBER 1929

KOUSSEVITZKY conducts the Boston Symphony in the first performance anywhere of Arnold BAX's *Second Symphony.*

"I put a great deal of time (and emotion) into the writing . . . [it] should be very broad indeed, with a kind of oppressive catastrophic mood." (From Bax's letter to Philip Hale, dated 22 November 1929)

22 DECEMBER 1929

Serge PROKOFIEV conducts in Paris the first performance of his *Divertimento,* op. 43, for orchestra, in four symphonic movements, in an idiom half-way between the candid stylization of his *Classical Symphony* and the evocative modernism of his *Scythian Suite.*

"It was called 'a little abstract.' Why? I could not understand. . . . I think now that it was my new conception of 'melody' which caused the impression of abstraction." (Prokofiev to Olin Downes in an interview, New York *Times,* 2 February 1930)

1930

13 JANUARY 1930

The Nose, first opera by the twenty-three-year-old Dmitri SHO-STAKOVITCH, to Gogol's fantastic tale of a nose, lost while shaving, incarnated in a government official, and eventually restored to the owner's face, the music in an extremely subtilized neo-Moussorgskian idiom, is produced in Leningrad.

18 JANUARY 1930

Dom André MOCQUEREAU, Benedictine father, successor of Dom POTHIER as editor of *Paléographie musicale,* which established the Gregorian tradition sanctioned by the papal *motu proprio* of 22 November 1903, and originator of the theory that Gregorian neumes possessed a definite rhythmic value, dies at Solesmes, France, his spiritual home, in his eighty-first year.

26 JANUARY 1930

The Mexican Orquesta Filarmonica inaugurates a series of free concerts for workers (*Conciertos para Trabajadores*).

11 FEBRUARY 1930

Edward Burlingame HILL completes the composition of his *Second Symphony* in four movements.

(This date is the final date of the ink score. The dates of composition of the movements are: (I) 9 Aug.–30 Oct. 1929; (II) 31 Oct.–5 Nov. 1929; (III) 6 Nov.–11 Nov. 1929; (IV) 12 Nov.–26 Nov. 1929. All these dates communicated by the composer)

14 FEBRUARY 1930

Arnold SCHOENBERG completes in Berlin the composition of his score for small orchestra, *Begleitungsmusik zu einer Lichtspielszene* (accompaniment to a cinema scene), in one continuous movement, subdivided into three cinematographically effective sections, along a fine scale of dynamics—*Drohende Gefahr; Angst; Katastrophe*—

in the strictest twelve-tone technique, with a two-bar period of the initial tone-row, E-flat, G-flat, D, E, C-sharp, C, B, A, B-flat, A-flat, G, F. (Date communicated by the composer)

25 FEBRUARY 1930

John Hays HAMMOND, JR., gives, in New York, the first demonstration of his invention, "Crea-Tone," a pianoforte capable of increasing or sustaining the tone.

14 MARCH 1930

Henry WOOD conducts in London the first performance of the *Third Symphony* of Arnold BAX, often referred to as a "Northern" symphony, because of its somber tone-color.

23 MARCH 1930

Achtung, Aufnahme! (Attention! Camera!), operatic sketch of film-studio life, by the German composer, Wilhelm GROSZ, is produced at the Frankfort Opera.

28 MARCH 1930

Walter PISTON, the Boston neo-classicist, conducts the Boston Symphony Orchestra in the first performance of his *Suite for Orchestra* in three movements, intended as a specimen of absolute music, based on older forms, but containing a definitely "American" section with a syncopated, sliding tune over the pianissimo vamp.

29 MARCH 1930

A week before his sixty-first birthday, Albert ROUSSEL completes his *Symphony in G,* op. 42, in four movements, written for the fiftieth anniversary of the Boston Symphony Orchestra. (Date at end of manuscript)

1 APRIL 1930

Cosima WAGNER, widow of WAGNER, daughter of LISZT, dies in Bayreuth in her ninety-third year, surviving WAGNER by forty-seven years and one and a half months.

12 APRIL 1930

Twenty months after Leoš JANÁČEK's death, his last opera, *The House of the Dead,* to Dostoievsky's autobiographical novel of the same name, written in a realistically dramatic style with an abundance of minor seconds in the harmony, ending with an apotheosis to Liberty, is performed for the first time at Brno. (Date from Daniel Muller, *Janáček,* Paris, 1930)

23 APRIL 1930

The New York Philharmonic Orchestra with TOSCANINI as conductor sails for a European tour.

23 APRIL 1930

Alban BERG gives a radio interview in Vienna on the subject: *"Was ist atonal?"* (*See* text in Part III)

29 APRIL 1930

Lo Straniero, opera in two acts, by Ildebrando PIZZETTI, the third part of the operatic triptych, *Debora, Fra Gherardo, Lo Straniero,* is given at the Royal Opera Theatre in Rome—the story of a virtuous parricide, pursued by the Furies, who finds and loses a biblical shepherd-king's beautiful daughter, set to music in a flowing modern Italian way, without attempting particularly Hebraic effects.

6 MAY 1930

Christopher Columbus, opera in two parts and 27 scenes by Darius MILHAUD—containing elements of Greek drama (the use of suasive chorus), mystery play (allegory), music drama (use of musical mottoes), expressionist technique (Columbus conversing with his second self), symbolism and modern newsreel methods (the use of motion pictures)—to the book of Paul Claudel, is produced at the Berlin State Opera.

25 MAY 1930

Transatlantic, opera of the machine age by the American composer, George ANTHEIL, is performed for the first time at the Frankfort Opera.

"In general the whole story is one of political corruption in the U.S.A.; a character something like J. P. Morgan (basso) who backs a presidential candidate only to have this candidate turn traitor to the powers of blackness. There is, of course, a love story, too; J. P. Morgan (let us say) uses a woman, a very beautiful one to try and induce our hero to come along to his way of thinking. But she loves our president-to-be and turns coat to J. P. Morgan, too. The whole thing shows the horrible whirlwind of 1927 in U.S.A.; a Happy End is practically pasted on the end of the opera to make it even more ironic; I wanted to have rose petals falling all over the stage at the end. A satire, and the first modern political opera." (From George Antheil's letter to the author)

2 JUNE 1930

Le Fou de la Dame, second stage-work by Marcel DELANNOY, a neo-medieval "chanson de geste" attempting to amalgamate all styles from Troubadour homophony to jazz, is produced at the Opéra-Comique in Paris.

4 JUNE 1930

Cantata for soprano, men's chorus, and orchestra, by Russian-born, Paris-bred not yet eighteen-year-old Igor MARKEVITCH, in a neo-contrapuntal style, admitting both clear tonal concords and frictional minor seconds, is performed in Paris for the first time.

5 JUNE 1930

An unknown clavier concerto in C minor by J. S. BACH is discovered in Eisenach.

25 JUNE 1930

A thousand years have passed since the death of the Benedictine monk, Hucbald, inventor of staff notation.

25 JUNE 1930

Kaikhosru SORABJI, half-Parsi, half-Spanish, British-born composer of music of extraordinary rhythmic and contrapuntal complexity, finishes the composition of his piano work, *Opus Clavicembalisticum,* in three parts with twelve subdivisions, two of

which have forty-four and eighty-one variations respectively, the
printed copy taking up two hundred and fifty-two pages—the longest piano work in modern music.

"The *Opus Clavicembalisticum* has been described as the greatest and
most important work for piano since the Art of Fugue, as indeed it is.
. . . I have no false modesty nor mock-humility in my make-up, so do
not be surprised at the calm way in which I recognize the importance
of my own work!!" (From Sorabji's letter to the author)

17 JULY 1930

Leopold AUER, celebrated violin pedagogue, trainer of a flock of
celebrated violinists chiefly via the St. Petersburg Conservatory,
dies at Loschwitz in his eighty-sixth year.

19 JULY 1930

Deems TAYLOR completes the composition of his second opera,
Peter Ibbetson. (Date on printed score)

4 AUGUST 1930

Siegfried WAGNER, little son of a great father, dies at Bayreuth, in
his sixty-second year, surviving his mother by four months and
three days.

15 AUGUST 1930

Igor STRAVINSKY completes the score of his *Symphony of Psalms,*
"composed for the glory of God and dedicated to the Boston Symphony on the occasion of the fiftieth anniversary of its existence,"
for chorus and orchestra minus all violins and violas, in three
linked movements marked by metronome indications and the
word "tempo":

(1) *quarter-note equals 92,* an accompanied chorale with an introduction
centering on a cadential E-minor chord; (2) *eighth-note equals 60,* a
four-part fugue with a subject of four principal notes within the range
of a major seventh, the *comes* being in the dominant; (3) *quarter-note
equals 48, Alleluia* for the chorus on five notes centering on C, accompanied by unison tonics and dominants, this slower tempo alternating
with the rapid tempo of eighty half-notes to a minute, the contrapuntal
texture being of the second, third, and fourth species, and, for the final

chorale, in the fifth species, with forty-eight half-notes to a minute, culminating in an augmentation for an eight-bar coda in C major. (Date in Stravinsky's *Chroniques de ma vie*, Paris, 1935)

1 SEPTEMBER 1930

The eighth Festival of the International Society for Contemporary Music opens in Liége with a program of wind-instrument music played by the First Regiment of Les Guides, including:

Fanfares for a Corrida by the Belgian Raymond MOULAERT; *Spiel* by Ernst TOCH; *Konzertmusik,* op. 41, in brilliant military-band style, by Paul HINDEMITH; *Pièce Symphonique* for piano and wind orchestra by the Liége-born Franckist composer and educator, Joseph JONGEN; *Dionysiaques* by Florent SCHMITT; *Symphony for Wind Instruments* (in memory of Debussy) by STRAVINSKY; *Danse Funambulesque* by Jules STRENS; and *Fireworks* by Maurice SCHOEMAKER.

2 SEPTEMBER 1930

At the second concert of the Liége Festival (ISCM) the following program of chamber music is given:

Musique pour Piano by the German-Czech Erhard MICHEL; an austere and contrapuntal *Septet* for violin, clarinet, viola, horn, cello, bassoon, and piano by Karel HÁBA, brother of the quarter-tonalist, Alois HÁBA; *Chansons Françaises* in a pleasing neo-Lullyan vein by the only woman of the French "Six," Germaine TAILLEFERRE; the neo-romantic *Sonata for Two Pianofortes* by Arnold BAX; and the *Second String Quartet* by the Belgian neo-polyphonist, Albert HUYBRECHTS.

3 SEPTEMBER 1930

At the third concert of the Liége Festival (ISCM) the following program of chamber music is given:

Quintet for flute, oboe, clarinet, horn, and bassoon, by the Czech polyphonist, K. B. JIRÁK; *Moralités non Légendaires* for voice and diverse instruments in a Dadaistic vein by the Belgian, Fernand QUINET; *Trio* for flute, violin, and cello by Albert ROUSSEL, at his best in mastery and elegance; *Quintet* for saxophone and strings by Karl STIMMER; and the cannily wrought neo-Pergolesian *Serenade* for clarinet, bassoon, trumpet, violin, and cello by Alfredo CASELLA.

4 SEPTEMBER 1930

At the fourth concert of the Liége Festival (ISCM) the following
program of orchestral music is given:

Music for Orchestra, op. 35, by the Swiss composer, Volkmar ANDREAE,
in a peculiar neo-Straussian vein, the non-programmatic title of the work
to the contrary notwithstanding; *Sinfonietta* by the Dutch-American
composer, Bernard WAGENAAR, in a neo-Beethovenian style, vigorous
and richly thematic; *Concerto for Viola* by the white hope of British
music, William WALTON; *Sinfonia Italiana* in an extravert cantabile
style by the Italian, Antonio VERETTI; *Rondo Burlesque* by Florent
SCHMITT; and *Poème de l'Espace,* discordant glorification of a transatlantic flight by the Belgian composer, Marcel POOT.

6 SEPTEMBER 1930

At the fifth and last concert of the Liége Festival (ISCM) the following program of orchestral music is given:

Praeludium, a contrapuntal neo-Bachian piece of *Augenmusik* by the
German "constructivist," Ernst PEPPING; *Start,* subtitled "symphonic allegro," descriptive of a sport event, by the Czech, Pavel BOŘKOVEC;
Chant Funèbre by the French composer of new music in old forms,
Jean RIVIER; *Temptation,* Gaelic pipe march by Henry GIBSON; a *Violin Concerto* by the Viennese musical scientist, Josef Matthias HAUER,
built on his mutually exclusive six-tone tropes; the hedonistic, ultra-
practical *Suite* by the German-Polish SCHREKER pupil, Karol RATHAUS;
Fantaisie by the Parisian-Rumanian, Marcel MIHALOVICI; and the
crushing orchestral *Steel Foundry* (with a suspended metal sheet shaken
for realistic onomatopoeia) by the Soviet enfant terrible, Alexandre
MOSSOLOV.

10–11 OCTOBER 1930

Sir George HENSCHEL, the first conductor of the Boston Symphony
Orchestra who conducted its first concert on 22 October 1881, directs the same program—save for Wagner's *Meistersinger* Prelude
which replaced Weber's *Jubel* Overture as the closing number—
at the opening pair of concerts in the fiftieth year of the Boston
Symphony Orchestra.

(Date and programs from M. A. DeWolfe Howe, *The Boston Symphony
Orchestra,* 1931)

12 OCTOBER 1930

Albert Roussel arrives in America on his first American tour.

20 OCTOBER 1930

Hitlerite students throw stink bombs at the Frankfort Opera House in protest against the "immoral" opera, *Mahagonny,* by Kurt Weill, and one Communist is killed by a beer stein during a post-theatrical argument.

24 OCTOBER 1930

Symphony in G Minor, in orthodox four movements, but in an idiom of ultimate contrapuntal and harmonic freedom, by Albert Roussel, written for the fiftieth anniversary of the Boston Symphony Orchestra, is performed for the first time anywhere by the Boston Symphony, Koussevitzky conducting.

7 NOVEMBER 1930

Metamorphoseon, Modi XII (Theme and Variations) by Ottorino Respighi, composed for the fiftieth anniversary of the Boston Symphony Orchestra, is performed for the first time anywhere by the Boston Symphony, Koussevitzky conducting.

12 NOVEMBER 1930

Karl Buecher, German political economist, who in his book *Arbeit und Rhythmus* gave the suggestion that music may have originated from rhythmic movements of the laborer at work, dies in Leipzig in his eighty-fourth year.

14 NOVEMBER 1930

The *Fourth Symphony* in orthodox four movements, in a free modulatory, but very tonal and diatonic style, by Serge Prokofiev, written for the fiftieth anniversary of the Boston Symphony Orchestra, is performed for the first time anywhere by the Boston Symphony, Koussevitzky conducting.

28 NOVEMBER 1930

Symphony No. 2, "Romantic," by the Nebraskan, Howard Han-

SON, composed for the fiftieth anniversary of the Boston Symphony Orchestra, is performed for the first time by the Boston Symphony, KOUSSEVITZKY conducting.

11 DECEMBER 1930

Seven principal concert bureaus of America announce a merger with the Columbia Broadcasting System, effective 1 January 1931, under the collective title of Columbia Concerts Corporation.

12 DECEMBER 1930

HONEGGER's first real unmitigated operetta, *Le Roi Pausole,* to Pierre Louys' licentious story with modern trimmings by Wille-metz, is produced at the Bouffes-Parisiennes, in Paris.

13 DECEMBER 1930

The Brussels Philharmonic Orchestra gives the world première of STRAVINSKY's *Symphony of Psalms,* as part of a festival of STRA-VINSKY's music.

17 DECEMBER 1930

Philip HESELTINE, English composer (under the pen-name of Peter Warlock) and writer on music, brilliant champion of hedonistic simplicity and epicurean gaiety in the arts, dies, a suicide by gas, in his London (Chelsea) apartment, at the age of thirty-six years, one month, and seventeen days.

(Date from the London *Times* obituary in the issue of 18 December 1930. Moser gives the erroneous date of 18 December)

"Shortly after seven o'clock on the morning of Wednesday, December 17th, a strong smell of gas was noticed to be coming from his flat, but when an attempt was made to obtain entrance there was no reply from within, and the door and windows were all shut and bolted. The police were called in and the door was broken open; he was discovered lying upon a couch, unconscious, fully clothed. On removal to St. Luke's Hospital he was found to be dead." (Cecil Gray, *Peter Warlock,* London, 1934)

19 DECEMBER 1930

The Boston Symphony Orchestra gives the first American performance of STRAVINSKY's *Symphony of Psalms,* under the direction of KOUSSEVITZKY.

"As originally arranged, Stravinsky's Symphony of Psalms was to be heard for the first times at the concerts of the Boston Symphony Orchestra (to which it is dedicated) on Friday and Saturday, December 12 and 13. The illness of Dr. Koussevitzky deferred production here until 19 and 20 December. Meantime the Philharmonic Society of Brussels had played and sung it on Saturday, 13 December, as an item in a 'Stravinsky Festival.' " (Boston *Evening Transcript,* 26 December 1930)

1931

5 FEBRUARY 1931

At the dedication of Severance Hall, the permanent home of the Cleveland Orchestra, *Evocation* by Charles Martin LOEFFLER, picturing the building of a temple of the Muses, in a half-archaizing, half-impressionistic idiom, written for the occasion, is performed for the first time.

7 FEBRUARY 1931

Peter Ibbetson, lyric drama in three acts by Deems TAYLOR, is produced by the Metropolitan Opera in New York.

"Deems Taylor Cheered at End of New Opera—Demonstration at Première of 'Peter Ibbetson' Before Distinguished Audience—Author Has Many Recalls—Damrosch Embraces Him at End of First Act." (Headlines in the New York *Herald Tribune*)

" 'Peter Ibbetson' Wins Great Ovation at World Premiere—Deems Taylor's Native Opera Is Greeted with 36 Curtain Calls at Metropolitan—A Beautiful Production—Vast Audience Deeply Moved by Du Maurier's Emotional Story and Some Wept.—300 in Performance" (Headlines in the New York *Times*)

13 FEBRUARY 1931

Symphony (without further indication of key or opus number) in three movements, virtually atonal with wide-spaced intervals for melodic framework, by Arthur HONEGGER, written for the fiftieth anniversary of the Boston Symphony Orchestra, is performed for the first time anywhere by the Boston Symphony, KOUSSEVITZKY conducting.

23 FEBRUARY 1931

Nellie MELBA, celebrated singer whose fame spread even into the realm of gastronomy (Peach Melba), dies in her native Melbourne, Australia, in her seventieth year.

24 FEBRUARY 1931

STRAVINSKY conducts the Paris première of his *Symphony of Psalms,* and the Columbia Phonograph Company records the entire work during the rehearsals.

19 MARCH 1931

The first American performance of Alban BERG's expressionist opera, *Wozzeck,* is given by the Philadelphia Grand Opera Company, Stokowski conducting.

"American Premiere of Berg's *Wozzeck*—Grim Horror-Haunted Music Drama Produced by Philadelphia Opera Company—Triumphs as Dramatist—Composer a Technical Master—Some of the Music Touches Emotional Heights." (Headlines in the New York *Times,* 20 March 1931)

"Public interest in the occasion was extraordinary. A roster of the audience would constitute a social and musical 'Who's Who in the Eastern United States.' Composers, conductors, concert artists, and musical journalists came from points within a circle whose radius measures hundreds of miles. A special train brought music lovers from New York. An artistic event assumed the importance of a big football match. . . . An artistic event of primary importance. There can be no doubt of that. The resistance which preliminary acclaim tends to set up was dissipated at once. This audience of connoisseurs paid homage to the genius of the composer. For once acquaintances greeted musical chroniclers in the intermissions not with 'what do you think of it?' but with 'I like it!' The success was general and overwhelming." (L. A. Sloper in the *Christian Science Monitor,* 21 March 1931)

25 MARCH 1931

Composers, members of the Russian Association of Proletarian Musicians, open their first convention in Moscow.

28 MARCH 1931

Half a century has passed since the death at St. Petersburg of Modest MOUSSORGSKY, the great musical realist, originator of prosodically designed vocal line in the opera and song, and restorer of old modality in a new free style.

(Grove, in the 1907 edition, states that Moussorgsky died on his forty-second birthday, 16/28 March 1881, but gives the year of Moussorgsky's birth as 1835 instead of 1839. That 1881 minus 1835 is not 42 should be apparent to anyone, yet the 1927 edition of Grove carries the same story. This is what may be called Public Error No. 1, the most unnecessary of all errors found in music dictionaries.

There is further confusion about the day of the month of Moussorgsky's birth. The Russian sources usually give 16 March, old style, a date also given in an autobiographical sketch prepared by Moussorgsky himself, and found in the archives of Vladimir Stassov. This document is not in Moussorgsky's hand, but he had made some corrections and additions, and let the date, 16 March, stand. There exists, however, incontrovertible evidence that Moussorgsky was born on the 9th of March 1839, old style, not the 16th. In the register of the Odigitriev Church in the Toropetzky District of the Pskov Government, there is the following entry under the year 1839: "Born on the 9th, and baptized on the 13th of the month of March, infant Modest. His parents are: Peter Alexeievitch Moussorgsky and his legitimate spouse, Julia Ivanovna, both from the village of Karevo." Follows a list of witnesses of the baptism, etc. Both the autobiographical sketch and the register of birth are reproduced in the January 1917 issue of the *Musicalny Sovremennik*. Thus, the date 9/21 March 1839 should be accepted as correct)

3 APRIL 1931

Konzertmusik for string and brass instruments in two movements, composed, in a free neo-romantic style, by Paul HINDEMITH, for the fiftieth anniversary of the Boston Symphony Orchestra, is performed by the Boston Symphony for the first time anywhere, KOUSSEVITZKY conducting.

4 APRIL 1931

George CHADWICK, American composer of symphonic and instrumental music in all genres, in an orthodox European neo-romantic manner endued with strong Americanisms, educator of a generation of American composers, dies in Boston in his seventy-seventh year.

5 APRIL 1931

Comedians, opera by Reinhold GLIÈRE, is produced at the Moscow State Opera.

26 APRIL 1931

Angul HAMMERICH, Danish music historian, brother of the Danish composer, Asger HAMERIK (who preferred this more Scandinavian spelling), dies in his native Copenhagen in his eighty-third year, outliving his brother by nearly eight years.

3 MAY 1931

Otto WINTER-HJELM, Norwegian composer, co-founder with Grieg of the first Norwegian Academy of Music in 1866, dies in the renamed city of his birth, then Christiania, now Oslo, at the age of ninety-three. (Date from *Totenschau, * Peters' *Jahrbuch,* 1931)

12 MAY 1931

Eugène YSAŸE, celebrated Belgian violinist in the grand tradition of the nineteenth century, dies in Brussels, in his seventy-third year.

14 MAY 1931

An unruly Fascist strikes TOSCANINI at his concert at Bologna for refusal to lead the orchestra in a performance of the Fascist hymn, *Giovinezza,* as a prelude to his program. (New York *Times,* 16 May 1931)

15 MAY 1931

The Festival Week of New Music opens in Munich with the first performance of *Comedy of Death,* opera by Francesco MALIPIERO, written in a broad contrapuntal, neo-Monteverdian style.

16 MAY 1931

Cress Ertrinkt, "school opera" in the neo-infantile idiom by FORT-NER, is produced at the Festival Week of New Music in Munich.

17 MAY 1931

Die Mutter, opera in quarter-tones by the Czech apostle of fractional tone systems, Alois HÁBA, is produced in first performance at the Munich Festival.

"My first quarter-tone opera is a demonstration of the fact that it is humanly possible to build large musical forms in an unthematic style. Harmonically I have used combinations ranging from two to twenty-four different sounds. Melodically I use multiples of quarter-tones: 3/4 tones, 5/4 tones, neutral thirds, sixths, fourths, and sevenths. This style may be defined as diatonic music of the quarter-tone system. For the première in Munich, the firm of August Foerster has built a new quarter-tone piano, Kohlert has constructed two new quarter-tone clarinets, Heckel has supplied two quarter-tone trumpets." (Alois Hába in *Anbruch,* May 1931)

18 MAY 1931

The syndicate of artists and musicians of Bologna, Italy, adopt a resolution condemning Toscanini's stand in refusing to conduct the Fascist hymn at his Bologna Concert as "absurd and unpatriotic."

18 MAY 1931

Entrata by the neo-academic Carl ORFF; *Concerto Grosso* by the neo-classicist Heinrich KAMINSKI; an oratorio by the reformed modernist, Werner EGK—Germans all—are performed at the Munich Festival.

19 MAY 1931

A *Chorkantate* by the Russian-German romanticist Vladimir VO-GEL is performed for the first time at the Munich Festival.

20 MAY 1931

La Rappresentazione di Anima e di Corpo, spiritual oratorio by CAVALIERI, is revived at the Munich Festival three hundred and thirty-one years after its original performance.

22 MAY 1931

At the concluding concert of the Festival Week of New Music at Munich, the *Lyric Cantata* by the Swiss neo-contrapuntist, Conrad BECK, is performed for the first time, as a companion piece to STRAVINSKY's *Oedipus Rex* and KŘENEK's *Nightingale* for coloratura soprano, two flutes, and strings.

3 JUNE 1931

Deep Forest, prelude for chamber orchestra written in an impressionistic fin-de-siècle manner by Mabel DANIELS, her op. 34, No. 1, is performed in New York for the first time by the Barrère Little Symphony, Georges Barrère conducting.

6 JUNE 1931

Under the auspices of the Pan-American Association of Composers, Nicolas SLONIMSKY conducts the first of the two concerts of American music at the Salle Gaveau in Paris, with the following program:

American Life, overture in an atonal jazz idiom by the Baltimore-born Schoenbergian, Adolph WEISS; *Three Places in New England:* (1) *Colonel Shaw and his Black Regiment,* subtle evocation, with no ethnological literalness; (2) *Putnam Park, Connecticut,* musicorama of American Revolution, with snatches of contemporary songs and marches in polymetric simultaneity; (3) *The Housatonic at Stockbridge,* an impressionist tone painting exceedingly fluid in rhythm within a set meter, by the precursor and pioneer, Charles E. Ives; *Men and Mountains,* quasiatonal Blake-inspired score by Carl RUGGLES; *Synchrony,* constructivist symphonic poem with "tone-clusters" of narrow-range intervals, by Henry COWELL (this performance being the first anywhere); and *La Rebambaramba,* based on Cuban Negro life with great profusion of native rhythms by the Cuban mulàtto composer, Amadeo ROLDÁN.

"It seems that polyrhythmic and polyharmonic experiments are conducted in America in a spirit more sane, more candid, and more youthful than here. One needs a certain savagery to move with easy step in this new domain of music administered with fist blows. With us, a heavy artistic heredity takes away from this spontaneous play a part of its joyous insouciance." (Émile Vuillermoz in *Excelsior,* Paris, 8 June 1931)

"Nicolas Slonimsky of Boston, indefatigable in furthering the cause of the extreme radical composers, has brought out in Paris orchestral compositions by Americans who are looked on by our conservatives as wild-eyed anarchists. . . . Are these Parisians to be blamed if they say that the American composers thus made known to them are restless experimenters, or followers of Europeans whose position in the musical world is not yet determined, men who show ingenuity chiefly by their rhythmic inventions and orchestral tricks; men who apparently have no melodic gift, or, having it, disdain it for the tiresome repetition and transformation of an insignificant pattern; who neglect the sensuous charm of stringed instruments and put their trust for startling effects in combinations of wind and percussion choirs?" (From Philip Hale's editorial, "Mr. Slonimsky in Paris," Boston *Herald*, 7 July 1931)

7 JUNE 1931

La Société Française de Musicologie of Paris is recognized by the government as an educational institute *"d'utilité publique."*

11 JUNE 1931

At the second Pan-American concert in Paris, the following program for chamber orchestra is given, Nicolas SLONIMSKY conducting:

Sones de Castilla, suite of Stravinsky-esque airs of old Spain by the Spanish composer, Pedro SANJUÁN; *Energia,* primitive and virile in its anti-aesthetical constructivism by the Mexican, Carlos CHAVEZ; *Préambule et Jeux* for harp and nine instruments by the Franco-American modernizer, Carlos SALZEDO; *Bembé,* Cuban movement in primitive discordant polyphony and polyrhythm by the Cuban, Alejandro CATURLA; *Three Canons* in dissonant counterpoint by Wallingford RIEGGER; and *Intégrales,* abstract music of condensed, static emotion by Edgar VARÈSE.

23 JUNE 1931

Amphion, ballet-melodrama by Arthur HONEGGER to the book of Paul Valéry, is produced at the Paris Opéra, with Ida Rubinstein dancing the principal part.

14 JULY 1931

Anna DVOŘÁK, widow of the composer, dies at her residence at Wysoka, having survived Dvořák by twenty-seven years and two and a half months.

21 JULY 1931

Hans Barth patents his quarter-tone piano.

"This instrument has two keyboards of eighty-eight notes each and appears to be much larger than the present-day piano. The upper keyboard is tuned to the regular international pitch and has the usual five black keys and seven white keys. The other keyboard is pitched a quarter-tone lower and the keys are five blue keys and seven red keys. The 'A,' a quarter-tone lower than the regular '440' pitch, is 427½ pitch. . . . The music written for this instrument at first sounds weird to the average listener, but after a while it gives one a new feeling of tone color never experienced before." (Date and information communicated by Hans Barth)

23 JULY 1931

The ninth annual Festival of the International Society for Contemporary Music opens at Oxford, England, with the following program of orchestral music:

Lyric Suite for small orchestra in orthodox four movements in a Scriabin-esque idiom and subtilized instrumentation, by the Soviet composer, Lev Knipper; *Pianoforte Sonata* in a continuous three-segmented movement, cumulatively built in a general neo-classical idiom of enlarged tonality, by the American, Roger Sessions; *String Trio* in an atonal constructivist idiom, by the Polish composer, Josef Koffler; *Ame en Peine* for unaccompanied chorus by Jean Huré, French composer who had died one and a half years before; *Three Unaccompanied Choruses* in a designedly austere non-contrapuntal style by the Schoenbergian composer and Byzantine scholar, Egon Wellesz; *Four Japanese Songs* for voice and orchestra in the "Tokyo scale" (with quarter-tones) and the hexatonic "peasant scale" by the Polish composer, Jan Maklakiewicz; and *Sinfonietta* in three movements, in an eighteenth-century style, by the Spanish composer, Ernesto Halffter.

24 JULY 1931

At the second concert of the Oxford Festival (ISCM) three ballets are produced:

Pomona by the British composer, Constant Lambert, in dance-suite form (conducted by the composer); *La Somnambule,* a grotesque dance, in an "absolute" form, with an abstract, symbolic scenario, by the Prague-born atonal neo-classicist, Erwin Schulhoff (conducted by the composer);

and *Job,* "being Blake's vision of the Book of Job," a "masque for dancing" by VAUGHAN WILLIAMS, re-orchestrated for theater orchestra by Constant LAMBERT, and conducted by him.

25 JULY 1931

At the Oxford Festival (ISCM) in an afternoon performance a
musical game for children by Paul HINDEMITH, his first piece of
kindergarten *Gebrauchsmusick,* in a neo-Haydnesque style, with
simple stage action, free from all allegory or symbolism, is presented under the title *Wir Bauen eine Stadt.*

In the evening concert, the following program is given:

String Quartet in four descriptive movements (Calme, Rhythmique,
Douloureux, Rigaudon) by the post-impressionist, now turning toward
absolute music, Marcel DELANNOY; *Sonatina* for pianoforte in three
movements, in delicate neo-classical vein, light of texture and ternary
in form, by the Viennese, Otto JOKL; *Sonatina* for flute and clarinet by
Jean CARTAN, French composer writing in concise, expressive style in a
general neo-classical direction; the ultra-chromatic, harmonically tense
and dynamically explosive *Second Sonata* for violin and piano by Eugene GOOSSENS; and a discursive *Piano Quintet* by the Italian composer,
Mario PILATI.

27 JULY 1931

As part of the ninth annual Festival of the ISCM, an orchestral concert of modern music is given in the Queen's Hall, London, with the following program:

Symphonic Music in a neo-classical "absolute" style by the Polish composer, Roman PALESTER; *Symphony* for small orchestra, op. 21, by Anton WEBERN, built on a series of twelve different notes subdivided into
two symmetrically disposed tropes, and orchestrated in WEBERN's customary attenuated manner, so that in some sections no instrument is allowed to play two thematic notes in succession, thus establishing the
principle of non-repetition of tone-color as well as of the twelve notes;
Rhapsody for orchestra by PIZZETTI's disciple, Virgilio MORTARI; *Second
Symphony* by the Russian cosmopolitan composer, Vladimir DUKELSKY,
in three movements, and in a neo-Glinka-esque stylized manner; *Music
for Orchestra,* non-programmatic in design, by Constant LAMBERT, conducted by the composer; and *An American in Paris,* a mock-nostalgic
jazzified symphonic poem by George GERSHWIN.

28 JULY 1931

As part of the ninth annual Festival of the ISCM, a second orchestral concert is given in the Queen's Hall, London, presenting the following program of orchestral music:

Three Symphonic Pieces by Juan José CASTRO, Argentine composer of Parisian training; *Three Symphonic Movements* by the Belgian, Fernand QUINET; *Polish Songs* for unaccompanied chorus by the Polish neo-romantic composer, Karol SZYMANOWSKI; *Song of the Wolves* for unaccompanied chorus by the Hungarian, Ferencz SZÁBO; *Benedicite* for soprano solo, chorus, and orchestra by VAUGHAN WILLIAMS; *Two Studies for Orchestra* (Ritmica funebre—Ritmica scherzosa) by the German-Russian, Vladimir VOGEL, written in an expansive sonorous style; and *Psalm 80* for chorus and orchestra by Albert ROUSSEL.

15 AUGUST 1931

The first annual Festival of Mountain White Folk Music ("White Top Folk") is held at Marion, Virginia.

21 AUGUST 1931

Moussorgsky, Letters and Documents, a collection of new material on MOUSSORGSKY's life, prepared and edited by Andrey RIMSKY-KORSAKOV, son of the composer and director of the music manuscript department of the Leningrad Public Library, is published by the State Music Publishers, Moscow. (Colophon date)

25 AUGUST 1931

Edward Burlingame HILL completes the composition of his *Concertino* for piano and orchestra. (Date communicated to the author by the composer)

6 SEPTEMBER 1931

Randall THOMPSON, New York-born composer, completes at Gstaad, Switzerland, four and a half months after his thirty-second birthday, his major opus, the *Second Symphony,* in four contrasting movements in a peculiarly subdued rhythmic and harmonic idiom, much in the manner of European neo-romantic composers.

3 OCTOBER 1931

Carl NIELSEN, the SIBELIUS of Denmark, composer of romantically expansive music (his third symphony is surnamed *Espansiva*) singularly compatible with austerity of form, dies at Copenhagen in his sixty-seventh year.

10 OCTOBER 1931

Belshazzar's Feast, oratorio for mixed choir, baritone, and orchestra by William WALTON, written in an effective neo-Handelian manner, is performed for the first time at the Leeds Festival in England.

22 OCTOBER 1931

Alfredo CASELLA completes at Olevano Romano the score of his opera, *La Donna Serpente* (begun in Rome on 16 October 1928), in a style of commedia dell'arte, spontaneously improvisatory, and with harmonies in a clear tonal idiom, pan-diatonically enriched.

23 OCTOBER 1931

Harold MORRIS, American composer, plays the solo part with the Boston Symphony Orchestra in the first performance anywhere of his *Piano Concerto* in an evocative somber post-impressionistic style, in three movements, of which the second is based on the *Negro Pilgrim Song.*

23 OCTOBER 1931

Igor STRAVINSKY conducts in Berlin the first performance, played by Samuel Dushkin, of his *Violin Concerto,* in three movements, in an oscillating major-minor mode, classical form, and quiet rhythm, except for the varimetric Finale recalling the *Danse Sacrale* of *Le Sacre du Printemps.*

13 NOVEMBER 1931

Edgar VARÈSE completes, in Paris, the score of *Ionisation,* written for instruments of percussion, friction, and sibilation, of indeterminate pitch (the kettle-drums being excluded), written in a sonata form, with the first subject given out by the *tambour militaire* (the while two sirens slide over the whole range in opposite directions like two harps glissando), the second by the *tutti* of percussion instruments, the development section being built on contrasting metal and wood percussion tone-color, and the coda (after an abridged recapitulation) introducing tubular chimes and low-register pianoforte tone-clusters (like pedal points).

19 NOVEMBER 1931

For the first time since the war, a French orchestra, the Orchestre Symphonique de Paris, under Pierre MONTEUX, gives a concert in Berlin, in a program of French music.

19 NOVEMBER 1931

Jack and the Beanstalk, "a fairy opera for the childlike" to the book of John Erskine, by the Russian-born American, Louis GRUENBERG, a modernistic score with suggestion substituted for naturalism (the cow's male voice, the giant's falsetto, the laying of the golden eggs in subtilized orchestral sonorities, etc.), is performed for the first time anywhere at the Juilliard School of Music in New York.

24 NOVEMBER 1931

Alban BERG's expressionist opera, *Wozzeck,* is performed in a New York première by the Philadelphia Opera Company, Leopold STOKOWSKI conducting.

"The evening was one not soon to be forgotten. An original and distinguished work of art, extraordinarily moving and sincere, was placed before us in the fullness of its power, its pity, and its truth—a work which raises in sympathetic minds that haunting question which was asked so long ago by Aeschylus, 'Ah! What is mortal life?' " (Lawrence Gilman in the New York *Herald Tribune,* 25 November 1931)

25 NOVEMBER 1931

Sonata for chamber choir, by the Dutch composer, Daniel RUYNE-MAN, with vocal instrumentation built on the differentiation of tone-color of various vowels, is performed for the first time in Vienna.

1 DECEMBER 1931

Marc DELMAS, French composer of the transition style, Prix de Rome winner of 1919, dies in Paris in his forty-seventh year.

2 DECEMBER 1931

Vincent d'INDY, French composer of romantic inspiration, whose music reflects nature through programmatic inference, and whose style is notable for his scrupulous avoidance of all unclean sonorities, dies in his native Paris in his eighty-first year.

8 DECEMBER 1931

Of Thee I Sing, political satire by George KAUFMAN, music by George GERSHWIN, is produced at the Majestic Theatre in Boston.

15 DECEMBER 1931

Igor MARKEVITCH, nineteen-and-a-half-year-old Russian-born Parisian composer, conducts the Orchestre Symphonique de Paris in the first performance of his ballet suite, *Rebus,* dedicated to the memory of DIAGHILEV, and containing the following movements:

Prelude, with two trumpets in strident concertanto; *Dance,* in clear neo-classical idiom; *Gigue,* cumulatively dynamic; *Variations,* in a continuous movement; *Fugue;* and *Parade of Vices,* the solution of the Rebus being: "Poverty is not a Vice!"

21 DECEMBER 1931

A Nous la Liberté, French "film sonore" by René Clair, with melodious quasi-popular incidental music by Georges AURIC, is shown at the Ermitage Theatre in Paris for the first time.

27 DECEMBER 1931

The Academy of Santa Cecilia in Rome confers honorary membership on Paul HINDEMITH, Zoltán KODÁLY, Albert ROUSSEL, and Georges ENESCO. (Date communicated by the Academy)

1932

5 JANUARY 1932

Maximilian, opera by Darius MILHAUD, based on the story of the Mexican Emperor and written in tense, strident harmonies punctuated by rhythmic ostinatos, is produced at the Paris Opéra.

6 JANUARY 1932

Paul WITTGENSTEIN, one-armed Austrian pianist (his right arm was amputated in a Russian hospital when he was a war prisoner), plays in Vienna the first performance anywhere of RAVEL's piano *Concerto* for the left hand alone, specially written for him.

14 JANUARY 1932

Eight days after the first performance in Vienna of his left-hand piano *Concerto,* RAVEL conducts in Paris, at a concert of his music, the first performance of his first piano *Concerto* for both hands (written before the left-hand *Concerto*), with Marguerite Long playing the solo part.

23 JANUARY 1932

Belkis, Queen of Sheba, "choreography in seven scenes" by Ottorino RESPIGHI, couched in an eclectic oriental idiom, including old modes, pentatonic tropes, as well as chromaticized "Eastern" tone-progressions, is produced at La Scala in Milan.

29 JANUARY 1932

Rhapsody No. 2 for orchestra, originally named *Rhapsody in Rivets,* by George GERSHWIN, written in a more austere manner than the first *Rhapsody (in Blue),* is performed for the first time anywhere (discounting a trial hearing in a studio of the National Broadcasting Company in New York City on 26 June 1931) by the Boston Symphony Orchestra, KOUSSEVITZKY conducting.

19 FEBRUARY 1932

Symphonic Ode, composed for the fiftieth anniversary of the Boston Symphony Orchestra (1931) by Aaron COPLAND, is performed for the first time anywhere by the Boston Symphony, KOUSSEVITZKY conducting.

20 FEBRUARY 1932

Henry SAYERS, author of *Ta-Ra-Ra-Boom-De-Ay,* dies in New York in his seventy-eighth year.

(Theodore Metz, author of the song *There'll Be a Hot Time in the Old Town Tonight,* also claimed the authorship of *Ta-Ra-Ra-Boom-De-Ay.* *Le Ménestrel* of 12 April 1921 reports the death in London of a Richard Morton, adding that he was the author of *Ta-Ra-Ra-Boom-De-Ay*)

25 FEBRUARY 1932

Sun-Treader, so named after Browning's line, "Sun-treader, light and life be thine forever," symphonic poem by the Vermonter, Carl RUGGLES, written in a poignant atonal idiom for a large orchestra in fives, unrelievedly tense from the first accelerated beats of the drum to the last C-major chord (stuffed with piercing chromatics between its third and its fifth), is performed for the first time anywhere in Paris by the Orchestre Symphonique de Paris, Nicolas SLONIMSKY conducting.

6 MARCH 1932

John Philip SOUSA, American "March King," dies at Reading, Pennsylvania, at the age of seventy-seven years and four months, almost forty years after the first concert of the Sousa Band at Plainfield, New Jersey, 26 September 1892.

10 MARCH 1932

A century has passed since the death at Evesham, England, of Muzio CLEMENTI.

10 MARCH 1932

Francesco MALIPIERO completes at Asolo, eight days before his fiftieth birthday, the composition of his *Violin Concerto* in three movements, written in a characteristic pan-diatonic tonality, the seven tones of the scale being superimposed freely on each other over a functional bass (thus the opening chord is C-G-E-A-D-G-B, functioning as C major).

12 MARCH 1932

The Congregation of the Council at the Vatican issues a decree discouraging the use of modern sacred music in Catholic churches and forbidding it when royalties to the composer or publisher are to be paid.

14 MARCH 1932

Congress of Arab music opens in Cairo, the discussion centering on the problem of establishing a standard scale.

16 MARCH 1932

Ottorino RESPIGHI conducts in New York the world première of his mystery-triptych, *Mary of Egypt,* a legend of sin and repentance in a neo-modal austere style.

16 MARCH 1932

The *Fourth Symphony* by Arnold BAX is performed for the first time anywhere by the San Francisco Symphony, Basil Cameron conducting.

17 MARCH 1932

Alfredo CASELLA conducts in Rome the first performance of his opera, *La Donna Serpente.*

18 MARCH 1932

Richard SPECHT, Austrian writer on music, author of a circumstantial two-volume biography-appreciation of Richard STRAUSS as well as of a book on BRAHMS, dies in his native Vienna in his sixty-second year.

24 MARCH 1932

Randall THOMPSON's *Second Symphony* is performed for the first time anywhere by the Rochester Philharmonic Orchestra, How-ard HANSON conducting.

26 MARCH 1932

Jean CARTAN, French composer of chamber music of fine texture and exquisite detail, disciple of Roussel, dies at the sanitarium of Bligny, a victim of tuberculosis, at the age of twenty-five years, three months, and twenty-five days.

31 MARCH 1932

Two centuries have passed since the birth at Rohrau of Joseph HAYDN.

31 MARCH 1932

H.P. (Horsepower), constructivist ballet by the Mexican, Carlos CHAVEZ, is produced, with stage design by Diego Rivera, by the Philadelphia Grand Opera Company, STOKOWSKI conducting.

2 APRIL 1932

Leopold STOKOWSKI conducts a radio-broadcast concert of the Philadelphia Orchestra in the following program of American music:

Pleasure-Dome of Kubla Khan, impressionist symphonic poem by Charles Tomlinson GRIFFES (dead six days short of twelve years before); constructivist *Synchrony* by Henry COWELL; *Virginia Reel,* by John POWELL; *Music for the Theatre* by Aaron COPLAND; *Nine Colors* by the Russian-born American impressionist-miniaturist, Louis GRUENBERG; *Atonal Fugue* (for eighteen violins), with a definite keynote, by the Russo-American, Arcady DUBENSKY; the third part of *Abraham Lincoln,* biographical symphony by the jazz composer and orchestrator, Robert Russell BENNETT; and *Suite* in a neo-classical idiom by the Bostonian, Walter PISTON.

15 APRIL 1932

Wilhelm FURTWAENGLER conducts the first of the two "Festkon-zerte" of the Berlin Philharmonic Orchestra on the occasion of its fiftieth anniversary in a program that includes, besides BACH's B-minor *Suite* and BRUCKNER's *Seventh Symphony,* the first per-

formance of a piece specially written by Paul HINDEMITH, entitled
Philharmonisches Konzert (Variationen fuer Orchester).

22 APRIL 1932

La Femme Nue, "veristic" opera by the French composer, Henri
FÉVRIER, is produced at the Paris Opéra-Comique.

23 APRIL 1932

The Council of People's Commissars publishes a decree dissolving
literary, artistic, and musical proletarian organizations, among
them the RAPM (Russian Association of Proletarian Musicians).

"7 o'clock in the evening. In the hall of the Collegium of the People's
Commissariat of Education there is an atmosphere of excitement—all the
composers and musical workers of Moscow and Leningrad are gathered
there. All ages and all wings of creative musical craft of Soviet culture
are represented, from Ippolitov-Ivanov to the leaders of the RAPM.
. . . Those assembled are grouped according to trends and tendencies.
There is restrained talk. On the serious faces, a question: what is going
to happen? It is apparent that something unusual is in the air. Possibly
a decisive battle. . . . Comrade Bubnov opens the discussion of problems of construction in Soviet musical culture, points out some breaks
in this field. He asks to talk frankly, to the bitter end. . . . Those present take the floor one after another, and attack the RAPM with extraordinary vehemence. Its theoretical, creative, tactical attitudes are
under fire. In many speeches there is rancour; theoretical contentions
give way to echoes of recent squabbles. Feelings run high. . . . It is
clear that the RAPM rule, which limits the sphere of creative work,
causes unhealthy conditions for the development of Soviet music. . . .
On 24 April, the Moscow papers publish the decree of the Central Committee announcing the dissolution of Proletarian art associations." (*Sovietskaya Musica,* No. 3, 1933, p. 132. See also the declaration of aims of
the RAPM in Part III)

30 APRIL–1 MAY 1932

The first Festival of Contemporary American Music is held at
Yaddo (the name being taken in memory of a child's labialized
pronunciation of "shadow"), private estate near Saratoga Springs,
New York, presenting eighteen chamber works in two evening
and one afternoon concerts:

Aaron COPLAND's *Variations* for piano; Walter PISTON's *Sonata* for flute and piano; Virgil THOMSON's songs with string quartet accompaniment; seven songs by Charles IVES, ranging from the evocative *Serenity* to the rollicking cowboy ballad *Charlie Rutlage;* songs by Paul BOWLES in a subtilized impressionistic mood; songs with string quartet accompaniment by Robert Russell BENNETT; *Piano Sonata* by Roger SESSIONS; the tersely effective *Sonata* for piano by Roy HARRIS; *Unidad* and *36* for piano in an "abstract" percussive style by the Mexican, Carlos CHAVEZ; *Suite* for flute unaccompanied in four movements, the last containing a series of thirty-six non-repeated notes, by Wallingford RIEGGER; *Four Diversions* for string quartet by Louis GRUENBERG; *Quartet* by Nicolai BEREZOWSKY; string quartets by Marc BLITZSTEIN, Israel CITKOWITZ, a racy quartet by the Mexican, Silvestro REVUELTAS; and piano pieces by Vivian FINE, Oscar LEVANT, and Henry BRANT, all three less than twenty years old.

1 MAY 1932

Five winning works by American composers, Philip JAMES, Max WALD, Carl EPPERT, Florence GALAJIKIAN, and Nicolai BEREZOW-SKY, selected from 573 manuscripts in a contest for the National Broadcasting Company's $5,000 prize, are broadcast under the direction of Eugene GOOSSENS, and the prize is awarded to a composition by Philip JAMES, entitled *Station WGZBX,* in four characteristic movements: *In the Lobby; Interference; A Slumber Hour; Mikestruck.*

2 MAY 1932

Columbia University announces the award of the Pulitzer Prize to George KAUFMAN and George GERSHWIN for their political satire, *Of Thee I Sing.*

"This award may seem unusual, but the play is unusual. . . . Its effect on the stage promises to be very considerable, because musical plays are always popular, and by injecting genuine satire and point into them, a very large public is reached." (From the statement by Columbia University)

9 MAY 1932

Emile HERZKA, head of the Universal Edition of Vienna, friend and champion of musicians of the vanguard, dies in Vienna in his sixty-fourth year.

1 JUNE 1932

Nicolas MIASKOVSKY's *Twelfth Symphony,* op. 35, in G minor, in three movements, dedicated to the fifteenth anniversary of the October Revolution, and known also as the "Collective Farm Symphony," is performed for the first time in Moscow, Albert Coates conducting.

(The *Twelfth Symphony* was completed 12 December 1931, orchestration finished 31 January 1932. These dates communicated by the composer)

"Already during my work on the *Tenth Symphony* I had an idea of writing several orchestral works based on song and dance material. . . . When the first call to collectivization of peasant agriculture was sounded, I was very much taken by this measure, which seemed most revolutionary in its consequences . . . almost instantly I conceived the musical image of a symphony about rural life, in three stages—before, during the struggle for the new order, and finally after the completion of that struggle. In the autumn of 1931 I began to work on my project but before that had time to write the *Eleventh Symphony* in which I voiced impressions of a more subjective character.

"The *Twelfth Symphony* turned out not quite according to my plans; in some respects it appeared schematic, although I did alter the formal scheme to express the subject matter. But, above all, I did not succeed in finding the proper idiom and form of the last movement. That part expresses my design only on its exterior, but is little convincing inwardly." (*Autobiographical Notes* by Miaskovsky in the *Sovietskaya Musica,* No. 6, 1936)

16 JUNE 1932

The tenth Festival of the International Society for Contemporary Music opens in Vienna with the following orchestral program:

Innominata, neo-classical work in dissonant counterpoint, by the Swiss, Conrad BECK, performed, by coincidence, on his thirty-first birthday; *Piano Concerto* in a vigorous rhythmic and diatonic style by the Russian expatriate composer, Nicolas LOPATNIKOV; *Overture to an Ancient Greek Tragedy,* based on the enharmonic mode, which includes quartertone intervals, by the Czech, Miroslav PONC, pupil of HÁBA; *Violin Concerto* by Karel HÁBA, brother of Alois, written in a discursive virtuoso manner without fractional tones; *Catalonian Melodies* by the Barcelona composer, Robert GERHARD; and *Bal Vénitien* in a style of slightly acidulated impressionism by the French composer, Claude DELVINCOURT.

17 JUNE 1932

At the second concert of the Vienna Festival (ISCM), the following program of chamber music is given:

Cantari alla Madrigalesca for string quartet in lyric neo-modal style by Francesco MALIPIERO; *Flute Sonata* by the Czech, Fidelio FINKE; *Viola Sonata* by Walter LEIGH of England; the catholic (from LISZT to jazz) *Piano Sonata* by the Austrian, Julius SCHLOSS; *Children's Cantata* in modernized church modes, by the Polish composer, Boleslaw WOYTOWICZ; and *Quintet for Wind Instruments,* a piece of abstract contrapuntal music by the Croatian composer, Josef MANDIC.

17 JUNE 1932

A monument to DEBUSSY is unveiled in Paris, and a concert of his works is conducted by GAUBERT, PIERNÉ, and TOSCANINI at the Champs-Élysées Theatre.

20 JUNE 1932

At the third concert of the Vienna Festival (ISCM), the following program of orchestral music is given:

Serenade for small orchestra by the Latvian-born Eduard ERDMANN, in a melodious neo-classical vein slightly touched with dissonance; *Piano Concerto* in percussive modern style by the German, Norbert VON HANNENHEIM; the vigorous, clear, and cunningly balanced *Violin Concerto* by the Pole, Jerzy FITELBERG; *Durch die Nacht,* song-cycle in an eclectic Germanic manner by Ernst KŘENEK; and a *Symphony for Brass* in a mock-serious jazzified fashion, by the Austrian, Hans JELINEK.

21 JUNE 1932

At the fourth, and last, concert of the Vienna Festival (ISCM), the following program of chamber music is given:

Quintet for oboe and strings in lyric, neo-Elizabethan light manner, by the English neo-romanticist, Arthur BLISS; a percussive, discordant, rhythmic *Kleine Sonate* for piano by the Czech, Karel REINER, pupil of HÁBA; *Serenade* by the Italian, Vittorio RIETI; *String Trio* in five movements, academically worked out, by the Austrian composer, Leopold SPINNER; *Eight Bagatelles* for string quartet and piano by the twenty-

year-old Parisian, Jean Françaix, in a hedonistic, brilliant neo-
Stravinskian manner; and *Nonet* for flute, oboe, clarinet, bassoon, horn,
and string quartet, in strong contrapuntal style by the Hungarian-
Parisian composer, Tibor HARSÁNYI. (On the same day, the Arbeiter-
Sinfonie, conducted by Anton von Webern, gives a program containing
SCHOENBERG's *Begleitungsmusik zu einer Lichtspielszene;* Alban BERG's
Drei Weinlieder to Baudelaire's words; and MAHLER's *Second Sym-
phony*)

15 JULY 1932

Four weeks after his fiftieth birthday, STRAVINSKY finishes the composition of the *Duo Concertant* for violin and piano.

"It is my love for the bucolic poets of antiquity and for the savant art
of their technique that determined the spirit and the form of my *Duo
Concertant*. The theme evolves through the five movements of my
piece, which form an integral whole and, so to say, a musical parallel to
ancient pastoral poetry." (Stravinsky, *Chroniques de ma vie,* Paris,
1935)

AUGUST 1932

Darius MILHAUD composes at Cauterets, France, a "musical story
for children," *A Propos de Bottes,* for a series "La Musique en
famille et à l'école," designed to serve the needs of every musical
man, woman, or child, very easy to play and to sing, but not without harmonic spice.

"The aim of this work is to put contemporary French musicians in
touch with amateurs of all ages. The taste for music must be encouraged
so that this sublime art may resume its place in the home. It seems that
amateurs who used to get together to play ensemble music have gradually abandoned this pastime so necessary for the development of musical culture. Mechanical music that has penetrated everywhere does not
give a pleasure similar to that felt by amateurs who like to play all by
themselves. It is necessary that these amateurs, without relinquishing the
masterpieces of the past, enter into contact with contemporary music.
It is incumbent upon composers to write all kinds of music, for amateurs as well as for children and schools. The music must be easy to perform, while preserving the character of our epoch and the personality
of the composer. We hope in this manner to create a constant collaboration between the amateurs and composers of today." (From Darius Milhaud's argument in the printed score)

1 AUGUST 1932

Composers of Leningrad form the Leningrad Union of Soviet Composers.

28 AUGUST 1932

The management of the Philadelphia Orchestra issues a statement to the effect that "debatable" new music will be avoided on the programs of the orchestra in order to keep a hold on the majority of its patrons.

28 AUGUST 1932

Jean NOUGUÈS, French composer of "veristic" operas, bordering on operettas, among them the popular *Quo Vadis,* dies in Paris in his fifty-eighth year.

13 SEPTEMBER 1932

Julius ROENTGEN, German composer, pianist, and educator, Director of the Amsterdam Tonkoonst Conservatory, dies at Utrecht, in his seventy-eighth year.

25 SEPTEMBER 1932

Jean CRAS, French composer of atmospheric quasi-impressionist music, disciple of Henri Duparc, dies in Paris in his fifty-fourth year.

27 SEPTEMBER 1932

Pierre DEGEYTER, composer of the *Internationale,* dies in Paris, eleven days before reaching eighty-four years of age.

29 SEPTEMBER 1932

Six months and twenty-six days after the death of Eugen D'ALBERT, his posthumous opera, *Dr. Wu,* is produced at the Dresden Opera.

1 OCTOBER 1932

Aulos, Chilean music monthly, begins publication at Santiago.

28 OCTOBER 1932

Igor STRAVINSKY plays with Samuel Dushkin the first performance of his *Duo Concertant* at a Rundfunk (radio) concert in Berlin.

31 OCTOBER 1932

Serge PROKOFIEV plays, with the Berlin Philharmonic Orchestra, the first performance anywhere of his *Piano Concerto, No. 5.*

6 NOVEMBER 1932

Symphony by Jean FRANÇAIX, twenty-year-old French composer, written in a fresh neo-classical vein with enough acidities, asperities, and rhythmic jostling to make it a distinctly twentieth-century piece, is performed in Paris for the first time by the Orchestre Symphonique de Paris, MONTEUX conducting.

10 NOVEMBER 1932

The *Second Symphony,* in four movements, by Bernard WAGENAAR is performed for the first time by the New York Philharmonic Orchestra, Toscanini conducting.

19 NOVEMBER 1932

Poker Flat, the third opera by the Czech composer, Jaromir WEIN-BERGER, in an Americanized dance manner, is produced at Brno.

25 NOVEMBER 1932

On his first American tour, Florent SCHMITT plays the piano part of his *Symphonie Concertante* for piano and orchestra at its first performance anywhere by the Boston Symphony Orchestra, KOUS-SEVITZKY conducting.

29 NOVEMBER 1932

Two days after the sixty-fifth birthday of Charles KOECHLIN, a festival of his music, all first performances, is given by the Orchestre Symphonique de Paris, Roger DESORMIÈRE conducting the following works: *Three Poems* after Kipling's *Jungle; Fugue in F Minor; Five Chorals in Medieval Modes;* and *Symphonic Fugue.*

29 NOVEMBER 1932

Three centuries have passed since the birth in Florence of Jean Baptiste LULLY (French spelling) or Lulli (Italian spelling). (The *Encyclopaedia Britannica* gives the wrong year, 1639, for Lully's birth)

DECEMBER 1932

The Lyre-Bird issues in Paris the first volume of the collected works of François COUPERIN, under the editorship of Maurice CAUCHIE.

"I have determined that an integral edition of Lully's works (Edition of the *Revue Musicale*) and of Couperin should be published first, for these two masters are known but in part, and their unpublished manuscripts constitute a legacy of French music which it is imperative to save from oblivion. . . . A similar preoccupation has drawn my choice towards the English Sonatas of John Blow and Purcell." (From the Preface to the first volume by Louise B. M. Dyer, founder of the Lyre-Bird Edition in Paris)

3 DECEMBER 1932

René LENORMAND, French composer-melodist, who created the form of French *Lied,* and founded the society, Le Lied en Tous Pays, dies in Paris in his eighty-seventh year.

11 DECEMBER 1932

The English Folk Dance Society, founded by Cecil Sharp, and the Folk Song Society are officially amalgamated under the name, "English Folk-Dance and Song Society," London.

(Arthur H. Fox-Strangways in his book *Cecil Sharp* cites this date as the "coming of age" of the society; the first issue of the annual *Journal of the English Folk-Dance and Song Society* is datelined December 1932; see, however, the catalogue card in the Boston Public Library, under *English Folk Dance Society,* London, which reads: "September 1, 1931, [sic] the *English Folk-Dance Society* merged with the *Folk Song Society* under the name, *The English Folk-Dance and Song Society,* London")

12 DECEMBER 1932

On the Banks of the Borysthenes, ballet by Serge PROKOFIEV, is performed for the first time at the Paris Opéra.

17 DECEMBER 1932

Ottorino Respighi, Giuseppe Mulé, Ildebrando Pizzetti, Riccardo Zandonai, Alberto Gasco, Alceo Toni, Riccardo Pick-Mangiagalli, Guido Guerrini, Gennaro Napoli, and Guido Zuffenato issue a manifesto deploring the "cerebrality" of modern music.

"We are against this art which cannot have and does not have any human content and desires to be merely a mechanical demonstration and a cerebral puzzle. In the musical world reigns the Biblical confusion of Babel. For twenty years the most diverse and disparate tendencies have been lumped together in a continual chaotic revolution. . . . A logical chain binds the past and the future—the romanticism of yesterday will again be the romanticism of tomorrow." (New York *Times,* 7 Jan. 1933)

28 DECEMBER 1932

Judge Woolsey of the United States District Court rules that the Pulitzer prize play, *Of Thee I Sing,* does not in any way plagiarize the revue *U.S.A. With Music,* copyrighted on 17 February 1930, by its authors, Lowenfeld and George Antheil.

30 DECEMBER 1932

Dmitri Shostakovitch writes, in Leningrad, the first of his twenty-four *Preludes* for piano in a free diatonic style, the framework being, in this particular piece, pure C major with dissonant melodic figuration.

(Dates of composition of the remaining twenty-three *Preludes* are: No. 2, 31 December 1932; No. 3, 1 January 1933; No. 4, 2 January 1933; No. 5, 4 January 1933; No. 6, 5 January 1933; No. 7, 7 January 1933; No. 8, 11 January 1933; No. 9, 14 January 1933; No. 10, 22 January 1933; No. 11, 27 January 1933; No. 12, 28 January 1933; No. 13, 3 January 1933; No. 14, 1 February 1933; No. 15, 2 February 1933; No. 16, 7 February 1933; No. 17, 11 February 1933; No. 18, 15 February 1933; No. 19, 21 February 1933; No. 20, 22 February 1933; No. 21, 24 February 1933; No. 22, 28 February 1933; No. 23, 1 March 1933; No. 24, 2 March 1933. The date, 31 January 1932 on the printed copy, for the second *Prelude,* is an obvious misprint for 31 December 1932)

1933

JANUARY 1933

The first part of the *Trésor de musique byzantine,* collection of liturgical chants of the Byzantine Church, composed and sung during the golden age of the Empire, is issued by the Lyre-Bird Press in Paris, under the editorship of Egon WELLESZ, Schoenberg disciple and Byzantine scholar. (Date of Preface)

6 JANUARY 1933

Vladimir DE PACHMANN, eccentric Russian-born pianist-Chopinist, dies in Riga, while establishing residence to divorce his fourth wife, in his eighty-fifth year.

7 JANUARY 1933

The Emperor Jones, opera in seven scenes, based on Eugene O'Neill's play, by Louis GRUENBERG, written with profusion of orchestral and rhythmic color, is produced by the Metropolitan Company in New York, with Lawrence Tibbett in the principal role.

"*The Emperor Jones* Triumphs as Opera—World Premiere of Gruenberg's Version of O'Neill's Play Hailed at Metropolitan—Tibbett Superb in Role—Drama Swift, Tense, Emotional, with Fantastical Music, and Spectacular Finale." (Headlines in the New York *Times*)

8 JANUARY 1933

The Academy of Santa Cecilia confers honorary membership on Eugene GOOSSENS, Karol SZYMANOWSKI, Florent SCHMITT, Josef SUK, and Gabriel PIERNÉ. (Date obtained by the author from the Academy)

10 JANUARY 1933

Edwin A. FLEISHER issues a privately printed catalogue of orchestral music of his music collection in the Free Library of Phila delphia, giving the instrumentation of hundreds of orchestral works and the dates of first performances of some. (Date of the Preface)

16 JANUARY 1933

The *Eleventh Symphony,* in B-flat minor, op. 34, by Nicolas MIASKOVSKY, in three movements, is performed for the first time in Moscow, Constantin Saradjev conducting.

(Composed from 10 September 1931 to 20 October 1931, orchestration completed 19 March 1932. Dates communicated by the composer)

19 JANUARY 1933

Rudolf GANZ conducts the Detroit Symphony Orchestra in the first performance of his *Animal Pictures,* character sketches written in a facile and pleasing manner, with some suggestive onomatopoeia.

12 FEBRUARY 1933

Lev KNIPPER conducts in the Red Banner Central House of the Red Army in Moscow the first performance of his *Third Symphony,* for large orchestra, chorus, and a military band, written in an optimistic major mode, partly based on Siberian folklore, and dedicated to the Far Eastern Army.

13 FEBRUARY 1933

Henri DUPARC, French composer of atmospheric songs of historic value as first examples of symphonic treatment of piano parts, dies in Paris in his eighty-sixth year, nearly half a century after he stopped composing.

21 FEBRUARY 1933

Carlos CHAVEZ is appointed Chief of the Department of Fine Arts of Mexico.

22 FEBRUARY 1933

Riccardo ZANDONAI conducts the first performance of his three-act opera buffa. *La Farsa Amorosa,* at the Royal Opera of Rome.

23 FEBRUARY 1933

The first issue of *Sovietskaya Musica,* Soviet periodical comparable with *Die Musik, La Revue musicale, Rivista musicale italiana,* and similar publications, rich in new material and elegantly put out, is published in Moscow, under the date-line, January–February 1933.

"Our periodical starts publication at a moment of extraordinary significance. The Soviet land, under the guidance of the party, its Central Committee, and the leader of the world proletariat, comrade Stalin, has completed the first five-year plan in four years, and is now entering the second five-year plan. . . . The decree of 23 April 1932 has aroused great enthusiasm among workers of the artistic front, among them musicians. The Union of Soviet Composers has the task of shaping this enthusiasm. . . . Our periodical must become one of the most important instruments of this leadership. . . . We will fight a relentless battle against the danger of the rightist interpretation of the decree of 23 April 1932 in the sense that the Central Committee has 'amnestied' all bourgeois idealistic theories. Under the pretense of study of Western-European technique, the rightist musicians are smuggling in the ideological baggage of the rotting bourgeois world, all these 'atonalities,' jazz harmonies, etc. . . . With the same conviction our periodical will fight all kinds of 'leftist' distortions of Marxism-Leninism, vulgarization, and pseudo-simplification, which was the practice and theory of the now liquidated Russian Association of Proletarian Musicians." (From the editorial article by N. Tcheliapov)

26 FEBRUARY 1933

Seventy-seven years and three months since he completed it, BIZET's youthful first *Symphony* in C major is performed for the first time in Paris, conducted by Felix Weingartner, from the manuscript found in the archives of the Paris Conservatory.

2 MARCH 1933

At a concert of works by LEV KNIPPER at the Moscow Conservatory, his *Fourth Symphony,* subtitled *Four Etudes for Orchestra; Improvisation, March, Aria, Finale,* is performed for the first time.

5 MARCH 1933

The *Violin Concerto* by Francesco MALIPIERO is performed for the first time anywhere by Viola Mitchell, with the Concertgebouw Orchestra in Amsterdam.

11 MARCH 1933

Carl EBERT, Director of the Berlin Civic Opera, and Fritz STIEDRY, conductor, are dismissed from their posts by order of Dr. Goebbels, as not meeting the requirements of the Aryan paragraph of the National Socialist statutes.

15 MARCH 1933

The National Socialist head of the Berlin Rundfunk forbids broadcasting of "Negro jazz."

16 MARCH 1933

The Leipzig authorities cancel a scheduled concert under the direction of Bruno WALTER, on the ground that a concert conducted by a Jew might endanger public order and security.

27 MARCH 1933

Mouvement Symphonique No. 3, by Arthur HONEGGER, without a programmatic subtitle (the first two "symphonic movements" being *Pacific 231* and *Rugby*), is performed for the first time anywhere by the Berlin Philharmonic, Wilhelm Furtwaengler conducting.

1 APRIL 1933

Arturo TOSCANINI, Walter DAMROSCH, Frank DAMROSCH, Serge KOUSSEVITZKY, Arthur BODANZKY, Harold BAUER, Ossip GABRILOVITCH, Alfred HERTZ, Charles Martin LOEFFLER, Fritz REINER, and Rubin GOLDMARK dispatch the following cable to the incumbent German Chancellor, urging him to stop racial and religious discrimination:

"Chancellor Adolf Hitler, Berlin, Germany. Your Excellency: The undersigned artists who live and execute their art in the United States of

America feel the moral obligation to appeal to your Excellency to put a stop to the persecutions of their colleagues in Germany for political or religious reasons. We beg you to consider that the artist all over the world is estimated for his talent alone and not for his national or religious convictions. . . . We are convinced that such persecutions as take place in Germany at present are not based on your instructions, and that it cannot possibly be your desire to damage the high cultural esteem Germany, until now, has been enjoying in the eyes of the whole civilized world. Hoping that our appeal in behalf of our colleagues will not be allowed to pass unheard, we are, Respectfully yours, etc."

"I am not enchanted over the idea of addressing as 'your Excellency' a man for whom I have not the slightest respect, neither do I think it quite truthful to say, 'We are convinced that such persecutions as take place in Germany at present are not based on your instructions,' whereas in reality I am thoroughly convinced that Hitler is personally responsible for all that is going on in Germany at the present time. I also want to make it clear that I am not in the least bit afraid to add my signature." (From a letter of Ossip Gabrilovitch, published in the New York *Times*, 2 April 1933, p. 29, col. 1)

4 APRIL 1933

The National Socialist commissarial head of the Radio Department issues the following order in connection with the protest of American musicians against racial and religious discrimination.

"According to newspaper reports, several conductors and musicians in the United States—Arturo Toscanini, Walter Damrosch, Frank Damrosch, Serge Koussevitzky, Arthur Bodanzky, Harold Bauer, Ossip Gabrilovitch, Alfred Hertz, Charles Loeffler, Fritz Reiner, and Rubin Goldmark—have lodged a complaint with the Chancellor because of the rejection of certain Jewish and Marxist fellow-musicians in Germany. . . . Pending clarification of this matter, I direct that the compositions and records of the afore-mentioned gentlemen shall no longer find a place on the programs of German broadcasters and also that no musical performance in which they in any wise have a part shall be received from concert halls or other senders."

5 APRIL 1933

The *Arctic Symphony* by Sergei VASSILENKO, based on Lapp and Eskimo folk tunes, is performed for the first time at a concert of his works in Moscow.

9 APRIL 1933

Sigfrid KARG-ELERT, German theorist and composer in divergent styles, from simple Lieder to atonal character sketches, chiefly known for textbooks for the organ, dies in Leipzig in his fifty-sixth year.

(Hull, Grove, Meyer's *Lexikon,* and Della Corte and Gatti, *Dizionario di musica,* give the wrong year of Karg-Elert's birth, 21 November 1879, instead of 1877. The correct date, 1877, is given by Riemann and Moser, and is further substantiated in a valedictory article in *Die Signale* of 23 November 1927, *Sigfrid Karg-Elert, zum 50 Geburtstage.* In English sources, the correct year is given in the program book of the Karg-Elert Festival, held in London from 5 May 1930 to 17 May 1930)

10 APRIL 1933

Dr. Goebbels, German Minister of Propaganda, rejects Wilhelm Furtwaengler's appeal in behalf of Jewish musicians and artists, specifically Otto Klemperer, Bruno Walter, and Max Reinhardt.

12 APRIL 1933

The *Second Concerto* for violin and orchestra, subtitled *The Prophets,* by M. CASTELNUOVO-TEDESCO, in three movements characteristic of the three prophets, Isaiah, Jeremiah, and Elijah, is performed for the first time anywhere by Jascha Heifetz with the New York Philharmonic Orchestra, Arturo Toscanini conducting.

23 APRIL 1933

Blair FAIRCHILD, American composer, resident since 1903 in Paris, where he settled after a short diplomatic career in the Near East, dies in Paris in his fifty-sixth year.

27 APRIL 1933

At the initiative of the International Music Bureau, the Moscow Radio Station organizes the first broadcast dedicated to the international revolutionary musical movement, presenting, among other works, the symphonic poems, *Class Struggle* and *November*

Seventh, by the Sovietized Hungarian, Ferencz SZÁBO, and *Symphonic Suite* by Hanns EISLER.

30 APRIL 1933

The International Music Congress opens in Florence in connection with the Florentine Musical May Festival.

7 MAY 1933

A century has passed since the birth in Hamburg of Johannes Brahms.

11 MAY 1933

Symphony by Youri SHAPORIN is performed for the first time by the Moscow Philharmonic Orchestra, Albert Coates conducting.

"My 'Symphony' was originally conceived as a piano concerto, but gradually outgrew that form. The embryonic sketches were made in 1926, and the symphony as a whole was completed in 1931–32. In this symphony I have tried to show the development of the fate of a human being in a great historical upheaval. It portrays the gradual transformation of individual consciousness in the process of acceptance of Revolution. The first part is the *Past*–that which is gone, and is no more. In this *Past,* however, there are seeds of revolutionary consciousness. It is reflected, thematically, in the first part of the symphony in which I use, in a modified form, a civil war song, 'Little Apple, whither are you rolling? If you go too far, you won't come back.' I treat this song in tragic tones. . . . The second part is called *Plyas* (Dance). . . . It is a realistic intermezzo with an emphasis on rhythmic power. . . . The third part is *Lullaby.* In it the feminine element seems to dominate. . . . The fourth part is the *March.* The thought behind the word *March* is that the revolution is an ever moving process." (From the composer's letter to the author, reproduced in 17th program book of the Boston Symphony Orchestra, season 1936–1937)

20 MAY 1933

Howard HANSON conducts at Ann Arbor, Michigan, the first presentation of his opera, *Merry Mount,* in concert form in anticipation of the stage production at the Metropolitan Opera.

24 MAY 1933

Ernst KRENEK completes the score of *Charles V,* his first composition in which the twelve-tone technique is consistently used.

25 MAY 1933

Walt Disney's Silly Symphony in technicolor, *The Three Little
Pigs,* is presented for the first time at Radio City Music Hall, New
York.

30 MAY 1933

Arnold SCHOENBERG and Franz SCHREKER are dismissed from the
faculty of the Prussian Academy of Arts by order of the German
Ministry of Education.

31 MAY 1933

Twenty-nine American composers form a Composers' Protective
Society, designed to combat the following common difficulties:

"1—The attitude which has reduced the composer to a minor position
in the modern musical world. 2—The usurpation of the dominant position in modern musical life by interpreters—instrumentalists, singers,
conductors. 3—The consequently unhealthy atmosphere for the nurturing
of new music—the apathy of the public, the limitations of the press, the
lack of organized encouragement of new music. 4—The concentration of
power in the hands of an average conductor—a self-confessed autocrat
—at whose mercy the average composer invariably is. 5—The exaggerated
attention bestowed upon a new reading of a familiar masterpiece, as
compared with the grudging, inadequate 'notice' of a new work. 6—The
operation of petty prejudices in directorial circles and nationalistic loy-
alties on the part of conductors, resulting frequently in the performances of inferior works which reflect discredit on the whole of modern
music. 7—The familiar practice of conductors and virtuosi in making up
their season's repertoire while abroad during the Summer months, with
the result that the American composer is deprived of the opportunity of
acquainting the public with his works via the programs of these artists
who provide the bulk of our musical activity during the Winter. 8—The
lack of opportunity for the composer (unless he is also an interpreter) to
earn a living through the serious pursuit of his profession. 9—The paucity
of informed discussion of new works in the periodical press as compared

with the attention devoted to new literature and painting." (New York *Times*, 1 June 1933)

5 JUNE 1933

Arturo TOSCANINI notifies the German government of his refusal to conduct at the Bayreuth Wagner Festival in view of discrimination against Jewish musicians in Germany.

6 JUNE 1933

The Fires of Paris, opera on a subject of the French Revolution, by Boris ASAFIEV, known as critic under the pseudonym, Igor GLEBOV, is produced at the Moscow State Opera.

9 JUNE 1933

The eleventh Festival of the International Society for Contemporary Music opens in Amsterdam with the following program:

Neo-classical *Suite for Orchestra* by Leo KAUFFMAN; *Fifteen Variations for String Orchestra*, on a twelve-note row, by a young Polish composer, Josef KOFFLER; *Pianoforte Concerto* in an iterative percussive style, by the not quite thirty-year-old Hungarian Bartók disciple, Paul KADOSA, with the composer at the piano; the *First Symphony* by the Dutch composer, Guillaume LANDRÉ, along neo-Flemish contrapuntal lines; and *Suite* for orchestra by the Czech composer, František BARTÓŠ.

10 JUNE 1933

At the ISCM Festival at Amsterdam, the Catalan composer Robert GERHARD conducts the following program:

His *Passacaglia* and *Chorale,* from a cantata based on a fourteen-note figure, serving alternately as an *ostinato* and *cantus firmus; Pater Noster* by Jean CARTAN, French composer who died young, a little over a year before; and *Belshazzar's Feast,* powerful neo-Handelian cantata by William WALTON. (This concert was originally scheduled to take place 11 June, according to advance programs)

11 JUNE 1933

At the ISCM Festival at Amsterdam, a concert of Dutch *a cappella* music is given, presenting choral works by the classical Flemish contrapuntists, Jacob Obrecht, Orlando Lasso, Jan Tollins, and

Sweelinck, in the first part; and by the modern Dutch composers, Bernard van den Sigtenhorst Meyer, J. N. Mul, and Willem Pijper in the second.

13 JUNE 1933

At the ISCM Festival at Amsterdam the following program of orchestral music is given:

A short *Second Symphony* by the Dutch composer, Bertus VAN LIER, in a complex neo-polyphonic style; *Five Orchestral Pieces,* in dissonant counterpoint by the young German, Edmund VON BORCK; neo-impressionistic *Concertino* for piano and orchestra by the half-French, half-Russian girl-composer, Marcelle DE MANZIARLY, with the composer at the piano; *Partita,* in a neo-classical optimistic style, by a representative of modern Italy, Goffredo PETRASSI; and *Theme and Variations* by a young Scotsman, Erik CHISHOLM.

14 JUNE 1933

Halewijn, expressionistic allegoric opera by Willem PIJPER, is presented at Amsterdam in the course of the ISCM Festival.

15 JUNE 1933

At the last concert of the ISCM Festival at Amsterdam, the following program of chamber music is given:

Terse and powerful *Piano Variations* by Aaron COPLAND; *Sonatina* for flute and clarinet by Juan Carlos PAZ of Buenos Aires; *Sonatina* for clarinet and piano by the Czech neo-polyphonist, Isa KREJCI; *Songs* by Ernst KŘENEK; *Three Songs* by the Ohio modernist, Ruth CRAWFORD, to Carl Sandburg's three poems, *Rat-Riddles* ("Why do you sneeze on Tuesdays?" to bass-drum accompaniment), *Prayers of Steel,* and *Tall Grass;* and a *Wind Quintet* by the twenty-four-year-old Yugoslavian composeress, Ljubrica MARIE.

1 JULY 1933

Arabella, a comedy of errors in the Vienna of 1860, by Richard STRAUSS, written in his light operetta style, is produced at the Dresden Opera.

6 JULY 1933

Robert KAJANUS, Finnish composer, conductor, and authoritative interpreter of Sibelius' works, dies at Helsingfors in his seventy-seventh year.

23 JULY 1933

Begleitungsmusik zu einer Lichtspielszene, Arnold SCHOENBERG's first symphonic work which portrays cinematic emotions as indicated in the subtitles, *Drohende Gefahr, Angst, Katastrophe,* is performed for the first time in the cinema capital by the Hollywood Bowl Orchestra, at a "Twilight" Sunday concert, Nicolas Slonimsky conducting.

24 JULY 1933

At a ceremony in a Paris synagogue, Arnold SCHOENBERG returns to the Hebrew faith, which he abandoned in 1921.

24 JULY 1933

Max SCHILLINGS, neo-Wagnerian German composer, whose synthetic style reflects influences of Wagnerian music drama, Pfitzner's symbolism, Italian verismo, and Viennese neo-romanticism, dies in Berlin in his sixty-sixth year.

30 JULY 1933

A Wagner Museum is opened at Triebschen, the villa near Lucerne where *Tristan und Isolde* was composed.

9 AUGUST 1933

The U.S.S.R. State Music Publishing House publishes the four-hand piano arrangement of a symphonic work, signed by Debussy, presumably composed during his sojourn in Moscow circa 1880, when he was domestic pianist to Madame von Meck, amateur musician and Tchaikovsky's financial benefactress. (Printer's date)

"The Debussy Symphony now published for the first time was found by the mathematician, C. S. Bogushevsky, who happened to buy a bound volume of four-hand arrangements of symphonic works among which he found a hand-written copy of an unknown work by Debussy, probably his autograph. On the title page was written in French: *Symphonie en Si —Andante—Air de Ballet—Final,* then follow a dedication and signature

without date: *Ach. Debussy*. The names in the title do not coincide with
the designations of the symphony itself which is subdivided not into
three, but into four sections: *Allegro ben marcato; Un poco piu lento;
Primo tempo; Le double plus lent*. It is to be supposed that besides this
symphony, Debussy wrote three more works, unknown to us, which form
a cycle with the present symphony. This work was probably written in
the late seventies or early eighties of the last century, during Debussy's
sojourn in Moscow. It reached us in the form of a four-hand arrangement,
doubtless Debussy's own. But it is also possible that the symphony was
never orchestrated and that the present form is not a transcription, but
the only authentic form." (From the Preface to the publication by N.
Jilaev)

13 AUGUST 1933

Paul HILLEMACHER, the elder of the two Hillemacher brothers,
composers of collective operas under the joint initials P. L. (Paul
and Lucien), dies in Versailles, in his eighty-first year, having
survived his younger partner-brother by over twenty-four years.

12 SEPTEMBER 1933

Two centuries have passed since the death of François Couperin.

13 SEPTEMBER 1933

Bronislaw HUBERMANN replies to Furtwaengler's invitation to continue his concert appearances in Germany, expressing the inner
impossibility to do so.

"Dear Friend, my attitude is based on the following fundamental objective human and ethical considerations: As far as the special realm of
the furtherance of the art of music is concerned, municipal and state
opera houses are an essential factor; yet no case has come to my attention
of the intended reinstatement of those orchestra conductors and music
teachers who were dismissed on account of their Jewish origin, their
differing political views or even their lack of interest in politics. . . .
You try to convince me by writing, 'Some one must make a beginning
to break down the wall that keeps us apart.' Yes, if it were only a wall
in the concert hall! It is not a question of violin concertos nor even
merely of the Jews; the issue is the elementary preconditions of our
European culture, the freedom of personality unhampered by fetters
of caste or race." (From the letter)

25 SEPTEMBER 1933

Two and a half centuries have passed since the birth of the father of contemporary harmony, Jean Philippe Rameau.

15 OCTOBER 1933

Twenty days after his twenty-seventh birthday, Dmitri SHOSTAKO-VITCH plays the piano part with the Leningrad Philharmonic in the first performance of his *Concerto* for piano and orchestra in four contrasting movements: optimistic *Allegro Moderato;* meditative *Lento;* short, transitional *Moderato;* and rollicking (*style pompier*), C-major *Allegro brio.*

23 OCTOBER 1933

The first volume covering the period 1876–1878 of the complete correspondence between Tchaikovsky and Madame von Meck, under the editorship of Nicolas Zhegin, Director of the Tchaikovsky Museum at Klin, and with his annotations, establishing for the first time the whole truth concerning Tchaikovsky's abnormal marriage, is published by the U.S.S.R. State Publishing House. (Printer's date)

31 OCTOBER 1933

Arnold SCHOENBERG arrives in America to teach at the Malkin Conservatory in Boston.

11 NOVEMBER 1933

The League of Composers presents in New York a concert of Arnold SCHOENBERG's chamber music, in celebration of his arrival in America.

11 NOVEMBER 1933

A century has passed since the birth in St. Petersburg of Alexander BORODIN, registered as the legitimate son of the serf butler, Borodin, but in fact the illegitimate son of the sixty-two-year-old prince, Luke Gedeonov, and twenty-five-year-old physician's wife, Avdotia Antonova.

(The date 30 October 1833, old style, **or** 11 November 1833, new style, is definitely established. The year 1834 given in most dictionaries is false)

15 NOVEMBER 1933

1929—A Satire, orchestral work depicting the emotions before and after the market crash by David Stanley SMITH, Dean of the Yale School of Music, is performed in New York for the first time anywhere.

15 NOVEMBER 1933

The establishment of the Reichsmusikkammer, affiliated with the German Ministry of Propaganda, is announced by Dr. Joseph Goebbels, and the following officers named: President, Richard STRAUSS; Vice-President, Paul GRAENER; General Music Director, Wilhelm FURTWAENGLER; members, Fritz STEIN, Gustav HAVEMANN; Secretary, Heinz IHLERT.

18 NOVEMBER 1933

The Philadelphia Symphony Orchestra, Leopold Stokowski conducting, makes the record of Dmitri SHOSTAKOVITCH's *First Symphony* on the day of recognition of the Soviet government by the United States.

(Date communicated to the author by Charles O'Connell, Director of the Artist Department of the Victor Company)

21 NOVEMBER 1933

Lionel DE LA LAURENCIE, French musicologist, editor of the *Encyclopèdie de la musique,* President of the French Society of Musicology, dies in Paris in his seventy-third year.

24 NOVEMBER 1933

Three movements from the symphonic poem, *Symphonie avec Hymne,* by Daniel LAZARUS, *Voyage Millénaire, Marche Funèbre,* and *Hymne,* in a characteristic idiom reflecting the archaic modes in modern dress, with saxophones in the orchestra, is performed for the first time anywhere by the St. Louis Symphony Orchestra, Vladimir Golschmann conducting.

29 NOVEMBER 1933

Francesco MALIPIERO completes at Asolo his *Sinfonia,* "in four movements like the four seasons," brief in duration (the *Lento— Autumn* is only fifty-one varimetric bars in length), in a neo-pastoral idiom, pan-diatonically ornamented.

12 DECEMBER 1933

Theodore Moses TOBANI, composer of the celebrated song, *Hearts and Flowers,* written in September 1893, dies in New York of apoplexy in his seventy-ninth year, survived by eight children.

15 DECEMBER 1933

Moon Trails, suite of four western sketches by Emerson WHIT-HORNE, is performed for the first time anywhere by the Boston Symphony Orchestra, Serge Koussevitzky conducting. (The score was completed 26 April 1933)

15 DECEMBER 1933

Carlos CHAVEZ conducts the Orquesta Filarmonica, Mexico City, in the first performance of his *Sinfonia de Antigona,* written in an austere idiom, making use of old Greek modes.

21 DECEMBER 1933

Paul HINDEMITH conducts in London a broadcast over the B. B. C. network of the first partial performance of his opera-symphony, *Mathis der Maler,* evocative of medieval art, and written in an extensive idiom ranging from ancient modes to the twelve-tone system, on the same program with his *Concerto* for piano and orchestra.

26 DECEMBER 1933

Dmitri KABALEVSKY completes in Moscow the composition of his choral *Third Symphony,* subtitled *Requiem,* and conceived as a symphonic song in memory of Lenin. (Date at end of printed score)

30 DECEMBER 1933

L. Dunton GREEN, English music critic, dies in an airplane disaster over Belgium, eight days after his sixty-first birthday.

31 DECEMBER 1933

An anti-jazz parade is held at Mohall, Ireland, with banners proclaiming "Down with jazz and paganism," and Sean MacEntee, Finance Minister, is denounced for his tolerance of jazz bands in the state broadcasting system.

1934

1 JANUARY 1934

The German State Philharmonic Orchestra of the German Soviet Republic of the Volga basin is established by decree of the Soviet government.

15 JANUARY 1934

The *Fifth Symphony* of Arnold BAX is performed for the first time by the London Philharmonic Orchestra, Beecham conducting.

16 JANUARY 1934

Madame Helena PADEREWSKA, wife of Paderewski, dies at Morges, Switzerland, in her seventy-fifth year.

21 JANUARY 1934

Dramatic Symphony, Lenin, by Vissarion SHEBALIN, for chorus, four soloists, narrator, and large orchestra, is performed for the first time by the Leningrad Philharmonic Orchestra.

21 JANUARY 1934

The Academy of Santa Cecilia in Rome confers honorary membership on Serge PROKOFIEV. (Date obtained by the author from the Academy)

22 JANUARY 1934

Lady Macbeth of the Mzensk District, grand opera in four acts and nine scenes to Leskov's quasi-Shakespearean story of a provincial uxoricide, by Dmitri SHOSTAKOVITCH, op. 29, is produced at the State Musical Theatre in Moscow.

"I started the composition of my opera, *Lady Macbeth of the Mzensk District,* late in 1930, and completed it in December 1932. I tried to make the musical language of the opera as simple as possible. I cannot agree with the theories once current here that the vocal line should be nothing more than speech with accentuated intonations. Opera is, before all, a vocal work. All vocal parts in my opera are built on broad cantilena, making use of all resources of the human voice, that richest musical instrument. The musical development follows a symphonic plan in continuous flow, with interruptions only at the end of each act. The musical interludes between the scenes serve as a continuation and development of the musical idea and illustrate the events of the drama." (D. Shostakovitch, *My Opera,* in the program book of the performance)

"Shostakovitch shows himself a ruthless satirist, ridiculing the cruelty of the merchant class, the stupidity of Russian priests, coarse soldiery, covetous bourgeoisie, corrupted lackeys, and noblemen. . . . From the musical point of view, Shostakovitch applies the method of 'lowering' of musical materials expressive of a given social type. He takes military marches, church music usage, ritual motives, and builds musical characterisation on this material. . . . Thus the scene at the police headquarters is treated with a deafening march by which the composer depicts the middle-class and the police. Under the mask of this stupid showy music, the animal image of the repellent Russian middle-class type is exposed to light." (A. Ostretzov, *The Music of the Opera, ibid.*)

"*Lady Macbeth of the Mzensk District,* later renamed *Katerina Ismailova,* the heroine's name, held our attention from the very first time that Shostakovitch played over the music at my house. All those present realized at once that we were confronted with a phenomenon of the highest creative order. The silence which lasted several minutes after he stopped playing was a sign of our emotion. No one cared to talk or to use common terms of praise. They would have been out of place here. . . . The opera was accepted without hesitation, and we, proud and happy to be the first to extend this act of recognition, signed the contract with Shostakovitch." (Boris Mordvinov, producer of the opera, *ibid.*)

26 JANUARY 1934

Symphony (1933) by Roy HARRIS, in three movements, is performed from manuscript by the Boston Symphony Orchestra, Koussevitzky conducting, seventeen days before the composer's thirty-sixth birthday.

"In the first movement I have tried to capture the mood of adventure and physical exuberance; in the second, of the pathos which seems to underlie all human existence; in the third, the mood of a positive will to power and action." (From Roy Harris' program note)

"The present encounters of Mr. Roy Harris, composer of music from the West with the symphonic public of Boston in the East must surely have pleasured him. . . . On Friday afternoon the symphony was played for the first time anywhere by a conductor and an orchestra whetted for the occasion. . . . Twice Mr. Harris was genuinely urged from his 'guest-seat' to the front of the stage, there to make acknowledgement to the conductor above and the audience before him. There were those present who believe themselves ear-witnesses to an event in the course of American music." (H. T. Parker in the Boston *Evening Transcript*, 27 January 1934)

8 FEBRUARY 1934

Four Saints in Three Acts, imaginative opera with affectedly simple music by Virgil THOMSON to Gertrude Stein's fantastically alogical libretto, is produced by the Society of Friends and Enemies of Modern Music, at Hartford, Connecticut, with a Negro cast in cellophane costumes.

10 FEBRUARY 1934

Merry Mount, opera by Howard HANSON from early colonial life in three acts and six scenes—*The Village (Midday); The Maypole (Afternoon); The Forest (Twilight); Bradford's Dream, The Hellish Rendezvous (Night); The Forest (Night); The Village (Night)* —is produced at the Metropolitan Opera in New York.

"Merry Mount World Premiere Is Acclaimed at Metropolitan—Opera of Puritans and Cavaliers Hailed As Lyric Protest." (Headlines in the New York *Herald Tribune)*

"Merry Mount Gets a Stirring Ovation—Reception Most Enthusiastic of 10 Years at Metropolitan." (Headlines in the New York *Times)*

"50 Curtain Calls Cap Opening of Merry Mount—Rochesterians Attend —Many Composers Present." (Headlines in the New York *Evening Post)*

"By Ballyhoo an Opera May Hardly Prevail—in Spite of Current Hubbub Merry Mount Remains Minor Stuff." (Headlines in the Boston *Evening Transcript*)

10 FEBRUARY 1934

First Symphony, op. 17, in orthodox four movements, by Louis GRUENBERG, composed in 1919 and revised in 1929, reaches belated first performance at a Boston Symphony concert, Koussevitzky conducting.

16 FEBRUARY 1934

Second Symphony by Nicolai BEREZOWSKY, in orthodox four movements, tonal, but with no designation of key, neo-romantic, but with no literary program, is performed for the first time from manuscript by the Boston Symphony Orchestra, Richard Burgin conducting.

23 FEBRUARY 1934

Sir Edward ELGAR, "laureate of English music," creator of a new national style of great dignity, impersonal beauty, and felicitous ardor, dies in London at the age of seventy-six years, eight months, and three weeks.

28 FEBRUARY 1934

Helen Retires, opera by George ANTHEIL to the libretto of John Erskine, is produced at the Juilliard School of Music in New York.

1 MARCH 1934

The first issue of *Revista brasiliera de musica*, trimestral magazine in the Portuguese language, is published in Rio de Janeiro.

2 MARCH 1934

Four Minutes and Twenty Seconds, for flute and string quartet, by Roy HARRIS, so named because it was expressly written to fill the extra side of the gramophone recording of his *Symphony (1933)*, is recorded by the Columbia Phonograph Company.

12 MARCH 1934

Mathis der Maler, symphony-suite by Paul HINDEMITH, in three movements descriptive of three pictures by Mathis—*Angelic Concert, Entombment,* and *The Temptation of Saint Anthony*—and conceived in the widest scope of musical resources from the medieval modes to the twelve-tone system, is performed for the first time in its entirety by the Berlin Philharmonic Orchestra, Furtwaengler conducting.

16 MARCH 1934

The Motion Picture Academy in Hollywood awards its certificate for the best animated cartoon to Walt Disney's Silly Symphony, *Three Little Pigs.*

16 MARCH 1934

Arnold SCHOENBERG makes his first American appearance as conductor with the Boston Symphony Orchestra, in his symphonic poem, *Pelleas und Melisande,* op. 5.

(Schoenberg was to be guest-conductor of the Boston Symphony at the concerts 12–13 January 1934, in a program of his works, but suffered a severe cold and was unable to appear)

20 MARCH 1934

The First Uzbek Symphony Orchestra gives its first concert at Tashkent, presenting the first performance of *Uzbekistan,* symphonic suite by IPPOLITOV-IVANOV, specially written for the occasion.

21 MARCH 1934

Franz SCHREKER, Monaco-born Vienna-bred German composer of effective theater music in a post-Wagnerian style, dies in Berlin two days before reaching his fifty-sixth birthday.

24 MARCH 1934

Dybbuk, opera to a Hebrew play on the subject of pathological possession by the spirit of the dead, by Ludovico ROCCA, written in a conventional Italianate style, is produced at La Scala in Milan.

24 MARCH 1934

La Favola del Figlio Cambiato, opera by Francesco MALIPIERO to Pirandello's play, is produced at Rome.

26 MARCH 1934

By Mussolini's order, Francesco MALIPIERO's opera, *La Favola del Figlio Cambiato,* produced two days before, is taken off the repertoire for reasons of "moral incongruity" in the story.

30 MARCH 1934

Henry Taylor PARKER, the H. T. P. of the Boston *Evening Transcript,* American music critic who wrote poems in prose for musical reviews and who fervidly encouraged all that is new and youthful in art, dies of pneumonia in Boston, a month before reaching his sixty-seventh birthday.

1 APRIL 1934

Die Musik, Germany's most scholarly musical monthly, becomes the official organ of Reichsjugendfuehrung and editorially pledges to serve the ideals of Hitler youth in art.

2 APRIL 1934

The twelfth Festival of the International Society for Contemporary Music opens in Florence with the following program of Italian orchestral music, arranged by the Italian section of the ISCM, Corporazione delle Musiche Nuove:

Symphony No. 2 by Franco ALFANO, written in the characteristic expansive and grandiloquent idiom of his operas; *Partita* by the thirty-year-old Luigi DALLAPICCOLA, representing a departure from the twelve-tone system of his earlier works and a trend toward neo-Casellan Scarlattianism; *Symphony* in four movements "like four seasons," in a tersely poetic idiom and economic instrumentation, by Francesco MALIPIERO; *Two Sicilian Songs,* by Giuseppe MULÉ; and the powerful *Introduction, Aria,* and *Toccata* by Alfredo CASELLA.

3 APRIL 1934

At the second concert of the ISCM Festival at Florence, the following program of chamber music is given:

String Quartet in a refined impressionist style by Henri MARTELLI; *Suite* for trumpet (mostly muted), bass clarinet, saxophone, and piano in a *style pompier*, with excursions into sophisticated vulgarity, by the twenty-four-year-old German expatriate, Rudolf HOLZMANN, replacing Hindemith who had withdrawn his previously scheduled work for political reasons; *Four Songs* on national tunes by the Serbian, Slavko OSTERC; vigorous and loud *Piano Sonata* by the young Dane, Knudage RIISAGER; Alban BERG's *Lyric Suite* for string quartet, written in a lofty poetic style within the twelve-tone system; and *Sonata* for two violins and cello, in a post-Stravinskian style, by the white hope of French music, Jean FRANÇAIX.

4 APRIL 1934

At the third concert of the ISCM Festival in Florence, the following program of orchestral music is given:

Arthur HONEGGER's *Mouvement Symphonique No. 3* (successor to the *Pacific* and *Rugby,* respectively symphonic movements No. 1 and No. 2), devoid of a programmatic subtitle or any acknowledged program; Maurice RAVEL's *Concerto* for left hand alone played by the one-armed pianist, Paul WITTGENSTEIN; *Rhapsody* for violin and orchestra by Béla BARTÓK; *Psalm* for soprano and orchestra by the twenty-two-year-old Parisian Russian, Igor MARKEVITCH, written in a strident neo-diatonic idiom, conducted by the composer, creating a sensation and shocking the audience into loud shouts of protest; *Turkmenia,* suite of middle-Asian dances in an effective rhythmic style by the Soviet composer, Boris SCHECHTER.

5 APRIL 1934

At the fourth concert of the ISCM Festival in Florence, the following program of chamber music is given:

Fantasy Quartet for oboe and strings by the twenty-year-old Englishman, Benjamin BRITTEN, in a poetic tonal style; *Piano Trio* by the Hungarian, Heinrich NEUGEBOREN; *Quartettino* for strings, in a gloomy introspective neo-Mahlerian manner by the Austrian, Leopold SPINNER; explosive *Sonata* for violin and piano by the Czech, Jaroslav JEZEK; *Five Lyric Pieces* in a neo-Wolfian manner by the Viennese Berg disciple, Hans Erich APOSTEL; *Cantata* for mezzo-soprano, flute, oboe d'amore, lute, viola d'amore, viola da gamba, and cello in a neo-archaic modal idiom by the Swiss, Richard STUERZENEGGER; and the smooth neo-classical *Sinfonietta* by the Swede, Lars-Erik LARSSON.

6 APRIL 1934

Union Pacific, ballet in five scenes by Nicolas NABOKOV, portraying the building of the transcontinental railroad, and making use of popular American tunes, is produced for the first time by the Monte Carlo Ballet at the Forrest Theatre, Philadelphia.

7 APRIL 1934

At the fifth and last concert of the ISCM Festival in Florence, the following program of Italian chamber music is given:

Second Quartet, in a simple, unaffected tonal style, by Mario LABROCA; *Concertino* for wind instruments, percussion, xylophone, and piano, in a hedonistic urban style by the twenty-year-old Venetian, Gino GORINI; *Songs* by CASTELNUOVO-TEDESCO; *Divertimento* for string trio, clarinet, bassoon, and trumpet, in five movements, by Riccardo NIELSEN of Bologna; and the dramatic and poetic *String Quartet* in D by Ildebrando PIZZETTI.

14 APRIL 1934

Symphonic Song by Serge PROKOFIEV, written in his new lyrico-heroic style, lucidly tonal and symmetrically constructed, is performed for the first time by the Moscow Philharmonic Orchestra.

22 APRIL 1934

All German singing societies are amalgamated into a German Saengerbund in conformity with the National Socialist principle of leadership.

26 APRIL 1934

Festival of the Workers, orchestral overture by Harl McDONALD, is performed for the first time at a youth concert of the Philadelphia Symphony Orchestra.

30 APRIL 1934

Igor STRAVINSKY conducts the first performance at the Paris Opéra of his *Persephone,* melodrama in three parts for orchestra, chorus, tenor, and a speaking voice, to a poem by André Gide.

"At the beginning of 1933, Mme. Ida Rubinstein had inquired whether I would consent to write the music for a poem by André Gide. I agreed in principle, and at the end of January André Gide joined me at Wiesbaden, where I happened to be staying. He showed me his poem, which was taken from the superb Homeric hymn to Demeter. The author expressed his willingness to make any modification in the text required by the music and under such conditions an agreement was quickly reached. A few months later I received the first part of the poem. I worked at the music of *Persephone* from May 1933 till I finished it at the end of the year." (Stravinsky, *Autobiography,* New York, 1936)

"*Persephone* is a sequel to *Oedipus Rex,* to the *Symphony of Psalms,* to the *Capriccio, Violin Concerto,* and the *Duo Concertant*—in short, to a progression from which the spectacular is absent. . . . I am on a perfectly sure road. There is nothing to discuss nor to criticize. One does not criticize anybody or anything that is functioning. A nose is not manufactured; a nose just is. Thus, too, my art." (Stravinsky's statement, translated from the original French, *Musical Times,* London, 1934)

4 MAY 1934

Shah-Senem, opera on native Azerbeidjan tunes by Reinhold GLIÈRE, is produced in Baku.

7 MAY 1934

Kykunkor, the Witch, African opera by Asadata Dafora HORTON of Sierra Leone, based on native African songs and rhythms, with a Negro cast and an orchestra of primitive percussion instruments, is produced at the Unity Theatre Studio in New York.

11 MAY 1934

Semiramis, ballet by Arthur HONEGGER, making use of Martenot's electrical instrument, ondes musicales, and *Oriane,* "tragédie dansée" by Florent SCHMITT, are performed for the first time at a ballet recital of Ida Rubinstein, at the Paris Opéra.

25 MAY 1934

Gustav HOLST, English composer of symphonic and choral works built on a large scale, and written in a neo-Handelian grandiose manner, dies in London in his sixtieth year.

JUNE 1934

Fernando LIUZZI completes his two-volume edition of documents and transcriptions of Italian medieval music, *La Lauda e i primordi della melodia italiana.*

(Date of the Preface. The inscription on the title-page "XIII E. F." means the thirteenth year of the Fascist Era, that is, the year 1934 of the Christian Era)

6 JUNE 1934

A Permanent Council for International Cooperation of Composers is founded in Wiesbaden after the Festival of German Music there with the following membership:

Richard STRAUSS; Emil REZNICEK (Germany); Friedrich BAYER (Austria); Emil HULLEBROCK (Belgium); Peder GRAM (Denmark); N. O. RAASTED (Denmark); Yrjö KILPINEN (Finland); Carol BÉRARD (France); Maurice BESLY (England); Adriano LUALDI (Italy); Ludomir RÓZYCKI (Poland); Adolf STREULI (Switzerland); Jaroslav KŘIČKA (Czechoslovakia); Kurt ATTERBERG (Sweden); and Jón LEIFS (Iceland).

9 JUNE 1934

Maschinenmensch, ballet of robots, music by Eugen ZÁDOR, is produced at the Landes-Theater in Braunschweig.

10 JUNE 1934

Francesco MALIPIERO completes at Asolo the composition of his *Concerto* for pianoforte and orchestra in one continuous movement, in a percussive instrumental style, with characteristic neoclassical diaphony. (Date at end of manuscript)

10 JUNE 1934

Frederick DELIUS, English composer of poetic music in all forms, often with literary allusions, dies at his French home, near Fontainebleau, in his seventy-second year, after a long period of infirmity and blindness.

10 JUNE 1934

Igor STRAVINSKY becomes a French citizen by decree of the French Ministry of Justice. (Date from *Le Journal officiel* for 1934, p. 5769, col. 3)

11 JUNE 1934

On his seventieth birthday, Richard STRAUSS receives a framed picture of Hitler with the following inscription: "Dem grossen Komponisten Richard Strauss in aufrichtiger Verehrung, Adolf Hitler"; also a framed picture of Dr. Goebbels with the inscription, "Dem grossen Meister der Töne in dankbarer Verehrung zum 70 Geburtstag."

15 JUNE 1934

Alfred BRUNEAU, prolific French composer of operas in an effective dramatic style and conventional nineteenth-century harmonic idiom, dies in Paris in his seventy-eighth year. (Moser's *Musik-Lexikon* gives in the *Nachtrag* the incorrect date 24 June 1934)

8 JULY 1934

Serge PROKOFIEV completes in Moscow the symphonic version of the suite, *Lieutenant Kije,* op. 60, based on the music for the film of that name, written in 1933. (Date communicated by the composer)

20 AUGUST 1934

Debussy's second wife, née Emma MOYSE, niece of the financier Osir, and formerly the wife of Monsieur Bardac, dies in Paris.

10 SEPTEMBER 1934

Sir George HENSCHEL, German-Polish singer-conductor, first leader of the Boston Symphony Orchestra, naturalized in England in 1890, and knighted in 1914, dies in Scotland in his eighty-fifth year.

12 SEPTEMBER 1934

In reply to queries, the Reichsmusikkammer officially denies that

Josef Weil, translator of the Dutch Thanksgiving hymn, *Wir treten zum Beten vor Gott den Gerechten,* was a Jew.

13 SEPTEMBER 1934

On the occasion of Arnold SCHOENBERG's sixtieth birthday, a dedicatory volume is published by Universal Edition, with a poem by Schoenberg himself, *Verbundenheit,* an anagrammatic poem by Alban Berg, spelling *Glaube, Hoffnung, und Liebe,* and articles by Anton von Webern, Alois Hába, Egon Wellesz, Erwin Stein, Darius Milhaud, Alexander Zemlinsky, Alma Mahler, Hans Erich Apostel, Paul Stefan, Willi Reich, Paul A. Pisk, David Josef Bach, and others.

"A Berlin paper has chosen to attach a special significance to Arnold Schoenberg's sixtieth birthday. It is true that Schoenberg has influenced a certain group of musicians who create, without exception, in an atmosphere alien to the world. . . . Schoenberg is a fanatic of Nihilism, of destruction. He places himself outside of all community. Whether we call his music twelve-tone music or atonal music or something else is immaterial. The point is that this music is given in sounds that do not mean anything to our ears. Even Jews reject this music." (*A Lance for Schoenberg* by Herbert Gerigk, in *Die Musik,* November 1934)

23 SEPTEMBER 1934

The second volume of the Tchaikovsky-von Meck correspondence, covering the period 1879–1881, is published in Moscow, edited by N. Zhegin, Director of the Tchaikovsky Museum in Klin.

28 SEPTEMBER 1934

The Council of People's Commissars of the U.S.S.R. publishes a statement decreeing that Soviet composers should be paid, as a fair average, from 10,000 to 12,000 rubles for an opera, 6,000 to 8,000 rubles for a symphony, 3,000 to 5,000 rubles for a chamber work, and 500 to 1,000 rubles for a mass song.

29 SEPTEMBER 1934

The Reichsmusikkammer issues an order prohibiting the use by artists and musicians of foreign-sounding names, and setting the date 31 October 1934 as final for changing such names back to the homely, even if Aryan, originals.

(Date from Heinz Ihlert, *Die Reichsmusikkammer,* Berlin, 1935)

29 SEPTEMBER 1934

Carlos CHAVEZ conducts in Mexico City the first performance of his *Sinfonia Proletaria (Llamadas),* a workers' symphony for chorus and small orchestra, written in an unadorned rhythmic style, alternating in duple and triple time.

12 OCTOBER 1934

Serge KOUSSEVITZKY conducts the Boston Symphony Orchestra in the first performance of his *Passacaglia on a Russian Theme.*

15-20 OCTOBER 1934

The Pageant of Labour is held at Crystal Palace, London, with a ballet in six episodes: (1) *Capital Enslaves the Worker;* (2) *Martyrdom of the Children;* (3) *Consolation of Philanthropy and Religion;* (4) *London Receives the Chartists;* (5) *The Triumph of the Trade Unions;* (6) *Fletcher Family, 1900,* with music by Alan BUSH, based on a system of musical mottoes for each characteristic trait or personage. (Dates and information from the original programs)

21 OCTOBER 1934

Hans Joachim MOSER completes his *Musik-Lexikon* in one volume of 1005 pages, containing biographical, theoretical, and historical information on music and musicians of all times, presented in a terse scholarly fashion.

22 OCTOBER 1934

Dane RUDHYAR, French-American composer, completes at Chamita, New Mexico, the piano score of his symphonic poem with recitation, *Paean to the Great Thunder,* the first of a trilogy, entitled *Cosmophony,* and designed to express stages of development of mystic consciousness. (Date communicated to the author by the composer)

24 OCTOBER 1934

Hugues PANASSIÉ completes in Paris his book in French, entitled *Le Jazz Hot,* the first historical treatise on jazz presented in a serious scholarly manner. (Date of Preface)

1 NOVEMBER 1934

An article in *Die Musik* discloses that the National Socialist Kulturgemeinde has, through its leader, Dr. Walter Strang, commissioned to both Rudolf WAGNER-REGENY and Julius WEISMANN new musical settings for *A Midsummer Night's Dream* to replace Mendelssohn's score. (These new scores came to performance respectively on 6 and 11 June 1935, during the Reichstagung of the National Socialist Kulturgemeinde at Düsseldorf)

"The National-Socialist Kulturgemeinde has discharged an important obligation of the National-Socialist Revolution in commissioning a new music to *A Midsummer Night's Dream* of Shakespeare. Mendelssohn's music is inadmissible in the third Reich, where the unshatterable laws of racial purity must be uncompromisingly maintained." (Wilhelm Herzog in *Die Musik,* 1 November 1934)

10 NOVEMBER 1934

Thirty years, six months, and nine days after the death of Antonin DVOŘÁK, the Post Office Department of Czechoslovakia issues a commemorative stamp, with Dvořák's image, value 50 kronen.

(Information obtained by the author from the philatelic division of the Prague Post Office)

15 NOVEMBER 1934

The *Thirteenth Symphony,* op. 36, in B minor, in one movement, by Nicolas MIASKOVSKY is performed for the first time anywhere by the Chicago Symphony, Frederick Stock conducting.

(The *Thirteenth Symphony* was completed 29 May 1933, orchestration finished 20 October 1933. These dates communicated by the composer)

"The necessity of some sort of discharge of accumulated subjective moods, unalterably inherent in my nature, and, in my age, impossible to eradicate, brought to life the *Thirteenth Symphony,* a very pessimistic work, which I, in my creative blindness, regarded as an emotional experience. It proved to be an error—true, the symphony was emotional enough, but its contents turned out to be rather peculiar. It has remained a page in my diary: I do not intend to make propaganda for it." (From *Autobiographical Notes* by Miaskovsky in *Sovietskaya Musica,* No. 6, 1934)

20 NOVEMBER 1934

Maximilian STEINBERG is appointed acting Director of the Leningrad Conservatory. (Date communicated to the author by Maximilian Steinberg)

25 NOVEMBER 1934

Concerto for piano and orchestra by Darius MILHAUD, in three movements (*Très Vif,* with some bitonal interplay in the middle section; *Barcarolle,* acridly chromatic and tenuously scored; and a *Finale*), is performed for the first time at the Concerts Pasdeloup in Paris, Marguerite Long playing the solo part, Albert Wolff conducting.

25 NOVEMBER 1934

Wilhelm FURTWAENGLER writes an article in the *Allgemeine Musikzeitung* in defense of Hindemith, declaring that musical Germany can ill afford to reject a musician of Hindemith's powers.

30 NOVEMBER 1934

Philip HALE, music critic and annotator whose writings, scattered over the pages of the Boston *Herald* and notes in the Boston Symphony program books, constitute a thesaurus of information and skeptical wisdom, dies at 1:30 p.m. in Boston, his home since 1889, in his eighty-first year.

30 NOVEMBER 1934

Suite from the opera, *Lulu,* by Alban BERG, to Wedekind's gruesome drama of unnatural love and murder, is performed for the first time at the Berlin State Opera, Erich Kleiber conducting.

"The accounts of the performance of Alban Berg's symphonic sketches from *Lulu* show the ideological confusion and lack of artistic instinct of the majority of the Berlin musical press. It is significant that one of the lowest foreign yellow publications, the *Neue Wiener Journal,* could quote many of the Berlin reviews which seemed quite in agreement with the emigrated *Musikjuden.* . . . Such criticisms ought to be made impossible in the age of directed public opinion, for they tend to confuse the mind and hamper the upbuilding of our culture. The German Press Union will do well to test the fitness of these writers for their task." (*Die Musik,* January 1935)

"The performance was a great success!! Only one voice protested from the gallery, with a shout, 'Heil Mozart.' " (*Ibid.*)

3 DECEMBER 1934

The *First Symphony* by William WALTON is given for the first time by the London Symphony Orchestra, Hamilton Harty conducting, without the as yet unwritten last movement.

4 DECEMBER 1934

Wilhelm FURTWAENGLER resigns as conductor of the Berlin Philharmonic, Deputy President of the Reich Chamber of Music, and as Director of the Berlin State Opera, as a result of the controversy connected with the elimination of Paul Hindemith from German musical life.

"State Counsellor Dr. Wilhelm Furtwaengler has asked the Minister of the Reich, Dr. Goebbels, to relieve him from his duties as Vice-President of the Reichsmusikkammer and conductor of the Berlin Philharmonic Orchestra. At the same time he requested the Prussian First Minister to release him from the post of Director at the Berlin State Opera. Both ministers have granted his requests." (Official statement)

"The *Hindemith Case* has widened itself into a *Furtwaengler Case.* In this question we find two opposite ideologies. The one side considers everything in the light of pure artistic endeavor. The other—the National-Socialist—realizes that an artist often represents political trends. . . . So when a man like Hindemith, after a few German beginnings, lives and works for fourteen years in Jewish company and feels himself at ease in that company; when he consorts almost exclusively with Jews, and is loved by them; when he, following the trend of the November Republic, commits the foulest perversion of German music, we have a right to reject him and his environment. The accomplishments of such an artist within the November Republic, and the laurels reaped by him in that now overthrown Republic, are by right of no value to our movement. . . . It is a great pity that so great an artist as Dr. Wilhelm Furtwaengler entered personally into this controversy and chose to identify himself with Hindemith's cause. . . . Herr Furtwaengler lingers in his nineteenth-century ideas and has manifestly lost all sense of the national struggle of our times." (Alfred Rosenberg, *Aesthetics or National Struggle?* in *Die Musik,* January 1935)

6 DECEMBER 1934

Dr. GOEBBELS, Minister of Propaganda of the Third Reich, delivers a thundering denunciation of the moral decay of "atonal composers," making an indignant reference to the bathtub aria in Hindemith's opera, *Neues vom Tage.*

"Technical mastery is not an excuse but an obligation. To misuse it for meaningless musical trifles is to besmirch true genius. Opportunity creates not only thieves, but also atonal musicians who in order to make a sensation exhibit on the stage nude women in the bathtub in the most disgusting and obscene situations, and further befoul these scenes with the most atrocious dissonance of musical impotence."

15 DECEMBER 1934

Franco PAOLANTONIO, Italian conductor of the opera at Rio de Janeiro, is shot and killed by a discharged musician during a rehearsal of the musical comedy, *Feodora.*

(Date from special cable to the New York *Times,* 16 December 1934. Peters' *Jahrbuch* for 1934 gives, in its *Totenschau* column, the erroneous date of 17 December 1934)

15 DECEMBER 1934

Jean FRANÇAIX plays the solo part in the first performance of his *Concertino* for piano and orchestra at a Concert Lamoureux in Paris, Jean Morel conducting.

20 DECEMBER 1934

Big Ben, variation fantasy on the Westminster chimes, by Ernst TOCH, curiously combining the tonal elements of the natural harmonic series with highly chromaticized counterpoint, is performed for the first time anywhere in Cambridge, Massachusetts, by the Boston Symphony Orchestra, Richard Burgin conducting.

25 DECEMBER 1934

The *Second Symphony* of Dmitri KABALEVSKY, in orthodox four movements with the Scherzo and Finale connected, is performed for the first time by the Moscow Philharmonic Orchestra, Albert Coates conducting.

(Composition finished in Moscow, 8 November 1934. Date at the end of the printed score)

26 DECEMBER 1934

Arnold SCHOENBERG completes in Hollywood the composition of his *Suite* for string orchestra, in five classical suite movements— *Largo-Allegro; Adagio; Minuet; Gavotte; Gigue*—in G major, the first key signature he has put on paper since 9 March 1907.

"I was incited to write this work by a musician who is a teacher at New York University and conducts a pupils' orchestra. He told me much that was most gratifying about these American orchestras of which there are many hundreds. This piece, therefore, will provide instructive examples of progressions which are possible within tonality to any genuine musician who knows his craft; an actual preparation, not only from a harmonic but also from a melodic, contrapuntal, and technical standpoint." (From Arnold Schoenberg's letter to Erwin Stein, November 1934)

31 DECEMBER 1934

The two thousandth performance of Gounod's *Faust* is given at the Paris Opéra.

1935

13 JANUARY 1935

Johnny Comes Marching Home, overture by Roy HARRIS, revised version, is performed for the first time by the Minneapolis Symphony Orchestra, Eugene Ormandy conducting, and a record is made during the performance by the Victor Gramophone Company.

16 JANUARY 1935

Pietro MASCAGNI conducts the première of his opera, *Nerone*, at La Scala in Milan.

22 JANUARY 1935

Heinrich SCHENKER, creator of the theory of *Urlinie*, according to which each work possesses an ultimately traceable fundamental melodic and harmonic thread, dies in Vienna in his sixty-seventh year.

23 JANUARY 1935

The Copenhagen radio station broadcasts a concert of Icelandic composers, including the *Icelandic Dances* and Overture, *Iceland*, by the Sólheimar-born German-bred neo-romanticist, Jón LEIFS.

28 JANUARY 1935

Michael IPPOLITOV-IVANOV, Russian composer of rhapsodic music, with programmatic ethnological or geographic titles, successor to the ideals of the Russian national school, dies in Moscow in his seventy-sixth year.

"The last days of the beloved Soviet composer were filled with social activity. 'My life has been an uninterrupted hymn to labor,' he wrote. 'I wish the life of our musical youth were also a hymn to labor.' . . . He died suddenly and without suffering in his sleep. His wife and constant friend, Varvara Mikhailovna Zarudnaya, found him dead at 2:30 a.m. on the 28 January 1935." (Sergei Bugoslavsky, *M. M. Ippolitov-Ivanov,* Moscow, 1936)

5 FEBRUARY 1935

Lady Macbeth of the Mzensk District, opera by Dmitri SHOSTA-KOVITCH, is performed for the first time in America, under the auspices of the League of Composers, at the Metropolitan Opera in New York, Rodzinsky conducting.

"It was one of the most distinguished audiences of the season. Leaders of society, business, finance, music, and the arts were in attendance.

Among those present were Mr. and Mrs. John D. Rockefeller, Jr., Mrs. Vincent Astor, Mrs. Cornelius Vanderbilt, Arturo Toscanini, Leopold Stokowski. . . . A line of standees stretched from the box office down Broadway twenty minutes before the curtain went up. Considering the snow and the cold, this offered a telling example of public interest in the production. It was a capacity." (The New York *Times*)

7 FEBRUARY 1935

In reply to Olin Downes' inquiry concerning the originals of his transcriptions of old music, Fritz KREISLER cables from Venice to the New York *Times* the confession of his innocuous fraud:

"The entire series labelled 'classical manuscripts' are my original compositions with the sole exception of the first eight bars from the Couperin Chanson Louis XIII, taken from a traditional melody. Necessity forced this course on me thirty years ago when I was desirous of enlarging my programs. I found it inexpedient and tactless to repeat my name endlessly on the programs."

8 FEBRUARY 1935

The Boston Symphony Orchestra, Serge Koussevitzky conducting, gives two American works for the first time: *Concerto Sinfonico* for piano and orchestra by Alexander STEINERT, with the composer at the piano; and *American Sketches* by Frederick CONVERSE, a symphonic suite in four characteristic movements: *Manhattan; The Father of Waters; Chicken Reel;* and *Bright Angel Trail.*

23 FEBRUARY 1935

Two and a half centuries have passed since the birth of HANDEL, in Halle, four weeks before the birth of Bach.

24 FEBRUARY 1935

The *Fourteenth Symphony,* op. 37, in C major, in five movements, by Nicolas MIASKOVSKY is performed for the first time by the Moscow Symphony Orchestra, V. Kubatzky conducting.

(The *Fourteenth Symphony* was completed 18 August 1933, the orchestration finished 11 October 1933. Dates communicated by the composer)

"I managed to make my *Fourteenth Symphony* sufficiently colorful and dynamically sharp, and, although I cannot boast of freshness or original- ity of its musical idiom, I think it possesses a vital spark." (*Autobiographi- cal Reflections on My Creative Path* by Miaskovsky in *Sovietskaya Mu- sica,* No. 6, 1936)

28 FEBRUARY 1935

Wilhelm FURTWAENGLER declares in a conversation with the Ger- man Minister of Propaganda that his article on Hindemith of 25 November 1934 was intended as purely musical in content, and that he regrets the political implications and encroachments on the domain which should belong exclusively to the Leader and Chancellor of the Reich, and to his ministers.

7 MARCH 1935

As a measure to reduce noise in New York City all organ grinders' licenses are abolished by the mayor's order.

14 MARCH 1935

Der Prinz von Homburg, the hundredth opus of Paul GRAENER, is produced for the first time at the Berlin State Opera House.

21 MARCH 1935

Two and a half centuries have passed since the birth at Eisenach of Johann Sebastian BACH.

3 APRIL 1935

Djemal RECHID, Turkish composer, plays the piano part in the first performance of his *Concerto Chromatique* for piano and orchestra, at the Ravag Radio Station in Vienna.

12 APRIL 1935

David Stanley SMITH conducts the Boston Symphony in the first performance of his *Epic Poem,* op. 55.

25 APRIL 1935

Wilhelm FURTWAENGLER resumes his post as conductor of the Berlin Philharmonic, after straightening out the difficulties with the National Socialist leadership.

17 MAY 1935

Paul Dukas, "the Degas of music," French composer of impressionistically rarefied music for orchestra, dies in Paris in his seventieth year, having destroyed in his last lucid moment all his unpublished manuscripts, a violin sonata, an overture, and an unfinished work intended for the fiftieth anniversary of the Boston Symphony.

18 MAY 1935

Arnold Schoenberg's *Suite* for string orchestra, in the five movements of the classical suite, is performed for the first time by the Los Angeles Philharmonic Orchestra, Otto Klemperer conducting.

19 MAY 1935

Charles Martin Loeffler, Alsace-born composer, resident in America since 1881, master of the impressionist musical palette, deeply influenced by Debussyst pictorialism, dies at his home in Medfield, near Boston, in his seventy-fifth year.

27 MAY 1935

A concert of works by Enrico Bossi, announced in Berlin by a Jewish choir and orchestra, is canceled by the municipal authorities.

28 MAY 1935

Jelka Rosen Delius, widow of Frederick Delius, dies in London, not quite a year after her husband's death.

29 MAY 1935

Josef Suk, Czech neo-romantic composer, Dvořák's son-in-law, and continuator in a modernized idiom of his musical precepts, dies at Benesovo in his sixty-second year.

8–10 JUNE 1935

The First Workers' Olympiad is held in Strasbourg, presenting programs of choral and orchestral music by workers' societies of Switzerland, Holland, England, Czechoslovakia, and France, sponsored by vanguard writers and composers of Europe and America, with the understandable exception of official Germany. (Dates and information from the original programs)

24 JUNE 1935

Die Schweigsame Frau, eleventh opera of Richard STRAUSS, to the book of Stefan Zweig, written in the style of Italian opera buffa, is produced at the Dresden Opera, thirteen days after Strauss' seventy-first birthday.

13 JULY 1935

Richard STRAUSS resigns his post as President of the German Reichsmusikkammer for reasons of age, rumor giving as the real reason his collaboration with Stefan Zweig, a Jew.

13 JULY 1935

Peter RAABE is appointed head of the Reichsmusikkammer, to succeed Richard Strauss, and Paul GRAENER is made President of the German Composers' Society.

27 JULY 1935

Nicolai SOKOLOFF is appointed head of the Music Project of the (U. S.) Federal Works Progress Administration.

1 AUGUST 1935

The Federal Music Project is established as a branch of the Emergency Relief Bureau to provide work for unemployed American musicians.

2 AUGUST 1935

Mikola KOLIADA, Ukranian Soviet composer, author of a symphonic poem, *The Siege of Tractorstroy*, depicting the drama of agricultural industrialization, perishes in a fall in the Caucasian mountains during a pleasure trip, in his twenty-ninth year.

11 AUGUST 1935

Four months and thirteen days before his untimely end, Alban BERG completes the composition of his last work, the *Concerto* for violin and orchestra, commissioned by the American violinist, Louis Krasner, and dedicated "to the memory of an angel," daughter of Mahler's widow by her second marriage, who died young.

30 AUGUST 1935

The Reichsmusikkammer decrees that non-Aryans shall not be employed in German orchestras.

1 SEPTEMBER 1935

Igor STRAVINSKY completes in Paris the composition of his *Concerto* for two pianos, in four movements. (The first movement was completed on 10 June 1935; the second on 13 July 1935)

1 SEPTEMBER 1935

The thirteenth Festival of the International Society for Contemporary Music opens at Prague with the following orchestral program:

Miserae by Karl Amadeus HARTMANN, in a brooding introspective mood, within an atonal idiom, but not in the twelve-tone system; *Concerto* for piano and wind orchestra by the Serbian, Slavko OSTERC, in a neo-Czernian style with a lyrical second movement; *Variations* for orchestra, op. 31, by Arnold SCHOENBERG, masterpiece of logical construction, as instructive, one might say, for effective and varied use of the twelve-tone system as Bach's *Kunst der Fuge* is instructive for fugal composition; *Concerto* for cello and orchestra by Karel HÁBA, the "semitone-minded" brother of the quarter-tonist, Alois Hába, written in the non-thematic system of composition, governed by a succession of moods and unrepeated mood-motifs; and *Second Symphony* by Vissarion SHEBALIN, in a fine rhapsodic fashion within the orthodox tonality and form.

"The Festival was originally to have been held in Karlsbad; and only at the beginning of July, after the orchestra had held a great many preparatory rehearsals, did the municipality decide that it could not undertake the financial responsibility. For a few days the Festival was officially declared off. Then came an offer from the International Music Bureau of Moscow to give the Festival in November 1935. In addition the hundred and twenty delegates and artists would receive free passage from the Russian frontier to Moscow and free hospitality during the Festival itself. The Czecho-Slovakian section, faced with this truly magnificent gesture, was able to awake local interest, with the effect that the municipality of Prague undertook the Festival. *Thus the Soviet Union saved the Festival."* (Alan Bush in the *Musical Times,* October 1935)

2 SEPTEMBER 1935

At the second concert of the ISCM Festival in Prague, the following program of chamber music is given:

Sonata for violin and piano in a lyrico-explosive archaico-modernistic idiom by the Dutch composer, Heink BADINGS; *Berceuse* for voice, flute, clarinet, and harp, in a neo-Moussorgskyan vein by the Polish composer, Boleslaw WOYTOWICZ; *Four Songs* for voice and string quartet by H. W. SUESSKIND of Czechoslovakia, in a fresh lyric style; *Concertino* for two pianos by Fidelio FINKE, in three characteristic archaizing movements: *Alla Marcia, Nocturno, Quodlibet; Dialectic* for string quartet by the British composer, Alan BUSH, in a complex polythematic idiom; *Divertimento in Four Studies* for soprano, flute, oboe, clarinet, viola, and cello by the modern Italian, Luigi DALLAPICCOLA, in a rationally lyric manner, depicting four emotions, melancholy, gaiety, joy, despair; and *Fantasy* for string orchestra in a neo-contrapuntal style by the Swiss composer, Willy BURKHARD.

2 SEPTEMBER 1935

George GERSHWIN completes in New York the composition of his opera, *Porgy and Bess,* his last important work, with arias expressive of the spirit of American jazz-song as Verdi's arias are expressive of Italian song. (Date communicated to the author by the composer)

4 SEPTEMBER 1935

At the third concert of the ISCM Festival in Prague, the following program of chamber music is given:

String Quartet by Sándor VERESS of Hungary, written in a synthetic Bartók-Kodály style; *Introduction and Allegro* for violin and eleven instruments by the Italian, Goffredo PETRASSI, in an optimistic neo-Scarlattian style, played under the composer's direction; *String Quartet* by the French composer, Raymond CHEVREUILLE, written according to the expressionistic theory of harmony-moods; *Concerto* for nine instruments by Anton VON WEBERN, op. 24, written in the twelve-tone system, and based on three-note themes, in the characteristic subtilized instrumentation of great economy of sonorous m ans; *Sonata for Harp* by Alexander JEMNITZ of Hungary, in an atonal, but not Schoenbergian style, playing upon the minutest tonal and dynamic effects; *Prelude, Interlude,* and *Fugue* for two violins by the Englishwoman, Elizabeth MACONCHY, in a neo-Bachian style; *Chaconne* and *Étude-Toccata* for piano by Vladimir VOGEL, in a difficult virtuoso style with neo-Busonian contrapuntal complexities; and *Wind Quintet* in a light effective form by young Alexander MOYZES of Czechoslovakia.

6 SEPTEMBER 1935

At the fourth concert of the ISCM Festival in Prague, the following program of orchestral music is given:

Poème Héroïque by the Belgian composer, Jef VAN DURME, in a neo-lyrical, pseudo-programmatic vein, within a modified tonality; *Symphony in A Major* in a dense Schmittian style, anchored to a definite tonality, by the French neo-romanticist, Pierre Octave FERROUD, less than a year before his tragic death; *Concerto* for piano and orchestra by Pavel BOŘKOVEC of Czechoslovakia, in a modernistic virtuoso style of the Prokofiev type; *Symphonic Suite* from the opera, *Lulu,* by Alban BERG, here played less than four months before his untimely death; and *The Path of Life,* symphonic fantasy for orchestra by Alois HÁBA, portraying, in his non-thematic style, the three anthroposophic forces of the universe, Christ, Lucifer, and Ahriman.

12 SEPTEMBER 1935

A century has elapsed since the bass tuba was patented by the Director of the Berlin Gardes du Corps-Musik, Wilhelm WIE-PRECHT.

24 SEPTEMBER 1935

The centenary of the death of Vincenzo BELLINI is celebrated in his native town, Catania, and throughout Italy.

30 SEPTEMBER 1935

Porgy and Bess, George GERSHWIN's last major work, is produced for the first time on any stage at the Colonial Theatre in Boston.

10 OCTOBER 1935

The *First Symphony,* op. 34, by the twenty-two-year-old Soviet composer, Tikhon KHRENNIKOV, in three movements, *Allegro, Adagio, Molto Allegro,* in a youthful rhythmic style, entirely tonal, is performed for the first time anywhere by the Moscow Radio Orchestra, George Sebastian conducting.

12 OCTOBER 1935

Eugen HADAMOWSKI, director of the German radio system, issues an order banning broadcasting of jazz music "to do away with the last remnants of the culture-Bolshevistic Jew."

19 OCTOBER 1935

The *Fourth Symphony* by Albert ROUSSEL, in four movements, an incisive *Allegro,* wistful *Adagio,* terse *Scherzo,* and graceful *Finale,* in a definitely tonal idiom, including the key signature, is performed for the first time anywhere at a Pasdeloup concert in Paris, Albert Wolff conducting.

22 OCTOBER 1935

Quiet Flows the Don, four-act opera to Sholohov's novel by the twenty-seven-year-old Soviet composer, Ivan DZERZHINSKY is produced in Leningrad.

(Date given on the title-page of the printed score, published July 1937. The Moscow production of the opera took place 8 January 1936)

"The success of the opera is explained by the fact that its dramatic backbone is firmly and persuasively built. There is no superfluous 'psychology,' annoying digging into the hero's soul, no leftist simplification in presentation of important social phenomena. Striving toward realistic truth of expression, Dzerzhinsky has naturally remained uncontaminated by the extreme usages of musical expressionism with its morbid exposure of psychic ills. At the same time he does not try to write an opera without heroes or to transfer the accent to the masses alone, as some Soviet opera composers are apt to do. *Quiet Flows the Don* is a better developed genre of historical opera than the propagandist type of other Soviet operas. . . . One of the opera's great qualities is the accessibility of its musical speech. The music is distinguished by its simplicity, expressive vigor, and fine characterization of the action. The composer does not resort to musical quotations from revolutionary songs but tries to re-create the style and the genre in agreement with historical truth. The folk-song intonations in the opera are a product of complex transformation of the material which lies at the foundation of popular song and dance. Naturalistic ethnology or artificial 'folkiness' is equally alien to the realistic method of Dzerzhinsky." (A. Ostretzov in the special program-book of the opera, published by the Bolshoi Theatre, Moscow, 1936)

28 OCTOBER 1935

The *Fifteenth Symphony,* op. 38, in D minor, in four movements, by Nicolas MIASKOVSKY is performed for the first time by the Radio Orchestra in Moscow, Leo Ginsberg conducting.

(The dates of completion of each movement are: 1st, 21 July 1933; 2nd, 18 May 1934; 3d, 17 September 1934; 4th, 15 October 1934. Orchestration completed 29 November 1934. All these dates communicated by the composer)

"Many praise my *Fifteenth Symphony* for its optimism and lyric emotion. But even that is not the language I seek to feel as an artist of the day. I do not know what this language should be, and I have no recipe for its creation; neither the trend toward folk-song nor urban melodies pure and simple will be the sole ingredients of the musical language of socialist realism." (Miaskovsky, *Autobiographical Notes* in *Sovietskaya Musica,* No. 6, 1936)

19 NOVEMBER 1935

Léon DU BOIS, Belgian composer of the "Walloon school," leaning toward the dramatic element of music, and since 1912 Director of the Conservatoire Royal in Brussels, dies there in his seventy-seventh year.

(Date communicated by the Secretary of the Conservatoire Royal in Brussels)

21 NOVEMBER 1935

Igor STRAVINSKY and his son, Sviatoslav, give the first performance of Stravinsky's *Concerto* for two pianos, without orchestral accompaniment, at the Salle Gaveau in Paris.

28 NOVEMBER 1935

The Italian Ministry for the Press and Propaganda issues an order forbidding performances in Italy of works by artists belonging to the sanctionist nations, in retaliation for their nations' condemnation, within the Council of the League of Nations, of Italian aggression in Ethiopia.

"The Ministry for the Press and Propaganda has communicated to dependent organs precise directions, aiming to establish the attitude that Italy would adopt toward the countries exercising sanctions, in the field of artistic production. On the basis of these instructions, as regards the legitimate prose theater, the production of authors belonging to the Sanctionist countries shall be eliminated from the repertory, an exception being made of Shakespeare and Shaw. Special provisions have been made for the French repertoire, mainly in response to homage to the attitude assumed by the great majority of French intellectuals toward Italy at the present moment. From the repertories of Opera Houses shall be eliminated the works of authors belonging to the Sanctionist countries, whereas, for French works, there will be merely a reduction in the number of those normally presented to Italian audiences. . . . In the concert field, in general, the whole repertoire of composers belonging to Sanctionist countries shall be eliminated from programmes, save a small percentage of French and Spanish symphonic chamber music. In the field of light music, however, all compositions of Sanctionist countries shall be eliminated. In accordance with the above provision regarding repertoires, prohibitions and limitations will be imposed regarding the activities in Italy of artists and conductors belonging to Sanctionist countries. In consequence, all artists of vaudeville, reviews, operettas, operas, the dance, and all concert givers and conductors, belonging to Sanctionist countries, will no longer be permitted to work in Italy, with exceptions that may be conceded from time to time to artists of French nationality. The productions of all living authors of Russian nationality furnished with White Russian passports may be performed without limitation of any sort, and all Russian artists having such passports may engage in professional activities in Italy. In the field of radio, Italian music and the music of nonsanctionist countries only shall be performed although a limited quantity of French music may be included in programmes. Rules similar to those regulating radio activities have been issued regarding cinema orchestras and public functions in general." (Exact text obtained from the Italian Ministry for the Press and Propaganda)

28 NOVEMBER 1935

Erich von Hornbostel, Vienna-born German musical scientist, founder of the phonographic method of comparative musicology, recorder of folk songs of primitive races, owner of the unique library of records of Polynesian, Javanese, American Indian, and other melodies of prime authenticity, which he gave to the Berlin University, dies in his fifty-ninth year in Cambridge, England, an exile of the Hitler regime as son of a Jewish mother and Aryan father.

30 NOVEMBER 1935

The Limpid Stream, ballet of the twenty-nine-year-old Dmitri SHOSTAKOVITCH, portraying in tones the life on a collective farm, is produced by the Moscow State Opera.

1 DECEMBER 1935

The *Second Violin Concerto,* op. 63, by Serge PROKOFIEV, completed in Baku on 16 August 1935, is performed in Madrid for the first time anywhere. (Dates communicated to the author by the composer)

9 DECEMBER 1935

Nina GRIEG, widow of Grieg, dies at Copenhagen, two weeks after reaching ninety years of age, outliving Grieg by twenty-eight years, three months, and five days.

12 DECEMBER 1935

La Spirale, new propaganda organization for modern music, gives its initial concert in the hall of the Schola Cantorum in Paris, presenting chamber music by Claire DELBOS, André JOLIVET, Paul LE FLEM, Jules LE FEBVRE, Edouard SCIORTINO, Georges MIGOT, DANIEL-LESUR, and Olivier MESSIAEN. (Date from the original program)

"The Committee of *La Spirale* proposes to promote contemporary music through concerts of French compositions and exchange concerts with composers of other countries. *La Spirale* will endeavor not so much to give first performances as to give repeated hearings of significant works. The organization has adopted the name *La Spirale,* because it finds the justification of its qualities in this title. A spiral is unlimited. It symbolizes the spirit of Progress for, while it is constantly attached to the center of origin, it traces none the less a new path with every turn." (From the declaration of the Committee of *La Spirale,* printed in the first program)

15 DECEMBER 1935

Roy HARRIS completes in New York the score of his *Symphony for Voices* on four poems of Walt Whitman, written for chorus unaccompanied, making use of rhythmic beats punctuated by explosive spoken sounds. (Date communicated to the author by the composer)

16 DECEMBER 1935

The administration of the Metropolitan Opera in New York rules that no paid applause shall be tolerated in the opera, and no claque leaders shall be allowed to enter into agreements of any sort with the artists.

24 DECEMBER 1935

Alban BERG, the romantic composer of Vienna, whose art penetrates deeply into human consciousness and whose devotion to his teacher, Arnold Schoenberg, contributes greatly to the enrichment of the twelve-tone system of composition, dies in Vienna at the age of fifty years and ten and a half months.

"In the first days of September, Berg was to participate in the Festival of the International Society for Contemporary Music, but had to cancel the trip at the last moment because of an abscess that developed on his back. The abscess was removed by surgical means and soon healed. Yet it was the beginning of his fatal illness. On 17 December 1935, Berg was brought to the hospital and operated on; a blood transfusion, performed on the 19th, brought about a slight improvement. He expressed a wish to thank the blood donor personally. After he saw him, a young smart Viennese boy, he turned to me and remarked with an undescribable expression, 'I only hope this will not make an operetta composer out of me!' On 22 December, the illness took a catastrophic turn: the heart refused to serve. . . . On 24 December 1935, fifteen minutes after one o'clock in the morning, he died in the arms of his wife." (Willi Reich, *Alban Berg*, Vienna, 1937)

1936

12 JANUARY 1936

Theodore METZ, composer of the celebrated song hit, *There'll Be a Hot Time in the Old Town Tonight,* dies in New York in his eighty-ninth year.

21 JANUARY 1936

Paul HINDEMITH writes in London, on the day after the death of King George V, *Funeral Music* for solo viola and string quartet accompaniment, to be performed in Queen's Hall on the following evening in place of his *Viola Concerto.*

25 JANUARY 1936

Florent SCHMITT is elected a member of the French Academy, having received more votes than his nearest rival, the recent French citizen, Igor Stravinsky.

26 JANUARY 1936

Ernest BLOCH completes at Châtel, Savoy, France, the full score of his *Voice in the Wilderness,* symphonic poem for orchestra with cello obbligato, in six movements. (Date at end of manuscript)

28 JANUARY 1936

An authoritative article, entitled *A Mess Instead of Music,* is published in *Pravda,* central organ of the ruling Communist party in U.S.S.R., condemning Shostakovitch's opera, *Lady Macbeth of the Mzensk District* as deliberately anti-melodic and subservient to Western modernism.

"With the cultural development in our country there has been increasing demand for good music. Never in history did composers have such grateful audiences as in our land. The popular masses want good songs and also good instrumental compositions, good operas. . . . Several theaters have presented the opera, *Lady Macbeth of the Mzensk District* by Shostakovitch to this new Soviet public. Officious music critics exalt this opera to the high heavens and spread its fame far and wide. The listener is from the very first bewildered by a stream of deliberately discordant sounds. Fragments of melody, beginnings of a musical phrase appear on the surface, are drowned, then emerge again to disappear once more in the roar. To follow this 'music' is difficult; to get anything out of it, impossible. . . . And so during the entire opera. On the stage singing is replaced by screaming. If the composer happens to chance on a simple and understandable melody, he, as if frightened by such calamity, rushes into the jungles of musical confusion, at times reaching complete cacophony. Expressiveness, required by the listeners, is replaced by frenzied rhythm. Noise expresses passion. . . . All this is not because the composer has no talent, not because of his inability to express simple and strong feeling in music. This music is deliberately turned inside out in order to destroy all resemblance with classical operatic music, with plain musical speech. This music which is based on the principle of negation of opera, similar to that governing the leftist art which denies simplicity in the theater, denies realism, understandable imagery, natural sound of speech. It is the extension of Meyerhold's most objectionable ideas into the realm of music. It is a leftist mess instead of human music. The stirring quality of good music is sacrificed in favor of petty-bourgeois formalist cerebration, with pretense of originality by means of cheap clowning. It is a game which may end very badly. . . . The danger of such aberration for Soviet music is clear. Leftist monstrosities in the opera have their origin in the same source as leftist monstrosities in art, in poetry, in pedagogy, in science. The petty-bourgeois 'innovations' lead to its severance from true art, from true science, from true literature. . . . While our critics and music critics, too, swear by the name of Socialist Realism, the stage serves us, in Shostakovitch's production, the coarsest kind of naturalism. Landlords and people are painted uniformly in their most beastly aspect. The predatory merchant woman, through murder coming in possession of wealth and power, is represented as a 'victim' of the bourgeois system. Leskov's story is given a meaning which it does not possess. . . . And all this is crude, primitive, vulgar. The music quacks, grunts, growls, suffocates itself in order to express the amatory scenes as naturalistically as possible. 'Love' is smeared all over the opera in the most vulgar manner. The merchant's bed occupies the central place of the stage. On it all 'problems' are solved. In the similarly naturalistic and coarse manner are presented the poisoning and the whipping. . . . The composer, apparently, does not set himself the task of listening to the desires and expectations of the Soviet public. He scrambles sounds to make them interesting to formalist-esthetes, who have lost all good taste. . . . Some critics call this glorification of merchant lust a satire. But there is no satire here. The author strives to attract the public to the coarse and vulgar passions and deeds of the merchant woman, Katherina Izmailova, using the entire arsenal of musical and dramatic expression. . . . *Lady Macbeth* enjoys fine success with the bourgeois audiences abroad. Does not the fact that this opera is messy and absolutely devoid of political connotations contribute to this success among the bourgeoisie, that it tickles the perverted tastes of the bourgeois audiences with its fidgeting, screaming, neurasthenic music?" (From the *Pravda* article)

4 FEBRUARY 1936

The Union of Soviet Composers votes to expel the composer, Alexandre MOSSOLOV, for staging drunken brawls in public places, beating up a waiter in a restaurant, and generally behaving "in the glorious old Russian style," and adopts the following resolution:

"In view of the fact that testimony of several comrades disclosed a picture of civic and moral decay in Mossolov's life, and seeing that his disgraceful behavior in the restaurant of the Press Building on the night of 31 January is not an isolated case, but represents one of numerous episodes that corroborate the above estimate of his character, the plenum of the Union of Soviet Composers, considering Mossolov's deeds incompatible with the honorable position of a Soviet composer, and disgraceful to the workers of Soviet music, unanimously resolves to expel Mossolov from the Union." (*Sovietskaya Musica*, No. 3, 1936)

6 FEBRUARY 1936

Three Shadows, (1) *Omen,* (2) *A Poet,* (3) *Grass—a Dirge,* poems for orchestra by Lazare SAMINSKY, are performed for the first time by the New York Philharmonic Orchestra, Hans Lange conducting.

8 FEBRUARY 1936

Julius Caesar, three-act opera by Francesco MALIPIERO, after Shakespeare, is produced at the Teatro Carlo Felice in Genoa.

10 FEBRUARY 1936

After two months and twelve days Italy rescinds the artistic ban against the sanctionist nations, and a circular letter to this effect is sent to all theaters.

"In reference to the circular of this ministry of date 29/11/1935 prod. 7644, circ. n. 10, containing counter-sanctionist provisions in the field of the theater, the following is communicated to you: Commencing the tenth of February, all provisions regarding foreign repertoires enumerated in the above-mentioned circular are abrogated. In regard to the *dramatic repertoire* the provision remains in force by which performances of all foreign works may take place only when, in addition to the 'censorship visa,' they are provided with special authorization issued by the Italian Society of Authors and Editors as provided for by the inspectorate of the theater. The provision regarding artists, conductors, and executants in general remains in force, there having been no modification of the rules in this respect. You are requested to see to it that the present provisions are duly applied. I shall appreciate a note of acknowledgment. The Minister [signature]." (The full text obtained from the Italian Ministry for the Press and Propaganda)

28 FEBRUARY 1936

Sixteen days after the thirty-eighth birthday of Roy HARRIS, two of his works are performed for the first time on the same day, in two American cities: *Second Symphony* in three movements by the Boston Symphony, Richard Burgin conducting; and *Prelude and Fugue* for strings by the Philadelphia Orchestra, Werner Janssen conducting.

28 FEBRUARY 1936

The management of the New York Philharmonic Orchestra announces the appointment of Wilhelm FURTWAENGLER for the season 1936–1937.

1 MARCH 1936

Die Musik issues a special anti-Semitic number, with articles with meaningful titles: *Mendelssohn, Mahler und wir; Der Jude als Musikfabrikant,* illustrated with pictures of Mendelssohn, Meyerbeer, Offenbach, Mahler, Schoenberg, Toch, Weill, and Klemperer, and prefaced with quotations from Adolf Hitler's scriptures on the subject of Jews in art.

6 MARCH 1936

Josef STRANSKY, Austrian-American conductor, dies in New York of a sudden heart attack in his sixty-fourth year.

6 MARCH 1936

Rubin GOLDMARK, New York-born nephew of the celebrated Karl Goldmark, and himself a composer of symphonic music of American flavor, dies in New York in his sixty-fourth year.

13 MARCH 1936

Oedipe, opera by Georges ENESCO, is produced at the Paris Opéra.

14 MARCH 1936

After a storm of opposition to the New York Philharmonic appointment of Wilhelm FURTWAENGLER, as a friend and abettor of the German National Socialist government, he declines the offer in the following cable from Luxor, Egypt.

"Political controversies disagreeable to me. Am not politician but exponent of German music, which belongs to all humanity regardless of politics. I propose postpone my season in the interests of Philharmonic Society and music until the public realizes that politics and music are apart."

18 MARCH 1936

A Theatre of People's Art, for propaganda of the musical creative output of the peoples of U.S.S.R., including recitals of native instrumentalists, is founded in Moscow.

21 MARCH 1936

Alexandre GLAZUNOV, the last great symphonist of old Russia, true heir to the tradition of Balakirev, Borodin, and Rimsky-Korsakov, master-contrapuntist and noble defender of established musical aesthetics, dies in Paris, at the age of seventy years, seven months, and eleven days.

25 MARCH 1936

Farkhad and Shirin, opera by V. A. USPENSKY, based on national Uzbek tunes, is produced at Tashkent. (Date from *Sovietskaya Musica,* No. 4, 1937)

26 MARCH 1936

A decade (ten days) of Music of National Defense, organized on the initiative of the Political Administration of the RKKA and the Union of Soviet Composers, ends in Moscow, having given, in four public concerts and three radio broadcasts, works by thirty-seven composers, among them first performances of Vissarion SHEBALIN's *Fourth Symphony,* commemorating the battle at Perekop, Crimea, in March 1920, and Lev KNIPPER's *Sixth Symphony,* dedicated to the Red Cavalry.

3–5 APRIL 1936

The first International Festival is given at Baden-Baden in un-
disguised opposition to the annual Festivals of the International
Society for Contemporary Music, presenting programs of works
by composers of eight nations:

Jean FRANÇAIX (France); Paul HOEFFER, Werner EGK, Wolfgang FORT-
NER, Paul GRAENER, Ernst PEPPING, Wilhelm MALER, Paul HINDEMITH,
Gerhard FROMMEL, WOLF-FERRARI, Max TRAPP (Germany); Francesco
MALIPIERO (Italy); Lars LARSSON (Sweden); Knudage RIISAGER (Den-
mark); Conrad BECK and Albert MOESCHINGER (Switzerland); Josip
SLAVENSKI (Yugoslavia); Petro PETRIDIS (Greece); and Igor STRAVINSKY.

4 APRIL 1936

Thirteen centuries have elapsed since the death of Isidor of
Seville, who said that never could musical sounds be reproduced
on paper in precise notation (*scribi non possunt*).

11 APRIL 1936

Two Symphonic Sketches by Otto LUENING are performed for the
first time anywhere at the "Popular Concert" of the New York
Philharmonic, Hans Lange conducting.

15 APRIL 1936

Musica viva, a trimonthly music magazine in four languages,
starts publication in Geneva under the editorship of Hermann
SCHERCHEN.

18 APRIL 1936

Ottorino RESPIGHI, rhapsodic composer of effective symphonic and
operatic music, virtuoso of pictorial orchestration, dies in Rome
at 6:10 a.m., at the age of fifty-six years, nine months, and nine
days.

19 APRIL 1936

The fourteenth Festival of the International Society for Contemporary Music opens at Barcelona with a Sunday morning
concert of the Municipal Band in the following program:

Three Symphonic Movements, Pastoral, Dance, Nuptial, by the Catalan composer, Josep M. RUERA, written for the wind instruments, in a neo-archaic style, making use of the Greek modes (conducted by the composer); *Devise,* by Vladimir VOGEL, based on a five-note motif-device and a march tune, the two subjects uniting in the Finale in sextuple counterpoint; *Joan of Os,* symphonic legend for soloists, chorus, and wind orchestra by the Catalan composer, Director of the Municipal Band of Barcelona, Ricard LAMOTE DE GRIGNON, written in the austere style of a medieval mystery (conducted by the composer); and *Dionysiaques,* symphonic poem of Florent SCHMITT.

On the evening of the same day an orchestral concert is given, with the following program:

Prelude and Fugue by the German neo-contrapuntist, Edmund VON BORCK; *Ariel,* ballet suite by the Catalan composer, Robert GERHARD, subdivided into four sections, expressive of four moods of the Shakespearean sprite; three fragments from the opera, *Carl V,* by Ernst KŘENEK; the world première of the *Violin Concerto* by Alban BERG, his last work, played by the American violinist, Louis Krasner, for whom it was written, and conducted by Scherchen in the absence of the previously announced conductor, Anton von Webern; and three fragments from BERG's opera, *Wozzeck.*

20 APRIL 1936

Czar Kalojan, national Bulgarian opera by the thirty-seven-year-old Bulgarian composer, Pantcho VLADIGEROV, is produced at Sofia, Bulgaria. (Date communicated by the composer)

20 APRIL 1936

At the ISCM Festival at Barcelona, the following program of chamber music is given:

Piano Sonata, op. 1, by the Viennese neo-romanticist, Ludwig ZENK, in one tripartite movement; *Four Psalms* for soprano and chamber orchestra by the Swiss neo-classicist, Robert BLUM; *Two Movements for String Quartet,* op. 1, by the New York-born Viennese composer, Mark BRUNSWICK, in a neo-classical idiom; *Five Berceuses* by the Slovak composer, Václav KAPRÁL, inspired by his memories of the lullabies his mother sang to him and his eleven brothers and sisters; and *Concertino da Camera,* for alto saxophone and small orchestra by Jacques IBERT, in three movements of which the second and third coalesce, written in the virtuoso manner of an eighteen-century solo piece.

21 APRIL 1936

At the ISCM Festival in Barcelona, the following program of chamber music is given:

Sonata for flute and piano in three movements, in a rational, classical, melodic style, by Walter PISTON; *Five Sonnets of Elizabeth Browning,* for soprano and string quartet in a symphonic *Lied* style by Egon WELLESZ; *Suite* for violin and piano in four movements, *March, Moto Perpetuo, Lullaby,* and *Waltz,* by the twenty-two-year-old Englishman, Benjamin BRITTEN, based on a four-note motto; *Quelques Airs de Clarisse Juranville,* for soprano, string quartet, and piano, the first piece of musical surrealism by the former self-acknowledged Dadaist, now aesthetic actionist, the Belgian, André SOURIS; *Les Ombres Perennes,* three movements for piano, approximating the sonata form, and evocatory of the shades of Bach, Handel, and Scarlatti, by the Catalan, Manuel BLANCAFORT; and the fifth *String Quartet* in five movements by Béla BARTÓK.

22 APRIL 1936

At the ISCM Festival in Barcelona, the following program of orchestral music is given:

Sun-Treader, with a motto from Browning, by the Vermonter, Carl RUGGLES, written in an intensely emotional atonal style; the fine-textured neo-classical *Fourth Symphony* by Albert ROUSSEL; *Concerto* for piano and orchestra in a neo-romantic style, quickened with percussive rhythm, by the Swiss composer Frank MARTIN; *Don Lindo de Almeria,* choreographic divertissement by Rodolfo HALFFTER, elder brother of Ernesto; *Concerto quasi una Fantasia* for violin and orchestra by the Parisian Rumanian, Marcel MIHALOVICI; and *Danse Polonaise,* based on Carpathian folk songs by Roman PALESTER.

23 APRIL 1936

At the ISCM Festival in Barcelona, the following program of orchestral music is given:

Overture, a piece of absolute music in a pan-diatonic idiom by the young Englishman, Lennox BERKELEY; *Symphony,* in two movements, in an atonal idiom, by Karl Alfred DEUTSCH, Austrian composer, resident in Paris; *Second Concerto* for violin and orchestra, op. 61, based on the mountain songs of Poland, by Karol SZYMANOWSKI; *Sinfonia* with piano concertante, by the Manila-born, erstwhile prodigy, FEDERICO ELIZALDE, in orthodox four movements; and *Overture* in a rhythmic neo-classical idiom by the Swede, Lars-Erik LARSSON.

24 APRIL 1936

Bernard VAN DIEREN, Dutch composer, resident in London since 1909, dies in London, in his fifty-second year.

25 APRIL 1936

Two months and twenty-three days before the Fascist rebellion in Spain, the Barcelona Festival of the ISCM ends with a concert of modern Spanish music, in the following program:

La Nochebuena del Diablo, cantata on the popular children's legend, by Oscar ESPLÁ; *Sonatina,* ballet in one act and five scenes by Ernesto HALFFTER; three dances from the ballet, *Three-Cornered Hat,* by Manuel DE FALLA; *Ballad* for piano and orchestra by Salvador BACARISSE; *Por el Rio Guadalquivir* by Joaquin TURINA; *Triana* by Isaac ALBÉNIZ, orchestrated by Arbós; *Initiation* from the *Liturgia Negra* by Pedro SANJUÁN, inspired by Cuban Negro ritual; *Sardana* by Juli GARRETA; fragment from *Goyescas* by Enrique GRANADOS; and *El Comte Arnau,* lyric poem for soloists, chorus, and orchestra by Felipe PEDRELL.

1 MAY 1936

The Wind Massive, an orchestra composed of 3,150 wind instruments and percussion players, is presented for the first time in Leningrad on the International Day.

2 MAY 1936

Petya and the Wolf, symphonic fairy tale for children, by Serge PROKOFIEV, is performed for the first time at a children's concert of the Moscow Philharmonic in the large hall of the Moscow Conservatory.

(The full score was completed in Moscow, 24 April 1936; the sketches, 15 April 1936. All these dates communicated by the composer)

7 MAY 1936

Franz WAGNER, Dresden pianist, gives the first air piano recital in history, playing a program of romantic music on the aluminum grand piano aboard the *Hindenburg,* during the airship's first transatlantic crossing.

13 MAY 1936

The last concert is given at the Augusteo of Rome, before its demolition to uncover Augustus' tomb on the site under the building.

(1,935 concerts have been given at the Augusteo, producing 940 Italian compositions, of which 531 were first performances, and 1,492 compositions by non-Italians)

27 MAY 1936

The Orquesta Sinfonica Nacional of Bogotá, Colombia, under the direction of Guillermo ESPINOSA, conductor, is formally established by a decree of the President of the Republic of Colombia.

3 JUNE 1936

La Jeune France, a new group of French young composers, presents at the Salle Gaveau, in Paris, a program of orchestral compositions by Olivier MESSIAEN, Yves BAUDRIER, André JOLIVET, and DANIEL-LESUR, and—in a sisterly-motherly capacity—Germaine TAILLE-FERRE.

"As the conditions of life become more and more hard, mechanical and impersonal, music must bring ceaselessly to those who love it its spiritual violence and its courageous reactions. *La Jeune France,* reaffirming the title once created by Berlioz, pursues the road upon which the master once took his obdurate course. This is a friendly group of four young French composers: Olivier Messiaen, Daniel-Lesur, Yves Baudrier, and André Jolivet. *La Jeune France* proposes the dissemination of works youthful, free, as far removed from revolutionary formulas as from academic formulas. . . . The tendencies of this group will be diverse; their only unqualified agreement is in the common desire to be satisfied with nothing less than sincerity, generosity and artistic good faith. Their aim is to create and to promote a living music. . . . At each concert *La Jeune France,* assembling an unbiased jury, will cause to be performed in the measure of its means one or several works characteristic of some interesting trend within the bounds of their aspirations. . . . They also hope to encourage the performance of the young French scores which have been allowed to languish through the indifference or the penury of official powers, and to continue in this century the music of the great composers of the past who have made French music one of the pure jewels of civilization." (The manifesto of the group printed in the program)

11 JUNE 1936

The Fountain of Bachtchisarai, opera to Pushkin's poem, by the Russian composer and critic, Boris ASAFIEV (Igor Glebov), is produced at the Moscow State Opera.

30 JUNE 1936

After a year and twelve days of intermittent work, Serge RACHMANINOV completes in New York the score of his *Third Symphony* in three movements, the first movement having been composed between 18 June and 22 August 1935; the second between 26 August and 18 September 1935; and the third between 6 and 30 June 1936. (Dates from Rachmaninov's letter to the author, dated 20 January 1937)

1 JULY 1936

The singers and stage hands of the Opéra-Comique in Paris start a sit-down strike after the last performance of the season, demanding the resignation of the director.

3 JULY 1936

One year, one month, and three weeks before his death, Albert ROUSSEL completes at Vasterival the full score of his *Rapsodie Flamande,* op. 56, based on popular Flemish tunes, his first work of a definitely native flavor. (Date at end of printed score)

10–25 JULY 1936

The first congress of Latin-American music is held at Rio de Janeiro, presenting concerts of Latin-American music.

11 JULY 1936

On the hundredth anniversary of the birth of the Brazilian national composer, Antonio Carlos GOMES, the Brazilian Post Office issues a set of stamps with musical quotations from Gomes' works, the first use of musical notes in philately.

(Grove, Riemann, Hull give the wrong year, 1839, of Gomes' birth; the accurate *Enciclopedia italiana* gives the correct date)

14–16 JULY 1936

On the occasion of the French national holiday, the first since the advent to power of a Socialist cabinet, Romain Rolland's plays, *Danton* and *The Fourteenth of July,* are presented in public performance at the Paris Arena, with incidental music, written by Albert ROUSSEL, Arthur HONEGGER, Jacques IBERT, Daniel LAZARUS, Darius MILHAUD, Georges AURIC, and Charles KOECHLIN.

16 JULY 1936

The third volume of the Tchaikovsky-von Meck correspondence, covering the last period, 1882–1890, is published in Moscow, edited and annotated by N. Zhegin, Director of the Tchaikovsky Museum in Klin. (Printer's date)

26 JULY 1936

Arnold SCHOENBERG completes in Hollywood the composition of his fourth *String Quartet,* op. 37, in four movements, within the frame of strict twelve-tone system, in lyrical melodic treatment. (Date communicated to the author by the composer)

10 AUGUST 1936

Julien TIERSOT, French composer and musicographer, pupil of Massenet and César Franck, dies in Paris in his eightieth year.

12 AUGUST 1936

Ignace PADEREWSKI rehearses for the first time as a cinema actor in a London film studio, playing the piano in his part in the film, *The Moonlight Sonata.*

16 AUGUST 1936

During the Berlin Olympiad, the first performances of the works by the winners of the Olympic prizes are given, with the following program:

Olympic Hymn by Richard STRAUSS, with a call-motif, "Olympia"; *Il Vincitore* by the Italian, Lino LIVIABELLA, in a glorified Verdi-Respighi manner; *Olympic Cantata, 1936,* by Kurt THOMAS, based on Protestant hymnology; *Olympic Festival Music* by Werner EGK, in an effective pictorial manner; and *Olympic Pledge* by Paul HOEFFER, in an eclectic neo-Handelian style.

17 AUGUST 1936

Pierre Octave FERROUD, French composer of symphonic and orchestral music in a vigorous rhythmic, neo-Schmittian style, is killed while motoring in Hungary, near Debregen, at the early age of thirty-six years, seven months, and eleven days.

29 AUGUST 1936

The National Bureau of Standards in Washington starts at 5 p.m., Eastern Standard Time, a broadcast, continued without interruption until 11:40 a.m. on the thirteenth of September, of the 440-cycle standard A for tuning purposes. (Information obtained by the author from the Bureau of Standards)

3 SEPTEMBER 1936

Nikita BALIEV, creator of the intimate cabaret, *Chauve-Souris,* dies in New York in his sixtieth year.

9 SEPTEMBER 1936

Carlos SALZEDO composes at Camden, Maine, a piece for harp alone, entitled *Scintillation,* in which he employs special effects invented by him, and named *Eolian Flux, Eolian chords*, and *gushing chords;* also brassy sounds produced by playing with the fingernails very close to the sounding boards. (Date at the end of the manuscript)

14 SEPTEMBER 1936

Ossip GABRILOVITCH, Russian-born pianist and, since 1918, conductor of the Detroit Symphony Orchestra, dies in Detroit at 7:30 in the morning, in his fifty-ninth year.

15 SEPTEMBER 1936

The Orchestre National de Belgique is founded in Brussels. (Date communicated by the Secretary of the Orchestre National)

15 SEPTEMBER 1936

The WPA Federal Music Project announces that from 1 January to 15 September fifteen WPA orchestras gave concerts before an attendance of 32,000,000 persons throughout the United States, and that 10,797 performances were given before 11,167,173 persons in July and August.

23 SEPTEMBER 1936

Ten days after his sixty-second birthday, Arnold SCHOENBERG completes in Hollywood the composition of his *Violin Concerto,* op. 36. (Date communicated to the author by Arnold Schoenberg)

4 OCTOBER 1936

Thirty-two years, five months, and three days after the death of Antonin DVOŘÁK, his early *First Symphony,* subtitled *The Bells of Zlonitz,* discovered in the Prague archives, is performed for the first time by the State Radio Orchestra of Czechoslovakia.

5 OCTOBER 1936

The newly organized State Symphony Orchestra of the U.S.S.R., formed of 130 best musicians, gives its first concert in Moscow under the direction of Erich Kleiber.

7 OCTOBER 1936

Forty unpublished songs of Hugo WOLF, mostly juvenilia discarded by the composer, are published by the Musikwissenschaftlicher Verlag. (Date in the publisher's advertisement)

12–17 OCTOBER 1936

The first Festival of the International Society for the Renascence of Catholic Liturgical Music is held at Frankfort, Germany, presenting contemporary sacred music by composers of twelve different nations.

22 OCTOBER 1936

Partita for Orchestra by Johann Nepomuk DAVID, in six parts, based on a single subject in four-fold appearance (direct, mirror, crab, and mirror-crab), is performed for the first time anywhere at a Gewandhaus Concert in Leipzig.

24 OCTOBER 1936

The music publishing industries of America appoint Joseph Mc-Kee, former acting Mayor of New York City, as "the arbiter of all matters pertaining to the fair conduct of business within the industry."

24 OCTOBER 1936

The *Sixteenth Symphony,* op. 39, in F major, by Nicolas MIASKOV-SKY, dedicated to Soviet aviation and reflecting in its four movements the optimism of progress, the gay spirit of youth, the solemnly mournful sentiments evoked by the loss of the giant plane, *Maxim Gorki,* and the broadness of Russian folk song, is performed for the first time at the Philharmonic Orchestra concert in Moscow, Eugen Szenkar conducting.

(The *Sixteenth Symphony* was composed between 12 October 1935 and 21 December 1935, orchestration completed 5 April 1936. Dates communicated by the composer)

29 OCTOBER 1936

Overture on Russian Themes, op. 72, by Serge PROKOFIEV, completed 25 September 1936, is performed for the first time in Moscow, Eugen Szenkar conducting. (Dates communicated by the composer)

4 NOVEMBER 1936

Filip LAZAR, Rumanian-Parisian composer of orchestral and chamber music in virtuoso style, with urban programmatic titles, or—in later years—of neo-classical leanings, dies in Paris in his forty-third year, of pneumonia contracted during a visit to the tomb of Pierre Octave Ferroud, who died two and a half months before.

5 NOVEMBER 1936

Charles Sanford TERRY, English musical scholar, historian, author of a treatise on Bach, editor of an exhaustive collection of Bach's chorales and hymns, dies at Aberdeen twelve days after his seventy-second birthday.

5 NOVEMBER 1936

John BARBIROLLI, London-born conductor, makes his first appearance with the Philharmonic Orchestra of New York.

6 NOVEMBER 1936

RACHMANINOV's *Third Symphony* in three movements is performed for the first time anywhere by the Philadelphia Orchestra, Stokowski conducting.

11 NOVEMBER 1936

Edward GERMAN, English composer of stage music in the light Sullivan-like manner, dies in London in his seventy-fifth year.

12 NOVEMBER 1936

Bogatyri (Heroes), an opera-farce with music by BORODIN, discovered in 1932 by Igor Glebov in the manuscript collection of the Leningrad Public Library, is produced by the Kamerny Theatre in Moscow, with a new libretto by the Soviet poet, Demian Biedny.

14 NOVEMBER 1936

The Council of People's Commissars orders discontinuance of performances of the opera, *Bogatyri*, as produced by the Kamerny Theatre in Moscow, on the grounds that the ridicule with which the libretto treats the objectively progressive act of Christianization of Russia in 988 is historically unjustifiable.

"In view of the fact that the opera-farce by Demian Biedny, produced by Tairov at the Kamerny Theatre in Moscow, making use of Borodin's music: (a) is an attempt to glorify the bandits of the Kiev Russia as positive revolutionary elements, which contradicts history and is false throughout in its political tendency; (b) blackens the heroes of Russian epics while they are in the popular imagination bearers of the heroic traits of the Russian people; (c) gives an anti-historic mocking presentation of the Christianization of Russia which was in reality a positive factor in the history of the Russian nation, as contributing to the relations of Slavic nations with nations of higher culture. . . . The Committee of Arts at the Council of People's Commissars resolves: *Bogatyri* is to be taken off the repertoire as alien to Soviet art." (*Pravda,* 14 November 1936)

17 NOVEMBER 1936

Ernestine SCHUMANN-HEINK, Prague-born American contralto singer, equally successful in simple *Lieder* as in Wagnerian and Straussian operatic roles, and, in her seventies, even in the motion pictures, dies in Hollywood at the age of seventy-five years, five months, and two days.

(Riemann, Moser, and Hull give the erroneous date of Madame Schumann-Heink's birth 15 July 1861, instead of 15 June. That the June date is correct is authenticated by the Associated Press dispatch from Hollywood of 15 June 1936, reporting an elaborate party staged for Mme. Schumann-Heink on her seventy-fifth birthday)

19 NOVEMBER 1936

At the Royal Philharmonic Society's concert in London, the gold medal is presented to Richard STRAUSS, during his sojourn in England.

19 NOVEMBER 1936

Pickwick, opera in three acts by Albert COATES, is presented for the first time on the second night of the season of the new British Opera Company, at Covent Garden, in London.

24 NOVEMBER 1936

The First Suite from the ballet, *Romeo and Juliet,* by Serge PROKOFIEV, is performed for the first time by the Moscow Philharmonic Orchestra.

(The music of the ballet was completed 8 September 1935, and two orchestral suites drawn from it during the summer and autumn of 1936. All these dates are communicated by the composer)

27 NOVEMBER 1936

By a decree of Dr. Joseph Goebbels, German Minister of Propaganda, critics in all fields of art are not allowed to praise or to blame, but merely to describe.

"Among professional critics who write their reviews in an objective business-like manner and who consider their role as that of mediators between the public and the artist, the order of Dr. Goebbels, to the effect that description *(Kunstbetrachtung)* be substituted for criticism, will find full agreement. The Germany of today lets artists and critics be comrades once more: servants of a common cause, workers for a common purpose." (Richard Ohlekopf in *Die Signale,* Berlin, 9 December 1936)

"What are the conditions of literary, artistic, and theatrical criticism in Germany? What compelled the Government to forbid to those younger than thirty to be critics? . . . Our country whose hymn is *Giovinezza* will not deny criticism to young people especially when one believes as we firmly do that young people are more capable of writing disinterested criticism than the old. Also it would be impossible, in a country where art thrives on polemics, to replace a critical review by 'objective accounts.' This, regardless of the fundamental question of whether any work of art can be objectively described. We are taught in school that any sentence, even such as 'This beefsteak is good' or 'The yolk of an egg is yellow,' is a judgment expressed in words. It appears all the more true since to vegetarians beefsteak is not good, and to us the yolk of egg is 'rosso' [red] whereas to the French it is 'jaune' [yellow]. . . ." (From the article *Abolire la critica?* in *La Tribuna,* Rome, 3 December 1936)

6 DECEMBER 1936

Igor STRAVINSKY completes in Paris the full score of his ballet, *The Card Party.* (Date at the end of the manuscript)

10 DECEMBER 1936

Eight days after his thirty-seventh birthday John BARBIROLLI, English conductor of the New York Philharmonic Orchestra, is re-engaged as permanent conductor for a term of three years.

10 DECEMBER 1936

Pinocchio Overture, based on a familiar children's story, by ERNST TOCH, is performed for the first time anywhere by the Los Angeles Philharmonic Orchestra, Otto Klemperer conducting.

15 DECEMBER 1936

The Dream of Wei Lien, Chinese ballet by a resident Russian composer, Aaron AVSHALAMOV, making use of Chinese melodies in Russianized harmonic and Germanized contrapuntal treatment, is produced at the Metropole Theatre in Shanghai, with a Chinese cast.

19 DECEMBER 1936

Joseph ACHRON plays the solo part in the first performance anywhere of his second *Concerto* for violin, with the Los Angeles Philharmonic Orchestra, Otto Klemperer conducting.

26 DECEMBER 1936

The first concert of the newly organized Palestine Symphony Orchestra, composed mostly of musicians driven out of Central Europe by neo-medieval racial discrimination, is given at Tel Aviv, conducted by Arturo Toscanini, and presenting music of Rossini, Brahms, Schubert, Mendelssohn, and Weber.

"The idea of organizing the orchestra originated with Mr. Huberman about a year ago, when he visited Palestine and decided to aid refugee German and Jewish musicians, many of whom are world-renowned. It was his untiring efforts of the past year that culminated in the phenomenal success of its first concert tonight. . . . Toscanini refused any remuneration, even traveling expenses. He said that at a time when forces were seeking the destruction of the Jewish people he felt it his duty to prove his sympathy with the Jews within his own domain of music. . . ." (New York *Times,* 27 December 1936)

31 DECEMBER 1936

Roy HARRIS completes in Princeton, New Jersey, the composition of his piano *Quintet.* (Date communicated to the author by Johanna Harris)

1937

2 JANUARY 1937

A century has passed since the birth of Mili BALAKIREV, genial Amphitryon of the Russian Mighty Five.

5 JANUARY 1937

Serge PROKOFIEV wins in a Paris court a lawsuit against Serge Lifar, the Russian dancer, for 30,000 francs due Prokofiev out of the 100,000 francs fee for the ballet *On the Banks of the Boris-thenes,* commissioned by Lifar, but found by critics and public to be deficient in artistic merit.

"Any person acquiring a musical work puts faith in the composer's talent. There is no reliable criterion for evaluation of the quality of a work of art which is received according to individual taste. History teaches us that the public is often mistaken in its reaction." (Excerpt from the judgment of the court)

13 JANUARY 1937

Kyor-Oglu (A Blind Man's Son), opera by the Azerbaidzhan composer Uzeir GADZHIBEKOV on the subject of the victorious peasant rebellion led by Kyor-Oglu whose father was blinded by the Turkish oppressors, is produced in Baku.

21 JANUARY 1937

Paul Sacher conducts the Basel Chamber Orchestra in the world première of *Music for Strings, Percussion and Celesta* by Béla BARTÓK in four movements: (1) a cyclical fugue (2) a modulatory movement wherein a highly chromatic subject on A is imitated by the dominant, then by the dominant of the dominant, by the dominant of the dominant of the dominant, and by the dominant of the dominant of the dominant of the dominant, until the remote key of E-flat is reached, and the theme is turned upside-down and sent back to the original A by way of a series of subdominants (3) a sonata movement in asymmetric rhythms

(4) a paradoxical rondo with a nonrecurring subject leading to a coda in which the fugue subject of the first movement is conformally expanded into a diatonic pattern.

21 JANUARY 1937

A Voice in the Wilderness, symphonic poem in six movements for orchestra and cello obbligato by Ernest BLOCH, the sections "bound together by a barely perceptible thematic relationship or reminiscence," with the cello having "an aggressive role, without endless displays of virtuosity, like the character in a drama," is performed for the first time by the Los Angeles Philharmonic, Klemperer conducting.

(The well-known passage in the Bible [Isaiah 40:3] from which the title is taken is actually a millennium-long misapprehension due to the absence of punctuation in ancient texts, and the real meaning is given in Powis Smith's "American Translation" of the Bible: "Hark! one calls: 'In the wilderness clear the way of the Lord. Make straight in the desert a highway for our God!' ")

21 JANUARY 1937

Third Symphony in three movements by Nicolai BEREZOWSKY, written in rhapsodic style within a clear tonal frame, is performed for the first time by the Rochester Philharmonic, José Iturbi conducting.

21 JANUARY 1937

Symphony in One Movement by Samuel BARBER, tri-thematically conceived so that the whole symphony becomes a triptych of contrasting sections, with ample use made of the contrapuntal devices of augmentation and diminution, is performed for the first time by the Cleveland Orchestra, Rodzinski conducting.

23 JANUARY 1937

Rembrandt van Rijn, opera in four acts and sixteen scenes, text and music by the Germanized Dane, Paul VON KLENAU, written in a neo-Wagnerian style on the subject of the painter's life, is produced on the same day in Berlin and Stuttgart.

25 JANUARY 1937

Second Symphony (Elegiaca) by Francesco MALIPIERO is performed for the first time by the Seattle Symphony Orchestra, Basil Cameron conducting.

"In regard to my *Second Symphony* I want to avoid confusion and misunderstanding. I wish to refer at once to the subtitle *Elegiaca.* This qualificative is an explanation how music that I wrote in the anxious and tragic months of the year 1936, a year full of sadness, yet remains outside of the events, and has elegiac character. This symphony is just music. . . . I wish to emphasize that in the term *elegiaca* there is no intention of program music." (Composer's note in the Seattle Symphony program book)

24 FEBRUARY 1937

Ten months and six days after the death of Ottorino RESPIGHI, his posthumous opera *Lucretia,* completed by his widow Elsa Olivieri Respighi, is produced in Milan.

2 MARCH 1937

Massimilla Doni, lyric opera by the Swiss composer Othmar SCHOECK to the subject of Balzac's novelette of the same name, is produced for the first time at the Dresden Opera.

10 MARCH 1937

L'Aiglon, opera to Rostand's imperial play about Napoleon's tubercular son, "the eaglet," with music by Arthur HONEGGER (Acts II, III and IV) and Jacques IBERT (Acts I and V), in a style midway between Wagnerian grandiloquence and Debussyan colorism, is produced at the Monte Carlo Opera.

12 MARCH 1937

Charles Marie WIDOR, the Nestor of French musicians, last pupil of Rossini, composer of orthodox music in all forms, the best of which are for his chosen instrument, the organ, Permanent Secretary of the Académie des Beaux-Arts, dies in Paris nineteen days after his ninety-third birthday.

19 MARCH 1937

Oedipus Rex of Sophocles, with music of Andrea Gabrieli (c. 1510-1586) arranged by Fernando Liuzzi (1884-1940), is performed in Sabratha, Italian Libya, at the inauguration of the Teatro Romano, reconstructed from the ruins of the old Roman theater.

20 MARCH 1937

Signorina Gioventù and *Nikotina,* two comic operas in the best pseudo-hedonistic Viennese tradition by the Czech composer Vitězslav Novák, are produced at the Prague Opera.

28 MARCH 1937

Karol Szymanowski, Polish composer of neo-Chopinesque music in a poetically coloristic vein, dies near Lausanne, Switzerland, in his fifty-fourth year.

(Inasmuch as Szymanowski died before midnight, the date should be as above, not 29 March as given out in newspaper dispatches. Date and hour of death specified in the Szymanowski number of *Muzyka,* 15 May 1937, p. 165)

1 APRIL 1937

Amelia Goes to the Ball, one-act opera buffa by the 25-year-old Italian-born American composer Gian-Carlo Menotti to his own libretto in Italian, originally entitled *Amalia al Ballo,* of a story of society women in Milan at the turn of the century, with a musical score in a gay Wolf-Ferrarian manner, is produced in an English translation at the Philadelphia Academy of Music, Fritz Reiner conducting.

8 APRIL 1937

Arthur Foote, American composer of ingratiatingly romantic music in various genres, dies in Boston at the age of eighty-four years, one month and three days.

"It is difficult to realize that Arthur Foote is no longer among us with his sunny smile and cheerful manner. . . . He always made everyone happy and at ease in his presence—the hallmark of a true gentleman. This broad humility appeared in his compositions which struck a note not likely soon to be duplicated." (Walter R. Spalding in a letter to the *Boston Evening Transcript*, 13 April 1937)

9 APRIL 1937

Five days before the composer's eightieth birthday the world première of Edgar Stillman KELLEY's symphony, *Gulliver, His Voyage to Lilliput,* is performed by the Cincinnati Symphony Orchestra, Goossens conducting.

10 APRIL 1937

Algernon ASHTON, British composer of twenty-four elaborate string quartets in all twenty-four keys, and writer of a record quantity of letters to the London press on every topic, with a special attention to the subject of neglected tombstones, dies in London in his seventy-eighth year.

10 APRIL 1937

At the eighth Festival of Chamber Music given at the Library of Congress, Washington, under the auspices of the Elizabeth Sprague Coolidge Foundation, Paul HINDEMITH makes his first American appearance, performing on a program of his own works his *Sonata for Viola Alone.*

11 APRIL 1937

At the Washington Festival of Chamber Music, Paul HINDEMITH plays the viola solo part, accompanied by a small orchestra conducted by Carlos Chávez, in the first American performance of his "concerto after folk songs," *Der Schwanendreher* in three movements, the third of which is a set of variations propounding a rhetorical question: *"Seid ihr nicht der Schwanendreher?"*

13 APRIL 1937

Music for strings in 1/6 tones by Alois HÁBA and his disciples is played for the first time in Prague at a concert of the music society *Pritomnost,* which means The Present.

21 APRIL 1937

The Second Hurricane by Aaron COPLAND, an American school opera especially designed for performance by boys and girls ranging in age from eight to eighteen, to a story about a dramatic rescue during a flood, is performed for the first time by a cast of 150 children at the Henry Street Music School in New York, Lehman Engel conducting.

27 APRIL 1937

STRAVINSKY conducts at the Metropolitan Opera House in New York the world première of his ballet *The Card Party* in three deals of straight poker (of which Stravinsky is a devotee), with the situation complicated at each deal "by the endless guiles of the perfidious Joker who believes himself invincible because of his ability to become any desired card": (1) First Deal: *Introduction, Pas d'action, Dance of the Joker, Little Waltz* (one player is out and two remain in the game with even straights); (2) Second Deal: *Introduction, March, Variations of the Four Queens, Variations of the Jack of Hearts and Coda, March and Ensemble* (three aces and a joker beat four queens); (3) Third Deal: *Introduction, Waltz-Minuet, Combat between Spades and Hearts, Triumph of the Hearts* (a struggle between three flushes, in which the joker at the head of a sequence of spades is beaten by a royal flush in hearts), to a musical score in a planned eclectic style of sophisticated commonplace redolent of Rossini, Delibes, Johann Strauss, Ravel, and also jazz.

1 MAY 1937

Two centuries have passed since the compilation of the first German music dictionary, Barnickel's *Kurzgefasstes Musikalisches Lexicon,* listing both the names of illustrious composers and musical terms in alphabetical order.

8 MAY 1937

On the eve of the first anniversary of the Italian Empire, Alfredo

CASELLA's opera *Il Deserto Tentato* (The Conquered Desert), evoking the Ethiopian conquest, is produced at the Florence May Festival.

"*Il Deserto Tentato,* mystery in one act, is a sort of lay oratorio in which the poet and the musician have endeavored to evoke the Ethiopian war, transferring it to an altogether unreal and mythical plane. . . . In highly poetical language it exalts the humanitarian mission of a great nation as it takes possession through the exploits of its aviators of a barren desert, bringing to it the civilization it has been awaiting since time began. The music is simple (at least in appearance), monumental, severe, with important choral participation. I shall add that this opera seems to me my best work." (From Casella's letter to the author, dated 1 June 1937)

12 MAY 1937

At the conclusion of the coronation of King George VI and Queen Elizabeth of England, the *Te Deum* composed for the occasion by VAUGHAN WILLIAMS on traditional themes treated in a free modulatory manner, is performed at Westminster Abbey in London.

(Date from *The Form and Order of the Service That Is To Be Performed and the Ceremonies That Are To Be Observed in the Coronation of Their Majesties King George VI and Queen Elizabeth in the Abbey Church of St. Peter Westminster on Wednesday, the 12th Day of May, 1937, with the Music To Be Sung, London, 1937*)

12 MAY 1937

Three months and twelve days after his seventy-fifth birthday, and fifty-two years, three months and two days after his first appearance as conductor on the same podium, Walter DAMROSCH conducts at the Metropolitan Opera House in New York the world première of his opera *The Man Without a Country* to Edward Everett Hale's patriotic story, refurbished, with added love interest, by Arthur Guiterman.

23 MAY 1937

Lenox Avenue, musical panorama of Harlem life by the Negro composer William Grant STILL, is broadcast over the Columbia network.

30 MAY 1937

The Moscow Radio Station arranges a special concert broadcast on short wave to a Soviet polar party on the ice floe in the vicinity of the North Pole.

31 MAY 1937

Cinco Piezas Breves for strings by Domingo SANTA CRUZ, Chilean composer of dissonantly contrapuntal neo-classical music, is performed by the Orquesta Sinfónica de Chile in Santiago.

2 JUNE 1937

Louis VIERNE, French organist and composer of melodious and harmonious pieces for his instrument, dies in his sixty-seventh year, while playing a concert of his works at Notre Dame in Paris where he was organist since 1900.

2 JUNE 1937

Hans VON WOLZOGEN, the German Wagnerian who originated the term *Leitmotiv* (Wagner's own term was *Grundthema*), dies at Bayreuth a few months before reaching his ninetieth birthday.

2 JUNE 1937

Two acts and two fragments of the third act of Alban BERG's uncompleted opera *Lulu* (to Wedekind's somber story of lust, perversion, and murder by disembowelment at the hands of Jack the Ripper) in which purity of the classical design (each scene is part of a symphonic suite) combines with a curious literalism of musical action (Lulu kills her last husband with five consecutive bullets on the ascending chromatics of the violins, C-sharp, D, E-flat, E, F), all within the framework of the strictest twelve-tone technique, are given for the first time at the Municipal Theater in Zurich.

5 JUNE 1937

The first television performance of an opera takes place when the BBC televises Act III of *Faust*.

"This was not a special television production but rather presentation by television of a regular performance. The first whole opera to be televised was *La Serva Padrona* on 23 December 1937. In the case of *Hansel and Gretel* the experiment was tried for the first time of having two casts. The singers were not seen, the acting casts were silent, and their movements consisted largely of miming specially devised for the music of the opera. The next special television production, again with two casts, was Act II of *Tristan* on 25 January 1938." (Information supplied by Assistant Director of Television of BBC)

5 JUNE 1937

At the age of eighty-one years, six months and a day, W. J. HENDERSON, American "reporter with a specialty, music," as he liked to style himself, kills himself in New York with a shot in the mouth to end the misery of illness and nerve exhaustion.

15 JUNE 1937

Checkmate, ballet by Arthur BLISS dramatizing a tensely played chess game in unblushingly luscious harmonies reinforced by frequent pedal points, is produced at the Champs-Elysées in Paris, Constant Lambert conducting.

16 JUNE 1937

The world première of Marc BLITZSTEIN's leftist opera-revue *The Cradle Will Rock* is given in New York in a makeshift performance, with the composer playing the piano and the singers placed in the audience, to circumvent the regulations of their union prohibiting stage appearance in an unlicensed show.

20 JUNE 1937

Walter PISTON conducts over the Columbia Broadcasting System the world première of his *Concertino* for piano and chamber orchestra, "an adventure of a musical idea," as he characterized it in his introductory radio speech.

21 JUNE 1937

Dreadnaught Potemkin, realistic opera by the Soviet composer

Oles TCHISHKO to the true story of a naval mutiny during the abortive Russian revolution of 1905, with such naturalistic touches as a line sung by a disgruntled sailor: "Our borscht is full of worms," is produced in Leningrad.

21 JUNE 1937

The fifteenth Festival of the International Society for Contemporary Music opens at the Paris Exposition of 1937 with the following program of chamber music:

Second String Quartet by Arthur HONEGGER; *Voice of Yamato* for soprano, two flutes, clarinet, bassoon and cello by the Japanese woman-composer Michigo TOYAMA; *Nonet* by the Czech, Karel REINER; *Duo* for flute and clarinet by the Catalan, Joaquin HOMS; *Morceau de Concert* for cello and piano by Alan BUSH, English leftist composer of propulsively rhythmic music; *Suite en Rocaille* for flute, violin, alto, cello and harp by the French post-impressionist Florent SCHMITT.

22 JUNE 1937

At the second concert of the Paris ISCM Festival the following program of orchestral music is presented:

Symphonie Concertante by Karol SZYMANOWSKI; *Concerto for Orchestra* by the Soviet neo-classicist Michael STAROKADOMSKY; *Fantasy for String Orchestra* by Norbert VON HANNENHEIM who was a delegate of pre-Hitler Germany at the ISCM Festival in Vienna in 1932, but changed his allegiance to Rumania after the Nazification of German music; *Second Concerto* for violin and orchestra by Jerzy FITELBERG; *Hommage à Babeuf,* for wind instruments and percussion by the Belgian, André SOURIS; *Symphonie Concertante* by the Swedish neo-romantic Hilding ROSENBERG; *Second Symphony* in a lyrical pandiatonic style by Francesco MALIPIERO.

23 JUNE 1937

At the third concert of the Paris ISCM Festival the Garde Republicaine of Paris gives an orchestral concert with the following program:

Prelude from the neo-Gallic *Suite in F* by Albert ROUSSEL; *Canción y Movimiento* by E. LOVREGLIO; *Gulliver chez Lilliput* by Gabriel PIERNÉ; *Chorale and March* by Alfredo CASELLA.

24 JUNE 1937

At the fourth concert of the Paris ISCM Festival the following program of chamber music is given:

Second String Quartet by the Hungarian, Sandor VERESS; *String Quartet* No. 9 by Darius MILHAUD; *Four Melodies* by the Austrian atonalist Hans Erich APOSTEL; *Trio* for piano, violin and cello by the Dutch neo-classicist Henk BADINGS. (*Two Pieces* for clarinet and piano by Peter SCHACHT were scheduled for this program, but withdrawn at the last moment by the composer in view of the unfavorable attitude of the Nazi Government towards German participation in ISCM Festivals)

24 JUNE 1937

Don Juan de Mañara, second opera by Eugene GOOSSENS, after Arnold Bennett's story in which Don Juan is depicted as a sensual idealist for whom "the alcove is the altar," in a musical style of sublimated naturalism (Don Juan's sensual hysteria is simulated by a staccato beat), is produced in London.

25 JUNE 1937

At the fifth concert of the Paris ISCM Festival the following program of orchestral music is presented:

Overture from the opera *Nova Zeme* (New Earth) by the Czech quartertonist Alois HÁBA; neo-hedonistic *Concerto* for piano and orchestra by Jean FRANÇAIX, self-styled representative of "La Jeune France"; *Passacaglia* by the Argentinian twelve-tonist Juan Carlos PAZ; two movements from the *German Symphony,* op. 56, by the expatriate Hanns EISLER, left-wing composer of twelve-tone music; *Concerto* for string quartet and orchestra by the Catalan, JOSEP VALLS; *Toccata* by the Serbian, Demetríj ZEBRE. (On the same day a presentation of quarter- and sixth-tone music was given by Alois HÁBA)

26 JUNE 1937

At the sixth and last concert of the Paris ISCM Festival the following program of chamber music is given:

Second String Quartet by Elizabeth MACONCHY of England; *Grimaces Rythmiques* for piano in a Satiesque vein by the Serbian, Miloje MILOJEVIC; *Il Paradiso è all'ombra delle Spade,* hymn for three pianos by Luigi DALLAPICCOLA, Italian twelve-tonist; *Divertimento* for small orchestra by the Swede, Lars-Erik LARSSON.

5 JULY 1937

Aram KHATCHATURIAN, 34-year-old Soviet-Armenian composer, plays the piano part, with the Moscow State Orchestra, in the world première of his worldlily virtuosistic *Piano Concerto,* showing off digitally deft arpeggiated technique and lyrically alluring quasi-oriental melodies.

11 JULY 1937

George GERSHWIN, American composer, creator of new urban folk music stimulating to the masses and professional musicians alike, whose career from humble beginnings to material and artistic recognition is unique in the world of music, dies in Hollywood at 10:35 a.m., following an operation on a cystic brain tumor, two and a half months before his thirty-ninth birthday.

"Music was to him not a mere matter of ability, it was the air he breathed, the dream that he dreamed. I grieve over the deplorable loss to music, for there is no doubt that he was a great composer." (Arnold Schoenberg in a speech at the Gershwin memorial radio hour, 9 p.m., 12 July 1937, from Hollywood)

17 JULY 1937

Juan José CASTRO, Argentinian composer of modernistic symphonic and stage music, conducts at the Teatro Colón in Buenos Aires the first performance of his cubistic ballet *Mekhano,* featuring a dance of the hammer, dance of seduction, and transfusion of robot blood (to the accompaniment of running passages in whole-tone scales).

17 JULY 1937

Gabriel PIERNÉ, French composer of songful operas and light symphonic pieces in an elegant Gallic style, dies in Brittany barely a month before his seventy-fourth birthday.

19 JULY 1937

By unanimous vote at a general meeting in Munich, the 76-year-old music society *Der Allgemeiner deutscher Musikverein* is dissolved, as alien to the totalitarian philosophy of the Third Reich and incompatible with the musical ideals of the Hitler Youth.

25 JULY 1937

Music for Radio, tantalizingly non-subjective piece by Aaron COPLAND, is performed as a commissioned work by the Columbia Broadcasting System Orchestra. (A national contest for a descriptive title of *Music for Radio* was held after this broadcast, and the winning title among those suggested by the radio listeners was *Saga of the Prairie*)

26 JULY 1937

A century has passed since the establishment, by a papal decree, of the French Congregation of the Order of St. Benedict at Solesmes, restorers of Gregorian plain-chant.

1 AUGUST 1937

Anti-Fascist Symphony for large orchestra, chorus and military band by the 28-year-old Soviet composer Boris MOKROUSOV is performed for the first time in Moscow.

8 AUGUST 1937

Time Suite by Roy HARRIS in six movements, reflecting the spirit of the world, from "Religion" to "Labor" and from "Philosophy" to "Broadway," is broadcast in a world première over the CBS network.

17 AUGUST 1937

A London Overture by John IRELAND, inspired by a bus conductor's cry of "Piccadilly!", topically literal, diatonic, gay, and unassuming, is performed for the first time at the Promenade Concerts in London, Sir Henry Wood conducting.

23 AUGUST 1937

Albert ROUSSEL, nobly poetic composer of France whose early

symphonic evocations of the Orient, where he had traveled as a marine officer, and whose later works of neo-classical texture established a new synthesis of impressionist, romantic, and neo-classical styles, dies in Royan in his sixty-ninth year.

"On 28 July, Roussel went to Royan, hoping to find there the much needed rest. On 13 August he was compelled to take to bed and interrupt the composition of his *Trio* for oboe, clarinet and bassoon. Of this Trio only the middle part was completed: it is a stirring swan song. Roussel bore valiantly the awful suffering caused by a heart attack. On Monday, 23 August, shortly before four o'clock in the afternoon, the great composer died." (From *Albert Roussel* by Arthur Hoerée, Paris, 1938)

23 AUGUST 1937

The Works Progress Administration announces that the Federal Music Project gave 4,360 programs, attended by 4,346,705 listeners, during the month of July 1937, and that the highest monthly attendance was reached in August 1936 with a total of 6,178,093 listeners.

27 AUGUST 1937

El Salón México, a symphonic sketch by Aaron COPLAND named after the popular night club in Mexico City, and based on the melodic material of urban Mexican folklore, is performed for the first time by the Orquesta Sinfónica de Mexico, Carlos Chávez conducting.

6 SEPTEMBER 1937

Henry HADLEY, American composer of operas and symphonies in which he put European technique and orthodox idiom to the service of American subject matter, dies in New York in his sixty-sixth year.

12 SEPTEMBER 1937

Partisan Days, ballet by Boris ASAFIEV on the subject of the civil war in Russia, is produced in Leningrad.

19 SEPTEMBER 1937

Howard HANSON conducts the CBS Orchestra in the first performance of three movements (without the *Finale*) of his *Third*

Symphony, "written in commemoration of the 300th anniversary of the first Swedish settlement on the shores of Delaware in 1638, and conceived as a tribute to the epic qualities of the Swedish pioneers in America," with their "rugged and turbulent character alternating with a religious mysticism." (A fourth movement, a brilliant *Finale,* was added to the Symphony later, and the work was performed in its entirety in a broadcast of the NBC Symphony Orchestra, 26 March 1938, the composer conducting. First concert performance was conducted by the composer with the Boston Symphony Orchestra on 3 November 1939)

22 SEPTEMBER 1937

Silvestre REVUELTAS, Mexican composer of impassioned music which combines intimate Mexicanism with a modernistic knack for effective dissonances, conducts in as yet uncaptured Madrid his deeply emotional score, *Homenaje a Federico García Lorca,* an homage to the Spanish poet murdered by the Fascists.

1 OCTOBER 1937

Eighteenth Symphony in C major, op. 42, by Nicolas MIASKOVSKY, the only living composer who has doubled the Beethoven number, is performed for the first time by the Philharmonic Orchestra in Moscow, Gauck conducting.

7 OCTOBER 1937

The Society of Recorder Players is incorporated in London, England, as a first step in the revival of the Shakespearean vertical flute, with Arnold DOLMETSCH, the inventor of the modern recorder, as president, and his son Carl as musical director.

17 OCTOBER 1937

Green Mansions, "non-visual opera" by Louis GRUENBERG to the novel of the same name by W. H. Hudson, with the musical tones intended to replace verbal description, so that trees, birds or snakes are to be made audible by sonorous technique, is performed for the first time in a broadcast over the Columbia network.

23 OCTOBER 1937

Soil Upturned, second opera by Ivan DZERZHINSKY, written to the Cossack epic of Sholohov, as a sequel to *Quiet Flows the Don,* is produced at the Bolshoi Theater in Moscow.

1 NOVEMBER 1937

The Soviet Committee of Arts decrees a new system of gradation in honoraria paid to artists for concert work, from 50 to 600 rubles, according to four categories of merit.

4 NOVEMBER 1937

After many a weary month of feverish research and painful collation of divergent data in reference works, the first edition of *Music Since 1900* by Nicolas SLONIMSKY, a chronological panorama of musical events since the turn of the century, is published by W. W. Norton & Co. in New York.

4 NOVEMBER 1937

First Symphony in A minor by Gardner READ in four movements, planned as a cyclical construction in which the three principal themes, explicitly stated in the first movement, are restated by virtually every instrument in the orchestra, and conceived in somber tone colors, with an ending on a chord of muted cellos and divided basses in the low register, is performed for the first time by the New York Philharmonic, Barbirolli conducting, as a prize-winning work ($1000) in a contest sponsored by the Philharmonic.

17 NOVEMBER 1937

A Lincoln Symphony by Daniel Gregory MASON, proponent of admittedly conservative trends in American music, set in four musico-biographical movements: (1) *The Candidate from Spring-*

field (2) *Massa Linkum* (3) *Old Abe's Yarns* (4) *1865,* is performed for the first time by the New York Philharmonic, Barbirolli conducting.

18 NOVEMBER 1937

Wallenstein, fourth opera by Jaromir WEINBERGER, dedicated to the Austrian Chancellor Schuschnigg, is produced at the Vienna State Opera.

21 NOVEMBER 1937

Fifth Symphony by Dmitri SHOSTAKOVITCH in four movements, conceived in the neo-Beethovenian spirit of classical universality of appeal, is performed for the first time by the Leningrad Philharmonic Orchestra.

"The subject of my Symphony is an individual in the making. The Symphony is conceived in a lyrical vein. The finale of the Symphony resolves the tense tragedy of the early movements on an optimistic plane. The question is raised sometimes whether tragedy should have a place in Soviet art, confusing tragedy with doom and pessimism. I believe that Soviet tragedy as a genre has every right to exist. But its contents must be suffused with a positive idea as in the life-asserting pathos of Shakespeare's tragedies." (From Shostakovitch's statement *My Creative Reply* in *Vetchernaya Moskva* of 25 January 1938)

"The Symphony consists of four movements. Each movement presents a complete formulation of psychological moods. At the same time, the Symphony is an artistic monolith. . . . There is a feeling of joy, of happiness: it is bubbling in the orchestra and it passes through the hall like a spring breeze. The audience feels grateful to the composer, the reactions of our Soviet listener to music ring true. The Soviet listener is incapable of absorbing decadent, somber, pessimistic art, but he responds enthusiastically to all that is joyful, optimistic, self-asserting. And the absorbing optimism of Shostakovitch was understood and accepted by the Soviet listener." (Alexei Tolstoy in *Izvestia*)

26 NOVEMBER 1937

Schumann's only *Violin Concerto,* composed between 21 September and 3 October 1853, but unpublished and unperformed owing to the express stipulation in the will of the violinist Joachim (who owned the manuscript) that the Concerto should not be performed until 100 years after Schumann's death, is brought to performance in Berlin nineteen years before the expiration of the term of Joachim's will.

"Before the performance of this Concerto takes place, a remarkable book will have been published and reviewed, *Horizons of Immortality* by Baron Erik Palmstierna. The last pages of this book contain a detailed account of spirit-messages that have been conveyed to Miss Jelly d'Aranyi expressing Schumann's personal wish that this Concerto should be produced. . . . I know how my friend Miss d'Aranyi has worked at the Schumann Concerto and at other music; and I assert my positive conviction that the spirit of Schumann is inspiring Jelly d'Aranyi's production of Schumann's posthumous *Violin Concerto.*" (Donald Tovey in a letter to the London *Times,* 24 September 1937. But Schumann's spirit did not reckon with the more tangible ponderabilities of the Nazi spirit. The Concerto was produced in Berlin not by d'Aranyi, but by an obscure Hitlerian violinist. After several performances in Europe and America the Concerto, not of Schumann's best, was relegated to the limbo)

26 NOVEMBER 1937

On the occasion of the seventy-fifth birthday of the dean of Argentinian composers, Alberto WILLIAMS (who owes his Saxon patronymic to his grandfather Benjamin Williams, of Exeter, England) , a concert of his works featuring the premières of his Sixth Symphony, surnamed *Death of the Comet,* and Symphony No. 7, *Eternal Repose,* is presented in Buenos Aires. (Actually the concert took place three days after his seventy-fifth birthday, for he was born on 23 November 1862)

3 DECEMBER 1937

Symphony No. 3 in G major by Edward Burlingame HILL in three movements, completed on 19 February 1937, with "no descriptive background, aiming merely to present musical ideas according to the traditional forms," and seasoned with delicate Parisian flavor in its instrumentation, is performed for the first time by the Boston Symphony Orchestra, Koussevitzky conducting.

16 DECEMBER 1937

Lambeth Walk, jaunty cockney dance in which partners are instructed to slap their knees, point thumbs over their shoulders (in hitch-hike fashion) while loudly yelling "Hoy!" and strut vulgarly, makes its sensational appearance in the London musical revue *Me and My Girl,* books and lyrics by Arthur Rose and Douglas Furber, music by Noel GAY. (1,065 performances were given in a continuous run up to 2 September 1939 when London theaters were shut down for the duration of World War II)

17 DECEMBER 1937

Seventeenth Symphony in G-sharp minor, op. 41, by Nicolas MIASKOVSKY in the orthodox four movements is performed for the first time in Moscow.

(Orchestrated from 14 April 1937 to 25 June 1937; piano score completed 11 February 1937. The *Eighteenth Symphony* was performed before the *Seventeenth Symphony,* on 1 October 1937)

18 DECEMBER 1937

Thirty-nine paintings by George GERSHWIN are shown at a memorial exhibition in New York.

"George had a way of regarding his painting and his music as almost interchangeable phenomena. They sprang, he felt, from the same Freudian elements in him—one emerging as sight, the other as sound. . . . There were, indeed, periods when the palette almost weaned him from the piano; when he willingly stopped composing to paint, and only grudgingly stopped painting to compose." (Frank Crowninshield in the exhibition catalogue)

18 DECEMBER 1937

Two centuries have passed since the death in Cremona, at the age of ninety-two, of the mirific violin maker Antonio STRADIVARIUS.

19 DECEMBER 1937

Forty-eight representative American composers assemble at the Beethoven Association in New York for the purpose of organizing the American Composers' Alliance, with the objective of protecting the economic rights of the composer in the fields not covered by ASCAP, and thus not necessarily in conflict with that organization.

21 DECEMBER 1937

A Boy Was Born, a choral set of six variations by the 24-year-old Benjamin BRITTEN, is broadcast in the world première by the BBC in London.

21 DECEMBER 1937

The Reichsmusikkammer establishes a music examining board in order to protect the German people against the influence of undesirable and deleterious music such as phonograph records played by Jews and Negroes.

25 DECEMBER 1937

The National Broadcasting Company Symphony Orchestra gives its first concert under the conductorship of Arturo TOSCANINI who has assumed permanent direction of this newly formed orchestra, after having refused to remain at the head of the New York Philharmonic.

28 DECEMBER 1937

Transatlantic radio photo transmission of music manuscript is used for the first time when, as a result of the loss in the mails of string parts to SIBELIUS' score *Origin of Fire,* scheduled for performance by the Boston Symphony Orchestra, the orchestra management arranges with the publishers Breitkopf and Härtel to transmit the missing parts from Leipzig by radio.

28 DECEMBER 1937

Maurice RAVEL, the "musical watchmaker," in whom delicate precision of tonal manipulation was marvelously complemental to the poetry of simple world-things, and whose coloristic evocations, pervaded with prismic light, have created a new art of subliminal expressiveness, dies in Paris of a brain ailment, eleven days after a futile operation, in his sixty-third year.

"Perhaps the brain rebelled against pitiless dominion, or perhaps the heart took revenge on the brain which, for too many long years of the life of a great artist, had kept it in subjection amounting to slavery." (Ildebrando Pizzetti in the memorial issue of *La Revue Musicale,* December 1938)

"The perfection of Ravelesque art may be compared to that of Chopin, Mozart, or Bach. Ravel recalls particularly the composer of *Nozze di Figaro* by this astounding combination of a child's soul with a musical technique of such plenitude that it is certainly not an exaggeration to call it magical." (Alfredo Casella, *ibidem*)

"From the political and cultural viewpoint, Hungary has for centuries suffered from the proximity of Germany. But young Hungarian musicians at the turn of this century were already directing themselves towards French culture. And that is why, from our Hungarian viewpoint, the genius of Ravel, side by side with that of Debussy, has such great significance." (Béla Bartók, *ibidem*)

"Maurice Ravel seemed to us one of those rare creators who in the domain of music had the power of revolutionizing the very foundations of their art while remaining faithful to the eternal laws which govern that art. . . . Among the many reasons for our admiration for Ravel, there is one which makes his memory sacred to us: One of our best composers, Emil Riadis (1890-1935), prematurely taken from us, was a fervent disciple and admirer of Ravel." (Manolis Kalomiris, director of the Athens Conservatory, *ibidem*)

"The great respect I have for Ravel's mastery increases my regret that I am not sufficiently informed about the details of his life to write a testimonial doing justice to the stature of your great composer." (Richard Strauss, *ibidem*)

"It has been said more than once in this journal that Roussel stands much nearer the soul of his people than Ravel. No wonder, considering that we learn from a reliable source that Maurice Ravel—really Ravelovitch—was a descendant of a family that had emigrated from the East, and so should be regarded as an *Urfranzösisch* composer." (*Signale,* Berlin, 9 March 1938)

"Ravex, Ravez, and Ravet are fairly current in Savoie. The form Ravel probably originates in a misreading of the final *t*. The hypothesis that the name can be traced back to the Jewish patronymic *Rabbele* is unfounded. Ravel's mother, née Marie Delouart, was born in 1840 in the Basses-Pyrénées, France, the descendant of a Basque family whose name was Deluarte or Eluarte." (M. D. Calvocoressi in the supplementary volume to Grove's Dictionary, 1940)

1938

5 JANUARY 1938

Songs of Our Day, nine choral pieces by Serge PROKOFIEV written in a new Soviet style of musical folksiness, are performed for the first time in Moscow.

6 JANUARY 1938

Filling Station, realistically automobilistic ballet by Virgil THOMSON, centered on the figure of a courteous filling station mechanic who welcomes a passing motorist in an immaculately clean gasoline palace, with a musical score in the vernacular, sounding "like all the familiar American tunes though there is no direct quotation," is produced by Ballet Caravan in Hartford, Connecticut.

13 JANUARY 1938

Symphony in G Minor by E. J. MOERAN, conceived in a neoromantic vein, is performed for the first time by the London Philharmonic, Leslie Heward conducting.

27 JANUARY 1938

Horoscope, astrological ballet by Constant LAMBERT with dances of the signs of the Zodiac (the prancing Leo, the waltzing Gemini, the meditative Virgo, and others) arranged in varied musical styles, some in dissonant harmonies, some in placid counterpoint, is produced in London. (An orchestral suite from this ballet was first performed at the London Promenade Concerts on 8 August 1938, the composer conducting)

3 FEBRUARY 1938

A Paris tribunal awards STRAVINSKY the symbolic sum of one franc in his suit against Warner Brothers for defamation of character in a film entitled *The Fire Bird,* in which a girl is se-

duced after her resistance is weakened and her virtue under-
mined by the playing of a phonograph record of Stravinsky's luxuriantly sensuous ballet suite of that name.

10 FEBRUARY 1938

Die Wirtin von Pinsk, opera on the subject of Napoleon's invasion of Russia, by Richard MOHAUPT, written in an enhanced
diatonic idiom often expanded into clear bitonality, is performed
for the first (and last) time at the Dresden Opera House.

"Since the performance of my *Symphonic Melodrama* on the radio I have
suffered more and more on account of my wife being Jewish. The great sensation produced by my opera *Die Wirtin von Pinsk* in Dresden was followed
by a protest against performance of my works. The opera was immediately
forbidden and a few months later an official ban was applied to all my
works." (From the composer's letter to the author, dated Berlin, 28 June
1938. Mohaupt and his wife came to the United States in 1939)

11 FEBRUARY 1938

Evocations, orchestral suite by Ernest BLOCH, composed between
1930 and 1937, and written in a decidedly orientalistic manner,
in three sections: a buddhistically serene *Contemplation,* pentatonically strident *Houang-Ti, God of War,* and tintinnabulat-
ingly bustling *Renouveau-Spring,* a tone-picture of Chinatown
in San Francisco, is performed for the first time by the San Francisco Symphony, Monteux conducting.

12 FEBRUARY 1938

The first part of *Pilgrimage and Passion of the Virgin Mary,*
oratorio by Nicolas TCHEREPNIN based on medieval Russian
chants in a nineteenth-century harmonic treatment, is performed
for the first time at the Pasdeloup Concerts in Paris.

13 FEBRUARY 1938

While listening to the radio broadcast of Tchaikovsky's Fourth
Symphony by the New York Philharmonic, Nicolas SLONIMSKY
discovers at 4:30 p.m. the formula of the "Grossmutterakkord,"

containing all the twelve tones (C, B, D-flat, B-flat, D, A, E-flat,
A-flat, E, G, F and G-flat, in this order) and eleven different intervals, the equidistant intervals from the central interval being
inversions of one another, and the central interval, the tritone,
being the inversion of itself, with even intervals forming an increasing arithmetical progression, and odd intervals a decreasing
one.

15 FEBRUARY 1938

The ashes of Teresa CARREÑO, Venezuelan pianist who died in
New York in 1917, are repatriated in Caracas by the Government
of Venezuela.

22 FEBRUARY 1938

Colas Breugnon, opera by Dmitri KABALEVSKY to Romain Rolland's story *Le Maître de Clamecy,* is produced in Leningrad.

4 MARCH 1938

Alan BUSH plays the piano part in the first performance, broadcast by the BBC Orchestra in London under the direction of Sir
Adrian Boult, of his *Piano Concerto* in four movements of reso-
lute, non-chromatic, rhythmic music, with a choral ending in
which the baritone solo and the male chorus deliver a musical
address of social significance.

16 MARCH 1938

Julietta, expressionist opera by Bohuslav MARTINU to the story
of a man who exteriorizes a girl in a dream so that vision becomes
attractive reality, is produced at the National Opera in Prague.

17 MARCH 1938

Ernst KRENEK plays the world première, with the Concertgebouw
Orchestra in Amsterdam, Bruno Walter conducting, of his *Second
Concerto for Piano and Orchestra* (composed between 25 May
1937 and 22 August 1937) in four movements without pause,
cast in the twelve-tone technique adopted by Krenek in 1931 as a

suitable method "to supply music (which by the nature of its
historical development has renounced the harmonic scaffolding
of tonality) with a new unifying device," and using the basic
series, D, F-sharp, A-sharp, C-sharp, B, C, E, G, G-sharp, A, E-flat,
straight, inverted, backwards, and backwards inverted, as well as
bunched in chords. (Krenek played the first American performance of this Concerto on 4 November 1938 with the Boston Symphony Orchestra, Richard Burgin conducting)

"I knew the concerto he was playing. It was written in a very modern idiom.
It was radical, atonal, aggressive music. I had been present when it had been
booed and hissed in Europe. The people next to me kept quiet. An old lady
was reading the program. After a little while she looked up and turned to
her husband. And now she said something that should put that unknown
Boston lady among the great thinkers of our time. 'Conditions,' the old lady
said, 'conditions in Europe must be dreadful.' " (H. W. Heinsheimer, *Menagerie in F Sharp*, New York, Doubleday & Co., Inc., 1947)

18 MARCH 1938

Cyril ROOTHAM, English composer of symphonic and instrumental music in a straightforward Elgarian tradition, dies in
Cambridge in his sixty-second year, leaving behind an unorches-
trated manuscript of his *Second Symphony* which he, unable to
move his hands, dictated Delius-like to his friends and pupils,
note by note.

24 MARCH 1938

De Snoek (The Pike), one-act comic opera dealing with the fishing trip of an inmate in a penologically advanced jail, by the
33-year-old Dutch composer Guillaume LANDRÉ, son and name-
sake of the 63-year-old dean of Dutch composers, Guillaume (or
Willem) Landré, is produced in Amsterdam.

24 MARCH 1938

A hymn-fanfare of "Greater Germany" entitled *Grossdeutschland
zum 10 April* (the day of of the Hitler "yes" plebiscite in Austria)
by Paul WINTER, Munich lieutenant and composer of the *Olym-
pia-Fanfare,* is performed for the first time over the Vienna Radio.

"I had the happiness to be a witness of the first journey of the Führer through his liberated homeland, and I have lived the indescribable stormy jubilation of the inspired Austrians in Linz and Vienna. On the day after the arrival of the Führer in the Austrian capital, as I rode back to Linz, I suddenly had the thought of this Fanfare as an expression of my great and profound joy over the events of these days and the magnificent consummation of Greater Germany." (Paul Winter in *Die Musik,* May 1938)

2 APRIL 1938

Quincy PORTER conducts the New York Philharmonic in the first performance of his *First Symphony* in three movements, "an attempt to find expression for feelings and emotions which the composer knew no other way of setting down," conceived as absolute music, aggressively rhythmic and not infrequently strident in harmony and counterpoint, lyric in melody and impressionistic in tone-color.

8 APRIL 1938

Walter PISTON conducts the Boston Symphony Orchestra in the first performance of his *First Symphony* (completed on 25 September 1937) in three movements, conceived as a neo-classical essay in absolute forms, devoid of any "pictorial, narrative, political or philosophical intent," with the principal theme-motto restated in the brass at the close of the symphony in grandiloquent C major.

11 APRIL 1938

The Society for the Preservation and Encouragement of Barber-Shop Quartet Singing in America is founded by O. C. Cash, oil man of Tulsa, Oklahoma.

"The Society for the Preservation and Encouragement of Barber-Shop Quartet Singing in America was organized on 11 April 1938. For a year or more I had been collecting the words to all the old barber shop favorites. I decided to have a meeting of twelve men that I knew in Tulsa who, on occasion, had been caught in the throes of a barber-shop chord. Much to my surprise on the meeting night, 35 men instead of 12 showed up. Each man originally notified had brought two or three cronies I did not know. All the old favorites were harmonized and it was impossible to get the brothers to take time off to eat the Dutch lunch that had been prepared. Someone inquired: 'When are we meeting again?' . . . Attendance doubled for the next three or four meetings, the newspapers wrote a story or two about it which was picked up by the AP and UP wire services, and within two months chapters were formed all the way from Hollywood, Bing Crosby, President, to New York, Mayor La Guardia, President." (From O. C. Cash's letter to the author, dated 11 April 1940)

(The biggest barber-shop quartet contest was held during the last week of July 1940 at the New York World's Fair. The first prize, consisting of four radio phonographs and home recording sets, was awarded by Mayor La Guardia, as chairman of SPEBSQSA, Chapter I, to the policemen of the Flat Four, who prevailed against other contestants, Melody Maulers, Frog Hollow Four, Chromatic Canaries, and the Phillips 6 Barflies, the latter being champion winners of the 1939 contest in Tulsa)

12 APRIL 1938

Feodor CHALIAPIN, Russia's great basso, whose fabulous life story, from peasant beginnings to glorious achievements in world capitals, constitutes one of the most legendary artistic biographies, dies in Paris in his sixty-fifth year, a few months before the planned celebration of the half-century since his first public appearance.

"His illness started last summer; old chronic diabetes aggravated by acute anemia. The doctors decided to resort to blood transfusions. The first was given by Chaliapin's wife Maria Valentinovna. Then the doctors called on Chaliapin's youngest daughter Dasia. For the third a professional blood donor named Chien was called. Chaliapin joked: 'His name is Chien. I'm afraid I'll start barking tomorrow.' But the transfusions were futile. In the morning of 12 April he lost consciousness and became delirious. He kept crying 'Where am I? In a Russian theater? To sing, I must breathe, but have no breath' . . . At 5:15 p.m. Chaliapin died." (From *Les Dernières Nouvelles*, Paris, 13 April 1938)

"Chaliapin has betrayed his people and traded his fatherland for round coin. Having lost contact with his native soil, Chaliapin during his sojourn abroad did not create a single new role. His great talent dried up long ago. He left nothing behind after his death, has not handed over to anyone his methods of work or his experience." (*Izvestia*, Moscow, 14 April 1938)

"Only those are dead that are forgotten. . . . This inscription I read in some cemetery. If the idea is right, Chaliapin will never die. He cannot die! For this miraculous artist with a truly fabulous gift is unforgettable. Forty-one years ago, almost from the very beginning of his career whose witness I was, he had been on a pedestal from which he never came down, never stumbled, to the last days of his life. All agreed in their admiration for him, plain mortals, eminent people, and the great. The same words, always and everywhere: extraordinary, astounding. And his great fame has spread over all the earth. In this, too, Chaliapin was unique, an artist whose recognition was general from his early days. General in the full sense of the word. Yes, Chaliapin was a giant. But for future generations he will be a legend." (Rachmaninov in a letter-tribute, in *Les Dernières Nouvelles*, Paris, 17 April 1938)

14 APRIL 1938

The Captive of the Caucasus, ballet to Pushkin's poem by Boris ASAFIEV, is produced in Leningrad.

22 APRIL 1938

Concerto for Organ and Orchestra by Leo SOWERBY in three movements, marked (1) vigorously and moderately fast (2) slowly and wistfully (3) boldly, with a magniloquent ending in C major in a resonant finale, is performed for the first time by the Boston Symphony Orchestra, Koussevitzky conducting, E. Power Biggs, soloist.

1 MAY 1938

The Reichsmusikkammer issues a decree forbidding all Aryan music instructors to teach pupils of Jewish extraction.

5 MAY 1938

Anthony and Cleopatra, opera to Shakespeare's drama by Francesco MALIPIERO in the medievalizing oratorio style, chaste in melody and stark in harmony, is produced at Florence during the Florentine May Festival.

6 MAY 1938

Under the direction of Gino Marinuzzi, an orchestra of 900 symphony musicians, 45 military bands and 111 choruses, totaling 10,000 in all, give an open air concert of operatic selections in Rome on the occasion of Hitler's visit to Mussolini.

8 MAY 1938

Dumbarton Oaks, a concerto for chamber orchestra by STRA-
VINSKY in three movements, named after the estate of Robert
Woods Bliss, characteristically reviving the classical tradition of
musical dedication to wealthy patrons, is performed at the Bliss
home in Washington under the direction of Nadia Boulanger.
(At the first Paris performance, 16 June 1938, the piece was
billed simply *Concerto,* without mention of the name of the
patron's estate)

"This *Concerto* sounds strangely dull, and abounds in scholastic devices and
commonplaces. Any vestige of imagination, any novel effect is systematically
eliminated. . . . Either this is the end of music, its mortal illness, or its radical
reincarnation and rejuvenation. There is no other alternative." (Boris Schloe-
zer in *Les Dernières Nouvelles,* Paris, 21 June 1938)

10 MAY 1938

Jeanne d'Arc au Bûcher, "a vast popular fresco" by Arthur HON-
EGGER (completed on 30 August 1935) , written as a modern *chanson de geste,* to a text by Paul Claudel, conceived along realistic
lines, with the culminating martyrdom climaxing a continuous
dramatic rise of emotional music and words, spoken and sung, is
performed for the first time in Basel in concert form, by the Basel
Chamber Orchestra, Paul Sacher conducting.

22 MAY 1938

An exhibition of "degenerate music" is opened at Düsseldorf in
order to prevent "the spread in Germany of the microbes of musical decomposition" and eradicate music of "Marxist, Bolshe-
vistic, Jewish, or any other un-German tendencies" under "such
slogans as atonal music and jazz."

22 MAY 1938

Ostmark-Overture by Otto BESCH, a jubilee piece, enlivened by
marching syncopation, intended to celebrate the transformation
of the Oesterreich of Johann Strauss into the Ostmark of Adolf

Hitler, is performed for the first time at the opening of the Düsseldorf Festival.

28 MAY 1938

Mathis der Maler, opera in seven scenes by Paul HINDEMITH, illustrating the story of the painter Mathis Gruenewald (1470-1531) against the background of the Peasants' War, and including the imaginative conversion of Mathis into St. Anthony, the subject of his own painting, couched in a tense contrapuntal idiom within an enhanced modal frame, is produced at Basel, Switzerland, after Hindemith has been declared definitely *persona non grata* in Nazi Germany.

28 MAY 1938

The first air-conditioned opera house is opened in Dessau, enabling singers and patrons to act and react in a pure atmosphere at prescribed temperature.

30 MAY 1938

The Incredible Flutist, ballet by Walter PISTON to an imaginative story about a versatile flutist in the circus band who can charm not only snakes but also snake charmers, with boisterous music in all moods, from mock-romantic to vulgarly Lisztian, and all idioms, from simple diatonic to twelve-tone themes, luxuriously orchestrated and further enhanced by shouting, is performed for the first time by the Boston Pops Orchestra, Arthur Fiedler conducting.

2 JUNE 1938

The Scarlet Letter, opera after Hawthorne's classic by Vittorio GIANNINI, is produced for the first time at the State Opera of Hamburg, Germany, with the composer's sister Dusolina singing the part of the young Salem matron whose unhallowed love for a Puritan clergyman was stigmatized with the embroidered initial A, for Adulteress.

12 JUNE 1938

One hundred and twenty-nine years after HAYDN's death, his

skull, which was stolen from his casket two days after his funeral, and later came into the possession of the Vienna Male Singing Society, is restored, in a solemn ceremony, to the rest of the body, at Eisenstadt.

17 JUNE 1938

The sixteenth Festival of the International Society for Contemporary Music opens in London with the following program of orchestral music:

Military Symphonietta by Vitezslava KAPRÁLOVA, 23-year-old daughter of the composer Vaclav Kaprál, conducted by herself, and dedicated to Beneš, President of Czechoslovakia, the title "military" being "not an appeal for war but rather for a conscious defensive attitude mobilizing physical feelings and enthusiasm for the preservation of national independence"; *Third Symphony* in four orthodox movements by the Polish atonalist Józef KOFFLER, who was to perish tragically four years hence in the destruction of the Warsaw ghetto; *Domini est Terra*, psalm for chorus and orchestra in a typical neo-classical manner by Lennox BERKELEY of England; *Das Augenlicht* for mixed choir and orchestra by Anton VON WEBERN, a profound and solemn incantation in an independent atonal style; *Jeanne d'Arc*, symphonic suite for orchestra in five movements by the French composer Manuel ROSENTHAL, representing a sort of anachronistic symphonic biography of the French virgin saint, concluding on a modified *Marseillaise* (the third movement was omitted at this performance) ; *Tres Ciudades* for voice and orchestra by the Spaniard, Julián BAUTISTA, to the words of Federico García Lorca; *Le Nouvel Age,* "Symphonie Concertante" by Igor MARKEVITCH, reviving the late eighteenth-century form of Concerto-Symphony.

18 JUNE 1938

At the second concert of the London ISCM Festival the following program of chamber music is given:

Quintet for flute, clarinet, violin, viola and cello by the Swede, Franz SYBERG; *String Quartet* by the anti-Nazi German composer Karl Amadeus HARTMANN; *Theme and Variations* for two violins by Alan RAWSTHORNE of England (the program book stated: "The composer is convinced that the theme appears in each variation") ; *String Quartet* by Karol RATHAUS of Austria; *Sonata* for violin and piano by the neo-classical German-American Werner JOSTEN; *String Quartet* by the Czech, Viktor ULLMAN; *Pianoforte Quintet* by the Berlin-born Spanish-Cuban, Joaquín NÍN-CULMELL.

19 JUNE 1938

At the third concert of the London ISCM Festival two old English operas are presented: *Venus and Adonis* by Dr. John Blow
(1649-1708), newly arranged by Anthony Lewis, and *The Ephe-
sian Matron* by Charles Dibdin (1745-1814).

20 JUNE 1938

At the fourth concert of the London ISCM Festival the following
program is presented:

Suite for strings and pianoforte by Willem Landré (Holland); two movements from *Suite* for female voices, oboe and strings by Peggy Glanville-
Hicks (Australia); *Variations* for string orchestra on a theme of Frank Bridge
by Benjamin Britten; *Music for Radio* by Frantisek Bartos (Czechoslovakia);
Concerto for trumpet and strings by Knudage Riisager (Denmark); *Cantata*
for soprano, chorus and pianoforte by Ernst Krenek; *Sonata* for two pianofortes and percussion by Béla Bartók.

22 JUNE 1938

At the fifth concert of the London ISCM Festival the following
program of chamber music is performed:

Two pieces from his *La Nativité du Seigneur* for organ solo, performed by
Olivier Messiaen; three movements from *Nonet* by the Lithuanian, Jeronimas
Kacinskás, in an a-thematic style; *Nachtklänge*, songs with wind quintet by
the Czech, Isa Krejčí; *Little Suite* for violin and piano by Bertus van Lier
(Holland); *Racconto* for flute, saxophone, bassoon and double bass by Jörgen
Bentzon (Denmark); *Two Songs for Soprano* with oboe, clarinet and bassoon
by Vojislav Vuckovic (Serbia); *Composition* for violin and viola by the
Swede, Sten Broman, a piece of absolute music in two-part counterpoint,
without double stops in either instrument; *Suite dans le Goût Espagnol* for
oboe, bassoon, trumpet and harpsichord by Roland Manuel.

22 JUNE 1938

Charles V, opera by Ernst Krenek in which historical facts are
symbolically interpreted as soul events, the music being entirely
constructed according to the twelve-tone technique of composition, is produced in Prague. (Krenek was not present at this performance because he could not risk flying over German territory
from London)

24 JUNE 1938

At the last concert of the London ISCM Festival the following
program of orchestral music is performed:
Concerto for Orchestra by the Italian, Riccardo NIELSEN, in strict neo-classical
style; *Mouvement Symphonique* by the Serbian, Slavko OSTERC, in chromatic
though not twelve-tone style, streamlined so as to eliminate all repeats or
sequences; *El Salón México* by Aaron COPLAND; *Aubade, Interlude, Dance* by
the Catalan, Robert GERHARD; excerpts from the opera *Mathis der Maler* by
Paul HINDEMITH; *Dances* for orchestra by the French composer Jean BINET;
fragments from the oratorio *Das Gesicht Jesajas* by the Swiss composer Willy
BURKHARD, in a linear style within a tonal frame.

21 JULY 1938

St. Francis, choreographic legend by Paul HINDEMITH (composition completed in Berlin on 5 February 1938), is performed in
London by the Ballet Russe of Monte Carlo. (A concert suite
drawn from the ballet is catalogued under the title *Nobilissima
Visione*)

24 JULY 1938

Der Friedenstag, Richard STRAUSS' one-act opera of war and
peace, the action taking place on the day of the Westphalian
Peace, 24 October 1648, is produced in Munich (most Strauss
operas received their world premières in Dresden) before an international audience, with excellent success and sixteen curtain
calls for the composer, but in pointed absence of Hitler and
Goebbels. (In his speech on 30 January 1940, Hitler spoke bit-
terly of the Westphalian Peace which chopped Germany into a
multitude of Reichs)

28 JULY 1938

Jack JUDGE, English popular song writer whose *Tipperary,* composed in 1912, was destined to become a bravely nostalgic war
song of the British Tommies, dies at West Bromwich at the age
of sixty.

29 JULY 1938

Third Symphony by Candelario HUÍZAR, strongly individual composer of Mexico who began composing in earnest at the age of

forty, is performed for the first time by the Orquesta Sinfónica de Mexico, Chávez conducting.

18 AUGUST 1938

Benjamin BRITTEN, 24-year-old boy wonder of the new British music, plays the piano part in the world première of his boisterously nonchalant *Piano Concerto* at the London Promenade Concerts, Sir Henry Wood conducting.

"The Concerto was conceived with the idea of exploiting various important characteristics of the pianoforte, such as its enormous compass, its percussive quality, and by its suitability for figuration; so that it is not by any means a symphony with pianoforte, but rather a bravura concerto with orchestra." (From the composer's program note)

1 SEPTEMBER 1938

Stchors, opera by Boris LIATOSHINSKY based on the life and heroic death of the Ukrainian division commander of that name, is produced at the Kiev Opera House.

3 SEPTEMBER 1938 ·

At the opening concert of the Nordic Music Festival in Copenhagen, Jon LEIFS, prime composer of Iceland, conducts the first performance of his music to the drama *Loftr.*

23 SEPTEMBER 1938

Aurelio GIORNI, Italian-American composer last seen the day before at 6:30 p.m., walking near the Housatonic River (in western Massachusetts) in a state of profound depression, vanishes in an obvious suicide attempt. (His body was recovered a few days later. When his *Symphony* was played by the National Orchestral Association in New York on 25 April 1938, the reviews were critical)

23 SEPTEMBER 1938

Phonograph records and full scores of Sibelius' *Finlandia,* Sousa's march *Stars and Stripes Forever* and a swing piece by Green, Galliard & Stewart, *Flat Foot Floogie,* are deposited, along with other samples of twentieth-century culture, in a Time Capsule, indestructible metal tube, buried underground in the area of the New York World's Fair, to be opened in A.D. 6938.

24 SEPTEMBER 1938

Béla BARTÓK completes in Budapest the composition of his *Three Contrasts* for violin, clarinet and piano, applying a modernized *scordatura,* in which a normally tuned violin alternates with one tuned G-sharp, D, A, and E-flat.

25 SEPTEMBER 1938

Eugenie SCHUMANN, Robert Schumann's last surviving daughter, dies in Berne, Switzerland, five weeks before her eighty-seventh birthday.

15 OCTOBER 1938

Daphne, bucolic tragedy in one act by Richard STRAUSS based on the myth of Apollo's frustrated love for man-fearing Daphne who is transformed into a laurel bush, is produced at the Dresden Opera under the direction of Karl Boehm to whom the opera is dedicated.

21 OCTOBER 1938

A suite in two sections, *Variations* and *Finale,* for string quartet and orchestra by Nicolai BEREZOWSKY, is performed for the first time by the Boston Symphony Orchestra, Koussevitzky conducting.

24 OCTOBER 1938

The Bach Society of New Jersey, in a letter to the Federal Communications Commission, protests against the syncopating of classical music, and especially Bach, by swing bands on the radio:

"Recently, on two occasions, we heard a jazz orchestra giving a rendition of Bach's *Toccata in D Minor.* All the beautiful fugue effects were destroyed by the savage slurring of the saxophone and the jungled discords of the clarinet. By no stretch of the imagination could such performances be tolerated except by people of no discrimination. As a group interested in bringing the best of

Bach's music to the people in our State, we must protest against the jazzing of Bach's music."

25 OCTOBER 1938

A century has elapsed since the birth in Paris of Georges BIZET, Gallic musician *par excellence* whose sunny Mediterranean muse outshone in the course of time the teutonically tenebrous genius of Wagner.

27 OCTOBER 1938

The Oxford Companion to Music, one-man, 1091-page, pictorial music dictionary compiled by Percy A. SCHOLES, the genial British scholar with a knack for writing descriptive prose on music in a detachedly scientific manner, whether the subject be church modes or chopsticks, is published by the Oxford University Press.

5 NOVEMBER 1938

Essay for Orchestra (No. 1) and *Adagio For Strings* by Samuel BARBER, the former representing a musical analogy of literary essay, and the latter a glorified exercise in writing for strings, are performed for the first time by the NBC Symphony Orchestra, Toscanini conducting.

11 NOVEMBER 1938

On the twentieth anniversary of the Armistice, Kate Smith, the amiable star of the radio, sings Irving BERLIN's anthem-like song *God Bless America,* originally composed in 1918 for a show *Yip Yip Yaphank* at Camp Upton, N. Y., where he was a draft sergeant, but never performed in public.

(On 29 November 1940, Alfred M. Aarons, an 80-year-old song writer, sued Irving Berlin and Kate Smith in a Federal court in Los Angeles, charging plagiarism from his own song *America, My Home So Fair,* copyrighted in 1918, and allegedly identical in parts with *God Bless America,* but failed to prove his case)

11 NOVEMBER 1938

Concerto for Violin by Edward Burlingame HILL, originally written in 1933 and revised in 1937, is performed for the first

time by the Boston Symphony Orchestra, Koussevitzky conducting, Ruth Posselt, soloist.

14 NOVEMBER 1938

MIASKOVSKY'S *Violin Concerto,* op. 44, in D minor, conceived in
a lyrico-dramatic style, with luscious harmonies hovering around
the tonic, is performed for the first time in Leningrad. (First
movement completed 1 June 1938; second movement composed
on 5-6 June; third movement 7-13 June; orchestrated from 8-20
July; dates communicated by composer)

21 NOVEMBER 1938

Ruby HELDER, woman tenor whose vocal chords were slightly
larger than normal, which resulted in the lowering of her voice
an octave down to the tenor's range, dies in Hollywood in her
forty-ninth year.

21 NOVEMBER 1938

Leopold GODOWSKY, pianist extraordinary and composer of clever
and difficult piano pieces with exotic or esoteric titles, whose
ready wit matched his agile fingers, dies in New York in his sixty-
ninth year.

24 NOVEMBER 1938

Werner EGK, German neo-romantic composer, conducts at the
Berlin Opera the first production of his opera *Peer Gynt.*

"The National Socialist press made an assault upon the work, spoke of 'Dreigroschenoper' plagiarism, of 'system' music, and declared it to be 'unfit for
the National Socialist outlook on the world.' And then something quite unexpected occurred: at one of the opera's more recent Berlin presentations
there appeared—a *deus ex machina,* so to speak—Führer Adolf Hitler himself.
The work pleased him extremely; he asked to have the composer introduced,
and is said to have made the statement that he was happy to have met such
talent. The direct result of this surprising change was the proposal of the
opera to the executive board of the Reich Music Festival (and thereby the
prospect of numerous productions throughout the Reich), and also the be-
stowal upon Egk of a government prize of 10,000 marks for his composition
of a new opera." (From an unsigned dispatch from Düsseldorf, Germany,
published in the *Christian Science Monitor,* 15 July 1939)

26 NOVEMBER 1938

Concerto for Cello and Orchestra by PROKOFIEV in three movements, completed in Moscow on 18 September 1938, in a revised version containing about fifty per cent of the original version made in Paris in 1934, and with a *Reminiscenza* to hook together the disparate sections of this half-Parisian, half-Soviet work, is performed for the first time in Moscow.

28 NOVEMBER 1938

Vano MURADELI, Soviet composer, native of the Caucasus, conducts the Moscow Philharmonic Orchestra in the first performance of his *Symphony in Memory of Kirov,* Soviet leader assassinated in 1934.

28 NOVEMBER 1938

The State Jazz Orchestra of the USSR is inaugurated in Moscow with a concert of jazzified pieces by TCHAIKOVSKY and RACHMANINOV, and a suite for jazz orchestra by SHOSTAKOVITCH written expressly for the occasion.

29 NOVEMBER 1938

A Poem About Stalin by Aram KHATCHATURIAN, written in a lyrical vein, with Caucasian overtones deferentially alluding to Stalin's origin, is performed for the first time at the Second Festival of Soviet Music in Moscow, with a choral ending to the words of the Caucasian poet Ashug Mirza:

"Leader of the country. —Higher than the mountains rises your glory among the people. —You have illumined the open spaces as does the sun. —Soon the world will open its eyes, and will raise your banner.—Ashug Mirza knows it, and that is why he sings so freely. —With a song of joy and work the wide lanes will soon resound. —Your name is ever with us like a banner, tovaristch Stalin!"

2 DECEMBER 1938

Concerto for piano and orchestra by Darius MILHAUD is performed for the first time by the Minneapolis Symphony Orchestra, with Mitropoulos performing both as conductor and pianist.

4 DECEMBER 1938

The Bishop of the Fejervar Diocese in Hungary decrees exclusion of the wedding marches from *Lohengrin* and *Midsummer Night's Dream* from all Catholic churches of his parish, alleging that Wagner's march presages the loosening of matrimonial ties, and that Mendelssohn's music accompanies the transformation of the bridegroom into an ass.

6 DECEMBER 1938

Mozart's newly discovered *Mass in B-flat* for solo voices, mixed chorus, two horns and string orchestra, restored from a set of parts found in the library in Zittau, allegedly written about the same time as *The Magic Flute,* is performed in Berlin for the first time after discovery.

11 DECEMBER 1938

Orquesta Sinfónica Nacional, the first full-fledged orchestra in Peru, is officially inaugurated in Lima, with the Austrian musician Theo Buchwald as conductor.

11 DECEMBER 1938

President Roosevelt dedicates the new Steinway piano installed in the East Room of the White House to replace the old-fashioned gold-cased instrument which occupied its place of honor since 1903, and expresses the hope that future Presidents will use the new instrument for the advancement of music. (He had no premonition at the time that his successor would be an amateur pianist)

12 DECEMBER 1938

The *International Cyclopedia of Music and Musicians,* the largest ever published single-volume music dictionary (2287 pages), edited by Oscar Thompson on a novel plan, with feature articles for greater composers, is published by Dodd, Mead & Co. in New York.

15 DECEMBER 1938

Joseph Szigeti and the Cleveland Orchestra, Mitropoulos conducting, give the world première of Ernest BLOCH's *Violin Concerto,* in three movements, the first, *Allegro,* of American-Indian
character, the second, *Andante,* in a dreamy folk-song manner,
and the last, *Deciso* and *Allegro Moderato,* a rhapsodic incantation, with the essential melodic scheme based on widely spaced
diatony.

16 DECEMBER 1938

Dédicaces for piano and orchestra and soprano voice by the ambi-
dextrous composer of popular and serious music, Vladimir Du-
KELSKY, set to a text by the French futurist Guillaume Apollinaire, and subdivided into five short movements, is performed
for the first time by the Boston Symphony Orchestra, Koussevitzky conducting.

16 DECEMBER 1938

An Outdoor Overture, ozonically refreshing and pandiatonically
pellucid orchestral piece by Aaron COPLAND designed for effort-
less music making by school orchestras, is performed for the first
time by the orchestra of the High School of Music and Art in New
York.

23 DECEMBER 1938

Boogie-Woogie, a new style of "swinging the 88" (playing the
piano) characterized by an *ostinato* bass, with the right hand
promenading over the keys in alluring arpeggios and scales, is
presented to the public for the first time at Carnegie Hall, at a
symposium concert "From Spirituals to Swing."

"The originator of boogie-woogie was Pine Top Smith of Chicago, who died
a few years ago after a barroom brawl. We don't know where his name came
from, but the music's name is based on an old phrase, 'pitch a boogie,' which
simply meant 'throw a party.' It was at 'houseparties' in the prohibition days
that boogie-woogie flourished; a crowd would gather around while the boogie-
woogie boys, who bore such names as Crippled Clarence and Toothpick, held
a little cutting session. (Maybe we ought to explain that cutting means trying to outplay your predecessor)" (*The New Yorker,* 31 December 1938)

"Boogie-woogie is a kind of blues piano playing in which the left hand drones a set bass phrase over and over, while the right hand goes to town with whatever variations the player can think up. Its form is identical with that of the classical *passacaglia,* a kind of dance music (of Spanish origin) that was old stuff to Bach's grandfather. Though boogie-woogie's mournful thump and clatter has long been heard in the humbler dives of New Orleans and Chicago, it was not taken up by the connoisseurs until 1938. In Manhattan the temple of boogie-woogie has been a subterranean leftist cabaret in Greenwich Village called Cafe Society. Its high priests: Negroes Albert Ammons, Pete Johnson, Meade Lux Lewis." (*Time,* 4 March 1940)

1939

5 JANUARY 1939

Voder, the first machine ever to produce the sound of the human voice, synthetized from primary hisses and buzzes, is demonstrated at the Franklin Institute in Philadelphia.

10 JANUARY 1939

Julius BITTNER, Austrian composer of operas, dies in Vienna, in his sixty-fifth year, after an amputation of both legs.

20 JANUARY 1939

John Kirkpatrick presents in New York the first integral performance of the Second Pianoforte Sonata, entitled *Concord, Mass., 1840-1860,* by the American musical transcendentalist Charles IVES, composed between 1909 and 1915, in four movements named after Concord's great writers: *Emerson* (based on material from an uncompleted *Emerson Piano Concerto,* at times profound and dissonant in texture, and again utterly simple and concordant) ; *Hawthorne* ("suggesting some of his wilder, fantastical adventures into the half-childlike, half-fairylike phantasmal realms," with clusters of notes played by using a strip of board 14¾ inches long to characterize his "Celestial Railroad") ; *The Al-*

cotts (based on the four-note motto from Beethoven's *Fifth Symphony,* as though played on "the little old spinet-piano Sophia Thoreau gave to the Alcott children") ; and *Thoreau* ("a transcendental tune of Concord") .

"This Sonata is exceptionally great music—it is, indeed, the greatest music composed by an American, and the most deeply and essentially American in impulse and implication." (Lawrence Gilman in the *New York Herald Tribune,* 21 January 1939)

23 JANUARY 1939

Alt-Danzig, orchestral suite by the German composer Georg VOL-LERTHUN glorifying the spirit of German Danzig, is broadcast over the Berlin radio network as part of an unsubtle propaganda campaign in favor of the reincorporating of Danzig with the German Reich.

1 FEBRUARY 1939

La Nina Boba (The Silly Girl) , opera buffa by WOLF-FERRARI, after Lope de Vega, is produced at La Scala in Milan.

2 FEBRUARY 1939

Novachord, musical instrument invented by Laurens HAMMOND, electronically operated so that the timbre of any instrument, from the Hawaiian guitar to the clavichord, from the piccolo to the trombone, and from the violin to the double-bass, can be reproduced, is demonstrated for the first time in the auditorium of the Department of Commerce in Washington.

3 FEBRUARY 1939

Cotillon, a suite of dances for orchestra by the Australian-born composer Arthur BENJAMIN based on the melodies in an old collection, *The Dancing Master* (London, 1719) , in nine dancing figures: (1) *Lord Hereford's Delight* (2) *Daphne's Delight* (3) *Marlborough's Victory* (4) *Love's Triumph* (5) *Jig It* (6) *The Charmer* (7) *Nymph Divine* (8) *The Tattler* (9) *Argyle,* is performed for the first time by the BBC Symphony Orchestra.

15 FEBRUARY 1939

Nineteenth Symphony in E-flat major, op. 46, for military band by Nicolas MIASKOVSKY, in four movements (composed between 3 and 26 January 1939) reflecting (1) folk dance and song (2) symphonized waltz (3) meditative repose (4) impetuous joy, is performed for the first time at the Comintern Radio Station in Moscow.

24 FEBRUARY 1939

Third Symphony by ROY HARRIS (actually his *Fourth,* the First having been discarded) in one continuous movement of five sections—tragic, lyric, pastoral, fugal, dramatic—with the first section taken *notatim* from a violin concerto written for Jascha Heifetz but not accepted by him for performance, is played for the first time by the Boston Symphony Orchestra, Koussevitzky conducting.

26 FEBRUARY 1939

Robert SANDERS, 32-year-old Chicagoan, conducts the New York Philharmonic in the first performance of his *Little Symphony in G,* the winner of the New York Philharmonic prize, in three movements, conceived as absolute music and traversing non-subjective attitudes varying from the funereally solemn to fanfarically virile.

27 FEBRUARY 1939

Mrs. Franklin D. Roosevelt resigns from the Daughters of the American Revolution in protest against the refusal of the DAR to permit Marian ANDERSON, Negro contralto, to give a recital in DAR-owned Constitution Hall in Washington.

(Barred from public halls, Marian Anderson gave an Easter Sunday open air concert in Lincoln Memorial Park on 9 April 1939 with 75,000 people in attendance, and with prominent political leaders, including Secretary Ickes and Mrs. Roosevelt, as sponsors. Marian Anderson appeared eventually in Constitution Hall on 7 January 1943)

27 FEBRUARY 1939

Life for the Czar, GLINKA's patriotic opera on the theme of the

· · MUSIC SINCE 1900 · ·

peasant Ivan Susanin's heroic deed in leading the Poles, bent on the assassination of the newly elected Czar Michael Romanov, to their and inevitably his own destruction in the wintry wilds near Kostroma, is revived on the Moscow stage, under the name *Ivan Susanin,* for the first time since the Revolution, with the Czar eliminated from the libretto, but with no changes in the music. (A preview of the opera was given on 21 February 1939 for a select audience, and another showing took place in Moscow on 24 February for the members of the Red Army and Navy)

2 MARCH 1939

Amadeo ROLDÁN, Cuban mulatto composer of propulsively aphrodisiac Afro-Cuban music palpitating with primitive rhythms (such as the ballet *Rebambaramba*) , dies in Havana of cancer, in his thirty-ninth year.

20 MARCH 1939

La Chartreuse de Parme, opera to Stendhal's famous story by Henri SAUGUET, in eleven scenes taking over four hours to perform, is produced at the Paris Opéra.

20 MARCH 1939

Violin Concerto by the Soviet neo-classicist Michael STAROKA-DOMSKY is performed for the first time in Moscow.

21 MARCH 1939

A century has passed since the birth of the mighty Russian, Modest MOUSSORGSKY, whose innovating genius advanced the frontiers of harmony and contributed powerfully to the creation of a truly national Russian music.

29 MARCH 1939

The Earl of Clarendon, Lord Chamberlain and Supervisor of the London stage, bans a song, *Even Hitler Had a Mother,* scheduled to be performed in a revue on April 20, as irreverent to the head of a foreign nation. (The ban was lifted and the song given in September 1939)

31 MARCH 1939

Joseph ACHRON plays the world première of his *Third Violin Concerto* with the Los Angeles Philharmonic Orchestra, Klemperer conducting.

1 APRIL 1939

Festival of Music for the People, designed to present music as an organizing force in the service of peace, freedom and work, opens in London in a program presenting a pageant, *Music and the People* in ten episodes, featuring 500 singers, 100 dancers and the People's Festival Wind Band, with music specially composed by Frederic AUSTIN, Alan BUSH, Erik CHISHOLM, Arnold COOKE, Christian DARNTON, Norman DEMUTH, Elizabeth LUTYENS, Elizabeth MACONCHY, Alan RAWSTHORNE, Edmund RUBBRA, Victor YATES and VAUGHAN WILLIAMS.

3 APRIL 1939

The second concert of the Festival of Music for the People is presented in London in the following program of choral music:

Two English Folk Songs by VAUGHAN WILLIAMS; *British Folk-Music Settings* by Percy GRAINGER; *Matra Pictures*, a set of Hungarian Folk-Songs by Zoltán KODÁLY; militantly satirical *Three Cantatas for Solo Voice with Instrumental Accompaniment* (1) *News from Vienna, 1938* (2) *Cantata of Exile* (3) *Prison House*, by Hanns EISLER; *Peace on Earth* for unaccompanied chorus by Arnold SCHOENBERG; and *Popular Tunes of the Day in USSR* by sundry Soviet composers, arranged for an orchestra of balalaikas.

5 APRIL 1939

The third concert of the Festival of Music for the People is presented in London in a program including:

Beethoven's *Egmont Overture;* the first performance of Benjamin BRITTEN's *Ballad of Heroes* for tenor solo, chorus and orchestra, written as a tribute to the men of the British Battalion, International Brigade, who fell fighting fascism in Spain; *Lento* and *Finale* from the *Concerto* for piano and orchestra, baritone solo and male chorus by Alan BUSH, with the innovation of a social

program note sung in the *Finale,* composer at the piano; and an optimisti-
cally eschatological cantata, *These Things Shall Be* by JOHN IRELAND.

5 APRIL 1939

Fifth Symphony by Alexandre GRETCHANINOV, the 75-year-old
Russian romanticist now living in America, is given in a world
première at a Youth Concert of the Philadelphia Orchestra, Stokowski conducting.

5 APRIL 1939

Ferruccio BURCO, prodigious boy maestro who, barely out of dia-
pers and into velvet pants, proceeded to conduct professional
orchestras, is born in Milan to Anna Gentile Burco, an opera
singer, and Claudio Burco, painter and aviator.

14 APRIL 1939

David Stanley SMITH conducts the Boston Symphony Orchestra
in the world première of his *Fourth Symphony,* composed in the
short time between 28 June and 9 August 1937 in Connecticut,
cast in the classical four movements, and integrated into an im-
peccably academic musical structure.

14 APRIL 1939

Four and a half months before Hitler's attack on Poland, the
seventeenth Festival of the International Society for Contemporary Music opens in Warsaw, presenting the following orchestral works:

Symphony by the 35-year-old Catalan, Josep VALLS, written in a polyrhythmically vitalized and metrically stylized native neo-Mediterranean manner
(the finale is a dance in 7/8 meter); *Five Orchestral Pieces* by Christian
DARNTON, all extremely short, lasting an average of 96 seconds each; *Epic
Legend* by the Belgian, Marcel POOT, designed as a twentieth-century counterpart of an old-fashioned romantic ballad; *Passacaglia-Chorale* by the Serbian modernist Slavko OSTERC; *Scherzo* and *Finale* from the *Violin Concerto*
by the half-Russian, half-German composer Vladimir VOGEL, based in part on
a 24-tone theme as the sum of a 12-tone row and its melodic inversion, followed by a double fugue paradoxically modeled with declared intention after

the plan of Mozart's overture to *The Magic Flute;* and *First Symphony* in D major by the French composer Jean RIVIER.

15 APRIL 1939

At the second concert of the Warsaw ISCM Festival the following program is presented:

Conrad BECK, *Kammerkantate;* Knudage RIISAGER, *Concertino* for saxophone and chamber orchestra; Francis POULENC, *Mass* in G major for unaccompanied mixed chorus; Milan RISTIC, *Suite* for four trombones in quarter-tones; Luigi DALLAPICCOLA, *Tre Laudi* for voice and chamber orchestra; André SOURIS, *Rengaines* for wind quintet; and Robert DE ROOS, *Five Etudes* for piano and orchestra.

16 APRIL 1939

At the third concert of the Warsaw ISCM Festival the following program of choral music by Polish composers is given: *Cantate Romantique* by Stanislaw WIECHOWICZ; *Cantata Ecclesiastica* by Michal KONDRACKI; and *Stabat Mater* by Karol SZYMANOWSKI.

16 APRIL 1939

The sounds of King Tut-ankh-amen's 22½-inch trumpet of silver and gold, and 19½-inch one of copper, are heard in a world radio broadcast after a silence of 3,297 years.

17 APRIL 1939

At the fourth concert of the Warsaw ISCM Festival the following program of chamber music is presented:

Elizabeth LUTYENS, *String Quartet;* Eugen SUCHON, *Sonatına* for violin and piano; Anton VON WEBERN, *String Quartet; Kojiro* KOBUNE (Japan), *String Quartet*; Alberto HEMSI (Egypt), *Coplas Sefardies* for voice and piano; Honorio SICCARDI (Argentina), *Two Songs;* Henk BADINGS, *String Quartet.*

20 APRIL 1939

At the Warsaw ISCM Festival the following program of chamber music is given:

Jerzy FITELBERG, *String Quartet;* Demetrij ZEBRE, *Trois Poèmes Lyriques* for violin and piano; Joaquin HOMS, *String Quartet;* Jozef ZAVÁDIL, *Petite Suite* for violin and piano; Piet KETTING, *Fugue* for piano; Vladimir POLIVKA, *String Quartet.*

21 APRIL 1939

The concluding concert of the Warsaw ISCM Festival presents the following orchestral works:

Twenty Variations in Symphonic Form by Boleslaw WOYTOWICZ (Poland); *Le Savetier et le Financier* for baritone and orchestra by Gaston BRENTA (Belgium); *Ostinato* for Orchestra by Lars-Erik LARSSON (Sweden); *Prelude and Invention* for string orchestra by the Parisian-Rumanian, Marcel MIHALOVICI; *Symphonic Studies* by Alan RAWSTHORNE (England); and *Overture* by Antoni SZALOWSKI (Poland).

22 APRIL 1939

The Old Maid and the Thief, opera buffa by Gian-Carlo ME-NOTTI in fourteen scenes depicting various happenings resulting from a welcome intrusion of a tramp ("tall and burly, black hair and curly, light complexion, Southern inflection") in a spinster's home ("somewhere in the United States"), with the subsequent transformation of the spinster into a thief to keep the handsome guest well provided and content, is performed for the first time by the National Broadcasting Company. (First stage performance was given by the Philadelphia Opera Company on 11 February 1941)

23 APRIL 1939

The Concertgebouw Orchestra in Amsterdam, Mengelberg conducting, Zoltán Szekely, soloist, presents the world première of the *Violin Concerto* by Béla BARTÓK, completed by him on 31 December 1938, and cast in three movements: (1) *Allegro non troppo,* opening in simple triad harmony in B major, and gradually evolving into a whole panorama of modern techniques, fluid polyharmonies, huddled chromatic clusters, broad modalities verging on pandiatonicism, undeveloped twelve-tone mottoes, rhythmic bounces in artful syncopation, runs in consecutive seconds, and the incidental use, in a long violin cadenza, of proximate quarter-tones in the vicinity of an open string (2) *Andante tranquillo,* melorhythmic variations on a folksong-like subject, subsequently detonalized by intervallic contractions and expansions, with a fugal stretto leading to a return of the simple theme (3) *Allegro molto,* a precipitate rondo, commencing with a broad quasi-classical subject which, atonally disfigured, procreates its own inversion, and is pitted against it in a clashing stretto, relieved temporarily by a fanfaric canon in proclamatory thematic fourths, until they pile up in quartal pillars, and are abruptly abandoned for a deafening drum crescendo, leading to a coda in which a self-inverting ostinato figuration forms a static underpinning for upcreeping chordal masses inexorably gravitating towards the central tonic B major, which, pierced by interference scales in frictional runs from C, eventually gains undisputed domination in a clear and unobstructed B major triad.

24 APRIL 1939

John Herbert FOULDS, English composer of romantic music with theosophic undertones, an early dabbler in quarter-tones and similar musical arcana, dies in Calcutta in his fifty-ninth year.

28 APRIL 1939

Paul Bunyan, ballet for puppets and solo dancers by the barely 18-year-old composer William BERGSMA (born in California on 1 April 1921), is performed for the first time in Rochester, Howard Hanson conducting.

30 APRIL 1939

The World's Fair opens in New York with a third-of-a-million dollar Music Hall, with Olin DOWNES as music director. (Downes resigned on 24 May 1939 when the Fair Administration announced cancellation of all performances of serious high-grade music and substitution of more popular entertainment)

12 MAY 1939

Luis A. DELGADILLO, Nicaragua's lone composer of symphonic and chamber music, conducts in Managua the intermittently existent Orquesta Sinfónica de Nicaragua in the first performance of his Nicaraguanistically colorful symphonic suites, *Escenas Pastoriles* and *Los Tincos.*

17 MAY 1939

Serge PROKOFIEV conducts in Moscow the world première of his cantata *Alexander Nevsky* (score completed on 7 February 1939), expanded from the incidental music to the film of the same name, in seven sections: (1) *Russia under the Mongolian Yoke* (Asiatic wails in a minor mode) (2) *Song About Alexander Nevsky* (commemorating the victory over the Swedes on the Neva River, for which Alexander received his surname) (3) *Teutonic Knights in Pskov* (chant to Latin words in a mock-Gregorian monotone) (4) *Arise, Russian People* (a nonchalantly virile marching song) (5) *Battle on Ice* (percussive glorification of the rout of the Teutonic Knights on the frozen surface of Lake Peipus, 5 April 1242) (6) *Field of the Dead* (modal lament) (7) *Alexander's Entry in Pskov* (chime-ringing glory-singing finale).

18 MAY 1939

The Devil and Daniel Webster by Douglas MOORE, a folk opera to the story, by Stephen Vincent Benét, of the Devil incarnated as Lawyer Scratch, from whom Daniel Webster, in ordinary procedure, redeems the soul of an unfortunate debtor, is produced in New York.

19 MAY 1939

Under the auspices of the Society of Friends and Enemies of Modern Music, Ernst KRENEK conducts in Hartford, Connecticut, his first major work written in America, *Eight-column Line,* a newspaper ballet in the twelve-tone technique, with the principal tone-row symbolizing the daily headline.

24 MAY 1939

Billy the Kid by Aaron COPLAND, nostalgic ballet on the life of the picaresque badman of the West (obit 1886), with stylized cowboy tunes used as raw material in the score, is produced by Ballet Caravan in New York. (A symphonic suite drawn from this ballet was performed for the first time by the Boston Symphony Orchestra on 30 January 1942)

25 MAY 1939

Violin Concerto by Harold Morris is performed for the first time by the NBC Symphony Orchestra, Frank Black conducting, Philip Frank, soloist.

31 MAY 1939

In the Storm, opera by Tikhon Khrennikov (formerly entitled *The Brothers*), from the Kulak Rebellion in the Tambov region in 1919-1921, with a love story of two young collectivists cast against the turbulent events of class struggle, written in a melodiously broad Russian neo-Tchaikovskian manner, is produced for the first time in Moscow.

2 JUNE 1939

Josef Reiter, Austrian composer of the Hitler Cantata *Festgesang an den Führer des deutschen Volkes,* written in a blatant fanfare style, dies in Vienna in his seventy-eighth year, unsung and unhonored by the Nazis themselves who never put the *Festgesang* in performance, although the vocal score was hopefully published by the Nazi-occupied Universal Edition.

9 JUNE 1939

The world première of the *Seventh Symphony* of Arnold Bax, dedicated to the American people, is given in New York under the direction of Sir Adrian Boult, along with the *Concerto for Oboe and Orchestra* by Eugene Goossens, with the composer's brother Leon as soloist.

10 JUNE 1939

Sir Adrian Boult conducts the New York Philharmonic, with Solomon as soloist, in the world première of the *Concerto* for piano and orchestra by Arthur Bliss, commissioned by the British Council for the British Week at the New York World's Fair, and dedicated "to the People of the United States of America," in three movements: (1) *Allegro con brio* (2) *Adagietto* (3) *Andante maestoso,* conceived in a grand pianistic manner, Lisztomorphic in its sonorous virtuosity, Chopinoid in its chromatic lyricism, and Rachmaninovistic in its chordal expansiveness.

17 JUNE 1939

The first Tartar opera, *Katchkin* (The Fugitive), on the subject of the Pugatchov rebellion, by the 27-year-old Tartar composer Nazib Dzhiganov, is produced at the opening of the new Tartar Opera Theater in Kazan.

23 JUNE 1939

Effective in the Fall of 1939, the marching cadence of the United States Army is reduced from 128 to 120 steps per minute by decree of the War Department.

18 JULY 1939

Manuel Palau conducts in Valencia the inaugural concert of the new Orquesta de Falange Española Tradicionalista in a program of classical and modern music.

24 JULY 1939

The Vienna municipality declares all personal estate and music rights of Johann Strauss, "the waltz king," the property of the city, depriving Strauss' non-Aryan stepdaughter of all rights to the inheritance, and overruling her attempt to prove she was a real daughter of Johann Strauss and, as such, an Aryan.

27 JULY 1939

Mario Castelnuovo-Tedesco, Italian composer of Jewish ancestry, arrives in New York as an immigrant from Italy that, following Hitler's ideas, has expelled her Jews from all liberal and artistic professions.

8 AUGUST 1939

The Italian Department of Education announces its decision in the matter of the use of French words for instrumental forms:

"just as *omelette* can be replaced by the Italian *frittata,* so *Ouver-ture* should be *Introduzione,* and *Suite, Sequenza.*"

28 AUGUST 1939

Chasca, lyric opera on a native Argentinian subject by Enrique M. CASELLA, is produced at Tucumán, Argentina, with the orchestra, composed of wind and percussion instruments, placed in three groups behind the scenery, and invisible to the spectators.

29 AUGUST 1939

The Lucerne Festival closes in the atmosphere of impending war, with a concert led by TOSCANINI, and with his son-in-law Vladimir Horowitz playing the Brahms *B-flat Piano Concerto.*

31 AUGUST 1939

Six and a quarter hours before Hitler's invasion of Poland, Arthur COHN, 28-year-old Philadelphia composer, completes at Yaddo, Saratoga Springs, New York, the composition of his *Four Symphonic Documents:* (1) *Oppression* (2) *Dictators* (3) *Exiles* (4) $\equiv$

"The final movement was completed on the last day of August at 6:30 p.m. The next day the Nazi soldiers invaded Poland (1 September at 5:45 a.m., German time), and with this definite catastrophic move in world affairs I erased the original text of the fourth movement (which title I shall never reveal) and refused to place any title in its stead—four parallel dashes were substituted. Let those who desire make their own title from the music." (From the composer's letter to the author)

8 SEPTEMBER 1939

Lawrence GILMAN, writer of impassioned prose on music, and unregenerate believer in the universal significance of the art of music, dies of a sixth heart attack, at his country place at Sugar Hill, New Hampshire, at 11:15 p.m.

11 SEPTEMBER 1939

Jimmy Kennedy and Michael Carr dish out the first ditty of a week-old war, *We're gonna hang out the washing on the Siegfried Line, if the Siegfried Line's still there,* a marching tune in 2/4 time, with a traditional 32-bar refrain. (Actually the Siegfried Line wasn't there, militarily speaking, when the Allied armies reached its location during the last stages of the war)

27 SEPTEMBER 1939

The initial eleven notes of Chopin's *A major Polonaise,* the identification motto of the Warsaw radio station, are sounded on the xylophone, for the last time before the surrender of the city to the Nazis.

6 OCTOBER 1939

American Festival Overture by William SCHUMAN, an animated musical fresco depicting 20th-century American life, with the initial three notes imitating "a call to play of New York kids, usually yelled on the syllables 'Wee-Awk-Eee,' to get the gang together for a game or a festive occasion of some sort," with an appropriately lank melodic line and eruptive rhythms, is performed for the first time by the Boston Symphony Orchestra, Koussevitzky conducting, at a special concert "in honor of the American composer," along with works by GERSHWIN *(Piano Concerto)*, Roy HARRIS *(Third Symphony)*, and Randall THOMPSON *(Second Symphony)*.

12 OCTOBER 1939

Variations and Fugue by the expatriate Czech composer Jaromir WEINBERGER on a tune *Under the Spreading Chestnut Tree* by William Sterndale Bennett (1816-1875), made famous when King George sang it at a boys' camp in October 1939, is performed for the first time by the New York Philharmonic, Barbirolli conducting. (The piece was originally scheduled for performance by the Royal Philharmonic Orchestra in London for 30 November 1939 but was canceled when the outbreak of the war forced suspension of the London orchestral season)

14 OCTOBER 1939

Broadcast Music, Inc. (BMI) is organized in New York City, "pursuant to a resolution to carry out the building of an alternate source of music suitable for broadcasting," in opposition to and competition with the hitherto practically monopolistic ASCAP.

25 OCTOBER 1939

The Colors of War by Bernard ROGERS is performed by the Rochester Philharmonic, Howard Hanson conducting.

31 OCTOBER 1939

Overture by Lev KNIPPER, dedicated to the "liberation of the Western Ukraine and White Russia" from Poland, the first symphonic work celebrating the event, is broadcast over the Moscow Radio.

2 NOVEMBER 1939

Mario CASTELNUOVO-TEDESCO gives the world première of his ingratiatingly pianistic *Second Piano Concerto* with the New York Philharmonic, Barbirolli conducting.

17 NOVEMBER 1939

Hans PFITZNER's *Kleine Sinfonie* for strings, eight woodwind instruments, trumpet, harp and cymbals, is performed for the first time at a concert by the Berlin Philharmonic in Hamburg, Furtwaengler conducting.

18 NOVEMBER 1939

The Third Soviet Music Festival opens in Moscow with the production of a patriotic symphony-cantata, *On the Field of Kulikov* by Youri SHAPORIN, glorifying the Russian victory over the Tartar chieftain Mamay in 1380, and conceived in an epically grandiose neo-Borodinian style; and a *Harp Concerto* by Alexander Mossolov, regenerate ultra-modernist chastened into a frame of mind appropriate for composition of harp music.

20 NOVEMBER 1939

Seventh Symphony by Lev KNIPPER in three movements, signalizing "the readiness of the Soviet people to answer, blow for blow, the agitation of warmongers," is performed for the first time at the Moscow Festival of Soviet Music, on the same program with PROKOFIEV's cantata *Alexander Nevsky* (originally produced in Moscow on 17 May 1939).

23 NOVEMBER 1939

Peacock Variations by Zoltán KODÁLY, a series of sixteen variations on the Hungarian theme, *Fly, Peacock, Fly,* composed for the fiftieth anniversary of the Concertgebouw Orchestra, is performed for the first time by that orchestra in Amsterdam, Mengelberg conducting.

25 NOVEMBER 1939

Emelian Pugatchov, oratorio by Marian KOVAL glorifying the peasant rebel executed on 11 January 1775 by Catherine the Great for impersonating her late husband Peter III (whom she had assassinated with the aid of her lovers), is produced at the Soviet Music Festival in Moscow.

3 DECEMBER 1939

Sixth Symphony by SHOSTAKOVITCH in three movements, *Largo, Allegro* and *Presto,* written in a romantically realistic style, is performed for the first time at the Soviet Music Festival in Moscow.

7 DECEMBER 1939

Violin Concerto by William WALTON, composed in a broad tonal style, with touches of instrumental virtuosity, is given its world première by Jascha Heifetz and the Cleveland Orchestra, Rodzinski conducting.

20 DECEMBER 1939

On Stalin's sixtieth birthday, PROKOFIEV's cantata *Zdravitza*

(Health Toast), written to words in Russian, Ukrainian, White-Russian, Kurd, Mari, and Mordva languages, is performed in Moscow, on the same program with MIASKOVSKY's *Salutatory Overture,* also composed for Stalin's birthday, and cast in the optimistic, flatless and sharpless key of C major.

22 DECEMBER 1939

Second Symphony by the Russian-American composer of cheerfully neo-classical music, Nicolas LOPATNIKOV, in the traditional four movements, is performed for the first time by the Boston Symphony Orchestra, Koussevitzky conducting.

23 DECEMBER 1939

Monte Ivnor, romantic opera by Lodovico ROCCA to the story of a heroic nation defending a mountain peak in an unnamed semi-Slavic country against an unnamed foe, is produced at the Teatro Reale in Rome.

1940

5 JANUARY 1940

The linking of radio stations by short wave instead of the customary telephone wires is successfully demonstrated by connecting the station WIXOJ near Worcester, Massachusetts, with New York by means of the "staticless" FM (Frequency Modulation) radio developed by Major Edwin H. Armstrong.

7 JANUARY 1940

Mrs. Effie Canning CARLTON, who in 1886, at the age of fifteen, composed *Rock-a-Bye, Baby,* the somnificent classic whose lulling cadences have induced countless millions of children to restful sleep, dies in Boston in her sixty-eighth year.

5 FEBRUARY 1940

Ernst BACON conducts the WPA Orchestra in Chicago in the first performance of his *Second Symphony.*

29 FEBRUARY 1940

Arnold DOLMETSCH, "Musical Confucius," restorer and interpreter of the glory of old instruments (in old German, Dolmetsch means Interpreter), and founder of the Haslemere Festivals where old and new music was played on the new-old instruments of his manufacture, dies in Surrey of influenza, five days after his eighty-second birthday.

1 MARCH 1940

La Danse des Morts, oratorio by Arthur HONEGGER to the poem of Paul Claudel, inspired by Holbein's cycle of drawings in the Historical Museum in Basel, fusing religious and dramatic elements, spoken psalmody and choral polyphony, into a grandiose musicorama in which the voice of Jehovah rouses the skeletons to a lugubrious orgy, with a finale in the spirit of a pandemoniac *quodlibet* in which *Pont d'Avignon* is contrapuntally pitted against *Carmagnole* and *Dies Irae,* is performed for the first time anywhere by the Basel Chamber Orchestra, Paul Sacher conducting.

3 MARCH 1940

Karl MUCK, "calm, undemonstrative, graceful, elegant, aristocratic" (as Philip Hale once described him) conductor, great in his Brahms and Wagner, supremely authoritative in other music, dies in Stuttgart in his eighty-first year.

7 MARCH 1940

Arthur SHEPHERD conducts the Cleveland Orchestra in the first performance of his *Second Symphony* (his first symphony, *Horizons,* was premièred by him, also with the Cleveland Orchestra, on 22 December 1927), in four classically orthodox movements, with some unorthodox materials (e.g., a Mexican cowboy song in the Scherzo) and modernistic rhythmic intricacies.

7 MARCH 1940

Pennsylvania Symphony by Charles Wakefield CADMAN, embodying the history of Pennsylvania from the days of the early settlers to the throbbing era of industrial boom (illustrated by banging an iron plate in the orchestra), is performed for the first time by the Los Angeles Philharmonic, Albert Coates conducting.

10 MARCH 1940

The first American telecast of an opera is made in New York, featuring a tabloid version of *Pagliacci* sung by Metropolitan Opera singers.

14 MARCH 1940

Violin Concerto by Paul HINDEMITH in three movements, written in an enhanced tonal style, with extensions into quartal melody and harmony and acute chromaticism, is performed for the first time by the Concertgebouw Orchestra in Amsterdam, Mengelberg conducting. (The American première of the Concerto, given on 19 April 1940 by the Boston Symphony Orchestra, Richard Burgin, soloist, Koussevitzky conducting, was marked "first performance" in the program book through an honest misapprehension)

14 MARCH 1940

Dame Kobold, comic opera by Kurt VON WOLFURT, 60-year-old Latvian-born composer, written in a neo-Rosenkavalierian manner, is performed for the first time at Kassel.

18 MARCH 1940

Concerto for Violin and Orchestra by Walter PISTON in three movements, an acridly energetic *Allegro,* reticently modal *Andantino,* and spiritedly rhythmed *Allegro,* cast in ternary tonality, D major—F minor—D major, is performed for the first time by

Ruth Posselt with the National Orchestral Association in New York, Leon Barzin conducting.

23 MARCH 1940

Anna, veteran white mare of the Metropolitan Opera House in New York, the mount of many a Radames, from Caruso down, dies of old age at the Pegasus Club, Rockleigh, New Jersey.

24 MARCH 1940

Professor Edouard BRANLY, inventor of the coherer, and the first man who sent a wireless communication from one room to another (he made a report of his experiment to the Académie des Sciences on 24 November 1890), dies in war-depressed Paris in his ninety-sixth year.

6 APRIL 1940

VILLA-LOBOS conducts in Rio de Janeiro the first complete performance of his opera *Izaht,* to a Parisian story of an apache girl who self-denyingly saves the fiancée of the viscount she loves, and an apache leader whose natural daughter that fiancée turns out to be, all this set to uninhibitedly tuneful music with heteroousianly Brazilian rhythms.

7 APRIL 1940

New York Skyline, "symphonic millimetrization" by the scientifically minded Brazilianist, VILLA-LOBOS, with its melody charted from a pre-Empire-State-Building panoramic view of New York City, is radiocast from Rio de Janeiro on the occasion of the opening of the Brazilian Pavilion at the New York World's Fair.

9 APRIL 1940

Stereophonic reproduction of recorded music from sound film, giving true-to-life spectrum of overtones, is demonstrated in public for the first time by the Bell Telephone Laboratories in Carnegie Hall, New York.

11 APRIL 1940

Moby Dick, dramatic cantata by Bernard HERRMANN, a sonorous glorification of Melville's cetacean hero, employing an appropriately leviathanic orchestra, including radio thunder drums, is performed for the first time by the New York Philharmonic, Barbirolli conducting.

12 APRIL 1940

Eugene GOOSSENS conducts the Cincinnati Symphony Orchestra in the world première of his first full-fledged *Symphony* in four movements, dedicated to "my colleagues of the Cincinnati Symphony Orchestra."

19 APRIL 1940

Concertino for String Orchestra by Edward Burlingame HILL in three neatly contrasting movements, in which the last represents a string orchestra as a concertizing quadruple soloist, is performed for the first time by the Boston Symphony Orchestra, Koussevitzky conducting.

25 APRIL 1940

Four choral movements from Roy HARRIS's *Folk-Song Symphony,* his *Fourth,* written "to bring about cultural cooperation and understanding between the high school, college and community choruses of our cities with their symphony orchestras," and based on American 19th-century ballad tunes (both urban and rural) of known and unknown authorship, are performed at the American Spring Festival in Rochester, Howard Hanson conducting. (The first complete performance of the *Folk-Song Symphony* was given by the Cleveland Orchestra, Rudolph Ringwall conducting, on 26 December 1940, with these subdivisions: (1) *Welcome Party* (2) *Western Cowboy* (3) *Interlude: Dance Tunes for Strings and Percussion* (4) *Mountaineer Love Song* (5) *Interlude: Dance Tunes for Full Orchestra* (6) *Negro Fantasy* (7) *Finale.* On 9 March 1941 the New York Philharmonic, Barbirolli conducting, presented the two orchestral Interludes from the *Folk-Song Symphony,* plus a specially composed middle Interlude in slow tempo)

28 APRIL 1940

Luisa TETRAZZINI, "the new Patti," Italian prima donna, ample of figure and mighty of lungs, who could pick up a carnation while holding a high C, and whose biography included a marriage to a gigolo with a subsequent scandal and divorce, dies at 8:30 a.m. in Milan, at the age of sixty-eight.

3 MAY 1940

One-cent Stephen FOSTER stamps and two-cent John Philip SOUSA stamps of the United States Composers series are placed on sale in Washington.

7 MAY 1940

The New York Song Writers' Protective Association votes, 372 to 24, against commercial lewdness in popular American music, and resolves to expel members purveying dirty songs for coin machines in loitering places, but reserves judgment on sophisticated Cafe Society songs with an optional double meaning, such as *She had to go and lose it at the Astor.*

7 MAY 1940

A century has passed since the birth of TCHAIKOVSKY, great Russian melodist whose infectious emotionalism and profound Russianism have endeared his music to Old Russia and New Russia alike. (The Soviet government decreed to commemorate the centenary by renaming a Moscow boulevard Tchaikovsky Boulevard, and to issue postage stamps with Tchaikovsky's picture)

13 MAY 1940

2,200,000 Victor HERBERT three-cent stamps are placed on sale on the first day of issue, in New York, and a like number of Edward MACDOWELL five-cent stamps are placed on sale at the MacDowell Colony in Peterborough, New Hampshire, along with ten-cent stamps with a picture of Ethelbert NEVIN.

Carlos CHÁVEZ conducts an ensemble of Mexican musicians at
the Museum of Modern Art in New York in a program of Mexican music, featuring his own composition *Xochipili-Macuilxo-
chitl* (the name of the Aztec god of music) .

The opera *Volo di Notte* by Luigi DALLAPICCOLA is produced in
Florence.

Carlton COOLEY plays the solo viola part in the world première of
his *Concertino* for viola and orchestra, broadcast by the NBC
Symphony Orchestra, Frank Black conducting, in three contrastful movements, in a harmonic idiom spiced with endurable bi-
tonalities.

Andrey Nicolaievitch RIMSKY-KORSAKOV, son and historiographer
of his father, the great Rimsky-Korsakov, dies of pneumonia in
Leningrad in his sixty-second year.

Amerindia, ballet by the foremost composer of Bolivia, José
María Velasco MAIDANA, glorifying "the new Indian of tomorrow," is produced in La Paz, an event described by the President
of Bolivia as "of transcendent significance in the history of Bolivia's artistic culture."

Frederick CONVERSE, New England composer of six symphonies
in a fine American romantic tradition, and of the symphonic
apotheosis of Ford's saga of mass production, *Flivver 10,000,000,*
dies at his home in Westwood, Massachusetts, in his sixty-ninth
year.

On his seventy-sixth birthday Richard STRAUSS hands over to the

Japanese Ambassador in Berlin the score of his *Festliches Präludium,* written for the 2600th anniversary of the Japanese dynasty, and accepted by the Mikado as a dedicatory work.

16 JUNE 1940

Vitězslava KAPRÁLOVÁ, 25-year-old Czech composer, daughter of Václav Kaprál (*ova* is the feminine ending in Czech names), dies in Montpellier, France, of tuberculosis, two years, less a day, after she conducted at the London ISCM Festival her pathetically unprophetic *Military Symphonietta,* designed to mobilize the spirit of national independence.

19 JUNE 1940

Maurice JAUBERT, 40-year-old composer of modernistically Gallic cinema music and Couperinesque chamber music, is killed in action during the last agonizing days of French military resistance.

23 JUNE 1940

Simeon Kotko, opera by Serge PROKOFIEV (originally entitled *I Am the Son of a People of Workers*) to the story of the civil war of 1918-1920 in the Ukraine, is produced in Moscow.

25 JUNE 1940

At the Lewisohn Stadium in New York, Artur Rodzinski conducts the first performances of three American works: *And They Lynched Him on a Tree* by the Negro composer William Grant STILL, scored for chorus, orchestra, contralto and narrator; *Challenge: 1940* by Roy HARRIS, written by him in four days, opening with a "song of despair" and followed by the robust chorus to the text of the Preamble of the Constitution of the United States; and *Ballad for Americans,* a "statement of democracy," words by John Latouche, music by Earl ROBINSON, first heard over the CBS network on 5 November 1939. (The concert was originally scheduled for 24 June 1940, but was postponed on account of rain)

5 JULY 1940

This is Our Time, cantata by William SCHUMAN, is performed at the Stadium Concerts by the New York Philharmonic Orchestra and workers' chorus of the People's Philharmonic Choral Society, comprising members of many trades, iron workers, house painters, carpenters, laundrymen and furriers, Rodzinski conducting. (The performance was originally scheduled for Independence Day, 4th of July, but rain forced postponement)

8 JULY 1940

The Berkshire Music Center opens at Lenox, Massachusetts, under the general direction of Serge Koussevitzky, as the outgrowth of the annual (since 1934) Berkshire Music Festivals.

10 JULY 1940

Sir Donald TOVEY, the hyper-cultured British music essayist and analyst, writer of finely chiseled metamusical prose, and incidentally a composer of romantic pieces of all descriptions, conductor and pianist, dies in Edinburgh a week before his sixty-fifth birthday.

12 JULY 1940

Panambi, ballet on the subject of an Indian legend by the 24-year-old Argentinian composer Alberto GINASTERA, is produced at the Teatro Colón in Buenos Aires. (A suite from this ballet was performed previously, on 2 November 1937)

26 JULY 1940

Ernst TOCH becomes an American citizen.

1 AUGUST 1940

Two centuries have elapsed since ARNE's imperially proud song *Rule, Britannia* was first heard in London.

4 AUGUST 1940

Twenty days after his arrival in New York from crushed France,

Darius MILHAUD conducts the first performance, broadcast over the Columbia network, of *Le Cortège funèbre,* a dirge composed by him in his native Aix-en-Provence during the last days of the Battle of France.

4 AUGUST 1940

Charles NAGINSKI, 31-year-old Egyptian-born, American-Jewish composer of brilliant eclectic gifts, drowns in the Housatonic River by accident, or, more likely, by design.

9 AUGUST 1940

Ferial by Manuel PONCE, a "symphonic divertissement" bearing on the title page the simple dedication, "A Mexico," and depicting in bright orchestral tones the Mexican fiesta, beginning with a scene at a church, and ending with a Mexican dance, is performed for the first time in Mexico City, Chávez conducting.

16 AUGUST 1940

As a result of investigations conducted by Harold Nicolson, Parliamentary Secretary to the Ministry of Information, it is announced that the playing of music by Chopin and Rachmaninov in munitions factories produces an increase of the output from 6 to 12 per cent.

27 AUGUST 1940

Prelude to The Great Dictator, arranged by Meredith WILLSON from the music to Charlie CHAPLIN's film, whistled and hummed by Chaplin himself and set down on paper by professionals, with the hero "Hynkel" represented by a hoarse trumpet, is performed for the first time at a concert by the San Francisco Symphony Orchestra on Treasure Island, the site of the World's Fair, Meredith Willson conducting, along with Willson's own *Second Symphony,* subtitled *The Missions of California.*

15 SEPTEMBER 1940

Stabat Mater for a ten-part chorus and organ, a newly-discovered work by Domenico SCARLATTI, in which, in contrast with most of his known music, he appears a true polyphonist, is performed for the first time on the opening day of the Siena Festival in Italy.

1 OCTOBER 1940

Nadezhda PLEVITSKAYA, once celebrated Russian singer of peasant songs, who sang for the Czar as willingly as for the Soviet Commissars, and had appeared in New York with Rachmaninov at the piano, dies in a prison cell in Rennes, France, where she was jailed for complicity in the kidnapping and murder of a Russian general.

5 OCTOBER 1940

Silvestre REVUELTAS, jovial 40-year-old composer of Mexico (he was born on the last day of the 1800's, 31 December 1899), firm believer in the political potency of music (his posthumous ballet *La Coronela* depicts a girl-colonel as a symbol of revolution in the days of the struggle against the Diaz dictatorship), dies in Mexico City of pneumonia, precipitated by alcoholism, at 12:10 past midnight (and thus, technically speaking, on 6 October), on the night of the performance of his last finished ballet *El Renacuajo Paseador* (Pollywog Promenading).

10 OCTOBER 1940

Frederick STOCK opens the Jubilee season of the Chicago Symphony Orchestra, celebrating its fiftieth anniversary with his own salutatory *Festival Fanfare,* with percussion aplenty, including the Schellenbaum, a luxuriantly ornate multiple pseudo-Turkish jingle, known as a "jingling johnny."

17 OCTOBER 1940

Darius MILHAUD conducts the Chicago Symphony Orchestra in the world première of his *First Symphony,* completed in Aix-en-Provence on 19 December 1939, and conceived in a broadly rhapsodic style, in four movements of varied moods.

18 OCTOBER 1940

A "social showing" (dress rehearsal) of the first Buriat-Mongol opera, *Enkhe, the Steel Giant* by M. FROLOV, an epical legend, with Borodin-like elaborations of Buriat-Mongol folk melos, is given in Moscow at the Buriat-Mongol Festival.

24 OCTOBER 1940

Symphony in C by John Alden CARPENTER in one quadripartite movement, written in a romantic style, with imaginative excursions into tonal impressionism, is performed for the first time by the Chicago Symphony Orchestra as a commissioned work for the orchestra's Jubilee year.

31 OCTOBER 1940

American Creed by Roy HARRIS, diptych for orchestra and chorus, conceived as a musical reply to rhetorical questions, "What do we believe? What do we want? What is the American way?," composed between 1 June and 11 August 1940, in two linked sections: (1) *Free to Dream* (2) *Free to Build,* is performed for the first time by the Chicago Symphony Orchestra, for whose fiftieth anniversary it was written, Stock conducting.

6 NOVEMBER 1940

After a long journey from Switzerland through Vichy-governed France and fascist Spain, in a flight from the "unbearable moral atmosphere of the European continent," the grand old man of Poland and music, PADEREWSKI, lands in New York on the S.S. *Excambion* from Lisbon.

7 NOVEMBER 1940

Igor STRAVINSKY conducts the Chicago Symphony Orchestra in the world première of his new *Symphony in C,* completed at Beverly Hills, California, on 19 August 1940, and dedicated to the Chicago Symphony Orchestra in a wording identical with that of his dedication of the *Symphony of Psalms* to the Boston

Symphony Orchestra ten years before: "This Symphony, composed for the glory of God, is dedicated to the Chicago Symphony Orchestra on the occasion of the fiftieth anniversary of
its existence," the work comprising four movements: (1) *Moderato alla breve,* in sonata form (2) *Larghetto concertante,* "simple, clear and tranquil" (3) *Allegretto,* "white music," in Stravinsky's words, comprising a *Minuet,* a *Passepied,* and a *Fugue*
(4) *Adagio, Tempo giusto,* in widely spaced harmonies, ending
in a "medieval" cadence with long chords, finally coming to rest
on a bitonal musical pillar, a G major triad reposing on the C
major sixth-chord.

7 NOVEMBER 1940

Sixth Symphony by Frederick CONVERSE is performed posthu-
mously for the first time by the Indianapolis Symphony Orchestra, Fabien Sevitzky conducting.

12 NOVEMBER 1940

Alejandro García CATURLA, primitivistic modernist of Cuban
music, composer of powerful music of Afro-Cuban inspiration, is
assassinated by two bullets in the chest, fired by a criminal whose
case Caturla, as district judge of his native town Remedios, held
under advisement.

13 NOVEMBER 1940

Fantasia, a cosmogonic "silly symphony" by Walt Disney, with
the musical score zeugmatically put together from cavalierly
apocopated classical and modern masterworks (abstract designs
for Bach's *Toccata and Fugue;* vesuviating mushroom dance to
Tchaikovsky's *Nutcracker;* Mickey Mouse as *The Sorcerer's Apprentice* of Dukas; mesozoic monsters disporting themselves in
the primordial slime for Stravinsky's *Le Sacre du Printemps;*
flirting centaurs and centaurettes for a tabloid extract from
Beethoven's *Pastoral* Symphony; alligators and hippopotamuses
joyfully splashing in African rivers to the music of Ponchi-
elli's *Dance of the Hours;* a witches' Sabbath for Moussorgsky's
Night on Bald Mountain; and an angelic apotheosis to Schu-

bert's *Ave Maria*), conducted by Stokowski, whose coat tails are occasionally pulled by Mickey Mouse, with Deems Taylor as an urbane commentator, opens at the Broadway Theater in New York at 9:11 p.m. (instead of the scheduled hour, 8:40), with a special "fantasound" equipment creating the illusion of realistically stereophonic reception. (An error of 90,000,000 years is made in the picturization of *Le Sacre* in which a giant Tyrannosaurus Rex of the Cretaceous period fights a Stegosaurus of the Jurassic period)

16 NOVEMBER 1940

At the Moscow Festival of Soviet Music, *Twenty-First Symphony* by Nicolas MIASKOVSKY, composed between 28 May and 1 July 1940, meditative in mood, and Russian in essence, symphonically contracted into one cyclic movement, is performed (ahead of his *Twentieth Symphony*) by the Moscow State Orchestra, Golovanov conducting, on the same program with first performances of the *Violin Concerto* by Aram KHATCHATURIAN, written in a lyrical Russian manner with touches of Caucasian rhythms, and fragments from the opera *Decembrists* by SHAPORIN. (Miaskovsky's *Twenty-First Symphony* was performed as a commissioned work by the Chicago Symphony Orchestra on 26 December 1940, under the title *Symphonie-Fantaisie*)

21 NOVEMBER 1940

Die Walkuere is brilliantly staged at the Moscow Opera House, the first Wagner opera produced in Russia sⁱnce 6 December 1925.

21 NOVEMBER 1940

Daniel AYALA, Mayan composer of neo-primitivistic music of Mexican flavor, conducts the orchestra of the University of Mexico in the first performance of the symphonic suite from his ballet *El Hombre Maya*, as a tribute to the composer's ancestral race.

23 NOVEMBER 1940

At the Moscow Festival of Soviet Music, SHOSTAKOVITCH plays

the piano part in the world première of his *Quintet* for piano and strings (which was to win him a Stalin prize of 100,000 rubles), in five movements: (1) *Prelude,* with a gigue flanked by the slow introduction and finale (2) *Fugue,* stately yet dynamic (3) *Scherzo,* in a boisterously Shostakovitchian manner (4) *Intermezzo,* gaunt yet passionate (5) *Finale,* toccata-like, lithesome and trottingly whimsical.

28 NOVEMBER 1940

Twentieth Symphony by Nicolas MIASKOVSKY in three movements (composed between 17 April and 23 May 1940, and orchestrated between 3 and 20 September 1940), is performed for the first time in Moscow.

5 DECEMBER 1940

Jan KUBELIK, "hyper-romantic violin virtuoso," and raven-locked darling of the feminine audiences at the turn of the century, dies in Prague at the age of sixty years and five months.

6 DECEMBER 1940

Concerto for Violin and Orchestra by Arnold SCHOENBERG, written in the twelve-tone technique, with a thematic tone-row (capable of forty-eight transformations) A, B-flat, E-flat, B, E, F-sharp, C, D-flat, G, A-flat, D and F, is performed for the first time anywhere by Louis Krasner and the Philadelphia Orchestra, Stokowski conducting.

"The *Concerto* combines the best sound effects of a hen yard at feeding time, a brisk morning in Chinatown, and practice hour at a busy conservatory. (*Philadelphia Record,* 7 December 1940)

"The violinist slithers his bow around, apparently at random, pauses to pluck at a string here, and poke at another there. While this is going on, the orchestra is busy playing a game that sounds like every man for himself." (*Philadelphia Inquirer,* 7 December 1940)

"For thirty years, bald, parchment-faced, Austrian-born Composer Arnold Schoenberg has written music so complicated that only he and a couple other fellows understand what it is all about. This music, which sounds to the uninitiated not only queer, but accidental, has been enjoyed by very few.

But it has thrown the world of music into a Kilkenny cat fight. One cat camp maintains that Schoenberg's music, like Einstein's theory, sounds queer because it is way over the average man's head; opponents swear that Schoenberg is pulling everybody's leg, including his own, and that his miscalled music is a gibberish of wrong notes. Gibberish or no, Arnold Schoenberg's music is fearfully difficult to play. The main difficulty is to get all of Schoenberg's wrong notes in the right places." (*Time*, 16 December 1940)

Rodriguez: A virtuoso recently told me that the *Concerto* is unplayable until violinists can grow a new fourth finger especially adapted to play on the same string at the same stop as three other fingers.
Schoenberg [laughing like a pleased child]: Yes, yes, that will be fine. The *Concerto* is extremely difficult, just as much for the head as for the hands. I am delighted to add another *unplayable* work to the repertoire. I want the *Concerto* to be difficult and I want the little finger to become longer. I can wait. (From a dialogue between José Rodriguez and Schoenberg in the anthology *Arnold Schoenberg*, 1937)

15 DECEMBER 1940

Kammersymphonie by Arnold SCHOENBERG in two movements, the first of which was composed as early as 1906, and reorchestrated in 1935 (completed on 18 April 1935), while the second was composed anew in 1940, is given its first performance in New York by the New Friends of Music, Fritz Stiedry conducting.

"The difficulties that Schoenberg faced were enormous. As he had meanwhile advanced to an entirely different level, he found that his personal contact with his work had been disrupted: it was remote from him from the point of view both of time and style. He solved his task in a brilliant way—he finished the symphony in his former style, but with his new technique developed by his compositions based on the chromatic scale. He used all his knowledge of musical development and orchestration he had acquired in recent years. So the work underwent a re-formation more far-reaching than, for instance, a classical work does when it is orchestrated by a modern composer. It was *Schoenberg interpreted by Schoenberg*." (From a program note by Schoenberg's pupil, and son-in-law, Felix Greissle)

15 DECEMBER 1940

Third Symphony by the British composer Edmund RUBBRA, written in the orthodox four movements, rhapsodically treated, is given for the first time in Manchester, Malcolm Sargent con-

ducting. (The first performance of Rubbra's *Symphony* was announced for 23 September 1940 in London but was canceled on
account of air raids)

24 DECEMBER 1940

The British Broadcasting Corporation broadcasts Christmas
carols from the ruins of the Coventry Cathedral, all but destroyed by air bombardment.

1941

1 JANUARY 1941

As a result of the non-renewal of contract between ASCAP
(American Society of Composers, Authors and Publishers) and
the radio networks, Cheerio, the trained canary who could sing
only a version of *Yankee Doodle,* protected by ASCAP, and
Sharkey, the trained seal whose only tune on the harmonica is
Where the River Shannon Flows, also an ASCAP property, are
prevented from appearing as guests on a radio program.

2 JANUARY 1941

Sinfonia Biblica by Nicolas NABOKOV, Russian composer living in
the United States, in four symbolic movements: (1) *Ecclesiasti-*
cus (Wisdom) (2) *Solomon* (Love) (3) *Absalom* (Fear) (4)
Hosannah (Praise), intended as "a piece of music first of all,
the Old Testament being the stimulus," with all themes interre-
lated so that the restless theme of Absalom's flight is a rhythmically accelerated intervallic inversion of the theme of Wisdom, is
performed for the first time by the New York Philharmonic,
Mitropoulos conducting.

3 JANUARY 1941

Three Symphonic Dances, orchestral suite by RACHMANINOV (originally planned as a triptych with the three sections entitled *Midday, Twilight,* and *Midnight,* but later changed to simple tempo indications) is performed for the first time by the Philadelphia Orchestra, Ormandy conducting.

5 JANUARY 1941

No For an Answer, second opera of social significance by Marc BLITZSTEIN (Blitzstein means lightning-stone), to Blitzstein's own story of a group of unemployed Greek waiters persecuted by the police, is performed for the first time at Mecca Auditorium in New York by the composer, acting as a one-man orchestra at the piano, and a chorus and soloists on the stage.

10 JANUARY 1941

Frank BRIDGE, British composer of rhapsodic pieces in all genres, and also slightly atonal chamber music, dies at his home in Eastbourne in his sixty-second year.

10 JANUARY 1941

Concerto for two pianos and orchestra by the Cyprus-born American composer Anis FULEIHAN is performed for the first time in Hempstead, New York.

12 JANUARY 1941

The Virgin of Sparta, short opera with narration by the dean of Greek composers, Manolis KALOMIRIS, is performed for the first time in Athens.

24 JANUARY 1941

Albert EINSTEIN presents a program of violin music at the Present Day Club in Princeton, at a benefit for the American Friends Service Committee for Refugee Children in England, playing the E minor *Sonata* by Mozart, and two pieces, *Old Indian Song* and *Russian Dance,* by Frida S. Bucky of New York.

24 JANUARY 1941

Concerto for Violin and Chamber Orchestra by Conrad BECK is performed for the first time by the Basel Chamber Orchestra, Paul Sacher conducting.

25 JANUARY 1941

Iver HOLTER, the Nestor of Norwegian composers, dies in Oslo six weeks after his ninetieth birthday.

28 JANUARY 1941

Quiet City, instrumental suite by Aaron COPLAND for trumpet, English horn and string orchestra, excerpted from the stage play of the same name, is presented by the Saidenberg Little Symphony in New York.

1 FEBRUARY 1941

Western Union and Postal Telegraph are forced to discontinue the use of *Happy Birthday to You* for their "singing telegrams," which song, included in the collection *Song Stories for the Kindergarten* by Patty S. and Mildred J. HILL, unexpectedly turns out to be a copyright property of Clayton F. Summy Co. of Chicago.

6 FEBRUARY 1941

Concerto for Orchestra by Zoltán KODÁLY, commissioned by the Chicago Symphony Orchestra, written in a strongly pronounced national Hungarian style, is given its world première in Chicago, Stock conducting.

7 FEBRUARY 1941

Concerto for Violin and Orchestra by Samuel BARBER, written in a luscious neo-romantic manner, furbished with occasional bitonal harmonies, is performed for the first time by the Philadelphia Orchestra, Ormandy conducting, Albert Spalding, soloist.

7 FEBRUARY 1941

Paul HINDEMITH's first major work composed in America, *Con-*

certo for Violoncello and Orchestra in three compact movements, conceived in an emphatic tonal style, and with clear regard for the right of the solo instrument to be heard, is performed for the first time by Gregor Piatigorsky and the Boston Symphony Orchestra, Koussevitzky conducting. (Dates of composition, marked on the manuscript: First movement, 30 June 1940; Second movement, 4 July 1940; Third movement, 9 September 1940, at Tanglewood in Lenox, Massachusetts)

9 FEBRUARY 1941

Morton GOULD conducts in New York the première of his *Spirituals for String Choir and Orchestra,* subtitled respectively *Proclamation, Sermon, A Little Bit of Sin, Protest,* and *Jubilee,* and designed to develop the entire gamut of American musical emotions from traditional religious hymns to profane jazz, with the employment of sandpaper blocks, wire brushes and vibraphone in the orchestra, for purposes of vernacular onomatopoeia.

15 FEBRUARY 1941

Guido ADLER, grand old man of musical scholarship, barely allowed to draw his days to a natural close without the catalysis of a concentration camp, dies in Vienna at the age of eighty-five years and three months.

20 FEBRUARY 1941

Four days before his sixty-fourth birthday Rudolph GANZ plays with the Chicago Symphony Orchestra, Stock conducting, the piano part in the world première of his *Piano Concerto,* in four movements of competently pianistic music, in which two themes of the Scherzo are intervallically derived from the numbers of Ganz's automobile licenses of 1940 (280893, in A minor) and of 1941 (501127, in A major).

21 FEBRUARY 1941

Eugene Goossens conducts the Cincinnati Symphony Orchestra

in a world première of the *First Symphony* by the Manila-born composer of acceptably melodic music, John HAUSSERMANN, in four movements, of which the third, "slow and mournful, was inspired by the news of Ravel's death."

22 FEBRUARY 1941

First Symphony by Paul CRESTON, New York-born composer whose real name is Joseph Guttoveggio, in four descriptive movements marked (1) *With majesty* (2) *With humor* (3) *With serenity* (4) *With gaiety,* is performed for the first time at the Brooklyn Academy of Music by the NYA Symphony Orchestra conducted by Fritz Mahler, nephew of Gustav Mahler, along with the following world premières: *Ballad of a Railroad Man* by Roy HARRIS; *Violin Concerto* by Henry BRANT; *Jazz Poem* by Randall THOMPSON; and *Latin-American Symphonette* by Morton GOULD (conducted by the composer), set in four stylized dance-rhythms, *Rumba, Tango, Guaracha,* and *Conga.*

23 FEBRUARY 1941

Piano Concerto by Mischa PORTNOFF, written in a pleasantly Chopinesque manner with some Prokofievian aftereffects, is performed for the first time by the New York Philharmonic, Nadia Reisenberg, soloist, Barbirolli conducting.

23 FEBRUARY 1941

Rebus by Frank BRIDGE, a symphonic movement illustrating the spread of a rumor, in which a clearly stated theme develops into something quite different from it—a sort of variations *ad absurdum,* is given its posthumous first performance by the London Philharmonic Orchestra, Sir Henry Wood conducting.

1 MARCH 1941

Seth Flint, the bugler who sounded the last bugle call at Appomattox (9 April 1865) ending the Civil War, dies at Worcester, N. Y., at the age of ninety-three.

6 MARCH 1941

Third Symphony by Leo SOWERBY in three movements: (1) *with vigor and drive* (2) *slowly, with warmth of expression* (3) *fast and with fiery energy* (score completed on 30 July 1940), is performed for the first time by the Chicago Symphony Orchestra, Stock conducting.

7 MARCH 1941

Camargo GUARNIERI, leading composer of young Brazil, conducts in São Paulo the first performance of his incisively exotic *Dansa Brasileira,* based on the rhythms of the Brazilian samba.

9 MARCH 1941

Carlos PEDRELL, Uruguayan-born composer of expertly contrived Hispanic songs and piano pieces, and nephew of the great musical Hispanist, Felipe Pedrell, dies in Paris, his adoptive home for decades, in his sixty-third year.

11 MARCH 1941

Sir Henry Walford DAVIES, the twentieth holder of the office of Master of the King's Musick since its creation under Charles II in 1660, whose duty was to arrange music for royal weddings, funerals and coronations, composer in his own right of numerous cantatas, choruses and songs, and, in later years, broadcaster (with "a perfect radio voice") of music talks for schools, dies at his home near Bristol in his seventy-second year.

12 MARCH 1941

Charles Sanford SKILTON, American composer of ingratiatingly bland Indian operas, Indian orchestral pieces, Indian cantatas, and Indian string quartets, dies in Lawrence, Kansas, in his seventy-third year.

12 MARCH 1941

George H. MENDELSSOHN, 29-year-old great-great-grandson of Felix Mendelssohn-Bartholdy, arrives in New York from his native

Hungary, with the expressed desire to volunteer for service in the United States Army.

23 MARCH 1941

Fantaisie Portugaise for orchestra by the half-German, half-Spanish composer Ernesto HALFFTER, long resident in Portugal, is performed for the first time in Paris.

27 MARCH 1941

Third Symphony by Alfredo CASELLA (begun in Rome on 8 October 1939, and completed in Siena, 24 August 1940), in four neo-classically conceived movements, is performed in a world première by the Chicago Symphony Orchestra, Stock conducting.

29 MARCH 1941

Sinfonia da Requiem by the 27-year-old British composer Benjamin BRITTEN in three parts: (1) *Lacrymosa,* "a slow marching lament in a persistent 6/8 rhythm with a strong tonal center on D" (2) *Dies Irae,* "a form of dance of death, with occasional moments of quiet marching rhythm" (3) *Requiem Aeternam,* performed for the first time by the New York Philharmonic, Barbirolli conducting.

31 MARCH 1941

Bohuslav MARTINU, Czech composer, arrives in New York.

11 APRIL 1941

Arnold SCHOENBERG becomes an American citizen.

12 APRIL 1941

Guillermo URIBE-HOLGUIN, 61-year-old Colombian composer, conducts the Orquesta Sinfónica Nacional in his native Bogotá, in the first performance of his symphonic poem *Bochica,* op. 73, based on the legend of the redemptor of Chibchas' sins, who caused floods to be formed into the geographically celebrated cataract of Tequendama.

20 APRIL 1941

Lorenzo the Magnificent, historic oratorio for soprano and orchestra by Igor MARKEVITCH, is conducted by the composer in the world première in Rome.

10 MAY 1941

Queen's Hall of London burns down as a result of incendiaries dropped during the night by the German air raiders.

"At 10 o'clock on the morning of Sunday, May 11th, 1941, the members of the London Philharmonic Orchestra arrived for the rehearsal. They found clouds of smoke pouring from the ruined building and 'water, water everywhere.' Many of them had left their instruments there overnight. Arrangements were then made to transfer the concert to the Duke's Hall of the Royal Academy of Music, and an emergency box-office was established at a table outside the wrecked building. At 3 o'clock that afternoon the concert was given as advertised, but unrehearsed and largely with borrowed instruments. Queen's Hall was gone; music carried on." (From *Queen's Hall,* 1893-1941, by Robert Elkin, London, 1943)

10 MAY 1941

Robert WARD, 23-year-old American composer of instrumental music in closely-knit classical contrapuntal texture, conducts the Juilliard Graduate School Orchestra in New York in the first performance of his *First Symphony* in three movements.

11 MAY 1941

At the inaugural concert in Atlantic City of the All-American Youth Orchestra, organized and conducted by Leopold Stokowski, Henry COWELL plays the piano part in the world première of his *Tales of the Countryside* in four movements, each composed in a different state of the Union: *Deep Tides* (written in California); *Exultation* (in New York); *The Harp of Life* (composed in Iowa cornfields); and *Country Reel* (written on a Kansas farm), conceived as Amero-Celtic folk-song inventions, with an occasional application of tone-clusters (pandiatonic and pan-pentatonic columns of notes, played with forearms and fists).

13 MAY 1941

Tarquin, "a new opera for the modern stage" by Ernst KRENEK (completed in Hollywood on 13 September 1940), is produced by the Experimental Theater at Vassar College, with the composer, as member of the faculty, playing the piano version of the score, originally written for clarinet, trumpet, violin, percussion and two pianos.

17 MAY 1941

The eighteenth Festival of the International Society for Contemporary Music, blacked out of Europe, opens in New York with a broadcast of chamber music over the Columbia network in a program including *Three Sonnets* from Shakespeare for voice and piano by Piet KETTING of Holland, and the miniaturistically brief *Third String Quartet* by Antoni SZALOWSKI of Poland.

18 MAY 1941

Les Illuminations, nine pieces by Benjamin BRITTEN, for tenor and string orchestra, to nine poems in the original French by Rimbaud (score completed on 25 October 1939, in Amityville, N. Y., where the composer was visiting), and *Prelude to a Tragedy* by Henk BADINGS of Holland are broadcast over the CBS network, as part of the eighteenth ISCM Festival.

19 MAY 1941

A concert of chamber music is presented at Columbia University as part of the eighteenth ISCM Festival:

Second String Quartet by Paul KADOSA of Hungary; *Psalm 54* for voice and piano by Stefan WOLPE, formerly of Germany, now living in New York; *Second Piano Sonata* by René LEIBOWITZ, the leading atonalist of France; *Divertimento for solo Flute* by the British composer William ALWYN; *String Quartet No. 4* by Jerzy FITELBERG.

20 MAY 1941

Bernard WAGENAAR conducts at Columbia University a broadcast performance of his *Triple Concerto* for flute, cello, harp and orchestra, as part of the eighteenth ISCM Festival.

21 MAY 1941

A chamber music concert of the eighteenth ISCM Festival is given at the New York Public Library:

Second String Quartet by Matyas SEIBER of Hungary; *Piano Sonata* by Viktor ULLMAN, formerly of Czechoslovakia; a pointillistically atonal *String Quartet* by Anton VON WEBERN (described in the program book as "independent," but still living in Vienna despite the fact that he was officially blacklisted and included among cultural bolshevists in a Hitlerite brochure, *Entartete Musik*) ; *Les Voix de Paul Verlaine à Anatole France* for voice, two pianos and two percussion instruments, written in a pointedly atonal idiom by Paul DESSAU (formerly of Germany), now living in New York; and neo-Regerian *Piano Pieces in Seven Parts,* composed by the pianist Artur SCHNABEL.

23 MAY 1941

A concert of chamber music by American and Latin-American composers is given at the Museum of Modern Art in New York as part of the eighteenth ISCM Festival:

Theme with Variations and Finale for violin and piano by the 24-year-old North Carolinian, Edward T. CONE, written in a prematurely mature style; *Three Songs* by Russel G. HARRIS; *Piece for String Quartet* by the Mexican composer Salvador CONTRERAS; *Theme and Variations* for cello and piano by Paul NORDOFF; *String Quartet* by Emil KOEHLER; *Music for Trio* (clarinet, saxophone and trumpet) written in the twelve-tone technique by the Argentinian modernist Juan Carlos PAZ; and *Música de Feria* for string quartet by the late national composer of Mexico, Silvestre REVUELTAS.

24 MAY 1941

As part of the eighteenth ISCM Festival a chamber music concert, including the first performance of the *Concerto for String Quartet* by Edmund PARTOS of Palestine, and *Second Quartet* by Zoltán KODÁLY, is broadcast over the Columbia network.

25 MAY 1941

The Columbia Broadcasting System presents three orchestral works as part of the eighteenth ISCM Festival:

Small Overture by Roman PALESTER of Poland, written in a gay, square-rhythmed, Prokofiev-like idiom; *Obertura Concertante* by Rodolfo HALFFTER,

Spanish composer living in Mexico; and *Hymnus, Der Tag und Die Nacht* by the Swiss composer Willy BURKHARD, written in an earnest neo-Lutheran style.

27 MAY 1941

Two Preludes for orchestra by the Mexican composer Blas GA-LINDO, and *Sinfonietta* for chamber orchestra by Charles NAGINSKI (mysteriously drowned in the Housatonic River on 4 August 1940) are broadcast at the concluding concert of the eighteenth ISCM Festival.

8 JUNE 1941

Nine-minute Overture, a bustling, neo-classically tonal piece of music, impregnated with some inter-tonal matter, by the 21-year-old Harold SHAPERO, receives the Prix de Rome, a purse of $1,000 to continue his study, and is broadcast twice (second time because of the sudden enthusiasm of the conductor, and also extra time left) on the program of the Columbia Broadcasting Symphony Orchestra, Howard Barlow conducting.

10 JUNE 1941

Concerto for organ, string orchestra and kettledrums by Francis POULENC is performed for the first time in Paris.

12 JUNE 1941

On the occasion of King George VI's official birthday (his real birthday is 14 December), Myra HESS, is named Dame Commander of the British Empire for her musical services in wartime (Dame Commander corresponding in rank to the male Knight Commander, next to the top rank of Dame Grand Cross).

27 JUNE 1941

The British Broadcasting Corporation radioes to the peoples of subjected Europe an invitation to use the Morse signal for the letter V—three short taps and one long—or the four notes of the Fate motive of Beethoven's *Fifth Symphony,* also meaning V in

Morse, to demonstrate their defiance whenever the Nazis are around.

(On 8 July 1941 the British Press Service said that the radio station at Hilversum, Holland, pointedly substituted a broadcast of the recording of the *Fifth Symphony* for a canceled program. The day of 20 July 1941 was declared by Churchill to be V day throughout the Nazi-conquered continent. The Nazis decided to steal the symbol rather than fight it, advertised the V sign as the initial letter of the German nonce word *Viktoria,* and featured broadcasts of the first four notes of Beethoven's *Fifth Symphony.* The same four notes were broadcast by the Westminster chimes in London)

29 JUNE 1941

Ignace Jan PADEREWSKI, magical pianist of bygone decades, composer of famous musical perennials, Polish patriot and statesman during the brief interval between Poland's resurrection and its transformation into a Pilsudski dictatorship, dies in New York at 11:45 p.m., at the age of eighty years, seven months and eleven days. (Upon President Roosevelt's instructions, Paderewski's body was laid to rest under the mast of the battleship *Maine* in Arlington Cemetery, there to await the liberation of Poland—but it still remained there in 1948 because of the opposition of Paderewski's former intimates to the return of his body to Poland under its post-war political regime)

4 JULY 1941

Jan SIBELIUS sends an appeal to America for understanding of Finland's international difficulties:

"In 1939 my fatherland was attacked by the bolsheviks. Enlightened American people then realized we were fighting not only for our freedom but for all western civilization and they gave us valuable assistance. Now that the barbaric hordes of the East are again attacking us in their attempt to bolshevize Europe, I am convinced that freedom-loving intelligent American people will rightly understand and appreciate the present situation, realizing that the bolshevization of Europe would annihilate freedom and civilization in this continent."

5 JULY 1941

Lorin MAAZEL, 11-year-old boy wonder, "a chubby little chap with a big shock of black hair and a round, earnest face" (born of American parents at Neuilly, France, on 6 March 1930), actually conducts from memory a concert of the NBC Symphony Orchestra in a grown-up program including a complete Mendelssohn symphony, and succeeds in maintaining a steady tempo throughout the performance.

6 JULY 1941

A week after the German invasion of Russia, Reinhold GLIÈRE addresses an appeal to American musicians:

"In this portentous hour, when savage Fascist bands have attacked my native land, I should like to greet all my colleagues beyond the ocean who are supporting the Soviet people in its struggle for humanism. We, Soviet composers, together with the people, are employing the medium of our art to help the Red Army wage its struggle against the brutal enemy. Together with the entire country we have put ourselves on a war footing. I have written a marching song, *Hitler's End Will Come.*"

10 JULY 1941

Tango, orchestral version of the violin piece of the same name by Igor STRAVINSKY, is performed for the first time at the summer Dell Concerts in Philadelphia under the direction of the "King of Swing" Benny Goodman, wielding a pencil instead of a baton.

18 JULY 1941

Concierto Argentino for piano and orchestra by Alberto GINASTERA is performed for the first time in Montevideo.

27 JULY 1941

Bernard HERRMANN, composer of scholarly as well as cinematically slick music, conducts the orchestra of the Columbia Broadcasting System in the world première of his *First Symphony.*

28 JULY 1941

"Defense Swing," a new ballroom dance in which the male advances with a shooting gesture, and the female throws up her hands in an instinctively defensive movement, is adopted at the sixth Annual Convention of the Dance Educators of America.

29 JULY 1941

El Indio, orchestral suite, nominally by the untutored Peruvian, Daniel Alomia ROBLES (1871-1942), integrated and orchestrated by the hypertutored German musician naturalized in Peru, Rudolph HOLZMANN, is performed for the first time by the Orquesta Sinfónica Nacional of Lima.

10 AUGUST 1941

Dean DIXON, 26-year-old Negro musician, the first member of his race to lead a major orchestra, conducts the New York Philharmonic at a Stadium Concert in a program of Brahms, Berlioz and Liszt.

7 SEPTEMBER 1941

Eleazar DE CARVALHO, 29-year-old Brazilian composer of Dutch-Indian extraction, conducts on Brazil's Independence Day the world première of his opera *Tiradentes,* "the tooth puller," to the life story of a revolutionary dentist of Brazil's war for independence, written in the style of a national folk opera, with orchestral interludes onomatopoetically evoking the animal sounds of the jungle.

30 SEPTEMBER 1941

Oscar Lorenzo FERNANDEZ, composer of intensely national Brazilian music, conducts in Rio de Janeiro the world première of his opera *Malazarte,* to the story of a legendary figure of Colonial Brazil, the Master of Evil Arts *(Malas artes)*, with the music following a modified system of leading motives in which the principal moods, Destiny, Seduction, Love, and Death, are thematically represented in the score.

4 OCTOBER 1941

Manuel PONCE, pioneer of Mexican national music, conducts in Montevideo, Uruguay, the world première of his *Concierto del Sur* (Concerto of the South) for guitar and orchestra, with Segovia, to whom the *Concerto* is dedicated, as soloist.

11 OCTOBER 1941

Nicolai BEREZOWSKY plays the solo part in the world première, with the Columbia Broadcasting Symphony Orchestra, of his *Concerto* for viola and orchestra.

17 OCTOBER 1941

Third Symphony by William SCHUMAN (completed on 11 January 1941) in four neo-classical movements, *Passacaglia, Fugue, Chorale,* and *Toccata,* subjected to oscillatory polyharmonies in fluid bitonality, is performed for the first time by the Boston Symphony Orchestra, Koussevitzky conducting. (Schuman's *First Symphony* was performed on 21 October 1936 by the Gotham Symphony Orchestra in New York; *Second Symphony* was performed on 25 May 1938 by the Greenwich Orchestra—he later withdrew it for revisions which, however, were never carried out)

17 OCTOBER 1941

Eugene Goossens conducts the Cincinnati Symphony Orchestra in a world première of *The Lincoln Symphony* by Jaromir WEINBERGER in four movements: (1) *The Hand on the Plough* (2) *Scherzo Héroique* (3) *O Captain! My Captain!* (4) *Deep River.*

19 OCTOBER 1941

Baal Shem (so named after the Jewish-Polish founder of the religious sect of Hassids) for violin and orchestra by Ernest BLOCH is performed for the first time by Joseph Szigeti and a WPA orchestra in New York.

21 OCTOBER 1941

Aaron COPLAND plays in Buenos Aires the world première of his *Piano Sonata* in three movements, based on the principle of evolving patterns, and presenting, in uncompromisingly severe tones, a study in balanced sonority, with acoustically stringent intervals serving as intensifiers of musical matter, and widely spaced chordal verticals marking moments of tonal rarefaction.

23 OCTOBER 1941

Plain Chant for Americans by William Grant STILL is performed for the first time by the New York Philharmonic.

31 OCTOBER 1941

Nicolas SLONIMSKY conducts in Buenos Aires the world première of his *Suite* in eight movements: *Jazzelette, A Penny for Your Thoughts, The Happy Farmer, Fugato, Anatomy of Melancholy, Bitonal March, Valse très sentimentale,* and *Typographical Errors,* written in the consonant counterpoint of mutually exclusive tone groups, and scored for flute (and piccolo), oboe, clarinet, assorted drums, typewriter with bell, and cat's meow (interchangeable, if a live cat is unobtainable, with a small lion's roar).

5 NOVEMBER 1941

Czech Rhapsody by Jaromir WEINBERGER is performed for the first time by the National Symphony Orchestra in Washington, Kindler conducting.

7 NOVEMBER 1941

Kormtchaia (Russian word for steerswoman, as applied to the guiding spirit of the Virgin Mary), by Arthur LOURIÉ, Russian composer now living in the United States, a religious symphony constructed on the principle of intervallic symbolism, is performed for the first time by the Boston Symphony Orchestra, Koussevitzky conducting.

14 NOVEMBER 1941

Rapsodie Polonaise by Alexandre TANSMAN, dedicated to the defenders of Warsaw, containing thematic allusions to the Polish and English national anthems, is performed for the first time by the St. Louis Symphony, Golschmann conducting.

14 NOVEMBER 1941

Concerto Grosso by Bohuslav MARTINU, originally scheduled for performance in Vienna in 1938, but canceled after the Anschluss; later announced for a première in Prague and squashed by Hitler's rape of Czechoslovakia; and again planned for a performance in May 1940 in Paris, but called off under the pressure of tragic military events in France, is finally performed in a world première by the Boston Symphony Orchestra, Koussevitzky conducting.

17 NOVEMBER 1941

Second Symphony by Virgil THOMSON in three movements: (1) *Allegro militaire* (2) *Andante* (3) *Allegro,* definitely neo-romantic in its inspiration, with "no formal exposition and no recapitulation in any of the movements, nothing but continuous variation and transformation of the musical material with which it starts," is performed for the first time in its entirety by the Seattle Symphony Orchestra, Sir Thomas Beecham conducting.

21 NOVEMBER 1941

Symphony in E-flat by Paul HINDEMITH in four movements (completed in New Haven on 15 December 1940), evolved in an artful system of fluid tonality, is performed for the first time by the Minneapolis Symphony Orchestra, Mitropoulos conducting.

21 NOVEMBER 1941

Second Symphony by Robert CASADESUS in the classical four movements, of which the third is an *Ecossaise* replacing a Scherzo, is performed for the first time by the Cincinnati Symphony Orchestra, Goossens conducting.

28 NOVEMBER 1941

Scottish Ballad for two pianos and orchestra by Benjamin BRIT-
TEN, thematically derived from old Scottish tunes, such as *Dun-
dee, the Flowers of the Forest* (a lament for the Scottish soldiers
who fell in the Battle of Flodden), and a *Reel,* is performed for
the first time anywhere by the Cincinnati Symphony Orchestra,
Goossens conducting, with Ethel Bartlett and Rae Robertson as
soloists.

3 DECEMBER 1941

Christian SINDING, the facile romanticist of Norwegian music,
and author of a piano perennial, *Rustles of Spring,* dies in Oslo
at the age of eighty-five.

9 DECEMBER 1941

For the first time since the Revolution, Tchaikovsky's patriotic
Overture 1812, in which the triumph of Russia over the invader
is vividly illustrated in magniloquent brasses, is performed in
Soviet Russia at the concert of a specially assembled Leningrad
orchestra.

15 DECEMBER 1941

The Tchaikovsky House-Museum in Klin is recaptured by the
Red Army.

"A pack of mad swine could not dirty the house as much as the Germans did.
They tore off the wooden panels and used them for fuel, while there was
plenty of wood in the courtyard. Fortunately, all the manuscripts, personal
books, the favorite piano, the writing desk, in a word all that was most valuable, had been evacuated in time. I saw with my own eyes a picture of
Beethoven torn down from the wall and carelessly thrown on a chair. Next
to it the Germans excreted on the floor. This is absolutely a fact. The German
officers and soldiers used the floor for a privy next to an excellent large portrait of Beethoven." (Eugene Petroff in *Izvestia,* 17 December 1941)

18 DECEMBER 1941

Darius MILHAUD plays, with the Chicago Symphony Orchestra,
the piano part in the world première of his *Second Concerto* for

piano and orchestra in three contrasting movements, with the *Finale* suggesting the rhythms of a rumba.

21 DECEMBER 1941

First Symphony in three movements by David DIAMOND, 26-year-old American composer of peculiarly subjective music within the framework of classical form, based on a motto of three notes which constitute the germ of the entire work, is performed for the first time by the New York Philharmonic, Mitropoulos conducting.

1942

1 JANUARY 1942

Concerto for piano and orchestra by Carlos CHÁVEZ in three movements, written in a flintily percussive manner, with lyrical passages suggestive of monastic austerity, and with but an occasional glimpse of Mexican folkways, is performed for the first time by the New York Philharmonic, Mitropoulos conducting, Eugene List, soloist.

6 JANUARY 1942

Emma CALVÉ, the celebrated Carmen of yore, dies in obscurity in France at the age of eighty-three. (She was born on 15 August 1858, as per her birth certificate, the majority of music dictionaries to the contrary notwithstanding)

6 JANUARY 1942

A Suite of *Eight Etudes for Orchestra* by Robert Russell BEN-NETT, intended to provide the orchestra and the conductor with "specific problems to overcome, in the same way that etudes for solo instruments present technical difficulties to the performer or student," with dedications respectively to Walter Damrosch,

Aldous Huxley, Noel Coward, "King" Carl Hubbell (the base-ball pitcher), to all Dictators, to the Grand Lama, to Eugene Speicher the painter, and to the Ladies, is performed for the first time at the concert of the Philadelphia Orchestra in New York.

7 JANUARY 1942

Statements for Orchestra, a suite by Aaron COPLAND in six brief sections: I Militant, II Cryptic, III Dogmatic, IV Subjective, V Jingo, VI Prophetic, explicitly named "as a help to the public in understanding what the composer had in mind when writing these pieces," is performed for the first time in its entirety by the New York Philharmonic, Mitropoulos conducting.

12 JANUARY 1942

Symphony-Ballad, op. 54, in B minor, in three movements by Nicolas MIASKOVSKY, based on Caucasian themes, and composed in Naltchik, Caucasus, in the autumn of 1941 as the Nazis neared the Caucasian mountain range, is performed for the first time in Tbilisi, capital of Georgia.

14 JANUARY 1942

Fred FISHER, composer of *When Irish Eyes Are Smiling,* and over a thousand other song hits, lyric writer, author and publisher, commits a lonely act of suicide by hanging, in New York, in his sixty-fifth year.

16 JANUARY 1942

The one-armed pianist Paul Wittgenstein plays the solo part with the Philadelphia Orchestra, Ormandy conducting, in the world première of Benjamin BRITTEN's *Diversions on a Theme,* op. 21, for pianoforte for left hand, and orchestra, written to "exploit and emphasize the single line approach," and consisting of eleven variations on a "simple musical theme."

Ouverture pour une Fête by Jacques IBERT is performed for the first time in Paris.

Jamaican Rumba by Arthur BENJAMIN, a rollicking stylization of the infectious Caribbean dance, is performed for the first time by the WOR broadcasting orchestra with Wallenstein conducting.

The Blood of the People, opera by Ivan DZERZHINSKY portraying the struggle of the war, with the Nazis characterized by puppet-like march-tunes, and the Soviet guerrillas by lyrically tense passages, with the concluding chorus chanting: "Rise, Soviet people, defend your native land; never will our people be in Fascist captivity," is produced in the town of Tchkalov by the company of the evacuated Leningrad Opera.

Fourth Symphony by William SCHUMAN in three movements (completed on 17 August 1941), conceived on a plan of enhanced tonality of pandiatonic and bitonal facture, with occasional explorations of chromatic potentialities in divergent motion, and with sprinklings of jazz-like showerlets vivifying the rhythmic pulse, is performed for the first time by the Cleveland Orchestra, Rodzinski conducting.

Concerto for violin with string orchestra, piano, and assorted percussion by Bohuslav MARTINU is performed for the first time by the Basel Chamber Orchestra under the direction of its founder, Paul Sacher.

STRAVINSKY conducts the Janssen Symphony Orchestra in Los Angeles in a world première of his *Danses Concertantes* in five movements, completed on 13 January 1942, and couched in a stylized *ottocento* manner, with the introductory march identically repeated in the fifth movement, the second movement being a *Pas d'Action,* the third, a theme with variations, and the fourth, a *Pas de Deux.*

10 FEBRUARY 1942

Felix POWELL, the composer of the hedonistic war song *Pack Up Your Troubles in Your Old Kit Bag and Smile, Smile, Smile,* unsmilingly shoots himself dead in Brighton, England.

10 FEBRUARY 1942

Ramuntcho, fourth opera by Deems TAYLOR, written in a broadly melodious, almost operettish manner, to the ultra-romantic story of Pierre Loti from the life of Basque smugglers (two Basque songs, sung in Basque, are included as well as a Basque game of *pelota*) wherein Ramuntcho, the contrabandist of illegitimate birth, falls in love with a girl from a non-smuggling family, with an unhappy ending ensuing when he goes into the army and she into a convent, is produced by the Philadelphia Opera Company. (A public dress rehearsal of *Ramuntcho* was given on 7 February 1942, which date might be technically regarded as first performance, except that the invited audience did not pay admission)

16 FEBRUARY 1942

Concerto for Violin and Orchestra by George DYSON, the well-grounded British traditionalist of the post-Elgarian school, is performed by the BBC, Sir Adrian Boult conducting.

17 FEBRUARY 1942

Oscar LEVANT, the ubiquitous musical wit of the radio and author of a self-accusingly titled book, *A Smattering of Ignorance,* plays the piano part in the world première of his surprisingly competent *Concerto in One Movement,* with the NBC Symphony Orchestra, Wallenstein conducting.

20 FEBRUARY 1942

The Metropolitan Opera Company stages in New York the world première of a one-act opera, *The Island God,* by the operatically deft Italian-American composer Gian-Carlo MENOTTI, to his own libretto dealing with a married couple cast off on an uninhabited island in the Mediterranean during World War II, and a Greek God roused from musty obsolescence in the ruins of a temple, with a total disaster overtaking everyone when a young fisherman, landing on the island, seduces the wife, the husband thereupon attacking the God, who strikes him down with an Olympian thunderbolt, and is thereby so weakened in his own low potential that he disintegrates back into his ontologically primordial nihility.

26 FEBRUARY 1942

David VAN VACTOR conducts the Chicago Symphony in a première of his *Gothic Impressions,* a set of twelve variations on an "aggressive" theme.

1 MARCH 1942

John CAGE, American experimenter in rhythmed sounds, conducts at the Chicago Arts Club the first performance of his meta-musical *Imaginary Landscape,* scored for an electrical oscillator, tin cans, buzzers of variable frequency, Balinese gongs, generator whine, plucked coil and marimbula.

1 MARCH 1942

Seventh Symphony by Dmitri SHOSTAKOVITCH, glorifying, in its four movements, the heroic city of Leningrad, and composed partly in Leningrad under siege (first movement was completed in Leningrad on 3 September 1941; second on 17 September; third on 29 September; and the last movement on 27 December 1941, in Kuibishev), is performed for the first time in Kuibishev (Samara) on the Volga, by the Bolshoi Theater orchestra, evacuated from Moscow, Samosud conducting.

"My *Seventh Symphony* is inspired by the great events of our patriotic war, but it is not battle music. The first movement is dedicated to the struggle, and the fourth to victory. . . . No more noble mission can be conceived than that which spurs us on to fight against the dark forces of Hitlerism. That is why the roar of the cannon does not keep the muses of our people from lifting their strong voices." (From Shostakovitch's statement)

5 MARCH 1942

First Symphony by Richard MOHAUPT in four movements interlinked by a common motto, is performed for the first time by the New York Philharmonic, Goossens conducting.

5 MARCH 1942

Suvorov, patriotic opera by Sergei VASSILENKO glorifying the deeds of the great Russian general of the Napoleonic era, and composed in the grandiloquent manner of the National School, is produced in Moscow.

15 MARCH 1942

King John, Shakespearian overture by Mario CASTELNUOVO-TEDESCO, is performed for the first time anywhere by the New York Philharmonic, Barbirolli conducting.

16 MARCH 1942

Strawberry Jam (Home Made), a modernistic caricature of a jam-session of a jazz band by Robert McBRIDE, is performed for the first time by the National Orchestral Association in New York.

16 MARCH 1942

Alexander VON ZEMLINSKY, Austrian composer of knowledgeably neo-romantic music, Schoenberg's first teacher, a resident in the United States since December 1938, dies at Larchmont, New York, at the age of sixty-nine.

20 MARCH 1942

Teodoro VALCÁRCEL, Titicaca-born Peruvian Indian composer of neo-Incan music, dies in Lima in his forty-second year.

28 MARCH 1942

During a night bombing attack, the Great Organ of the Marien-
kirche in Lübeck, at which Buxtehude presided from 1668 to his
death, and Bach played in 1705, is destroyed in the ruins of the
church itself.

29 MARCH 1942

Solomon and Balkis, one-act opera by Randall THOMPSON,
adapted from Kipling's story, *The Butterfly That Stamped,* and
dealing with Solomon's difficulties with his 999 wives constantly
quarreling among themselves, and a magical butterfly that by
stamping its feet can cause Solomon's palace to crumble, scored
for an utilitarianly small orchestra, and couched in mock-Han-
delian harmonies with quasi-oriental chromaticism for the characterization of Balkis, the Queen of Sheba, is performed for the
first time over the Columbia network, Howard Barlow conducting. (The first stage performance was given at Harvard University, 14 April 1942)

9 APRIL 1942

Fourth Symphony by Alexander GRETCHANINOV, 77-year-old
composer of symphonies and operas in a grand Russian style, is
performed for the first time by the New York Philharmonic,
Barbirolli conducting.

11 APRIL 1942

Henry PRUNIÈRES, urbane and scholarly historian of French music, dies at Nanterre, near Paris, at the age of fifty-five.

16 APRIL 1942

Second Essay for orchestra by Samuel BARBER, intended to parallel in music the literary form of an essay, is performed for the
first time by the New York Philharmonic, Bruno Walter conducting.

17 APRIL 1942

Concerto for violin and orchestra, by Nicolas LOPATNIKOV, Russian-born, German-bred, Americanized composer of strongly-knit

contrapuntal music in a modernistic manner, in three movements, of which the second is Russian in spirit and lyrical in mood, is performed for the first time by the Boston Symphony Orchestra, Koussevitzky conducting, Richard Burgin, soloist.

22 APRIL 1942

On his tour of the United States, Francisco MIGNONE, the neoromantic Brazilian, conducts the NBC Symphony Orchestra in New York in the first performance of his *Festival of Churches,* depicting, in its four movements, four cathedrals of Brazil.

24 APRIL 1942

Concerto for Voice and Orchestra in four movements by the Manila-born composer John HAUSSERMANN, in which the voice is treated as a wordless instrument, is performed for the first time anywhere by the Cincinnati Symphony Orchestra, Goossens conducting.

30 APRIL 1942

Concerto for violoncello and orchestra by 27-year-old David DIAMOND, written in a tensely rhapsodic manner with uncompromising dissonances stridently striding across the score, is performed in Rochester, Hanson conducting, Luigi Silva, soloist.

2 MAY 1942

Ernst BACON conducts at the Spartanburg, South Carolina, Music Festival the first performance of his opera *A Tree on the Plains,* abounding in genuine Americanisms and homespun songs, such as a hitch-hiking ditty or a chewing gum ballad.

7 MAY 1942

Felix WEINGARTNER, Austrian conductor, impassioned interpreter of classical masterpieces, dies at Winterthur, Switzerland, in his seventy-ninth year.

14 MAY 1942

A Lincoln Portrait by Aaron COPLAND, completed on 16 April 1942, a symphonic poem with narration, from Lincoln's sayings— "This is what Abe Lincoln said,"—and musical quotations from two songs of Lincoln's time, *Camptown Races* and *The Pesky Sarpent,* is performed for the first time by the Cincinnati Symphony Orchestra, Kostelanetz conducting.

"The composition is roughly divided into three sections. In the opening section I wanted to suggest something of the mysterious sense of fatality that surrounds Lincoln's personality. Also, near the end of that section, something of his gentleness and simplicity of spirit. The quick middle section briefly sketches in the background of the times he lived in. This merges into the concluding section where my sole purpose was to draw a simple but impressive frame about the words of Lincoln himself." (From Copland's statement)

23 MAY 1942

Paul Sacher conducts the Basel Chamber Orchestra in a world première of HONEGGER's *Symphony* for string orchestra, his Second, completed in October 1941 in Nazi-darkened Paris, and set in three movements: (1) *Molto moderato,* with a drone of three diresomely somber notes in the violas and a kinetically charged atonal fugato as an alternating motive (2) *Adagio mesto,* a chromatic lament in the ever-mournful violas, relieved by a diatonic chant in the violins (3) *Vivace non troppo* (with the first violins in six sharps for the initial twenty-two measures, but none in the other string parts), a rendingly discordant gigue, concluding with a neo-Lutheran chorale in the high strings optionally reinforced by a trumpet, and finally coming to rest on a pandiatonically enriched (+ B + E) D major chord.

12 JUNE 1942

Walter LEIGH, English composer of tasteful neo-Brittanic music in a cheerfully diatonic manner, is killed in Libya in a tank battle with the German forces.

26 JUNE 1942

Concerto for violin and orchestra in four movements by the anti-

Fascist composer Rodolfo HALFFTER, since 1939 resident in Mexico, is performed for the first time by Samuel Dushkin with the Orquesta Sinfónica de Mexico, Chávez conducting.

27 JUNE 1942

Epic March, a war piece for orchestra by John IRELAND, is performed in London by the BBC orchestra, Sir Henry Wood conducting.

3 JULY 1942

Harl McDONALD, manager of the Philadelphia Orchestra and symphonic composer in his own right, conducts the National Symphony Orchestra in Washington, D. C., in a première of his symphonic poem *Bataan,* descriptive, in a cinematically illustrative manner, of the dramatic ordeal of American men on Bataan Peninsula in the Philippines.

14 JULY 1942

My Toy Balloon, variations on a Brazilian folk tune by Nicolas SLONIMSKY, is performed at the Boston Pops, Arthur Fiedler conducting, with some unusual and perhaps undignified sound effects, such as the popping with hatpins of toy balloons attached to the musicians' stands.

14 JULY 1942

Newsreel "in five shots" by William SCHUMAN, originally written as a high-school piece for band of class A difficulty, and featuring in cinematically changing sequence a quadrupedally galloping *Horse-Race,* a mock-sentimentally waltzing *Fashion Show,* a primitivistically ferocious *Tribal Dance,* syncopatingly grimacing *Monkeys at the Zoo,* and a circensianly blatant *Parade,* is performed for the first time in a version for large orchestra at the Stadium Concerts in New York, Smallens conducting.

18 JULY 1942

VILLA-LOBOS conducts in Rio de Janeiro his formidable *Chôros*

No. 11, scored for piano and large orchestra, and picturing, in its pandemoniac turmoil, the unity in diversity of the Brazilian landscape.

19 JULY 1942

Hawaiian Festival Overture by the Hawaiian composer Dai-keong LEE, with thematic material based on tetratonic melos of native hues, is performed for the first time by the New York Philharmonic at the Stadium Concerts, Efrem Kurtz conducting.

20 JULY 1942

Symphony-Suite No. 23, op. 56, in three movements by Nicolas MIASKOVSKY, based on Caucasian themes, and composed in Tbilisi in December 1941, is performed for the first time by the Moscow Radio Orchestra.

1 AUGUST 1942

The nineteenth Festival of the International Society for Contemporary Music opens at the Greek Theater, San Francisco, with the following program of music played by the Northern California WPA Symphony Orchestra:

Divertimento for String Orchestra by Béla BARTÓK; *Concerto for Viola and Orchestra* by Nicolai BEREZOWSKY; *Canon and Fugue* for string orchestra by Wallingford RIEGGER; *Concerto for Piano and Orchestra* by Karol RATHAUS, with E. Robert Schmitz as soloist; *Symphonic Sketch on Three American Folk Tunes (Kentucky Moonshine, Little Brown Jug and Sucking Cider Through a Straw)* by Arthur KREUTZ.

2 AUGUST 1942

At the second concert of the San Francisco ISCM Festival the following program of music is presented by the California Youth Orchestra of Mills College students:

Concerto for Small Orchestra by Robert PALMER; *Sinfonietta* by Stanley BATE, English composer living in the United States; *Suite for String Orchestra* by Felix LABUNSKI; *Sinfonietta,* op. 27, by Nicolas LOPATNIKOV.

3 AUGUST 1942

At the third concert of the San Francisco ISCM Festival the

Budapest String Quartet plays the following program: *Introduction and Scherzo* by Norman SUCKLING; *Informal Music* No. 2 by Normand LOCKWOOD; *Divertimento* by Frederic BALAZS; and *Fifth Quartet* by Alexandre TANSMAN.

5 AUGUST 1942

At the fourth program of the San Francisco ISCM Festival at the Hall for Chamber Music, Mills College, Darius Milhaud gives a talk on the French Six, with the *Concerto for Two Pianos* by Francis POULENC, and *Le Boeuf sur le toit,* a bitonal palimpsest depicting a Paris night club, by MILHAUD, as musical illustrations.

6 AUGUST 1942

At the fifth concert of the San Francisco ISCM Festival the following program of chamber music is presented:

Sonata for Oboe and Piano by the Russian-Argentine composer Jacobo FICHER; *Sonata de Primavera* by the Argentine composer of neo-romantic music; José María CASTRO; *Prelude, Allegro,* and *Pastorale* for clarinet and viola by the English violist Rebecca CLARKE; *Three Songs,* to religious texts, by the Yugoslav-born André SINGER; and *Sonatina for Oboe, Clarinet and Piano* by the 23-year-old pupil of Milhaud, Donald FULLER.

7 AUGUST 1942

At the sixth concert of the San Francisco ISCM Festival the following program of chamber music is presented:

Sonatina for violin and piano by the 30-year-old Milhaud-trained composer, Charles JONES; the atonal *Six Little Piano Pieces,* op. 19, by SCHOENBERG; Ernest BLOCH's *Poems of the Sea* for piano; *Three Songs* by Carlos CHÁVEZ; Ernest BLOCH's *Piano Sonata; Music for Children* by the Argentine neo-romanticist Luis GIANNEO; *Seven Miniatures on Brazilian Folk Themes* by the Ravelesque Brazilian composer Fructuoso VIANNA; and *Toccata* for piano by a 37-year-old Austrian disciple of Alban Berg, Jacques DE MENASCE, living in New York since 1941.

7 AUGUST 1942

As a guest conductor of the Orquesta Sinfónica de Mexico, Dimitri Mitropoulos conducts the first performance of the *Fourth Symphony* by the 54-year-old Mexican composer Candelario

Huízar, cast in the traditional four movements, with thematic material inspired by folksongs of the Mexican countryside.

8 AUGUST 1942

Les Animaux Modèles, ballet by Francis Poulenc, is produced at the Paris Opéra.

8 AUGUST 1942

In the seventh program of the San Francisco ISCM Festival the following concert of orchestral music is performed by the Janssen Symphony Orchestra of Los Angeles, Werner Janssen conductor:

Fanfare, Chorale and Finale for brass instruments by Godfrey Turner; *Sinfonia da Requiem,* op. 20, by Benjamin Britten, commissioned by the Japanese Government through the British Council for Cultural Relations with Other Countries, and originally intended as a jubilee piece to celebrate the 2600th anniversary of the Japanese dynasty, but rejected by Japan as over-Christian in nature; *Concerto du Loup* by Vittorio Rieti (the *Loup* in the title being not a wolf, but a French river); *Folk Tunes of Castile* by Pedro Sanjuán; and a one-movement *Concerto for Orchestra* by the 26-year-old Chicagoan, Ellis Kohs.

9 AUGUST 1942

In the eighth program of the San Francisco ISCM Festival the following concert of orchestral music is performed by the Janssen Symphony Orchestra of Los Angeles, Werner Janssen conducting:

Prelude to a Holiday by the Australian-born Arthur Benjamin, conductor of the Vancouver Symphony Orchestra in Canada since 1940; *Symphony in E-flat* by Paul Hindemith, now professor of music at Yale University; *Concerto for Chamber Orchestra* by the neo-classical modernist David Diamond; and *Allegro Symphonique* by the Belgian, Marcel Poot, founder of a modernistic group known as Synthesists.

14 AUGUST 1942

Fourth Symphony by the British composer Edmund Rubbra is performed for the first time at the London Promenade concerts.

22 AUGUST 1942

Henry Eichheim, American composer of orientalistic music clothed in Scriabinesque harmonies, with pentatonic tintinnabulations effected by authentic Chinese, Burmese, Siamese, and Balinese drumlets, dies in Santa Barbara, California, in his seventy-third year.

8 SEPTEMBER 1942

João Gomes DE ARAUJO, the Nestor of Brazilian composers, author of sundry Italianate operas in an earnest quasi-Verdian manner, dies in São Paulo a month and three days after his ninety-sixth birthday.

23 SEPTEMBER 1942

Benjamin BRITTEN's setting of *Seven Sonnets by Michelangelo* for voice and piano is performed for the first time at one of the Boosey & Hawkes concerts in London.

27 SEPTEMBER 1942

Alec TEMPLETON, Welsh-born blind pianist, plays the first performance of his *Concertino Lirico* with the CBS Symphony Orchestra, Bernard Herrmann conducting.

9 OCTOBER 1942

A Fanfare for Airmen by Bernard WAGENAAR is trumpeted as a musical salute to the Air Corps by the Cincinnati Symphony Orchestra, Goossens conducting.

15 OCTOBER 1942

Leningrad, suite for chorus and orchestra by Dmitri SHOSTAKO-VITCH, written as a tribute to the courage of Leningrad citizens during the siege, is performed for the first time in Moscow.

16 OCTOBER 1942

Rodeo, one-act ballet by Aaron COPLAND, a pleasantly new-fashioned musical stereopticon of the Wild West, to the story of a cowbelle who outdid the cowboys in bronco busting, and so was shunned at dance parties until she found her masculine match, is produced by the Ballet Russe de Monte Carlo in New York. (An orchestral suite from this ballet was performed for the first time by the New York Philharmonic on 22 June 1943, at the Stadium Concerts, Alexander Smallens conducting)

16 OCTOBER 1942

Fanfare for Russia by Deems TAYLOR, based upon the Russian folk song *Dubinushka* ("The Little Cudgel"), is proffered by the Cincinnati Symphony Orchestra, Goossens conducting, as a token of admiration for Russian tenacity in the face of the Nazi march to the Volga.

20 OCTOBER 1942

Frederick STOCK, German-American conductor excelling in clearly delineated renditions of symphonic masterpieces, dies three weeks before his seventieth birthday, in Chicago, where he conducted the Chicago Symphony Orchestra since 1910.

22 OCTOBER 1942

Second Symphony by John Alden CARPENTER in three movements, with some authentic Algerian tunes in its thematic material (Carpenter had visited Algiers upon his retirement as vice-president of the Carpenter Railway and Ship Supplies Co.), is performed for the first time by the New York Philharmonic, Bruno Walter conducting.

23 OCTOBER 1942

A Fanfare for the Fighting French by Walter PISTON is played by the Cincinnati Symphony, Goossens conducting, as a gesture of admiration for the unconquerable French nation.

30 OCTOBER 1942

A Fanfare to the Forces of Our Latin American Allies by Henry COWELL, written as a hemispheric good-neighbor salutation, is radioed by the Cincinnati Symphony Orchestra, Goossens conducting.

1 NOVEMBER 1942

A Lincoln Legend, a symphonic paragraph by Morton GOULD,

ambidextrously gifted composer of serious and popular music, is performed for the first time by the NBC Symphony Orchestra.

3 NOVEMBER 1942

The Opera Cloak, melodiously old-fashioned opera by Walter DAMROSCH, to the story of a lonesome seamstress slaving away in New York, who finds a passionate love letter in the pocket of an opera cloak left for repairs, and in her vicarious excitement rings a fire alarm, with a happy denouement vouchsafed when a handsome fireman climbs a ladder into the window of her room, takes her out to a dance, and she dons the mended opera cloak, is performed for the first time by the New York Opera Company.

5 NOVEMBER 1942

George M. COHAN, song and dance man, the "Yankee Doodle Dandy" of the vaudeville stage, and author of the patriotic song of the First World War, *Over There,* dies of cancer in New York, in the sixty-fifth year of his life, and fifty-fourth of his stage career. (A motion picture portraying his life, with James Cagney as Cohan, was shown to him in New York five months before his death)

13 NOVEMBER 1942

The *First Symphony* by Bohuslav MARTINU, in the classical four movements, treated as an expansion of a string quintet, and shunning all purely coloristic schemes, with the harmonic texture employing parallel fourths and seconds in chromatic runs and canonic imitation, and sonorous pedal points serving as a basis for euphonious bitonality, is performed for the first time by the Boston Symphony Orchestra, Koussevitzky conducting.

18 NOVEMBER 1942

A millennium has elapsed since the death of ODO DE CLUGNY, the Benedictine monk who first expanded the hexachordal system of the ancients into a continuous scale of notes from A to G, and who made a definite distinction between B flat (*b rotundum* from its shape later developed into the modern flat sign) and b natural (*b quadratum* which evolved into the modern natural sign) .

27 NOVEMBER 1942

A Fanfare for Paratroopers by Paul CRESTON is sounded by the Cincinnati Symphony Orchestra, Goossens conducting, as one of the several salutatory flourishes to members of the armed forces on the ground, on the seven seas, in the air, and, as in this case, in mid-air.

27 NOVEMBER 1942

Two of the three movements of the *Cantata de los Rios de Chile* for chorus and orchestra by the "Chilean Hindemith," Domingo SANTA CRUZ, descriptive of the great mountain stream Maipo and the mighty mount Aconcagua, couched in an austerely contrapuntal idiom, with half-hidden references to local background (an imitation of a Chilean policeman's whistle is cited in the oboe part) , are performed in Santiago.

28 NOVEMBER 1942

Hymn to St. Cecilia for chorus by Benjamin BRITTEN is broadcast in a first performance by the BBC singers in London.

9 DECEMBER 1942

Gayane ballet by Aram KHATCHATURIAN, descriptive of the life on a Soviet collective farm in the Caucasus, so named after the heroine of the story who foils the villainies of her anti-Soviet husband, and after the latter is liquidated, marries the liquidator, featuring a series of quasi-oriental dances (*Saber Dance*, with its chromatically repetitive rhythmic drive, has become particularly popular) , is produced in the town of Molotov, renamed in honor of the Soviet Minister of Foreign Affairs from its ancient name Perm, in the northeast of European Russia.

9 DECEMBER 1942

Festival Overture by Alexandre GRETCHANINOV, couched in proclamatory sonorities of the grand old school of Russian music, is performed for the first time by the Indianapolis Symphony Orchestra, Sevitzky conducting.

11 DECEMBER 1942

Fanfare de la Liberté, a musical tribute by Darius MILHAUD to the ever-living spirit of France, is given for the first time by the Cincinnati Symphony Orchestra, Goossens conducting.

18 DECEMBER 1942

Fanfare for American Heroes, a musical proclamation for Americans of all races and creeds by William Grant STILL, is intoned by the Cincinnati Symphony Orchestra, Goossens conducting.

31 DECEMBER 1942

Fourth Symphony in B minor by Arne OLDBERG, in the orthodox four movements, written in a pleasing neo-Schumannesque manner, is performed for the first time by the Chicago Symphony Orchestra, Hans Lange conducting.

1943

10 JANUARY 1943

Second Symphony in C minor by Tikhon KHRENNIKOV, expressing "the irresistible will to defeat the fascist foe," and depicting in its four movements the maturing of the Soviet man, lament for the innocent war victims, energetic spirit of the young Soviet fighters, and the conquering military impulse, is performed for the first time in Moscow (the Finale was later revised, and the new version performed in Moscow on 9 June 1944).

13 JANUARY 1943

Concerto for piano and small orchestra by William SCHUMAN (completed by him on 18 July 1942) is performed for the first time by the Saidenberg Little Symphony in New York.

15 JANUARY 1943

Fanfare for France by Virgil THOMSON is offered by the Cincinnati Symphony, Goossens conducting.

19 JANUARY 1943

The Shoestring Opera Company, a non-profit membership corporation formed "to demonstrate that artistic, dramatic music can be presented without the prohibitive cost of present-day grand opera," opens its first season with a performance of *Tales of Hoffmann* at Hunter College in New York.

"Shoestring. Colloq. a very small amount of money or capital used to start or carry on an enterprise or business." (The American College Dictionary)

21 JANUARY 1943

1941, symphonic suite by PROKOFIEV in three movements: *Battle, At Night,* and *For the Brotherhood of Nations,* is performed for the first time at Sverdlovsk.

22 JANUARY 1943

Fanfare for Freedom by Morton GOULD is proclaimed by the Cincinnati Symphony Orchestra, Goossens conducting.

29 JANUARY 1943

Fanfare for Airmen by Leo SOWERBY is trumpeted by the Cincinnati Symphony Orchestra, Goossens conducting.

1 FEBRUARY 1943

RACHMANINOV becomes an American citizen.

2 FEBRUARY 1943

Alexandre TANSMAN conducts the National Symphony Orchestra of Washington, D. C., in the first performance of his *Fifth Symphony.*

5 FEBRUARY 1943

Fanfare for Poland by Harl McDONALD is sounded for the first time by the Cincinnati Symphony, Goossens conducting.

13 FEBRUARY 1943

Prayer in Time of War by William SCHUMAN is proffered by the Pittsburgh Symphony, Reiner conducting.

17 FEBRUARY 1943

Music for Movies, instrumental suite by Aaron COPLAND, is performed for the first time by the Saidenberg Little Symphony in New York.

26 FEBRUARY 1943

Fanfare for the Medical Corps by Anis FULEIHAN is administered by the Cincinnati Symphony, Goossens conducting.

26 FEBRUARY 1943

On the twenty-fifth anniversary of the founding of the Red Army, Koussevitzky conducts the Boston Symphony in the world première of the *Fifth Symphony* by Roy HARRIS in three movements: *Prelude, Chorale,* and *Fugue,* dedicated to Russia in the following inscription in the score: "As an American citizen I am proud to dedicate my *Fifth Symphony* to the heroic and freedom-loving people of our great ally, the Union of Soviet Socialist Republics, as a tribute to their strength in war, their stanch idealism for world peace, their ability to cope with stark materialistic problems of world order without losing a passionate belief in the fundamental importance of the arts."

28 FEBRUARY 1943

American Epic: 1620, a tone poem for orchestra by Bainbridge CRIST, is performed for the first time by the National Symphony Orchestra, Kindler conducting.

5 MARCH 1943

First Symphony by Morton GOULD is performed for the first time by the Pittsburgh Symphony Orchestra.

5 MARCH 1943

Fanfare for the American Soldier by Felix BOROWSKI is presented by the Cincinnati Symphony Orchestra, Goossens conducting.

12 MARCH 1943

Fanfare for the Common Man by Aaron COPLAND is blown by the Cincinnati Symphony Orchestra, Goossens conducting.

19 MARCH 1943

Violin Concerto in G minor by the musical Janus, Vladimir DUKELSKY (on Broadway, Vernon Duke), in three movements, the first having "certain earmarks of the sonata form without being written in that form at all," the second, "a melancholy waltz," and the third, a theme with variations, is performed for the first time by the Boston Symphony Orchestra, Richard Burgin conducting, Ruth Posselt, soloist.

23 MARCH 1943

Joseph SCHILLINGER, Russian musical scientist who, in his theomachian ardor, devised a leviathanically panmusical Schillinger System which treats music as a technology of sound, and proposed to train composers as mechanical engineers, dies in New York in his forty-eighth year, at the culmination of an astonishingly successful teaching career during which a whole pleiad of Broadway celebrities, from Gershwin down, flocked to his gadget-filled Park Avenue suite in quest of superior musical knowledge.

26 MARCH 1943

A Free Song, Secular Cantata No. 2 for chorus and orchestra by
William SCHUMAN (completed on 16 October 1942), to the text
taken from three poems by Walt Whitman, commencing with
the words: "Too Long, America," and concluding with the "Song
of the Banner," couched in a propulsive rhythmic style as a twentieth-century counterpart of old Handelian forms, is performed
for the first time anywhere by the Boston Symphony Orchestra,
Koussevitzky conducting.

27 MARCH 1943

Music for the Marines by David VAN VACTOR is played by the
Indianapolis Symphony Orchestra.

28 MARCH 1943

Serge RACHMANINOV, the towering giant of the golden age of
Russian music, whose emotional Concertos and Preludes are the
perennials of pianism around the globe, dies of cancer and pneumonia, at Beverly Hills, California, at 1:30 a.m., four days before
his seventieth birthday.

2 APRIL 1943

Fanfare for the Signal Corps by Howard HANSON, one of the
many tributes to the armed forces by American composers, is
presented by the Cincinnati Symphony Orchestra, Goossens conducting.

4 APRIL 1943

Raoul LAPARRA, French composer of hispanistic operas, is killed
in an American air raid upon the Renault works near Paris, in
his sixty-seventh year.

12 APRIL 1943

Prelude and Fugue for orchestra by Arcady DUBENSKY, written
in effective Russian counterpoint, is performed for the first time
by the Boston Symphony Orchestra, Koussevitzky conducting.

The Testament of Freedom by Randall THOMPSON for men's voices, piano and orchestra, written for the 200th anniversary of the University of Virginia at Charlottesville, to a text from the writings of Thomas Jefferson, the University's founder, with a musical score conceived in the spirit of new simplicity, leaving not a discord untamed in its triumphantly diatonic C major harmony, is presented for the first time by the Virginia Glee Club, Stephen Tuttle conducting, the composer at the piano.

16 APRIL 1943

Eugene GOOSSENS concludes a season's series of fanfares for the armed forces, conducting the Cincinnati Symphony Orchestra in the first performance of his own *Fanfare for the Merchant Marine,* based on two eighteenth-century tunes associated with sailors and ships, "The Roast Beef of Old England," and "Heart of Oak."

29 APRIL 1943

Joseph ACHRON, Russian-born composer of Hebraic violin pieces and, more important, of numerous works in an individually modernistic idiom, dies in Hollywood two weeks before his fifty-seventh birthday.

12 MAY 1943

Albert STOESSEL, 48-year-old conductor and composer, drops dead of heart failure, while conducting a performance of *Dunkirk,* ballad-poem by Walter DAMROSCH, at the National Institute of Arts and Letters in New York.

14 MAY 1943

Kurt HUBER, German musicologist, specialist in folk music, is beheaded in Munich by the Nazis on a charge of participation in student demonstrations.

1 JUNE 1943

In defiance of the Nazi ban on Milhaud as a non-Aryan émigré,

MILHAUD's *Scaramouche* is performed on the sly, at the École Normale de Musique in Paris, disguised in the program as Mous-Arechac (anagram of Scaramouche) by Hamid-al-Usurid (anagram of Darius Milhaud).

24 JUNE 1943

VAUGHAN WILLIAMS conducts at the London Promenade Concerts the world première of his *Fifth Symphony* in D major, in four movements: *Allegro, Scherzo, Romanza,* and *Passacaglia,* dedicated "in sincere flattery" to Sibelius, with some material taken from an unfinished opera *Pilgrim's Progress,* and with the slow movement bearing an epigraph from Bunyan (about Christian's seeing the Cross at the Sepulchre).

30 JUNE 1943

The first band concert ever to be given on Kiriwina Island in the South Pacific arouses the natives to frenzied delight.

8 JULY 1943

Lennox BERKELEY conducts at the Promenade Concerts in London the world première of his *Symphony* in four movements.

19 AUGUST 1943

Ernest MOERAN plays the solo part in the first performance of his *Rhapsody* for piano and orchestra at the London Promenade Concerts.

20 AUGUST 1943

Violin Concerto by the Mexican national composer Manuel PONCE in three movements, of which the second is derived from Ponce's celebrated song *Estrellita,* is performed for the first time by the Orquesta Sinfónica de Mexico, Chávez conducting.

25 SEPTEMBER 1943

A Hugo Wolf House Museum is opened (not without Nazi-foisted pomp) at Windischgräz (Slovenjgradec), in the house where Hugo WOLF was born. (It was dispersed after the war and a doctor's office was established there in 1946)

26 SEPTEMBER 1943

The Four Freedoms, symphonic suite by Robert Russell BEN-NETT, wherein Freedom of Speech is exemplified by the musical portrait of a street orator; Freedom of Worship by a religiously hymnal chorale; Freedom from Want by a merry dance tune, and Freedom from Fear by a lullaby, developing into a march, is performed for the first time by the NBC Symphony Orchestra, Frank Black conducting.

8 OCTOBER 1943

Ode in Three Parts by STRAVINSKY, *Eulogy, Eclogue, Epitaph,* "a chant," dedicated to the memory of Mme. Koussevitzky as "an appreciation of her spiritual contribution to the art of the eminent conductor, in which the second part is a kind of *concert champêtre,* suggesting out-of-door music, an idea cherished by Natalie Koussevitzky," is performed for the first time by the Boston Symphony Orchestra, Koussevitzky conducting.

9 OCTOBER 1943

Italo MONTEMEZZI conducts in New York the first performance of his opera *L'Incantesimo* (Enchantment), broadcast over the NBC network.

14 OCTOBER 1943

Frontiers, a symphonic scroll by Paul CRESTON picturing "the westward American migration achieved through the vision, constancy and indomitable spirit of the pioneers," with three distinct sections marking "the vision, the trek, the achievement," is performed for the first time by the Toronto Symphony Orchestra, Kostelanetz conducting.

15 OCTOBER 1943

Serenade for tenor, horn and string orchestra, a song-sequence by Benjamin BRITTEN to poems by Tennyson, Blake, Ben Jonson, Keats, and others, is performed for the first time in London.

15 OCTOBER 1943

The Prairie, an orchestral suite by the 21-year-old Berlin-born, American composer Lukas Foss, extracted from his cantata of the same name to the poem of Carl Sandburg, with fanfare-like sonorities suggesting "vast open landscapes, and lots of fresh air," is performed for the first time by the Boston Symphony Orchestra, Koussevitzky conducting. (The cantata was performed in its entirety in New York, on 15 May 1944, by the Collegiate Chorale, Robert Shaw conducting)

17 OCTOBER 1943

Invasion, a short tone-poem by Bernard ROGERS, expressive of the anxious waiting for the allied landing in Western Europe, and cast in ominously somber harmonies, is performed by the New York Philharmonic, Rodzinski conducting.

22 OCTOBER 1943

Nicolai BEREZOWSKY conducts the Boston Symphony Orchestra in the world première of his *Fourth Symphony* in four movements, couched in a freely interpreted idea of rhapsodic symphony, with thematic retrospection at strategic musical points serving for structural unity.

28 OCTOBER 1943

On the twenty-fifth anniversary of the foundation of Czechoslovakia, two orchestral works by Bohuslav MARTINU are performed, one in New York, the other in Cleveland: *Memorial to Lidice,* a tribute to the Czech village martyred by the Nazis, played by the New York Philharmonic, Rodzinski conducting; and the *Second Symphony* (composed between 29 June and 24 July 1943), dedicated to the Czech colony of Cleveland, and played by the Cleveland Orchestra, Erich Leinsdorf conducting.

29 OCTOBER 1943

A symphonic version of *Commando March* by Samuel BARBER, originally composed for military band and performed by the Army Air Force band at Atlantic City, New Jersey, in April, 1943, and also used in American short-wave propaganda broadcasts throughout the world, is performed for the first time by the Boston Symphony Orchestra, Koussevitzky conducting.

29 OCTOBER 1943

Paul HINDEMITH's ballet overture *Cupid and Psyche,* to "the old Apuleius story, as far as it is depicted in the paintings at the Villa Farnesina in Rome," is performed for the first time by the Philadelphia Orchestra, Ormandy conducting.

29 OCTOBER 1943

Percy GOETSCHIUS, grand old man of American musical pedagogy, sincere believer in the immutable tenets of Germanic classicism (he used to call the C major scale "God's own scale," but was liberally tolerant of new-fangled musical lunacies, from Debussy down to Alban Berg), dies in Manchester, New Hampshire, at the patriarchal age of ninety.

4 NOVEMBER 1943

One-hour-long *Eighth Symphony* by Dmitri SHOSTAKOVITCH in four movements, couched in a characteristically Shostakovitchian manner with solemnly somber slow movements, slowly rising dynamics, gigglingly bouncing violin tunes, and magniloquently proclamatory cadential brasses, is performed for the first time by the Moscow State Orchestra.

5 NOVEMBER 1943

Concerto for Two Pianos by Bohuslav MARTINU in three movements, based on native Czech melodies, is performed for the first time by the Philadelphia Orchestra, Ormandy conducting, Pierre Luboshutz and Genia Nemenoff, soloists.

11 NOVEMBER 1943

André PIRRO, profoundest Bach scholar of France, penetrating esthetician of classical music, dies in Paris in his seventy-third year.

12 NOVEMBER 1943

Symphony for Strings by William SCHUMAN (completed on 31 July 1943) in three movements: (1) *Molto agitato ed energico,* based on a theme played in unison by violins on the G string (2) *Larghissimo,* employing a novel effect of fortissimo on muted strings in bitonal triad harmony (3) *Presto leggiero,* in a jazzily syncopated manner, is performed for the first time by the Boston Symphony Orchestra, Koussevitzky conducting.

14 NOVEMBER 1943

Leonard BERNSTEIN, 25-year-old native of Lawrence, Massachusetts, makes a spectacular debut as associate conductor of the New York Philharmonic, when he is called at 24-hour notice to pinch-hit for Bruno Walter, acquitting himself sensationally in a challengingly tough program including Strauss' *Don Quixote,* and an artfully tangled set of variations by the Hollywoodized Hungarian composer Miklós ROSZA.

"There are many variations of one of the six best stories in the world: the young corporal takes over the platoon when all the officers are down; the captain, with the dead admiral at his side, signals the fleet to go ahead; the young actress, fresh from Corinth or Ashtabula, steps into the star's role; the junior clerk, alone in the office, makes the instantaneous decision that saves the firm from ruin. The adventure of Leonard Bernstein, 25-year-old assistant conductor of the Philharmonic, who blithely mounted the podium at Carnegie Sunday afternoon when Conductor Bruno Walter became ill, belongs in the list. The corporals and captains must be brave, the young actress beautiful and talented, the clerk quick on his feet. Likewise, Mr. Bernstein had to have something approaching genius to make full use of his opportunity. It's a good American success story. The warm, friendly triumph of it filled Carnegie Hall and spread far over the air waves." (*A Story Old and Ever New,* Editorial in the *New York Times,* 16 November 1943)

17 NOVEMBER 1943

The Anxious Bugler by John Alden CARPENTER, describing the emotions of "any boy anywhere, who finds himself a soldier," is performed for the first time by the New York Philharmonic, Rodzinski conducting.

Soldiers on the Town, humorous march for orchestra by Nicolai BEREZOWSKY, "an attempt to portray soldiers on leave on a week-end pass anywhere, any town," is performed for the first time by the New York Philharmonic, Rodzinski conducting.

Gardner READ conducts the Boston Symphony Orchestra in the first performance of his *Second Symphony* in three movements, cast in somber Sibelian colors, with hidden rhythmic energies periodically released in frenetic explosions.

Three centuries have passed since the death in Venice of Claudio MONTEVERDI, the first great composer of operas in which instruments were contrapuntally combined and blended with voices.

Howard HANSON conducts the Boston Symphony Orchestra in the first performance of his *Fourth Symphony,* the *Requiem,* dedicated to the memory of his father, and written in solemnly sonorous style, with the movements named after the parts of the Requiem service, *Kyrie, Requiescat, Dies Irae,* and *Lux Aeterna.*

The stockrooms and the building of the great German publishing firm Breitkopf and Härtel are destroyed in an air raid on Leipzig (some plates were later recovered in the ruins; manuscripts and other unique objects had been hidden away at the outbreak of the war, and so saved from destruction).

8 DECEMBER 1943

Twenty-Fourth Symphony by Nicolas MIASKOVSKY (composed between 10 June and 20 July 1943; orchestrated between 8 August and 3 September 1943) in three movements is performed for the first time by the Moscow State Orchestra.

16 DECEMBER 1943

Bernard HERRMANN conducts the New York Philharmonic in the first performance of his *For the Fallen,* "a berceuse for those who lie asleep on the many alien battlefields of this war," with a quotation from Handel's *Messiah* in the coda, "He shall feed his flock like a shepherd."

23 DECEMBER 1943

Deems TAYLOR conducts the New York Philharmonic in a performance of his variations for orchestra, *Marco Takes a Walk,* on the same program with a performance of Nicolai BEREZOWSKY's *A Christmas Festival Overture,* based on Ukrainian Christmas carols, Barlow conducting.

30 DECEMBER 1943

March in Time of War, by Roy HARRIS, dedicated to the American composers in the armed services, and written around the folk song *True Love, Don't Weep,* is performed for the first time by the New York Philharmonic, Rodzinski conducting.

30 DECEMBER 1943

Second Symphony by Aram KHATCHATURIAN, written in an energetic rhythmic manner, with interludes of Caucasian lyricism, is performed for the first time in Moscow.

31 DECEMBER 1943

Concerto for violin and orchestra by Bohuslav MARTINU, in three movements of neo-romantically tense music, is performed for the first time by the Boston Symphony Orchestra, Mischa Elman (for whom the *Concerto* was written) as soloist, Koussevitzky conducting.

1944

5 JANUARY 1944

A symphonic paragraph, *In Memoriam: The Colored Soldiers Who Died for Democracy* by William Grant STILL, one of a series of compositions commissioned by the League of Composers, in dedication to an aspect of World War II, is performed for the first time by the New York Philharmonic, Rodzinski conducting.

8 JANUARY 1944

Wiktor LABUNSKI conducts the St. Louis Symphony Orchestra in the first performance of *Canzone* and *Scherzo* from his *Symphony in G Minor,* the *Canzone* based on three themes in the style of American folk songs.

14 JANUARY 1944

STRAVINSKY conducts the Boston Symphony Orchestra in the first performance of his *Four Norwegian Moods* (originally designed as incidental music for a film about Norway), composed "without any assumption of ethnological authenticity," using Norwegian folk tunes "only as a rhythmic and melodic basis," and the orchestral version of his *Circus Polka,* originally written for an elephant ballet at the Ringling Brothers Circus, and using a misharmonized tune from Schubert's *Military March.*

20 JANUARY 1944

Symphonic Metamorphosis on Themes of Carl Maria von Weber by Paul HINDEMITH in four movements: (1) *Allegro* (from four-hand piano music of Weber) (2) *Turandot-Scherzo* (from Weber's incidental music to Schiller's play of that name) (3) *An-dantino* (4) *March,* titivated by contrapuntal ornamentation, and rhythmically diversified by a sizeable battery of percussion, is performed for the first time by the New York Philharmonic, Rodzinski conducting.

27 JANUARY 1944

Concerto for Saxophone and Orchestra by Paul CRESTON in three movements marked respectively (1) Energetic (2) Meditative and (3) Rhythmic, is performed for the first time by the New York Philharmonic, Vincent Abato, saxophonist, William Steinberg conducting.

28 JANUARY 1944

Leonard BERNSTEIN conducts the Pittsburgh Symphony Orchestra in the first performance of his symphony, *Jeremiah,* in three movements: *Prophecy, Profanation, Lamentation,* profoundly immersed in Judaic music, designed "to parallel in feeling the intensity of the prophet's pleas with his people," and embodying both the reverently ritual and orgiastically primitive elements of the Hebrew tradition, with the voice of the prophet appearing in a vocal solo at the conclusion of the symphony, chanting the original Hebrew text.

1 FEBRUARY 1944

M. D. CALVOCORESSI, cosmopolitan Russian-born, French-educated, English music essayist of Greek extraction, dies in Chelsea, England, in his sixty-seventh year.

6 FEBRUARY 1944

Arnold SCHOENBERG's *Piano Concerto,* completed in California on 30 December 1942, and written in the twelve-tone series, E-flat, B-flat, D, F, E, C, F-sharp, G-sharp, C-sharp, A, B, and G, is performed for the first time by Steuermann with the NBC Symphony Orchestra in New York, Stokowski conducting.

7 FEBRUARY 1944

Lina CAVALIERI, the lyric soprano, once famous for her 19th-century beauty, perishes tragically in Florence, when her suburban villa is hit by a bomb during an American air raid.

8 FEBRUARY 1944

Violin Concerto by the Soviet symphonist LEV KNIPPER (whose choral ending in the *Fourth Symphony* has become a Russian folk song, *Poliushko,* known also as *Meadowlands*) is performed for the first time in Moscow.

12 FEBRUARY 1944

Colonial Pageant by Tibor SERLY, orchestral suite utilizing some tunes from "the music that Washington knew," is performed for the first time by the Buffalo Philharmonic, Franco Autori conducting.

13 FEBRUARY 1944

A luxuriantly sonorous *Fourth Symphony* by George ANTHEIL, the *enfant terrible* of the Parisian era of American music, now repatriated in Hollywood, is performed by Stokowski and the NBC Symphony Orchestra.

14 FEBRUARY 1944

Concerto for violin and orchestra by Robert Russell BENNETT is performed for the first time by the National Orchestral Association in New York, Louis Kaufman, soloist, Leon Barzin conducting.

15 FEBRUARY 1944

Ludus Tonalis by Paul HINDEMITH, a piano suite of twelve fugues, twelve interludes, a Prelude and a Postlude, which latter are crab inversions of each other, so that the Prelude played upside-down is identical with the Postlude (allowing for non-retroactive accidentals), and vice versa, is performed for the first time in the series of Composers' Concerts at the University of Chicago.

16 FEBRUARY 1944

Edmund VON BORCK, German composer of neo-classical instrumental music in a strongly linear contrapuntal and dynamically contrastful manner, is killed during the fighting in Italy near Nettuno, four days before his thirty-eighth birthday.

17 FEBRUARY 1944

William Billings Overture by William SCHUMAN, built on themes from three choral works "by America's first professional composer, William Billings," is performed for the first time by the New York Philharmonic, Rodzinski conducting.

19 FEBRUARY 1944

Nicolas MEDTNER, old-worldly Russian composer of romantic piano pieces, plays with the London Philharmonic Orchestra, Sir Adrian Boult conducting, the world première of his *Third Piano Concerto,* ascetically contrapuntal in texture, but vivaciously rhythmic in pianistic technique.

19 FEBRUARY 1944

Burnet TUTHILL conducts the St. Louis Symphony Orchestra in the first performance of his orchestral rhapsody *Come Seven,* intended not as "a musical description of the well-known gutter game," but reflecting "an attempt to compose in seven rhythm," with an ending succumbing to the desirability of a throw of eleven after a seven in a crap game, and so written in 11/8 meter.

23 FEBRUARY 1944

Ode to the Red Army, words by John Masefield, Poet Laureate, written in honor of the valiant Russian soldiers ("Though flanks were turned and center gone—You stood for home and struggled on—And now you reap reward; the line—Comes west again; the foes decline.—O hope, burn on; O star, still shine"), with music by Sir Arnold BAX, is sung in Albert Hall, London, on the twenty-sixth anniversary of the Red Army.

25 FEBRUARY 1944

Missa Oecumenica for soli, chorus, organ and orchestra by Alexandre GRETCHANINOV in six sections: *Kyrie, Gloria, Credo, Sanctus, Benedictus,* and *Agnus Dei,* "inspired by the idea of the oecumenic (universal) significance of the church" and intended "to combine the musical character of the East and West," is performed for the first time by the Boston Symphony Orchestra, Koussevitzky conducting.

25 FEBRUARY 1944

Eugene GOOSSENS conducts the Cincinnati Symphony Orchestra in the world première of his *Phantasy-Concerto,* "a four-movement piano concerto in miniature," with José Iturbi as soloist.

1 MARCH 1944

Hudson River Legend, ballet by Joseph WAGNER to Washington Irving's story of supernatural doings in colonial America, with a modernistic score featuring among other things a Geometry Dance, is performed by the Boston Civic Symphony Orchestra, Arthur Fiedler conducting.

3 MARCH 1944

Second Symphony by Samuel BARBER in three movements, composed at the Army Air Field in Fort Worth, Texas, and dedicated to the Army Air Forces, featuring in the second movement an electrical tone generator simulating, in its rhythm, the code signal of a radio beam, with a spirally mounting theme in the finale expressing the rapid upward flight, is performed for the first time by the Boston Symphony Orchestra, Koussevitzky conducting.

(Barber revised this Symphony in 1947, eliminating all programmatic allusions, and in this "absolute" form the Symphony was performed for the first time at the Curtis Institute of Music in Philadelphia on 5 January 1949, and by the Philadelphia Orchestra on 21 January 1949)

5 MARCH 1944

Second Symphony by Walter PISTON in three movements, a bi-thematically classical *Moderato,* a coaxingly lyrical *Adagio,* and a trithematically proclamatory *Allegro,* with subsurface Americanisms audible despite the composer's rejection of conscious musical nationalism ("Is the Dust Bowl more American than, say, a corner in the Boston Athenaeum? . . . The composer cannot afford the wild-goose chase of trying to be more American than he is"), is performed for the first time, as a commissioned work, by the National Symphony Orchestra in Washington, Kindler conducting.

15 MARCH 1944

A marching song, with music by the Red Army band leader ALEX-ANDROV, originally composed as a "Hymn to the Bolshevik Party," and then revised with a new set of words stressing the national rather than the international aspect, is proclaimed the official anthem of the USSR.

18 MARCH 1944

A century has passed since the birth of Nicolas RIMSKY-KORSAKOV, the great limner of gorgeously Russian operas and luminously orientalistic symphonic music. (Born 6 March 1844, old style, at 4:53 p.m.)

19 MARCH 1944

A Child of Our Time, a modern cantata by the English "young Turk" of music, Michael TIPPETT, in three parts describing respectively (1) the general state of affairs in the world as it affects individuals, minorities, social classes and races (2) the conflict of personal fate with elemental social forces (3) synthesis of a Man's shadow with a Man's light (all with reference to the shooting of a German diplomat in Paris by a Jewish boy refugee in November 1938), is performed for the first time by the London Philharmonic.

21 MARCH 1944

PROKOFIEV's war cantata *Ballad of a Boy Who Remained Unknown,* to the story of a young Soviet partisan who blew up the Nazi staff automobile in a village where his mother and sister had been murdered by the invaders, is performed for the first time in Moscow.

Fancy Free, a fancifully modernistic ballet with music by Leonard BERNSTEIN, is produced by the Ballet Theater in New York.

Violin Concerto by Luis GIANNEO, Argentinian composer of effective music in an engagingly Gallic vein, is performed for the first time in Buenos Aires.

Sixth Symphony by Roy HARRIS in four meaningful movements subtitled *Awakening, Conflict, Dedication,* and *Affirmation,* with programmatic allusions to Abraham Lincoln (symbolically, the score was completed on Lincoln's birthday, 12 February 1944, which was also the composer's birthday, his forty-sixth), is performed for the first time by the Boston Symphony Orchestra, Koussevitzky conducting.

"The shadow of Abe Lincoln has hovered over my life from childhood. This was, I suppose, inevitable, for the very simple reason that my birthday fell on the national holiday honoring Lincoln's birth, which meant that, on that day, school was dismissed. And so in seeking to compose a symphony worthy of our great national crisis, I too have turned to one of the great moments in the history of our nation for guidance." (From composer's statement)

A Tale of the Battle for the Russian Land by Youri SHAPORIN, patriotic cantata depicting in epic tones the awesome chronology of the Nazi invasion, is performed for the first time in Moscow.

Cécile CHAMINADE, French composer of unpretentiously semiclassical and—to the unfastidious ear—ingratiatingly attractive piano pieces with charmingly descriptive titles, dies in war-darkened Monte Carlo in her eighty-seventh year.

24 APRIL 1944

P. Kilian KIRCHHOFF, learned analyst of Byzantine hymnography, translator of all the Kanons and Stichera of the Byzantine Triodion and Pentekostarion, is executed in Brandenburg by the Nazis because he had said privately that Hitler was bringing doom to Germany.

27 APRIL 1944

Night Flight, wartime tone-poem for orchestra by Gardner READ, is performed for the first time by the Rochester Philharmonic, Hanson conducting.

6 MAY 1944

Carl ENGEL, Paris-born and Berlin-educated musicologist, second editor of the *Musical Quarterly,* and composer of some expertly contrived quasi-impressionistic pieces for piano, instruments, and voice, dies at the age of sixty in New York.

"When I depart for other regions, I expect to leave behind a lot of what belongs under unfinished business. My attempt at finishing here one of these numerous businesses before the frost sets in, must at best seem rather sketchy. For, in all candor, the old indolence holds me back. All I can do is to open the door and invite more intrepid explorers to enter the room for speculation." (From Engel's premonitory article in the January 1942 issue of the *Musical Quarterly*)

8 MAY 1944

Dame Ethel May SMYTH, British composer of dignified oratorios, operas, and instrumental music distinguished by calm assurance of mastery over the tonal ingredients, dies at the age of eighty-six in Woking, Surrey.

12 MAY 1944

The Passion by Bernard ROGERS, religious oratorio in six scenes, from Christ's entry into Jerusalem (in percussive march time) to the last prayer on the Cross (in a voice of agonizing monotone, with flattened notes in non-tempered pitch), culminating in a quintal chord pillar composed of all twelve notes of the cycle of fifths, from low C to high F, is performed for the first time at the May Festival in Cincinnati, Goossens conducting.

Leone SINIGAGLIA, Italian composer of appealing symphonic and operatic music with folksy Lombardian melorhythms, dies in Turin at the age of seventy-five.

16 MAY 1944

4 JUNE 1944

Symphony on Marching Tunes by Morton GOULD, a quasi-symphonic concatenation of Americanistic rhythms, is performed for the first time at the Lewisohn Stadium in New York.

10 JUNE 1944

Sir Henry COWARD, the Nestor of English choral conductors, and author of a standard treatise on choral singing, dies at Sheffield at the age of ninety-four years and six months.

12 JUNE 1944

Riccardo ZANDONAI, Italian composer of numerous operas in a luxuriantly grandoperatic manner, dies in Pesaro at the age of sixty-one.

30 JUNE 1944

A performance of *Götterdämmerung* is given at the Vienna Opera House, concluding with symbolic irony the last season in the glorious old monument of imperial splendor before its utter destruction in the air raid of 12 March 1945.

19 AUGUST 1944

Sir Henry WOOD, English symphonic and choral conductor, indefatigable champion of British music, who, in the words of Arnold Bax "has been esteemed a national institution . . . , purified and enriched the musical taste of at least two generations," dies in London in his seventy-sixth year, a few days before the last concert of the fiftieth season of the Promenade Concerts which he had conducted since their foundation in 1895. (Public concerts were interrupted in the summer of 1944 on account of the V-I bombardment, but broadcasts were continued from the BBC studios)

3 SEPTEMBER 1944

Theme and Variations according to the Four Temperaments (Melancholic, Sanguine, Phlegmatic, and Choleric), by Paul HINDEMITH, scored for chamber orchestra and piano, and conceived as a modern revival of the romantic program suite, is performed for the first time by an ensemble of Boston Symphony players, Richard Burgin conducting, in Boston.

3 SEPTEMBER 1944

Franz DRDLA, composer of successful violin pieces, one of which, a *Serenade,* became a fiddler's perennial, dies in Vienna in his seventy-sixth year.

7 SEPTEMBER 1944

Eduardo SANCHEZ DE FUENTES, the grand old man of Cuban music, composer of some celebrated Habaneras, and codifier of basic melorhythmic elements of Cuban popular music, dies in Havana in his seventieth year.

8 OCTOBER 1944

Samuel BARBER's *Capricorn Concerto* for flute, oboe, trumpet and strings, so named after the composer's house at Mt. Kisco, New York, is performed for the first time by the Saidenberg Little Symphony in New York.

13 OCTOBER 1944

Second Symphony by David DIAMOND, in four movements of quasi-romantic inspiration, containing moments of somber dejection alternating with passages of rhythmically carefree music, is performed for the first time by the Boston Symphony Orchestra, Koussevitzky conducting.

"It was in no way my intention to have the musical substance represent specific emotional reactions or to conjure up programmatic fantasies. I have a horror of anything as prosaic as that. My emotional life and reactions to certain events and situations have worked hand in hand with purely abstract musical conception and manipulation of material; and it was always the material that remained foremostly important to me in my working stages." (From composer's statement)

17 OCTOBER 1944

Letter from Home by Aaron COPLAND, intended "to convey emotional reactions associated with the reading of a letter from home," is performed for the first time by Paul Whiteman and the Philco Radio Orchestra. (A version for full orchestra of *Letter from Home* was presented by the Cleveland Orchestra, Szell conducting, on 27 February 1947)

20 OCTOBER 1944

Theme and Variations for Orchestra, op. 43b (op. 43a is ditto for band) by SCHOENBERG, bearing an unarguably definite key signature in G major, with a march-like theme non-atonally transfigured in seven variations, and a *Finale* "using motival and harmonic features of the theme, thus producing new themes of contrasting character and mood," is performed for the first time by the Boston Symphony Orchestra, Koussevitzky conducting.

"When I had finished my first *Kammersymphonie,* op. 9, I told my friends: 'Now I have established my style. I know now how I have to compose.' But my next work showed a great deviation from this style; it was a first step toward my present style. My destiny had forced me in this direction—I was not destined to continue in the manner of *Transfigured Night* or *Gurrelieder* or even *Pelléas and Mélisande.* The Supreme Commander had ordered me on a harder road. But a longing to return to the older style was always vigorous in me; and from time to time I had to yield to that urge. This is how and why I sometimes write tonal music. To me stylistic differences of this nature are not of a special importance. I do not know which of my compositions are better; I like them all, because I liked them when I wrote them." (From Schoenberg's article published in the *New York Times,* 19 December 1948, under the heading, *One Always Returns*)

21 OCTOBER 1944

Fugue on a Victory Tune by Walter PISTON, in the stately style of a military march, one of a long series of wartime music pieces commissioned by the League of Composers, is performed by the New York Philharmonic, Rodzinski conducting.

22 OCTOBER 1944

Chant de Libération for baritone, chorus and orchestra by Arthur

Honegger (composed during the Nazi Occupation in 1942) is performed two months after the liberation of Paris, at the Concerts du Conservatoire, Charles Münch conducting.

24 OCTOBER 1944

A Stopwatch and an Ordnance Map for men's chorus and kettle-drums, a realistic piece of wartime life by Samuel Barber, is performed for the first time in Columbus, Ohio.

24 OCTOBER 1944

Gabriel Grovlez, French composer of impressionistic pieces in various instrumental genres, dies in Paris at the age of sixty-five.

30 OCTOBER 1944

Martha Graham and her dance group present in Washington the first production of *Appalachian Spring* by Aaron Copland (so named after a poem by Stephen Crane, though bearing no relevance to it), scored for thirteen instruments, and divided into seven musical tableaux, unsatirically portraying in tonally pellucid triad harmonies the bride, the groom, the revivalist, and the elders, thus unfolding a vivid musicorama of American ways. with the last section based on a Shaker song: "When true simplicity is gained—To bow and to bend we shan't be ashamed— To turn, turn will be our delight—Till by turning, twining we come round right." (A symphonic suite drawn from this ballet was first performed by the New York Philharmonic on 4 October 1945, and on the next day, by the Boston Symphony Orchestra and the Cleveland Orchestra)

1 NOVEMBER 1944

Manuel Rosenthal, French composer of the soberly modernistic school, conducts in Paris the first performance of his neo-ecclesiastical oratorio *Saint Francis of Assisi,* written in 1939, consisting of ten chronologically descriptive sections, *Prayer, Youth, The Kiss of the Leper, Saint Clara, Sermon to the Birds, Hymn to*

the Sun, Angelic Kithara, Grand Miracle of the Stigmata, Death,
and *Angels' Chorus,* and scored for orchestra with chorus, vibraphone, and an electronic instrument, "les ondes Martenot."

11 NOVEMBER 1944

Ozark Set by Elie SIEGMEISTER, descriptive of the life of the common people in the Ozark mountains of Missouri and Arkansas, in
four movements: *Morning in the Hills, Camp Meeting, Lazy
Afternoon* and *Saturday Night,* infused with Americanistic melorhythms and spiced with endurable dissonances, is performed for
the first time by the Minneapolis Symphony Orchestra, Mitropoulos conducting.

12 NOVEMBER 1944

Edgar Stillman KELLEY, American composer of descriptive music
for orchestra, and engagingly old-fashioned operettas, dies in
New York at the age of eighty-seven years and eight months.

17 NOVEMBER 1944

Virgil THOMSON conducts the Philadelphia Orchestra in the first
performance of a suite from his *Portraits,* featuring *Bugles and
Birds* (Picasso), *Cantabile for Strings* (a Russian painter), *Tango
Lullaby* (a young girl), *Fugue* (conductor Smallens), and *Percussion Piece* (a California lady long resident in Massachusetts).

"They are all drawn from life. The subject sits for his likeness as he would
for a painter; and the music is composed in front of him, usually at one
sitting. Orchestral scoring is later worked out in detail. The musical style of
the pieces varies with the personality of the subject. Sometimes it is harmonious, sometimes dissonant, sometimes straightforwardly tuneful, sometimes
thematically or contrapuntally developed. An effort has been made to catch
in all cases a likeness recognizable to persons acquainted with the sitter."
(Virgil Thomson in the program notes)

23 NOVEMBER 1944

Ode to Napoleon, op. 41b, by Arnold SCHOENBERG, to Byron's
poem, scored for string orchestra, piano and rhythmic narration,
and composed according to a reformed twelve-tone technique,

with the symmetrical motto of an ascending fourth and a descending minor second, thrice repeated, characterizing a presumptuous dictator, and a motto of fifths, by symbolic inversion, depicting the democratic spirit of George Washington, is performed for the first time by the New York Philharmonic, Rodzinski conducting.

23 NOVEMBER 1944

Alfredo CASELLA completes in Rome the composition of his *Solemn Mass for Peace*, begun 1 June 1944, when the flight of the Germans from Italy presaged the end of the war.

"The drama of the war, racial suffering (my wife is a Jewess), and finally a long and painful illness necessitating two operations, were the circumstances that determined in this composition a certain change of style, a final deepening of an art that has cost me more than thirty years of arduous work." (From Casella's statement)

24 NOVEMBER 1944

Rounds for String Orchestra by David DIAMOND ("The work is spherical—that is why I call it 'Rounds'") in three movements played without pause, with the middle section, *Adagio,* "acting as a resting point between the two fast movements," is performed for the first time as a commissioned work by the Minneapolis Symphony Orchestra, Mitropoulos conducting.

1 DECEMBER 1944

Concerto for violin and orchestra by Louis GRUENBERG, in three movements: (1) *Rhapsody,* to be played "with simple dignity" (2) *Lento,* "with simplicity and warmth," where the violin croons two Negro spirituals, "Oh, Holy Lord" and "Massa Jesus" and (3) a fast movement, "Lively and with good humor," imitating a hill-billy fiddler and a small-town religious revival meeting, with some snatches from "Arkansaw Traveler," is performed for the first time anywhere by Jascha Heifetz, for whom the *Concerto* was written, and the Philadelphia Orchestra, Ormandy conducting.

Concerto for Orchestra by Béla BARTÓK, completed by him on 8
October 1943 during recuperation from his next-to-last illness, in
five movements: (1) *Introduction,* in a sternly ascetic manner
(2) *Game of Pairs* (so named because woodwinds are paired at
specific intervals, bassoons in sixths, oboes in thirds, clarinets in
sevenths, flutes in fifths, muted trumpets in major seconds) (3)
Elegy, "a lugubrious death song" (4) *Interrupted Intermezzo,* derived from two asymmetrically rhythmic themes, the return of
which is interrupted by a fluid songful episode (5) *Finale,* symbolic of "life-assertion," with a persistently repetitive fugal subject developed in single, double and triple augmentation, single,
double and triple diminution, and *stretti* in quadruple counterpoint, climaxing in a grandiose coda, is performed for the first
time, as a commissioned work, by the Boston Symphony Orchestra, Koussevitzky conducting.

Nocturne, from the orchestral suite *Decatur at Algiers* by George
ANTHEIL, "a colored picture from an American boy's treasured
and thumb-worn book of naval heroes," with the thematic material a composite of orientalistic tunes and typical American
motives, is performed for the first time by the St. Louis Symphony
Orchestra, Golschmann conducting.

Side Show by William SCHUMAN, a cinematically projected piece
of symphonic Americana, is performed for the first time by the
Pittsburgh Symphony Orchestra, Reiner conducting.

Sinfonia Tripartita by Vittorio RIETI, dedicated to Stravinsky,
but composed in a neo-Scarlattian vein, is performed for the first
time by the St. Louis Symphony Orchestra, Golschmann conducting.

24 DECEMBER 1944

Mrs. H. H. A. BEACH, first American woman composer of competent symphonic and other pieces, dies in New York at the age of seventy-seven.

30 DECEMBER 1944

Vit NEJEDLY, 32-year-old Czech composer of three symphonies, is killed near Dukla, Slovakia, fighting in a resistance movement against the Nazi occupiers.

30 DECEMBER 1944

Romain ROLLAND, great French writer, author of *Jean Christophe,* and a singularly imaginative historian of music, dies at his home in Vézelay, France, at the age of seventy-eight.

1945

5 JANUARY 1945

Feast During the Plague, symphonic suite with chorus and soprano soloist by the Russian-French-American composer Arthur Vincent LOURIÉ, to a Pushkin story of romantic love and death during the Black Plague in Florence, with a musical score in the pandiatonic idiom of the Stravinskian school, is performed for the first time by the Boston Symphony Orchestra, Koussevitzky conducting.

13 JANUARY 1945

Serge PROKOFIEV conducts in Moscow an all-Prokofiev symphony concert featuring the world première of his *Fifth Symphony,* op. 100, "a symphony about the spirit of man," composed in one month during the summer of 1944, and set in the optimistic key of B-flat major, in four movements of fervidly Russian lyricism and bouncingly Prokofievian exuberance.

19 JANUARY 1945

Festive Overture by William Grant STILL, bristling with sonorous fanfares executed on muted trumpets and bolstered with a generously equipped battery of percussion, xylophone and marimba, is performed for the first time, as a prize-winning work of the orchestra's Jubilee Contest, by the Cincinnati Symphony Orchestra, Goossens conducting.

24 JANUARY 1945

Ernst KRENEK becomes a citizen of the United States.

26 JANUARY 1945

Violin Concerto by Willy BURKHARD, Swiss composer of tautly contrapuntal neo-Lutheran music, is performed for the first time in Zurich by the orchestra of the Collegium Musicum, Paul Sacher conducting.

26 JANUARY 1945

Concerto for Harp and Orchestra by Nicolai BEREZOWSKY in three movements, of which the first is based on the Nativity hymn *Intonent hodie voces ecclesiae,* second, a cradle song, third, orientalistic in its melorhythmic scheme, is performed for the first time by the Philadelphia Orchestra, Edna Phillips, harpist, Ormandy conducting.

1 FEBRUARY 1945

Concerto for Orchestra by Morton GOULD in three movements marked (1) *Moderately fast, with drive and vigor* (2) *Slowly, with stately lyricism* and (3) *Fast, with gusto,* boisterously Americanistic in thematic derivation, with a suggestion of boogie-woogie in the finale, is performed by the Cleveland Orchestra, Golschmann conducting.

3 FEBRUARY 1945

STRAVINSKY conducts the New York Philharmonic in the first performance of his *Scènes de Ballet,* written in a neo-Delibian manner, "patterned after the forms of the classical dance, free of any given literary or dramatic argument," comprising eleven terpsichorean poses.

4 FEBRUARY 1945

Symphony in G, by Lukas Foss, cast in a broadly inclusive style ranging from neo-Handelian chordal staticism to vernacular jazzification, is performed for the first time by the Pittsburgh Symphony Orchestra, Reiner conducting.

15 FEBRUARY 1945

Second Symphony by Paul CRESTON, "conceived as an apotheosis of the two foundations of all music: song and dance," in two movements: (1) *Introduction and Song* (2) *Interlude and Dance,* is performed for the first time by the New York Philharmonic, Rodzinski conducting.

22 FEBRUARY 1945

Virgil THOMSON conducts the New York Philharmonic in the first performance of his *Symphony on a Hymn Tune,* derived from two pentatonic tunes of the Southern Baptists, *How Firm a Foundation* and *Yes, Jesus Loves Me,* in four movements: (1) *Introduction* (as a "conversational passage for solo instruments and pairs of instruments followed by a statement of the hymn tune in half-in and half-out-of-focus harmonization") and *Allegro,* "a succession (and superposition) of dance-like passages derived from the main theme," ending with a heteroousian cadenza for piccolo, violin, cello and trombone (2) *Andante,* a series of variations, featuring an imitation of a distant locomotive whistle simulated by a simultaneous run of brass glissando gliding upwards to a landing on a D-major triad (3) *Allegretto,* "a passacaglia of marked rhythmic character on the hymn-tune bass" (4) *Finale,* "a canzona on a part of the main theme."

23 FEBRUARY 1945

On his second visit to the United States, VILLA-LOBOS conducts the Boston Symphony in the world première of his *Chôros No. 12,* composed for a mastodontic orchestra plus an assortment of Brazilian shakers and drumlets, a *chôros* being "a new form of musical composition in which are synthesized the different modalities of Brazilian, Indian and popular music."

26 FEBRUARY 1945

Concerto for the electronic instrument Theremin and orchestra by Anis FULEIHAN, is performed by the New York City Symphony Orchestra, Stokowski conducting, Clara Rockmore, soloist.

2 MARCH 1945

Music for English Horn and Orchestra by Edward Burlingame HILL, who confesses to being "intimidated" by the "classic examples of the expressive treatment of that nostalgic instrument," in two sections separated by a contrasting episode, with a piano part as a background, is performed for the first time by the Boston Symphony Orchestra, Koussevitzky conducting, Louis Speyer, soloist, on the same program with the first performance of *Concertino* for orchestra by Nicolas LOPATNIKOV in three sections: *Toccata, Elegietta,* and *Finale,* written in a Russianized neoclassical manner.

2 MARCH 1945

Alfred EINSTEIN, the German musicologist whose all-embracing scholarship extends from micromusical scrutiny of the classics to universal concepts of musico-historical philosophy, becomes an American citizen.

5 MARCH 1945

Rudolf KAREL, Czech composer of profoundly national music for instruments and voices, dies in a concentration camp at Teresin.

12 MARCH 1945

During an American air raid, five bombs hit the Vienna Opera

House, three falling on the stage and smashing the iron curtain separating the stage from the orchestra, one exploding above the right proscenium box, and one bursting in the Operngasse, opening a gap of 120 square yards in the left side of the building, and leaving it a heap of twisted debris.

14 MARCH 1945

Francisco BRAGA, the Massenet of Brazil, composer of pleasantly dulcet operas in a songfully Gallic manner, dies in Rio de Janeiro, four weeks before his seventy-seventh birthday.

15 MARCH 1945

Ode to Those Who Will Not Return by Lukas Foss, a musical homage to war victims, is performed for the first time by the New York Philharmonic, Szell conducting.

16 MARCH 1945

Concerto for Violin and Orchestra by Harl McDONALD in three movements, written in a simple neo-Mendelssohnian manner, is performed for the first time by the Philadelphia Orchestra, Ormandy conducting, Alexander Hilsberg, soloist.

21 MARCH 1945

Samuel FEINBERG, neo-romantic Russian composer of Scriabinesque music, plays with the State Orchestra in Moscow the world première of his *Second Piano Concerto,* for which he received a Stalin prize.

21 MARCH 1945

Fantasia for Viola and Orchestra, "the most difficult piece ever written for the viola," by John KLENNER, spontaneously taught composer of modern tear-jerkers, such as *Heartaches,* is performed for the first time by the New York Chamber Orchestra.

23 MARCH 1945

An orchestral set, *Variations on a Theme by Eugene Goossens,* by ten American composers: Paul CRESTON, Aaron COPLAND, Deems TAYLOR, Howard HANSON, William SCHUMAN, Walter PISTON, Roy HARRIS, Anis FULEIHAN, Bernard ROGERS and Ernest BLOCH, is performed by the Cincinnati Symphony Orchestra, Goossens conducting, on the occasion of the orchestra's Golden Jubilee.

25 MARCH 1945

Figure Humaine, cantata by Francis POULENC composed during the Nazi occupation of France, is given its world première by the BBC in London, which was, in Poulenc's words, "the unfailing source of hope during the German occupation."

12 APRIL 1945

Peter RAABE, German music scholar who in 1935 succeeded Richard Strauss as President of the inglorious Reichsmusikkammer, and wrote a brochure on the flowering of the art of music in the Third Reich, dies in Weimar in his seventy-third year, amid the intellectual and physical ruins of his Germany.

"Peter Raabe died on 12 April 1945, on the day of the entry of the American troops into Weimar. He certainly did not die by suicide (as was rumored); he was ill for weeks, and perhaps for years before, broken down by his long fight against the administration imposed upon him, with whose views he could not bring himself into accord, and which despite his efforts refused to relieve him from his office. I myself was present at his sickbed a few days before his death, and spoke at his burial." (Letter, dated 24 July 1947, from Prof. Dr. Wahl, Director of the Goethe Museum in Weimar)

14 APRIL 1945

Dai-keong LEE, 29-year-old Hawaiian composer now with the Fifth Air Force in the Pacific, conducts the Australian Broadcasting Orchestra in Sydney in the world première of his *First Symphony,* written in an un-Hawaiian, anti-romantic, pro-Hindemith style scorning any illustratively tropical adumbrations.

20 APRIL 1945

Fables, symphonic suite, after Aesop, for narrator and orchestra by the Philadelphia composer Vincent PERSICHETTI, picturing in a series of illustrative orchestral sketches (1) The Fox and the Grapes (2) The Wolf and the Ass (3) The Hare and the Tortoise (4) The Cat and the Fox (5) A Raven and a Swan (6) The Monkey and the Camel, is performed for the first time by the Philadelphia Orchestra, Ormandy conducting.

28 APRIL 1945

Characters from Hans Christian Andersen, descriptive suite for orchestra by Bernard ROGERS, is performed for the first time by the Rochester Philharmonic, Hanson conducting.

8 MAY 1945

Thanksgiving for Victory by VAUGHAN WILLIAMS for speaker, chorus and orchestra, to the words from Shakespeare's *Henry V,* the Bible, and Kipling, is broadcast by the BBC on Victory-in-Europe Day.

12 MAY 1945

The First Annual Festival of Contemporary American Music, "sponsored by the Alice M. Ditson Fund, and devoted to the performance of significant chamber and orchestral compositions by contemporary American composers," opens at Columbia University in New York with an afternoon concert by the NBC Symphony Orchestra, Howard Hanson conducting the following program: *Rounds for Strings* by David DIAMOND; *Fourth Symphony* by Howard HANSON (Pulitzer Prize Award, 1943); *Concerto* for saxophone and orchestra by Henry BRANT; and *Second Symphony* by Walter PISTON.

(In the evening of 12 May, a concert of chamber music was given, programming *First String Quartet* by Robert PALMER; *Water Music for String Quartet* by Robert Russell BENNETT; and *Second String Quartet* by William BERGSMA. On 13 May the following program of chamber music was given: *Second String Quartet* by Frederick JACOBI; *Quintet* for oboe and string quartet by Robert MCBRIDE; *Six from Ohio* for oboe, violin, viola and cello by Alvin ETLER; and *String Quartet* by Wallingford RIEGGER. On 14 May a special performance for out-of-town guests was presented of *The Scarecrow,* chamber opera in two acts by Normand LOCKWOOD, first performed on 9 May 1945 at Columbia University)

18 MAY 1945

Vladimir HELFERT, scholarly historian of Czech music, dies in Prague a few days after the liberation, from the effects of disease and malnutrition contracted during his long incarceration in the Teresin concentration camp.

7 JUNE 1945

Peter Grimes, opera by Benjamin BRITTEN to the macabre story of a morbidly sadistic fisherman driven to suicide by village gossip after consecutive accidental deaths of his two boy apprentices, conceived on a tense expressionistic plan, with tonal harmonics recurrently intensified by discordant stridencies, and with uninhibited use in the text of such hitherto unoperatic expressions as "bitch" and "hell," is produced at the Sadler's Wells Theater in London at its reopening after the War.

13 JUNE 1945

Suite Française by Darius MILHAUD, written for band in 1944, and representing five nostalgic musical postcards of Normandy, Brittany, Ile-de-France, Alsace-Lorraine, and Provence, where the Allied armies battled after invasion, is performed for the first time by the Goldman Band in New York.

26 JUNE 1945

Nicolas TCHEREPNIN, epigone of the great Russian National School, author of effective ballet music, dies at Issy-les-Moulineaux, near Paris, at the age of seventy-two.

3 JULY 1945

Oscar THOMPSON, enlightened and witty American writer on musical matters, progressively-minded music critic and lexicographer, dies in New York in his fifty-eighth year.

3 JULY 1945

As a gesture of Soviet-American good will and friendship, the

State Symphony Orchestra in Moscow presents a concert of American symphonic music in a program including *Ode to Friendship* by Roy HARRIS, *March in Memoriam* by Wallingford RIEGGER, Samuel BARBER's *Essay for Orchestra,* Elie SIEGMEISTER's *Ozark Set,* and GERSHWIN's *Rhapsody in Blue.*

14 JULY 1945

The Allied Authorities in Germany issue an order forbidding the singing or playing of any military music or National Socialist songs.

31 JULY 1945

VAUGHAN WILLIAMS conducts at the Promenade Concerts in London the first performance of his symphonic suite *The Story of a Flemish Farm,* composed of excerpts from a cinema score, to the story of Belgian airmen who at the beginning of the German invasion managed to hide their national flag and carry it to England.

2 AUGUST 1945

Pietro MASCAGNI, Italian opera composer who in his youth wrote his lone opera of enduring fame, *Cavalleria Rusticana,* which set off the flowering of operatic realism, dies in Rome at the age of eighty-one years and eight months.

5 AUGUST 1945

Emil VON REZNICEK, Czech-Austrian composer of pleasantly lyrical and occasionally animated Germanic music, dies in devastated Berlin at the age of eighty-five.

23 AUGUST 1945

Leo BORCHARD, conductor of the Berlin Philharmonic Orchestra, is accidentally shot and killed by an American sentry in occupied Berlin when the driver of the automobile in which he was riding ignored the order to stop.

1 SEPTEMBER 1945

Grünewald, symphonic poem by the Polish composer Jan MAK-
LAKIEWICZ, glorifying in martial tones the battle of 1410 in which
the Teutonic Knights were utterly routed by Polish armies on
the field of Grünewald (known also as the battle of Tannen-
berg), is performed for the first time by the Cracow Philharmonic.

15 SEPTEMBER 1945

On leaving the house of his son-in-law in Mittersill, near Salzburg, Anton VON WEBERN, 62-year-old Austrian composer of mi-
cromusically subtilized instrumental works, is accidentally killed
by an American sentinel in consequence of his failure to obey a
misinterpreted signal to stop.

16 SEPTEMBER 1945

John MCCORMACK, golden-voiced Irish tenor whose heartstring-
tugging singing moved millions, dies near Dublin at the age of
sixty-one.

26 SEPTEMBER 1945

Béla BARTÓK, great composer of modern Hungary who developed
a technique of composition exploring the outermost frontiers of
musical tones and rhythms, and also collected and classified the
folk songs of his native Transylvania and adjacent regions, dies
in New York of leukemia, at the age of sixty-four.

"The man whose music had elemental sweep, barbaric rhythm and penetrating force, never weighed more than 116 pounds and sometimes as little as 90.
His constant battle with ill health started as a youth when he had lung
trouble. His body remained delicate and other difficulties—asthma, skin trouble, stomach disorders and fever—made their appearance. The fever increased
and in the spring of 1944 it was diagnosed as leukemia. In September 1945
there was an abrupt rise in his white cell count, and the doctors knew he was
near the end. He died on 26 September 1945, shortly before noon. ASCAP
paid the funeral expenses, for, following the tradition set by so many other
great composers, Bartók left no estate save the boundless wealth of his music."
(Erno Balogh in *Musical Digest,* September 1947)

(Bartók's body was cremated and the ashes kept in parcel No. 470 of the
Ferncliff Cemetery near Hartsdale, N. Y., sans headstone, sans marker, sans

everything. Not until the third anniversary of Bartók's death was this mortuary anonymity broken, and a memorial tablet placed on his grave)

12 OCTOBER 1945

Third Symphony by Bohuslav MARTINU in three movements, is performed for the first time by the Boston Symphony Orchestra, Koussevitzky conducting.

26 OCTOBER 1945

Suite Symphonique by Ernest BLOCH in three movements: (1) *Overture* (2) *Passacaglia* (3) *Finale,* culminating in "a grotesque sardonic fugue," is performed for the first time by the Philadelphia Orchestra, Monteux conducting.

27 OCTOBER 1945

Harvest for harp, vibraphone and strings by Morton GOULD, employing a chordal contrapuntal technique leading to mild polytonality, with materials of cheerful folk song character suitable for singing at harvest time, is performed for the first time by the St. Louis Symphony Orchestra, Golschmann conducting.

30 OCTOBER 1945

Victory Overture by Reinhold GLIÈRE (originally written for band and performed in Moscow on 22 February 1945 without the word Victory in the title) is performed in a version for large orchestra for the first time in Moscow.

2 NOVEMBER 1945

Piano Concerto in F major by Gian-Carlo MENOTTI in three movements, influenced by the Italian pre-romantic instrumental style, notably that of Domenico Scarlatti, is performed for the first time by the Boston Symphony Orchestra, Richard Burgin conducting, Rudolf Firkušny, soloist.

3 NOVEMBER 1945

Ninth Symphony by SHOSTAKOVITCH (completed on 30 August 1945, at the Composers' Rest Home near Ivanovo), the shortest of his symphonic productions, in five miniature movements, of which the last three, *Presto, Largo* and *Allegretto,* are integrated into an uninterrupted section, bristling with familiar clichés of Shostakovitchian technique, march-like rhythms, giggling glissandos of the strings, elegiac episodes between fast movements, the whole giving the impression of a joyous postlude to exertions of war, is performed for the first time at the opening concert of the season of the Leningrad Philharmonic.

10 NOVEMBER 1945

Ode to the End of War by PROKOFIEV, scored for a triumphantly grandiose orchestra of woodwinds, brass, percussion, four pianos, eight harps, and sixteen double-basses, but no violins, cellos, or violas, is performed for the first time in Moscow.

11 NOVEMBER 1945

Jerome KERN, American composer of nostalgically appealing light operas and musical revues, dies in New York at the age of sixty years and ten months.

16 NOVEMBER 1945

Suite for Violin and Orchestra by Darius MILHAUD, in three sections: (1) *Gigues* (2) *Sailor Song* and (3) *Hornpipes,* written in a candidly virtuoso manner, with thematic material taken from anonymous 18th-century melodies, is performed for the first time by the Philadelphia Orchestra, Ormandy conducting, Zino Francescatti, violinist.

21 NOVEMBER 1945

Cinderella, ballet by PROKOFIEV (composition, interrupted by the war, was completed in 1943 in the town of Molotov, renamed from Perm, in the Urals) written to an earthy Russian version of the universal dream-fulfillment fairy tale, *Masha Chernushka* (literally "Little Mary, the Dirty-Black One"), with a musical score in the traditional manner of the Russian classical ballet, featuring a *pas de deux* for Masha, a mazurka for the desirable prince, waltzes for the rest, with twenty arias and songs super-added, making it an opera-ballet, is performed for the first time in Moscow.

29 NOVEMBER 1945

The Seven Ages, symphonic suite by John Alden CARPENTER, from the famous lines spoken by Jaques in Shakespeare's *As You Like It,* in seven musical episodes, ending with "sans eyes, sans taste, sans everything," is performed for the first time by the New York Philharmonic, Rodzinski conducting.

30 NOVEMBER 1945

Fourth Symphony by Bohuslav MARTINU in the classical four movements, marked with neo-romantic intensity and spangled with quasi-bitonal sonorities, is performed for the first time by the Philadelphia Orchestra, Ormandy conducting.

6 DECEMBER 1945

Darius MILHAUD conducts the New York Philharmonic in the world première of his Caribbean diptych *Le Bal Martiniquais* in two divisions, *Chanson Créole* and *Biguine,* on folk themes of the island of Martinique, with the thematic material derived from his little suite for piano and voice, *La libération des Antilles,* a setting to poems by the islanders expressing their joy at the liberation of the French West Indies from Vichy rule.

8 DECEMBER 1945

Alexander SILOTI, Russian pianist, pupil of Liszt and teacher of Rachmaninov, dies in New York at the age of eighty-two.

14 DECEMBER 1945

Tobias MATTHAY, famous piano pedagogue and originator of the

Matthay system of solid and reliable piano technique, dies in Haslemere, England, at the age of eighty-seven.

28 DECEMBER 1945

STRAVINSKY becomes an American citizen, renouncing allegiance to France whose citizen he had become on 10 June 1934.

1946

4 JANUARY 1946

Concerto for Violoncello and Orchestra by Vladimir DUKELSKY in three movements, in rapidly changing moods from spasmodically rhythmic to mock-lyrical, with overpoweringly difficult violoncellistic tricks in a grandiosely expansive C major finale, is performed for the first time by Gregor Piatigorsky with the Boston Symphony Orchestra, Koussevitzky conducting.

10 JANUARY 1946

Harry VON TILZER (real name, Harry Gumm), untutored composer of hundreds of sentimental ballads, and originator of the term "Tin Pan Alley" (he used to practice on a piano with paper laid on the strings so that it sounded like a tin pan), dies a lonely death in a Broadway hotel in New York at the age of seventy-three.

24 JANUARY 1946

STRAVINSKY conducts the New York Philharmonic in the world première of his *Symphony in Three Movements*, (1) *Overture* (2) *Andante* (3) *Con moto,* the first movement approximating a rhythmically diversified toccata, the second, a terse concertino, and the third, a self-conscious reversion to Stravinsky's early style, with its unsymmetric gasps of suspenseful silence, walled by concrete columns of static sound.

25 JANUARY 1946

Metamorphoses by Richard STRAUSS, composed in a month between 13 March 1945 and 12 April 1945, for twenty-three solo string instruments, inscribed *In Memoriam,* and containing thematic quotations from Beethoven's Funeral March in the *Eroica,* as a dirge on the death of the German State, is performed for the first time in Zurich, Switzerland, Paul Sacher conducting.

29 JANUARY 1946

Andrés SÁS, the Paris-born Peruvian composer, conducts in Viña del Mar, Chile, the first performance of his ballet *La Señora del Pueblo.*

4 FEBRUARY 1946

Trois Petites Liturgies de Présence Divine by Olivier MESSIAEN, conceived in pseudo-orientalistically neo-ecclesiastic manner, is performed for the first time in Paris.

6 FEBRUARY 1946

Oswald KABASTA, Austrian conductor, commits suicide in Munich, in fear of imminent denazification proceedings, and in the consciousness of being guilty of more than passive cultural aid to the Nazi cause.

8 FEBRUARY 1946

Third Concerto for piano and orchestra by Béla BARTÓK, his last work written out shortly before his death, is performed for the first time by the Philadelphia Orchestra, Ormandy conducting, Gyorgy Sandor, pianist.

"The *Concerto* for piano and orchestra, his third, was scored fully with the exception of the last seventeen measures, which were sketched in a kind of musical shorthand used by Bartók. These last seventeen measures were deciphered and scored by his friend and colleague, Tibor Serly. Bartók worked feverishly to the very last to complete the *Concerto,* and it was touching to note that he had prematurely scrawled in pencil the Hungarian word *vege—* the end—on the last bar of his sketch copy as though he were desperately aiming to reach it. On no other score had he ever written the word." (From program notes by Tibor Serly)

17 FEBRUARY 1946

Danzón Cubano by Aaron COPLAND, a stylized Afro-Cuban dance, with syncopation sharpened to a fine point, and with metric apocopes further accentuating the rhythm, is performed for the first time in its symphonic version by the Baltimore Symphony Orchestra, Reginald Stewart conducting. (It was performed in its original form, for two pianos, by Copland and Bernstein on 17 December 1942 at a concert of the League of Composers in New York)

21 FEBRUARY 1946

Roy HARRIS conducts the New York Philharmonic in the first performance of his miniature suite for orchestra, *Memories of a Child's Sunday,* dedicated "To little Richard Rodzinski, aged one and a little bit," in three sections: (1) *Bells,* "meant to evoke glad memory of having heard bells as a child" (2) *Dreams,* dealing "with the psychological states of a child's slumber, especially that fitful slumber which children are apt to have in mid-afternoon, when the savage dreams of atavistic emotions often frighten them into crying out as though in great fear" (3) *Play Hours,* "a memory of unconcerned play—animal spirits."

23 MARCH 1946

Airborne, modern oratorio by Marc BLITZSTEIN, depicting in twelve temporal stages the history of human flight, mythological and real, from Icarus to the airmen of World War II, written in a dramatically terse, percussive style, with brassy triads in close harmony punctuating the brusquely declarative text of the narration, is performed for the first time by the New York City Symphony, Leonard Bernstein conducting.

25 MARCH 1946

Ebony Concerto by STRAVINSKY for clarinet and swing band, so titled after the swing name "ebony stick" for clarinet, and contrived in an appropriately fidgety rhythmic manner, with fitful instrumental wheezes creating a stimulatingly neurotic mood, is performed for the first time by Woody Herman's Band in Carnegie Hall, New York.

5 APRIL 1946

Concerto for Violoncello and Orchestra by Samuel BARBER in three movements, written in a cheerfully modernistic style, with a moderately pyrotechnical display of violoncellistic passage work, and marked allusions to jazz rhythms, is performed for the first time by the Boston Symphony Orchestra, Koussevitzky conducting, Raya Garbousova, soloist.

5 APRIL 1946

Vincent YOUMANS, American composer of many a pretty ditty and rememberable tune, including the perennial *Tea for Two*, dies of consumption in Denver at the age of forty-seven.

11 APRIL 1946

In Memory of Franklin Delano Roosevelt, an orchestral elegy by Bernard ROGERS, is performed by the New York Philharmonic, Rodzinski conducting, on the eve of the first anniversary of Roosevelt's death.

20 APRIL 1946

Deirdre of the Sorrows, the first Canadian grand opera, dealing with a Celtic love triangle in Ulster *ca.* A.D. 1, composed by Healey WILLAN, himself an Ulster Celt, is given in a world première by the Canadian Broadcasting Corporation in Toronto.

5 MAY 1946

Second Symphony in A major by Douglas MOORE, in the classical four movements, "an attempt to write in clear objective modified classical style, with emphasis on rhythmic and melodic momentum," with "no underlying program, although the second movement was suggested by a short poem of James Joyce," is performed for the first time anywhere by the Paris Radio Orchestra, Robert Lawrence conducting.

8 MAY 1946

The Medium, dramatic opera by Gian-Carlo MENOTTI to his own libretto dealing with a fake medium who suddenly feels the physical touch of otherworldly limbs and goes berserk, killing her deaf-mute assistant, with music in a highly effective neo-Puccinian style, with some extra modernities thrown in to heighten the tension, is performed for the first time in New York. (In January 1948, the National Spiritualist Association protested against a Chicago production of *The Medium,* claiming that it would "serve to discredit honest and sincere mediums of the Spiritualist Religion at the time of its 100th birthday")

10 MAY 1946

Serpent Heart, ballet with music by Samuel BARBER and choreography by Martha Graham to a Freudianistically mythological story of possessive and destructive love "which feeds upon itself like a serpent heart," with the principal characters symbolically listed as One Like Medea, and One Like Jason, is performed for the first time at the opening program of the Second Annual Festival of Contemporary American Music at Columbia University. (A symphonic suite from *Serpent Heart* was performed for the first time on 5 December 1947 by the Philadelphia Orchestra, Ormandy conducting, under the title *Medea*)

17 MAY 1946

Petite Symphonie Concertante for harp, cembalo, piano and two small string orchestras by the 55-year-old Swiss composer Frank MARTIN in four movements, conceived in an elegantly neo-classical style, with the application of a modified twelve-tone technique in melodic construction, coloristically vivified by touches of impressionistic azure, is performed for the first time by the orchestra of the Collegium Musicum in Zurich, Paul Sacher conducting.

20 MAY 1946

Lazare SAMINSKY conducts in New York the first performance of his *Requiem,* composed in memory of his wife, who was a poet and novelist.

1 JUNE 1946

Leo SLEZAK, Wagnerian tenor and screen comedian, whose witticisms made comic history in Vienna (once when the mechanical swan in the last act of *Lohengrin* departed without waiting for him, Slezak inquired in a matter-of-fact way, "When does the next swan leave?") , dies on his estate in Egern on Lake Tegernsee in his seventy-third year.

21 JUNE 1946

Heinrich KAMINSKI, German composer of neo-Lutheran choral music and instrumental works written in a severe manner of modern Germanic counterpoint, dies at Ried near Benediktbeuern, two weeks before his sixtieth birthday.

21 JUNE 1946

Vergilii Aeneis, heroic symphony for voices and orchestra, by Francesco MALIPIERO, is performed for the first time in Turin.

7 JULY 1946

After four years of interruption because of war, the International Society for Contemporary Music resumes its annual activities with the opening of the twentieth Festival in London with the following program of orchestral music :

Stadtpfeifermusik by Richard MOHAUPT, a gay utilitarian score of town piper's music; *Three Symphonic Preludes* by Elizabeth LUTYENS; *Piano Concerto* by Robert DE ROOS of Holland; *Second Symphony* by Elsa BARRAINE of France; and *Ode to the End of War* by Serge PROKOFIEV.

8 JULY 1946

The second concert of the twentieth ISCM Festival in London presents the following program:

Fifth String Quartet by Jerzy FITELBERG; *Sonatina* for clarinet and piano by the Swiss impressionist Albert MOESCHINGER; *Songs from Captivity* for chorus and percussion by Luigi DALLAPICCOLA; *Sonata* for two pianos by STRAVINSKY (first performed on 8 August 1944 at a "Concert with Commentaries" given

by Nadia Boulanger at Indiana University) ; and *String Quartet* in E-flat by
Paul HINDEMITH.

10 JULY 1946

The third concert of the twentieth ISCM Festival in London is
given in the following program:

Seventh String Quartet by Ernst KRENEK; *Suite* for violin and piano by Jozef
ZAVADIL of Czechoslovakia; *Quatuor pour la Fin du Temps* for clarinet, cello
and piano by Olivier MESSIAEN; and *Ode to Napoleon* for reciter, string quartet and piano by SCHOENBERG.

12 JULY 1946

The fourth concert of the twentieth ISCM Festival in London is
presented in the following program:

Symphony for String Orchestra by William SCHUMAN; *Five Folk-Tunes* for
children's voices and instruments by Andrzej PANUFNIK of Poland; *Cantata*
for soprano, chorus and orchestra by Anton VON WEBERN; and *Divertimento
No. 2* for string orchestra and solo trumpet by Tibor HARSÁNYI.

12 JULY 1946

The Rape of Lucretia, non-Shakespearian opera in two acts of
two scenes each, by Britain's most successful twentieth-century
opera composer Benjamin BRITTEN, to the libretto of a French
version of the celebrated rape case of 509 B.C., and the first presentation of a woman's violation on the operatic or any other
stage (with an outspoken dialogue containing such lines as "let
me rise to my first sepulchre, which is your thighs . . . give me
my birth again out of your loins of pain," and warnings of the
female chorus: "Go, Tarquinius, before your nearness tempts
Lucretia to yield to your strong maleness") , with an economically
reduced chamber opera score for eight singers and seventeen solo
instruments, conceived in a characteristically Brittenish manner
wherein elements of atonal expressionism are cunningly fused
with statically pedal-pointed tonal polyharmonies, and dramatic
directness is secured by emphatic but spaciously measured rhythmic propulsion, is produced for the first time at the Glyndebourne Festival in England.

14 JULY 1946

The fifth concert of the twentieth Festival of the ISCM is given in London in the following program:

Cortèges for orchestra by Alan RAWSTHORNE; *Nocturne* for orchestra by Raymond LOUCHEUR of France; *Violin Concerto* by Roman PALESTER; *Concerto for Orchestra* by Béla BARTÓK.

21 JULY 1946

Sunday in Brooklyn, a gay orchestral piece of sabbatical music by the Brooklyn composer Elie SIEGMEISTER, is performed on an NBC broadcast.

21 JULY 1946

Paul ROSENFELD, "Happy voyager in the arts," American writer and keen appraiser of musical values, dies in New York at the age of fifty-six.

25 JULY 1946

GRETCHANINOV becomes an American citizen.

2 AUGUST 1946

Ernst KURTH, Viennese music scholar who promulgated a cogent theory of linear counterpoint which deeply influenced musicians in Germany, Russia, and elsewhere, dies at the age of sixty in Berne, Switzerland, where he settled in 1912.

12 AUGUST 1946

The Mikado, flippant operetta by GILBERT and SULLIVAN, making fun of Japan's Emperor-worship, and heretofore taboo in Japan, is produced for the first time in Tokyo by the Special Services Detachment of General Headquarters of the American Army of Occupation, with a new overture on oriental themes written by Klaus PRINGSHEIM, German musician long resident in Japan, who also supplied some new music for the entrance of the Mikado in the second act. (The first performance was scheduled for 22 July 1946, and the *New York Times* and other newspapers actually reported it as having taken place on that date, but the première

had to be postponed because of hot weather which made the
wearing of heavy ceremonial robes uncomfortable)

"Previous to beginning production, there was considerable discussion as to
the propriety of doing the operetta. Permission was finally obtained and production was begun in May 1946. The principals were all members of the
United States Armed Forces with the exception of the women's roles which
were sung by the Civilian Actress Technicians, American women employed in
the Special Services Soldier Show Program. In the chorus all the first tenors
and basses were American. With the exception of two, the women's chorus of
nineteen was entirely Japanese, professionals from the Japanese Victor Recording Company. The Corps de Ballet was entirely Japanese, trained in
authentic Japanese dance patterns. Sixteen performances were given and the
show closed on 25 August. . . . At no time was any performance open to the
Japanese public. However, on 11 August at 10 a.m. a dress rehearsal was
held. Invitations and passes were issued to one hundred and eleven Japanese
artists, singers, theater producers, newspaper editors and columnists. These
were the only Japanese authorized at any time to see *The Mikado.*" (From a
letter, dated 14 May 1948, to the author from Gerald J. Cameron, Executive
Officer of the Entertainment & Recreation Branch of the United States Army)

17 AUGUST 1946

Symphonie Liturgique by Arthur HONEGGER, in three movements subtitled *Dies Irae* (in apocalyptically strident chromatics,
devoid of any thematic allusion to the traditional chant, with
giant intervallic strides suggesting an atonal Doomsday); *De
Profundis Clamavi* (in dejected low tones, tortuously and tortur-
ously rising to shrill heights of polytonal anxiety); and *Dona
Nobis Pacem* (an imploring prayer for peace, against the rumble
of distant drums of war, with a diatonic hopefulness dashed
again and again by chromatic bursts of despair), is performed
for the first time in Zurich under the direction of Charles Münch,
to whom the score is dedicated.

18 AUGUST 1946

Corrobboree, suite from the primitivistic ballet by the 42-year-old
Australian composer John ANTILL, representing in its four sections the ceremonial dances of antipodean aborigines: (1) Welcome Ceremony (2) Dance to the Evening Star (3) Rain Dance

(4) Procession of Totems and Fire Ceremony, is performed for the first time by the Sydney Symphony Orchestra, Goossens conducting. (The American première of *Corrobboree* was given by Goossens with the Cincinnati Symphony Orchestra on 23 November 1946)

3 SEPTEMBER 1946

Moriz ROSENTHAL, the "little giant" of the piano, and the one but last (the last being the Portuguese pianist da Motta, who died on 31 May 1948) pupil of Liszt, dies in New York at the age of eighty-three.

3 SEPTEMBER 1946

Missouri Suite for string orchestra by the Missouri-born Richard DU PAGE in four picturesque movements: *Little Dixie, City Life, Swampeast* and *Hill Country*, is performed for the first time at the Saratoga Spa Music Festival.

4 SEPTEMBER 1946

Paul LINCKE, composer of numerous Germanic operettas and a perennial of semi-classical music, *The Glow Worm*, dies at Klausthal-Sellerfeld, near Goettingen, in his eightieth year.

9 SEPTEMBER 1946

Little Symphony for String Orchestra by Richard HAGGERTY, written in an effectively neo-Prokofievian mold, is performed for the first time at the Saratoga Spa Music Festival.

27 SEPTEMBER 1946

The Cracow Philharmonic presents the first performance of two Polish works: *Second Symphony* by the Parisian-trained Boleslaw WOYTOWICZ, and *Concerto for String Orchestra* by the 42-year-old neo-Polonist, Tadeusz KASSERN, in four classically built movements, written in a trenchantly fugal style with generous cadenzas for the soloists in each section.

7 OCTOBER 1946

Two centuries have elapsed since the birth in Boston of William
BILLINGS, the first professionally competent American composer
who created the new art of "fuguing tunes" (which gave rise,
through an imaginative misspelling, to "fudging" tunes of the
hill country in Kentucky and Tennessee).

8 OCTOBER 1946

Heitor VILLA-LOBOS conducts in Rio de Janeiro the first performances of his *Piano Concerto, Fantasia* for cello and orchestra, and
the tone-poem *Madonna* (composed in 1945 for the Koussevitzky Music Foundation; it had its first American performance
on 26 December 1947 by the Boston Symphony Orchestra).

8 OCTOBER 1946

RCA Victor presses its billionth recording: John Philip SOUSA's
Stars and Stripes Forever.

10 OCTOBER 1946

Musique de Table by the French composer Manuel ROSENTHAL,
written in 1942 as the ironic expression of an irrepressible desire
for unobtainable food delicacies, with eight sections marked by
names of a paradisiacally yummy menu: (1) *Salade russe* (2)
Eels in Red Wine (3) *Quenelles lyonnaise* (4) *Beef Tenderloin*
(5) *Mixed Fresh Vegetables* (6) *Loin of Venison* (7) *Salade de
saison* and (8) *Fromage de montagne,* all set to music impressionistically suggestive of anticipatory salivation, but becoming
quite raucous in depicting more substantial foods, is performed
for the first time in America by the New York Philharmonic,
Rodzinski conducting.

11 OCTOBER 1946

Fifty years have elapsed since the death in Vienna of the frustrated genius of Wagnerian symphonism, Anton BRUCKNER.

16 OCTOBER 1946

Sir Granville BANTOCK, English composer of brobdingnagian oratorios in lilliputianly orthodox harmonies, such as *Omar Khayyam* in three huge sections, and an unfinished set of twenty-four symphonic poems to Southey's *Curse of Kehama* (only two were written), dies in London at the age of seventy-eight.

18 OCTOBER 1946

Third Symphony by Aaron COPLAND in four movements, each characterizing a definite mood: (1) *Molto moderato,* with simple expression (2) *Allegro molto* (3) *Andantino quasi allegretto* (4) *Molto deliberato* (Fanfare) ; *allegro risoluto* (the opening fanfare in the finale being derived from Copland's *Fanfare for the Common Man*) , the whole representing the measured maturity of Copland's creative mind (which led Virgil Thomson to write an editorial "Copland as a Great Man") , and cast in the idiom of absolute music so that "any reference to jazz or folk material is purely unconscious," is performed for the first time by the Boston Symphony Orchestra, Koussevitzky conducting.

22 OCTOBER 1946

Sinfonietta by the Belgian composer Marcel POOT, a member of seven Belgian musicians who call themselves *Synthétistes,* whose music is a synthesized product of classical forms and modern devices, is performed for the first time anywhere by the Chicago Symphony Orchestra, Defauw conducting.

24 OCTOBER 1946

At the Ballet Theater in New York, Leonard BERNSTEIN conducts his *Facsimile,* a chortlingly neurotic ballet with rambunctiously modernistic music to an existentialistically ironic story of intermingled passions and mutual frustrations of two men and one woman.

25 OCTOBER 1946

Three days before the fiftieth birthday of Howard Hanson, the

American composer and director of the Eastman School of Music
in Rochester, hospitable incubator and launching platform for
hundreds of young American composers, a symphonic tribute by
Roy HARRIS ("a confrère who had himself benefited greatly from
Hanson's generosity toward his contemporaries") based on a
theme from Hanson's *Third Symphony*, and entitled *Celebration*,
with a fanciful harmonization of *Happy Birthday to You* in a
brassy coda, is performed by the Boston Symphony Orchestra,
Koussevitzky conducting.

30 OCTOBER 1946

Concerto for violoncello and orchestra by Aram KHATCHATURIAN,
written in an unabashedly chromatic style, with orientalistic passage work, is performed for the first time in Moscow.

2 NOVEMBER 1946

Fantasy on Down East Spirituals by Arthur SHEPHERD, "an excursion into the realm of American folk tunes," making use specifically of the following, "Experience," "The End of the World,"
"Last Trumpet," and "Sweet Messenger," is performed for the
first time by the Indianapolis Symphony Orchestra, Sevitzky conducting.

5 NOVEMBER 1946

Sigismond STOJOWSKI, 77-year-old Polish pianist and teacher (he
was born on 14 May 1869, not 1870, as all dictionaries have it),
dies in New York, where he had lived for forty years.

10 NOVEMBER 1946

Second Symphony by Eugene GOOSSENS is performed for the first
time by the BBC in London.

13 NOVEMBER 1946

Pantomime by Lukas Foss, written originally as a ballet, with the
simple harmonic foundation of shifting major triads as a genera-

tor of principal thematic patterns, is performed for the first time by the Baltimore Symphony Orchestra, Reginald Stewart conducting.

14 NOVEMBER 1946

Fifth Symphony by Guy ROPARTZ, 82-year-old French composer of pleasantly Franckian music, is performed for the first time in Paris, Charles Münch conducting.

14 NOVEMBER 1946

Manuel DE FALLA, great Spanish composer of tensely hispanic music with percussive undertones of orgiastic polyrhythmy, dies nine days before his seventieth birthday at Alta Gracia, Argentina, where he settled in 1938.

15 NOVEMBER 1946

On his first visit to the United States, Zoltán KODÁLY, foremost living composer of Hungary, conducts the Pittsburgh Symphony Orchestra in his *Dances of Galanta,* written in a neo-Magyar manner, with rhythm and color reflecting the spirit of native folk songs.

18 NOVEMBER 1946

Ode to the Milky Way by the ambimusical symphonic Broadwayist, Vladimir DUKELSKY, "a kind of musical monologue of a man stretched out on the deck of a transport and looking up at the Milky Way" (assuming there is no moon), is performed for the first time by the New York City Symphony Orchestra, Leonard Bernstein conducting.

22 NOVEMBER 1946

Third Piano Concerto by Ernst KRENEK in five movements, in which the piano is used antiphonally with various sections of the orchestra, and cast in an enhanced tonality, without the application of the twelve-tone system adopted by Krenek for the past decade and a half, with some experimental effects (at one point the soloist silently presses down on the keys and plays glissandos on the strings inside the piano) , and occasional digressions into jazz, is performed for the first time anywhere by the Minneapolis Symphony Orchestra, played and conducted from memory by Dimitri Mitropoulos.

24 NOVEMBER 1946

Seventeen days before his seventieth birthday Alfonso Broqua, Uruguayan composer of operas and songs in a sensitively Hispano-American manner, dies in Paris where he had settled in 1903.

27 NOVEMBER 1946

Nicolas Lopatnikov plays the piano part in the world première of his *Second Piano Concerto,* with the CBS Symphony Orchestra, Berezowsky conducting.

28 NOVEMBER 1946

Second Concerto for violoncello and orchestra by Darius Mil-haud, in three mood movements: (1) *Gai* (2) *Tendre* (3) *Alerte,* is performed for the first time by the New York Philharmonic, Rodzinski conducting, Edmund Kurtz, soloist.

29 NOVEMBER 1946

Camargo Guarnieri (who does not use his given middle name Mozart, feeling that it would be presumptuous) , Brazilian composer of colorful music in native rhythms, conducts the Boston Symphony Orchestra in the world première of his *Symphony* in three movements, marked, according to mood, tempo and design: (1) *Rude* (2) *Profundo* (3) *Radioso,* of which the first is close to sonata form, the second is thematically developed from ecclesiastical chants tinged with Brazilian tone colors, and the third reflects the melorhythmic figures of folk songs in northeast Brazil.

5 DECEMBER 1946

On his first visit to the United States, Manuel Rosenthal, French composer of epicurean orchestral pieces, conducts the New York

Philharmonic in a program featuring his own gustatorily color-istic *Fête du Vin* (originally written for the Paris Exposition of 1937 as a musical tribute to French wines), his orchestration of Lully's *Noces Villageoises,* and *Piano Concerto* by Henri BAR-RAUD, E. Robert Schmitz, soloist.

6 DECEMBER 1946

Maximilian STEINBERG, Russian composer of finely wrought vocal and symphonic music, son-in-law of Rimsky-Korsakov, and for many years director of the Leningrad Conservatory, and teacher of a generation of new Russian composers, among them Shosta-kovitch, dies in Leningrad at the age of sixty-three.

9 DECEMBER 1946

Joaquín NÍN-CULMELL, Berlin-born Cuban composer, plays the piano in the world première of his *Concerto* for piano and or-chestra, with the Rochester Philharmonic, at Williamstown, Mas-sachusetts.

11 DECEMBER 1946

Sérénade à Angelique by Arthur HONEGGER, a fanciful sketch for small orchestra wherein a declaration of love for Angélique, pro-pounded by a solo trombone *cantabile,* is scornfully spurned in a discordant objurgation, is performed for the first time by the Paris Radio Orchestra.

13 DECEMBER 1946

First Symphony by the internationally celebrated pianist and pedagogue Artur SCHNABEL in four movements: (1) *Molto mode-rato* (2) *Vivace* (3) *Largo con devozione e solennità* (4) *Allegro molto e con brio,* cast in an uncompromisingly atonal idiom of dissonant counterpoint with the main themes containing tone-rows of non-repeated notes (in one theme as many as eleven), but stopping short of the twelve-tone system (Schnabel has stated that his *Symphony* "is in no way related" to that system), is per-formed for the first time by the Minneapolis Symphony Orchestra, Mitropoulos conducting, and preceded, to assuage the audience in advance, by an unquestionably classical rendition by Schnabel of Beethoven's *Fourth Piano Concerto.*

13 DECEMBER 1946

Three Cyprus Serenades, orchestral triptych by the Cyprus-born American composer Anis FULEIHAN, marked by Hellenistically expressive melorhythms, "without the addition of too much mustard," is performed for the first time by the Philadelphia Orchestra, Ormandy conducting.

14 DECEMBER 1946

During the celebration of the 800th anniversary of the foundation of Moscow, a patriotic cantata, *Moscow,* by Vissarion SHEBALIN, scored for soloists, mixed chorus, orchestra, organ and church bells, designed in a grand style of Russian homophony in massive sonorities, glorifying, in its five movements, the city of Moscow and its people ("seven times seven roads, seven times seven blue rivers, the whole earth's pathway, the whole earth's fame, honor and glory from century to century, all lead, all have come to the wondrous city of Moscow") is performed at the Moscow Conservatory.

17 DECEMBER 1946

An artists' tribunal in Berlin acquits Germany's No. 1 orchestral conductor Wilhelm FURTWAENGLER of the taint of Hitlerism.

"What kept me in Germany was my anxiety to preserve German music in its integrity. I could not do that from abroad. When Thomas Mann asks, 'How can Beethoven be played in Himmler's Germany,' I reply: 'Where was the music of Beethoven more needed than in Himmler's Germany?' I could not, therefore, quit Germany in her hour of greatest need, and I do not regret not having done so." (From Furtwaengler's statement to the press)

19 DECEMBER 1946

Norman DELLO JOIO, New York-born composer of Neapolitan extraction, plays, with the New York Philharmonic Orchestra,

Szell conducting, the piano part in the world première of his *Ricercari* in three movements, characterized by acrid neo-classicism and rhythmic verve, alluding to the original etymology of the title, from *ricercare,* to search.

20 DECEMBER 1946

Darius MILHAUD conducts the Boston Symphony Orchestra in the world première of his *Second Symphony* in five movements descriptive of the quality of mood rather than tempo or form: (1) *Paisible* (pacific, despite some belligerent activities of the piccolo and the trumpet), (2) *Mystérieux* (with some tonal hugger-mugger high up in the violins), (3) *Douloureux* (in which ineffable sadness is roared in *fff*), (4) *Avec Sérénité* (in jig time) and (5) *Allélouia* (a fugal finale with ecclesiastical undertones).

21 DECEMBER 1946

Minstrel Show by Morton GOULD, "a musical impression of the old minstrel tunes," with characteristic slide trombone and banjo effects, plus sandpaper blocks to imitate a soft-shoe dance, is performed for the first time by the Indianapolis Symphony, Sevitzky conducting.

22 DECEMBER 1946

A Bell Overture by Gardner READ, an essay in bell sonorities, from the tubular chimes to Russian sleighbells, with an additional assortment of ethereal clinks in the celesta and attenuated flageolet tones in the harp, is performed for the first time by the Cleveland Orchestra, Ringwall conducting.

27 DECEMBER 1946

Charles Münch, Alsatian conductor, makes his American debut with the Boston Symphony Orchestra (of which he is conductor-elect as of October 1949), conducting a program of French music including *Sonata a due* by Maurice JAUBERT, who lost his life in the last days of French military resistance, on 19 June 1940;

ROUSSEL's *Bacchus et Ariane;* HONEGGER's *Symphony for String Orchestra* (which is his *Second Symphony,* premièred by the Basel Chamber Orchestra on 23 May 1942), and SAINT-SAENS' *Third Symphony.*

28 DECEMBER 1946

Carrie Jacobs BOND, 84-year-old widow who stirred American hearts with artlessly sentimental ditties such as *The End of a Perfect Day,* which she published herself on borrowed money, and which sold over five million copies, dies in Glendale, California, and is buried in the Forest Lawn Memorial Court of Honor, Hollywood's Westminster Abbey.

30 DECEMBER 1946

Charles Wakefield CADMAN, American composer of melodious songs of which *At Dawning,* originally rejected by fourteen publishers, became a perennial semi-classical best-seller, and also of some pentatonically Indian music, dies in Los Angeles six days after his sixty-fifth birthday.

1947

7 JANUARY 1947

L'Oro, opera by Ildebrando PIZZETTI, has its world première at La Scala in Milan.

9 JANUARY 1947

Second Symphony by Roger SESSIONS in four movements, with these tempo indications (serving as clues to "what is sometimes called the emotional content") : (1) *Molto agitato; Tranquillo e misterioso; Molto agitato* (2) *Allegretto capriccioso* (3) *Adagio, tranquillo ed espressivo* (4) *Allegramente,* dedicated to the mem-

ory of President Roosevelt, and written in a highly charged harmonic, contrapuntal and rhythmic idiom (as much a challenge
to untutored ears as Roosevelt's political ideas were a challenge
to horse-and-buggy minds), is performed for the first time anywhere by the San Francisco Symphony Orchestra, Monteux conducting.

9 JANUARY 1947

Street Scene, a dramatic folk opera to the play by Elmer Rice,
with music by Kurt WEILL portraying in idiomatically functional
tones the life in a New York tenement district, is produced in
New York.

11 JANUARY 1947

The Warrior, opera by Bernard ROGERS, "a drama in which the
characters speak musically," to the Biblical story of Samson and
Delilah, cast in an advanced non-operatic style midway between
the impressionism of Debussy and atonalism of the Viennese
school, is produced by the Metropolitan Opera in New York, the
first opera by an American-born composer at the Metropolitan
since the production of *Peter Ibbetson* by Deems Taylor in 1931.

18 JANUARY 1947

Prairie Legend, "a midwestern set" by Elie SIEGMEISTER, "inspired
by the quietness and simple beauty of endless fields and the
black earth," is performed for the first time in its entirety by the
New York Philharmonic, Stokowski conducting. (The second
part, *Harvest Evening,* was performed on 29 December 1946 by
the New York Philharmonic, Stokowski conducting)

21 JANUARY 1947

Paul Sacher conducts the Basel Chamber Orchestra in a gala
concert on the occasion of the twentieth anniversary of its formation, in a program featuring world premières of three works especially written for it:

Toccata e due Canzoni by Bohuslav MARTINU; *Concerto in D* for string orchestra in three movements, *Vivace, Arioso, Rondo,* by STRAVINSKY, in his

austerest chiaroscuro manner; and the *Fourth Symphony* by Arthur HONEGGER, subtitled, to honor the occasion, *Deliciae Basilienses,* conceived in a tonal atmosphere of intimate and folksy charm, in three movements: (1) *Lento misterioso,* in subdued colors of a meaningful instrumental confabulation (2) *Larghetto,* built upon a freely modified rustic Swiss tune "Z'Basel an mim Rhy" and (3) *Allegro-Finale,* a rhythmic tripartite Rondo, Passacaglia, and Fugue, eventuating in a fife fanfare, with a coda of six measures of barely audible chorale.

21 JANUARY 1947

The Denver Symphony Orchestra, Saul Caston conducting, with Johana Harris and Max Lanner, pianists, gives the world premi-ère of the *Concerto* for two pianos and orchestra by Roy HARRIS, divided into three movements: (1) *Toccata,* written to exploit "the technical resources of the piano" (2) *Variations on a Cho-rale,* in which "the variation style is treated in such a way as to knit the whole work together into a large, expanding, organic form" and (3) *Dance,* in the form of a freely-designed double fugue.

26 JANUARY 1947

Grace MOORE, operatic star of America and Europe, is killed in an airplane crash two minutes after the takeoff from Copenhagen on a flight to Stockholm.

28 JANUARY 1947

The Birthday of the Infanta, suite in seven sections to Oscar Wilde's sentimentally sophisticated tale, by the Italian neo-ro-mantic composer Mario CASTELNUOVO-TEDESCO, now living in Hollywood, is performed for the first time by the New Orleans Symphony, Freccia conducting.

28 JANUARY 1947

Reynaldo HAHN, Venezuela-born, Paris-bred composer of pleas-ingly impressionistic stage music, dies in Paris in his seventy-second year.

2 FEBRUARY 1947

Symphonia Serena by Paul HINDEMITH in four movements, in-cluding a paraphrase of an obscure Beethoven march, a colloquy between two sections of a string orchestra, a recitative in which one violin plays backstage, and a multithematic finale, is performed for the first time as a commissioned work by the Dallas Symphony Orchestra, Antal Dorati conducting.

3 FEBRUARY 1947

Artur RODZINSKI resigns in a huff from his post as conductor of the New York Philharmonic in protest against the monopolistic policies of the manager Arthur Judson, and shortly afterwards accepts an appointment as conductor of the Chicago Symphony Orchestra, without a formal contract, stating to the press: "I know I will be able to work with them without conflict, and that is something that was not always true of my association with the Philharmonic."

9 FEBRUARY 1947

Concerto in D for violin and orchestra by the whilom bad-boy of music, George ANTHEIL, and now a reformed composer of acceptable music, is performed for the first time anywhere by the Dallas Symphony, Dorati conducting.

15 FEBRUARY 1947

Violin Concerto in D major in three movements by Erich Wolfgang KORNGOLD, who in his *Wunderkind* days early in the century was hailed as a new Mozart (his given name Wolfgang symbolizes this kinship), is given its première by Jascha Heifetz and the St. Louis Symphony Orchestra, Golschmann conducting.

"The work was contemplated for a Caruso of the violin rather than for a Paganini. It is needless to say how delighted I am to have my *Concerto* performed by Caruso and Paganini in one person: Jascha Heifetz." (From the composer's statement)

16 FEBRUARY 1947

Morton GOULD, composer of semi-classical hits as well as symphonic non-hits, conducts the Dallas Symphony Orchestra in the première of his *Third Symphony,* completed on 27 January 1947 (the composer notes on the manuscript: "including diapering and

taking care of Ricky") , in four variegated movements, with principal motto-themes derived from a pre-determined intervallic
pattern, the instrumentation emphasizing extreme contrasts
(such as a conspicuous bass drum antithetically employed in episodes featuring the flutes) , and the mood ranging from rhapsodic
and intense to affable waltztime to sardonic humor to fugal
austerity. (The last movement was completely revised as a passacaglia, and the new version performed for the first time by the
New York Philharmonic, Mitropoulos conducting, on 28 October
1948)

18 FEBRUARY 1947

Gian-Carlo MENOTTI conducts in New York the première of his
one-act opera *The Telephone,* to his own libretto, subtitled
L'Amour à trois, the third actor of the triangle being the telephone itself (which raucously rings every time the timorously
amorous suitor is about to open his mouth, until he decides to
propose by telephone from the corner drugstore) , set to a neo-
Mozartian score pleasingly modernized by palatable non-har-
monic tones. (A revised version of Menotti's companion opera
The Medium, originally produced on 8 May 1946, was performed
on the same bill)

19 FEBRUARY 1947

Robert Russell BENNETT conducts the Knoxville Symphony Orchestra in the first performance of his *A Dry Weather Legend,* a
folksy piece for flute and orchestra (with the regular conductor
Lamar Stringfield acting as flutist) , to a West Virginia tale of a
rabbit barred from drinking water from a well he refused to help
dig.

27 FEBRUARY 1947

Concerto for Piano and Orchestra by Paul HINDEMITH, completed on 29 November 1945, in three movements, of which the
last is a medley on a medieval dance, *Tre Fontane,* written in a
characteristic manner of eclectic neo-classicism, basically tonal
but sonorously reinforced by chromatic progressions, is performed

for the first time by the Cleveland Orchestra, Szell conducting, Sanromá, soloist.

27 FEBRUARY 1947

Third Symphony by the 24-year-old Pennsylvanian, Peter MEN-NIN, in the classical three movements, with a vimful first and vigorous third movement contrasted with lyrical "voice-weaving" in the slow middle movement, is performed for the first time by the New York Philharmonic, Walter Hendl conducting.

5 MARCH 1947

Alfredo CASELLA, scholarly animator of new Italian music, cultured composer of expertly constructed symphonic poems in a modernistically vernacular vein, and penetrating analyst of old and new musical civilizations, dies in Rome at the age of sixtyfour.

7 MARCH 1947

Symphony in B-flat by Mark BRUNSWICK in three movements, emphatically tonal but couched in the idiom of strongly dissonant counterpoint, is performed for the first time by the Minneapolis Symphony Orchestra, Mitropoulos conducting.

7 MARCH 1947

The Song of Songs, biblical "solo cantata" by Lukas Foss to text from the Song of Solomon, in four sections, (1) *Awake, O North Wind* (2) *Come, My Beloved* (3) *By Night on My Bed* and (4) *Set Me as a Seal Upon Thine Heart,* cast in an idiom of neo-ecclesiastical modernity, with fugal elements and arioso forms in free alternation with recitative, is performed for the first time by the Boston Symphony Orchestra, Koussevitzky conducting, Ellabelle Davis, Negro soprano (to whom the work is dedicated), soloist.

11 MARCH 1947

First Symphony by Cecil EFFINGER of Colorado, in three connected movements, the first in variation form, the second a scherzo, and the last a fugue, with musical material derived from the protracted melody of the opening, with lyrical digressions mitigating and edulcorating the austerity of strongly woven polyharmony, is performed for the first time by the Denver Symphony Orchestra, Saul Caston conducting.

15 MARCH 1947

Twenty-fifth Symphony by Nicolas MIASKOVSKY is performed for the first time in Moscow.

19 MARCH 1947

Minotaur, ballet by the pandiatonically-minded neo-classicist Elliott CARTER, is produced by Ballet Society in New York.

19 MARCH 1947

Willem PIJPER, Dutch composer of coloristic symphonies and impressionistic chamber music, dies at Leidschendam in his fifty-third year.

21 MARCH 1947

Robert CASADESUS plays the piano part in the world première by the Minneapolis Symphony Orchestra, Mitropoulos conducting, of his *Concerto in E Major* in three classical movements, with pleasurably titillatory disharmonies spicing an otherwise traditional pianistic score.

1 APRIL 1947

Europa und der Stier, opera by a mythical Siegfried SITZPLATZ, conjured up by simultaneous playing of different phonograph records in heteroousian disharmony with singing commercials, is presented "for the first and last time" on April Fool's Day by radio station WQXR in New York.

11 APRIL 1947

The Santa Fe Time Table for mixed chorus *a cappella* by Ernst KRENEK, to a text monodically intoning the names of railroad stations on the Santa Fe Railroad, from Albuquerque to Los

Angeles, is performed for the first time at the University of Chicago, along with first performances of Krenek's *Trio* for violin, clarinet and piano; *Sonata* for unaccompanied viola; *Violin Sonata;* and his *Seventh String Quartet,* with the composer officiating as pianist and conductor.

18 APRIL 1947

The Trial of Lucullus, one-act opera by Roger SESSIONS to the text of a radio play by Bertolt Brecht symbolizing the defeated pride of a dictatorial aggressor, with the music delineating in sharp accents and strong dissonant counterpoint the characters on the stage, is produced for the first time at the University of California in Berkeley.

26 APRIL 1947

Symphony in A by John POWELL is performed for the first time by the Detroit Symphony Orchestra, Krueger conducting.

1 MAY 1947

Violin Concerto by Herbert INCH is performed for the first time by the Rochester Philharmonic, Hanson conducting, Jacques Gordon, soloist.

1 MAY 1947

A three-day Symposium on Music Criticism opens at Harvard University, established "to help the new army of listeners by providing them with a greater number of competent guides," and "to initiate a fundamental reexamination of the principles of music criticism," with speeches by eminent writers on music, and first performances of commissioned works: *Third String Quartet* by Walter PISTON; *String Trio,* op. 45, in one movement, by Arnold SCHOENBERG; *Sixth String Quartet* by Bohuslav MARTINU.

2 MAY 1947

On the second day of the Harvard Symposium on Music Criticism three choral works are presented for the first time: *Appare-*

bit Repentina Dies, a setting to a medieval poem, for mixed chorus and brasses by Paul HINDEMITH; *La Terra,* after Virgil's Georgics, for chorus and organ by Francesco MALIPIERO; and *In the Beginning,* to the words from Genesis, for mezzo-soprano and chorus by Aaron COPLAND.

3 MAY 1947

The Harvard Symposium of Music Criticism is concluded with appropriately musicophilic speeches, and a dance program by Martha Graham featuring the première of *Night Journey,* a Freudianistic ballet dealing with incestuous involvement in a mirifically dextrorse umbilical cord, to a metamusically contrived score by William SCHUMAN piquantly spiced with eruptively accented disharmonies.

5 MAY 1947

Charles IVES, unique American composer who anticipated the modern harmonic and rhythmic idioms of the twentieth century long before their reputed protagonists, receives belated recognition in the form of the Pulitzer Prize, awarded to him for his *Third Symphony,* written thirty-six years before, and first performed in New York on 5 April 1946 by the New York Little Symphony, Lou Harrison conducting.

7 MAY 1947

The Mother of Us All, opera in three acts and eight scenes by the subtle symphonizer of sophisticated simplicities, Virgil THOMSON, to a text by Gertrude Stein (she called the work, before a single note was put on music paper, "the greatest American tragic opera"), outlining the life story of the American pioneer of women's suffrage, Susan B. Anthony, and miscechronistically lumping together such assorted personalities as Lillian Russell, Ulysses S. Grant, Daniel Webster, as well as two characters designated as Gertrude S. and Virgil T., supposed to "supply comment and interpretation," with a musical score abounding in sublimated melodic Americanisms ("jamais de banalité, le plus possible de lieux communs," as the composer put it), is produced for the first time at Columbia University in New York, Otto Luening conducting.

12 MAY 1947

At the opening concert of the Third Annual Festival of Contemporary American Music at Columbia University, Nicolai BERE-ZOWSKY conducts the première of his oratorio *Gilgamesh,* musical setting of a Babylonian poem inscribed on clay tablets in 1750 B.C. and recounting the tale of liberal King Gilgamesh who refused to appease a Sumerian dictator, scored for orchestra, chorus, four solo singers and a narrator, and pitched to a tense neo-primitivistic expressiveness perilously close to the ripping of the tonal seams of the tempered system.

25 MAY 1947

Johannes WOLF, the great German musical medievalist, dies at the age of seventy-eight in Munich (his unique library of documents and copies of medieval manuscripts was destroyed in Berlin in an air raid on 22 November 1943).

29 MAY 1947

The twenty-first Festival of the International Society for Contemporary Music opens in Copenhagen with the following program of symphonic music:

Fifth Symphony by the 37-year-old Dane, Vagn HOLMBOE; *Variations Symphoniques* by the 53-year-old Belgian, Jean ABSIL (conceived as a monothematic symphony in three parts and twelve variations); *Concerto for String Orchestra* by Sweden's most productive composer, Hilding ROSENBERG; *De Profundis* by Vitezslav NOVÁK (first performed in Brno on 20 November 1941 as a mute lamentation over the sufferings of Czechoslovakia); and *Galdres-latten,* symphonic dance by the Norwegian, Harald SAEVERUD, inspired, according to the composer's statement, by the incredibly potent spirit of his great-grandfather who was a village fiddler and maker of fiddles.

31 MAY 1947

At the second concert of the twenty-first ISCM Festival in Copenhagen the following program of chamber music is presented:

Second String Quartet in one movement by the Swiss neo-medievalist, Willy Burkhard; *Toccata* for two pianos by Anton Heiller of Vienna; *Trio for Two Violins and Viola* by Gyorgy Kósa of Hungary; *Piano Sonata* by Jan Kapr of Czechoslovakia; *Sextet* for wind instruments and piano by Herman Koppel of Denmark.

1 JUNE 1947

At the third concert of the twenty-first ISCM Festival in Copenhagen the following program of chamber music is presented:

Trio for Strings by Karl Birger Blomdahl of Sweden; *Piano Sonata* by Aaron Copland, devised as a calculated study in thematic patterns and percussively pianistic sonoritics; *Second Violin Sonata* by Prokofiev, written in his newly wise, ironically lyrical vein (in a postcard, dated 3 February 1948, to the *Musical Digest,* Bernard Shaw described this Sonata as "a humorous masterpiece of authentic violin music," unaware of the fact that Prokofiev originally wrote it for the flute, later arranging it for violin) ; Hindemithish *Partita for Piano* by Niels Viggo Bentzon of Denmark; and *Second String Quartet* by the London-born, neo-classical Hebraist, Benjamin Frankel.

2 JUNE 1947

At the fourth concert of the twenty-first ISCM Festival in Copenhagen the following program is presented:

Serenades for piano, twelve wind instruments, double-bass and percussion by David van de Woestyne (Belgium) ; *Concerto* for clarinet and strings by the neo-Elizabethan, Elizabeth Maconchy; *Duae fugae novem compositae sonis quattuor sine nomine vocibus* by Adone Zecchi (Italy) on a nine-note theme and scored in four parts for unnamed instruments or voices; *Sonetto di Michelangelo* for chamber orchestra by Fartein Valen (Norway) ; *Concerto* for bassoon and orchestra by Michal Spisak (Poland) ; and *Preludes joyeux* by Camille Schmit (Belgium) .

2 JUNE 1947

Concerto for accordion and orchestra by Roy Harris, first of its kind to be written in serious symphonic style, in two sections, *Passacaglia* and *Dance,* treating the accordion like an oboe in lyric solo episodes, and like a full-blown folk organ in opulent orchestral passages, is performed for the first time by the NBC Symphony Orchestra, the composer conducting.

2 JUNE 1947

Herman DAREWSKI, Russian-born composer, inventor of the system of Kiddie Music Notation, with the notes of the scale designated by names of animals (he taught this method to Princess Elizabeth, heiress-apparent to the British throne), dies in London at the age of sixty-four.

3 JUNE 1947

At the fifth concert of the twenty-first ISCM Festival in Copenhagen the following program of chamber music is presented:

Arcana Musae Dona by Rudolf ESCHER (Holland), combining urbane impressionism with conscious neo-medievalism; *Trio* for oboe, clarinet and bassoon by Klement SLAVICKY (Czechoslovakia); *Second String Quartet* by Ernest BLOCH, marked by passionate expressiveness in a modernistically acrid technique; *Sonata for Piano* by André JOLIVET, 41-year-old member of the group "La Jeune France"; and three choral works, *Cade la sera, Ululate,* and *Recordare Domine* by Ildebrando PIZZETTI, erstwhile chromaticist, and now neo-ecclesiastical diatonicist.

4 JUNE 1947

At the sixth and last concert of the twenty-first ISCM Festival in Copenhagen the following program is presented:

Sinfonia breve in five movements by Gosta NYSTROEM (Sweden); *Spoon River Anthology* by Gino NEGRI (Italy) to words from the American classic of Edgar Lee Masters, scored for soloists, chorus and orchestra; *Petite Symphonie Concertante* by the Swiss neo-classicist Frank MARTIN; and a ballet suite from *Don Quixote* by Roberto GERHARD, Spanish-Catalan expatriate living in London.

10 JUNE 1947

Les Mamelles de Tirésias, opéra-burlesque by Francis POULENC, is produced at the Opéra Comique in Paris, to an existentialist libretto of Claude Rostand portraying the heroine's struggle to divest herself of *mamelles,* which eventually float away as two balloons, one red and one blue, and explode when a match is applied to them, as a sequel to which demammification she assumes the masculine name Tirésias, whereupon her husband retaliates by a reciprocally transsexual transvestitism, with a happy ending provided when both assume their original sexes to the strains of a "metamorphosis waltz," and urge the audience to proliferate fruitfully for the sake of the demographic rehabilitation of France: "faites des enfants, vous qui n'en faisiez guère."

16 JUNE 1947

Bronislaw HUBERMAN, Polish-born violinist excelling in soulful virtuosity, dies at Nant-sur-Corsier, Switzerland, in his sixty-fifth year.

20 JUNE 1947

Benjamin BRITTEN conducts at the Glyndebourne Festival in England the first performance of his fourth opera *Albert Herring*, after Maupassant, but with its locale transferred to an English town, and recounting the merry contretemps that befall Albert Herring, a shy and virtuous citizen crowned as May King by default when local girls fail to meet a chastity qualification, and disgraced in his turn by an embarrassingly realistic frame-up by a female, set to a musical score of appropriate levity, with a thematic allusion to the love-potion motive in *Tristan*, for a scene in which Herring drinks what he believes to be tepid lemonade but turns out to be sparkling champagne.

20 JUNE 1947

Lemonade Opera, a cooperative enterprise so named after the thirst-quenching beverage customarily served in theaters during the intermission period, opens its first season in New York with an appropriately effervescent performance of Mozart's *Don Giovanni*.

25 JUNE 1947

Symphony No. 5½ by the Democriteanly cachinnigenous Missourian, Don Gillis, so named because it was written while marking time between the integer-numbered symphonies No. 5 and No. 6, and subtitled *Symphony for Fun*, in four movements: *Perpetual Emotion, Spiritual, Scherzophrenia,* and *Conclusion*, is performed for the first time at the Boston Pops, Arthur Fiedler conducting.

6 AUGUST 1947

Danton's Death, opera by the 29-year-old Austrian, Gottfried EINEM, to the story of the French Revolution as reflected in the personal fates of Danton and Desmoulins, and designed in an eclectic musical style (waggish listeners remarked: "Nicht von Einem, sondern von Vielen"), is produced at the Salzburg Festival.

6 OCTOBER 1947

Leevi MADETOJA, Finnish composer of operas and symphonic poems in the somber tone colors of a Sibelian palette, dies in Helsinki in his sixty-first year.

10 OCTOBER 1947

Vladimir DUKELSKY's *Third Symphony* in E major in three movements, ranging in mood from bucolic sophistication to fugally fused funerealities to elegiacally Elysian solemnities, is performed in a world première by the Radio Orchestra in Brussels.

20 OCTOBER 1947

Thomas K. Scherman conducts in New York the first of eight concerts of the Little Orchestra Society founded by him with the twofold purpose (1) to encourage modern composers by providing an outlet for their works (2) to perform neglected masterpieces of the past, with the following world premières presented during the first season: David DIAMOND's neo-Prokofievian music for *Romeo and Juliet; Concerto* for harp and orchestra in a brisk, neo-classical manner by Norman DELLO JOIO; *Farm Journal* by the smiling philosopher of music, Douglas MOORE, featuring such scenes as *Up Early, Sunday Clothes, Lamplight* and *Harvest Song;* and sundry pieces by Leclair, Enesco, Busoni and others.

24 OCTOBER 1947

Short Symphony by Henry COWELL, his fourth, in four movements, with identifying subtitles: (1) *Hymn* (2) *Ballad* (3)

Dance (4) *Fuguing Tune,* Americanistic in material, including original hymnlike tunes, Irish-American jigs, ballad melodies and stylizations of fuguing tunes developed from the shaped-note style of the old collection *Southern Harmony* (1854), is performed for the first time by the Boston Symphony Orchestra, Koussevitzky conducting.

24 OCTOBER 1947

Seventh Symphony by Alexandre TANSMAN in four movements, conceived in a lyrical style and diversified by playful episodes on the piccolo, xylophone and strings in harmonics, is performed for the first time by the St. Louis Symphony Orchestra, Golschmann conducting.

30 OCTOBER 1947

Leopold Stokowski conducts the New York Philharmonic in the première of *Symphony* by Elie SIEGMEISTER, in the classical four movements, "dealing with the spirit, the struggle, the hope of man, without using any actual folk tunes, although some sections have the feeling of American song and dance."

4 NOVEMBER 1947

A century has passed since the death of Felix MENDELSSOHN, the "happy musician," whose facile melodism and programmatic sentimentalism charmed and captivated the hearts of Victorian Europe.

7 NOVEMBER 1947

Great Friendship, opera by the Georgian composer Vano MURADELI depicting the Caucasian civil war in 1918-1920, is performed for the first (and last) time at the Moscow Opera, arousing criticism of Communist party officials as being chaotic, cacophonous and un-Soviet in its esthetics and politics.

20 NOVEMBER 1947

In an encyclical letter of Pope Pius XII, *Mediator Dei,* a new and more liberal view (as compared with *Motu Proprio* of 1903) regarding the use of post-Gregorian music by non-ecclesiastical composers is announced, allowing the inclusion in Catholic worship of "modern music and singing . . . if they are not profane and do not spring from a desire of achieving extraordinary and unusual effects," reaffirming the importance of Gregorian chant, "which the Roman Church considers her own as handed down from antiquity and kept under her close tutelage," and further urging "that the faithful attend the sacred ceremonies not as if they were outsiders or mute onlookers, but . . . fully appreciate the beauty of the liturgy and take part in the sacred ceremonies, alternating their voices with the priest and the choir, according to the prescribed norms." (Full text in the section *Letters and Documents*)

21 NOVEMBER 1947

Third Symphony by Vincent PERSICHETTI, 32-year-old Philadelphian, in four movements marked, according to their musical moods, (1) *Somber* (2) *Spirited* (3) *Singing* (4) *Fast and Brilliant,* commencing with a thematic minimum of two syncopated figurations and evolving towards a full-chorded chorale in the finale, is performed for the first time by the Philadelphia Orchestra, Ormandy conducting.

25 NOVEMBER 1947

A waterproof Irish harp manufactured by Melville Clark of Syracuse, New York, with non-poppable pre-shrunk non-fraying weatherproof pitch-perfect nylon strings, is demonstrated by Elaine Vito of the NBC Symphony Orchestra, plunging into a glass tank with it, and playing a few arpeggios under water in a fine liquid tone, after overcoming the Archimedean tendency to float.

27 NOVEMBER 1947

Fourth Symphony by Ernst KRENEK in three movements, the inner meaning of which is a materialization of an Ideal, "pure and sufficient unto itself, detached from life's reality," which reality "soon makes itself felt in the shape of disturbing and menacing elements," until "in a final dramatic struggle these forces are defeated and the Ideal is successfully integrated into the Here and Now," written in the twelve-tone technique to secure "a very high amount of logical coherence and intelligible significance," is performed for the first time by the New York Philharmonic, Mitropoulos conducting.

28 NOVEMBER 1947

Efrem ZIMBALIST gives the first performance of his *Concerto* for violin and orchestra in C-sharp minor, in three movements of lusciously Tchaikovskian fiddling, with the Philadelphia Orchestra, Ormandy conducting.

14 DECEMBER 1947

Trilogy by Utah's composer Leroy ROBERTSON, an impressionistic tone-poem inspired by "viewing the high plateaus of the Wasatch Range while tending sheep," with one passage picturing "the oldtimers who spit tobacco into brass spittoons," the score that won an all-time high prize of $25,000 donated by the chemical magnate Henry Reichold of Detroit (Robertson spelled his name backwards, Nostrebor, as a nom de plume for the contest), is performed in a world première by the Detroit Symphony Orchestra.

15 DECEMBER 1947

Werner Janssen conducts the Portland, Oregon, Symphony Orchestra in the first performance of *Genesis,* a setting for orchestra, voices and narrator, of the opening passage from the Bible, by six composers (SCHOENBERG, STRAVINSKY, TOCH, MILHAUD, CASTEL-NUOVO-TEDESCO, TANSMAN) and one Hollywood musician, Nathaniel SHILKRET, who commissioned the work.

25 DECEMBER 1947

PROKOFIEV's *Sixth Symphony* in a definitely designated (and for symphonies very rare) key of E-flat minor, in three movements:

(1) *Allegro agitato,* "lyrical at times, austere at others" (2) *Largo,* "bright-colored and full of song" (3) *Finale,* "rapid, in a major mode, with austere reminiscences of the first movement," is performed for the first time in Moscow.

1948

1 JANUARY 1948

Willem LANDRÉ, Dutch composer of carefully wrought and contrapuntally impeccable instrumental and vocal music, inheritor of the Diepenbrock tradition of austere romanticism, dies at Eindhoven at the age of seventy-three.

2 JANUARY 1948

The Return of Pushkin, elegy in three parts by Nicolas NABOKOV for voice and orchestra, to a Pushkin poem of homesickness, written in a pleasingly nostalgic old-Russian vein, is performed for the first time by the Boston Symphony Orchestra, Koussevitzky conducting, Marina Koshetz (daughter of Nina Koshetz), soloist.

9 JANUARY 1948

Third Symphony by Walter PISTON in four straightforward movements: (1) *Andantino* (2) *Allegro* (3) *Adagio* (4) *Allegro,* eminently tonal in essence (the composer designates the movements as being respectively in Tonality C, Tonality F, Tonality G, Tonality C), and built in linked "phases" of thematic development, is performed for the first time by the Boston Symphony Orchestra, Koussevitzky conducting.

13 JANUARY 1948

The board of trustees of the Chicago Symphony Orchestra curtly dismisses its conductor Artur Rodzinski (now in the middle of his first season), charging him with "last-minute program changes causing confusion in rehearsals, staging of operatic productions in place of regular concerts, exceeding the budget by $30,000 and attempting to secure a three-year contract."

21 JANUARY 1948

Ermanno WOLF-FERRARI, Italian opera composer whose entertaining sketch *Secret of Suzanne* (the secret is the shocking realization that Suzanne indulges in cigarette smoking) established a new type of modern opera buffa, dies in Venice nine days after his seventy-second birthday.

23 JANUARY 1948

Fourth Symphony by David DIAMOND, his "smallest large symphony," in three movements: (1) *Allegretto* (2) *Andante* (3) *Allegro,* paralleling the concepts of life and death, "I, a continual sleep; II, the alternation between sleeping and waking; III, eternal waking, birth being the passing from I to II, and death the transition from II to III," is performed for the first time by the Boston Symphony Orchestra, Leonard Bernstein conducting.

25 JANUARY 1948

Second Symphony by Robert WARD, 30-year-old American composer of music in "older forms treated in a new way," in three movements subtitled (1) *Fast and energetic* (2) *Slowly* (3) *Fast,* is performed for the first time by the National Symphony Orchestra in Washington, Kindler conducting.

29 JANUARY 1948

Roy HARRIS conducts the Indianapolis Symphony Orchestra in the first performance of his short philosophical tone-poem *Quest,* a "tension piece," in which a vigorously rhythmed idea is relentlessly driven forward, undergoing the process of rhythmic diminution and dynamic tightening until a tonal catharsis is finally achieved.

30 JANUARY 1948

Symphony for Classical Orchestra by the 27-year-old Harold SHA-
PERO of Lynn, Massachusetts, premeditatedly cast in the traditional four movements, with deliberate emphasis on the sense of
tonality, climaxed in a luxuriant display of B-flat major chords,
is performed for the first time by the Boston Symphony Orchestra,
Bernstein conducting.

8 FEBRUARY 1948

Symphonie expiatoire by Henri SAUGUET, composed in 1944-1946
"to relieve one's conscience, to expiate in the original sense of
the word," dedicated "to the innocent victims of the war, and
reflecting the helplessness during the Nazi occupation of France,"
cast in four movements, the last of which is a "berceuse des
morts," is performed for the first time in Paris.

10 FEBRUARY 1948

The Central Committee of the Communist Party of the USSR in
Moscow publishes a stern resolution denouncing "decadent formalism" (meaning formulism, adherence to cerebral formulas in
art) in Soviet music, and specifically naming SHOSTAKOVITCH,
PROKOFIEV and KHATCHATURIAN as delinquents, and MIASKOVSKY
and SHEBALIN as inculcators of inharmonious music in the educational institutions of the Soviet Union. (Full text in the section
Letters and Documents)

22 FEBRUARY 1948

Wilhelm FURTWAENGLER conducts the Berlin Philharmonic in the
first performance of his own *Second Symphony.*

24 FEBRUARY 1948

The Seine at Night, symphonic poem by the transsequanic Missourian, Virgil THOMSON, the "Lutecian Maro" who "wrote in
Paris music that was always, in one way or another, about Kansas

City," is performed for the first time by the Kansas City Phil-harmonic, Efrem Kurtz conducting.

27 FEBRUARY 1948

Fourth Symphony, subtitled *In Memoriam,* by Francesco MALI-PIERO in four movements, alternately proclamatory, funereal, pas-toral, and pathos-laden, in which "the musical dissonance is lin-ear and is developed with that logic which was spontaneous in Italian music," and set in a broad frame of serene pandiatonicism, is performed for the first time anywhere as a commissioned work by the Boston Symphony Orchestra, Koussevitzky conducting.

29 FEBRUARY 1948

Concerto for Violin and Orchestra by David DIAMOND is per-formed for the first time by the Vancouver Symphony Orchestra, Jacques Singer conducting.

13 MARCH 1948

The Houston Symphony Orchestra, Frederick Fennell conduct-ing, gives the world première of the *Third Symphony* by Harold MORRIS, subtitled *Amaranth* (after a poem of that name by Ed-win A. Robinson, but not connected with it in subject matter, the spiritual meaning of the word being a flower that never fades), in four movements expressive of (1) joy and freedom (2) play and humor (3) exaltation (4) triumph, written in a keyless tonality centripetally gravitating toward the pivotal C, which is the last and the first keynote of the work.

15 MARCH 1948

Czinka Panna, opera by Zoltán KODÁLY to a story of the gypsy girl who played an inspiring part in the 1703 revolution in Hun-gary led by Rákóczi against the Hapsburg domination, is pro-duced at the Budapest Opera.

20 MARCH 1948

Five days before his eighty-first birthday, TOSCANINI, conducting the NBC Symphony Orchestra in an all-Wagner program, is televised over the WNBT television network in New York hooked up with other stations in Washington, Philadelphia, Schenectady and Buffalo. (This was to be the first telecast of a major symphony orchestra concert, but Toscanini went on the video screen at 6:30 p.m., and CBS got ahead of NBC by an hour, televising a concert of the Philadelphia Orchestra, Ormandy conducting, piped to New York by coaxial cable)

23 MARCH 1948

Hilding ROSENBERG, Swedish composer of massively sonorous vocal works, conducts in Stockholm the first performance of the final portion of his eight-hour-long opera-oratorio *Joseph and His Brethren,* written to the story from Thomas Mann's biblical novel *Joseph.*

26 MARCH 1948

Hanns EISLER, composer of atonal symphonies as well as eminently tonal mass songs, since 1942 a writer of background music for Hollywood films, leaves the United States as a "voluntary deportee," as a result of the actions of the House Committee on Un-American Activities alleging that he had "perjured his way in and out of the United States at will, going to Soviet Russia and other countries when he pleased."

1 APRIL 1948

Symphony in C by Frederick JACOBI in three movements, intended as the exposition of "anti-obscurantist" music that "should give pleasure and not try to solve philosophical problems," is performed for the first time by the San Francisco Symphony, Monteux conducting.

2 APRIL 1948

The new Turkish State Opera House opens in Ankara with a

program of music by Turkish composers: a symphony by Kemal
KAZIM; and one scene from the opera *Kerem* by Ahmed Adnan
SAYGUN, to a Tristanesque story of Kerem's love for a beauteous
Turkish maiden, with a score in a modern idiom devoid of con-
ventional orientalities.

4 APRIL 1948

Duett-Concertino for clarinet, bassoon, string orchestra and harp
by Richard STRAUSS, composed in Montreux in 1947, and built
upon a contrast between the "gay clarinet" and the "sad bassoon,"
is performed for the first time over the Lugano, Switzerland,
radio.

9 APRIL 1948

Saga of the Mississippi by Harl McDONALD, an alluvial diptych
in two sections: (1) *Prehistoric Mississippi*, in a slothfully modal
vein (2) *Father of Waters*, with thematic material developed
from a Canadian-Indian fishing call, later syncopated into a ne-
groid tune, and some Gregorianistic chants as identifying mottoes
for proselytizing Jesuit priests, is performed for the first time by
the Philadelphia Orchestra, Ormandy conducting.

9 APRIL 1948

Knoxville, Summer of 1915 by Samuel BARBER (to a poem of
James Agee), with the legend: "We are talking now of summer
evenings in Knoxville, Tennessee, at the time when I lived there
so successfully disguised to myself as a child," metempsychotically
conjuring up the simple life of a relatively recent past, with a
sophisticatedly sentimental score for soprano and orchestra
marked by a slightly off-pitch melodiousness, is performed for the
first time by the Boston Symphony Orchestra, Koussevitzky conducting, Eleanor Steber, soloist.

15 APRIL 1948

Rhapsody for Orchestra by Artur SCHNABEL, written in a quasi-
atonal idiom, is performed for the first time by the Cleveland
Orchestra, Szell conducting.

21 APRIL 1948

The Royal Philharmonic Society of London, under the direction of Sir Adrian Boult, presents the world première of the *Sixth Symphony* by the 75-year-old dean of British composers, VAUGHAN WILLIAMS, in four connected movements so that "each of the first three has its tail attached to the head of its neighbour," (1) *Allegro* (2) *Moderato* (3) *Scherzo* (4) *Epilogue,* written in a robustly triadic idiom of moderate modernity, scored for a large orchestra including a saxophone and non-pitched percussion, richly overladen with proclamatory brass and energized with cross-rhythms in orderly syncopation, the whole subordinated to the commanding unity of the principal key of E minor, in which the work opens brassily and closes stringfully.

22 APRIL 1948

Fall River Legend, ballet to the story of the celebrated Lizzie Borden parricide case ("Lizzie Borden took her axe and gave her mother forty whacks"), with music by Morton GOULD ranging from New England hymnology to stylized social dances and sophisticatedly folksy balladry, is produced by Ballet Theater in New York.

24 APRIL 1948

Manuel PONCE, pioneer of musical Mexicanism, composer of impressionistic symphonic poems, and of *Estrellita,* which has virtually become a Latin-American folk song (Ponce never collected any royalties from it owing to a faulty copyright) dies in Mexico City at the age of sixty-one.

25 APRIL 1948

Third Symphony by the German neo-romanticist Ernst PEPPING in four movements subtitled *Morning, Afternoon, Evening, Night,* in which a passacaglia theme of the morning is inverted on the noon axis to depict the evening, is performed for the first time by the Berlin Philharmonic.

25 APRIL 1948

Wonsik LIM conducts the Korea Symphony Orchestra in Seoul in the first performance of his *Korean Dance Fantasy* and the Korean première of *Village Music* by Douglas MOORE.

28 APRIL 1948

Ballet Society of New York presents the world première of *Orpheus* by STRAVINSKY, cast in a Hellenistic style and neo-Gluckian mood, mitigated by some Bachian and Tchaikovskian undertones, with a mannered melodiousness in static homophony, disrupted here and there by darkening chordal complexes (such as a forebodingly inharmonious G-sharp in the bass of the opening A minor triad) and vesuviating suddenly in a rhythmic eruption to illustrate the dance of the Bacchantes.

2 MAY 1948

Arthur Henry Fox STRANGWAYS, learned British musicologist, specialist in Hindu music, dies in Dinton, near Salisbury, England, in his eighty-ninth year.

4 MAY 1948

Fourth Symphony by Bernard ROGERS, composed in the autumn of 1945 "to trace a line leading from darkness and despair to eventual hope and affirmation," in four movements, the first, "a battle fantasy" (expanded from the orchestral movement *Invasion* first performed by the New York Philharmonic on 17 October 1943) ; the second, a *Eulogy,* opening with an unaccompanied trumpet solo; the third, a *Fugue,* and the fourth, *Epilogue,* is performed for the first time by the Rochester Philharmonic Orchestra, Hanson conducting. (*Third Symphony* by Bernard Rogers was performed for the first time on 10 March 1938, by the Rochester Philharmonic, Hanson conducting)

5 MAY 1948

At the opening of the Fourth Annual Festival of Contemporary

Music at Columbia University, Otto LUENING conducts a belated world première of his opera *Evangeline* in three acts and eight scenes, composed sixteen years previously to Longfellow's celebrated poem, with a musical score embodying all the ethnic and religious elements implied in the diversity of the period, Lutheran hymns, Gregorian chants, and Indian calls.

9 MAY 1948

Experimental Theater in New York presents the first performance of *Ballet Ballads,* a new synthetic art show, with lyrics by John Latouche and music by Jerome MOROSS, esemplastically fusing instruments and voices, dance and lighting effects, into an American-flavored product, in three scenes: a folksy fresco in a "Bible belt setting," *Susannah and the Elders;* a terpsichorean marijuana dreamer, *Willie the Weeper* ("It's twelve-tone Willie with his sexy sax"); and the lives and loves of a frontier cowboy, *The Eccentricities of Davey Crockett,* who fishes a toothsome mermaid out of the Tennessee River, catches Halley's Comet by the tail, goes to Congress, and moves to Texas, finally to be killed at the Alamo.

13 MAY 1948

The Hospital, musico-medical suite by Dr. Herman M. PARRIS of Philadelphia, descriptive of a young woman's appendectomy, in ten spirited movements, featuring a nurse *(Allegro e amabile),* a pre-operation prayer *(Andantino),* operating room *(Allegro* realistically followed by *Molto agitato),* anesthesia *(Presto!),* in a musical style half-way between Handel and Gershwin via Dvořák, is performed for the first time by the Doctors' Orchestral Society in New York.

13 MAY 1948

Mass for Men's Voices and Organ by Roy HARRIS, "composed for the Catholic people of America," is performed for the first time at the Columbia University Festival in New York. (The work was originally intended for performance at St. Patrick's Cathedral in New York, but was called off by its officials in protest against

Harris's interview published in the *New York Times* of 15 February 1948, headlined COMPOSING FOR CASH—HARRIS PROVES COMPOSER CAN GET PAID FOR WORK, containing an oblique reference to a Mass scheduled to be performed at Eastertime at St. Patrick's Cathedral, implying that this work, too, was written for cash, which it wasn't)

16 MAY 1948

Third Symphony by Wallingford RIEGGER in four movements, fugal in essence, employing a modified twelve-tone technique, with rhythmic patterns and instrumental sonorities as integral elements of the interconnected whole, is performed for the first time by the CBS Symphony Orchestra, Dean Dixon conducting, on the same program with the première of Quincy PORTER's *Concerto for Viola and Orchestra*. (Riegger's Symphony was voted by the Music Critics Circle of New York "the symphonic work of most outstanding excellence composed by an American citizen and played for the first time in this city during the music season 1947-1948")

18 MAY 1948

The Princess and the Vagabond, short opera by Isadore FREED to a pre-Shakespearian tale of "The Taming of the Shrew," cast in an Irish locale, with a score built on simple modal harmony occasionally burnished with modernistic inflections, is performed for the first time as part of the Hartford, Connecticut, Music Symposium.

20 MAY 1948

Darius MILHAUD conducts in Paris the world première of his *Fourth Symphony* in four movements, with the notation at the end of the score reflecting his travels: "Pacific Ocean, Atlantic Ocean, August-September, 1947; orchestrated at Genval and Aix-en-Provence, October-December, 1947."

29 MAY 1948

The Second International Congress of Composers and Musicologists, gathered in Prague, issues a declaration in which they call on the musical world to remedy faults in contemporary music, both serious and light, and to surmount the ideological crisis inherent in the clash between serious music that grows over-intellectual, thus losing contact with the masses, and light music that cultivates banality and commonplace, thus lowering the musical taste of the mass listener. (Complete text of the Declaration is found in the section *Letters and Documents*)

31 MAY 1948

José Vianna DA MOTTA, Portuguese pianist, the last surviving pupil of Liszt, dies in Lisbon at the age of eighty.

5 JUNE 1948

The twenty-second Festival of the International Society for Contemporary Music opens in Amsterdam with the following program played by the Concertgebouw Orchestra:

Concerto for Orchestra by Raymond CHEVREUILLE of Belgium in four movements, written in an idiom of "tonal sentiment," but not without sporadic spurts of atonality; *Second Violin Concerto* by the Dutch neo-classicist Sem DRESDEN; and *Fifth Symphony* by Francesco MALIPIERO in four movements, in an emotionally romanticized neo-Vivaldian style approximating the spirit of the Italian concerto, with two pianos in the score as a twentieth-century counterpart of the cembalo. (*Second Symphony* by Miloslav KABELÁC of Czechoslovakia was programmed but not performed)

6 JUNE 1948

Christus Rex for double choir and organ, and the first part from a *Sinfonia* for organ by Hendrik ANDRIESSEN of Holland are presented at a morning concert of the Amsterdam ISCM Festival, followed in the afternoon by a demonstration of the Gamelan Orchestra from Java conducted by Bernard Yzerdraat, and, in the evening, a presentation of RAVEL's pseudo-Hispanic lyric comedy *L'Heure Espagnole*.

7 JUNE 1948

At the Amsterdam ISCM Festival the following all-Dutch program is played by the Concertgebouw Orchestra:

Little Suite on the notes E-F by Willem LANDRÉ (1874-1948), with the thematic two notes serving as nuclear motifs for six "symphonic epigrams," written in a tense chromatic style and first performed in Rotterdam on 11 June 1943; *Sinfonia Sacra In Memoriam Patris* by Willem Landré's son, Guillaume LANDRÉ, written as a devotional dedication shortly after his father's death; *Sinfonia piccola* by Léon ORTHEL, written in an aggressively polyrhythmic style, in six sections without pause, and first performed in Rotterdam on 31 October 1941; *Six Symphonic Epigrams* by Willem PIJPER (1894-1947), a set of remote variations on a 16th-century Dutch song; and *Symphonic Variations* by Henk BADINGS, written in 1936, in a modernistic neo-classical idiom of melorhythmically angular intervallic facture. (Daniel RUYNEMAN's *Amphitryon Overture* was programmed but not performed)

8 JUNE 1948

At a denazification court in Munich, Richard STRAUSS is cleared of charges of having been an accessory to the Nazi movement.

8 JUNE 1948

At the Amsterdam ISCM Festival the following program of chamber music is presented:

Trio in four movements by Klaus EGGE, Norwegian composer of strongly knit polyphonic music; *Put Away the Flutes* for tenor, flute, oboe and string quartet by Humphrey SEARLE of England, to a poem by the Irish poet W. R. Rodgers, written during World War II to illustrate the psychological renunciation in wartime: "Put away the flutes into their careful clefts, and cut the violins that like ivy climb flat to their very roots"; *Sonata* for two pianos by Hans HENKEMANS of Holland; *Sonatina* for oboe and piano by Antoni SZALOWSKI of Poland; *Eight Poems by Michelangelo* by the Swiss cellist Richard STURZENEGGER, designed as "a group of musical sculptures"; and *Quintet* for wind instruments by Finn HOFFDING of Denmark.

9 JUNE 1948

Six hundred and sixty-four years after the guest appearance in Hamelin of the fabled Pied Piper, the BBC broadcasts an audition of a flute, invented by John Heywood, whose sound, imitating the mating call of rats, makes use of rodent sex appeal to destroy them but, unlike the fluting of the Pied Piper of 1284, is harmless to children.

9 JUNE 1948

At the Amsterdam ISCM Festival the following program is presented by the Concertgebouw Orchestra:

Second Symphony by Roger SESSIONS in four movements of tensely wrought polyphony; *Violin Concerto* by Karl Birger BLOMDAHL of Sweden; *Symphonic Etudes* for piano and orchestra by the Przemyslite, Artur MALAWSKI (first performed on 30 April 1948 in Sopot, Poland) in six sections, written in a luscious quasi-Rachmaninovian virtuosistic manner; and *Musique pour l'Esprit en Deuil* by the Dutch composer Rudolf ESCHER, composed during the war years but not given its mournful title until 1945 (first performed by the Concertgebouw Orchestra in Amsterdam on 19 January 1947), and written in a somberly melodic style emotionalized by recurrent dynamic upsurges and sonorous climaxes in a score which includes a large percussion section, xylophone, bells, piano and two harps.

10 JUNE 1948

At the Amsterdam ISCM Festival the following program of chamber music is given:

Three Songs for soprano by Sandor JEMNITZ, Hungarian composer of pointedly atonal music; *Concertino da Camera* for flute, clarinet, bassoon and piano by Peggy GLANVILLE-HICKS; *4 Poemas Gallegos* for voice, flute, oboe, clarinet, viola, cello and harp by Julian BAUTISTA, Spanish composer now living in Argentina; and *Quintet* for wind instruments by the Czechoslovakian, Stepan LUCKY, who was a political prisoner in Nazi concentration camps, and whose predilection lies in experimental forms including quartertones. (*Primavera* for harp, flute and strings by Charles KOECHLIN of France was on the program but was called off due to lack of rehearsal time)

12 JUNE 1948

At the concluding concert of the Amsterdam ISCM Festival the following program is given by the Residentie Orchestra:

40th May, parachronistically titled orchestral suite in three movements by the Austro-Parisian composer Alexander SPITZMUELLER, written ostensibly for "the birthday of a beloved friend," in an imbricatingly linear counterpoint, trickily arranged in reversible canons; *Lullaby* for twenty-nine strings and two harps by Andrzej PANUFNIK of Poland, based on a folk song pointillized by cross rhythms, and titivated with quarter-tone glissandos; *Violin Concerto* in one movement of dodecatonic technique by Fartein VALEN of Norway, 60-year-old composer whose early years were spent in sub-equatorial Madagascar; *Horn Concerto* by Elizabeth LUTYENS; *Sinfonietta* in three movements by Walter PISTON, first performed in Boston on 10 May 1941.

Columbia Records, jointly with CBS and Philco, gives the first public demonstration for the press of LP (long playing) Microgroove, a non-breakable 12-inch vinylite disc, capable of playing for forty-five minutes, developed by Dr. Peter Goldmark, Director of CBS Engineering Research and Development Laboratories.

A Modern Music Festival is presented in Tokyo by the Toho Symphony Orchestra in a program of Japanese and American music including the overture *When Johnny Comes Marching Home* by Roy HARRIS, *El Salón México* by Aaron COPLAND, *Violin Concerto* by the 34-year-old Japanese composer Akira IFUKBE, and *Piano Concerto* by another Japanese musician, Fumio HAYASAKA.

George Templeton STRONG, 92-year-old American composer who, discouraged by the general lack of interest in native music, left America in 1892 and settled in Switzerland where he took up water color painting, dies in Geneva of unexorcisably terminal old age.

First Symphony by Arthur BENJAMIN, written "to reflect the feelings, the hopes and despairs of the times," and cast in an appropriately grim and somber mood, is performed for the first time at the Cheltenham Festival of Contemporary British Music, Barbirolli conducting.

Benjamin BRITTEN conducts at the Cheltenham Festival of Contemporary British Music the first performance of his modernized version of Gay's *Beggar's Opera,* with the 200-year-old tunes of Johann Christoph Pepusch pepped up, sometimes fugally telescoped, and new contrapuntal blood pumped into the quaint old music body.

15 JULY 1948

Down in the Valley, folk opera (so named after a Kentucky mountain song) by the Americanized German expressionist Kurt WEILL to the story of a condemned murderer who killed his old sweetheart's new beau, is produced at Indiana University.

24 JULY 1948

Saint Nicolas, cantata by Benjamin BRITTEN, is performed for the first time at the Aldeburgh Festival in England.

26 JULY 1948

Patriarch Alexei of the Russian Orthodox Church issues a statement condemning the "worldliness" in Russian church music and suggesting that a religious censor be appointed to see that suitable compositions, and no others, are sung in Russian churches.

26 JULY 1948

Magdalena, "a musical adventure" for the stage by VILLA-LOBOS, dealing with the amours of an equatorial dictator and a Parisian cocotte along the banks of the Colombian river Magdalena, and the theft of the statue of the Holy Virgin by the unconverted Indian fiancé of a converted Indian girl, set to languorous music (some of which is from other Villa-Lobos scores, such as a Chorale from his *Bachianas Brasileiras*) and abounding in chromatic humidity, with colorful monotony artfully mitigated by mechanistic effects (a broken-down pianola accompanies a frenetic jungle dance; an old Ford is cranked up to raucously polyharmonic sforzandos), is given its world première in Los Angeles.

29 JULY 1948

STRAVINSKY files, in a Los Angeles court, a lawsuit for a quarter million dollars against Leeds Music Corporation for using his name as the composer of *Summer Moon,* a defaced and premodulated version of a theme from Stravinsky's *Fire-Bird* published as a torch song with an appropriately mawkish text, and thereby damaging his standing as a "world famous composer of serious and sincere music."

At the opening of the American Dance Festival on the campus of Connecticut College in New London, Martha Graham presents the first performance of *Wilderness Stair,* ballet by Norman DELLO JOIO, subtitled "Diversion of Angels," cupidophilously portraying "games, flights, fancies, configurations of the lover's intention" in its choreography, and neo-classically gay in its musical score.

Le vin herbé, secular oratorio by the Swiss composer Frank MARTIN, a new conception of the Tristan theme, in three scenes, *Le philtre, La forêt du Morois, La mort,* scored for an utilitarianly economic ensemble of twelve voices, seven string instruments and piano, and cast in an individualized twelve-tone technique, "une sorte de mathématique *sui generis,* où les valeurs sont remplacées par des notes, et les fonctions par des rapports de tonalité," is produced at the Salzburg Music Festival.

An excerpt from the symphonic poem *Eloise* by Ernest Clyde SALISBURY, former inmate of the Wayne County General Hospital in the town of Eloise, Michigan (after which the piece was named), where he was treated for chronic alcoholism and manic depression by the musical therapist Dr. Ira M. ALTSHULER, who also helped him in supplying Tchaikovskian themes as material for his work, is performed for the first time by the Detroit Symphony Orchestra, Valter Poole conducting, at the Michigan State Fairgrounds, as a demonstration of confidence in mental hospitals which, in the composer's own words, "done me good."

Oscar Lorenzo FERNANDEZ, the "Brasileirissimo" composer of nostalgically poetic and sophisticatedly tropical music in all genres and forms, dies in his native Rio de Janeiro at the age of fifty.

27 AUGUST 1948

Oley SPEAKS, Ohio-born musician who began his career as a railroad office clerk, then became a baritone singer, and finally composer of fabulously successful songs, such as *On the Road to Mandalay* and *Sylvia,* dies in New York at the age of seventy-four.

19 SEPTEMBER 1948

The Tempest, Shakespearian opera by Kurt ATTERBERG with a realistically alliterative tempest tone-painted in the overture, is performed for the first time at the Stockholm Opera.

22 SEPTEMBER 1948

Four centuries have elapsed since the establishment in Dresden of the Court Chapel of vocalists (later augmented by instrumentalists, thus forming one of the earliest musical groups approximating the modern ensemble of performers), with Johann WALTHER, Lutheran church composer and pioneer hymnologist, as leader.

30 SEPTEMBER 1948

A Stradivarius violin is buried in the coffin with its owner, Louisa Terzi of Los Angeles, who won the violin at an international music contest in Milan in 1888, and willed that the instrument should go with her to the grave.

10 OCTOBER 1948

Siegmund VON HAUSEGGER, German composer of feudally Teutonic, Wagnerously ponderous, Nietzscheanly forensic symphonic poems and operas, dies in the war-scarred, de-Teutonized Munich, in his seventy-seventh year, his whilom grandeurs utterly faded, forgotten, and still.

11 OCTOBER 1948

175,000 Muscovites and 130,000 Leningraders crowd the twenty-eight cinemas of the two cities to see the Soviet film *Young Guard,* to Fadeev's novel about Russian partisan heroes, score by SHOSTAKOVITCH, "clear, realistic, and emotionally powerful music," according to *Pravda.*

14 OCTOBER 1948

The Orchestre National de France, 101-man strong, under the direction of Charles Münch, conductor-elect of the Boston Symphony Orchestra, presents its first concert of a series of forty-one appearances on its American tour (the first by a French orchestra since 1919), at Bridgeport, Connecticut, in a program of French music plus a specially written American work, a terse, contrapuntally knit *Toccata* by Walter PISTON.

24 OCTOBER 1948

Sinfonietta by Francis POULENC, written in his newly neo-classical vein, is given in a world première by the BBC Orchestra in London, Desormière conducting.

24 OCTOBER 1948

Franz LEHAR, the supreme fashioner of Viennese operettas from the easy pre-1914 world of merry widows, gypsy lovers, and Balkan princes expensively romancing in plush Paris, dies at 2:45 p.m., of the combined effects of cancer, double pneumonia, gastric ulcers, and heart disease, in his Upper-Austrian home, at Bad Ischl, in his seventy-eighth year.

27 OCTOBER 1948

Mass for boy sopranos and altos and ten wind instruments by STRAVINSKY is performed for the first time by La Scala Orchestra in Milan, Ansermet conducting.

4 NOVEMBER 1948

SCHOENBERG'S cantata *A Survivor of Warsaw* for narrator,

men's chorus and orchestra, with a text in English by Schoenberg himself, describing the horrors of a Nazi concentration camp, with chillingly realistic interpolations in German, shouting commands of the brutalitarian in charge, and a concluding prayer in Hebrew, is performed for the first time by the Albuquerque Civic Symphony Orchestra, Kurt Frederick conducting.

12 NOVEMBER 1948

Umberto GIORDANO, Italian composer who at the age of twenty-eight wrote his only successful opera *Andrea Chénier,* mellifluously melodramatizing the melancholy life of the guillotined French poet, dies in Milan in his eighty-second year.

13 NOVEMBER 1948

Arnold SCHOENBERG addresses an indignant letter to the editors of the *Saturday Review of Literature* protesting against the unlicensed use of his brainchild, the method of composition in twelve tones, in Thomas Mann's musicosophical novel *Doctor Faustus* featuring a mythical German composer of twelve-tone music, Adrian Leverkühn (1885-1943), realistically accoutred with a biographical chronology, analysis of imaginary works, and replete with technical details and musicotheoretical discussions.

"In his novel *Doctor Faustus,* Thomas Mann has taken advantage of my literary property. He has produced a fictitious composer as the hero of his book; and in order to lend him qualities a hero needs to arouse people's interest, he made him the creator of what one erroneously calls my 'system of twelve tones,' which I call 'method of composing with twelve tones.'

"He did this without my permission and even without my knowledge. In other words, he borrowed it in the absence of the proprietor. The supposition of one reviewer, that he obtained information about this technique from Bruno Walter and Stravinsky, is probably wrong; because Walter does not know anything of composition with twelve tones, and Stravinsky does not take any interest in it.

"I have still not read the book itself, though in the meantime Mann had sent me a German copy, with a handwritten dedication, 'To A. Schoenberg, dem Eigentlichen.' As one need not tell me that I am an 'Eigentlicher,' a real one, it was clear that he wanted to tell me that his Leverkühn is an impersonation of myself.

"Leverkühn is depicted, from beginning to end, as a lunatic. I am seventy-four and I am not yet insane, and I have never acquired the disease from which this insanity stems. I consider this an insult.

"When Mrs. Mahler-Werfel discovered this misuse of my property, she told Mann that this was my theory, whereupon he said: 'Oh, does one notice that? Then perhaps Mr. Schoenberg will be angry!' This proves that he was conscious of his guilt, and knew it was a violation of an author's right.

"Finally I sent him a letter and showed him the possible consequences of ascribing my creation to another person which, in spite of being fictitious, is represented like a living man, whose biography is told by his friend Serenus Zeitblom.

"One knows the superficiality and monomania of some historians who ignore facts if they do not fit in their hypotheses. Thus I quoted from an encyclopedia of the year 2060, a little article in which my theory was attributed to Thomas Mann, because of his Leverkühn.

"Much pressure by Mrs. Mahler-Werfel had still to be exerted to make Mann promise that every forthcoming copy of *Doctor Faustus* will carry a note giving me credit for the twelve-notes composition. I was satisfied by this promise, because I wanted to be noble to a man who was awarded the Nobel Prize.

"But Mr. Mann was not as generous as I, who had given him good chance to free himself from the ugly aspect of a pirate. He gave an explanation: a few lines which he hid at the end of the book on a place on a page where no one ever would see it. Besides, he added a new crime to his first, in the attempt to belittle me: He calls me '*a* (a!) *contemporary* composer and theoretician.' Of course, in two or three decades, one will know which of the two was the other's contemporary." (From Schoenberg's letter, published in the *Saturday Review of Literature* of 1 January 1949)

"Arnold Schoenberg's letter both astonished and grieved me. If his acquaintance with the book were not based exclusively on the gossip of meddling scandal mongers, he would know that my efforts to give the central figure of the novel 'qualities a hero needs to arouse people's interest' were neither limited to the transfer of Schoenberg's 'method of composing with twelve tones,' nor was this characteristic the most important one.

"It is quite untrue that it required 'much pressure' to induce me to give him due credit. As soon as I understood his concern I gave instructions to include in all translations, as well as in the German original, the statement which now appears in the English edition of *Doctor Faustus*. The statement does not raise the question who is whose contemporary. If Schoenberg wishes, we shall, all of us, consider it our greatest and proudest claim to be his contemporaries.

"Instead of accepting my book with a satisfied smile as a piece of contemporary literature that testifies to his tremendous influence upon the musical culture of the era, Schoenberg regards it as an act of rape and insult. It is a sad spectacle to see a man of great worth, whose all-too-understandable hypersensitivity grows out of a life suspended between glorification and neglect, almost wilfully yield to delusions of persecution and of being robbed, and involve himself in rancorous bickering. It is my sincere hope and wish that he may rise above bitterness and suspicion and that he may find peace in the assurance of his greatness and glory!" (From Thomas Mann's reply to Schoenberg in the *Saturday Review of Literature* of 1 January 1949)

23 NOVEMBER 1948

Second Symphony in E major by Ernst VON DOHNÁNYI, scored for a hugely inflated orchestra and, in the words of the London *Times,* "brimming over with the exuberant ripeness of decadent romanticism," is given its world première by the Chelsea Symphony Orchestra in London, Norman Del Mar conducting. (Dohnányi had left Hungary in 1948 when disputed evidence indicated that he was not too unfriendly with the Nazis during their heyday, and, after a cautiously inconspicuous tour in the United States, went to settle in Tucumán, Argentina, as a teacher)

26 NOVEMBER 1948

The Philadelphia Orchestra, Ormandy conducting, gives the first performance of Virgil THOMSON's Suite for Orchestra from incidental music for the film *Louisiana Story,* in four sections: (1) Pastoral—The Bayou and the Marsh Buggy (2) Chorale—The Derrick Arrives (3) Passacaglia—Robbing the Alligator's Nest (4) Fugue—Boy Fights Alligator, with local color provided by authentic regional melodies, and structural interest maintained by the application of the twelve-tone technique in four mutually exclusive triads, and the use in the Alligator Fugue of the tritone as the basic interval of the modulational scheme.

8 DECEMBER 1948

Lucifer, neo-medieval opera-cantata-mimodrama by Claude DELVINCOURT, 60-year-old French composer and director of the Paris Conservatory, with mutely mimed action on the stage sententiously commented upon by a chorus seated in the orchestra pit,

to the symbolistically embellished biblical story of the fall of angels and the first human murder (the original title of the opera
was *The Mystery of Cain*), is produced at the Grand Opéra in
Paris.

13 DECEMBER 1948

A symphonic diptych, *Elegy and Paean* for viola and orchestra,
by Roy Harris, with new-fangled "luminous" timbres produced
by microphonically magnified sound of a lidless grand piano
hidden from the audience, is performed for the first time by the
Houston Symphony Orchestra, Efrem Kurtz conducting, Prim-
rose, soloist.

29 DECEMBER 1948

The Union of Soviet Composers closes a nine-day discussion of
Soviet music written after the Resolution of the Central Committee of 10 February 1948, commending some composers for their
musical Sovietism, condemning others (particularly Prokofiev)
for the traces of unregenerate formalism in their works, and
concluding with this sentiment enunciated by Tikhon Khrennikov: "Only Bolshevik art, the mighty lever of our national enlightenment in the spirit of communism, is capable of truthfully
reflecting the greatness of the Lenino-Stalinist epoch."

"The music of composers mentioned in the Resolution of the Central Committee of the All-Union Soviet Communist Party (Bolsheviks) as representatives of the formalistic movement, naturally attracted the interest of the
plenum of the Union of Soviet Composers. Among the new works by these
composers the most successful were Shostakovitch's music for the film *Young
Guard,* and several choral works by Muradeli. Their endeavor to enter the
path of realistic creativeness and their partial successes in this, are demonstrated in Khatchaturian's music for the film about Lenin, Miaskovsky's Symphony on Russian themes, and Shebalin's Seventh Quartet. The plenum con-
cedes that the creative reorientation of these composers proceeds very slowly
as revealed by the presence of some unliquidated formalistic elements in their
music. Defeated ideologically, formalism still lives in the music of Soviet
composers. This is demonstrated by the new opera of Prokofiev, *Tale of a
Real Man.* In the modernistic, anti-melodic music of his opera, in the treatment of the Soviet people, the composer remains on his old positions, condemned by the Party and by Soviet Society. The spiritual world of the Soviet
man who performs miracles of valor and heroism for the love of his Father-

land, does not attract the composer's attention. He is still interested only in the external sharpness of stage action and naturalistic details." (Tikhon Khrennikov, Secretary General of the Union of Soviet Composers, in his article, *Soviet Music in Its New Stage,* in *Pravda,* 4 January 1949)

31 DECEMBER 1948

Recordare by Lukas Foss, a non-programmatic orchestral thren-ody begun on 30 January 1948 under the impact of Gandhi's assassination, with an initial theme trifurcating into (1) a nar-row-gauge anguished melody, (2) an elegiacally pastoral motive, and (3) a kinetically rhythmic passage (as an outcry of surviving energy), sectionally demarcated by softly plagal cadential divi-sions, and ending in a dirge of quasi-percussive sonorities, is per-formed for the first time by the Boston Symphony Orchestra, composer conducting; on the same program, Howard HANSON conducts the first performance of his *Piano Concerto,* Firkušny, soloist, in four brief movements of well-contrasted moods, from plagal serenities to energizingly syncopated motricities.

Part Three

LETTERS AND DOCUMENTS

Motu Proprio *of Pope Pius X on Sacred Music*

INSTRUCTION ON SACRED MUSIC

I

GENERAL PRINCIPLES

§ 1. Sacred music, being a complementary part of the solemn liturgy, participates in the general scope of the liturgy, which is the glory of God and the sanctification and edification of the faithful. It contributes to the decorum and the splendor of the ecclesiastical ceremonies, and since its principal office is to clothe with suitable melody the liturgical text proposed for the understanding of the faithful, its proper aim is to add greater efficacy to the text, in order that through it the faithful may be the more easily moved to devotion and better disposed for the reception of the fruits of grace belonging to the celebration of the most holy mysteries.

§ 2. Sacred music should consequently possess, in the highest degree, the qualities proper to the liturgy, and in particular *sanctity* and *goodness of form*, which will spontaneously produce the final quality of *universality*.

It must be *holy*, and must, therefore, exclude all profanity not only in itself, but in the manner in which it is presented by those who execute it.

It must be *true art*, for otherwise it will be impossible for it to exercise on the minds of those who listen to it that efficacy which the Church aims at obtaining in admitting into her liturgy the art of musical sounds.

But it must, at the same time, be *universal* in the sense that while every nation is permitted to admit into its ecclesiastical compositions those special forms which may be said to constitute its native music, still these forms must be subordinated in such a manner to the general characteristics of sacred music that nobody of any nation may receive an impression other than good on hearing them.

629

II

THE DIFFERENT KINDS OF SACRED MUSIC

§ 3. These qualities are to be found, in the highest degree, in Gregorian Chant, which is, consequently, the Chant proper to the Roman Church, the only chant she has inherited from the ancient fathers, which she has jealously guarded for centuries in her liturgical codices, which she directly proposes to the faithful as her own, which she prescribes exclusively for some parts of the liturgy, and which the most recent studies have so happily restored to their integrity and purity.

On these grounds Gregorian Chant has always been regarded as the supreme model for sacred music, so that it is fully legitimate to lay down the following rule: *the more closely a composition for Church approaches in its movement, inspiration and savor the Gregorian form, the more sacred and liturgical it becomes; and the more out of harmony it is with that supreme model, the less worthy it is of the temple.*

The ancient traditional Gregorian Chant must, therefore, in a large measure be restored to the functions of public worship, and the fact must be accepted by all that an ecclesiastical function loses none of its solemnity when accompanied by this music alone.

Special efforts are to be made to restore the use of the Gregorian Chant by the people, so that the faithful may again take a more active part in the ecclesiastical offices, as was the case in ancient times.

§ 4. The above-mentioned qualities are also possessed in an excellent degree by Classic Polyphony, especially of the Roman School, which reached its greatest perfection in the sixteenth century, owing to the works of Pierluigi da Palestrina, and continued subsequently to produce compositions of excellent quality from a liturgical and musical standpoint. Classic Polyphony agrees admirably with Gregorian Chant, the supreme model of all sacred music, and hence it has been found worthy of a place side by side with Gregorian Chant, in the more solemn functions of the Church, such as those of the Pontifical Chapel. This, too, must therefore be restored largely in ecclesiastical functions, especially in the more important basilicas, in cathedrals, and in the churches and chapels of seminaries and other ecclesiastical institutions in which the necessary means are usually not lacking.

§ 5. The Church has always recognized and favored the progress of the arts, admitting to the service of religion everything good and beautiful discovered by genius in the course of ages—always, however, with due regard to the liturgical laws. Consequently modern music is also admitted to the Church, since it, too, furnishes compositions of such excellence, sobriety and gravity, that they are in no way unworthy of the liturgical functions.

Still, since modern music has risen mainly to serve profane uses, greater care must be taken with regard to it, in order that the musical compositions of modern style which are admitted in the Church may contain nothing profane, be free from reminiscences of motifs adopted in the theatres, and be not fashioned even in their external forms after the manner of profane pieces.

§ 6. Among the different kinds of modern music, that which appears less suitable for accompanying the functions of public worship is the theatrical style, which was in the greatest vogue, especially in Italy, during the last century. This of its very nature is diametrically opposed to Gregorian Chant and classic polyphony, and therefore to the most important law of all good sacred music. Besides the intrinsic structure, the rhythm and what is known as the *conventionalism* of this style adapt themselves but badly to the requirements of true liturgical music.

III

THE LITURGICAL TEXT

§ 7. The language proper to the Roman Church is Latin. Hence it is forbidden to sing anything whatever in the vernacular in solemn liturgical functions—much more to sing in the vernacular the variable or common parts of the Mass and Office.

§ 8. As the texts that may be rendered in music, and the order in which they are to be rendered, are determined for every liturgical function, it is not lawful to confuse this order or to change the prescribed texts for others selected at will, or to omit them either entirely or even in part, unless when the rubrics allow that some versicles of the text be supplied with the organ, while these versicles are simply recited in the choir. However, it is permissible, according to the custom of the Roman Church, to sing a motet to the Blessed Sacrament after the *Benedictus* in a Solemn Mass. It is also permitted, after the Offertory prescribed for the Mass has been sung, to execute during the time that remains a brief motet to words approved by the Church.

§ 9. The liturgical text must be sung as it is in the books, without alteration or inversion of the words, without undue repetition, without breaking syllables, and always in a manner intelligible to the faithful who listen.

IV

EXTERNAL FORM OF THE SACRED COMPOSITIONS

§ 10. The different parts of the Mass and the Office must retain, even musically, that particular concept and form which ecclesiastical tradition has assigned to them, and which is admirably brought out by

Gregorian Chant. The method of composing an *introit*, a *gradual*, an *antiphon*, a *psalm*, a *hymn*, a *Gloria in excelsis*, etc., must therefore be distinct from one another.

§ 11. In particular the following rules are to be observed:

(a) The *Kyrie*, *Gloria*, *Credo*, etc., of the Mass must preserve the unity of composition proper to their text. It is not lawful, therefore, to compose them in separate movements, in such a way that each of these movements form a complete composition in itself, and be capable of being detached from the rest and substituted by another.

(b) In the office of Vespers it should be the rule to follow the *Caeremoniale Episcoporum*, which prescribes Gregorian Chant for the psalmody and permits figured music for the versicles of the *Gloria Patri* and the hymn.

It will nevertheless be lawful on greater solemnities to alternate the Gregorian Chant of the choir with the so-called *falsi-bordoni* or with verses similarly composed in a proper manner.

It is also permissible occasionally to render single psalms in their entirety in music, provided the form proper to psalmody be preserved in such compositions; that is to say, provided the singers seem to be psalmodising among themselves, either with new motifs or with those taken from Gregorian Chant or based upon it.

The psalms known as *di concerto* are therefore forever excluded and prohibited.

(c) In the hymns of the Church the traditional form of the hymn is preserved. It is not lawful, therefore, to compose, for instance, a *Tantum ergo* in such wise that the first strophe presents a romanza, a cavatina, an adagio and the *Genitori* an allegro.

(d) The antiphons of the Vespers must be as a rule rendered with the Gregorian melody proper to each. Should they, however, in some special case be sung in figured music, they must never have either the form of a concert melody or the fullness of a motet or a cantata.

V

THE SINGERS

§ 12. With the exception of the melodies proper to the celebrant at the altar and to the ministers, which must be always sung in Gregorian Chant, and without accompaniment of the organ, all the rest of the liturgical chant belongs to the choir of levites, and, therefore, singers in church, even when they are laymen, are really taking the place of the ecclesiastical choir. Hence the music rendered by them must, at least for the greater part, retain the character of choral music.

By this it is not to be understood that solos are entirely excluded.

But solo singing should never predominate to such an extent as to have the greater part of the liturgical chant executed in that manner; the solo phrase should have the character or hint of a melodic projection (*spunto*), and be strictly bound up with the rest of the choral composition.

§ 13. On the same principle it follows that singers in church have a real liturgical office, and that therefore women, being incapable of exercising such office, cannot be admitted to form part of the choir. Whenever, then, it is desired to employ the acute voices of sopranos and contraltos, these parts must be taken by boys, according to the most ancient usage of the Church.

§ 14. Finally, only men of known piety and probity of life are to be admitted to form part of the choir of a church, and these men should by their modest and devout bearing during the liturgical functions show that they are worthy of the holy office they exercise. It will also be fitting that singers while singing in church wear the ecclesiastical habit and surplice, and that they be hidden behind gratings when the choir is excessively open to the public gaze.

VI

ORGAN AND INSTRUMENTS

§ 15. Although the music proper to the Church is purely vocal music, music with the accompaniment of the organ is also permitted. In some special cases, within due limits and with proper safeguards, other instruments may be allowed, but never without the special permission of the Ordinary, according to prescriptions of the *Caeremoniale Episcoporum*.

§ 16. As the singing should always have the principal place, the organ or other instrument should merely sustain and never oppress it.

§ 17. It is not permitted to have the chant preceded by long preludes or to interrupt it with intermezzo pieces.

§ 18. The sound of the organ as an accompaniment to the chant in preludes, interludes, and the like must be not only governed by the special nature of the instrument, but must participate in all the qualities proper to sacred music as above enumerated.

§ 19. The employment of the piano is forbidden in church, as is also that of noisy or frivolous instruments such as drums, cymbals, bells and the like.

§ 20. It is strictly forbidden to have bands play in church, and only in special cases with the consent of the Ordinary will it be permissible to admit wind instruments, limited in number, judiciously used, and proportioned to the size of the place—provided the composition and accompaniment be written in grave and suitable style, and conform in all respects to that proper to the organ.

§ 21. In processions outside the church the Ordinary may give permission for a band, provided no profane pieces be executed. It would be desirable in such cases that the band confine itself to accompanying some spiritual canticle sung in Latin or in the vernacular by the singers and the pious associations which take part in the procession.

VII

THE LENGTH OF THE LITURGICAL CHANT

§ 22. It is not lawful to keep the priest at the altar waiting on account of the chant or the music for a length of time not allowed by the liturgy. According to the ecclesiastical prescriptions the *Sanctus* of the Mass should be over before the elevation, and therefore the priest must here have regard for the singers. The *Gloria* and the *Credo* ought, according to the Gregorian tradition, to be relatively short.

§ 23. In general it must be considered a very grave abuse when the liturgy in ecclesiastical functions is made to appear secondary to and in a manner at the service of the music, for the music is merely a part of the liturgy and its humble handmaid.

VIII

PRINCIPAL MEANS

§ 24. For the exact execution of what has been herein laid down, the Bishops, if they have not already done so, are to institute in their dioceses a special Commission composed of persons really competent in sacred music, and to this Commission let them entrust in the manner they find most suitable the task of watching over the music executed in their churches. Nor are they to see merely that the music is good in itself, but also that it is adapted to the powers of the singers and be always well executed.

§ 25. In seminaries of clerics and in ecclesiastical institutions let the above-mentioned traditional Gregorian Chant be cultivated by all with diligence and love, according to the Tridentine prescriptions, and let the superiors be liberal of encouragement and praise toward their young subjects. In like manner let a Schola Cantorum be established, whenever possible, among the clerics for the execution of sacred polyphony and of good liturgical music.

§ 26. In the ordinary lessons of Liturgy, Morals, Canon Law given to the students of theology, let care be taken to touch on those points which regard more directly the principles and laws of sacred music, and let an attempt be made to complete the doctrine with some particular instruction in the aesthetic side of sacred art, so that the clerics may not leave the seminary ignorant of all those subjects so necessary to a full ecclesiastical education.

§ 27. Let care be taken to restore, at least in the principal churches, the ancient *Scholae Cantorum,* as has been done with excellent fruit in a great many places. It is not difficult for a zealous clergy to institute such *Scholae* even in smaller churches and country parishes—nay, in these last the pastors will find a very easy means of gathering around them both children and adults, to their own profit and the edification of the people.

§ 28. Let efforts be made to support and promote, in the best way possible, the higher schools of sacred music where these already exist, and to help in founding them where they do not. It is of the utmost importance that the Church herself provide for the instruction of her choirmasters, organists, and singers, according to the true principles of sacred art.

IX

CONCLUSION

§ 29. Finally, it is recommended to choirmasters, singers, members of the clergy, superiors of seminaries, ecclesiastical institutions, and religious communities, parish priests and rectors of churches, canons of collegiate churches and cathedrals, and, above all, to the diocesan ordinaries to favor with all zeal these prudent reforms, long desired and demanded with united voice by all; so that the authority of the Church, which herself has repeatedly proposed them, and now inculcates them, may not fall into contempt.

Given from Our Apostolic Palace at the Vatican, on day of the Virgin and Martyr, St. Cecilia, November 22, 1903, in the first year of Our Pontificate.

PIUS X, POPE

The Black List
of
Disapproved Music

At the Convention of the Society of St. Gregory of America, held in Rochester, New York, May 4–6, 1922, the publication of a list of music not in accordance with the MOTU PROPRIO was authorized. The works of the following composers and the particular compositions listed below are clearly antagonistic to the principles enunciated in the document issued by Pope Pius X.

In preparing this section it was considered sufficient to mention the titles of only a few of the "most popular" of the objectionable Hymnals, Choir-Books, etc., still to be found in so many choir lofts.

It would be manifestly impossible to print a complete list of all the works which fall under this head. The purpose of the Society is to draw attention to the type of composition which is clearly opposed to the principles of the MOTU PROPRIO.

All the Masses by the following composers:

ASHMALL	GENERALI	MARZO
BATTMANN	GIORZA	MERCADANTE
BORDESE	KALLIWODA	MERLIER
BROWN (WILL. M. S.)	LA HACHE	MILLARD
CONCONE	LAMBILLOTTE	PONIATOWSKI
CORINI	LEJEAL	SILAS
DURAND	LEONARD	STEARNS
FARMER	LEPREVOST	TURNER
GANSS	LOESCH	WIEGAND

Of CHARLES GOUNOD's, the following Masses:

St. Cecilia   Sacred Heart   De Paques (No. 3)

The musical value of the religious compositions of MOZART, JOSEPH HAYDN, SCHUBERT, G. ROSSINI,* C. M. VON WEBER does not enter into the question. The exception taken is their purely liturgical unfitness according to the principles declared in the MOTU PROPRIO.

* Not to be confused with Rev. Carlo Rossini, whose compositions stand approved.

All the Vespers and Psalms, by

ALDEGA	GIORZA	MODERATI
BRIZZI	LEJEAL	STEARNS
CAPOCCI	MARZO	WIEGAND
CERRUTI	McCABE	ZINGARELLI
CORINI	MERCADANTE	
GENERALI	MILLARD	

The Requiem Masses by

CHERUBINI   MADONNA   GIORZA   OHNEWALD

Hymn- and Choir-Books

ST. BASIL'S HYMNAL
(All editions to date, December, 1931)
BERGE HYMNALS
CANTICA PUERORUM, Eduardo Marzo
LAUS ET PRECES, Eduardo Marzo
COLLECTION FOR SODALISTS, A. H. RoSewig
CONCENTUS SACRI, A. H. RoSewig
CATHOLIC CHOIR BOOK, P. Giorza
CATHOLIC CHOIR MANUAL, G. M. Wynne
SALVE, VOLUME I, P. Giorza
GLORIA, VOLUME II, P. Giorza

LAUS DEO, VOLUME III, P. Giorza
THE CHAPEL HYMN BOOK
CATHOLIC YOUTH'S HYMN BOOK, Christian Brothers
MAY CHIMES, Srs. Notre Dame
PETER'S CLASS BOOK
PETER'S CATHOLIC HARMONIST
PETER'S CATHOLIC HARP
PETER'S SODALITY HYMN BOOK
SUNDAY SCHOOL HYMN BOOK
VADE MECUM, Kelly
WERNER'S COLLECTION OF SEVEN PIECES
WREATH OF MARY

MISCELLANEOUS DISAPPROVED MUSIC

STABAT MATER—G. ROSSINI

All of Rossini's compositions should be excluded from the Catholic choir. These works are unchurchly, to say the least. The "Stabat Mater" is most objectionable from a liturgical standpoint.

REGINA COELI—P. GIORZA

All compositions by P. Giorza should be eliminated from the repertoire of the Catholic choirs. The composer wrote any number of "Ballets." He did not change his style one iota when he put sacred words to these utterly secular melodies. The worst example of this "Ballet" style in church is the setting of the "Regina Coeli," which, sad to relate, is still sung in many of our churches.

JESU DEI VIVI—G. VERDI

Taken from the opera "Attila." This number is another favorite among Catholic choirs. Verdi did not write this for use in the Church, but for one of his operas. He would have been the first to object to its use in its present form, since it is neither fitting nor appropriate.

The AVE MARIAS by

LUZZI, MILLARD, VERDI, BACH-GOUNOD, MASCAGNI, LAMBILLOTTE, KAHN, ETC.

All arrangements and adaptations of Operatic Melodies, such as Sextet from "Lucia di Lammermoor," Quartet from "Rigoletto," arias from "Tannhäuser," "Lohengrin," "Othello," etc.

SALVE REGINA, C. Henshaw-Dana

BORDESE'S COMPOSITIONS . . . ALL

Songs in English, such as
    The End of a Perfect Day
    Face to Face
    Beautiful Isle of Somewhere
    O Promise Me
    I Love You Truly
    There's a Beautiful Land on High
    Good Night, Sweet Jesus
    Wedding Marches
        From "Lohengrin"—R. Wagner
        From "Midsummer Night's Dream"—F. Mendelssohn

NOTE: The Society of St. Gregory, at its convention held in Rochester, New York, May 4–6, 1922, registered an emphatic protest against the efforts made by certain publishers of Catholic Church Music to create an impression that "revised editions" of Masses by Mozart, Haydn, Schubert, Weber, Gounod, Millard, Giorza, Farmer, Kalliwoda and other composers of the operatic school were edited to conform to the requirements of the MOTU PROPRIO.

Because a certain number of repetitions have been eliminated from these unacceptable works it does not follow that they are metamorphosed, through this process, into liturgical compositions. No amount of revision, editing or truncating can create a devotional composition out of a work that is intrinsically secular in character. Pope Pius X, in his MOTU PROPRIO, made clear the distinction between the secular and the sacred style.

The attempt of certain publishers to "hoodwink" a gullible public by using in an indiscriminate manner the caption "In accordance with the MOTU PROPRIO" deserves the condemnation of every friend of liturgical art. A flagrant example of this attempt to pull wool over the eyes of the innocent is found in the publication of the popular song "Silver Threads Among the Gold" as an "Ave Maris Stella" under the caption "In accordance with the MOTU PROPRIO."

What the Society of St. Gregory has condemned in the way of unliturgical music applies to those so-called Revised Hymnals which have merited the disapproval of the authorities simply because the compilers and editors have chosen to disregard the very plain recommendations contained in the MOTU PROPRIO.

Three Anti-Modernist Poems: 1884, 1909, 1924

I

DIRECTIONS FOR COMPOSING A WAGNER OVERTURE

(From an American newspaper, *ca.* 1884)

A sharp, where you'd expect a natural.
A natural, where you'd expect a sharp.
No rule observe but the exceptional
And then (first happy thought) bring in a Harp!

No bar a sequence to the bar behind,
No bar a prelude to the next that comes.
Which follows which, you really needn't mind:—
But (second happy thought!) bring in your Drums!

For harmonies, let wild discords pass;
Let key be blent with key in hideous hash;
Then (for last happy thought!) bring in your Brass!
And clang, clash, clatter—clatter, clang and clash.

A Sufferer

2

(From the New York *World,* inspired by some music of
Richard Strauss, *ca.* January 1909)

Hark! from the pit a fearsome sound
    That makes your blood run cold.
Symphonic cyclones rush around—
    And the worst is yet untold.

No—they unchain those dogs of war,
    The wild sarrusophones,
A double-bass E-flat to roar
    Whilst crunching dead men's bones.

The muted tuba's dismal groan
  Uprising from the gloom
And answered by the heckelphone,
  Suggest the crack of doom.

Oh, mama! is this the earthquake zone?
  What ho, there! stand from under!
Or is that the tonitruone
  Just imitating thunder?

Nay, fear not, little one, because
  Of this sublime rough-house;
'Tis modern opera by the laws
  Of Master Richard Strauss.

Singers? they're scarcely heard nor seen—
  In yon back seat they sit,
The day of Song is past, I ween;
  The orchestra is it.

3

(From the Boston *Herald,* February 1924, inspired by Stravinsky's
Sacre du Printemps)

Who wrote this fiendish "Rite of Spring,"
What right had he to write the thing,
Against our helpless ears to fling
Its crash, clash, cling, clang, bing, bang, bing?

And then to call it "Rite of Spring,"
The season when on joyous wing
The birds melodious carols sing
And harmony's in everything!

He who could write the "Rite of Spring"
If I be right, by right should swing!

The Art of Noises

FUTURIST MANIFESTO

MY DEAR BALILLA PRATELLA, GREAT FUTURIST COMPOSER:
In the crowded Costanzi Theater, in Rome, while I was listening with my futurist friends Marinetti, Boccioni, and Balla to the orchestral performance of your overwhelming MUSICA FUTURISTA, there came to my mind the idea of a new art: the Art of Noises, a logical consequence of your marvelous innovations.

Life in ancient times was silent. In the nineteenth century, with the invention of machines, Noise was born. Today Noise is triumphant, and reigns supreme over the senses of men. For many centuries life evolved in silence, or, at the most, with but a muted sound. The loudest noises that interrupted this silence were neither violent nor prolonged nor varied, since—if we overlook such exceptional phenomena as hurricanes, tempests, avalanches, waterfalls—nature is silent.

Noises being so scarce, the first *musical sounds* which man succeeded in drawing from a hollow reed or from a stretched string were a new, astonishing, miraculous discovery. By primitive peoples musical sound was ascribed to the gods, regarded as holy, and entrusted to the sole care of the priests, who made use of it to enrich their rites with mystery. Thus was born the conception of musical sound as a thing having an independent existence, a thing different from life and unconnected with it. From this conception resulted an idea of music as a world of fantasy superimposed upon reality, a world inviolate and sacred. It will be readily understood how this idea of music must inevitably have impeded its progress, as compared with that of the other arts. The Greeks themselves—with their theory of music (systematized mathematically by Pythagoras) which permitted the use of a few consonant intervals only—greatly limited music's scope and excluded all possibility of harmony, of which they knew nothing.

The Middle Ages, with their modifications of the Greek tetrachord system, with their Gregorian chants and their folk songs, enriched the art of music. Yet they continued to regard music from the point of view of *linear development in time*—a narrow view of the art which lasted several centuries and which persists in the more complicated polyph-

642

ony of the Flemish contrapuntists. The *chord* did not exist: the flow of the individual parts was never subordinated to the agreeable effect produced at any given moment by the ensemble of those parts. In a word, the medieval conception of music was horizontal, not vertical. An interest in the simultaneous union of different sounds, that is, in the chord as a complex sound, developed gradually, passing from the perfect consonance, with a few passing dissonances, to the complicated and persistent dissonances which characterize the music of today.

The art of music at first sought and achieved purity and sweetness of sound; later, it blended diverse sounds, but always with intent to caress the ear with suave harmonies. Today, growing ever more complicated, it seeks those combinations of sounds that fall most dissonantly, strangely, and harshly upon the ear. We thus approach nearer and nearer to the *music of noise*.

This musical evolution parallels the growing multiplicity of machines, which everywhere are assisting mankind. Not only amid the clamor of great cities but even in the countryside, which until yesterday was ordinarily quiet, the machine today has created so many varieties and combinations of noise that pure musical sound—with its poverty and its monotony—no longer awakens any emotion in the hearer.

To excite and exalt our senses, music continued to develop toward the most complex polyphony and the greatest variety of orchestral timbres, or colors, devising the most complicated successions of dissonant chords and preparing in a general way for the creation of MUSICAL NOISE. This evolution toward noise was hitherto impossible. An eighteenth-century ear could not have endured the dissonant intensity of certain chords produced by our modern orchestras—triple the size of the orchestras of that day. But our own ears—trained as they are by the modern world, so rich in variegated noises—not only enjoy these dissonances but demand more and more violent acoustic emotions.

Moreover, musical sound is too limited in qualitative variety of timbre. The most complicated of orchestras reduce themselves to four or five classes of instruments differing in timbre: instruments played with the bow, plucked instruments, brass winds, wood winds, and percussion instruments. So that modern music, in its attempts to produce new kinds of timbre, struggles vainly within this little circle.

We must break out of this narrow circle of pure musical sounds, and conquer the infinite variety of noise-sounds.

Everyone will recognize that every musical sound carries with it an incrustation of familiar and stale sense associations, which predispose the hearer to boredom, despite all the efforts of innovating musicians. We futurists have all deeply loved the music of the great composers. Beethoven and Wagner for many years wrung our hearts. But now we are satiated with them and derive much greater pleasure from ideally combining the noises of street-cars, internal-combustion engines, automobiles, and busy crowds than from re-hearing, for example, the "Eroica" or the "Pastorale."

We cannot see the immense apparatus of the modern orchestra without being profoundly disappointed by its feeble acoustic achievements. Is there anything more absurd than to see twenty men breaking their necks to multiply the meowling of a violin? All this will naturally infuriate the musicomaniacs and perhaps disturb the somnolent atmosphere of our concert halls. Let us enter, as futurists, into one of these institutions for musical anemia. The first measure assails your ear with the boredom of the already-heard and causes you to anticipate the boredom of the measure to come. Thus we sip, from measure to measure, two or three different sorts of boredom, while we await an unusual emotion that never arrives. Meanwhile we are revolted by the monotony of the sensations experienced, combined with the idiotic religious excitement of the listeners, Buddhistically intoxicated by the thousandth repetition of their hypocritical and artificial ecstasy. Away! Let us be gone, since we shall not much longer succeed in restraining a desire to create a new musical realism by a generous distribution of sonorous blows and slaps, leaping nimbly over violins, pianofortes, contrabasses, and groaning organs. Away!

The objection cannot be raised that all noise is loud and disagreeable. I need scarcely enumerate all the small and delicate noises which are pleasing to the ear. To be convinced of their surprising variety one need only think of the rumbling of thunder, the howling of the wind, the roar of a waterfall, the gurgling of a brook, the rustling of leaves, the receding clatter of a horse's hoofs, the bumping of a wagon over cobblestones, and the deep, solemn breathing of a city at night, all the noises made by wild and domesticated animals, and all those that the human mouth can produce, apart from speaking or singing.

Let us wander through a great modern city with our ears more attentive than our eyes, and distinguish the sounds of water, air, or gas in metal pipes, the purring of motors (which breathe and pulsate with an indubitable animalism), the throbbing of valves, the pounding of pistons, the screeching of gears, the clatter of streetcars on their rails, the cracking of whips, the flapping of awnings and flags. We shall amuse ourselves by orchestrating in our minds the noise of the metal shutters of store windows, the slamming of doors, the bustle and shuffle of crowds, the multitudinous uproar of railroad stations, forges, mills, printing presses, power stations, and underground railways.

Nor should the new noises of modern warfare be forgotten. Recently the poet Marinetti, in a letter from the trenches of Adrianopolis, de-

scribed to me in admirably unfettered language the orchestra of a great
battle:

"*every 5 seconds siege guns splitting the belly of space with a* TZANG-
TUMB-TUUUMB *chord revolt of 500 echos to tear it to shreds and
scatter it to infinity In the center of these* TZANG-TUMB-TUUUMB
*spied out breadth 50 square kilometers leap reports knife-thrusts rapid-
fire batteries Violence ferocity regularity this deep bass ascending the
strange agitated insane high-pitched notes of battle Fury panting breath
eyes ears nostrils open! watching! straining! what joy to see hear smell
everything everything taratatata of the machine guns frantically screaming amid bites blows traak-traak whipcracks pic-pac pum-tumb strange
goings-on leaps height 200 meters of the infantry Down down at the bottom of the orchestra stirring up pools oxen buffaloes goads wagons pluff
plaff rearing of horses flic flac tzing tzing shaak hilarious neighing iiiiii
stamping clanking 3 Bulgarian battalions on the march croooc-craaac
(lento) Shumi Maritza or Karvavena* TZANG-TUMB-TUUUMB *toc-
toctoctoc* (rapidissimo) *crooc-craac* (lento) *officers' yells resounding like
sheets of brass bang here crack there* BOOM *ching chak* (presto) *chacha-
cha-cha-chak up down back forth all around above look out for your
head chak good shot! Flames flames flames flames flames collapse of the
forts over behind the smoke Shukri Pasha talks to 27 forts over the
telephone in Turkish in German Hallo! Ibrahim!! Rudolf! Hallo!
Hallo, actors playlists echos prompters scenarios of smoke forests applause smell of hay mud dung my feet are frozen numb smell of salt-
peter smell of putrefaction Timpani flutes clarinets everywhere low
high birds chirping beatitudes shade* cheep-cheep-cheep *breezes verdure herds*
dong-dang-dong-ding-baaaa *the lunatics are assaulting the musicians of the
orchestra the latter soundly thrashed play on Great uproar don't cancel the concert more precision dividing into smaller more minute
sounds fragments of echos in the theater area 300 square kilometers Rivers Maritza Tundja stretch out Rudopi Mountains standing up erect
boxes balconies 2000 shrapnel spraying exploding snow-white hand-
kerchiefs full of gold* srrrrrrrr-TUMB-TUMB *2000 hand-grenades hurled
shearing off black-haired heads with their splinters* TZANG-srrrrrr-
TUMB-TZANG-TUMB-TUUUMB *the orchestra of the noises of war
swells beneath a long-held note of silence in high heaven gilded spherical balloon which surveys the shooting , , .*"

**We must fix the pitch and regulate the harmonies and rhythms of
these extraordinarily varied sounds.** To fix the pitch of noises does not
mean to take away from them all the irregularity of tempo and intensity
that characterizes their vibrations, but rather to give definite gradation
or pitch to the stronger and more predominant of these vibrations.
Indeed, noise is differentiated from musical sound merely in that the

vibrations that produce it are confused and irregular, both in tempo and in intensity. **Every noise has a note—sometimes even a chord— that predominates in the ensemble of its irregular vibrations.** Because of this characteristic note it becomes possible to fix the pitch of a given noise, that is, to give it not a single pitch but a variety of pitches, with-out losing its characteristic quality—its distinguishing timbre. Thus cer-tain noises produced by rotary motion may offer a complete ascending or descending chromatic scale by merely increasing or decreasing the speed of the motion.

Every manifestation of life is accompanied by noise. Noise is there-fore familiar to our ears and has the power to remind us immediately of life itself. Musical sound, a thing extraneous to life and independ-ent of it, an occasional and unnecessary adjunct, has become for our ears what a too familiar face is to our eyes. Noise, on the other hand, which comes to us confused and irregular as life itself, never reveals itself wholly but reserves for us innumerable surprises. We are con-vinced, therefore, that by selecting, co-ordinating, and controlling noises we shall enrich mankind with a new and unsuspected source of pleasure. Despite the fact that it is characteristic of sound to remind us brutally of life, **the Art of Noises must not limit itself to reproductive imitation.** It will reach its greatest emotional power through the purely acoustic enjoyment which the inspiration of the artist will contrive to evoke from combinations of noises.

These are the futurist orchestra's six families of noises, which we shall soon produce mechanically:

1	2	3	4	5	6
Booms Thunder-claps Explo-sions Crashes Splashes Roars	Whistles Hisses Snorts	Whispers Murmurs Mutter-ings Bustling noises Gurgles	Screams Screeches Rustlings Buzzes Crack-lings Sounds ob-tained by friction	Noises obtained by per-cussion on metals, wood, stone, terra-cotta, etc.	Voices of animals and men: Shouts Shrieks Groans Howls Laughs Wheezes Sobs

In this list we have included the most characteristic fundamental noises; the others are but combinations of these.

The rhythmic movements within a single noise are of infinite va-riety. There is always, as in a musical note, a predominant rhythm, but around this may be perceived numerous secondary rhythms.

CONCLUSIONS

1.—Futurist musicians must constantly broaden and enrich the field of sound. This is a need of our senses. Indeed, we note in present-day composers of genius a tendency toward the most complex dissonances. Moving further and further away from pure musical sound, they have almost reached the *noise-sound*. This need and this tendency can only be satisfied *by the supplementary use of noise and its substitution for musical sounds*.

2.—Futurist musicians must substitute for the limited variety of timbres of the orchestral instruments of the day the infinite variety of the timbres of noises, reproduced by suitable mechanisms.

3.—The musician's sensibility, liberating itself from facile, traditional rhythm, must find in noises the way to amplify and renew itself, since each noise offers a union of the most diverse rhythms, in addition to the predominant rhythm.

4.—Since every noise has in its irregular vibrations a general, predominating tone, it will be easy to obtain, in constructing the instruments which imitate it, a sufficiently wide variety of tones, semitones, and quarter-tones. This variety of tones will not deprive any single noise of its characteristic timbre but will merely increase its tessitura, or extension.

5.—The practical difficulties in the construction of these instruments are not serious. Once the mechanical principle producing a given noise is found, one may vary its pitch by applying the general laws of acoustics. For example, in instruments employing rotary motion the speed of rotation will be increased or diminished; in others, the size or tension of the sounding parts will be varied.

6.—Not by means of a succession of noises imitating those of real life, but through a fanciful blending of these varied timbres and rhythms, will the new orchestra obtain the most complex and novel sound effects. Hence every instrument must be capable of varying its pitch and must have a fairly extensive range.

7.—There is an infinite variety of noises. If, today, with perhaps a thousand different kinds of machines, we can distinguish a thousand different noises, tomorrow, as the number of new machines is multiplied, we shall be able to distinguish ten, twenty, or thirty thousand different noises, not merely to be imitated but to be combined as our fancy dictates.

8.—Let us therefore invite young musicians of genius and audacity to listen attentively to all noises, so that they may understand the varied rhythms of which they are composed, their principal tone, and their secondary tones. Then, comparing the varied timbres of noises with those of musical tones, they will be convinced how much more numerous are the former than the latter. Out of this will come not merely an understanding of noises, but even a taste and an enthusiasm for them. Our increased perceptivity, which has already acquired futurist eyes, will then have futurist ears. Thus the motors and machines of our industrial cities may some day be intelligently pitched, so as to make of every factory an intoxicating orchestra of noises.

I submit these statements, my dear Pratella, to your futuristic genius, and invite you to discuss them with me. I am not a professional musician; I have therefore no acoustic prejudices and no works to defend. I am a futurist painter projecting into an art he loves and has studied his desire to renovate all things. Being therefore more audacious than a professional musician could be, caring nought for my seeming incompetence, and convinced that audacity makes all things lawful and all things possible, I have imagined a great renovation of music through the Art of Noises.

Luigi Russolo

MILAN, *11 March 1913*
(Translated from the Italian by Stephen Somervell)

Society for Private Musical Performances in Vienna

(A STATEMENT OF AIMS, WRITTEN BY ALBAN BERG)

The Society was founded in November, 1918, for the purpose of enabling Arnold Schoenberg to carry out his plan to give artists and music-lovers a real and exact knowledge of modern music.

The attitude of the public toward modern music is affected to an immense degree by the circumstance that the impression it receives from that music is inevitably one of obscurity. Aim, tendency, intention, scope and manner of expression, value, essence, and goal, all are obscure; most performances of it lack clarity; and specially lacking in lucidity is the public's consciousness of its own needs and wishes. All works are therefore valued, considered, judged, and lauded, or else misjudged, attacked, and rejected, exclusively upon the basis of one effect which all convey equally—that of obscurity.

This situation can in the long run satisfy no one whose opinion is worthy of consideration, neither the serious composer nor the thoughtful member of an audience. To bring light into this darkness and thus fulfill a justifiable need and desire was one of the motives that led Arnold Schoenberg to found this society.

To attain this goal three things are necessary:

1. Clear, well-rehearsed performances.
2. Frequent repetitions.
3. The performances must be removed from the corrupting influence of publicity; that is, they must not be directed toward the winning of competitions and must be unaccompanied by applause, or demonstrations of disapproval.

Herein lies the essential difference revealed by a comparison of the Society's aims with those of the everyday concert world, from which it is quite distinct in principle. Although it may be possible, in preparing a work for performance, to get along with the strictly limited and always insufficient number of rehearsals hitherto available, for better or worse (usually the latter), yet for the Society the number of rehearsals allotted to works to be performed will be limited only by the attainment of the greatest possible clarity and by the fulfillment of all the composer's intentions as revealed in his work. And if the attainment of these minimum requirements for good performance should necessitate a number of rehearsals that cannot be afforded (as was the case, for example, with a symphony of Mahler, which received its first performance after twelve four-hour rehearsals and was repeated after two more), then the work concerned should not, and will not, be performed by the Society.

In the rehearsal of new works, the performers will be chosen preferably from among the younger and less well-known artists, who place themselves at the Society's disposal out of interest in the cause; artists of high-priced reputation will be used only so far as the music demands and permits; and moreover that kind of virtuosity will be shunned which makes of the work to be performed not the end in itself but merely a means to an end which is not the Society's, namely, the display of irrelevant virtuosity and individuality, and the attainment of a purely personal success. Such things will be rendered automatically impossible by the exclusion (already mentioned) of all demonstrations of applause, disapproval, and thanks. The only success that an artist can have here is that (which should be most important to him) of having made the work, and therewith its composer, intelligible.

While such thoroughly rehearsed performances are a guarantee that each work will be enabled to make itself rightly understood, an even more effective means to this end is given to the Society through the innovation of weekly meetings * and by frequent repetitions of every work. Moreover, to ensure equal attendance at each meeting, the program will not be made known beforehand.

Only through the fulfillment of these two requirements—thorough preparation and frequent repetition—can clarity take the place of the obscurity which used to be the only impression remaining after a solitary performance; only thus can an audience establish an attitude towards a modern work that bears any relation to its composer's intention, completely absorb its style and idiom, and achieve that intimacy that is to be gained only through direct study—an intimacy with which the concert-going public can be credited only with respect to the most frequently performed classics.

The third condition for the attainment of the aims of the Society is that the performances shall be in all respects private; that guests (foreign visitors excepted) shall not be admitted, and that members shall be obligated to abstain from giving any public report of the performances and other activities of the Society, and especially to write or inspire no criticisms, notices, or discussions of them in periodicals.

This rule, that the sessions shall not be publicized, is made necessary by the semi-pedagogic activities of the Society and is in harmony with

* At that time, every Sunday morning from 10 to 12, in the Society's small concert hall.

its tendency to benefit musical works solely through good performance and thus simply through the good effect made by the music itself.
Propaganda for works and their composers is not the aim of the Society.

For this reason no school shall receive preference and only the worth-
less shall be excluded; for the rest, all modern music—from that of
Mahler and Strauss to the newest, which practically never, or, at most,
rarely, is to be heard—will be performed.

In general the Society strives to choose for performance such works
as show their composers' most characteristic and, if possible, most pleasing sides. In addition to songs, pianoforte pieces, chamber music, and
short choral pieces, even orchestral works will be considered, although
the latter—since the Society has not yet the means to perform them in
their original form—can be given only in good and well-rehearsed 4-
hand and 8-hand arrangements. But the necessity becomes a virtue. In
this manner it is possible to hear and judge a modern orchestral work
divested of all the sound-effects and other sensuous aids that only an
orchestra can furnish. Thus the old reproach is robbed of its force—
that this music owes its power to its more or less opulent and effective
instrumentation and lacks the qualities that were hitherto considered
characteristic of good music—melody, richness of harmony, polyphony,
perfection of form, architecture, etc.

A second advantage of this manner of music-making lies in the concert style of the performance of these arrangements. Since there is no
question of a substitute for the orchestra but of so rearranging the orchestral work for the piano that it may be regarded, and should in fact
be listened to, as an independent work and as a pianoforte composition,
all the characteristic qualities and individualities of the piano are used,
all the pianistic possibilities exploited. And it happens that in this reproduction—with different tone quality—of orchestral music, almost
nothing is lost. Indeed, these very works, through the sureness of their
instrumentation, the aptness of their instinctively chosen tone-colors,
are best able to elicit from the piano tonal effects that far exceed its
usual expressive possibilities.

At the first nine meetings, the following works were performed:

Béla Bartók, 14 Bagatelles, Op. 6 (twice)

Alban Berg, Piano Sonata, Op. 1

Claude Debussy, Two Song Cycles: Proses Lyriques (twice) and Fêtes
galantes (twice); Trois Nocturnes pour orchestre, arr. for 2 pianos
4 hands by Maurice Ravel (twice)

Josef Hauer, Nomos in seven parts, Op. 1, and Nomos in five parts,
Op. 2

Gustav Mahler, 7th Symphony, arr. for piano 4 hands (twice); Five
songs from "Des Knaben Wunderhorn" (twice)

Hans Pfitzner, Five Songs, Op. 26

Max Reger, Introduction, Passacaglia, and Fugue for 2 pianos 4 hands,
Op. 96 (twice); Sonata for piano and 'cello in A minor, Op. 118
(twice)

Franz Schreker, Vorspiel zu einem Drama, arr. for piano 4 hands (twice)

Alexander Scriabin, Sonata for piano No. 4 (twice); Sonata for piano
No. 7 (twice)

Richard Strauss, Don Quixote, Op. 35, arr. for 2 pianos 4 hands (twice)

Igor Stravinsky, Trois pièces faciles and Cinq pièces faciles pour piano
à 4 mains (twice)

Anton von Webern, Passacaglia for orchestra, Op. 1, arr. for 2 pianos
6 hands

Alexander von Zemlinsky, Four Songs, Op. 8

The following works are in rehearsal and are (among others) planned
for performance:

Alban Berg, Vier Lieder, Op. 2

Julius Bittner, Sonata for piano and 'cello

Ferruccio Busoni, Six Elegies for piano

Gustave Charpentier, Poèmes Chantés, for solo voice and chorus

Claude Debussy, La Mer, 3 esquisses symphoniques, arr. for 2 pianos
4 hands

Fidelio Finke, Piano pieces

Egon Kornauth, Violin sonata

E. W. Korngold, Violin sonata, Op. 6

Gustave Mahler, 6th Symphony, arr. for piano 4 hands by A. von Zemlinsky

Viteslav Novak, Erotikon, piano pieces

Hans Pfitzner, Piano quintet in F minor, Op. 23

Maurice Ravel, Two Hebrew Songs

Max Reger, Suite for 'cello, Op. 131c; Sonata for violin and piano,
Op. 139, Sonata for clarinet and piano, in B minor, Op. 107

Franz Schreker, Kammersymphonie, arr. for 2 pianos 4 hands

Cyril Scott, Sonata for violin and piano, Op. 57

Richard Strauss, Symphonia domestica, Op. 53, arr. for 2 pianos 4
hands

Igor Stravinsky, Berceuses du chat, Chansons avec ensemble, Pribaoutki,
Chansons plaisantes

Josef Suk, "Erlebtes und Erträumtes," piano pieces; "Ein Sommer-
märchen," symphonic poem arr. for piano 4 hands

Anton von Webern, "Entflieht auf leichten Kähnen," mixed chorus a
capella, Op. 2

Karl Weigl, String quartet in E major

Alexander von Zemlinsky, Six Songs (Maeterlinck), Op. 13; 2nd String
Quartet, Op. 15

Finally it should be mentioned that, in addition to the performances listed, there were lectures and other meetings serving the purposes of the Society. The financial means for accomplishing these ends were obtained in the following ways:

1. Through the regular membership dues.
2. Through voluntary contributions over and above these dues.
3. Through occasional voluntary gifts from non-members.

Following are the official membership rates:

The weekly evening meetings of the Society count as concerts to which members subscribe for a season. The subscription rates for the selected category of seats may be paid in advance for the whole season, or in quarterly, monthly, or even weekly installments, although the member obligates himself to pay all the installments for a complete season. In addition, upon joining the Society and at the beginning of each season, introductory fees must be paid, their amount varying with the location of the seats.

There are four categories of seats. The least expensive (IV) cost 1 Krone a week; the next (III) 2 Kronen; the next (II) 3 Kronen; the first category is reserved for those who voluntarily pay more.

In accordance with these rates, membership dues are as follows:

		a) 52 Weekly Rates		b) 12 Monthly Rates		c) Quarterly Rates	
annually		Intro-ductory	Weekly	Intro-ductory	Monthly	Intro-ductory	Quarterly
		Kr.	Kr.	Kr.	Kr.	Kr.	Kr.
4th category	60.	8.	1.	6.	4.50	6,	13.50
3d "	120.	16.	2.	12.	9.	12.	27.
2nd "	180.	24.	3.	18.	13.50	18.	40.50
1st "	300.	34.	5.	30.	22.50	30.	67.50
or	400.	36.	7.	40.	30.	40.	90.
or	500.	40.	9.	80.	35.	80.	105.
etc.							

This grading of dues was devised in order to share the considerable expenses of the Society equitably and in proportion to the ability of members to pay. It is naturally expected that those who are in a position to make greater sacrifices will avail themselves of the first two categories.

Upon joining this Society, members must fill in and mail the appended form, declaring knowledge of and willingness to abide by the statutes.

16 February 1919   President:
                                                    Arnold Schoenberg

EXTRACT FROM THE STATUTES

4. Any person of honorable and unblemished character and willing to accept the regulations may become a member.

6. The members of the Society are obligated
   a) to further the aims of the Society and to avoid acts prejudicial to them.
   b) to pay membership dues for the current year, even in case of premature cessation of membership.
   c) not to injure the cause served by the Society.

8. The direction of the Society consists of
   a) the President, Arnold Schoenberg, the duration of whose tenure is not limited;
   b) a committee of from ten to twenty (chairman, secretary, etc.) chosen by the General Assembly in agreement with the President.

9. The President has a completely free hand in the direction of the Society. He decides upon the kind and amount of the expenditures necessary to the work of the Society: fees paid to participants and the committee members specified in section 10, rental of halls, payment for lectures, administrative expenses, etc. He has also the right to remit wholly or in part the dues of worthy and needy members.

12. All decisions of the General Assembly, including elections, changes in statutes, dissolution of the Society, etc., require for their validity the consent of the President.

(Translated from the German by Stephen Somervell)

The Ideological Platform of the Russian Association of Proletarian Musicians

MUSIC AND THE CLASSES

(This is the third and last formulation of the platform of the RAPM, adopted in 1929. The first formulation was published in the magazine *Musikalnaya Nov*, No. 12, 1924; the second in No. 1 of the magazine *Music and October* for 1926. The RAPM was dissolved by government decree 23 April 1932.)

Reflecting the general evolution of class society, the music of the past evolved along two main paths: on the one hand the music of the toilers, the exploited, and the oppressed classes (the so-called folk music), on the other hand the feudal bourgeois music, which comprises virtually the entire bulk of written "cultured" music.

The position of this or that class at a given historical moment determines the development of these two musical cultures.

The brilliant spread of the musical culture of the ruling classes was determined by its possession of the tools of material, technical culture in the domain of everyday life as in that of the special musical field (complicated musical instruments, special technique of their manufacture, special educational institutes, music printing, etc.).

On the contrary, the music of the oppressed and exploited classes, despite its deep musical significance, remains at a primitive stage as far as cultural, technical and material means are concerned.

The above conditions give the ruling classes the possibility of utilizing the creative forces of the exploited masses. At certain moments of history musicians of the ruling classes address themselves to the art of the oppressed classes and, taking their most valuable possession, nourish their own music entirely with the vitalizing juice of folk music.

The bourgeoisie of the period of well-developed capitalism exerts, as a ruling class, profound moral influence on all strata and classes of the population, systematically poisoning the worker's mind. This influence is shown in the ideology of a certain fraction of the working masses and in their everyday life, as a result of which we find tendencies of degeneration and disintegration in the artistic tastes of some of its members. In the field of music this degeneration follows on the one hand the line of urban romance, on the other that of religious petty bourgeois estheticism, and very recently, the erotic dance of the contemporary capitalist city (fox-trot, Charleston, jazz music, etc.).

Since the emergence of social differentiation and stratification in the country, similar tendencies may be noted in folk music; having undergone the influence mentioned above, it becomes contaminated with songs alien to its nature (all sorts of "patriotic," "religious" songs and also those mentioned above), and, inasmuch as it reflects the psychology of different social strata in the country (on the one hand that of toilers, workers, on the other hand that of the exploiting parasitical elements), it ceases to be uniform.

While defining the class nature of one or another musical composition, it is imperative to consider its ideological emotional content expressed by corresponding sonorous material.

MUSICAL CULTURE OF THE PAST

During the bourgeois revolution and its struggle with remnants of feudal society, the bourgeoisie appeared as the bearer of economic and cultural progress, and its ideologists, among them composers, expressed the aspirations of a great majority of the population. At that time the bounds of cultural intercourse among men were comparatively wide and the bourgeois artists reflected the views of this wide community. This could not but affect in a beneficial way the artistic output of the bourgeois artists, inasmuch as inspiration, enthusiasm, and creative power increase in the direct ratio to the number of recipients among the popular masses.

The creative production of composers reflecting active and heroic sentiments of the revolutionary bourgeoisie, compared to the rest of the musical legacy, appears nearest to the psychology and world outlook of the contemporary proletariat, inasmuch as it possesses a more realistic, a more objective attitude.

This musical legacy, representing the best in musical culture of the past, has also evolved the highest type of musical form. The creative production of Beethoven and Moussorgsky may be cited as specimens of this highly-developed culture.

Bourgeois music in its latest period (that of the entrance of capitalism into its highest stage, financial capitalism) has reflected the process of general decay and disintegration of bourgeois culture. During this period music begins to cultivate decadent moods, and engages in the following pursuits:

a. Cultivation of sensual and pathologically erotic moods emerging as a result of narrowing interests of a bourgeoisie degenerating morally and physically; cultivation of musical materials reflecting primitive psychology of the nations whose cultural evolution has stopped at early stages ("barbarism," specific "colonial" exotic music, etc.).
b. Mysticism, feeling of oppressiveness as a premonition on the part of the bourgeoisie of the impending social catastrophe and the end of bourgeois rule.
c. Reproduction in a musical work of the movement of the contemporary capitalist city with its milling humanity and industry. This naturalistic streak in contemporary music is a symptom of its decay and, of the inner devastation of the bourgeoisie, the inadequacy of its ideological-emotional world to serve as a "means of communication among men" and inspiration for composers. Hence, the so-called "emotionalist" trends in music and, specifically, urbanist music that reduces itself to a more or less successful reproduction of noises.
d. Cultivation of primitive coarse subjects as a means, on the part of the bourgeoisie, to slow up the process of degeneration and to fight the proletariat that threatens "anarchy" for the bourgeoisie after the Revolution.

The decadent subject-matter of bourgeois music determines its form. Under the influence of decadent moods the inner meaning of music becomes diluted; technical elements gain ascendancy and music splits into factions according to its formal elements. In contemporary decadent bourgeois music the most characteristic elements are:

a. Hypertrophy of harmonic, vertical concepts, resulting in utter monotony and poverty of metrical, rhythmical design, which leads towards distortion of the musical phrase and loss of dynamic power, and disappearance of melos that causes the vocal crisis of bourgeois opera.
b. Hypertrophy of the polyphonic principle, accompanied by complete negation of the modal groundwork of music (so-called linear music).
c. The pursuance of alogical spasmodic rhythms.
d. The striving towards so-called absolute self-dependent "constructivistic" music, mechanistically built, and claiming to produce an emotional response of a predetermined nature. The school of composition inculcating this attitude (the so-called theory of "manufacture" of musical compositions) contributes to the complete disappearance of creative urge, replaced by dead mechanical schematicism.

During this last period the bourgeoisie, disguising its class interests under convenient slogans, makes claim to "objective," formal, technical "attainments," rejects the legacy of the classical past, and promotes "novelty," "contemporaneity" and "progress" in a narrow, formal, technical sense. These trends in contemporary bourgeois music, symptomatic of the psychological distress of the bourgeoisie, are a direct result of its decay and degeneration.

THE PROLETARIAN REVOLUTION AND THE CONTEMPORARY SITUATION ON THE MUSICO-IDEOLOGICAL FRONT

A long chain of circumstances prevents the proletariat from mastering the fine arts, music and literature, and from producing their own protagonists in the arts, and specifically in music. These circumstances are:

First, the proletariat has begun the social revolution not waiting for the complete development of its culture within the framework of capitalistic society (despite the fact that the process of cultural development has started long before the acquisition of power by the proletariat, and that in certain fields proletarian culture has attained great heights).

Second, the social revolution of the proletariat has started in a land whose working class was at a very low cultural level.

Third, a great deal of creative power has been spent during a long civil war, and an industrial upbuilding accompanied by the greatest difficulties.

In view of this and many other circumstances the proletariat which exercises hegemony in social policy and general economy, does not exercise this hegemony in cultural pursuits, and, in particular, in the arts.

The absence at this moment of the hegemony of the proletariat in the arts gives the opportunity to ideologists of intermediate and even openly inimical social strata to pursue their artistic aims along bourgeois lines and even influence the policies of proletarian institutions by foisting their ideology on them. The NEP [New Economical Policy] and the numerous bureaucratic distortions of the Soviet State apparatus contribute to the process of this insidious penetration. Besides, a great majority of proletarian artistic groups, in contrast with the proletariat which openly proclaims the class character of its artistic organizations, strives to conceal this affiliation under the guise of societies "scientific," "interpretative," "creative" and such, while actually serving enemy ideology. In music, for instance, the reactionary character of the right wing of musical society and its connection with the bureaucratic circles of the old regime force this group to maintain secret solidarity without forming any open organizations.

Social organizations and trends existing in music reflect on the one hand the general class differentiation and the existence of social stratification among these classes, on the other hand the various peripeteia of class struggle, uniting and disuniting, as they do, the heterogeneous social formations.

At the present time there exist among musicians the following trends reflecting the ideology of fundamental social groups:

a. A group of musicians that has been formed under the influence of the bureaucratic circles of the old regime, sponsors of art and music.

At the present time this group, in view of absence of all connection with living art in all fields, has completely degenerated into a dead and retrograde epigonism incapable of contributing anything vital to music. Members of this group have managed, however, to entrench themselves in several important educational institutions.

b. A comparatively significant force, represented by a so-called group of "contemporaries" that reflects the ideology of the one-time "vanguard" young Russian bourgeoisie and bourgeois intelligentsia and that defends the tenets of modern decadent bourgeois art.

The vitality and significance of this group stand in undeniable connection with the presence in the economy of our land, along with a socialistic section, of a comparatively strong capitalist current productive of bourgeois ideology. In some measure the ideology of this group is sustained by the penetration into the U.S.S.R. of bourgeois influences from the capitalist countries.

c. In the course of the next few years there must be expected a rise of the intermediate strata and classes, the village and city intelligentsia. Being a motley conglomeration of heterogeneous phenomena, this grouping requires that we discriminate in passing judgment on them. Along with sincere and honest companion-of-the-road citizenry striving to understand the proletariat and reflect its world outlook in its creative production and musical activity, there exist here certain grossly adaptationist trends that do not go beyond outward exhibitionistic "revolutionariness," and are essentially alien or even inimical to the proletariat.

d. In the course of the last five years there has been considerable progress of proletarian art contributing to penetration of proletarian influence among the artistic intelligentsia.

This proletarian group of musicians is potentially strong, thanks to its connection with a class now in the vanguard of history.

RAPM

The non-enforcement of hegemony of the proletariat in the divers ideological fields and specifically in the domain of art cannot, of course, continue for any considerable time. After the very first successes in the task of economic recuperation, the proletariat will assemble and solidify its cultural powers to repel the petty-bourgeois influences and heighten the cultural level of the masses, in which there is observable a huge growth of independent activity, not solely in the political and economical fields but also in general culture. Voluntary proletarian organizations have contributed to this growth in no small measure and are at the same time a determining factor in this growth. Such are, in the domain of the arts, the Associations of Proletarian Artists, organizations historically given to the proletariat as conscious expressions of the historical process.

The fundamental task of the Proletarian Artistic Associations is to establish the hegemony of the proletariat in various fields of the arts.

In the domain of music, such an organization is embodied in the Russian Association of Proletarian Musicians (RAPM) which unites musicians active in the proletarian advance-guards on the various sections of the front of class war, among them on the musico-ideological section.

The ultimate aim of the RAPM is extension of the hegemony of the proletariat to the music field. At present it sets the following concrete tasks:

- a. Extension of the proletarian Communist influence to the musical masses, re-education and reorganization of these masses in order to direct their work and creative talents towards Socialist upbuilding.
- b. Creation of Marxist musicology and Marxist musical criticism, critical absorption of the musical culture of the past and of contemporary musical literature from the viewpoint of the proletariat.
- c. Demonstration of proletarian musical creative productions and creation of necessary conditions for complete development and growth of proletarian music.

Toward the accomplishment of these tasks the RAPM

- a. poses at its open meetings the most urgent problems in the domain of creative work, Marxist musicology, mass action and pedagogical musical work;
- b. expounds, through the medium of the Soviet professional and party press, and also the organs of the RAPM, its fundamental ideas, heightens the social, scientific-musical and artistic level of the musical masses, analyzes and gives a musico-sociological evaluation of musical literature, pointing out the path of new musical work in city and country;
- c. while helping the working and peasant masses to create their own music, organizes musical education of these masses for which purpose it encourages proletarianization of music schools and formation of music-teaching cadres in the conservatories, and also discusses in special conferences, problems of method in musical work among the masses and the individual circles in workers' clubs;
- d. poses and discusses the problems of formation of new interpretative ways and begins the work of sanitation of our concert masses, organizing its own exemplary choral and orchestral collectives, and also groups of individual performers.

In its interrelations with various groupings of musicians, the RAPM is guided by the general policy of the proletariat and the party in relation toward various social categories. Neither the circumstance that the working class has already acquired power, nor the special character of musical problems deters the proletariat from fighting against ideological influences opposed to the proletariat on the musical front. As to the intermediate, the so-called companion-of-the-road groupings, the RAPM deems it necessary and useful to attract these groups unquestioningly into creative, scientific and educational work in the domain of music and to utilize them in practical work.

"While weeding out the antiproletarian and the counter-revolutionary elements and fighting the ideology of the new bourgeoisie among some of the companions-of-the-road, it is imperative to exercise tolerance towards the intermediate ideological forms, patiently helping them to form comradely relationship with the cultural powers of Communism." (From the resolution of the Central Committee of the All-Russian Communist party on the party policy in literature)

In their creative work, composers, members of the Association of Proletarian Musicians, strive above all to reflect the rich, full-blooded psychology of the proletariat, as historically the most advanced, and dialectically the most sensitive and understanding class.

Following the dialectical and not the mechanistic laws of evolution, composers, members of the RAPM, strive to create gradually new musical forms and a new style born of its artistic subject matter.

The interrelation of content and form is regarded by the RAPM as a dialectical unity.

Thus, while not accepting any form of contemporary bourgeois music that in its content is opposed to the proletariat, the RAPM proclaims the slogan of learning the craft first of all from those among composers of the past who reflected in their creative output the subject matter close to the revolutionary ideas of the proletariat.

New musical forms are created and will be created by the proletariat. Proletarian music must "penetrate into the innermost masses of workmen and peasants, unite the thought and the will of these masses and raise them" for further struggle and construction, organizing their class consciousness in the direction of the ultimate victory of the proletariat as builder of Communist society.

(Translated from the Russian by Nicolas Slonimsky)

Futurist Manifesto of Aeromusic

SYNTHETIC, GEOMETRIC, CURATIVE

Our futurist temperament, accelerated by the dynamic quality of mechanical civilization, has attained a hypersensitivity thirsting after essence, speed, and trenchant decision.

Long declamations, hesitating analyses and endless trains of words-lamentations-and-bells die in boredom for the ears of those who are swiftly rising in the air.

The futurist movement, created by a synthesis of Italian innovators inspired with originality and speed, has taught and continues to teach the religion of speed, that is, the attempt to synthesize the world from above.

For, beyond all prosody, beyond free verse and outside the bonds of syntax, we have been able to obtain the synthesis and the synoptic simultaneity of unconstrained tables of words of a new poetry. Furthermore, we shall create a new futurist aeromusic whose law is synthesis—brevity beyond all music.

Music, by its very nature sensuous, enveloping, penetrating and persisting in the nerves after the fashion of a vapor or a perfume, tends towards analysis, while showing itself apt at summing up all the infinity of sensations in a stirring moment—thanks to its harmonic densities.

As futurist poets and musicians

a) We condemn music for music's sake which borders fatally on the fetishism of a set form, on virtuosity or technicism. Virtuosity and technicism have alienated Bach, Beethoven and Chopin from synthesis, and they have confined their genius in a maniacal pursuit of musical architecture and of music for music's sake, scattering and chilling the stirring ardor, the themes and the "finds" in the midst of tiresome development and depressing repetitions.

b) We condemn the custom of setting to music "pastist" poems and subjects, the kind that composers, with their usual incompetence, are fatally bound to choose.

Only synthesis of free words can enable music to fuse with poetry.

c) We condemn imitation of classical music. In art, every return is a defeat, or disguised impotence. We must invent, that is to say, extract a personal musical emotion from life.

d) We condemn the use of popular songs, which has led spirits as perspicacious and cultivated as Stravinsky and most inspired talents, as Pratella and Malipiero, away from synthesis in an artificial and monotonous primitivism.

e) We condemn imitations of jazz and negro music, killed by rhythmic uniformity and the absence of inspired composers, long Puccini-esque lamentation asthmatically interrupted by slaps and by the syncopated tom-tom of railway trains.

Futurist music, a synthetic expression of great economic, erotic, heroic, aviational, mechanical dynamism, will be a curative music.

We shall have the following types of syntheses, which will enable us to live sanely in speed, to fly, and to win in the greatest war of tomorrow.

Sonorous block of feelings. Decisive crash. Spatial harmony. Howling interrogation. Decision framed by notes. The regularity of the air motor. The caprice of the air motor. Compenetration of gay notes. Triangle of songs suspended at a thousand metres. Musical ascension. Fresh fan of notes over the sea. Aerial simultaneity of harmonies. Anti-human and anti-impressionist expression of the forces of nature. Coupling of echoes.

Italian musicians, be futurists, rejuvenate the souls of your listeners by swift musical syntheses (not exceeding a minute), thunderously arousing the optimistic and active pride of living in the great Italy of Mussolini, which will henceforth be at the head of the Machine Age!

F. T. Marinetti

Maestro Giuntini

(From the Italian monthly magazine, *Stile futurista*, August 1934)

History of the Dalcroze Method of Eurythmics

Émile Jaques-Dalcroze was born in Vienna on 6 July, 1865, of Swiss parents. He came to Geneva at the age of eight, where he was to attend the College, then the University, and meanwhile—most important —the Conservatory of Music. Later he went to Vienna, and then to Paris where he studied with Leo Délibes. A year's engagement as conductor of a theater orchestra in Algiers gave him the opportunity to study the rhythms of Arabian music. He returned to Vienna to study under Fuchs and Bruckner. In 1892 he became a professor of harmony at the conservatory in Geneva, and it was here that his musical activities were thenceforward localized.

1st period—Geneva, 1903–1910

It was as a professor of solfège at the Conservatory of Geneva that Jaques-Dalcroze became interested in the difficulty his students had in singing accurately. In an attempt to correct this fault, he began to make them walk in rhythm. This formed the basis of the exercise known as "stepping the time-values" ("faire des pas") which has slowly developed into eurythmics.

It was in 1903 that the first "steps" were taken. In 1904 Dalcroze continued to improve and elaborate his exercises, although the refusal of the Conservatory to accept his ideas had forced him to give private lessons. In 1905 the Conservatory allowed him to give his first demonstration (15 April), and on the first of July he expounded the principles of his method before a Conference held at Soleure (VI Tagung der Schweizerischen Tonkünstler). In spite of this, official institutions still denied him their support, and he continued to give private courses, constantly attracting more and more pupils.

After frequent conferences and demonstrations, the study of eurythmics was introduced into the conservatories at Zurich and Basel (autumn of 1905 and spring of 1906).

The first summer class took place between 23 August and 8 September 1906, at Geneva, with 77 enrollments. It was followed by three more, also in Geneva: from 1 to 15 August 1907 (115 students); 1–15 August 1908 (130 students); and 2–16 August 1909 (140 students).

Meanwhile Dalcroze and several of his pupils were giving demonstrations outside Switzerland, and in 1907 a course of eurythmics was opened at Paris and at Brussels. The year 1907 also witnessed the first meeting of the Society of Eurythmics (Société de Gymnastique Rythmique) at Geneva.

In 1908 conferences and demonstrations took place in Berlin, Dresden, Munich, and Husum. In 1909 other courses were started and the demonstrations increased, including Paris, Heidelberg, and Vienna.

The method was launched. In 1910, at the beginning of the year, Dalcroze gave other demonstrations at Paris and Brussels, then in Berlin, Leipzig, and Dresden. As a result of this last visit he was offered the Institut de Dresde-Hellerau, so that he might have a place in which to put his theory into practice, and on 3 October Dalcroze and fifteen of his pupils left Geneva for Hellerau.

2nd Period—Hellerau, 1910–1914

Jaques-Dalcroze arrived in Dresden in October 1910, and it was in this city, at Ständehaus, that the first lessons were given. The cornerstone of the buildings of Hellerau was laid on 26 April 1911, and in November of the same year began a course in eurythmics. But it was in 1912 that Hellerau, garden city of Europe built by Germany's greatest architects, was fittingly dedicated. In June and July of that year the great Festival of Jaques-Dalcroze took place, with a musical program composed of Gluck's *Orpheus* and *Echo et Narcisse* by Dalcroze himself. It was a landmark in the history of the art: 4141 people came from Germany and other countries to take part in the celebration. The second Festival was held a year later. *Orpheus* was performed in its entirety, and more than 5000 people attended.

It is difficult to convey an impression of the brilliance of this period in the history of Hellerau. All the artists of Europe were there at one time or another, including such outstanding figures as Paul Claudel, Karl Storck, Bernard Shaw, Prince Wolkonsky (Director of the Imperial Theatres of Russia), Adolphe Appia, Nijinsky, as well as all the stars of Diaghilev's Ballet Russe, Max Reinhardt, and many others.

The history of eurythmics was not concentrated, however, at Hellerau. In 1913 alone, Dalcroze gave demonstrations in six cities of Germany and seventeen cities outside, while other professors were introducing his method in 36 other cities. Foreign governments sent commissions to Hellerau to study this new educational system. Dalcroze was invited to present his innovation at the International Congress of Physical Education at Paris; before the royal family of Belgium; and at the International Congress of Music Professors at Berlin.

In Europe and elsewhere the study of eurythmics was growing; 23 cities (9 countries) introduced it into their public schools, and 19 cities (7 countries) into their Conservatories of Music. There are Dalcroze schools in Berlin, Breslau, Budapest, Dresden, Frankfort, Kiev, London, Moscow, Nürnberg, St. Petersburg, Prague, Warsaw, and Vienna; and eurythmics is taught in 127 cities of the following countries: Germany, America, England, Austria, Belgium, Spain, Finland, France, Holland, Hungary, Italy, Poland, Russia, Sweden, and Switzerland.

The year 1914 marks the end of the splendid activity of Hellerau. On 4 February, Wolf Dohrn, the great organizer of the Institute, died as the result of a mountain-climbing accident. At the beginning of the year Jaques-Dalcroze had come to Geneva to direct the preparations for the great "Fête de Juin." The war came, and he never returned to Hellerau.

3rd Period—Geneva, 1915-1935

After several months of confusion, when all hope had been lost of reorganizing a center for eurythmics, the Institute of Geneva was finally opened (12 October 1915). In spite of the war, its enrollment for the first year included 397 pupils, representing 16 nationalities.

Everywhere there was a similar effort to keep the new movement alive. In Switzerland eurythmics was taught in fourteen cities, and included in the curricula of the conservatories at Berne, Basel, and Zurich.

In England there were 1392 pupils in March, 1916; and all during the war Dalcroze continued, in spite of the danger of crossing the Channel, to visit the English schools.

Although there was no large school in France at this time, there was a Club de Gymnastique Rythmique at 52 rue de Vaugirard, Paris.

In the United States instruction was now given in seven cities, beginning in 1915 with the first Jaques-Dalcroze Institute.

Sweden, Holland, and Russia continued the work and sent reports to Geneva. Each year one or the other of these countries distinguished itself by an increase in the number of students or by expansion into more and more cities.

In 1919 Geneva held its first postwar summer course, which has been followed by many others, and relations were renewed with Germany.

In 1926 the first Congrès du Rythme was held in Geneva, a huge demonstration which held out great hope for the future of eurythmics. In August of the same year was founded the International Union of Professors of the Jaques-Dalcroze Method. On this occasion the approximate number of pupils throughout the world was estimated at 22,700.

In 1927, Dalcroze was invited to Frankfort to give conferences and demonstrations at the International Exposition of Music. It marked his triumphal return to Germany, and the press welcomed him with great enthusiasm.

The United States announced in 1927 that 22 cities had courses in eurythmics; and in 1929 England counted 5574 pupils divided among 144 schools.

From 1915 to 1935 more than 125 demonstrations were given in Switzerland; from 1920 to 1935 Dalcroze gave more than sixty demonstrations in nine other countries.

Eurythmics can be said to exist in more than thirty countries, among which are South Africa, Germany, England, Australia, Austria, Belgium, Canada, Chile, Denmark, Egypt, Spain, United States, Finland, France, Greece, Holland, Italy, Ireland, Japan, Lithuania, Morocco, the Natale, Norway, New Zealand, Palestine, Poland, Portugal, Russia, Sweden, Switzerland, Czechoslovakia, and Yugoslavia.

From 1915 to 1934 the Institute at Geneva had 7253 pupils, representing forty-six nationalities.

(From the *Association Jaques-Dalcroze* at Geneva)

From Bernard Shaw

4, WHITEHALL COURT (130) LONDON, S.W.1.
PHONE: WHITEHALL 3160.
TELEGRAMS: SOCIALIST, PARL-LONDON.

2nd September 1936

DEAR SIR,

Within my lifetime there has been a complete liberation of modulation from its old rules. All the composers, great and small, have now availed themselves fully of this. New modes have been tried, like the whole-tone (or organ tuner's) scale of Debussy; and the obsolete modes have been played with a little. But all this music was in terms of some tonality or other, however sudden and frequent its modulations and transitions might be. And the harmonic practice was so free that the scale became a 12 note scale with nothing of the old tonality left but a keynote. Still, as long as there was a keynote there was no fundamental difference between Bach and Richard Strauss.

Schönberg tried to get loose from the keynote by writing pieces in listening to which you could not guess which was to be the final chord, because there was no tonal cadence. The revolutionary young composers rushed in at this new game and dropped key signatures; so that their scores were a mass of accidentals; but Schönberg exhausted the fun of this and relapsed more and more into tonality. This drift is apparent in all the big composers now. It is hard to say that the symphonies of Sibelius are in this key or that; but when we come to know his symphonies by heart as we know those of Mozart and Beethoven they will appear as tonal to us as Elgar's.

In short the post-Wagnerian anarchy is falling into order as all anarchies do pretty soon; and I expect soon to hear the Wagnerian flood of endless melody getting embanked in the melodic *design* of Bach and Handel.

Faithfully,

G. BERNARD SHAW

Nicolas Slonimsky Esq.
238 Hemenway Street
Boston
Massachusetts
   U.S. America.

A Letter from the President of the Composers' League in Japan on Contemporary Japanese Music

MR. N. SLONIMSKY. BOSTON.
DEAR SIR!

I am a master of Hacsoh-ha composer's Society. I have read your letter with great rejoice. Hacsoh-ha is a group of my students, so all members are yet young about 20 years old, because I am yet 30 years. They have no interesting national compositions in their past. I have also no works in pure Japanese style. We Japanese composers, now and past, are studying Europian Harmony and Theory.

Ofcourse, we have a earnest desire to complete our pure national music in future. We have many mystic melodies and wonderful scales in past, but we have no theories now and past. So we must at first, anyhow, study the perfect theories by West. We young Japanese composer is trying every test to using our old scales on our work. But non of them succes about it.

It is necessary to Japan, or it is a duty of Japanese composers, to complete a work and theories about it. We must compose or find new Japanese pure music in Western high style, in its instrumentation, systems and theorical elements.

Every group of Japanese composers or privatly earnestly trying this new work, but non of them complete it.

For instance, I send my score "Thema and Variations" for string trio to you. You will find easily from it only a Europian music, not a Japanese colour you needed. I know you will disappointed after reading my score. There will exist only a imitation of Western music.

I am very sorry, that you must wait a complete Japanese works in future; four or five years after. I believe that we will complete it recently.

Mr. Yokota, Nakano, Hirai are all my student and they are yet poor as young, so this time I will not send their works to you. But, I have

669

many students about 150 members, and I will heartily send you when they will complete it.

Many thanks to your kind letter to our Japanese composer in far East. We feel so many happies that we are musician, such a international artist. Please remember me and teach us as long as possible. I have a riliance on my hard will to complete our new National music.

My honourable conductor! please encourage me hereafter. Good by!

from your
Taijiro Goh

Tokyo Imperial Academy of Music
Ueno, Tokyo, Japan
22 March 1936

What Is Atonality?

(A radio talk given by Alban Berg on the Vienna *Rundfunk*, 23 April 1930,
and printed under the title *"Was ist atonal?"* in *23*, the music magazine edited
by Willi Reich, No. 26/27, Vienna, 8 June 1936)

Interlocutor: Well, my dear Herr Berg, let's begin!

Alban Berg: You begin, then. I'd rather have the last word.

Int.: Are you so sure of your ground?

Berg: As sure as anyone can be who for a quarter-century has taken part in the development of a new art—sure, that is, not only through understanding and experience, but—what is more—through faith.

Int.: Fine! It will be simplest, then, to start at once with the title of our dialogue: What is atonality?

Berg: It is not so easy to answer that question with a formula that would also serve as a definition. When this expression was used for the first time—probably in some newspaper criticism—it could naturally only have been, as the word plainly says, to describe a kind of music the harmonic course of which did not correspond to the laws of tonality previously recognized.

Int.: Which means: In the beginning was the Word, or rather, a word, which should compensate for the helplessness with which people faced a new phenomenon.

Berg: Yes, that, but more too: This designation of "atonal" was doubtless intended to disparage, as were words like arhythmic, amelodic, asymmetric, which came up at the same time. But while these words were merely convenient designations for specific cases, the word "atonal"—I must add, unfortunately—came to stand collectively for music of which it was assumed not only that it had no harmonic center (to use tonality in Rameau's sense), but was also devoid of all other musical attributes such as melos, rhythm, form in part and whole; so that today the designation as good as signifies a music that is no music, and is used to imply the exact opposite of what has heretofore been considered music.

Int.: Aha, a reproach! And a fair one, I confess. But now tell me yourself, Herr Berg, does not such a distinction indeed exist, and

671

does not the negation of relationship to a given tonic lead in fact to the collapse of the whole edifice of music?

Berg: Before I answer that, I would like to say this: Even if this so-called atonal music cannot, harmonically speaking, be brought into relation with a major-minor harmonic system—still, surely, there was music even before that system in its turn came into existence. . . .

Int.: . . . and what a beautiful and imaginative music!

Berg: . . . so it doesn't follow that there may not, at least considering the chromatic scale and the new chord-forms arising out of it, be discovered in the "atonal" compositions of the last quarter-century a harmonic center which would naturally not be identical with the old tonic. . . . We already have today in the "composition in twelve tónes related only to each other" which Schoenberg has been the first to practice, a system that yields nothing in organization and control of material to the old harmonic order.

Int.: You mean the so-called twelve-tone rows? Won't you tell us something more about them in this connection?

Berg: Not now; it would lead too far afield. Let us confine ourselves to this notion of "atonality."

Int.: Agreed. But you have not yet answered my question whether there does not indeed exist a distinction such as that implied in the word between earlier music and that of today, and so whether the giving up of relationship to a keynote, a tonic, has not indeed unsettled the whole structure of music?

Berg: Now that we have agreed that the negation of major and minor tonality does not necessarily bring about harmonic anarchy, I can answer that question much more easily. Even if certain harmonic possibilities are lost through abandonment of major and minor, all the other qualities we demand of a true and genuine music still remain.

Int.: Which, for instance?

Berg: They are not to be so quickly listed, and I would like to go into that more closely—indeed, I must do so, because the point in question is to show that this idea of atonality, which originally related quite exclusively to the harmonic aspect, has now become, as aforesaid, a collective expression for music that is no music.

Int.: No music? I find that expression too strong; nor have I heard it before. I believe that what the opponents of atonal music are most concerned with is to emphasize the implied antithesis to so-called "beautiful" music.

Berg: That view you take from me. Anyhow, this collective term "atonality" is intended to repudiate everything that has heretofore made up the content of music. I have already mentioned such words as arhythmic, amelodic, asymmetric, and could name a dozen more expressions derogatory of modern music: like cacophony and manufactured music, which are already half forgotten, or the more recent ones like linear music, constructivism, the new factuality, polytonality, machine music, etc. These terms, which may perhaps properly apply in individual special instances, have all been brought under one hat to give today the illusory concept of an "atonal" music, to which those who admit no justification for this music cling with great persistence, purposing in this single word to deny to the new music everything that, as we said, has heretofore constituted music, and hence its right to exist at all.

Int.: You take too black a view, Herr Berg! You might have been entirely justified in that statement of the case of a while ago. But today people know that atonal music for its own sake can be fascinating, inevitably in some cases—where there is true art! Our problem is only to show whether atonal music may really be called musical in the same sense as all earlier music. That is, to show, as you have said, whether if only the harmonic foundation has changed, all the other elements of former music are still present in the new.

Berg: That I declare they are, and I could prove it to you in every measure of a modern score. Prove above all—to begin with the most important—that in this music, as in any other, the melody, the principal voice, the theme, is fundamental, that the course of the music is in a sense determined by it.

Int.: But is melody in the traditional sense at all possible in atonal music?

Berg: Yes, of course, even vocal melody.

Int.: Well, so far as song is concerned, Herr Berg, atonal music surely does follow a new path. There is certainly something in it that has never been heard before, I would almost like to say, something temporarily shocking.

Berg: Only as concerns harmony: on that we agree. But it is quite wrong to regard this new melodic line as taking a path entirely new, as you declare, in comparison with the usual characteristics of melodic procedure, or even as never before heard and shocking. Nor is this true of a vocal line, even if it is marked with what someone recently described as intervals of an instrumental chromaticism, distorted, jagged, wide-spaced; nor that it thereby totally disregards the requirements of the human voice.

Int.: I never said that, but I cannot help feeling that vocal melody and melody in general does seem never to have been treated like that before.

Berg: That is just what I am objecting to. I maintain on the contrary that vocal melody, even as described, yes, caricatured, in these terms, *has always existed,* especially in German music; and I further maintain that this so-called atonal music, at least in so far as it has emanated from Vienna, has also in this respect naturally adhered to the masterworks of German music and not —with all due respect—to Italian bel-canto opera. Melody that is linked with harmony rich in progressions, which is almost the same thing as being bold, may naturally, so long as one doesn't understand the harmonic implications, seem "distorted"—which is no less the case with a thoroughly chromatic style of writing, and for which there are hundreds of examples in Wagner. But take rather a melody of Schubert, from the famous song *"Letzte Hoffnung."* Is that distorted enough for you? [Berg here gives further examples—from Schubert: *"Wasserfluth,"* bars 11/12, *"Der stürmische Morgen,"* bars 4/8, 15/18; and from Mozart, *Don Juan* in particular—to show that even in the classics vocal melody may be constantly on the move, expressive in all registers, animated and yet capable of declamation—indeed, an ideal instrument.] But you will also see by these examples from the classics that it has nothing to do with atonality if a melody, even in opera-music, departs from the voluptuous tenderness of Italian cantilena—an element you will furthermore seek in vain in Bach, whose melodic potency nobody will deny.

Int.: Granted. But there seems to be another point in which the melody of this so-called atonal music differs from that of earlier music. I mean the asymmetrical structure of melodic periods.

Berg: You probably miss in our music the two- and four-bar periodicity as we know it in the Viennese classicists and all the romantics, including Wagner. Your observation is correct, but you perhaps overlook the fact that such metrical symmetry is peculiar to this epoch, whereas in Bach, for example, it is only to be found in his more homophonic works and the suites that derive from dance-music. But even in the Viennese classics, and especially in Mozart and Schubert, we observe again and again—and quite particularly in their most masterly works—efforts to break away from the restraints of this square symmetry. [Here Berg cites examples from *Figaro.*]

This art of asymmetric melodic construction developed still further in the course of the nineteenth century (just think of Brahms . . . *"Vergebliches Ständchen," "Am Sonntagmorgen,"* or *"Immer leiser wird mein Schlummer"*), and while the four-bar period preponderates in Wagner and his followers (they clung to this earlier style-factor in favor of other innovations, notably in the harmonic field), even at this time there is a very clear tendency to give up the two- and four-bar form. A direct line runs here from Mozart through Schubert and Brahms to Reger and Schoenberg. And it is perhaps not without interest to point out that both Reger and Schoenberg, when they discussed the asymmetry of their melodic periods, pointed out that these follow the prose of the spoken word, while strictly square-rhythmed melody follows, rather, metrical speech, verse-form. Yet, as with prose itself, unsymmetrical melodies may be no less logically constructed than symmetrical melodies. They too have their half and full cadences, rest and high points, caesuras and bridges, introductory and concluding moments which, because of their directional character, may be compared with modulations and cadences. To recognize all this is to feel in them melody in the truest sense of the word.

Int.:   . . . and perhaps even find them beautiful.

Berg: Quite right! But let us go on: This freedom of melodic construction is naturally accompanied by freedom of rhythmic organization. Because the rhythm of this music has undergone a loosening process—let us say through contraction, extension, overlapping of note-values, shifting of strong beats, as we see it quite particularly in Brahms—does not mean that the laws of rhythm are dispensed with; and the term "arhythmic" for this treatment, which after all represents just another refinement of the artist's means, is just as silly as "amelodic." This rhythmic treatment is particularly conditioned too by the multilinearity of the new music; we seem, indeed, to be finding ourselves in a time which very much resembles Bach's. For as that period, through Bach himself, wrought a change from pure polyphony and the imitative style (and the concept of the church modes), to a style of writing built on major-minor harmony, so now we are passing out of the harmonic era, which really dominated the whole Viennese classic period and the nineteenth century, slowly but incessantly into an era of preponderantly polyphonic character. This tendency to polyphony in so-called atonal music is a further mark of all true music and is not to be dismissed just because it has been nicknamed "linear structure."

Int.:   Now I think we have arrived at a most important point.

Berg: Yes, at counterpoint!

Int.:   Right! The essence of polyphony of course consists in the inter-ordination and subordination of voices, voices, that is, which have a life of their own. Here again we are dealing with the harmonic aspect; I mean, the individual lives of all the voices give rise to a second, a new life, that of the collective sound. . . .

Berg: . . . which is of course not accidental, but consciously built and heard.

Int.: Now that is just what surprises me. Then is that elemental interplay of atonal voices, which seem to me to lack any such essential contrast as would give rise to a strong internal life, also achieved by conscious construction, or is it the play of some admittedly highly inspired chance?

Berg: That question—to be brief and not too theoretical—I can answer with a truth won from experience, an experience that springs not only from my own creative work but from that of other artists to whom their art is as sacred as it is to me (so anachronistic are we of the "atonal" Viennese school!). Not a measure in this music of ours—no matter how complicated its harmonic, rhythmic, and contrapuntal texture—but has been subjected to the sharpest control of the outer and the inner ear, and for the meaning of which, in itself and in its place in the whole, we do not take the artistic responsibility quite as much as in the case of some very simple form—as a simple motive or a simple harmonic progression—the logic of which is at once clear to the layman.

Int.: That explanation seems to me to make sense. But if so, it almost seems as though the word "atonal" must be a misnomer for this whole tendency in music.

Berg: Why, that's what I've been saying the whole time, trying to make it clear to you.

Int.: But then you, that is, your music, must somehow have some relation to the *formal* elements of earlier music too? If my guess is correct, this very music—the word "atonal" doesn't sound right after what we've said—strives to keep in close touch with older forms?

Berg: With form itself; and is it any wonder then that we should turn back to the older forms as well? Is this not a further proof of how conscious contemporary practice is of the entire wealth of music's resources? We have just seen that this is the case in all serious music. And since this wealth of resources is apparent in every branch of our music simultaneously—I mean, in its harmonic development, in its free melodic construction, in its rhythmic variety, in its preference for polyphony and the contrapuntal style, and finally in its use of all the formal possibilities established through centuries of musical development— . . . no one can reproach us with our art and tag it as "atonal," a name that has become almost a byword of abuse.

Int.: Now you have made an important declaration, Herr Berg. I am somewhat relieved, for even I thought that the word "atonal," whencesoever it came, had given rise to a passing theory foreign to the natural course of musical development.

Berg: That would suit the opponents of this new music of ours, for then they would be right about the implications which really lie in the word "atonal," which is equivalent to anti-musical, ugly, uninspired, ill-sounding and destructive; and they would furthermore be justified in bemoaning such anarchy in tones, such ruination of music's heritage, our helpless state of deracination. I tell you, this whole hue and cry for tonality comes not so much from a yearning for a keynote relationship as from a yearning for familiar concords—let us say it frankly, for the common triads. And I believe it is fair to state that no music, provided only it contains enough of these triads, will ever arouse opposition even if it breaks all the holy commandments of tonality.

Int.: So it is still sacred to you, after all, good old tonality?

Berg: Were it not, how could such as we—despite the scepticism of our generation—maintain faith in a new art for which Antichrist himself could not have thought up a more diabolical appellation than that word "atonal"!

(Translated from the German by M. D. Herter Norton)

Gebrauchsmusik *and* Gemeinschaftsmusik

(From a letter to the author from B. Schott's Sons, dated Mainz, 16 June 1936)

The word *Gebrauchsmusik* seems to have come into use in the post-war period. It is hard to define its meaning exactly. With the mechanization of music through radio and gramophone, with the increasingly organized musical life in Germany, and also owing to political circumstances, many composers, some on their own initiative, some because they were commissioned, began writing music for special purposes. The most obvious examples were compositions for the radio and musical illustrations for films; in brief, all compositions which called for no independent value in themselves but served only a special use (*Gebrauch*). When the expression *Gebrauchsmusik* was first used it is not possible to establish. It is not an official description, such as might head a section of a catalogue; its opposite would be art music, concert music, absolute music.

With *Gemeinschaftsmusik* the case is somewhat different. The post-war trend towards a polyphonic style gave rise to a new type of music-making, cultivated especially by the youth, and distinguished from the usual orchestral styles in that every voice has an importance of its own, i.e., all voices are equal, forming a new *Gemeinschaft* (community) in which new joy is found. This was true not only of instrumental music but also of all sorts of vocal music or the combination of both. In this connection we speak of "activating" the listener; as distinguished from the old "middle-class concert life," the main emphasis in the new youth is put less on listening to compositions written for the concert hall than on making music themselves. Correspondingly, it is no longer the virtuoso who plays the leading role, but the group, the community. This group arose, as we said above, out of the spirit of the new music itself and would not have been possible had not the composers of the day been turning always further from the romantic style, back to the *Spielmusik* of the middle ages and of the eighteenth century.

As a leader of modern music Hindemith was probably the first important composer to write for these purposes. He published such compositions under the title of *Das Neue Werk* in 1927 [Schott], so that it is justifiable to regard this time as approximately the birth-hour of the concept of *Gemeinschaftsmusik*. The expression must have been first used in Schott's catalogue about this time.

We understand that in the United States *Gemeinschaftsmusik* is translated by "sociable music." We no longer use this expression in our catalogues but speak instead of *Sing- und Spielmusik* (music to be sung and played), which seems to correspond better to the spirit of the music than the former term. We believe that the word *Gemeinschafts-musik* went out of fashion with the political turn in Germany in 1933, perhaps because it came into being in the era just preceding.

Letter from Arnold Schoenberg on the Origin of the Twelve-Tone Method of Composition

DEAR MR. SLONIMSKY:

The "Method of composing with twelve tones" had many "first steps" (*Vorversuche*). The first step happened about December 1914 or at the beginning of 1915 when I sketched a symphony, the last part of which became later the "Jakobsleiter," but which never has been continued. The Scherzo of this symphony was based on a theme consisting of the twelve tones. But this was only one of the themes. I was still far away from the idea to use such a basic theme as a unifying means for a whole work.

After that I was always occupied with the aim to base the structure of my music *consciously* on a unifying idea, which produced not only all the other ideas but regulated also their accompaniment and the chords, the "harmonies." There were many attempts to achieve that. But very little of it was finished or published.

As an example of such attempts I may mention the piano pieces op. 23. Here I arrived at a technique which I called (for myself) "composing with tones," a very vague term, but it meant something to me. Namely: In contrast to the ordinary way of using a motive, I used it already almost in the manner of a "basic set of twelve tones." I built other motives and themes from it, and also accompaniments and other chords —but the theme did not consist of twelve tones. Another example of this kind of aim for unity is my "Serenade." In this work you can find many examples of this kind. But the best one is the "Variationen," the third movement. The theme consists of a succession of fourteen tones, but only eleven different ones, and these fourteen tones are permanently used in the whole movement. With lesser strictness still I use the tones of the first two measures in "Tanzszene."

The fourth movement, "Sonett," is a real "composition with twelve tones." The technique is here relatively primitive, because it was one of the first works written strictly in harmony with this method, though it was not the very first—there were some movements of the "Suite for Piano" which I composed in the fall of 1921. Here I became suddenly

680

conscious of the real meaning of my aim: unity and regularity, which unconsciously had led me this way.

As you see, it was neither a straight way nor was it caused by mannerism, as it often happens with revolutions in art. I personally hate to be called a revolutionist, which I am not. What I did was neither revolution nor anarchy. I possessed from my very first start a thoroughly developed sense of form and a strong aversion for exaggeration. There is no falling into order, because there was never disorder. There is no falling at all, but on the contrary, there is an ascending to higher and better order.

ARNOLD SCHOENBERG

Hollywood, California
3 June 1937

Mediator Dei *of Pope Pius XII on the Sacred Liturgy*

§191. As regards music, let the clear and guiding norms of the Apostolic See be scrupulously observed. Gregorian chant, which the Roman Church considers her own as handed down from antiquity and kept under her close tutelage, is proposed to the faithful as belonging to them also. In certain parts of the liturgy the Church definitely prescribes it; it makes the celebration of the sacred mysteries not only more dignified and solemn but helps very much to increase the faith and devotion of the congregation. For this reason, Our predecessors of immortal memory, Pius X and Pius XI, decreed—and We are happy to confirm with Our authority the norms laid down by them—that in seminaries and religious institutes, Gregorian chant be diligently and zealously promoted, and moreover that the old *Scholæ Cantorum* be restored, at least in the principal churches. This has already been done with happy results in not a few places.

GREGORIAN CHANT AND CONGREGATIONAL SINGING

§192. Besides, "so that the faithful take a more active part in divine worship, let Gregorian chant be restored to popular use in the parts proper to the people. Indeed it is very necessary that the faithful attend the sacred ceremonies not as if they were outsiders or mute onlookers, but let them fully appreciate the beauty of the liturgy and take part in the sacred ceremonies, alternating their voices with the priest and the choir, according to the prescribed norms. If, please God, this is done, it will not happen that the congregation hardly ever or only in a low murmur answer the prayers in Latin or in the vernacular." A congregation that is devoutly present at the sacrifice, in which our Saviour together with His children redeemed with His sacred blood sings the nuptial hymn of His immense love, cannot keep silent, for "song befits the lover" and, as the ancient saying has it, "he who sings well prays twice." Thus, the Church militant, faithful as well as clergy, joins in the hymns of the Church triumphant and with the choirs of angels and, all together, sing a wondrous and eternal hymn of praise to the most Holy Trinity in keeping with words of the preface, "with whom our voices, too, thou wouldst bid to be admitted."

§193. It cannot be said that modern music and singing should be entirely excluded from Catholic worship. For, if they are not profane nor unbecoming to the sacredness of the place and function, and do not spring from a desire of achieving extraordinary and unusual effects, then our churches must admit them since they can contribute in no small way to the splendor of the sacred ceremonies, can lift the mind to higher things and foster true devotion of soul.

§194. We also exhort you, Venerable Brethren, to promote with care congregational singing, and to see to its accurate execution with all due dignity, since it easily stirs up and arouses the faith and piety of large gatherings of the faithful. Let the full harmonious singing of our people rise to heaven like the bursting of a thunderous sea and let them testify by the melody of their song to the unity of their hearts and minds, as become brothers and the children of the same Father.

§211. Given at Castel Gandolfo, near Rome, on the 20th day of November in the year 1947, the 9th of Our Pontificate.

PIUS XII

SOVIET MUSICAL POLICY, 1948

Resolution of the Central Committee of the All-Union Communist Party (Bolsheviks) of 10 February 1948

The Central Committee of the All-Union Communist Party (Bolsheviks) considers that the opera *Great Friendship* (music by Muradeli, libretto by Mdivani), produced by the Bolshoi Theater of the Union of Soviet Socialist Republics on the Thirtieth Anniversary of the October Revolution, is a defective anti-artistic work, in its music and its libretto.

The basic defects of the opera are rooted, first of all, in the music. The music of the opera is inexpressive and weak. It has not a single memorable melody or aria. It is confused and discordant; it is built on continuous dissonances, and ear-splitting combinations of sounds. Occasional lines and scenes, making a pretense of melodiousness, are suddenly interrupted by discordant noises, alien to a normal human ear, which produce a depressing effect on the listener. There is no organic connection between the music and the stage action. The vocal part of the opera, choruses, solos, and ensembles, make a distressing impression. As a result, the resources of the orchestra and the singers remain unused.

The composer did not take advantage of the richness of folk melodies, songs, refrains and dance airs, so abundant in the art of the nations of the USSR, and especially in the art of the nations of North Caucasus, where the action represented in the opera takes place.

In the pursuit of false "originality" in his music, the composer Muradeli ignored the best traditions of classical opera in general, and particularly of Russian classical opera distinguished by inner substantiality, melodic richness, breadth of range, national spirit, and elegant, attractive and clear musical form, the qualities which made Russian operas the best in the world, an art beloved by and accessible to broad strata of the people.

The libretto of the opera is historically false and artificial; it pretends to represent the struggle for the establishment of Soviet power and amity of nations in North Caucasus in 1918-1920. In this opera the wrong impression is created that such Caucasian nations as the Georgians and Osetins were at that time inimical to the Russian people, which is historically false inasmuch as the obstacle blocking the establishment of the friendship of nations during that period in North Caucasus were the Ingushs and Chechens.

The Central Committee of the All-Union Communist Party (Bolsheviks) considers that the fiasco of Muradeli's opera is the result of the fallacious, and, for the art of a Soviet composer, fatal formalistic path taken by Comrade Muradeli.

As was demonstrated at the conference of Soviet musicians, held in the Central Committee of the All-Union Communist Party (Bolsheviks), the fiasco of Muradeli's opera is not an isolated case, but is closely connected with a precarious condition of contemporary Soviet music and with the spread among Soviet musicians of formalistic tendencies.

As far back as 1936, in connection with the appearance of the opera by D. Shostakovitch, *Lady Macbeth of the District of Mzensk, Pravda,* the organ of the Central Committee of the All-Union Communist Party (Bolsheviks), subjected to sharp criticism the anti-national formalistic distortions in the music of Shostakovitch, and exposed the harm and danger of this trend for the destinies of the development of Soviet music. *Pravda,* acting upon the instructions of the Central Committee of the All-Union Communist Party (Bolsheviks), clearly formulated the demands presented by the Soviet people to their composers.

Despite these warnings, and despite the directives given by the Central Committee of the All-Union Communist Party (Bolsheviks) in its resolutions regarding the magazines *Zvezda* and *Leningrad,* the cinema film *Great Life,* and measures for improvement of the repertoire of dramatic theaters, no reorientation of any kind was made in Soviet music. Occasional successes of some Soviet composers in the field of song writing that received recognition and attained wide popularity in our country, in film music, etc., do not alter the general picture of the situation. Particularly bad are the conditions in symphonic and operatic production, with reference to composers who adhere to the formalistic anti-national movement. This movement has found its fullest expression in the works of composers such as Comrades Shostakovitch, Prokofiev, Khatchaturian, Shebalin, Popov, Miaskovsky, and others, in whose music formalistic distortions, and anti-democratic tendencies which are alien to the Soviet people and its artistic tastes, are represented with particular obviousness. The characteristic features of this music are the negation of basic principles of classical music; the preachment of atonality, dissonances and disharmony, supposedly representative of "progress" and "modernism" in the development of musical forms; the rejection of such all-important concepts of musical composition as melody, and the infatuation with the confused, neuropathological combinations which transform music into cacophony, into a chaotic agglomeration of sounds. This music is strongly reminiscent of the spirit of contemporary modernistic bourgeois music of Europe and America, reflecting the dissolution of bourgeois culture, a complete negation of musical art, its impasse.

An essential trait of the formalistic movement is also the rejection of polyphonic music and polyphonic singing, based on simultaneous combination and development of a series of independent melodic lines, and the cultivation of a monotonous type of unison music and song, often without words, in violation of the system of many-voiced singing harmony peculiar to our people, all of which leads to impoverishment and decline of music.

Trampling upon the best traditions of Russian and western classical music, rejecting these traditions as supposedly "obsolete," "old-fashioned," and "conservative"; haughtily snubbing those composers who are conscientiously trying to absorb and develop the concepts of classical music as adherents of "primitive traditionalism" and "epigonism," many Soviet composers, in their pursuit after a false conception of novelty, have in their music torn themselves away from the ideals and artistic tastes of the Soviet people, have cloistered themselves in a narrow circle of specialists and musical epicures, have debased the lofty social role of music and narrowed its significance, limiting it to the gratification of the perverted tastes of esthetizing egocentrics.

The formalistic movement in Soviet music has engendered among some Soviet composers a one-sided cultivation of complex forms of instrumental wordless symphonic music, and a supercilious attitude towards such musical genres as opera, choral music, popular music for small orchestras, national instruments, vocal ensembles, etc.

All this inevitably leads to a loss of fundamentals of vocal culture and dramatic mastery, so that the composers forget how to write for the people, as evidenced by the fact that no Soviet operas comparable to Russian classical operas have been produced in recent years.

The break between some Soviet musicians and the people has led to the formulation of the corrupt "theory" that the people fail to understand the music of many contemporary Soviet composers because they have not "grown up" enough to appreciate their intricate compositions; that they will understand it a few centuries hence, and that one should not be embarrassed if some musical works do not find an audience. This thoroughly individualistic and radically anti-national theory has contributed even more to the segregation of some composers and musicologists from the people, from the criticism of Soviet society, and has driven them into their shells.

The cultivation of all these and similar views causes the greatest harm to Soviet musical art. A tolerant attitude toward these views means the spread among those active in Soviet musical culture of tendencies alien to it, leading to an impasse in musical development, to the liquidation of musical art.

The fallacious, anti-national, formalistic tendency in Soviet music exerts a pernicious influence on the preparatory study and education of young composers in our conservatories, especially in the Moscow Conservatory (Director Comrade Shebalin) where the formalistic tendency is predominant. Students are not inculcated in the respect for best traditions of Russian and western classical music; they are not brought up to love national art and democratic musical forms. The creative output of many students of our conservatories consists in blind imitation of the music of Shostakovitch, Prokofiev, and others.

The Central Committee of the All-Union Communist Party (Bolsheviks) finds an altogether intolerable situation in Soviet music criticism. The leading posts among critics are occupied by opponents of Russian realistic music and adherents of decadent formalistic music. Every new work by Prokofiev, Shostakovitch, Miaskovsky, Shebalin, is acclaimed by these critics as "a new victory of Soviet music" and they glorify in this music its subjectivism, constructivism, extreme individualism, and technical complications of the idiom, i.e., exactly that which should be subjected to criticism. Instead of combating the harmful views and theories alien to the principles of socialist realism, music critics promote them, hailing the composers who share these false artistic concepts as the advance guard in art.

Musical criticism has ceased to express the opinion of Soviet society, the opinion of the nation, and has become a mouthpiece of individual composers. Some music critics, instead of writing objective criticisms, have begun, because of personal friendship, to fawn upon this or that musical leader, glorifying their works in every conceivable way.

All this means that a section of Soviet composers has not yet outlived the vestiges of bourgeois ideology, nourished by the influence of contemporary decadent western European and American music.

The Central Committee of the All-Union Communist Party (Bolsheviks) considers that this unfavorable situation on the front of Soviet music has resulted from the incorrect line in Soviet music, pursued by the Committee of the Fine Arts attached to the Council of Ministers of the USSR, and the Organizational Committee of the Union of Soviet Composers.

The Committee of the Fine Arts of the Council of Ministers of the USSR (Comrade Khraptchenko) and the Organizational Committee of the Union of Soviet Composers (Comrade Khatchaturian), have failed to propagandize realistic concepts in Soviet music, the basis of which is the recognition of the tremendous progressive role of classical heritage, and especially of traditions of the Russian musical school, the utilization of this heritage and promotion of its further development, combining high ideational values with the artistic perfection of musical form, the genuineness and realism of music, its profound organic connection with the people, and with the people's musical and vocal art; a high professional mastery, and at the same time simplicity and accessibility of musical works—instead of all this, they have actually encouraged the formalistic movement alien to the Soviet people.

The Organizational Committee of the Union of Soviet Composers has become the tool of a group of composers-formalists, the hotbed of formalistic distortions. The Organizational Committee has created a suffocating atmosphere in which creative discussions are absent. The leaders of the Organizational Committee, and the musicologists grouped around them, heap praise upon anti-realistic, modernistic products undeserving of support, whereas works distinguished by their realistic character and by an effort to continue and to develop the classical heritage, are declared of secondary importance, remain unnoticed and are ignored. Composers who flaunt their "advanced" and "arch-revolutionary" ideas in music act in the Organizational Committee as proponents of the most backward and provincial conservatism, revealing a supercilious intolerance towards the slightest manifestations of criticism.

The Central Committee of the All-Union Communist Party (Bolsheviks) considers that the atmosphere, and the attitude towards the problems of Soviet music, created in the Committee of the Fine Arts at the Council of Ministers of the USSR and in the Organizational Committee of the Union of Soviet Composers, cannot be tolerated any longer, for they inflict the greatest harm upon the development of Soviet music. In recent years the cultural demands and the standard of artistic taste of the Soviet people have grown to an extraordinary degree. The Soviet people expect from their composers products of high quality in all forms, in opera, in symphonic music, in vocal art, in choral and dance music. In our country, composers are given unlimited opportunities, and all necessary conditions have been created for a genuine flowering of musical culture. Soviet composers have a listening audience such as no composer ever knew in the past. It would be unforgivable not to take advantage of all these richest potentialities, and not to direct one's creative efforts along the correct realistic path.

The Central Committee of the All-Union Communist Party (Bolsheviks) resolves:

(1) To condemn the formalistic movement in Soviet music as anti-national and leading to liquidation of music.

(2) To urge the Department of Propaganda and Agitation of the Central Committee and the Committee of the Fine Arts to correct the situation in Soviet music, to liquidate the defects pointed out in the present Resolution of the Central Committee, and to secure the development of Soviet music in the realistic direction.

(3) To call upon Soviet composers to realize fully the lofty requirements of the Soviet people upon musical art, to sweep from their path all that weakens our music and hinders its development, and assure an upsurge of creative work that will advance Soviet musical culture so as to lead to the creation in all fields of music of high-quality works worthy of the Soviet people.

(4) To approve organizational measures of the corresponding Party and Soviet organs, designed to improve the state of musical affairs.

MEETING OF SOVIET MUSICIANS IN MOSCOW, 17-26 FEBRUARY 1948

Speech of A. A. Zhdanov

Comrades, the Central Committee of the All-Union Communist Party (Bolsheviks) has decided to assemble a conference of Soviet musicians for the following reasons.

Recently the Central Committee took part in the social preview of the new opera by Comrade Muradeli, *Great Friendship*. You can well imagine with what attention and interest the Central Committee anticipated the very fact of the appearance of a new Soviet opera. Unforunately, the hopes of the Central Committee were not justified. The opera *Great Friendship* turned out to be a failure.

What were, in the opinion of the Central Committee, the reasons, and what were the circumstances which led to the bankruptcy of this opera? What are the basic defects of this opera?

Speaking of the basic defects of the opera, one must first of all mention its music. In the music of this opera there is not a single memorable melody. The music does not reach the listener. It is not by accident that a rather considerable and sufficiently qualified audience, consisting of no fewer than five hundred people, did not respond during the performance to any part of the opera.

The music of the opera turned out to be very poor. The substitution of inharmonious and at the same time noisy improvisations for melody transformed the opera into a chaotic assortment of screeching sounds. The resources of the orchestra in the opera are utilized to a very limited extent. Throughout a major portion of the opera, the musical accompaniment consists of but a few instruments, and only once in a while, sometimes in the most unexpected places, the whole orchestral ensemble enters in stormy, discordant, and often cacophonic interventions, getting on the nerves of the listener and violently perturbing his mood. This disharmony, this lack of correspondence between the music and the actions, moods, and events, represented on the stage in the course of the opera, produces a depressing effect. A drum intrudes on the most lyrical moments of intimate sentiments; on the other hand, in the scenes of fighting and excitement, when the action on the stage portrays heroic events, the music for some reason becomes soft and lyrical. This creates a break between the musical accompaniment and the moods which the artists are supposed to reflect on the stage.

Despite the fact that the opera treats a very interesting period, the epoch of the establishment of Soviet power in North Caucasus, with all the complexity of its multinational society, and the diversity of forms of class struggle, demanding an adequate picture of the eventful life of the nations of North Caucasus, the music of the opera is alien to the national art of the peoples of North Caucasus.

When Cossacks are on the stage (and they play an important role in the opera), their appearance is not signalized in the music or in the singing by anything characteristic of the Cossacks, of their songs and their music. The same is true in regard to the people of the mountains. If the action includes the dancing of a Lezghinka, its melody does not remind us of any popular rhythms of the Lezghinka. In his pursuit of originality, the composer introduces his own music for the Lezghinka, an unimpressive, tedious music, which is much poorer, much less attractive than the traditional popular music of the Lezghinka.

The pretense of originality permeates the entire score of the opera. The music produces, I should say, a stultifying impression on the listener. Some stanzas and scenes of a lyrical or semi-melodious nature, or those that pretend to be melodious, are suddenly interrupted by noise and shrieking in fortissimo, reminding us of the noise on a building lot, at the moment when excavators, stone crushers and cement mixers go into action. These noises, alien to the normal human ear, demoralize the listener.

A few words regarding the vocal part of the opera: choral, solo, and ensemble singing. Here, too, one must mention the poverty of the entire vocal line of the opera. They say that this opera has complex singing melodies. We do not find it so. The vocal part of the opera is poor, and cannot stand a critical comparison with that wealth of melody and breadth of range to which we are accustomed in the classical operas. In this opera the largest orchestral capacities of the Bolshoi Theater and the magnificent vocal abilities of its singers are left unused. This is a great error. It isn't right to bury the talents of the singers of the Bolshoi Theater, giving them the range of half an octave, or two thirds of an octave, when they can sing two octaves. One should not impoverish art, and this opera represents the impoverishment, the drying-up of art, musical as well as vocal art.

The Committee of the Fine Arts, and particularly its chairman Comrade Khraptchenko, holds the chief responsibility for this affair. He widely publicized the opera *Great Friendship*. More than that, even before the opera was reviewed and approved by listeners, it was announced for production in a number of cities, in Sverdlovsk, Riga, and Leningrad. In the Moscow Bolshoi Theater alone, according to the Committee's statement, six hundred thousand rubles were spent on its production.

This means that the Committee of the Fine Arts, having passed a bad opera for a good one, not only proved itself incompetent in the task of leadership in art, but demonstrated its irresponsibility in having induced the State to expend large sums of money without justification.

If the Central Committee of the All-Union Communist Party (Bolsheviks) is not correct in defending the realistic direction and classical heritage in music, let it be said openly. It may be that the old musical norms have outlived their time; perhaps they should be rejected and be replaced by a new, more progressive direction. One must declare it openly, without hiding in the corner, and without smuggling anti-democratic formalism in music as contraband under the slogan of supposed devotion to the classics, and loyalty to the ideals of socialist realism. It is bad, it is not quite honest. One must be frank and declare outright whatever Soviet musicians have to say on this question. It would be dangerous, and downright fatal for the interest of the development of Soviet art, if the repudiation of the cultural heritage of the past, and the adoption of degraded music, were cloaked in a toga of supposedly genuine Soviet music. Here we must call things by their true names.

Declaration of Tikhon Khrennikov

The Central Committee of our Party in its Resolution of 10 February 1948 severely branded the anti-democratic formalistic tendencies in Soviet music. The immediate reason for the intervention of the supreme Party organs into musical affairs was the new opera *Great Friendship* by Muradeli, staged by the Bolshoi Theater of the USSR in the days of the thirtieth anniversary of the October Revolution.

It was established that repeated directives of the Party on the problems of art were not carried out by the majority of Soviet composers. All the conversations about "reconstruction," about switching of composers to folkways, to realism, remained empty declarations. Almost all composers who worked in the field of large forms kept aloof from the people, and did not enjoy popularity with the broad audiences. The people knew only songs, marches and film music, but remained indifferent towards most symphonic and chamber music. Concerts in which Soviet symphonic novelties were performed were attended very poorly, whereas classical programs almost invariably filled the hall. Soviet people, in their letters to concert organizations and to the Radio Committee, often voiced their perplexity and at times their protests against the incomprehensible and complicated music of a number of Soviet composers.

The leading figures of our Party and the Central Committee of the All-Union Communist Party (Bolsheviks) have frequently expressed themselves on the subject of Soviet art, directing its development along the path of Socialist realism, and cleansing it of harmful influences and alien ideology. Let us recall the words of V. I. Lenin on the tasks of Soviet art, his appeals in favor of a folk direction in art, his defense of Russian classical heritage against the assaults of the Association of Proletarian Culture; let us further recall the conferences of the Committee for Agitation and Propaganda at the Central Committee of the All-Union Communist Party (Bolsheviks) on the problem of music, held in 1925 and 1929 at the peak of the activity of the Association for Contemporary Music; the Resolution of the Central Committee of the All-Union Communist Party (Bolsheviks) of 23 April 1932 regarding the reorientation of literary and artistic organizations; the articles in the newspaper *Pravda,* "Confusion Instead of Music," and "Ballet Falsification" in 1936; the resolutions of the Central Committee of the All-Union Communist Party in 1946 concerning the periodicals *Zvezda* and *Leningrad,* the film *Great Life,* and the repertory of the drama theaters. We cannot fail to mention the utterances of Comrade Zhdanov at the philosophical discussions of June 1947, and particularly the principal thesis of his declaration: the thesis of the intransigent struggle for the purity of Soviet ideology as the most advanced and the most progressive in the world.

Among the directives of the Central Committee of the All-Union Communist Party (Bolsheviks) dealing with art, the Resolution on Muradeli's opera *Great Friendship* is particularly important for the destinies of Soviet music. This Resolution deals a decisive blow to the anti-democratic formalist movement which has spread in Soviet music. It administers a crushing blow to modernist art as a whole. At the same time this Resolution directs Soviet music onto the path of realism leading to the development and integration of the best traditions of musical classicism and musical art of the nations of the USSR, the path of truly democratic art, the creation of which the Soviet people expects from its composers.

The Central Committee of the All-Union Communist Party (Bolsheviks) points out in its Resolution that formalistic distortions and anti-democratic tendencies have found their fullest expression in the works of such composers as Shostakovitch, Prokofiev, Khatchaturian, Popov, Miaskovsky, Shebalin, and others. In the music of these composers we witness a revival of anti-realistic decadent influences calculated to destroy the principles of classical music. These tendencies are peculiar to the bourgeois movement of the era of imperialism: the rejection of melodiousness in music, neglect of vocal forms, infatuation with rhythmic and orchestral effects, the piling-up of noisy ear-splitting harmonies, intentional illogicality and unemotionality of music. All these tendencies lead in actual fact to the liquidation of music as one of the strongest expressions of human feelings and thoughts.

In Soviet music, particularly during the last three or four years, there has been increasingly noticeable a break between the listener and musical art. Indicative in this respect is the fiasco with the public of the majority of works written by Soviet composers in recent years: Muradeli's opera *Great Friendship;* Prokofiev's *Festive Poem,* his cantata *Blossom Forth the Mighty Land* and the *Sixth Symphony;* Miaskovsky's *Pathetic Overture* and the cantata *Kremlin at Night;* Shostakovitch's *Poem of Fatherland;* Khatchaturian's *Symphonie-Poème,* and others.

In the music of the majority of Soviet composers there is noted an over-emphasis on purely abstract instrumental forms, not characteristic of the classical Russian movement in music, and a lack of interest in program music on concrete subjects of Soviet life. Exaggerated attention is given to chamber music written for a handful of connoisseurs, while ignoring such mass consumption forms as the opera.

The composers became engrossed in formalistic experimentation with artificially inflated and impracticable orchestral combinations (such as the inclusion of twenty-four trumpets in Khatchaturian's *Symphonie-Poème,* or the incredible scoring for sixteen double-basses, eight harps, four pianos, to the exclusion of the rest of the string instruments, in Prokofiev's *Ode on the End of War*). Such music could not be performed by any of the provincial orchestras; and the gala performances in the Moscow Philharmonic evoked nothing but bewilderment among the listeners by the irrational use of orchestral sonorities, at times actually causing physical suffering. Musical instruments were not used in their natural medium. Thus, the piano was converted into a percussion instrument (as in the fist blows on the keyboard in Prokofiev's *Sixth Sonata*); the violin was transformed from a songful, tender instrument into a grunting, percussive one. The clarity and logic of harmonic progressions were sacrificed in favor of intentional complexity of acoustical combinations; natural chords were turned into "timbre-sounds," into blots and inkspots of sound.

A peculiar writing in code, abstractness of the musical language, often reflected images and emotions alien to Soviet realistic art—expressionistic tenseness, neuroticism, escape into a region of abnormal, repulsive, and pathological phenomena. This defect is noticeable in many pages of Shostakovitch's *Eighth* and *Ninth Symphonies,* and the *Piano Sonatas* of Prokofiev. One of the means of escape from reality was also the "neo-classical" tendency in the music of Shostakovitch and his imitators, the resurrection of melodic turns and mannerisms of Bach, Handel, Haydn, and other composers, which were reproduced in a decadently distorted manner.

The musical art of the people and, above all, Russian folk songs were not favored by the aforementioned composers. When occasionally they turned toward folk melodies they arranged them in an overcomplex decadent manner alien to folk art (as in Popov's *Third Symphony on Spanish Themes,* and in some arrangements of Russian folk songs by Prokofiev).

All these creative faults are typical expressions of formalism.

Formalism is a revelation of emptiness and lack of ideas in art. The rejection of ideas in art leads to the preachment of "art for art's sake," to a cult of "pure" form, a cult of technical devices as a goal in itself, a hypertrophy of certain elements of the musical speech at the price of a loss of integrity and harmoniousness of art.

The Resolution of the Central Committee of the All-Union Communist Party (Bolsheviks) indicates that one of the traits of formalist music is the rejection of singing polyphony and a retreat towards a cerebral, dry, artificial counterpoint in the so-called linear style, or else the adoption of primitive unison writing.

The cultivation of form as a goal in art leads in the end to the disintegration of form itself and to the loss of high-quality professional mastery.

As Comrade Zhdanov has profoundly pointed out, the philosophical background of these views is subjective idealism. The artist imagines himself to be the appraiser and final judge of his art. He cares little about the listening human society. Personal caprice, a random whim, an extreme inconsiderateness, and the subjectivism of the isolated author are sharply contrasted with the requirements and expectations of his environment: "This is the way I feel, and I don't care what my listeners think about it."

Comrade Zhdanov has said in this connection that if an artist does not expect to be understood by his contemporaries, it leads to desolation, to an impasse. If a true artist, says Comrade Zhdanov, finds that his work is not understood by the listeners, he must figure out first of all why he failed to please the people, why the people cannot understand him.

The theory and practice of formalism is a complete negation of democratic aspirations of the Russian classical composers and of the progressive representatives of music criticism. Great musicians of the past addressed their art to a contemporary audience, to their people, and not to their remote descendants.

Soviet composers of the formalistic persuasion ignored these progressive traditions of Russian classicism. It is not by accident that Comrade Zhdanov said to the composers-formalists present at the conference in the Central Committee: "One must admit that the landlord Glinka, the government clerk Serov and the member of nobility Stasov were more democratic than you are."

The anti-democratic formalistic direction of Soviet music is closely connected with the bourgeois decadent music of the contemporary West and the modernistic music of pre-revolutionary Russia.

The present musical art of western Europe and America reflects the universal dissolution and spiritual impoverishment of bourgeois culture. One cannot name a single composer of the West who is not infected with formalistic diseases, subjectivism and mysticism, and lack of ideological principles. The apostle of reactionary forces in bourgeois music, Igor Stravinsky, with equal impartiality writes a Catholic Mass in a stylized decadent style, or jazz pieces for the circus. The latest musical "genius" of contemporary France, Olivier Messiaen, writes mystical music on subjects from the Bible and medieval Catholic works. Contemporary operas of the German composers Hindemith, Krenek, Alban Berg, the Englishman Britten, the American Menotti, are a conglomeration of wild harmonies, far removed from natural human song. In this music there is frankly proclaimed a reversion to the primitive savage cultures of prehistoric society; eroticism is glorified along with psychopathology, sexual perversion, amorality and the shamelessness of the contemporary bourgeois heroes of the twentieth century.

In the well-known opera by Krenek, *Sprung über den Schatten,* nearly all the characters are absolutely amoral individuals. In that opera there is even a special chorus of sexual psychopaths-masochists. In the opera by the German composer Max Brand, *Machinist Hopkins,* the principal characters are murderers and erotomaniacs. Machinist Hopkins himself is a vile fascist caricature of a leader in a workers' movement, and is represented as a lustful beast, a base exploiter of women.

In Hindemith's *Sancta Susanna* religious erotomania is portrayed with repulsive naturalism. Similar pathology characterizes the neurotic operas of Alban Berg, and, among recent operas, *The Medium* by Gian-Carlo Menotti which enjoys tremendous success with the bourgeois public in America. The central character of this opera is a professional swindler, a woman spiritualist who suffers from alcoholism, and in addition is a murderess.

In Russian music formalistic ideas flourished particularly during the reaction after the Revolution of 1905. Among characteristic examples of decadent art in music are Stravinsky's *Le Sacre du Printemps,* Prokofiev's *Buffoon,* and a number of other works by these composers. The man who inspired and commissioned the majority of these works was Serge Diaghilev, one of the most prominent ideologists of Russian modernism.

Diaghilev was the organizer of a modernistic group of artists, known as "The World of Art." He urged artists and musicians to sever connections with the great realistic traditions of Russian art: "Down with the traditions of the Mighty Five, of Tchaikovsky. They are obsolete and limited national phenomena; it is time to merge Russian art in a common European culture"— such was the frank and cynical slogan of Diaghilev and other representatives of the modernistic camp.

The modernist element in Russian music is the revelation of frank sycophancy before the Western music market, a desire to gain favor with the foreign audience, to titillate the nerves of the surfeited bourgeois listener-snob with exotic Russian "Asianism."

For Diaghilev's ballet in Paris, Stravinsky wrote *Petrouchka, Le Sacre du Printemps, Les Noces,* the opera *Le Rossignol,* and Prokofiev wrote his ballet *The Buffoon,* and other works.

The principal goal of the composers of these works is to escape from the contemporary world of humanity into the world of abstraction. Stravinsky himself, in his article, "What I Wished to Express in *Le Sacre du Printemps*" (*Music*, monthly magazine, 1913), writes: "I evoke neither human joy nor human sadness; I move towards a greater abstraction." His reversion to the images of "primordial earth" he explains by a desire to reflect "that fear which lives in every sensitive soul in contact with mysterious forces." This reversion to antediluvian barbaric images, the depiction of savagery and bestial instincts of a prehistoric man, of a Scythian, is found in some poems of the Russian writers of the bourgeois-modernistic type. In these poems, there is sounded an alarm before the "coming Ham," the plebeian who must come and destroy the beauty and the well-being of the bourgeois regime. In *Le Sacre du Printemps* Stravinsky expressed these moods in boisterous, chaotic, intentionally coarse, screaming sonorities. "Rhythm and motion, not the element of feeling, are the foundations of musical art," asserted Stravinsky. With Diaghilev's blessings Stravinsky uses, in *Petrouchka* and *Les Noces*, some elements of Russian life to mock at Russian customs and to please the European spectator by the express emphasis on Russian "Asianism," crudity, animal instincts, sexual motives. Ancient folk strains are here grotesquely distorted, twisted, and are served as if reflected in a crooked mirror. These so-called "irony and grotesque" are in evidence also in Prokofiev's ballet *The Buffoon*, in which the "exoticism" of old Russian folkways is relished in a decadent manner. The musical language of this work is related to the above-named ballets of Stravinsky. The continuation of the same line of "Russian grotesque" is seen in Stravinsky's comic opera "after Pushkin," *Mavra*, written in 1922. From this opera there is a direct line to the two defective operas by Shostakovitch, *The Nose* and *Lady Macbeth*.

Paralleling this line Stravinsky and other new composers of the West, such as Hindemith in Germany, launched in the 1920's a "new" slogan (actually it is closely connected with the first line) : "back to Bach!" This meant that in a number of works there were revived polyphonic devices mechanically transplanted from Bach. They were ornamented by "new" harmonies, transforming the whole thing into cacophony. This reversion to Bach led to the composition by Stravinsky of the so-called *Symphony of Psalms*, in which there are stridently combined the old Bachian devices of polyphonic writing with the ear-splitting "contemporary" harmonies. The meaning of this mixture is well expressed in the composer's dedication of this Symphony: "Dedicated to the Almighty Lord and to the American Philharmonic Society."*

The music of Soviet composers of the 1920's and 1930's offers numerous instances of formalistic tendencies in Soviet music: Shostakovitch: opera *The Nose, Second Symphony, Third Symphony;* Prokofiev: the ballets *The Prodi-*

---

* The inscription in the score of Stravinsky's *Symphony of Psalms* reads: "Composed for the glory of God and dedicated to the Boston Symphony on the occasion of the fiftieth anniversary of its existence."

gal Son, *On the Boristhenes, Pas d'acier,* the opera *The Flaming Angel, Third Symphony, Fourth Symphony, Fifth Piano Concerto, Fifth Piano Sonata;* Mossolov: *Iron Foundry, Newspaper Advertisements;* Knipper: the opera *North Wind, Tales of a Porcelain Buddha;* Deshevov: the opera *Ice and Steel;* Miaskovsky: *Tenth Symphony, Thirteenth Symphony, Third Piano Sonata, Fourth Piano Sonata;* Feinberg: *Piano Sonatas, First Piano Concerto;* Shebalin: *Lenin Symphony, Second Symphony;* Popov: *First Symphony;* Liatoshinsky: *Second Symphony,* songs; Boelza: *First Symphony, Second Symphony,* songs; Polovinkin: *Telescopes* for orchestra, *Accidents* for piano; Litinsky: Quartets and Sonatas; Stcherbatchev: *Third Symphony,* etc.

The formalistic element in music is particularly strong in the *Eighth Symphony,* the *Ninth Symphony,* and the *Second Piano Sonata* by Shostakovitch; in the *Sixth Symphony,* the opera *War and Peace,* and a number of piano works by Prokofiev; in *Symphonie-Poème* by Khatchaturian; in the Quartet and String Trio by Shebalin, and in the *Third Symphony* by Popov. In Miaskovsky's music we find a one-sided preoccupation with instrumental music and a lack of interest for vocal and operatic music, which had a detrimental effect on the melodic idiom of his instrumental compositions, particularly the *Third Piano Sonata* and the *Fourth Piano Sonata,* written in the 1920's, but newly revised by the composer in recent years.

The influence of formalism is strongly felt in the creative work of young composers. The imitation of negative traits of the music by Shostakovitch and Prokofiev, the infatuation with decadent thematics, exoticism and mysticism became almost a routine phenomenon in the creative output of the young generation of Soviet composers.

Formalistic distortions are also strongly reflected in the education of young composers in conservatories, particularly in the Moscow Conservatory. This is obviously connected with the fact that some composers mentioned in the Resolution of the Central Committee of the All-Union Communist Party (Bolsheviks) as representative of the formalistic movement (Shostakovitch, Shebalin and Miaskovsky) are professors of the Moscow Conservatory, and Shebalin is its director.

The almost total contamination of young composers with the harmful influence of western music, the imitation of negative qualities of Soviet composers belonging to the formalist school, neglect of the traditions of musical classicism, particularly Russian classicism, and of the art of the nations of the USSR, testifies to the fact that the formalist movement plays a decisive role in the education of the young cadres of composers.

The Central Committee of the All-Union Communist Party (Bolsheviks) notes an altogether intolerable condition of Soviet music criticism. Our critics have lost the most important quality of Russian progressive criticism. They have ceased to fight for the high aspirations of art, for the ideals of realistic and democratic art.

The orientation towards Stravinsky as the most progressive phenomenon in contemporary music is found in the treatise of A. Ogolevetz, *Introduction to Contemporary Musical Thought.* In essence the entire "theory" of A. Ogolevetz is, objectively speaking, a theoretical support of formalism, and is an anti-Leninist and anti-Marxist work.

The musical departments of the periodical, *Soviet Art,* and other newspapers, and the monthly *Sovietskaya Musica* did not fight for the ideals of democratic art but lent their pages to apologists for the formalist movement. The Committee of Fine Arts has often shown the inclination to stifle even the most timid attempts to criticize the formalist movement. Thus, at the personal directive of Comrade Khraptchenko, chairman of the Committee of Fine Arts, critical articles about the *Ninth Symphony* of Shostakovitch (among them an article by Keldysh strongly condemning this Symphony) were not allowed for publication in *Sovietskaya Musica.*

The policy of the Committee of Fine Arts, the Organizational Committee, and the Musical Fund, in the Section for Promotion and Propaganda of Soviet music, reflected above all the interests of the formalist school. Thus, the Musical Fund published the obviously fallacious formalistic compositions of the type of the *Second Symphony* of Boelza and the *Fourth Symphony* of Shostakovitch, not to mention numerous editions of different versions of works by a narrow group of composers of the formalist school.

The Committee on Fine Arts did not take suitable measures toward the development of Soviet music in the realistic direction; it failed to promote the composition of operas, choral music, popular music for small orchestras, music for national instruments, vocal ensembles, etc. Commissions given to composers by the Committee of Fine Arts did not direct Soviet music along the correct path. The system of commissions was basically a form of material security for the leading group of composers of the formalist school. The major part of State commissions for the year 1947 was taken up by abstract, textless, instrumental forms. Prokofiev alone received eight commissions, among them one for the preparation of a "new" version of his *Fourth Symphony* derived from his ballet *The Prodigal Son,* which was condemned by Soviet society.

The decisive role in the Music Section of the Committee for Stalin Prizes was played by the same composers, representatives of the formalist movement. Some products of decadent art, which failed to find recognition with the general public, were nominated for a prize on the basis of a hearing by the narrow circle of specialists. Almost every new work by "leading" composers was automatically promoted as a prize work, year after year.

Soviet composers must reject as useless and harmful garbage all the relics of bourgeois formalism in musical art. They must understand that the creation of high-quality works in the domain of the opera, symphonic music, song-writing, choral and dance music, is possible only by following the principles of socialist realism.

Our duty is to mobilize all our creative strength and to give a worthy response, in the shortest possible time, to this appeal of our Party, to the appeal of our great leader Comrade STALIN.

A Statement by Vano Muradeli

The Central Committee of our Party in its historic Revolution has subjected my opera *Great Friendship* to a just and severe criticism.

The Resolution establishes the fact that my opera is an anti-artistic composition, corrupt both from the musical and political standpoint. I fully agree with this absolutely correct evaluation of my opera.

A. A. Zhdanov, in his historic report to the General Assembly of Soviet Composers, exposed in clear terms the false formalistic tendencies in my opera *Great Friendship*.

The speech of Zhdanov will remain forever in my memory as an impassioned appeal to Soviet composers to serve our people with honesty and devotion, and to fight determinedly and unswervingly for the great ideals of building up Communist society in our country.

Addressing the Union of Soviet Composers, I wish to state the causes of my major creative errors. There are several reasons for my failure. I shall attempt to analyze them in full.

(1) Although I have been a convinced exponent of composition inspired by folk songs, I was unable to pursue this realistic path. Instead, attracted by false innovations, I have accepted the formalistic techniques of musical modernism.

(2) My isolation from other composers, which was a result of my "aristocratic" position in the Organizational Committee, deprived me of the opportunity of heeding their Bolshevik criticism, and receiving their professional advice.

(3) I have not made adequate study, and have not acquired sufficient professional knowledge of the operatic heritage of the great Russian and Western classics.

(4) Having been completely engrossed in the composition of my opera, I neglected to work on the improvement of my ideological political education.

(5) My over-confidence and self-complacency, my exaggerated preoccupation with professional activities, carelessness and haste, resulted in retarding the progress of my work.

(6) I failed to pay attention to the voice of the people and to their ideological and spiritual requirements. I lost the sense of true actuality and its vital imperatives. My opera *Great Friendship* failed to portray the life of the

people, or its art, in any of its native phases. This shows that I have lost contact with the life of our people.

I grew up in the atmosphere of folk music. My first compositions hardly differed from simple songs of the people. In my later works—*Four Georgian Songs, Symphonic Dance,* and *Ten Heroic Songs*—I again turned for inspiration to these sources of people's music.

How could it have happened that I failed to introduce a single folk song in the score of my opera? It seems strange and almost incredible to me, and can be explained only as a manifestation of my inherent snobbishness. Apart from that, I did not possess sufficient mastery and craftsmanship for writing a large operatic work and building a music drama. In a number of places in my opera I indulged in technical tricks to obtain novel effects. Thus my opera was deprived of natural feeling and logical development.

There is no justification for these techniques in my opera, for the absence of folk songs, for the over-elaborateness, and at times crudity of my musical language. All this deprives my opera of the sense of reality, leading me towards a false formalistic path.

I have before me a definite task, to realize fully and unequivocally the seriousness of my creative errors, and to correct these errors with ideological honesty in my future works. The Resolution of the Central Committee of the All-Union Communist Party (Bolsheviks) is a new and vivid manifestation of interest and solicitude shown by our Party for the destinies of Soviet socialist culture. This historic Resolution constitutes for Soviet composers a clear creative program presaging a mighty uplift of Soviet musical culture. I will try with all my heart to earn the right to continue my devoted service to our Soviet music.

Oral Statement of Dmitri Shostakovitch

As we look back on the road traversed by our art, it becomes quite clear to us that every time that the Party corrects errors of a creative artist and points out the deviations in his work, or else severely condemns a certain tendency in Soviet art, it invariably brings beneficial results for Soviet art and for individual artists.

The directives of the Central Committee of the All-Union Communist Party (Bolsheviks) are inspired by the desire to raise the standard and the significance of art in the development of our Soviet society.

When in 1936 the Central organ of our Party, *Pravda,* severely condemned my opera *Lady Macbeth of the District of Mzensk* and pointed out my serious aberrations, my formalism, this creative failure affected me profoundly. I gave it a great deal of thought, trying hard to derive from it all the necessary lessons. It seemed to me that in the years following, my art began to develop in a new direction. I strove to provide an answer in my work to the great and stirring problems that faced the whole Soviet land, the whole Soviet people. It seemed to me that to a certain extent I managed to eradicate the pernicious elements pointed out in *Pravda:* the over-complication of the musical language, the elaboration of musical thought, etc.

This severe but just criticism by the Party made me study more intensely the works of the Russian classics and Russian national art. In that light I regarded my work on Moussorgsky's opera *Boris Godunov* when I worked on its orchestration and on its editing.

As I look back mentally at all I have written after *Lady Macbeth,* it seems to me that in my symphonic works and chamber music there appeared elements new to my art, which when developed should have given me the opportunity of finding a path to the heart of the Soviet people. However, this did not materialize. I now can clearly see that I overestimated the thoroughness of my artistic reconstruction; certain negative characteristics peculiar to my musical thought prevented me from making the turn that seemed to be indicated in a number of my works of recent years. I again deviated in the direction of formalism, and began to speak a language incomprehensible to the people.

Now, when the Party and our entire nation, speaking through the Resolution of the Central Committee of the All-Union Communist Party (Bolsheviks), condemn this tendency in my music, I know that the Party is right; I know that the Party shows solicitude for Soviet art and for me as a Soviet composer.

All the resolutions of the Central Committee of the All-Union Communist Party (Bolsheviks) regarding the art of recent years, and particularly the Resolution of 10 February 1948 in regard to the opera *Great Friendship,* point out to Soviet artists that a tremendous national uplift is now taking place in our country, our great Soviet nation.

Some Soviet artists, and among them myself, attempted to give expression in their works to this great national uplift. But between my subjective intentions and objective results there was an appalling gap.

The absence, in my works, of the interpretation of folk art, that great spirit by which our people lives, has been with utmost clarity and definiteness pointed out by the Central Committee of the All-Union Communist Party (Bolsheviks).

I am deeply grateful for it and for all the criticism contained in the Resolution.

All the directives of the Central Committee of the All-Union Communist Party (Bolsheviks), and in particular those that concern me personally, I accept as a stern but paternal solicitude for us, Soviet artists.

Work—arduous, creative, joyous work on new compositions which will find their path to the heart of the Soviet people, which will be understandable to the people, loved by them, and which will be organically connected with the people's art, developed and enriched by the great traditions of Russian classicism—this will be a fitting response to the Resolution of the Central Committee of the All-Union Communist Party (Bolsheviks).

In my *Poem of Fatherland* I attempted to create a symphonic work infused with songfulness and melodiousness. It proved to be unsuccessful.

On the basis of the principles clearly given in the Resolution of the Central Committee of the All-Union Communist Party (Bolsheviks), I shall try again and again to create symphonic works close to the spirit of the people from the standpoint of ideological subject matter, musical language and form.

I shall still more determinedly work on the musical depiction of the images of the heroic Soviet people.

I am now at work on the music for a cinema film, *Young Guard,* and I have begun an opera of the same title. I hope that in these compositions I shall partially achieve the aims of which I spoke here.

Some of my songs have attained a certain popularity among the people. Now, equipped with the directives of the Central Committee of the All-Union Communist Party (Bolsheviks), I shall again and again try to create Soviet mass songs.

I have no doubt whatsoever that Soviet music is on the eve of a tremendous creative uplift. This uplift will develop on the basis of the realization in the art of Soviet composers of the wise and just directives of the Central Committee of the All-Union Communist Party (Bolsheviks).

I appeal to all composers to bend their efforts to the task of the realization of this remarkable Resolution.

Oral Statement of Aram Khatchaturian

The Resolution of the Central Committee of the All-Union Communist Party (Bolsheviks) is the expression of the will of our people and fully reflects the opinion of the Soviet people regarding our music.

The Resolution of the Central Committee of the All-Union Communist Party (Bolsheviks) brings liberation to us, Soviet musicians. Indeed one feels as if we have thrown off the chains that have held us for many years. Despite my depressed moral state (for understandable reasons), I have a feeling of joy and satisfaction.

We feel easier, more free; there is before us a clear path, a road for Soviet music to pursue its swift progress. I see this path clearly, and I have only one desire, to correct by creative work all my previous errors.

How could it happen that I have come to formalism in my art? I made use of many folk songs, particularly my native Armenian songs. I have also used other national songs, Russian, Ukrainian, Georgian, Uzbekian, Turkmenian, and Tartar songs. I wrote a number of compositions based on these songs.

I have always declared that I do not recognize non-melodic music; I have always maintained that melody is the foundation of musical composition. But despite the fact that I stood on these seemingly correct creative positions, I have committed formalistic errors.

I see two reasons for these errors. The first is my preoccupation with technique. I have often been reproached for my insufficient technical equipment. This was reflected in my consciousness. My desire to achieve a complete technical mastery imperceptibly resulted in an over-emphasis on technique, which is particularly evident in my *Symphonie-Poème*.

I have reached formalism because of my cultivation of abstract technique.

When music critics and musicologists were telling me that it was about time for me to go beyond the national confines, to renounce the supposedly narrow stylistic direction of my music, I listened attentively to these ideas. I failed to repudiate these harmful creative positions in time. In recent years I have moved farther and farther away from my native Armenian element; I wanted to be cosmopolitan.

Andrey Adreyevitch Zhdanov in his statement at the meeting in the Central Committee of the Party said that internationalism in music can develop only on the basis of enrichment and flowering of national music, and not by erasing the national elements.

Creative errors and formalistic leanings in our music could not but influence my work in the Organizational Committee, which became a hotbed of formalism. It could not fight formalism with members who either fully or partly stood on formalistic positions, or else were sympathizers. As the principal leader of the Organizational Committee, I had every opportunity to inaugurate and lead the struggle with this phenomenon in music. But I failed to do so.

I turned out to be a poor leader, and my methods of work in the Organizational Committee were undemocratic. In recent years I stood aloof from our composers' life. Members of the Organizational Committee became "grands seigneurs" proud of their "creative achievements," and as a result found themselves generals without an army. Criticism and self-criticism in the Organizational Committee were stifled.

The Resolution of the Central Committee declares that the Organizational Committee maintained a suffocating atmosphere, devoid of all creative discussion. One of the chief reasons interfering with the work of the Organizational Committee was a lack of unity among its members. We were preoccupied with petty quarrels and our personal interrelations. We forgot that we were appointed to guide the Union of Soviet Composers, that we were expected to lead all other composers. Hypocritically paying compliments to one another, we, the members of the Organizational Committee, actually were highly antagonistic to each other.

I accept full responsibility for the unfavorable situation on the front of Soviet music, which was created as a result of the incorrect line in the domain of Soviet music, established by the Organizational Committee.

I wish to point out another very serious danger. I want to warn those comrades who, like myself, hoped that their music, which is not understood by the people today, will be understood by the future generations tomorrow. It is a fatal theory. In our country, millions of people, the entire Soviet nation, are now arbiters of music. What can be higher and nobler than writing music understandable to our people and to give joy by our creative art to millions?

I urge all Soviet composers, and above all, Shostakovitch, Prokofiev, Shebalin, Popov, Miaskovsky, and Muradeli, to answer the stern but just Resolution of the Central Committee of the All-Union Communist Party (Bolsheviks) by a decisive reorientation of their musical views, and to prove by their artistic production the thoroughness and the sincerity of their reorientation.

Our principal task is now to unite on the basis of the Resolution of the Central Committee, to work as much as possible, and as well as possible, and to prove by deeds that Soviet composers are marching in the vanguard of victorious Soviet culture.

Letter from Prokofiev to Khrennikov

The state of my health prevents me from attending the General Assembly of Soviet Composers. I therefore wish to express my ideas in regard to the Resolution of the Central Committee of the All-Union Communist Party (Bolsheviks) of 10 February 1948, in the present letter. I request that you read it at the Assembly if you find it expedient.

The Resolution of the Central Committee of the All-Union Communist Party of 10 February 1948, has separated decayed tissue in the composers' creative production from the healthy part. No matter how painful it may be for many composers, myself included, I welcome the Resolution of the Central Committee of the All-Union Communist Party (Bolsheviks) which establishes the necessary conditions for the return to health of the whole organism of Soviet music. The Resolution is particularly important because it demonstrates that the formalist movement is alien to the Soviet people, that it leads to impoverishment and decline of music. It points out with ultimate clarity the aims that Soviet composers must attain to be of the greatest service to the Soviet people.

As far as I am concerned, elements of formalism were peculiar to my music as long as fifteen or twenty years ago. Apparently the infection caught from contact with some western ideas. When formalistic errors in Shostakovitch's opera *Lady Macbeth of the District of Mzensk* were exposed by *Pravda*, I gave a great deal of thought to creative devices in my own music, and came to the conclusion that such a method of composition is faulty.

As a result, I began a search for a clearer and more meaningful language. In several of my subsequent works—*Alexander Nevsky, A Toast to Stalin, Romeo and Juliet, Fifth Symphony*—I strove to free myself from elements of formalism and, it seems to me, succeeded to a certain degree. The existence of formalism in some of my works is probably explained by a certain self-complacency, an insufficient realization of the fact that it is completely unwanted by our people. The Resolution has shaken to the core the social consciousness of our composers, and it has become clear what type of music is needed by our people, and the ways of the eradication of the formalist disease have also become clear.

I have never questioned the importance of melody. I love melody, and I regard it as the most important element in music. I have worked on the improvement of its quality in my compositions for many years. To find a melody instantly understandable even to the uninitiated listener, and at the same time an original one, is the most difficult task for a composer. Here he is beset by a great multitude of dangers: he may fall into the trivial or the banal, or into the rehashing of something already written by him. In this respect, composition of complex melodies is much easier. It may also happen that a composer, fussing over his melody for a long time, and revising it, unwittingly makes it over-refined and complicated, and departs from simplicity. Undoubtedly, I fell into this trap, too, in the process of my work. One must be particularly vigilant to make sure that the melody retains its simplicity without becoming cheap, saccharine, or imitative. It is easy to say, but not so easy to accomplish. All my efforts will be henceforth concentrated to make these words not only a recipe, but to carry them out in my subsequent works.

I must admit that I, too, have indulged in atonality, but I also must say that I have felt an attraction towards tonal music for a considerable time, after I clearly realized that the construction of a musical work tonally is like erecting a building on a solid foundation, while a construction without tonality is like building on sand. Besides, tonal and diatonic music lends many more possibilities than atonal and chromatic music, which is evident from the impasse reached by Schoenberg and his disciples. In some of my works in recent years there are sporadic atonal moments. Without much sympathy, I nevertheless made use of this device, mainly for the sake of contrast, in order to bring tonal passages to the fore. In the future I hope to get rid of this mannerism.

In my operatic production I have been often criticized for the predominance of recitative over cantilena. I like the theater as such, and I believe that a person who attends the opera has a right to expect not only auditory, but also visual impressions; or else he would go to a concert and not to the opera. But every action on the stage is closely associated with recitative; on the other hand, cantilena induces a certain immobility on the stage. I recall the painful experience of watching the action in some of Wagner's operas, when during a whole act, lasting nearly an hour, not a single person moved on the stage. This fear of immobility prevented me from dwelling on cantilena too long. In connection with the Resolution, I thought over this problem with great care, and came to the conclusion that every operatic libretto has elements demanding the use of the recitative, while other elements imperatively require a treatment in the arioso style. But there are also sections (and these sections take up considerable space, adding up perhaps to one-half of the entire opera) which the composer may treat as he wishes, either as a recitative or as an arioso. Let us consider, for example, the scene of Tatiana's letter from *Eugene Onegin*. It would have been quite simple to write most of it in the form of a recitative, but Tchaikovsky preferred cantilena, and so made the letter scene into a sort of aria, which has this additional advantage that it is accompanied by stage action, giving satisfaction not only to the ear but also to the eye. This is the direction which I intend to take in my new opera on a contemporary Soviet subject, *A Tale of a Real Man* by Polevoy.

I am highly gratified that the Resolution has pointed out the desirability of polyphony, particularly in choral and ensemble singing. This is indeed an interesting task for a composer, promising a great pleasure to the listener. In my above-mentioned opera, I intend to introduce trios, duets, and contrapuntally developed choruses, for which I will make use of some interesting northern Russian folk songs. Lucid melody, and as far as possible, a simple harmonic language, are elements which I intend to use in my opera.*

In conclusion, I should like to express my gratitude to our Party for the precise directives of the Resolution, which will help me in my search of a musical language, accessible and natural to our people, worthy of our people and of our great country.

---

* Prokofiev's hopes were not fulfilled. During the discussion at the General Assembly of Soviet Composers held in Moscow between 21 and 29 December 1948, Khrennikov characterized Prokofiev's opera as "modernistic and anti-melodic," and added that at its performance in concert form in Leningrad the opera "aroused indignation and sharp protests."

A Letter to Stalin

Dear Joseph Vissarionovitch:

The composers and musicologists of the Soviet capital, assembled for the discussion of the historic Resolution of the Central Committee of the All-Union Communist Party (Bolsheviks) of 10 February 1948 regarding the opera by Muradeli, *Great Friendship,* send to you, our beloved leader and teacher, a warm salute and wishes for good health.

We are tremendously grateful to the Central Committee of the All-Union Communist Party (Bolsheviks) and personally to you, dear Comrade Stalin, for the severe but profoundly just criticism of the present state of Soviet music, and for the interest which you and the Central Committee of our Party have shown for the progress of Soviet music, and for us, Soviet musicians.

The conference of Soviet musicians with the Central Committee of the All-Union Communist Party (Bolsheviks), and particularly the speech of Comrade Zhdanov, and the Resolution of the Central Committee of the All-Union Communist Party (Bolsheviks) of 10 February 1948, are events of historical significance; the extraordinarily powerful, profound and precise analysis of the contemporary state of Soviet music, the clear directives for the elimination of defects in Soviet music give us inestimable help, a testimony of the great power and prophetic vision of the Communist Party.

We, composers and musicologists of the city of Moscow, recognize the complete justice of the Party's criticism of Soviet music, which is now freeing itself from the deadening impact of bourgeois-formalist routine, from the influence of decadence.

It is obvious to us that, having entered the path of formalistic pseudo-modernism, the representatives of the movement condemned in the Resolution of the Central Committee of the All-Union Communist Party (Bolsheviks) have disassociated themselves from folk music and song, have forgotten the musical language of their native land, have debased themselves to the point of subjecting their talents to models and dogmas of western European and American modernism. Confronted with the Soviet people, whose voice sounds in every line of the Resolution of the Central Committee of the All-Union Communist Party (Bolsheviks), we admit that many of us have forgotten the great traditions of Russian musical realism. The words of the great genius, Glinka, who declared "Music is created by the people, and we, artists, only arrange it," have not found their adequate expression in the art of Soviet composers. As a result, the national element has been ignored in our operatic and symphonic production, and the fallacious "theory," subjectively idealistic in its essence. has been circulated to prove that broad masses of listeners are supposedly not "grown up" enough to understand contemporary music.

For us, Soviet musicians, it is all the more painful to realize that we have failed to draw correct and logical conclusions from the warnings that have been repeatedly sounded by our Party whenever Soviet music has deviated from its true realistic path. The articles, *Confusion Instead of Music* and *Ballet Falsification,* published in *Pravda* twelve years ago, the Resolutions of the Central Committee of the All-Union Communist Party (Bolsheviks) concerning the magazines *Zvezda* and *Leningrad,* and the motion picture *Great Love,* and the article, *Regarding the Repertory of Dramatic Theatres and Measures for Its Improvement,* were not followed, as it was with profound justice pointed out in the Resolution of the Central Committee of the All-Union Communist Party (Bolsheviks), by any reorientation in Soviet music. Soviet composers and critics have failed to appreciate duly the timely and precise directives of the Central Committee of the All-Union Communist Party (Bolsheviks), and so have caused the heaviest detriment to Soviet musical culture. Only their lack of contact with the life of the nation can account for the fact that our composers were unable to evaluate in full the colossal and unprecedented growth of artistic tastes and requirements of the broad popular masses, and for that reason were unable to satisfy these tastes and requirements of the great Soviet people.

Your personal suggestions, dear Joseph Vissarionovitch, regarding the task of building the Soviet classical opera, given by you in your talk with the composer Dzerzhinsky in connection with his opera, *Quiet Flows the Don,* remain a fighting program of our creative effort. We shall bend every effort to apply our knowledge and our artistic mastery and to produce vivid realistic music reflecting the life and struggles of the Soviet people.

The creative isolationism of composers must be ended once and for all. There is no place for bourgeois individualism in the musical art of a country where the artist is given every opportunity for a full development of his creative individuality, where he is surrounded with solicitude and care, of which the artists of bourgeois countries dare not even dream. In no country has a composer such an audience as in our land.

The Soviet artist is the servant of the people. This is the first conclusion that all Soviet composers and musicologists ought to make, and the creative art of every Soviet musician must be subordinated entirely to this lofty democratic principle. Not for the snobs should sound our music, but for our whole great people.

We assure you, our beloved leader and teacher, that the appeals of the Central Committee of the All-Union Communist Party (Bolsheviks) addressed to us, Soviet musicians, will become a fighting program of our creative art. We shall give all our strength to the new and unparalleledly great flowering of Soviet musical art.

We give to you and to the whole Soviet people a sworn pledge that we shall direct our work along the path of socialist realism, tirelessly laboring to create, in all musical forms, models worthy of our great epoch, striving to make our music beloved by the whole great Soviet people, so that the great ideas that inspire our nation in its universally historic deeds of valor shall find living and vivid expression in our art.

Long live the Lenin-Stalin people, the nation-worker, nation-victor that has earned the right for the most progressive socialist art in the world!

Long live the Lenin-Stalin Central Committee of the All-Union Communist Party (Bolsheviks) !

Long live our leader and teacher, father of the nation, great STALIN!

Letter of Protest from Four Soviet Composers

To the Editor of *Izvestia:*

American newspapers have reported the release of the film *The Iron Curtain.* We know that this film pursues the aim of slandering our homeland, of fanning enmity and hatred for the Soviet people, in order to please the enemies of world peace and security.

With deep indignation we have learned from a report of the *New York Times* that excerpts from our musical works are being used in this film.

Needless to say, none of us ever gave, or could have given, his consent for the use of our music in any form whatsoever in the picture *The Iron Curtain.*

Knowing beforehand that Soviet composers would indignantly reject any such offer, the agents of the American Twentieth Century-Fox Corporation resorted to a swindling trick in order to steal our music for their outrageous picture. American reactionaries decided to supplement, by the theft of our works, the anti-Soviet forgeries on which their film is based.

The fact that these gentlemen enjoy full opportunity for political blackmail, that they ignore elementary rights of composers in making unwarranted use of their creative work, proves once more that manners and morals exist in the United States under which the rights of the individual, freedom of art, and democratic principles, to which allegiance is solemnly vowed, are in reality most unceremoniously trampled underfoot.

While expressing categorical protest against such methods, against this cynical infringement on the freedom of art, we resolutely insist that our music be removed from the film *The Iron Curtain.*

D. Shostakovitch, S. Prokofiev
A. Khatchaturian, N. Miaskovsky

April 1948

Declaration of the Second International Congress of Composers and Musicologists in Prague, 29 May 1948

We, composers and musicologists of different countries, gathered at the Second International Congress of Composers and Musicologists in Prague from 20 May to 29 May 1948, organized by the Union of Czech Composers, have, after discussions and conferences lasting for ten days, unanimously agreed on the following declaration.

Music and musical life of our epoch are undergoing a profound crisis. This crisis is characterized by the sharp conflict between so-called serious music and so-called light music.

So-called serious music is becoming increasingly individualistic and subjective in its content, and increasingly complex and constructivistic in its form.

So-called light music is becoming increasingly banal, impersonal, and standardized; in many countries it is made the object of a monopolized commercial industry, and becomes a piece of merchandise.

So-called serious music has lost the proper balance of its individual musical elements. In some cases, rhythmic and harmonic elements are over-emphasized, and the melodic elements rejected; in others, formally constructivistic elements are the determinants; or else, the logical development of the musical thought is replaced by a formless melodization and esthetizing imitation of old contrapuntal writing. But no formal ingenuities can conceal the ideational vacuity of the majority of these works.

On the other hand, so-called light music confines itself exclusively to primitive melodies, entirely ignoring all other elements. It is usually based on the most vulgar, most commonplace melodic formulas, exemplified particularly by American popular music.

These tendencies, supposedly opposite, are in reality two sides of the same nefarious phenomenon, and are conditioned by the same social process.

The more evident these defects are in contemporary serious music, the more complex its form and subjective contents, the smaller is its audience, while vulgar popular music penetrates deeper and deeper the musical life of different countries and peoples, contributing to the debasement and banality of perception of its many millions of listeners and perverting their musical tastes.

We, the delegates gathered at the Second International Congress of Composers and Musicologists in Prague, note that this situation is particularly inadmissible in our time when new social forms are being created, and when human culture enters a new era, posing before the creative artist new and urgent tasks.

The International Congress does not intend to give any concrete recipes or instructions for writing music; it is understood that each nation must find its own ways and methods. However, the reasons and the essence of the contemporary crisis in music ought to be understood by all, and we must apply a united effort to solve it.

A successful solution of the crisis in contemporary music seems to be possible under the following conditions:

(1) If composers renounce in their art the tendencies of extreme subjectivism; then their music would express great, new, and progressive ideas and aspirations of the popular masses and progressive ideals of contemporary life.

(2) If creative artists turn decisively towards national culture of their lands and become its true defenders against the cosmopolitan tendencies of contemporary life, for true internationalism in music is attained only on the basis of the strengthening of national culture.

(3) If the attention of composers is directed first of all towards musical forms that are most concrete in their contents, particularly, operas, oratorios, cantatas, songs, mass choruses, etc.

(4) If composers and music critics become active and practical workers in the musical education of their peoples.

The Congress urges composers of the whole world to write music in which high artistic qualities combine with creative individuality and deep and genuine folk art.

The Congress considers that exchange of experience and ideas among progressive composers and musicologists of all nations is now an acute and urgent necessity. To achieve this, progressive musicians must unite their forces, first of all in their own countries, which ought to lead in the nearest future to the formation of a union of progressive composers and musicologists of all countries.

The Congress states its conviction that such an association of progressive composers and musicologists of all countries, by arduous and determined work will solve the protracted contemporary musical crisis, and will restore to music its lofty and noble role in society. Only under such conditions will music become a mighty factor in the solution of the great historic tasks facing all progressive mankind.

For the Praesidium of the Second International Congress of Composers and Musicologists in Prague:

A. Estrella (Brazil) ; V. Stojanov (Bulgaria) ; St. Lucky, A. Kypta, A. Sychra, Jar. Tomásek (Czechoslovakia) ; Roland de Candé (France) ; M. Flothuis, M. Rebling (Holland) ; O. Danon, N. Devcic (Yugoslavia) ; Denés Bartha (Hungary) ; Zofia Lissa (Poland) ; Hanns Eisler (Austria) ; A. Mendelsohn (Rumania) ; Tikhon Khrennikov, Boris Yarustovsky, Youri Shaporin (USSR) ; Georges Bernand (Switzerland) ; Alan Bush, Bernard Stevens (Great Britain) .

(Translations from the Russian by Nicolas Slonimsky)

ALPHABETICAL INDEX
TO DESCRIPTIVE CHRONOLOGY

Crawford, Ruth, 18
  Prayers of Steel, 365; *Rat-Riddles*,
  365; *Tall Grass*, 365
"Crea-Tone," 322
Creston, Paul
  Fanfare for Paratroopers, 527;
  Frontiers, 535; *Goossens Vars.*, 560;
  Sax. Conc., 542; *1st Sym.*, 497; *2d
  Sym.*, 558
Crippled Clarence, 460
Crist, Bainbridge
  American Epic: 1920, 531
Crooning, 18
Crosby, Bing, 447
Crowninshield, Frank, 439
Crump, E. H., 118
Cui, César, 38, 83, 102, 184
Curtis Institute of Music, 545
Czapski, Stanislaw, 296
Czar Nicholas, 177, 182
Czerny, Carl, 163, 164, 394

Dada Almanach (Berlin), 167, 169
Dadaism, 166, 167, 168, 326, 409
Dalcroze, see Jaques-Dalcroze
Dall'Abaco, Evaristo Felice, 7
Dallapiccola, Luigi, 39, 42
  Divertimento, 395; *Paradiso*, 431;
  Partita, 376; *Songs from Captivi-
  ty*, 574; *Tre Laudi*, 467; *Volo di
  Notte*, 485
Dallas Sym. Orch., 589, 590
Da Motta, José Vianna, 614
Damrosch, Frank, 359
Damrosch, Walter, 180, 182, 258, 283,
  303, 308, 309, 330, 359, 360, 512
  Cyrano, 133; *Dunkirk*, 533; *Man
  Without a Country*, 427; *Opera
  Cloak*, 526
Dance Educators of America, 506
Dandelot, Arthur, 132, 221
Daniel-Lesur, 85, 400, 411
Danielou, J., 286
Daniels, Mabel
  Deep Forest, 335
Dannreuther, Edward, 50
Darewski, Herman, 597
Dargomizhsky, 34

Darnton, Christian
  5 *Orch. Pcs.*, 465; *Music & the
  People*, 465
Darrieux, Marcel, 240
Daudet, Léon, 176
Daughters of Am. Revolution, 463
Dauriac, Lionel, 5, 159
David, Johann Nepomuk
  Partita for Orchestra, 415
Davidenko, Alexander, 261
Debussy, Chouchou, 197
Debussy, Claude, 16, 31, 32, 35, 54, 77,
  80, 89, 107, 136, 139, 145, 159, 160,
  178, 185, 187, 216, 350, 381, 392, 423,
  537, 588
  L'après-midi, 78, 144; *Children's
  Corner*, 83, 197; *Clar. Rhap.*, 144;
  Estampes, 38; *Etudes*, 163; *Damoi-
  selle Elue*, 27; *Fêtes*, 12; *Flûte de
  Pan*, 227; *Ibéria*, 86, 98; *Images*, 86,
  99, 144; *Martyre de St. Sébastien*,
  112, 114; *La Mer*, 51, 55, 78, 81, 144;
  Nocturnes, 12, 19; *Nuages*, 12; *Pel-
  léas*, 24-29, 79, 202; *Pour le Pf.*, 58;
  Rondes de Printemps, 99; *Sax.
  Rhap.*, 196 *SQ*, 267; *Sym.*, 366; *Vln.
  Sonata*, 177; *Voiles*, 102
Defauw, Désiré, 580
"Defense Swing," 505
Degas, 392
Degeyter, Adolphe, 231
Degeyter, Pierre, 352
  The Internationale, 231, 352
De Koven, Reginald, 201
Delage, Maurice
  Seven Hai-Kais, 314
de la Mare, Walter, 225
Delannoy, Marcel
  Eventail de Jeanne, 312; *Fou de la
  Dame*, 313, 324; *Poirier de Misère*,
  285; *SQ*, 338
Delbos, Claire, 400
Delgadillo, Luis A.
  Escenas Pastoriles, 469; *Tincos*, 469
Delibes, Léo, 184, 221, 426, 558
Delius, Frederick, 380, 392, 445
  Brigg Fair, 77, 318; *Dance Rhap.*

NOTES

NOTES

NOTES

NOTES

NOTES

NOTES

A NOTE ON THE MANUFACTURE OF THIS BOOK

The text of this book was composed on the Linotype and Monotype in Baskerville, a type designed by the calligrapher and printer to Cambridge University, John Baskerville (1707-1775) of Birmingham. Baskerville is a classical type-face noted for its beauty and legibility. Its sharp precision of outline is best seen on a smooth surface paper, such as Warren's Publishers' English Finish supplied by the Canfield Paper Company, New York. The Third Edition of Music Since 1900 *was set up and printed by the Belgrave Press, New York; and bound by Chas. H. Bohn & Co., Inc., New York.*